Why Do You Need This New Edition?

If you're wondering why you should buy this new edition of *The Fourth Genre*, here are a few great reasons!

1 **Twenty-six of the seventy-four selections are new,** ensuring you have access to the latest forms, fresh topics, and emerging writers.

2 New readings feature extremely current topics such as the decline of personal blogs, the rise of the quarter-life crisis, and one writer's experience in Afghanistan, giving you the chance to **bring topics important to you outside of school into your academic work.**

3 New essays and memoirs authored for the web show how composing styles differ from print to electronic publication, better enabling you to **adapt your own writing style depending on whether your work will be read digitally or in print.**

4 New short and lyric essays present experimental forms, offering you the chance to **expand the range of texts you compose and add cutting edge genres to your writing repertoire.**

5 Younger writers are better represented in this new edition to **show you the kinds of topics and issues you can call on from your own experiences** as you write your own nonfiction.

6 A new discussion in the Introduction titled "The Contentious Issue of Truth" explores ethics and truthfulness in writing that should strive to be honest and creative, **helping you avoid mistakes made by writers recently outed for penning falsified memoirs or sloppy reporting.**

7 New selections are drawn from varied sources that include magazines like *Esquire*; Internet publications such as Brevity and Guilt & Pleasure; journals like *The Seneca Review*, *River Teeth*, and *Fourth Genre*; and the anthology *Generation What?* to **provide you with engaging course material authored for varied audiences and purposes.**

PEARSON

The Fourth Genre

Contemporary Writers of/on Creative Nonfiction

FIFTH EDITION

Robert L. Root, Jr.
Central Michigan University

Michael Steinberg
Michigan State University

Longman

New York San Francisco Boston
London Toronto Sydney Tokyo Singapore Madrid
Mexico City Munich Paris Cape Town Hong Kong Montreal

Acquisitions Editor: Lauren A. Finn
Senior Supplements Editor: Donna Campion
Marketing Manager: Sandra McGuire
Production Manager: Ellen MacElree
Project Coordination, Text Design, and Electronic Page Makeup: Nesbitt Graphics, Inc.
Senior Cover Design Manager: Nancy Danahy
Cover Designer: Nancy Sacks
Cover Images: Clockwise, starting from upper right: © Andrew Lewis/istockphoto;
ges, Inc.; © Caroline Woodham/Digital
s; © Kosinus/istockphoto.
ng

al, grateful acknowledgment is made to the
are hereby made part of this copyright page.

ation Data

f/on creative nonfiction / [compiled by]
h ed.

ndex.

ge literature. 4. Reportage
. Steinberg, Michael, 1940-

2008043574

3 4 5 6 7 8 9 10—BRR—13 12 11 10

Longman
is an imprint of

ISBN 13: 978-0-205-63241-1
www.pearsonhighered.com   ISBN 10: 0-205-63241-6

The essay is a notoriously flexible and adaptable form. It possesses the freedom to move anywhere, in all directions. It acts as if all objects were equally near the center and as if "all subjects are linked to one another" (Montaigne) by free association. This freedom can be daunting, not only for the novice essayist confronting such latitude but for the critic attempting to pin down its formal properties.

—*Phillip Lopate*

Admirers of nailed-down definitions and tidy categories may not like to hear it, but all writers and readers are full-time imaginers, all prose is imaginative, and fiction and nonfiction are just two anarchic shades of ink swirling around the same mysterious well. Those of us who would tell a story can only dip in our pens. We can never claim full certainty as to which shade of ink we're using.

—*David James Duncan*

The boundaries of creative nonfiction will always be as fluid as water.

—*Mary Clearman Blew*

Don't spread it around, but it's a sweet time to be an essayist.

—*Joseph Epstein*

Contents

Alternative Contents: Subgenres of Creative Nonfiction   xi

Preface: Beginning the Conversation   xv

Introduction: Creative Nonfiction, The Fourth Genre   xxiii

PART 1 *Writing Creative Nonfiction*   1

Angela M. Balcita, "Dumpling"   5

Jo Ann Beard, "Out There"   10

Robin Black, "The Answer That Increasingly Appeals"   15

Mary Clearman Blew, "The Unwanted Child"   23

Lisa Groen Braner, "Soundtrack"   34

John Calderazzo, "Lost on Colfax Avenue"   37

Shari Caudron, "Befriending Barbie"   38

Lisa D. Chavez, "Independence Day, Manley Hot Springs, Alaska"   49

Steven Church, "I'm Just Getting to the Disturbing Part"   56

Judith Ortiz Cofer, "Silent Dancing"   64

Meghan Daum, "On the Fringes of the Physical World"   71

J. D. Dolan, "Pool, A Love Story"   80

Matt Farwell, "Welcome to Afghanistan"   89

Hillary Frank, "The Color of Monday"   95

Dagoberto Gilb, "Northeast Direct"   100

Adam Gopnick, "The People on the Bus"   104

Vivian Gornick, "On the Bus"   110

Emily Gould, "The Death of the Personal Blog"   114

Patricia Hampl, "Red Sky at Morning"   116

Richard Hoffman, "Neighbors"   120

Pico Iyer, "Where Worlds Collide"   128

Jennifer Kahn, "Stripped for Parts"   138

Nicole Lamy, "Life in Motion"   144

Jonathan Lethem, "13,1977, 21"   149

Phillip Lopate, "Portrait of My Body"   155

Nancy Lord, "I Met a Man Who Has Seen the Ivory-Billed Woodpecker and This Is What He Told Me"   163

Bret Lott, "Brothers"   166

Jared Jacang Maher, "Listen to the Sounds of the House"   170

Debra Marquart, "Some Things About That Day"   177

John McPhee, "The Search for Marvin Gardens"   179

Tom Montgomery-Fate, "In Plain Sight"   188

Michele Morano, "Grammar Lessons: The Subjunctive Mood"   192

Susan Orlean, "Lifelike"   203

Michelle Otero, "Quinto Sol"   210

Carol Paik, "A Few Things I Know About Softball"   212

Kate Petersen, "To All Those Who Say Write What You Know"   221

Wendy Rawlings, "Virtually Romance: A Discourse on Love in the Information Age"   223

Chet Raymo, "Celebrating Creation"   233

Richard Rodriguez, "Disappointment"   237

Robert L. Root, Jr, "Knowing Where You've Been"   247

Scott Russell Sanders, "Cloud Crossing"   254

Mimi Schwartz, "My Father Always Said"   260

Michael Steinberg, "Chin Music"   268

Kate Torgovnick, "How I Became a Bed-Maker"   278

Susan Allen Toth, "Going to the Movies"   283

Erika Vidal, "Undressing Victoria"   286

Christine White, "Reflection Rag: Uncle Joe, Roberto Clemente and I"   298

PART 2 *Talking About Creative Nonfiction*   315

Jocelyn Bartkevicius, "The Landscape of Nonfiction"   317

Mary Clearman Blew, "The Art of Memoir"   324

Patricia Foster, "The Intelligent Heart"   328

Vivian Gornick, "A Narrator Leaps Past Journalism"   331

Patricia Hampl, "Memory and Imagination"   334

Steven Harvey, "The Art of Self"   344

Sonya Huber-Humes, "The Real Who, What, Where, Why of Journalism"   346

Tracy Kidder, "Courting the Approval of the Dead"   350

Judith Kitchen, "Mending Wall"   364

Phillip Lopate, "What Happened to the Personal Essay?"   368

Dustin Michael, "Advice to My Friend Beth's Undergraduate
     Nonfiction Students"   376

Brenda Miller, " 'Brenda Miller Has a Cold,' or, How the Lyric
     Essay Happens"   378

Michael Pearson, "The Other Creative Writing"   385

Robert L. Root, Jr., "Collage, Montage, Mosaic, Vignette,
     Episode, Segment"   390

Scott Russell Sanders, "The Singular First Person"   402

Mimi Schwartz, "Memoir? Fiction? Where's The Line?"   411

Peggy Shumaker, "Prose Poems, Paragraphs, Brief Lyric Nonfiction"   417

Michael Steinberg, "Finding the Inner Story in Memoirs and
     Personal Essays"   420

Marianna Torgovnick, "Experimental Critical Writing"   424

PART 3 *Composing Creative Nonfiction*   429

Emily Chase, "Warping Time with Montaigne"   433

Emily Chase, "Notes from a Journey toward 'Warping Time'"   439

Mary Elizabeth Pope, "Teacher Training"   447

Mary Elizabeth Pope, "Composing 'Teacher Training'"   453

Maureen Stanton, "Zion"   461

Maureen Stanton, "On Writing 'Zion'"   469

**Alternative Contents: Approaches to Writing and Discussing
     Creative Nonfiction   475**

Notes on Authors   480

Credits   483

Index   487

Alternative Contents

Subgenres of Creative Nonfiction

PARTS 1 AND 3   *Forms of Creative Nonfiction*

Memoir

Angela M. Balcita, "Dumpling" 5

Mary Clearman Blew, "The Unwanted Child" 23

Lisa D. Chavez, "Independence Day, Manley Hot Springs, Alaska" 49

Judith Ortiz Cofer, "Silent Dancing" 64

J. D. Dolan, "Pool, A Love Story" 80

Vivian Gornick, "On the Bus" 110

Patricia Hampl, "Red Sky at Morning" 116

Bret Lott, "Brothers" 166

Mimi Schwartz, "My Father Always Said" 260

Maureen Stanton, "Zion" 461

Michael Steinberg, "Chin Music" 268

Essay

Jo Ann Beard, "Out There" 10

Steven Church, "I'm Just Getting to the Disturbing Part" 56

Meghan Daum, "On the Fringes of the Physical World" 71

Matt Farwell, "Welcome to Afghanistan" 89

Hillary Frank, "The Color of Monday" 95

Dagoberto Gilb, "Northeast Direct" 100

Vivian Gornick, "On the Bus" 110

Richard Hoffman, "Neighbors"   120

Phillip Lopate, "Portrait of My Body"   155

Jared Jacang Maher, "Listen to the Sounds of the House"   170

Tom Montgomery-Fate, "In Plain Sight"   188

Mary Elizabeth Pope, "Teacher Training"   447

Scott Russell Sanders, "Cloud Crossing"   254

Kate Torgovnick, "How I Became a Bed-Maker"   278

Erika Vidal, "Undressing Victoria"   286

Segmented and Lyric Essays and Memoirs

Robin Black, "The Answer That Increasingly Appeals"   15

Mary Clearman Blew, "The Unwanted Child"   324

Lisa Groen Braner, "Soundtrack"   34

Judith Ortiz Cofer, "Silent Dancing"   64

Nicole Lamy, "Life in Motion"   144

Jonathan Lethem, "13,1977, 21"   149

Nancy Lord, "I Met a Man Who Has Seen the Ivory-Billed Woodpecker and This Is What He Told Me"   163

Michelle Morano, "Grammar Lessons: The Subjunctive Mood"   192

Kate Petersen, "To All Those Who Say Write What You Know"   221

Carol Paik, "A Few Things I Know About Softball"   212

Mary Elizabeth Pope, "Teacher Training"   447

Wendy Rawlings, "Virtually Romance: A Discourse on Love in the Information Age"   223

Robert L. Root, Jr., "Knowing Where You've Been"   247

Susan Allen Toth, "Going to the Movies"   283

Christine White, "Reflection Rag: Uncle Joe, Roberto Clemente and I"   298

Cultural Criticism/Literary Journalism

Shari Caudron, "Befriending Barbie"   38

Emily Chase, "Warping Time with Montaigne"   433

Adam Gopnick, "The People on the Bus"   104

Emily Gould, "The Death of Personal Blogs"   114

Pico Iyer, "Where Worlds Collide"   128

Jennifer Kahn, "Stripped for Parts"   138

Jonathan Lethem, "13, 1977, 21"   149

John McPhee, "The Search for Marvin Gardens"   179

Susan Orlean, "Lifelike"   203

Chet Raymo, "Celebrating Creation"   233

Richard Rodriguez, "Disappointment"   237

Erika Vidal, "Undressing Victoria"   286

Short Essays

Lisa Groen Braner, "Soundtrack"   34

John Calderazzo, "Lost on Colfax Avenue"   37

Nancy Lord, "I Met a Man Who Has Seen the Ivory-Billed Woodpecker and This Is What He Told Me"   163

Debra Marquart, "Some Things About That Day"   177

Michelle Otero, "Quinto Sol"   210

Kate Petersen, "To All Those Who Say Write What You Know"   221

PARTS 2 AND 3 Processes and Criticism of Creative Nonfiction

Memoir

Mary Clearman Blew, "The Art of Memoir"   324

Vivian Gornick, "A Narrator Leaps Past Journalism"   331

Patricia Hampl, "Memory and Imagination"   334

Mimi Schwartz, "Memoir? Fiction? Where's The Line?"   411

Michael Steinberg, "Finding the Inner Story in Memoirs and Personal Essays"   420

Essay

Patricia Foster, "The Intelligent Heart"   328

Steven Harvey, "The Art of Self"   344

Judith Kitchen, "Mending Wall"   364

Phillip Lopate, "What Happened to the Personal Essay?"   368

Brenda Miller, " 'Brenda Miller Has a Cold', or How the Lyric Essay Happens"   378

Scott Russell Sanders, "The Singular First Person"   402

Michael Steinberg, "Finding the Inner Story in Memoirs and Personal Essays"   420

Writing

Emily Chase, "Notes from a Journey toward 'Warping Time'"   439

Vivian Gornick, "A Narrator Leaps Past Journalism"   331

Dustin Michael, "Advice to My Friend Beth's Undergraduate Nonfiction Students"   376

Mary Elizabeth Pope, "Composing 'Teacher Training'"   453

Robert L. Root, Jr., "Collage, Montage, Mosaic, Vignette, Episode, Segment"   390

Maureen Stanton, "On Writing 'Zion'"   469

Michael Steinberg, "Finding the Inner Story in Memoirs and Personal Essays"   420

Genre Issues

Jocelyn Bartkevicius, "The Landscape of Nonfiction"   317

Vivian Gornick, "A Narrator Leaps Past Journalism"   331

Sonya Hubert-Humes, "The Real Who, What, Where, Why of Journalism"   346

Tracy Kidder, "Courting the Approval of the Dead"   350

Michael Pearson, "The Other Creative Writing"   385

Robert L. Root, Jr., "Collage, Montage, Mosaic, Vignette, Episode, Segment"   390

Mimi Schwartz, "Memoir? Fiction? Where's the Line?"   411

Peggy Shumaker, "Prose Poems, Paragraphs, Brief Lyric Nonfiction"   417

Marianna Torgovnick, "Experimental Critical Writing"   424

Preface

Beginning the Conversation

Our Approach

Rationale and Overview

The Fourth Genre, Fifth Edition, is an anthology devoted to contemporary works of creative nonfiction. The readings in all three sections encompass the genre's full spectrum: personal essays, memoirs, literary journalism, and academic/cultural criticism. Creative nonfiction is the kind of literary writing that regularly appears in small magazines, reviews, and journals such as *The Georgia Review*, *The Missouri Review*, and *The American Scholar*, in trade magazines such as *Harper's* and *The New Yorker*, in print and online journals focused on creative nonfiction such as *Fourth Genre*, *River Teeth*, *Creative Nonfiction*, *Brevity*, and *Under the Sun*, and in book-length essay and memoir collections. One of the hallmarks of this form is that the boundaries between subgenres are quite expansive. That's because its writers often braid narrative telling with fictional and poetic techniques and combine portraiture and self-reflection with reportage and critical analysis. In that regard *The Fourth Genre* highlights the elasticity and versatility of this still-evolving genre.

We also see creative nonfiction as the subject that binds together the three disparate strands in most English departments: literature, creative writing, and composition. Traditionally, the study of literature has been centered on analysis and interpretation in three genres—poetry, fiction, and drama; the study of creative writing has also focused on those genres; and composition has become the domain of nonfiction. We believe that this unnatural separation can be bridged by acknowledging creative nonfiction as the fourth genre. That is, we think of creative nonfiction simultaneously as a form of literature, as a goal of creative writing, and as the aesthetic impulse in composition.

This book, then, attempts to present creative nonfiction in a framework that emphasizes its keystone status.

- It is a reader for writers of creative nonfiction, providing a range of samples of the forms and strategies practiced by many contemporary writers.

- It is an anthology for students of nonfiction literature, providing not only examples of its variety but also theoretical and critical responses to the form by critics, teachers, and the writers themselves.
- It is a collection for students of composing practices, providing reflections on the forms and strategies by the essayists, memoirists, literary journalists, cultural critics, poets, and novelists who write creative nonfiction.

These specifications make *The Fourth Genre* most suitable for courses in composition, creative writing, and genre literature. And, not coincidentally, these are the courses in which we ourselves used the book in its classroom-testing stages.

The fact that each of us was simultaneously asked to develop courses in creative nonfiction at different universities also says something about the emergence of the fourth genre from neglect in past decades. Anthologies and collections of personal essays, nature writing, literary journalism, cultural criticism, travel writing, and memoirs have proliferated in recent years, and literary magazines have begun to include creative nonfiction and the essay among the forms they regularly publish. Workshops in creative nonfiction have also been included for strands of writer's conferences and writer's workshops, and individual conferences have been organized solely around "writing the self," "environmental writing," and "travel writing." *The Fourth Genre*, therefore, represents our attempt to compile a contemporary anthology/reader that approaches creative nonfiction from a number of perspectives, trying not to let our efforts prescribe its boundaries or place limits on its possibilities.

Creative nonfiction encompasses a variety of styles, sensibilities, and forms. Its writers share a common desire to speak in a singular voice as active participants in their own experiences. This impulse often overlaps with the writer's need to mediate that experience by serving as a witness/correspondent, thus creating a unique synergy. As a result, creative nonfictionists may write to establish or define an identity, to explore and chronicle personal discoveries and changes, to examine personal conflicts, to interrogate their opinions, and to connect themselves to a larger heritage and community. Given this context, the style, focus, and structure of each work may vary. Any given piece can be lyrical, expository, meditative, informational, reflective, self-interrogative, exploratory, analytical, and/or whimsical. Moreover, a work's structure might be a traditional "linear" narrative or it may create its own disjunctive and segmented form.

To take advantage of the genre's flexibility, as well as of its emphasis on the writer's presence and voice, we have chosen readings that are representative, accessible, and challenging to students in advanced composition and creative writing workshops, as well as to students in genre-specific literature courses. We assume that student readers will be asked to write their own creative nonfiction, and that, at the same time, they will be developing a personal/critical theory that reflects the genre's possibilities.

Perhaps our most vital concern is to initiate a writer-to-reader conversation on and about creative nonfiction. Therefore, we've designed the book to be interactive by dividing it into three separate yet interconnected sections: a representative anthology of personal essays, memoirs, works of literary journalism, and personal/cultural criticism as currently practiced by recognized and emerging writers; a gathering of essays and articles that centers on more general matters of craft, definition, and theory; and a section in which four emergent writers discuss how their accompanying works of creative nonfiction were composed.

This organization encourages student writers to learn their craft the way most successful writers have learned theirs: by reading what other writers have written, by picking up tips and ideas from writers about the way they write, and by applying to their own writing specific strategies culled from the readings.

Selections and Organization

The Fourth Genre's most distinctive features are the range and scope of the readings and the interconnectedness of the three sections. In selecting these particular works, we have tried to maintain a balance between writing that is serious and informal, rigorous and pleasurable. In all instances, our criteria was that the writings be stimulating and that they have literary worth; that they be wide ranging in subject and form, familiar at times and challenging at others; and that they be strong examples of the kind of thought-provoking and authentic writing that is being done in the genre today.

In addition, several other considerations have guided our choices, perhaps the most compelling of which was our desire to counterbalance the recent creative nonfiction anthologies and manuals that identify the genre as equivalent to literary journalism. Such books tend to place little emphasis on the personal, autobiographical, and "literary" impulses (discovery, exploration, reflection) that generate much of the writing that we would call *creative nonfiction*. While we think of this genre as broad and inclusive, we feel that creative nonfiction's identity is more closely connected to the spirit of Montaigne's work than it is to matters of subject, reportage, and research. That is to say, Montaigne's essays were first and foremost intimate and *personal*, and he actively cultivated self-exploration and self-discovery. As such, his writings express the digressions, meanderings, meditations, ruminations, and speculations that characterize a singular, idiosyncratic mind at work. As Montaigne himself says, "It is myself I portray."

This point of view is not meant to duck the issue of self-examination as it extends to larger connections and broader subjects. Quite the contrary. In fact, we believe along with cultural critic Mariana Torgovnick that "All writing about self and culture is personal in that writers and critics find some of their richest material in experience. . . . Often our search for personal meaning is precisely what generates our passion and curiosity for the subjects we research and write about." It is this kind of curiosity and self-exploration that marks the majority of pieces in this book—be they personal essays, memoirs, reportage, or academic criticism—or a commingling of more than one of those subgenres.

Other concerns that guided our choices were:

- to interest aspiring writers and curious readers who come to this genre from an assortment of academic disciplines
- to spotlight representative, accessible writers from a variety of fields—literature,

science, nature writing, women's studies, journalism, rhetoric and composition, and cultural studies among them
• to offer readings that remind us of the breadth and possibilities of this continually evolving genre

To these ends, we present the reader with a broad range of pieces, as well as essays and articles by writers and teachers about the forms in which they work. Along with pieces by established writers, we've tried to select works that are less frequently taught and anthologized—provocative writing that we think will stimulate fresh and enthusiastic responses from students and teachers. In choosing these particular readings, we're hoping that *The Fourth Genre* will generate numerous alternatives for using creative nonfiction in the classroom.

Part 1, Writing Creative Nonfiction, is an anthology/sampler of contemporary creative nonfiction. It is intended to showcase the variety of voices and personas, the flexibility and expansiveness, and the range of subject matter and structures that creative nonfiction is able to embrace. Part 1 is also a representative mix of thematic explorations, self-portraitures, investigations into subject matter and ideas, and intimate personal discoveries and disclosures. Not only do the specific subjects change as they are taken up by different writers, but the techniques each writer uses to explore his/her subject can vary widely. Some writers use straightforward narrative and reportage, others blend narrative telling with fictional techniques such as scenes, characters, and dialogue. Still others explore their subjects in more lyrical, discursive, or poetic ways.

However diverse these approaches might be, the individual pieces are marked by the distinctiveness of the author's presence, no matter whether he or she is the center of the piece or an observer-reporter. Therefore, in all the writings in this section we witness the mind of the writer as he or she attempts to examine what Mariana Torgovnick describes as "some strongly felt experience, deeply held conviction, long-term interest, or problem that has irritated the mind."

In Part 2, Talking About Creative Nonfiction, we have chosen essays by working writers and teachers who are as passionate about discussing matters of craft as they are articulate in explaining their theories about the nature of creative nonfiction. Because several of these authors have also written pieces that appear in Part 1, we invite the reader to pair self-selected works to see what kinds of strategies, theories, and perspectives the writers have developed. In addition, we also suggest that both teachers and students explore how the essays in Part 1 can serve as examples of the kinds of theoretical stances that the writers and teachers in Part 2 advocate.

Another way to approach the writing in Part 2 is to view it as a writer's conversation about the possibilities and limits of the genre. Consider, for example, the differing views on literal and invented truth in memoir as proposed by Mary Clearman Blew, Patricia Hampl, and Mimi Schwartz; or compare Phillip Lopate's idea of the personal essay as a more "self-interrogative form" with Scott Russell Sander's notion of the essayist as "the singular first-person"; or examine Mariana Torgovnick's passionate approach to using the personal voice in academic writing with Vivian Gornick's distinction about the memoirist's use of materials familiar to journalists.

You can also use this section of the book to probe more deeply into the assortment of composing strategies—i.e., the use of differing narrative stances and personas; the employment of disjunctive and segmented mosaics; and the pointedly fictional and poetical techniques that memoirists, personal essayists, literary journalists, and cultural critics adopt in their writings.

All of these perspectives, then, anchor the genre in the notions, theories, and designs of working writers, many of whom are also writing teachers. As such, they give the reader an "inside" and personal look at the various ways the genre is evolving, and at the same time they offer a broader, more inclusive view of how contemporary creative nonfiction is being written and defined.

In Part 3, Composing Creative Nonfiction, three writers add their voices to the conversation in an attempt to help the student (and teacher) bridge the gap between experienced and emergent writers. In addition to the pieces themselves, Maureen Stanton, Mary Elizabeth Pope, and Emily Chase discuss their composing processes, sharing decisions on the drafts and revisions that their works-in-progress have undergone. In so doing, they focus our attention on the writing process itself.

We created this section not only to give aspiring student writers an inside look at how these pieces evolved, but also to demonstrate the many possibilities that characterize this genre. We also think that student writers will benefit greatly from paying attention to the disclosures from emerging writers, especially as these writers supplement and reinforce the readings in Parts 1 and 2. In addition, the cross-references among all three sections open up the conversation further by revealing additional aspects of its texts and authors. And finally, by pairing the emerging writer's works with their own comments about their work, we are encouraging and reinforcing the kind of dialogue established in Parts 1 and 2.

Essentially then, Part 1 is an anthology *of* creative nonfiction, Part 2 an anthology *on* creative nonfiction, and Part 3 a shorter collection *of and about* the writing of creative nonfiction.

The readings in all three sections, and the book's interactive organization, therefore, express why we think that creative nonfiction is the most accessible and personal of all four literary genres, as well as why we believe that the time is ripe for extending this dialogue to curious and interested students.

Apparatus

In keeping with the spirit of the genre's flexibility, we have provided a minimum of editorial apparatus. We assume that teachers will mix and match whatever readings suit their inclinations and teaching designs. And rather than impose a thematic, historical, or subgeneric interpretation on its users, or lock the book into a pattern based on our course designs, we prefer to emphasize the genre's multiple dimensions and possibilities. Moreover, in keeping with our intent to acquaint students (and teachers) with the rich body of work that's being produced in creative nonfiction today, we've tried to make this anthology as flexible and user friendly as possible. We want to give students permission to think of themselves as apprentice/fellow writers, to urge them to experience their writing as an inside out activity, and finally to guide them in learning to read in more "writerly" ways.

That said, along with this Preface we have provided some guidelines and rationales for using the book. The Introduction, for example, offers an expanded discussion of why creative nonfiction is the fourth genre. It also contains a detailed explanation of what we think are the five main elements of creative non-fiction. In the section on Writers, Readers, and the Fourth Genre, we talk about the personal connections between writer and reader, while offering specific examples of why we think of creative nonfiction as both a literary and transactional genre. Here we also discuss creative nonfiction as a genre that pushes at boundaries, as well as a genre in which practitioners write primarily to connect themselves in more intimate, expressive, and personal ways with their readers. In the section entitled Joining the Conversation, we expand on the notion of why we designed *The Fourth Genre* as an inclusive, ongoing conversation about the art and craft of writing creative nonfiction. Moreover, in the introductions to all three sections—Part 1's anthology, Part 2's readings about the genre, and Part 3's dialogue on composing processes—we offer overviews of each section, as well as suggestions for using the book interactively.

Another apparatus is contained in the book's three tables of contents—all of which suggest alternative ways to read and teach *The Fourth Genre*. The table of contents at the front of the book is organized alphabetically to give teachers and students the option of deciding what readings they will match up or pair with one another. Subgenres of Creative Nonfiction, the first alternative table of contents, cross references the readings from Parts 1 and 3 according to Forms of Creative Nonfiction, and categorizes the Part 2 and Part 3 readings under the heading of Processes and Criticism of Creative Nonfiction. Approaches to Writing and Discussing Creative Nonfiction, the second alternative table of contents, catego-rizes the readings according to special focus and theme. All of these, of course, are meant to be suggestive rather than prescriptive; any number of these readings could fit into multiple categories and we hope readers will pair and compare readings on their own, as well as follow our suggestions. We have also provided brief Notes on Authors as an aid to further reading.

Supplements

Instructor's Manual

In addition to the guidelines within the text, we have written a comprehensive and detailed instructor's manual. It gives specific teaching suggestions and expla-nations for using the book in three different classroom settings. More specifically, it offers an assortment of options for organizing the materials in composition, cre-ative writing, and literary genre courses. In all instances we've included brief dis-cussions of the readings as creative nonfiction, as well as suggestions for pairing or clustering selections according to subgenres, compatible themes, and issues of craft. We've also designed questions that offer different perspectives on the read-ings and that address matters of composing. Finally, we've provided a variety of writing prompts and suggestions for dealing with students' writing in all three classroom settings.

Please Note: The instructor's manual is available online at www. Pearsonhighered.com.

mycomplab | The NEW MyCompLab Website

The new MyCompLab integrates the market-leading instruction, multimedia tutorials, and exercises for writing, grammar and research that users have come to identify with the program with a new online composing space and new assessment tools. The result is a revolutionary application that offers a seamless and flexible teaching and learning environment built specifically for writers. Created after years of extensive research and in partnership with composition faculty and students across the country, the new MyCompLab provides help for writers in the context of their writing, with instructor and peer commenting functionality, proven tutorials and exercises for writing, grammar and research, an e-portfolio, an assignment-builder, a bibliography tool, tutoring services, and a gradebook and course management organization created specifically for writing classes. Visit www.mycomplab.com for more information.

Acknowledgments

The paths by which the two of us have come to creative nonfiction are familiar ones to many writers and teachers. Writing has played an important role in both of our lives. It has been the subject of college courses and post-college workshops in poetry, fiction, drama, essay, environmental writing, film writing, and professional writing. It has been the preoccupation that has produced both published and unpublished work in a variety of forms—creative nonfiction, of course, but also poetry, fiction, drama, sports journalism, and radio commentary. As it does for so many other writers, the habit of writing colors the way we approach almost every thing we do in life.

We also have been teachers for most of our adult lives, particularly of writing courses and courses on the teaching of composition. Happily, the center of our teaching and our scholarship alike has been the study of and immersion in the activity that energizes our nonacademic lives.

This book had its genesis in courses in creative nonfiction we initiated in Western Michigan University's MFA/PhD program, Michigan State University's American Studies graduate program, and Central Michigan University's Composition and Communication Master's program. As we designed these courses and consulted with one another, we agreed to encourage our students to write essays that covered a range of contemporary creative nonfiction and to give them a range of strategies with which to do that. Moreover, we invited them into the genre by asking them to consider not only what contemporary writers were publishing but also what those same writers themselves were saying about the kind of work they do. As an ongoing activity, we continued to share our own work-in-progress with our students and to "publish" anthologies of student writing within the classes.

And so we have come to this book attempting to center creative nonfiction, to keep ourselves centered on it as writers and teachers and students of the fourth genre ourselves, and to invite further speculation about it by readers, writers, and teachers interested in how we write, think about, and teach creative nonfiction now.

Along the way we have been aided in our growth as writers and development as teachers of creative nonfiction by an array of colleagues, students, and teachers, as well by both our partners. In particular we should acknowledge the following:

For Michael Steinberg: The students in English 631 at Western Michigan University, and Shirley Clay Scott, former English Chair at Western, who gave me the opportunity to develop the MFA/PhD program's first creative nonfiction workshop; the students in American Studies 891 at Michigan State University, and Peter Levine, the program's director, and David Cooper, the former acting director, for allowing me free rein in designing my course; Donald Murray, whose writing and teaching has inspired my own; Skip Renker, who provided valuable input and advice when I needed it; Doug Noverr, my department chair, and Pat McConeghy, associate dean of Arts and Letters, both of whom granted me release time from teaching to complete this book; Barbara Hope, the director of the Stonecoast Writer's Conference, who over the course of three summers gave me the opportunity to develop a creative nonfiction workshop in conjunction with five wonderful colleagues: Phyllis Barber, David Bradley, Stephen Dunn, David Huddle, and Syd Lea. My special thanks to them for showing me how it's done. Thanks as well to Dr. Sam Plyler, who kept the faith throughout this project. And finally to Carole Berk Steinberg, my gratitude, as always, for her unconditional support and unflagging encouragement.

For Robert Root: The students in English 601 and English 593 at Central Michigan University, who first responded to these readings and wrote so many memorable essays themselves, in particular Carol Sanford, Mary Beth Pope, Sandra Smith, Emily Chase, and Amy Hough; the clerical staff in the Department of English at CMU, headed by Carol Swan and Carole Pasche, particularly the student assistants who worked on this manuscript, Jennifer Baars, Kelli S. Fedewa, Star Ittu, and Gretchen M. Morley; Becky Wildfong, Tom Root, and Caroline Root, good writers all; and Susan Root, whose understanding and support make all burdens lighter.

We would also like to take this opportunity to thank the following reviewers of the manuscript for this edition: Thomas DeMarchi, Florida Gulf Coast University; Michael DePalma, University of New Hampshire; Sharon L. Emmons, Portland Community College, Sylvania; Erica D. Galioto, Shippensburg University; Claudia Jannone, University of South Florida; and Toni Jensen, Chatham College.

We are grateful for the expert guidance of our initial editor, Eben Ludlow, for the continued support of our current editor, Lauren Finn, and for the recommendations and advice of reviewers of previous editions of the anthology as well as to teachers, students, and readers who have informally shared their responses to readings with us at conferences and workshops and in classrooms and hallways.

Robert L. Root, Jr.
Michael Steinberg

Introduction

Creative Nonfiction, the Fourth Genre

Creative nonfiction is the fourth genre. This assumption, declared in the title of the book, needs a little explaining. Usually literature has been divided into three major genres or types: poetry, drama, and fiction. Poets, dramatists, and novelists might arrange this trio in a different order but the idea of three literary genres has, until very recently, dominated introductory courses in literature, generic divisions in literature textbooks, and categories of literature in bookstores. Everything that couldn't be classified in one of these genres or some subgenre belonging to them (epic poetry, horror novels) was classified as "nonfiction," even though, as Jocelyn Bartkevicius points out elsewhere in this collection, they could also be classified as "nonpoetry" just as well. Unfortunately, this classification system suggests that everything that is nonfiction should also be considered nonliterature, a suggestion that is, well, nonsense.

We refer to creative or literary nonfiction as the fourth genre as a way of reminding readers that literary genres are not limited to three; we certainly do not intend the term to indicate ranking of the genres but rather to indicate their equality. It would be better to have a more succinct, exclusive term for the genre. Writers have been composing literary forms of nonfiction for centuries, even if only recently have they begun to use the terms *creative nonfiction* or *literary nonfiction* to separate it from the nonliterary forms of nonfiction. And, after all, although it is creative or imaginative or literary, it is still its being nonfiction that distinguishes it from the other literary genres.

The shape of creative nonfiction is, in Robert Atwan's phrase, "malleable," in O. B. Hardison's, "Protean." Perhaps we can picture its throbbing, pulsing, mercurial existence as locations on a series of intersecting lines connecting the poles of the personal and the public, the diary and the report, the informal and the formal, the marginalia and the academic article, the imaginative and the expository. Creative nonfiction essays would be located on these lines somewhere within the boundaries set by neighboring genres, not only "the three creative genres" of fiction, poetry, and drama but also the "expressive" genres of diary, journal, and autobiography and the "objective" genres of traditional (as opposed to literary) journalism, criticism, polemic, and technical writing. It may be fair to say that creative nonfiction centers in the essay but continually strains against the boundaries of other genres, endeavoring to push them back and to expand its own space without altering its own identity.

The Elements of Creative Nonfiction

Yet despite all the elusiveness and malleability of the genre and the variety of its shapes, structures, and attitudes, works of creative nonfiction share a number of common elements, although they may not all be present all the time in uniform proportions. The most pronounced common elements of creative nonfiction are *personal presence, self-discovery and self-exploration, veracity, flexibility of form*, and *literary approaches to nonfiction*.

Personal Presence

Writers of creative nonfiction tend to make their personal presence felt in the writing. Whatever the subject matter may be—and it can be almost anything—most creative nonfiction writing (as Rosellen Brown says of the essay) "presents itself, if not as precisely true, then as an emanation of an identifiable speaking voice making statements for which it takes responsibility" (5). In such writing the reader encounters "a persona through whose unique vision experience or information will be filtered, perhaps distorted, perhaps questioned"; the writer's voice creates an identity that "will cast a shadow as dense and ambiguous as that of an imaginary protagonist. The self is surely a created character" (5).

Throughout the various forms of creative nonfiction, whether the subject is the writer's self (as perhaps in personal essays and memoirs) or an objective, observed reality outside the self (as perhaps in nature essays and personal cultural criticism), the reader is taken on a journey into the mind and personality of the writer. Some writers directly engage in interrogations of the self by unequivocally examining and confronting their own memories, prejudices, fears, even weaknesses. Others are more meditative and speculative, using the occasion of remembered or observed experience to connect to issues that extend beyond the self and to celebrate or question those connections. Still others establish greater distance from their subjects, take more of an observer's role than a participant's role, yet even as they stand along the sidelines we are aware of their presence, because their voice is personal, individual, not omniscient.

This sense of the author's presence is a familiar element of essays and memoirs, of course. These center on the author's private reflections and experiences. As essayist Phillip Lopate writes,

> The hallmark of the personal essay is its intimacy. The writer seems to be speaking directly into your ear, confiding everything from gossip to wisdom. Through sharing thoughts, memories, desires, complaints, and whimsies, the

personal essayist sets up a relationship with the reader, a dialogue—a friendship, if you will, based on identification, understanding, testiness, and companionship. (xxiii)

But personal presence can also pull subject-oriented writing (principally journalistic and academic writing) into the realm of creative nonfiction. Arguing a need
for "writerly models for writing about culture," Marianna Torgovnick insists,
"Writing about culture is personal. Writers find their material in experience as
well as books, and they leave a personal imprint on their subjects. They must feel
free to explore the autobiographical motivation for their work, for often this motivation is precisely what generates writers' interests in their topics" (3). Including
this personal voice in cultural criticism surrenders some of the authority—or the
pretense of authority—generally found in academic writing, but substitutes for it
the authority of apparent candor or personal honesty. What Rosellen Brown
writes of the personal essayist is applicable to all creative nonfiction writers: "The
complex delight of the essayist's voice is that it can admit to bewilderment without losing its authority" (7). This sense of personal presence is one of the most
forceful elements of creative nonfiction.

Self-Discovery and Self-Exploration

As many writers in this book suggest—either directly or indirectly—this genre encourages self-discovery, self-exploration, and surprise. Often, the writer "is on a
journey of discovery, often unasked for and unplanned," Rosellen Brown writes.
"The essayist is an explorer, whereas the fiction writer is a landed inhabitant" (7).
Phillip Lopate speaks of self-discovery that takes place in essays as writing that
"not only monitors the self but helps it gel. The essay is an enactment of the creation
of the self" (xliv). This genre grants writers permission to explore without knowing
where they'll end up, to be tentative, speculative, reflective. Because writing creative nonfiction so often reveals and expresses the writer's mind at work and play,
the genre permits us to chart the more whimsical, nonrational twists and turns of
our own imaginations and psyches. More frequently than not, the subject matter becomes the catalyst or trigger for some personal journey or inquiry or self-interrogation. Writers who seem most at home with this genre are those who like to delve
and to inquire, to question, to explore, probe, meditate, analyze, turn things over,
brood, worry—all of which creative nonfiction allows, even encourages.

Such interests may seem at first glance appropriate only to a narrow range of
"confessional writing," but in much of the best creative nonfiction, writers use self-
disclosure as a way of opening their writing to a more expansive exploration. This
genre, then, is a good choice for writers who like to reach for connections that extend beyond the purely personal. As W. Scott Olson writes, "As the world becomes more problematic, it is in the little excursions and small observations that
we can discover ourselves, that we can make an honest connection with others,
that we can remind ourselves of what it means to belong to one another" (viii).

Flexibility of Form

One of the most exciting elements of creative nonfiction is the way in which contemporary writers "stretch the limits of the form" and "are developing a [nonfiction] prose that lives along the borders of fiction and poetry" (Atwan x). Contemporary creative nonfiction uses the full range of style and structure available to other literary and nonliterary forms. Most often, readers have noticed the use of fictional devices in creative nonfiction, particularly in what is termed "the nonfiction novel" or in certain examples of literary journalism, which Mark Kramer has defined as "extended digressive narrative nonfiction" (21). Rosellen Brown, who refers to the personal essay as a "nonfiction narrative," believes it is "every bit as much an imaginative construction as a short story" and that "it must use some, if not all, of the techniques of fiction: plot, characterization, physical atmosphere, thematic complexity, stylistic appropriateness, psychological open-endedness" (5).

And yet, while narrative elements may frequently play a part in creative nonfiction, the genre often works with lyrical, dramatic, meditative, expository, and argumentative elements as well. As Annie Dillard says, "The essay can do everything a poem can do, and everything a short story can do—everything but fake it" (xvii). It can also do everything a diary, a journal, a critical article, an editorial, a feature, and a report can do.

Moreover, perhaps more frequently than in other genres, creative nonfiction writers are likely to innovate and experiment with structure. They draw not only on narrative chronology and linear presentation but also on nonlinear, "disjunctive," or associative strategies. They use different angles and perspectives to illuminate a point or explore an idea, drawing on visual and cinematic techniques such as collages, mosaics, montages, and jump cuts. They can leap backward and forward in time, ignoring chronology of events to emphasize nonsequential connections and parallels; they can structure the essay around rooms in a house or cards in a Tarot deck; they can interrupt exposition or narrative with passages from journals and letters or scenes from home movies. Part of the excitement of the genre is its openness to creative forms as well as to creative contents, its invitation to experiment and push at boundaries between genres, and its ability to draw upon an unlimited range of literary techniques.

Veracity

Because it sometimes draws on the material of autobiography, history, journalism, biology, ecology, travel writing, medicine, and any number of other subjects, creative nonfiction is reliably factual, firmly anchored in real experience, whether the author has lived it or observed and recorded it. As essayist and memoirist Annie Dillard writes, "The elements in any nonfiction should be true not only artistically—the connects must hold at base and must be veracious, for that is the convention and the covenant between the nonfiction writer and his reader" ("Introduction," xvii). Like the rest of us, the nonfiction writer, she says, "thinks about actual things. He can make sense of them analytically or artistically. In either case he renders the real world coherent and meaningful, even if only bits of it, and even if that coherence and meaning reside only inside small texts" (xvii). For critic Barbara Lounsbery, who is principally speaking of literary journalism, factuality is central, by which she means: "Documentable subject matter chosen from the real world as opposed to 'invented' from the writer's mind"; she adds that "anything in the natural world is game for the nonfiction artist's attention" (xiii).

But factuality or veracity is a trickier element than it seems. As David James Duncan observes,

> We see into our memories in much the way that we see across the floor of a sunbaked desert: everything we conjure, every object, creature, or event we perceive in there, is distorted, before it reaches us, by mirages created by subjectivity, time, and distance. . . . The best that a would-be nonfiction writer can do is use imperfect language to invoke imperfectly remembered events based on imperfect perceptions. (55)

Artistry needs some latitude; self-disclosure may be too risky to be total, particularly where it involves disclosure of others. Just as Thoreau compressed two years at Walden Pond into one to get the focus he needed for his great book, creative nonfiction writers sometimes alter the accuracy of events in order to achieve the accuracy of interpretation. Some of this is inadvertent—the great challenge of memoir writing is knowing how much of what we remember is reliable and accepting the likelihood that we are "inventing the truth." "You can't put together a memoir without cannibalizing your own life for parts," Annie Dillard writes in "To Fashion a Text." "The work battens on your memories. And it replaces them" (70). Memories blur over time and edit themselves into different forms that others who had the same experience might not recognize. Finding the language to describe experience sometimes alters it, and your description of the experience becomes the memory, the way a photograph does. At the least we may feel a need to omit the irrelevant detail or protect the privacy of others not as committed to our self-disclosure as we are. The truth may not necessarily be veracious enough to take into court or into a laboratory; it need only be veracious enough to satisfy the writer's purpose and the art of the writing.

Literary Approaches to Language

The language of creative nonfiction is as literary, as imaginative, as that of other literary genres and is similarly used for lyrical, narrative, and dramatic effects. What separates creative nonfiction from "noncreative nonfiction" (if we can be forgiven the use of that term for a moment to categorize all nonfiction outside this genre) is not only "the unique and subjective focus, concept, context and point of view in which the information is presented and defined" (Gutkind v–vi) but also the ways in which language serves the subject. This is partly what Chris Anderson is alluding to when he writes that certain essays and journalism are not

THE CONTENTIOUS ISSUE OF "TRUTH"

Partly due to occasional revelations of dishonesty, prevarication, and outright fraud in some works of nonfiction and partly due to varied interpretations of what "creative nonfiction" really is, the issue of "truth" is discussed and debated more often in regard to the fourth genre than in regard to other genres. The first issue is easily addressed: no one defines "creative" as "dishonest" or "fraudulent" and no one encourages nonfictionists to be dishonest or fraudulent. The second issue is more problematic: If you approach creative nonfiction as if it were a scholarly, journalistic, scientific, or historical genre, then you likely emphasize verifiable factuality—that is, the use of evidence that can be independently corroborated or confirmed by anyone investigating the accuracy of the assertions or reportage. In regard to those subgenres or branches of nonfiction, there is no argument; the difficulty emerges only when applied to "creative nonfiction," the branch of nonfiction that includes memoirs, essays, literary journalism, and personal cultural criticism. Creative nonfiction need not be academic or journalistic and, more to the point, need not rely on verifiable factuality—that is, it usually draws on experiences, emotions, memories, and interpretations which are, by their very nature, impossible to corroborate or confirm by an independent investigator.

For example, how can you verify whether Annie Dillard ever locked gazes with a weasel as she declares she did in "Living Like Weasels"? You can look up her reference to Ernest Thompson Seton and track down his eagle story, perhaps, but other than interrogating Dillard herself or finding an inadvertent videotape of her and the weasel, as in an episode of *CSI*, you simply have to take her word that the event happened. The same thing is true of Dagoberto Gilb's story of seeing a man reading his novel in a train car where a weak battery on Gilb's computer made him sit near the only electrical outlet in the car. Think of the difficulty of tracking all those little facts down, including the train schedule, the date of the experience, the text Gilb typed on the computer. As Robert Atwan observes in his foreword to *The Best American Essays 2006*, "the unverifiable world is vast and accommodating." He encourages readers to ask themselves: "If a report of something is wholly unverifiable, should we even concern ourselves with the issue of truth?" It's a rhetorical question: the answer is no.

That said, we should also consider a further aspect of the fourth genre. Because another approach to it is from the direction of literature, with its emphasis on narrative, dialogue, character, and lyricism—in other words, drawing on aspects of fiction, drama, and poetry—the issue of truth is often raised in regard to how much liberty the writer has taken with the "facts." All nonfiction writers have to decide on the pertinence or relevance of particular evidence to the kind of work they hope to write; they have to be selective about what they include and what they exclude. Something is always left out of every piece of writing, and the writer always has to make choices about what difference those acts of omission will make. Some information merely distracts or, even worse, disengages the reader from the primary focus of the writing; it is better left out. For example, since so much of literary nonfiction is about personal experience rather than public events, rigorous identification of all participants, including the most tangential bystander, may divert attention from the purpose of relating the experience in the first place.

All writing also performs acts of commission—deliberately altering experiences and events to narrow focus on those elements the writer most wants the reader to attend to, to remember, to see as significant. The acts of omission are inevitable and less problematic than the acts of commission, since they may involve altering facts or inventing information. Some of these are minor and, by now, routine: Memoir, reportage, and ethnographic research frequently disguise the identity of witnesses and participants on ethical grounds, as well as grounds of relevance. Readers may not need to identify real-life individuals and authors have to decide whether to expose private lives to public scrutiny. Name changes are common acts of commission.

More troublesome, to some readers, are an author's conflation of time—by representing something that took place over several days as taking place in one or two—and the use of composite characters—characters composed of two or more other characters to create a third, who never actually existed. These would surely be unacceptable in noncreative nonfiction, but in more literary forms, and within certain limits in those forms, they are not. Memoirists often see memoir as a form of literature rather than a form of history or journalism. As Vivian Gornick explained about her having "made a composite out of the elements of two or more incidents" and "played loose with time [by] relating incidents that were chronologically out of order," she did these things "for the purpose of moving the narrative forward" and "for the sake of narrative development." She emphasizes that "none [of the incidents] . . . had been fabricated." Gornick's distinction—that she has fashioned her material, not fabricated it—is an important one.

The lines of demarcation between truth and fact, or between fashion and fabrication, are difficult to locate absolutely. Writers of the fourth genre walk those lines more delicately than those in other forms, but in the end they endeavor to represent the unverifiable world in which we all live as truthfully as they can.

literary (x), and what Barbara Lounsbery means by claiming that, no matter how well the other elements of a nonfiction work are achieved, "it may still fail the standards of literary nonfiction if its language is dull or diffuse" (xv). When Annie Dillard turned from writing poetry to writing literary nonfiction, she

was delighted to find that nonfiction prose can also carry meaning in its structures and, like poetry, can tolerate all sorts of figurative language, as well as al-
literation and even rhyme. The range of rhythms in prose is larger and grander
than it is in poetry, and it can handle discursive ideas and plain information as
well as character and story. It can do everything. I felt as though I had
switched from a single reed instrument to a full orchestra. ("To Fashion"
74–75)

When the writer of poetry or fiction turns to creative nonfiction, as poet Mary
Karr does in her memoir *The Liar's Club*, or poet Garrett Hongo does in his memoir, *Volcano*, they bring with them the literary language possible in those other
genres and are able to use it.

But poets and novelists aren't the only ones drawing on literary techniques in
nonfiction. Some journalists have taken so literary an approach to their reportage
that they have created a writing form that straddles literature and journalism, and
often can be identified as a form of creative nonfiction. In addition, a number of
primarily academic writers have sought a more personal perspective in the cultural criticism they write. They have made the language of their academic discourse more expansive, more intimate, more literary, allowing the reader to share
their subjective reactions to the ideas and experiences they discuss. Like Thoreau,
they retain rather than omit "the *I*, or first person," acknowledging, as he did, that
we "commonly do not remember that it is, after all, always the first person that is
speaking" (3). By doing so they do not simply present their information or opinions but also extend *themselves* toward the reader and draw the reader closer. In
essence, they move the written work beyond presentation into conversation.

The writer in creative nonfiction is often the reader's guide, pointing out the
sights along the way, the places of interest where special attention is required. In
such writing the reader is treated like a spectator or an audience. But often the
writer is the reader's surrogate, inviting her to share the author's space in imagination and to respond to the experience as if she is living it. In such writing the reader
is treated like a participant. In creative nonfiction, then, in addition to exploring the
information being presented—the ways various ideas, events, or scenes connect to
one another and relate to some overarching theme or concept or premise—the
reader also has to examine the role the writer takes in the work. The writer's role
and the structure of the writing are not as predictable in creative nonfiction as they
are in other forms, such as the news article or the academic research paper, the sermon or the lecture. The structure of the essay or article may be experimental or unexpected, an attempt to generate literary form out of subject matter instead of trying
to wedge subject matter into an all-purpose literary form. When it departs from linear, tightly unified forms to achieve its purpose, contemporary creative nonfiction
doesn't simply meander or ramble like the traditional essay ("My Style and my
mind alike go roaming," Montaigne said); instead, it moves in jump cuts, flash-
backs, flash-forwards, concentric or parallel or tangential strands. Readers sometimes have to let the works themselves tell them how they should be read.

Writers, Readers, and the Fourth Genre

The interaction between the writer and the genre the writer works in influences the outcome of the work. Writers of other nonfiction forms such as criticism, journalism, scholarship, or technical and professional writing tend to leave themselves out of the work and to view the work as a means to an end; they want to explain, report, inform, or propose. For them the text they produce is a vehicle, a container or a package, to transport information and ideas to someone else, the intended readers. Some people have referred to these forms as *transactional writing.* Writers of other literary forms such as poetry, fiction, and drama tend to put themselves in the work and to view the work as an end in itself; they want to reflect, explore, speculate, imagine, and discover, and the text they create is a structure, an anchored shape like a sculpture or a monument or a building, to which interested readers are drawn. The result is often called *poetic* or *creative writing.* Writers of creative nonfiction by definition share the qualities of both groups of writers, and the work they create reflects varying measures of both kinds of writing.

Many creative nonfiction writers in this book joined this conversation from the direction of their writing in other literary genres. Experienced poets or fictionists, they came to the fourth genre by way of personal essays and memoirs, nonfiction forms compatible with the desire for lyric and narrative expression, the desire to give voice to memory and meditation and acts of emotional and intellectual discovery. They came to it not only because of a need to write nonfiction but also because of a desire for creative expression. Similarly, creative nonfiction is also written by critics, journalists, and scholars who approach their writing the way essayists and memoirists do—that is, by inhabiting the work and by approaching it from a literary perspective more than (or as much as) from a critical, reportorial, or scholarly perspective.

We don't necessarily see sharply definable boundaries here, whose coordinates we can map precisely—neighboring nonfiction forms often share the same terrain for a long distance on either side of their common border. Yet, just as when you're traveling you don't need precise knowledge of geography or topography to sense that you're not in Kansas (or Vermont or California) anymore, so in reading you can also sense when a text is a work of "literary" nonfiction and not the "transactional" forms usual to journalism, scholarship, or criticism.

Because nonfiction in general has sometimes, mistakenly, been regarded as if it were an arid, barren wasteland of nonliterature surrounding lush, fertile oases of literature, it is important to make this clear: a great deal of nonfiction has always been literary, and it is the contemporary writers of literary or creative forms of nonfiction who are the focus of this book. The nonliterary forms of nonfiction are not our focus, but in some of those forms it is frequently difficult to notice when a writer slips over the border into the literary form. To make it easier to talk about creative nonfiction, then, we urge you to see it centered in the approaches taken by the essayist and memoirist and spiraling outward toward aesthetically oriented critics and literary journalists.

Working Definitions

Readers frequently ask us to be more specific about the definition we'd apply to creative nonfiction and the distinctions we'd make among the various forms. In spite of our insistence that it's impossible, even counterproductive, to try to pin down subgenres and that definitions are better intuited from examining texts than delineating characteristics, for the purposes of discussion about the genre we do have some working definitions in mind. As long as readers remember that we're not attempting to make absolute distinctions among forms, and that we can argue for placing most texts in multiple categories (note the repetition of titles in various categories in our alternative tables of content), we'll offer here some provisional descriptions that might help clarify distinctions.

First of all, we think of nonfiction as *the written expression of, reflection upon, and/or interpretation of observed, perceived, or recollected experience*. As a genre of literature made up of such writing, it includes such subgenres as the personal essay, the memoir, narrative reportage, and expressive critical writing; its borders with other reality-based genres and forms (such as journalism, criticism, history, etc.) are fluid and malleable. We would place nonfiction works on a line stretching from the most informative to the most literary. Works of creative nonfiction tend to concentrate more heavily, but not exclusively, on the literary end of that line. As a result, we might think in terms of four major categories:

- *Essay*—an author's engagement in prose with a subject or an experience; it becomes a personal essay when the author's own individual, idiosyncratic self, worldview, or experience is essential to the writing. The "plot" of the personal essay is the arc of the writer's thinking—that is, his or her reflections, reactions, speculations, associations, confusions—all of which are being employed in the service of trying to make sense of a topic, an experience, or a situation that perplexes and preoccupies the writer (e.g., Dagoberto Gilb's "Northeast Direct" and Vivian Gornick's "On the Bus").
- *Memoir*—a record of and reflection upon past events that the author experienced or witnessed. It is generally more concentrated or focused in time or circumstances than an autobiography would be. Literary memoir, in particular, tends to express how the writer's past history has helped shape his or her present self (e.g., Judith Ortiz Cofer's "Silent Dancing" or Mimi Schwartz's "My Father Always Said").
- *Cultural criticism*—an investigation of or reaction to or interpretation of specific artifacts or aspects of the culture—artistic, social, historic, political, etc. It becomes personal (and becomes creative nonfiction, though it may also be called "narrative scholarship" or "personal academic discourse") when the investigator is up front about his or her individual involvement with or experience of the topic (e.g., Richard Rodriguez "Disappointment" or Chet Raymo's "Celebrating Creation").
- *Journalism*—a report on public events or current affairs or occurrences of general public interest; it becomes literary journalism when the author includes

his or her own perspective or behavior as part of the reportage or elects to use the techniques of literature (those of fiction, poetry, drama, film, memoir) as a means of presenting the reportage (e.g., Pico Iyer's "Where Worlds Collide" or John McPhee's "The Search for Marvin Gardens").

In practice, as many of the works in this anthology illustrate, any of these categories can spill over into any or all of the others, fuse together, blend, and dance back and forth across boundaries.

Reading Creative Nonfiction

Readers come to creative nonfiction with different expectations from those they bring to the other genres. At the core of those expectations may be, in a sense, the hope of becoming engaged in a conversation. Much fiction, drama, poetry, and film is presented as performance, as entertainment essentially enclosed within itself—we are usually expected to appreciate or admire its creators' artistry whether or not we are encouraged to acknowledge their intensity or insight. Much nonliterary nonfiction (various forms of journalism and academic writing, for example) is presented as a transaction delivering information, sometimes objective, sometimes argumentative—we are usually expected to receive or accept their creators' knowledge or data the way we would a lecture or a news broadcast. Creative nonfiction, which is simultaneously literary and transactional, integrates these discourse aims: it brings artistry to information and actuality to imagination, and it draws upon the expressive aim that lies below the surface in all writing. Expressive writing breaks the surface most notably in personal writing like journals, diaries, and letters, but it has connected with the reader most prominently in the personal or familiar essay. Other forms of writing have at center personal impulse, the need for expression, but the essay has traditionally been the outlet by which that impulse finds public voice.

Readers turn to creative nonfiction to find a place to connect to the personal voice, to connect not to art or knowledge alone but to another mind. This means that writers too have a place to connect, a genre that gives them permission to speak in the first person singular, not only about their knowledge and their beliefs but also about their uncertainties and their passions, not only about where they stand but also about the ways they arrived there, not only about the worlds they have either imagined or documented but also about the worlds they have experienced or inhabit now. Creative nonfiction may be the genre in which both reader and writer feel most connected to one another.

Joining the Conversation

We think of *The Fourth Genre* as an inclusive, ongoing conversation about the art and craft of writing creative nonfiction. We want to exemplify and describe this evolving genre, allow it to define itself and preserve its vital elasticity, and avoid arbitrary and imprecise subcategorizing and classifying. Unlike conversations in real life, a conversation in an anthology allows only one speaker at a time to speak and no one is interrupted by anyone else. The reader is the one who has to make the individual speakers connect. We've tried to make the conversation a little easier to follow by putting the speakers in different rooms. The people who simply share their own examples of creative nonfiction have the largest room, at the front of the anthology, where the writing more or less speaks for itself. The people who have ideas and opinions about the nature of this genre, the kinds of writing it contains and the kinds of writers who produce it, have another room, where both those write creative nonfiction and those who study or examine it have their opportunities to speak. In the final room are those who attempt to explain how they wrote their own specific examples of creative nonfiction—the circumstances of composition, the tribulations of drafting and revising—where the conversation focuses on the composing processes of working writers.

In real life you wouldn't be able to hear all the speakers in this conversation, but in an anthology you can, because the speakers wait until you get to them before they speak. In spite of the layout of the place, you should feel free to wander back and forth among the rooms, following someone else's recommendations or your own inclinations and intuitions. Naturally, we encourage you to join the conversation, provide your own examples, discuss your own ideas of genre, theory, and technique, share your own composing processes.

Read selections in Part 1, Writing Creative Nonfiction, *to get a sense of the range of contemporary creative nonfiction.* The writers here reveal the variety of voices and personas, the flexibility and expansiveness, and the breadth of subject matter and structures creative nonfiction may adopt. It is a representative blend. It includes examples of the personal essay, the memoir, the travel essay, the nature essay, the lyric essay, literary journalism, and personal cultural criticism. (See the Alternative Table of Contents on Subgenres of Creative Nonfiction for further subdivisions and categories.) These selections also present a range of forms and structures, from the narrative and the lyrical to the discursive and the reportorial, from the traditional (chronology or argument) to the individual and unconventional (unique arrangements of segments or organization around a pattern).

Many of these works demonstrate the futility of labels, qualifying easily under the genre heading of creative nonfiction for personal presence, literary language, and other defining elements but straddling the boundaries of two or more subgenres, perhaps simultaneously literary journalism and personal essay, travel narrative and environmental reporting, memoir and cultural criticism. Instead they model the intimate relationship between form and content in creative nonfiction. Perhaps they will also suggest to you ways to invent forms that serve your own ends as a writer.

Read selections in Part 2, Talking About Creative Nonfiction, *to get a sense of what writers, critics, and scholars have to say about the nature of creative nonfiction and its various subgenres.* Many of the authors in this section have also written selections in Part 1. They take the form personally, sometimes discussing their own personal motives and composing strategies, sometimes the elements of the form they work in. As some of them point out, the tradition of essayist/critic goes back centuries, to the work of Montaigne, Addison and Steele, Lamb and Hazlitt, and as this genre re-emerges, it is contemporary practitioners, for the most part—the people who write and teach creative nonfiction—who are setting the terms of this conversation. This section mixes thoughts, opinions, speculations, critiques, theories, and assertions by working writers about the art and craft of their genre.

Many of the Part 2 pieces can be paired with essays in Part 1. Writing in Part 1 often serves as examples of the more theoretical positions in Part 2; writing in Part 2 often gives new perspective on writing in Part 1. So you can compare memoirs with the memoirists' discussion of the form, essays with the essayists' reflections on being essayists, cultural criticism with the critics' justifications for personal academic writing.

Other authors also give us insight into the forms and issues of creative nonfiction—the art of the memoir or of literary journalism, the elements of the disjunctive form or the question of truthfulness in nonfiction texts. Such essays attempt to give a personal perspective to a critical speculation on the forms in which the writers are working. They ground the genre in the behaviors and motives of working writers rather than in disembodied theories of literature or composing. They give the reader the opportunity to step back from the individual readings and take a longer view of process and text.

Read selections in Part 3, Composing Creative Nonfiction, *for a sense of the work habits, craft techniques, and serendipity they use to create a work of creative nonfiction.* Here, in commentary written especially for this anthology, several writers discuss their composing processes for specific works, also reproduced in this section. They share drafts, explain revisions, and map the motives for changes in their works-in-progress. They focus our attention in this conversation on the most fundamental aspect of the work, the composing itself, and bring us to the place where the reader can continue the conversation as a writer. If Part 1 gives us examples of the variety of creative nonfiction, and Part 2 gives us a lively discussion of the practices and products of the genre, Part 3 gives us a chance to sit at the shoulder of the writer herself and follow her through the twists and turns of creation. These writers reflect in their practices the ways writers in other parts of the book created their own selections. By example they suggest ideas and strategies that we can use in our own composing processes.

We think the fourth genre is the most accessible and urgent genre. It may not be necessary to read all three parts of the book or to read all selections in the parts you do read to get a sense of what creative nonfiction is about. We hope the book is flexible enough that readers can get what they want from it by coming at it from a number of different directions. Yet readers who do read in all three parts will get a fuller understanding of the breadth and power of this genre. And because the time is particularly right for other writers to join this conversation, we hope that wide reading in this book will help spur your writing of creative nonfiction and give you a writer's perspective on the art and craft of the fourth genre.

Robert L. Root, Jr.
Michael Steinberg

Works Cited

Anderson, Chris. "Introduction: Literary Nonfiction and Composition." *Literary Nonfiction: Theory, Criticism, Pedagogy*. Ed. Chris Anderson. Carbondale: Southern Illinois University Press, 1989. ix–xxvi.

Atwan, Robert. "Foreword." *The Best American Essays 1988*. Boston: Ticknor & Fields, 1988. ix–xi.

Brown, Rosellen. "Introduction." *Ploughshares* 20:2/3 (Fall 1994): 5–8.

Dillard, Annie. "Introduction." *The Best American Essays 1988*. Boston: Ticknor & Fields, 1988. xiii–xxii.

———. "To Fashion a Text." *Inventing the Truth: The Art and Craft of Memoir*. Ed. William Zinsser. Boston: Houghton-Mifflin, 1987. 53–76.

Duncan, David James. "Nonfiction = Fiction." *Orion* 15:3 (Summer 1996): 55–57.

Gornick, Vivian. "A Memoirist Defends Her Words." http://archive.salon.com/books/feature/2003/08/12/memoir—writing/index.html.

Gutkind, Lee. "From the Editor." *Creative Nonfiction* 1:1 (1993): v–vi.

Hongo, Garrett. *Volcano: A Memoir of Hawai'i*. New York: Knopf, 1995.

Karr, Mary. *The Liar's Club: A Memoir*. New York: Viking Penguin, 1995.

Kramer, Mark. "Breakable Rules for Literary Journalists." *Literary Journalism*. Ed. Norman Sims and Mark Kramer. New York: Ballantine, 1995. 21–34.

Lopate, Phillip. "Introduction." *The Art of the Personal Essay: An Anthology from the Classical Era to the Present*. New York: Anchor/Doubleday, 1994. xxiii–liv.

Lounsbery, Barbara. *The Art of Fact: Contemporary Artists of Nonfiction*. Contributions to the Study of World Literature, No. 35. New York: Greenwood Press, 1990.

Montaigne, Michel de. *The Complete Works*. Trans. Donald M. Frame. Stanford: Stanford University Press, 1957. 761.

Olson, W. Scott. "Introduction." *Old Friends, New Neighbors: A Celebration of the American Essay*. Ed. W. Scott Olson. *American Literary Review* 5:2 (Fall 1994): v–viii.

Thoreau, Henry David. *Walden*. Ed. J. Lyndon Shanley. Princeton: Princeton University Press, 1973. 3

Torgovnick, Marianna. "Introduction." *Eloquent Obsessions: Writing Cultural Criticism*. Ed. Marianna Torgovnick. Durham: Duke University Press, 1994.

Part 1

Writing Creative Nonfiction

Contemporary creative nonfiction, like any other literary genre, offers a great deal of latitude to writers in terms of what they are able to do in the form. "There are as many kinds of essays as there are human attitudes or poses," the great American essayist E. B. White once observed. "The essayist rises in the morning and, if he has work to do, selects his garb from an unusually extensive wardrobe: he can pull on any sort of shirt, be any sort of person, according to his mood or his subject matter—philosopher, scold, jester, raconteur, confidant, devil's advocate, enthusiast" (vii). In general the observation is appropriate for the whole range of creative nonfiction.

This section of the book samples widely from the range of contemporary creative nonfiction. Its selections reveal the variety of voices and personas, the flexibility and expansiveness, and the range of subject matter and structures creative nonfiction may adopt. It is a representative blend, demonstrating the malleability of the genre. Some pieces are fairly straightforward examples of the traditional personal essay, such as Dagoberto Gilb tracing a random encounter on a train and Phillip Lopate rambling discursively over the subject of his own body. Others center on nature or environmental or ecological topics but vary their approaches; Nancy Lord fashions a brief lyric essay from a conversation with a man who claims to have seen the ivory-billed woodpecker, Tom Montgomery-Fate tells us what he observes of ecological change during a walk along a familiar river, and Scott Russell Sanders muses on the beauty and power of nature on a hike with his infant son. Some examples of literary journalism center on different approaches to examining place, as Pico Iyer does with Los Angeles International Airport and John McPhee does with Atlantic City, or the activities of people, as Shari Caudron does with Barbie collectors and Susan Orlean does with taxidermists. The personal approach to cultural criticism allows Richard Rodriguez to ponder what California has become and Chet Raymo to explore the intersection of science and religion.

The range of approaches within a subgrouping suggests the flexibility of the form, the ways writers use creative nonfiction not as a vessel to be filled with meaning but rather as a way of constructing a shape appropriate to the meaning they create by writing. The ways that Mary Clearman Blew, Judith Ortiz Cofer, and Angela Balcita present their remembrances of parents and of childhood vary as much as their experiences growing up did. The techniques with which other writers present the past vary as well. For example, Jo Ann Beard uses a highly fictional technique to record her disturbing encounter on a highway, Jonathan Lethem gives us a series of moments from his obsessive viewing of *Star Wars*, and Kate Petersen writes about what she knows as a lyric essay rather than as a personal narrative. These readings suggest that the writer's feeling about the subject has more to do with the way the final version reads than any arbitrary set of generic guidelines. Even as we hint at the variety of the pieces in this part of the book, we have to acknowledge the futility of labels. Most of the selections can be classified a number of different ways. For example, Michael Steinberg's "Chin Music" is not only about an adolescent passion for baseball but also about the limits of compromise to achieve one's goals as well as the way memories help him reach a decision about his own teaching. Here, as in so many of these readings, we discover again that it is not a uniform structure or organization that links these selections but the common thread of the writer's personal presence, some times at considerable remove in essays not obviously about personal experience yet nevertheless there, examining subject matter in the light of personal inquiry.

A number of these pieces are what we term *segmented essays*, pieces that try out nonlinear patterns or structures. Lisa Groen Braner's short review of her life is scored with its soundtrack; Mary Clearman Blew's essay weaves among different family members and different times and events to piece together elements of family history; Nicole Lamy presents a series of snapshots as a history of places she's lived. Such structures let us see how intimately form and content are connected in creative nonfiction, and how they can be invented to serve the ends of the author. Moreover, they help extend our understanding of the range of writing creative nonfictionists do.

"What happened to the writer is not what matters; what matters is the large sense that the writer is able to *make* of what happened," Vivian Gornick once observed, writing about the author's presence in memoirs. "The narrator in a memoir is an instrument of illumination, but it's the writing itself that provides revelation" (5). These selections suggest to us the possibilities of form, structure, voice, persona, approach, presentation, ways of describing what happened, ways of making sense of what happened. Reading widely in Part 1 will not only give you a solid sense of what we write when we write creative nonfiction but also open up your own possibilities for subject matter and design. Reading other writers triggers our own memories and our own speculations. We don't so much imitate others' subjects and structures as use them as a bridge to our resources and inventions.

Part 1, Writing Creative Nonfiction, is in effect a mini-anthology of contemporary writing. As such it is complemented by the other two parts of the book, and we invite you to explore those other sections in connection with your reading in this part. For example, when reading the memoirs by Mary Clearman Blew and Patricia Hampl in Part 1, you may want to read their essays about the memoir in

Part 2, a section where writers talk about creative nonfiction, and/or Maureen Stanton's selections about memoir in Part 3, which pairs writers' essays with articles explaining how they wrote them. Or you might follow up Chet Raymo's essay on the Gallarus Oratory in Part 1 by reading Marianna Torgovnick's article about personal academic writing in Part 2 and Emily Chase's pair of readings in Part 3, a literary essay and an account of writing the literary essay. There are many possibilities for interaction among these three sections of the book.

Writers always find it helpful to see what other writers are doing, to hear them talk about how they are doing it, and to free-associate with their own memories and reflections from the ideas and stories that others share. Those who read these selections with a writer's eye will discover insights and perspectives that will serve their own writing well.

Works Cited

Gornick, Vivian. "The Memoir Boom." *Women's Review of Books* 13: 10–11 (July 1996): 5.
White, E. B. "Foreword." *Essays of E. B. White*. New York: HarperCollins, 1997.

Dumpling

Angela M. Balcita

My mother is serious. She looks into my eyes demanding my attention. "One cup rice, two cup water, put all in rice cooker, press button." She turns toward the simple, white machine.

"For how long?" I ask her. But I already know; I've watched her make rice a million times. It's done when the big cloud of steam shrinks to just a puff, when the bubbling turns into a gurgle.

"Oh, you know, like twenty minute," she says, "Til is puffy and little sticky. That how we like it, right?" When she says *we*, she's not just talking about me and her, not just talking about our family. *We* means *we Filipinos.* "You know those Americans, they eat potatoes every night. Pasta, even!"

She continues, "Okay, next is—"

But I'm already gone—out the front door and down the street where I will ride bikes, make believe and play tag.

From the porch, my mother yells, "Okay, *anak*, but tomorrow, you cook!" I cringe at the sound of her voice. Her heavy accent bounces off the long line of identical houses, off the corrugated roofs, over the broad green lawns.

The summer is extraordinarily hot, and I'm spending too much time in the sun. My mother can tell by the color of my skin, which has turned a few shades darker than its usual brown. The neighborhood girls are amazed by how dark I get without burning. We sprawl in the wet grass like dogs. They touch my dark arms and my shiny shins, all warm from absorbing the heat of the sun. The blond girl with the braids can't stop looking at me. She's older, lives in the house behind ours. She has kissed, at least, one boy I know of. She asks me, "You mean you don't get sunburned at all?"

"No," I say, not quite sure what *sunburned* means, "I don't think so."

Her soft bubble gum lips swell slightly in a circle when she replies, "Oh." Her straight teeth are as clean as her chalky complexion. She shows me where the

5

sun has made her skin the color of strawberries. "Here, see my shoulders, see the tops of my feet." Grass pokes out between her orange painted toenails. "That's neat that you don't burn. You get so tanned."

My mother, however, does not approve. It's an American thing. "Is low class," she says. "Back home, the field workers are dark." Her skin, lighter than mine, is pale like butter, smooth as cream. "Don't let yourself get *uling, anak*." *Uling*, the Filipino word for *charcoal*, is the color she's afraid my skin will turn. To prevent this, she has decided that this summer will be spent in the kitchen learning to cook. It is the summer after my Barbie phase, the summer before I start to like boys. I am not at all intrigued by the idea of cooking, and I whine my way through my second lesson.

"Empanadas—you like, right?" she asks, her eyes searching for hope. Yes, I do. The small purses of baked dough filled with meat and raisins are perfect treats for little hands like mine. Of course, I like them. But in protest, I shrug indifferently.

"Okay, you know, we need meat, peas, raisins . . ." she recites the ingredients as half her body sticks out of the fridge. From what I can see, her form is completely different from my skinny, undeveloped frame. She is short and plump. Her body curves in places mine does not: around the hips, down her legs. Her face is wide and pale, her eyes thinner than mine. My boyish legs are slim, my arms awkward. Everyone says I take after my father.

The heat from the skillet makes the kitchen unbearably warm. I pose in front of the window above the sink. Outside, the sun seems to be heating everything, too. The pavement on the driveway looks sticky and moist, too dangerous to walk on with bare feet. I try to ignore my mother mumbling behind me, and the sweet smell of the onions caramelizing, and the rich, nutty aroma of beef simmering in the pan. I try to ignore the growl in my stomach. "In the fridge, *anak*," she calls to me, "there is some dough. Can you get it?" I turn around to find her with one hand on her hip, the other holding a spatula over the pot on the stove. I think she looks like a professional, like she knows what she's doing, like maybe this could be her job if she had one.

The pasty dough is stiff from resting in the fridge. "How are we going to make anything from this?" I ask her. "It's like a rock."

"I show you," she says. Taking the dough from me, she throws it down on the counter. With the heel of her hand she pushes the center of the clump down, then pulls its sides up with her fingers. "*Ay, anak*, is not too hard." She does this repeatedly and swiftly, talking the whole time. "We make it flat, and we make circles for the *empanadas*. Feel it. Is not so hard, no?" The pastry, now warm and soft, feels like clay in my hands. I grab at its swollen pockets of air. It curls within my fingers with ease and delicacy. It is elastic, like skin, when I pinch it. She tells me to roll it out with the pin, cut out the thin disks with the cookie cutter. "Flat like paper, 'kay?" she says. I use all my effort to push and roll out the dough. So much that my palms stick to the wood of the pin. I use the sharp, metal cookie cutter to press out little circles. They come cleanly away.

She turns to the iron pot cooling over the stove. "Okay, now you like extra raisins, right? The raisins are good but, you make sure the meat has pepper.

Or else, is no good." She tastes a small amount of the meat, nodding after she swallows. "Okay, is good." She holds out some for me to try. I bite in, recognizing all the flavors that pass over my tongue: the fruitiness of the raisins, the freshness of the tiny green peas, the pepper on the meat. She's right. The pepper adds enough spice to tingle in my mouth.

She pushes the pot closer to me and puts the spoon in my hand. I try to remember what empanadas look like. Filling a disk with a spoonful of mixture, I fold the center to make a half moon. On the open side, I crimp the dough with a series of little folds to make a seam.

"You know is good when you fit eighteen folds," my mother says. She is watching me. I feel her there, nodding with my every move.

I do eighteen folds on my first try and glance at her for approval. "Good, *anak*," she says. When she smiles, her small eyes disappear into straight black lines and her smooth white cheeks engulf her entire face.

By August, I start to sense that the season will end soon. The ice cream trucks will be replaced with school buses. My play clothes will dissolve into uniforms. The heart of my summer nights outside will drift from the low-lit, softly humming skies to the smooth, rounded cushions of the living room sofa. But when school finally starts, neither excitement nor anxiety hit me. I do not worry about the homework, or the newness of a classroom on the third floor. I sit in class all day thinking about what I will cook when I get home.

Sio Pao. My last lesson. The dumpling is a symbol of perfection. If it's made right, it will be perfectly round, perfectly white, smooth and shiny.

"The trick is the dough," my mother says. She squints with intensity. "You sift flour good, you knead dough good, you be okay." Gently rocking the flour in a mesh sieve, she blows white powder in the air. She hums while she sifts. She pours water into the bowl of flour, and blending those ingredients together, her bony hands slowly produce an airy ball of dough. She lays that on the counter. She starts to knead it, working her arms low, her shoulders rising and falling with all her weight.

"Now you help," and she pulls me towards her. Both our hands are working intensely into the pillow of white. I can feel the muscles in my forearms stretch and tighten. Before long, our hands are the same, the same skinny fingers, the same longish nails, the same joints and knuckles.

"You pull the dough away like this," she says, grabbing a fistful. She pokes her finger into the center of the small ball to make an indentation. "You put the meat in here," she says, "and one slice of hard-boiled egg. Mmmm, so good with egg, right?"

When all the balls are filled, we set them on the counter to rise. "Now, to steam," she says. My mother takes a tall bamboo steamer from behind the pantry door. It looks ancient. The wooden edges are frayed, and the rim has blackened with heat and use. She places it above a pot of boiling water. Immediately, the vapor rises through the grid inside the steamer.

When the dough balls are ready to be cooked, she leans over the steamer, and places one inside. The vapor rises around her face, through her hair. I want to tell her that she looks like an angel, like she's breaking through a cloud. But, instead, I tell her she looks like a witch making her brew.

She laughs. "If I am, you are, too, right?" She snorts a bit when she laughs. Her nose stretches flatly over her face. I place the rest of the dumplings inside for steaming. After they have all cooked, we take one out, and it is perfect. Its surface is shiny with no blemishes. It smells fresh and moist. I hold it up for her to look at.

"Wow, *anak*, how nice," she says. "You did it." There is a delight in her eyes, something I feel good about seeing. The idea suddenly comes to me that a dumpling this perfect should be shared, or at least shown off.

"I will bring it for lunch tomorrow," I tell her.

"Yes," she says, nodding, happy I am happy.

I wait all day for lunch. In the cafeteria, the long rectangular tables are covered with Ziploc bags and drink boxes. At first, the rustling never seems to stop. But patiently I wait for the perfect moment to unleash my special treat . . . my baby . . . my Sio Pao!

"What's that?" The boy sitting across from me is the first person to notice. His red hair shoots out from the back of his head like a fan.

"It's Sio Pao," I say proudly. "I made it myself." The white dumpling is tightly wrapped in cellophane to display its complete roundness.

"Is it like a Hostess snowball?" another boy asks. "You know, with coconut and stuff."

"No, it's filled with meat and egg."

"Eeeewwwww," small voices cry in unison.

"Where'd you get it?" the redhead asks.

"I told you I made it."

The girl next to me leans over and sniffs. "It smells weird," she says.

A singular, piercing voice calls out, "It's chink food!"

It is silent for a moment. Then, slowly, a chorus of giggles begin. Little ones that ring on and on. I feel the heat under my skin slowly climb up my face. My hands and armpits feel tingly and wet.

"Mike, that's not nice," my best friend's voice cuts through the laughter. I can only focus on her wide green eyes and the tiny freckles sprinkled over her nose. She tries to save me, but it doesn't help. I feel naked, or like I've peed myself and I stink.

I eat my Sio Pao in silence and quickly, not finishing the entire dumpling. The rest of the afternoon is endless.

When I get home, my mother is in the kitchen. Her hair is pulled back showing the gray in her roots. "Well, *anak*, how was your day?" She extends her hand to touch my hair, but I swerve to avoid her.

"Fine," I say, and walk past her to the living room.

"What we make tonight, huh?" she asks, smiling. Her voice is soft and comforting, but all I hear is her accent, her broken sentences, her unfinished words.

"Nothing," I say.

"*Anak*, what wrong?"

"Nothing," I snap back, "I don't want any of your chink food. I don't want anything." My voice is unbelievably loud, louder than I mean it to be. It vibrates against the hallway walls and in my ears. "Why can't you cook normal food?"

And with that, I have the strength to look into her face. The skin between her eyebrows is wrinkled; she's trying to understand. Her small eyes are open, glassy and unclear. It would be easy to look away now, but I try to stand my ground, to stay strong, to keep looking at her.

"Why, *anak*?" It's all she can say. She searches my face for some sign. But I don't want to talk about it.

"Forget it." I turn around, defiantly. Walking away, I leave her standing there stunned and alone.

Upstairs in my room, silence crawls around me. The bed feels larger than I remember, even though I'm sure I've grown an inch taller this year. I think she'll probably come and save me. I think if I wait long enough she'll come up here with something to eat or she'll persuade me down to dinner. I wait forever. Eventually, I fall asleep.

The windows are dark when I wake. My room has grown cooler, and other than that, the only thing I can feel is hunger.

Downstairs, dinner has been eaten without me. In the living room, my mother does not turn away from the TV show she is watching. She does not stir at my arrival. From behind, I stare into her black curtain of hair. If I stare long enough, she'll feel me there. Maybe she didn't hear me come in. I clear my throat, and cough pathetically. But she never turns around.

There are Japanese eggplants on the kitchen table, rice and fish. My older brother is the only one left finishing his plate. "Mom says if you don't want to eat what we eat, then you can get food somewhere else," he says, with no hint of sympathy.

I go outside, and listen to the sounds of our street. There are lightning bugs dotting the air in front of the house. They are green and sparkling. I think maybe I can stay out here and look at them forever, but then I remember that they'll be gone in a week.

Out There

Jo Ann Beard

It isn't even eight A.M. and I'm hot. My rear end is welded to the seat just like it was yesterday. I'm fifty miles from the motel and about a thousand and a half from home, in a little white Mazda with 140,000 miles on it and no rust. I'm all alone in Alabama, with only a cooler and a tape deck for company. It's already in the high 80s. Yesterday, coming up from the keys through Florida, I had a day-long anxiety attack that I decided last night was really heat prostration. I was a cinder with a brain; I was actually whimpering. I kept thinking I saw alligators at the edge of the highway.

There were about four hundred exploded armadillos, too, but I got used to them. They were real, and real dead. The alligators weren't real or dead, but they may have been after me. I'm running away from running away from home.

I bolted four weeks ago, leaving my husband to tend the dogs and tool around town on his bicycle. He doesn't love me anymore, it's both trite and true. He does love himself, though. He's begun wearing cologne and staring into the mirror for long minutes, trying out smiles. He's become a politician. After thirteen years he came to realize that the more successful he got, the less he loved me. That's how he put it, late one night. He won that screaming match. He said, gently and sadly, "I feel sort of embarrassed of you."

I said, "Of what? The way I look? The way I act?"

And he said, softly, "Everything, sort of."

And it was true. Well, I decided to take a trip to Florida. I sat on my haunches in Key West for four weeks, writing and seething and striking up conversations with strangers. I had my thirty-fifth birthday there, weeping into a basket of shrimp. I drank beer and had long involved dreams about cigarettes, I wrote nearly fifty pages on my novel. It's in my trunk at this very moment, dead and decomposing. Boy, do I need a cup of coffee.

There's not much happening this early in the morning. The highway looks interminable again. So far, no alligators. I have a box of seashells in my back seat and I reach back and get a fluted one, pale gray with a pearly interior, to put on the dashboard. I can do everything while I'm driving. At the end of this trip I will have driven 3,999 miles all alone, me and the windshield, me and the radio, me and the creepy alligators. Don't ask me why I didn't get that last mile in, driving around the block a few times or getting a tiny bit lost once. I didn't though, and there you have it. Four thousand sounds like a lot more than 3,999 does; I feel sort of embarrassed for myself.

My window is broken, the crank fell off in Tallahassee on the way down. In order to roll it up or down I have to put the crank back on and turn it slowly and carefully, using one hand to push up the glass. So, mostly I leave it down. I baked like a biscuit yesterday, my left arm is so brown it looks like a branch. Today I'm wearing a long-sleeved white shirt to protect myself. I compromised on wearing long sleeves by going naked underneath it. It's actually cooler this way, compared to yesterday when I drove in my swimming suit top with my hair stuck up like a fountain on top of my head. Plus, I'm having a nervous breakdown. I've got that wild-eyed look.

A little four-lane blacktop running through the Alabama countryside, that's what I'm on. It's pretty, too, better than Florida, which was billboards and condos built on old dump sites. This is like driving between rolling emerald carpets. You can't see the two lanes going in the opposite direction because there's a screen of trees. I'm starting to get in a good mood again. The best was Georgia, coming down. Willow trees and red dirt and snakes stretched out alongside the road. I kept thinking, That looks like a *rope*, and then it would be a huge snake. A few miles later I would think, That looks like a *snake*, and it would be some snarl of something dropped off a truck.

Little convenience store, stuck out in the middle of nothing, a stain on the carpet. I'm gassing it up, getting some coffee. My white shirt is gaping open and I have nothing on underneath it, but who cares, I'll never see these people again. What do I care what Alabama thinks about me. This is a new and unusual attitude for me. I'm practicing being snotty, in anticipation of being dumped by my husband when I get back to Iowa.

I swagger from the gas pump to the store, I don't even care if my boobs are roaming around inside my shirt, if my hair is a freaky snarl, if I look defiant and uppity. There's nothing to be embarrassed of. I bring my coffee cup along and fill it at the counter. Various men, oldish and grungy, sit at tables eating eggs with wadded-up toast. They stare at me carefully while they chew. I ignore them and pay the woman at the counter. She's smoking a cigarette so I envy her.

"Great day, huh?" I ask her. She counts out my change.

"It is, honey," she says. She reaches for her cigarette and takes a puff, blows it up above my head. "Wish I wudn't in *here*."

"Well, it's getting hotter by the minute," I tell her. I've adopted an accent in just four weeks, an intermittent drawl that makes me think I'm not who everyone thinks I am.

"Y'all think this's hot?" she says idly. "*This* ain't hot."

When I leave, the men are still staring at me in a sullen way. I get in, rearrange all my junk so I have everything handy that I need, choose a Neil Young tape and pop it in the deck, fasten the belt, and then move back out on the highway. Back to the emerald carpet and the road home. Iowa is creeping toward me like a panther.

All I do is sing when I drive. Sing and drink: coffee, Coke, water, juice, coffee. And think. I sing and drink and think. On the way down I would sing, drink, think, and weep uncontrollably, but I'm past that now. Now I suffer bouts of free-floating hostility, which is much better. I plan to use it when I get home.

A car swings up alongside me so I pause in my singing until it goes past. People who sing in their cars always cheer me up, but I'd rather not be caught doing it. On the road, we're all singing, picking our noses, embarrassing ourselves wildly; it gets tiresome. I pause and hum, but the car sticks alongside me so I glance over. It's a guy. He grins and makes a lewd gesture with his mouth. I don't even want to say what it is, it's that disgusting. Tongue darting in and out, quickly. A python testing its food.

I hate this kind of thing. Who do they think they are, these men? I've had my fill of it. I give him the finger, slowly and deliberately. He picked the wrong day to mess with me, I think to myself. I take a sip of coffee.

He's still there.

I glance over briefly and he's making the gesture with his tongue again. I can't believe this. He's from the convenience store, I realize. He has on a fishing hat with lures stuck in it. I saw him back there, but I can't remember if he was sitting with the other men or by himself. He's big, overweight, and dirty, wearing a thin unbuttoned shirt and the terrible fishing hat. His passenger-side window is down. He begins screaming at me.

He followed me from that convenience store. The road is endless, in front there is nothing, no cars, no anything, behind is the same. Just road and grass and trees. The other two lanes are still invisible behind their screen of trees. I'm all alone out here. With him. He's screaming and screaming at me, reaching out his right arm like he's throttling me. I speed up. He speeds up, too, next to me. We're only a few feet apart, my window won't roll up.

He's got slobber on his face and there's no one in either direction. I slam on my brakes and for an instant he's ahead of me, I can breathe, then he slams on his brakes and we're next to each other again. I can't even repeat what he's screaming at me. He's telling me, amid the hot wind and poor Neil Young, what he wants to do to me. He wants to kill me. He's screaming and screaming, I can't look over.

I stare straight ahead through the windshield, hands at ten and two. The front end of his car is moving into my lane. He's saying he'll cut me with a knife, how he'll do it, all that. I can't listen. The front end of his Impala is about four inches from my white Mazda, my little car. This is really my husband's car, my beloved's. My Volkswagen died a lingering death a few months ago. There is no husband, there is no Volkswagen, there is nothing. There isn't even a Jo Ann right now. Whatever I am is sitting here clenched, hands on the wheel, I've stopped being her, now I'm something else. I'm absolutely terrified. He won't stop screaming it, over and over, what he's going to do.

I refuse to give him an inch. I will not move one inch over. If I do he'll have me off the road in an instant. I will not move. I speed up, he speeds up, I slow down, he slows down, I can see him out of the corner of my eye, driving with one hand, reaching like he's grabbing me with the other. "You whore," he screams at me. "I'll *kill* you, I'll *kill* you, I'll *kill* you . . . "

He'll kill me.

If I give him an inch, he'll shove me off the road and get his hands on me, then the end will begin in some unimaginable, unspeakable style that will be all his. I'll be an actor in his drama. We're going too fast, I've got the pedal pressed up to 80 and it's wobbling, his old Impala can probably go 140 on a straightaway like this. There will be blood, he won't want me to die quickly.

I will not lose control. I will ride it out. I cannot let him push me over onto the gravel. His car noses less than two inches from mine; I'm getting rattled. My God, he can almost reach me through his window, he's moved over in his seat, driving just with the left hand, the right is grabbing the hot air. I move over to the edge of my seat, toward the center of the car, carefully, without swerving.

In the rearview mirror a speck appears. Don't look, watch your front end. I glance up again; it's a truck. He can't get me. It's a trucker. Without looking at him I jerk my thumb backward to show him. He screams and screams and screams. He's not leaving. Suddenly a road appears on the right, a dirty and rutted thing leading off into the trees. He hits the brakes, drops behind, and takes it. In my rearview mirror I see that the license plate on the front of his car is buried in dried mud. That road is where he was hoping to push me. He wanted to push my car off the highway and get me on that road. He was hoping to kill me. He was hoping to do what maniacs, furious men, do to women alongside roads, in woods. I can't stop pressing too hard on the gas pedal. I'm at 85 now, and my leg is shaking uncontrollably, coffee is spilled all over the passenger seat, the atlas is wet, Neil Young is still howling on the tape deck. By force of will, I slow down to 65, eject the tape, and wait for the truck to overtake me. When it does, when it comes up alongside me. I don't look over at all, I keep my eyes straight ahead. As it moves in front of me I speed up enough to stay two car lengths behind it. It says *England* on the back, ornate red letters outlined in black. England.

That guy chased me on purpose, he *hated* me, with more passion than anyone has ever felt for me. Ever. Out there are all those decomposing bodies, all those disappeared daughters, discovered by joggers and hunters, their bodies long abandoned, the memory of final desperate moments lingering on the leaves, the trees, the mindless stumps and mushrooms. Images taped to tollbooth windows, faces pressed into the dirt alongside a path somewhere.

I want out of Alabama, I want to be in England. The air is still a blast furnace. I want to roll my window up, but I'd have to stop and get the crank out and lift it by hand. I'm too scared. He's out there still, waiting behind the screen of trees. I have to follow England until I'm out of Alabama. Green car, old Impala, unreadable license plate, lots of rust. Seat covers made out of that spongy stuff, something standing on the dashboard, a coffee cup or a sad Jesus. The fishing hat with a sweat ring around it right above the brim. Lures with feathers and barbs.

I've never been so close to so much hatred in my whole life. *He wanted to kill me.* Think of England, with its white cows and broken-toothed farmers and dark green pastures. Think of the Beatles. I'm hugging the truck so closely now I'm almost under it. Me, of all people, he wanted to kill. Me. Everywhere I go I'm finding out new things about myself. Each way I turn, there it is. It's Jo Ann he wanted to kill.

By noon I want to kill him. I took a right somewhere and got onto the interstate, had the nerve to pee in a rest area, adrenaline running like an engine inside me, my keys threaded through my fingers in case anyone tried anything. I didn't do anything to earn it, I realize. His anger. I didn't do anything. Unless you count giving him the finger, which I don't. *He* earned that.

As it turned out, my husband couldn't bring himself to leave me when I got back to Iowa, so I waited awhile, and watched, then disentangled myself. History: We each got ten photo albums and six trays of slides. We took a lot of pictures in thirteen years. In the early years he looks stoned and contented, distant; in the later years he looks straight and slightly worried. In that last year he only appears by chance, near the edges, a blur of suffering, almost out of frame.

Just before we split, when we were driving somewhere, I told him about the guy in the green car. "Wow," he said. Then he turned up the radio, checked his image in the rearview mirror, and smiled sincerely at the passing landscape.

The Answer That Increasingly Appeals

Robin Black

A phenomenon that fascinates me:
Patina.

A fragment of something I wrote on that subject:
"Are we taking the patina approach?"
"Yes."
It was the only way.

I lived in fear of every scrape, of every drop of water on our new, much too expensive leather chair—until he asked and I answered and we took the patina approach. We held our eyes screwed shut for just about one year, the official period of mourning in many religions (mine to name but one), until each individual scratch and every stain just disappeared, merging into something wonderful.

A short period of endurance. In retrospect. For something so lovely.
(Forgiveness itself, as I now understand.)
It takes your breath away.

A funny question:
What exactly is my religion?

9:34 a.m. Nov. 7, voice mail message left by me:
"Rabbi, hi. My name is Robin Black, Robin Black Goldberg. My husband, Richard, and I are members of the synagogue, yours, and our daughter Elizabeth is having a bat mitzvah this coming April. Becoming a bat mitzvah this April. I guess that I'm calling because I am feeling some conflict about this due in part, maybe entirely, to the fact that my father, who is dying right now, isn't Jewish. My mother is.

"Anyway, we were wondering if we could come in to talk to you about this. Just us. Not Elizabeth. I am really not looking to dump my ambivalence on her. To burden her. Our phone number is 555-1429, and if we could come in, maybe just to sort some of this through, I would really appreciate that."

9:42 a.m. Nov. 7, overstatement to my husband made by me:
"Sometimes I feel that I am the bravest person I have ever met."

9:47 a.m. Nov. 7, deceptively complex thing my brother says to me on the phone:
"There's actually a new book out called *The Half-Jewish Book* that I was going to buy you for Christmas, but it costs twenty-five dollars. In fact, I was wondering if maybe this Christmas we could just skip grown-up gifts altogether."

9:47 a.m. Nov. 7, my immediate response:
"Actually, I could really use some presents this year."

My most prized possession:
The handsewn Christmas stocking my grandmother made for me. It's velvet, a deep red that I have never been able to match. Edged in green satin ribbon and covered with miniature toys. A half-inch frying pan with quarter-inch fried eggs. An impossibly small pair of scissors, which actually do cut. And jingle bells. There's a little baby doll girl attached to the center of the front, and when you lay the stocking flat her eyes fall shut. But when the stocking is hung, her eyes open wide. They're blue, just like mine. I liked knowing as a child that the doll was hanging there to watch Santa Claus when he arrived. I named her Robin, after myself.

6:03 p.m. Nov. 7, snippet of conversation between my husband and me:
"The rabbi didn't return my call, by the way. I guess my spiritual crisis can just wait."
"Well, I'm not trying to excuse the guy, but generally Monday is their day off. They work weekends, you know."
"Oh. No. I didn't know."

10:12 a.m. Nov. 8, snippet of my telephone conversation with the rabbi:
"So, I don't know, I assume, Rabbi, that this isn't uncommon. People who are mixed. Having mixed feelings. You've dealt with this kind of thing before, I assume?"
"Well, yes. Though usually it's been resolved by now."
"Oh."
"But why don't you and Richard come in and we'll see where we go from here."
"Thank you. That would be great."

Reason my father is concerned about authorizing anyone to pull the plug:
Fear of eternal damnation as a result of assisting in his own suicide, which is a mortal sin.

Helpful hint from me to you:

The proportions on the Manischewitz Matzo Meal box are wrong. In their matzo ball recipe. You want to put in a lot more liquid than they say. Twice as much. And you want to let the mixture get back up to room temperature after you have refrigerated it. And you want to refrigerate it for longer than they say. And sometimes, for reasons I will never understand, you may have to let them cook for up to three times as long as you think. Even if you have done absolutely everything else right.

4:32 p.m. Nov. 8, statement made by me to Elizabeth that documents my ambivalence about not burdening Elizabeth with my ambivalence:

"We're going to meet with the rabbi on Friday to discuss my feelings about your bat mitzvah."

Something about Elizabeth that started when she was ten, the meaning of which I do not understand:

She won't eat pork.

Way she handled this when we were in Italy, where just about every sauce contains pork:

Asked her parents loudly at every meal: "Is this pig?"

Something that I like about myself:

Despite enormous temptation, born of tremendous inconvenience (not to mention irritation) I have never misled Elizabeth about whether something we were eating was or was not pig. And never will.

Precise cost, tax excluded, of The Half-Jewish Book: A Celebration:

USA $22.95
CANADA $32.95

A request for advice:

To Whom It May Concern,

I have a question. I am in need of some advice.

I am meeting with my rabbi this coming Friday to discuss with him the ambivalence I feel as a half-Jew/half-Southern Methodist in having my daughter bat mitzvahed this coming spring. In having her become a bat mitzvah, that is. My husband will also be at this meeting. I do not know the rabbi at all, but he is about our age, either side of forty. I assume that he is a spiritual person, at least I hope that he is, and I hope that he is an intelligent person as well. Because I think that the problem I am struggling with is a complex one, quicksilver, a matter of balance and of shades of identity.

I have chosen to raise my daughter as a Jew for two reasons. The first is that it is important to my husband that she be raised that way—though to be fair, he would be fair. He's not a bully on matters like this. Or anything, in fact. Not at all. But I like giving him this. The second reason is that I want her to have somewhere to turn in times of loss. I want her to have a spiritual home to come home to. When life hurts her. If she chooses to. I don't have a home like that, and when I have been hit hard, hit with grief, I have longed for that. I have felt at sea.

I think that it's too late for me, but this is a gift of sorts that I want to give to her.

So my question is, on Friday, for this meeting, what should I wear? Seriously. This isn't the punch line. I don't know what the right thing is to wear. I've never met with a rabbi before.

Question Elizabeth will ask when my father dies:
"Am I allowed to say kaddish for Grandfather even though he wasn't Jewish?"

Authority with which I will say, "Of course":

Circa 1975, my mother on the subject of organized religion:
"It's all horseshit."

Throughout my childhood, my father on the subject of organized religion:
"If I really wanted to be rich, filthy rich, wealthy beyond all dreams of avarice, and did not believe in the Lord, Jesus Christ, which I most certainly do, I would make up a religion and just watch the money come pouring in."

After her heart attack, my mother, again, on the subject of religion:
"I know it's all horseshit, but are you comfortable promising me that someone will say kaddish for me when I am gone?"

Principle by which my cabinets are organized:
One cabinet is for food and one for ingredients. Some things, like dried beans and like sugar, are hard to categorize, but there are only two cabinets to look in. So nothing that we store is truly lost.

11:57 a.m. Nov. 10, driving to see the rabbi, nicest thing my husband has ever said:
"I love you, you know."

Rhetorical question I must never ask Elizabeth again:
"Do you have any idea what this is costing us?"

11:59 a.m. Nov 10, emotion that overwhelms me as we enter the synagogue hand in hand:
Sadness.

What I am wearing:
A black skirt and a black turtleneck. My earrings are made of miniature compasses that actually work, and my brooch is a teeny, tiny triptych of an Italian landscape. They all sort of go together because both the triptych and the compasses are framed in gold.

Number of minutes late the rabbi is for our meeting:
Twelve.

Noon to 12:12 p.m. Nov. 10, thing I try to do for twelve minutes:

Not to think the rabbi is keeping us waiting because he thinks that I am a bad Jew.

Letter I will never send:

To the Authors of *The Half-Jewish Book: A Celebration:*

First I would like to thank you. For celebrating me. Because I think that you're correct and it isn't done nearly enough. In my opinion. And thank you as well for making a few other points. Like that half-Jews are also half–something else. That the other half isn't just a blank. That's a very important observation and one that I agree does get lost in the shuffle all too often.

But now I have a terrible confession to make: I hated your book. First of all, there's no index, which is a pain in the ass, but that isn't my main issue here. I only mention the index problem because after I read it, something struck me as odd and I went to look up "religion" in the index. And there wasn't one. "Religion" or "religious observance" or "practices of mourning." Anything like that. But there was no index, and I'm pretty sure, having flipped through the pages again and read the chapter headings, absolutely no discussion of how half-Jews might comfortably handle issues of loss and of mourning. What the role of ritual is. No real examination of the pain that might be inherent for some of us in having nowhere obvious to turn. Because, while I do leave room here for individual choice, there does appear to be, judging from history and all, a pretty strong and common human pull toward wanting to believe. And toward wanting to know what it is that you believe. And what you don't.

And even toward belonging to a community that shares at least some of your beliefs. And that can help you, I don't know, perform rituals without thinking them through. Without having to make decisions about it all the time.

Is that a crime?

I personally find that an impossible thing to have.

Because every step toward one half is a step away from the other.

So I do agree with your basic premise, that there's a need to stop treating us all like the problem children of the Judeo-Christian era, but who's kidding whom here?

Simple, it is not.

Reason I will never send that letter:

I really haven't figured out why I hated their book so much. And it was kind of nice of them to celebrate me. And, as it turns out, I'm not particularly articulate on the subject of their book. Not yet.

Occasions for the grief that left me feeling at sea:

I lost two pregnancies, two babies I very much wanted to have.

12:25 p.m. Nov. 10, thing my husband accuses me of being, in front of the rabbi, that I deny:

Angry.

12:42 p.m. Nov. 10, statement I hear coming out of my own mouth:
"I feel like I am betraying my father. At a particularly inopportune time."

12:47 p.m. Nov. 10, thing the rabbi accuses me of being, in front of my husband, that I deny:
Angry.

How I feel at being accused of being angry:
Well, angry. Of course.

Snippet of conversation I have had with Elizabeth, time and time again:
Her: Why do I have to go to Hebrew School?
Me: Because nobody made me go.
Her: That doesn't make any sense.
Me: (sigh) I don't care what you do when you grow up. Honestly. I just want you to make whatever decisions you make from the inside. The inside of something.
Her: You make it sound so simple. Do you know even what we actually do?
Me: Humor me. I'm a mother. I'm allowed to make mistakes. Maybe this is another one.
Her: I don't think it's a mistake.
Me: So what's the problem?
Her: It's just boring, that's all.

What I have written so far of the speech I hoped to give at Elizabeth's bat mitzvah:
Just about thirteen years ago, when I was new to mothering, and was very close to drowning in the joy of having you, somebody, a friend, watching how I reveled in your every moment, said this to me. She said: Enjoy these days, because you know, the very first step that your child takes is taken away from you.

At the time, I thought that she was very wise, and maybe she was. And her wisdom wounded me, because all that I could feel was the completeness I knew in pressing you to my skin. So this image of your leaving me was painful for me, because it did ring true. And as it turns out, as I now see, it is true that with each day, with every new challenge you take on and meet so well, you do take steps away from being the baby I nestled against myself. You have likes and dislikes that differ from mine. You shed with every passing second another need you have for me. As you gain competence, strength, independence, tastes of your own. These qualities you have so beautifully acquired, and that you carry with you so gracefully.

But now I also know that even in her wisdom, my advisor left out the other side. The other view that I have gained, not from wisdom but through experience. The salve, the balm, the reason why every mother is not inevitably doomed to grief. For with each step that my baby girl takes away from me, a woman takes a step in my direction. A beautiful, competent, strong, brilliant, complex, compelling young woman who is my own. You are no further from me now, my love, than you were when you were first born. No further from me now than you were the moment before you were born. You are as close to me now when you stand beside me as you were pressed onto me, an infant, soft and sleeping, sprawled across my chest.

The number of pieces into which my heart breaks when I learn that there is no time allotted for the mother to speak:
　　　How many pieces are there?

12:41 p.m. Nov. 10, what my husband says as my eyes begin to fill:
　　　"Are you sure, Rabbi? It would be a really great way for her to feel involved."

One of many reasons I love my husband:
　　　Moments like that.

12:41 p.m. Nov. 10, the rabbi's response:
　　　"I'm afraid that isn't possible."

12:43 p.m. Nov. 10, obvious thing that suddenly occurs to me for the first time:
　　　This bat mitzvah isn't about me.

Reason my mother stopped lighting Shabbos candles when I was eight years old:
　　　She realized that she was just going through the motions, just reduplicating the customs of her home, and that she didn't believe in the ritual itself.

Two things Elizabeth invariably does at take-off in a plane:
　　　Prays in Hebrew.
　　　Holds tight onto her mother's hand.

12:56 p.m. Nov. 10, the one thing I know for sure:
　　　I want to go home.

Letter I may actually send someday:
　　　Dear Rabbi,
　　　It may not have looked like it to you at the time, but meeting with you when we did was actually a tremendous help to me. I actually had to eat some fairly good-size crow with my husband afterward. He had said seeing you might be helpful. I, well to be frank, I scoffed.
　　　I think that what you said to me that helped the most was . . .

Reason that that sentence never ends:
　　　I don't really understand why it helped. And to the extent that I think it did, it had nothing to do with him. And I just don't think you can say that in a letter of that kind. A thank-you note to your rabbi.
　　　In fact I think this is just another letter I will never send.

What I will do while my husband recites the parental blessings in Hebrew:
> Stand next to him. Hold his hand. And keep my lips sealed.

Question to ponder:
> If the rabbi had told me I'm a bad Jew, why would I care?

Fact that also needs to be pondered:
> I would care. I would care a great deal.

Question that persists:
> But why?

Odds that someday I will talk to a Christian minister about settling this sense of dislocation in myself:
> Fifty-fifty.

The most likely reason that my father will not be attending Elizabeth's bat mitzvah:
> He will be dead.

What it looks like when someone draws their dying breath:
> I can only tell you what my mother's mother looked like. I went to the door of her room, to check on her, because we knew that she wasn't going to last much longer. I loved her very much. She taught me how to cook. And when I saw her chest move up and then move down I thought to myself, Well, she's okay; and I stood there, in her doorway, relieved and safe because it hadn't happened yet. She lay buried deep in blankets, nothing much left of her, her long hair splayed out gray across a pink pillow case. And as I leaned against the doorjamb, the side with the mezuzah fastened there, watching her I slowly realized that her chest had never risen after that, and that what I had just witnessed was her death.

What my daughter eats when I have scrambled eggs and bacon:
> Scrambled eggs.

Where I am left to turn when I am in pain:
> Here. There.
> And everywhere.

A funny question, repeated one more time:
> What exactly is my religion?

Answer that increasingly appeals:
> The Patina Approach:
> A short period of endurance
> For something that is so lovely
> It takes your breath away.

The Unwanted Child

Mary Clearman Blew

December 1958. I lie on my back on an examination table in a Missoula clinic while the middle-aged doctor whose name I found in the Yellow Pages inserts his speculum and takes a look. He turns to the sink and washes his hands.

"Yes, you're pregnant," he says. "Congratulations, Mommy."

His confirmation settles over me like a fog that won't lift. Myself I can manage for, but for myself and *it?*

After I get dressed, he says, "I'll want to see you again in a month, Mommy."

If he calls me Mommy again, I will break his glasses and grind them in his face, grind them until he has no face. I will kick him right in his obscene fat paunch. I will bury my foot in his disgusting flesh.

I walk through the glass doors and between the shoveled banks of snow to the parking lot where my young husband waits in the car.

"You're not, are you?" he says.

"Yes."

"Yes, you're not?"

"Yes, I am! Jeez!"

His feelings are hurt. But he persists: "I just don't think you are. I just don't see how you could be."

He has a theory on the correct use of condoms, a theory considerably more flexible than the one outlined by the doctor I visited just before our marriage three months ago, and which he has been arguing with increasing anxiety ever since I missed my second period. I stare out the car window at the back of the clinic while he expounds on his theory for the zillionth time. What difference does it make now? Why can't he shut up? If I have to listen to him much longer, I will kill him, too.

At last, even his arguments wear thin against the irrefutable fact. As he turns the key in the ignition his eyes are deep with fear.

"But I'll stand by you," he promises.

Why get married at eighteen?

When you get married, you can move into married student housing. It's a shambles, it's a complex of converted World War II barracks known as the Strips, it's so sorry the wind blows through the cracks around the windows and it lacks hot-water heaters and electric stoves, but at least it's not the dormitory, which is otherwise the required residence of all women at the University of Montana. Although no such regulations apply to male students, single women must be signed in and ready for bed check by ten o'clock on weeknights and one on weekends. No alcohol, no phones in rooms. Women must not be reported on campus in slacks or shorts (unless they can prove they are on their way to a physical education class), and on Sundays they may not appear except in heels, hose, and hat. A curious side effect of marriage, however, is that the responsibility for one's virtue is automatically transferred from the dean of women to one's husband. Miss Maurine Clow never does bed checks or beer checks in the Strips.

When you get married, you can quit making out in the back seat of a parked car and go to bed in a bed. All young women in 1958 like sex. Maybe their mothers had headaches or hang-ups, but *they* are normal, healthy women with normal, healthy desires, and they know the joy they will find in their husbands' arms will—well, be better than making out, which, though none of us will admit it, is getting to be boring. We spend hours shivering with our clothes off in cars parked in Pattee Canyon in subzero weather, groping and being groped and feeling embarrassed when other cars crunch by in the snow, full of onlookers with craning necks, and worrying about the classes we're not attending because making out takes so much time. We are normal, healthy women with normal, healthy desires if we have to die to prove it. Nobody has ever said out loud that she would like to go to bed and *get it over with* and get on with something else.

There's another reason for getting married at eighteen, but it's more complicated.

By getting married I have eluded Dean Maurine Clow only to fall into the hands of in-laws.

"We have to tell the folks," my husband insists. "They'll want to know."

His letter elicits the predictable long-distance phone call from them. I make him answer it. While he talks to them I rattle dishes in the kitchen, knowing exactly how they look, his momma and his daddy in their suffocating Helena living room hung with mounted elk antlers and religious calendars, their heads together over the phone, their faces wreathed in big grins at his news.

"They want to talk to you," he says finally. Then, "Come on!"

I take the phone with fear and hatred. "Hello?"

"Well!!!" My mother-in-law's voice carols over the miles. "I guess this is finally the end of college for you!"

A week after Christmas I lean against the sink in my mother's kitchen at the ranch and watch her wash clothes.

She uses a Maytag washing machine with a wringer and a monotonous, daylong chugging motor which, she often says, is a damn sight better than a washboard. She starts by filling the tub with boiling water and soap flakes. Then she agitates her whites for twenty minutes, fishes them out with her big fork, and feeds them sheet by sheet into the wringer. After she rinses them by hand, she reverses the wringer, and feeds them back through, creased and steaming hot, and carries them out to the clothesline to freeze dry. By this time the water in the tub has cooled off enough for the coloreds. She'll keep running through her loads until she's down to the blue jeans and the water is thick and greasy. My mother has spent twenty-five years of Mondays on the washing.

I know I have to tell her I'm pregnant.

She's talking about college, she's quoting my grandmother, who believes that every woman should be self-sufficient. Even though I'm married now, even though I had finished only one year at the University of Montana before I got married, my grandmother has agreed to go on lending me what I need for tuition and books. Unlike my in-laws, who have not hesitated to tell me I should go to work as a typist or a waitress to support my husband through college (after all, he will be supporting me for the rest of my life), my grandmother believes I should get my own credentials.

My mother and grandmother talk about a teaching certificate as if it were a gold ring which, if I could just grab it, would entitle the two of them to draw a long breath of relief. Normally I hate to listen to their talk. They don't even know you can't get a two-year teaching certificate now, you have to go the full four years.

But beyond the certificate question, college has become something that I never expected and cannot explain: not something to grab and have done with but a door opening, a glimpse of an endless passage and professors who occasionally beckon from far ahead—like lovely, elderly Marguerite Ephron, who lately has been leading four or five of us through the *Aeneid*. Latin class has been my sanctuary for the past few months; Latin has been my solace from conflict that otherwise has left me as steamed and agitated as my mother's whites, now churning away in the Maytag; Latin in part because it is taught by Mrs. Ephron, always serene, endlessly patient, mercilessly thorough, who teaches at the university while Mr. Ephron works at home, in a basement full of typewriters with special keyboards, on the translations of obscure clay tablets.

So I've been accepting my grandmother's money under false pretenses. I'm not going to spend my life teaching around Fergus County the way she did, the way my mother would have if she hadn't married my father. I've married my husband under false pretenses, too; he's a good fly-fishing Helena boy who has no idea in the world of becoming a Mr. Ephron. But, subversive as a foundling in a fairy tale, I have tried to explain none of my new aspirations to my mother or grandmother or, least of all, my husband and his parents, who are mightily distressed as it is by my borrowing money for my own education.

"—and it's all got to be paid back, you'll be starting your lives in *debt!*"

"—the important thing is to get *him* through, *he's* the one who's got to go out and face the world!"

"—what on earth do you think you'll do with your education?"

And now all the argument is pointless, the question of teaching certificate over quest for identity, the importance of my husband's future over mine, the relentless struggle with the in-laws over what is most mine, my self. I'm done for, knocked out of the running by the application of a faulty condom theory.

"Mom," I blurt, "I'm pregnant."

She gasps. And before she can let out that breath, a frame of memory freezes with her in it, poised over her rinse tub, looking at me through the rising steam and the grinding wringer. Right now I'm much too miserable to wonder what she sees when she looks at me: her oldest daughter, her bookish child, the daydreamer, the one she usually can't stand, the one who takes everything too seriously, who will never learn to take no for an answer. Thin and strong and blue-jeaned, bespectacled and crop-haired, this girl could pass for fifteen right now and won't be able to buy beer in grocery stores for years without showing her driver's license. This girl who is too miserable to look her mother in the face, who otherwise might see in her mother's eyes the years of blight and disappointment. She does hear what her mother says:

"Oh, Mary, no!"

My mother was an unwanted child. The fourth daughter of a homesteading family racked by drought and debt, she was only a year old when the sister nearest her in age died of a cancerous tumor. She was only two years old when the fifth and last child, the cherished boy, was born. She was never studious like her older sisters nor, of course, was she a boy, and she was never able to find her own ground to stand on until she married.

Growing up, I heard her version often, for my mother was given to a kind of continuous oral interpretation of herself and her situation. Standing over the sink or stove, hoeing the garden, running her sewing machine with the permanent angry line deepening between her eyes, she talked. Unlike the stories our grandmothers told, which, like fairy tales, narrated the events of the past but avoided psychological speculation ("Great-great-aunt Somebody-or-other was home alone making soap when the Indians came, so she waited until they got close enough, and then she threw a ladle of lye on them . . ."), my mother's dwelt on the motives behind the darkest family impulses.

"Ma never should have had me. It was her own fault. She never should have had me if she didn't want me."

"But then you wouldn't have been born!" I interrupted, horrified at the thought of not being.

"Wouldn't have mattered to me," she said. "I'd never have known the difference."

What I cannot remember today is whom my mother was telling her story to. Our grandmothers told their stories to my little sisters and me, to entertain us, but my mother's bitter words flowed past us like a river current past small, ignored onlookers who eavesdropped from its shores. I remember her words, compulsive, repetitive, spilling out over her work—for she was always working—and I was awed by her courage. What could be less comprehensible than not wanting to be? More fearsome than annihilation?

Nor can I remember enough about the circumstances of my mother's life during the late 1940s and the early 1950s to know why she was so angry, why she was so compelled to deconstruct her childhood. Her lot was not easy. She had married into a close-knit family that kept to itself. She had her husband's mother on her hands all her life, and on top of the normal isolation and hard work of a ranch wife of those years, she had to provide home schooling for her children.

And my father's health was precarious, and the ranch was failing. The reality of that closed life along the river bottom became more and more attenuated by the outward reality of banks and interest rates and the shifting course of agribusiness. She was touchy with money worries. She saw the circumstances of her sisters' lives grow easier as her own grew harder. Perhaps these were reasons enough for rage.

I recall my mother in her middle thirties through the telescoped eye of the child which distorts the intentions of parents and enlarges them to giants. Of course she was larger than life. Unlike my father, with his spectrum of ailments, she was never sick. She was never hospitalized in her life for any reason but childbirth, never came down with anything worse than a cold. She lugged the armloads of wood and buckets of water and slops and ashes that came with cooking and washing and ironing in a kitchen with a wood range and no plumbing; she provided the endless starchy meals of roast meat and potatoes and gravy; she kept salads on her table and fresh or home-canned vegetables at a time when iceberg lettuce was a town affectation.

She was clear-skinned, with large gray eyes that often seemed fixed on some point far beyond our familiar slopes and cutbanks. And even allowing for the child's telescoped eye, she was a tall woman who thought of herself as oversized. She was the tallest of her sisters. "*As big as Doris* is what they used to say about me!"

Bigness to her was a curse. "You big ox!" she would fling at me over some altercation with my little sister. True to the imperative that is handed down through the generations, I in turn bought my clothes two sizes too large for years.

All adult ranch women were fat. I remember hardly a woman out of her teens in those years who was not fat. The few exceptions were the women who had, virtually, become a third sex by taking on men's work in the fields and corrals; they might stay as skinny and tough in their Levis as hired hands.

But women who remained women baked cakes and cream pies and breads and sweet rolls with the eggs from their own chickens and the milk and butter and cream from the cows they milked, and they ate heavily from appetite and from fatigue and from the monotony of their isolation. They wore starched cotton print dresses and starched aprons and walked ponderously beside their whiplash husbands. My mother, unless she was going to be riding or helping in the hayfields, always wore those shapeless, starched dresses she sewed herself, always cut from the same pattern, always layered over with an apron.

What was she so angry about? Why was her forehead kneaded permanently into a frown? It was a revelation for me one afternoon when she answered a knock at the screen door, and she smiled, and her voice lifted to greet an old friend of hers and my father's from their single days. Color rose in her face, and she looked pretty as she told him where he could find my father. Was that how outsiders always saw her?

Other ranch women seemed cheerful enough on the rare occasions when they came in out of the gumbo. Spying on them as they sat on benches in the shade outside the horticulture house at the county fair or visited in the cabs of trucks at rodeos, I wondered if these women, too, were angry when they were alone with only their children to observe them. What secrets lay behind those vast placid, smiling faces, and what stories could their children tell?

My mother believed that her mother had loved her brother best and her older sisters next best. "He was always The Boy and they were The Girls, and Ma was proud of how well they did in school," she explained again and again to the walls, the stove, the floor she was mopping, "and I was just Doris. I was average."

Knowing how my grandmother had misjudged my mother, I felt guilty about how much I longed for her visits. I loved my grandmother and her fresh supply of stories about the children who went to the schools she taught, the games they played, and the books they read. School for me was an emblem of the world outside our creek-bottom meadows and fenced mountain slopes. At eight, I was still being taught at home; our gumbo road was impassable for most of the school months, and my father preferred that we be kept safe from contact with "them damn town kids," as he called them. Subversively I begged my grandmother to repeat her stories again and again, and I tried to imagine what it must be like to see other children every day and to have a real desk and real lessons. Other than my little sister, my playmates were mostly cats. But my grandmother brought with her the breath of elsewhere.

My mother's resentment whitened in intensity during the weeks before a visit from my grandmother, smoldered during the visit itself, and flared up again as soon as my grandmother was safely down the road to her next school. "I wonder if she ever realizes she wouldn't even have any grandchildren if I hadn't got married and had some kids! *The Girls* never had any kids! Some people should never have kids! Some people should never get married!"

With a child's logic, I thought she was talking about me. I thought I was responsible for her anger. I was preoccupied for a long time with a story I had read about a fisherman who was granted three wishes; he had used his wishes badly, but I was sure I could do better, given the chance. I thought a lot about how I would use three wishes, how I would use their potential for lifting me out of the present.

"What would you wish for, if you had three wishes?" I prodded my mother.

She turned her faraway gray eyes on me, as though she had not been ranting about The Girls the moment before. "I'd wish you'd be good," she said.

That was what she always said, no matter how often I asked her. With everything under the sun to wish for, that unfailing answer was a perplexity and a worry.

I was my grandmother's namesake, and I was a bookworm like my mother's older sisters. Nobody could pry my nose out of a book to do my chores, even though I was marked to be the outdoor-working child, even though I was supposed to be my father's boy.

Other signs that I was not a boy arose to trouble us both and account, I thought, for my mother's one wish.

"Mary's getting a butt on her just like a girl," she remarked one night as I climbed out of the tub. Alarmed, I craned my neck to see what had changed about my eight-year-old buttocks.

"Next thing, you'll be mooning in the mirror and wanting to pluck your eyebrows like the rest of 'em," she said.

"I will not," I said doubtfully.

I could find no way through the contradiction. On the one hand, I was a boy (except that I also was a bookworm), and my chores were always in the barns and corrals, never the kitchen. *You don't know how to cook on a wood stove?* my mother-in-law was to cry in disbelief. *And you grew up on a ranch?*

To act like a boy was approved; to cry or show fear was to invite ridicule. *Sissy! Big bellercalf!* On the other hand, I was scolded for hanging around the men, the way ranch boys did. I was not a boy (my buttocks, my vanity). What was I?

"Your dad's boy," my mother answered comfortingly when I asked her. She named a woman I knew. "Just like Hazel. Her dad can't get along without her."

Hazel was a tough, shy woman who rode fences and pulled calves and took no interest in the country dances or the "running around" her sisters did on weekends. Hazel never used lipstick or permed her hair; she wore it cut almost like a man's. Seen at the occasional rodeo or bull sale in her decently pressed pearl-button shirt and new Levis, she stuck close to her dad. Like me, Hazel apparently was not permitted to hang around the men.

What Hazel did not seem interested in was any kind of fun, and a great resolve arose in me that, whatever I was, I was going to have . . . whatever it was. I would get married, even if I wasn't supposed to.

But my mother had another, darker reason to be angry with me, and I knew it. The reason had broken over me suddenly the summer I was seven and had been playing, on warm afternoons, in a rain barrel full of water. Splashing around, elbows and knees knocking against the side of the barrel, I enjoyed the rare sensation of being wet all over. My little sister, four, came and stood on tiptoe to watch. It occurred to me to boost her into the barrel with me.

My mother burst out of the kitchen door and snatched her back.

"What are you trying to do, kill her?" she shouted.

I stared back at her, wet, dumbfounded.

Her eyes blazed over me, her brows knotted at their worst. "And after you'd drowned her, I suppose you'd have slunk off to hide somewhere until it was all over!"

It had never crossed my mind to kill my sister, or that my mother might think I wanted to. (Although I had, once, drowned a setting of baby chicks in a rain barrel.) But that afternoon, dripping in my underpants, goose-bumped and ashamed, I watched her carry my sister into the house and then I did go off to hide until it was, somehow, all over, for she never mentioned it at dinner.

The chicks had been balls of yellow fuzz, and I had been three. I wanted them to swim. I can just remember catching a chick and holding it in the water until it stopped squirming and then laying it down to catch a fresh one. I didn't stop until I had drowned the whole dozen and laid them out in a sodden yellow row.

What the mind refuses to allow to surface is characterized by a suspicious absence. Of detail, of associations. Memories skirt the edge of nothing. There is for me about this incident that suspicious absence. What is being withheld?

Had I, for instance, given my mother cause to believe I might harm my sister? Children have done such harm, and worse. What can be submerged deeper, denied more vehemently, than the murderous impulse? At four, my sister was a tender, trusting little girl with my mother's wide gray eyes and brows. A younger sister of an older sister. A good girl. Mommy's girl.

What do I really know about my mother's feelings toward her own dead sister? Kathryn's dolls had been put away; my mother was never allowed to touch them.

"I'll never, never love one of my kids more than another!" she screamed at my father in one of her afternoons of white rage. The context is missing.

During the good years, when cattle prices were high enough to pay the year's bills and a little extra, my mother bought wallpaper out of a catalog and stuck it to her lumpy walls. She enameled her kitchen white, and she sewed narrow strips of cloth she called "drapes" to hang at the sides of her windows. She bought a stiff tight cylinder of linoleum at Sears, Roebuck in town and hauled it home in the back of the pickup and unrolled it in a shiny flowered oblong in the middle of her splintery front room floor.

Occasionally I would find her sitting in her front room on her "davenport," which she had saved for and bought used, her lap full of sewing and her forehead relaxed out of its knot. For a moment there was her room around her as she wanted it to look: the clutter subdued, the new linoleum mopped and quivering under the chair legs that held down its corners, the tension of the opposing floral patterns of wallpaper, drapes, and slipcovers held in brief, illusory harmony by the force of her vision.

How hard she tried for her daughters! Over the slow thirty miles of gumbo and gravel we drove to town every summer for dentist appointments at a time when pulling teeth was still a more common remedy than filling them, when our own father and his mother wore false teeth before they were forty.

During the good years, we drove the thirty miles for piano lessons. An upright Kimball was purchased and hauled home in the back of the pickup. Its carved oak leaves and ivories dominated the front room, where she found time to "sit with us" every day as we practiced. With a pencil she pointed out the notes she had learned to read during her five scant quarters in normal school, and made us read them aloud. "F sharp!" she would scream over the throb of the Maytag in the kitchen as one of us pounded away.

She carped about bookworms, but she located the dim old Carnegie library in town and got library cards for us even though, as country kids, we weren't strictly entitled to them. After that, trips home from town with sacks of groceries included armloads of library books. Against certain strictures, she could be counted on. When, in my teens, I came home with my account of the new book the librarian kept in her desk drawer and refused to check out to me, my mother straightened her back as I knew she would. "She thinks she can tell one of my kids what she can read and what she can't read?"

On our next visit to the library, she marched up the stone steps and into the mote-filled sanctum with me.

The white-haired librarian glanced up inquiringly.

"You got *From Here to Eternity*?"

The librarian looked at me, then at my mother. Without a word she reached into her drawer and took out a heavy volume. She stamped it and handed it to my mother, who handed it to me.

How did she determine that books and dentistry and piano lessons were necessities for her daughters, and what battles did she fight for them as slipping cattle prices put even a gallon of white enamel paint or a sheet of new linoleum beyond her reach?

Disaster followed disaster on the ranch. An entire season's hay crop lost to a combination of ancient machinery that would not hold together and heavy rains that would not let up. A whole year's calf crop lost because the cows had been pastured in timber that had been logged, and when they ate the pine needles from the downed tops, they spontaneously aborted. As my father grew less and less able to face the reality of the downward spiral, what could she hope to hold together with her pathetic floral drapes and floral slipcovers?

Bundled in coats and overshoes in the premature February dark, our white breaths as one, my mother and I huddle in the shadow of the chicken house. By moonlight we watch the white-tailed deer that have slipped down out of the timber to feed from the haystack a scant fifty yards away. Cautiously I raise my father's rifle to my shoulder. I'm not all that good a marksman, I hate the inevitable explosive crack, but I brace myself on the corner of the chicken house and sight carefully and remember to squeeze. Ka-crack!

Eight taupe shapes shoot up their heads and spring for cover. A single mound remains in the snow near the haystack. By the time my mother and I have climbed through the fence and trudged up to the haystack, all movement from the doe is reflexive. "Nice and fat," says my mother.

Working together with our butcher knives, we lop off her scent glands and slit her and gut her and save the heart and liver in a bucket for breakfast. Then, each taking a leg, we drag her down the field, under the fence, around the chicken house and into the kitchen, where we will skin her out and butcher her.

We are two mid-twentieth-century women putting meat on the table for the next few weeks. Neither of us has ever had a hunting license, and if we did, hunting season is

*long closed, but we're serene about what we're doing. "Eating our hay, aren't they?" says
my mother. "We're entitled to a little venison. The main thing is not to tell anybody what
we're doing."*

And the pregnant eighteen-year-old? What about her?

In June of 1959 she sits up in the hospital bed, holding in her arms a small
warm scrap whose temples are deeply dented from the forceps. She cannot remember birthing him, only the long hours alone before the anesthetic took over.
She feels little this morning, only a dull worry about the money, money, money
for college in the fall.

The in-laws are a steady, insistent, increasingly frantic chorus of disapproval
over her plans. *But, Mary! Tiny babies have to be kept warm!* her mother-in-law keeps
repeating, pathetically, ever since she was told about Mary's plans for fall quarter.

*But, Mary! How can you expect to go to college and take good care of a husband and
a baby?*

Finally, *We're going to put our foot down!*

She knows that somehow she has got to extricate herself from these sappy
folks. About the baby, she feels only a mild curiosity. Life where there was none
before. The rise and fall of his tiny chest. She has him on her hands now. She must
take care of him.

Why not an abortion?

Because the thought never crossed her mind. Another suspicious absence,
another void for memory to skirt. What she knew about abortion was passed
around the midnight parties in the girls' dormitory: *You drink one part turpentine
with two parts sugar. Or was it the other way around? . . . two parts turpentine to one
part sugar. You drink gin in a hot bath . . .*

She has always hated the smell of gin. It reminds her of the pine needles her
father's cattle ate, and how their calves were born shallow-breathed and shriveled, and how they died. She knows a young married woman who begged her
husband to hit her in the stomach and abort their fourth child.

Once, in her eighth month, the doctor had shot her a look across his table. "If
you don't want this baby," he said, "I know plenty of people who do."

"I want it," she lied.

No, but really. What is to become of this eighteen-year-old and her baby?

Well, she's read all the sentimental literature they shove on the high school
girls. She knows how the plot is supposed to turn out.

Basically, she has two choices.

One, she can invest all her hopes for her own future in this sleeping scrap.
*Son, it was always my dream to climb to the stars. Now the tears of joy spring at the sight
of you with your college diploma . . .*

Even at eighteen, this lilylicking is enough to make her sick.

Or two, she can abandon the baby and the husband and become really
successful and really evil. This is the more attractive version of the plot, but she
doesn't really believe in it. Nobody she knows has tried it. It seems as out of reach
from ordinary daylight Montana as Joan Crawford or the Duchess of Windsor or

the moon. As she lies propped up in bed with the sleeping scrap in her arms, looking out over the dusty downtown rooftops settling into noon in the waning Eisenhower years, she knows very well that Joan Crawford will never play the story of her life.

What, then? What choice is left to her?

What outcome could possibly be worth all this uproar? Her husband is on the verge of tears these days; he's only twenty himself, and he had no idea what trouble he was marrying into, his parents pleading and arguing and threatening, even his brothers and their wives chiming in with their opinions, even the minister getting into it, even the neighbors; and meanwhile his wife's grandmother firing off red-hot letters from her side, meanwhile his wife's mother refusing to budge an inch—united, those two women are as formidable as a pair of rhinoceroses, though of course he has no idea in the world what it took to unite them.

All this widening emotional vortex over whether or not one Montana girl will finish college. What kind of genius would she have to be to justify it all? Will it be enough that, thirty years later, she will have read approximately 16,250 freshman English essays out of an estimated lifetime total of 32,000?

Will it be enough, over the years, that she remembers the frozen frame of her mother's face over the rinse tub that day after Christmas in 1958 and wonders whether she can do as much for her son as was done for her? Or that she often wonders whether she really lied when she said, *I want it?*

Will it be enough? What else is there?

Soundtrack

Lisa Groen Braner

1968

He sings a Beatles song, "Hey Jude," when I am just a baby. It plays on the radio. There are four master composers that begin with the letter B, he tells me later: Beethoven, Brahms, Bach, and the Beatles. My dad sings the Beatles.

1974

I listen to Julie Andrews in my bedroom, scratch the needle across the black plastic and turn up the volume. My sister and I dance and sing about spoons of sugar and flying kites. The baby with fuzzy hair bounces and smiles in my mom's arms—our new sister.

1981

On a spring day after school, I walk home with a boy who plays guitar. He's an eighth-grader with Jimi Hendrix hands. When he plays "Fire" I feel it, watching him strum, sing, and stir. Electric.

1984

Whenever you get scared up here, Dad says, just sing James Brown. Point your skis downhill and sing "I Feel Good." So I do. I ski the powder and sing—tips under snow, around the trees and through the clouds—close behind him.

1990

"The Sky Is Crying" in my empty college apartment. In a room of two chairs, a table, my roommate's stereo, and a glass of wine, my first love shatters. The crack in my heart widens with each blue note B. B. breaks open, spilling Merlot all over the white carpet.

1993

In the workaday world of subway stops and newspapers, I lose myself. One morning, a song rises up in the station. A hidden man sings words that fall on me like raindrops in a desert—"Wade in the Water." I leave my job and start writing.

1994

My future husband and I walk together through the Tuileries. A love song plays, Billy Joel, against Paris twilight. It's a cold June and the crepes warm our hands as we walk past Notre Dame, over the Seine, onto a lamplit street.

1997

No heartbeat, says the doctor. No baby. I didn't hear much after that. As I drive home from the hospital, Mary Chapin Carpenter sings about trouble, sorrow, and choosing to fly. I pack her words away somewhere to play them back later when I can listen.

1998

My newborn son likes it when I sing "Rock-a-Bye-Baby." He locks eyes with me at my breast, smiling at the sudden song. Milk spills from his mouth and rolls down his chin, onto the collar of his clean pajamas. He forgets about the milk when I sing.

2000

I stand in an old pew swaying to a hymn I've never heard before while my new-born daughter sleeps on my shoulder. The words stop in my throat. "Precious Lord, take my hand." I sink into the sound and feel buoyant, helped to stand.

2006

I try to sing "Blue Bayou" for my dad, as I do for my children at night. I know the lyrics, the melody, but my voice won't carry today, not for him lying there dying. The song wavers flat. He is too tired and polite to protest. I stop and sit next to him. It's hard to sing when you're crying, I tell him. Without moving he nods his head yes and understands.

Lost on Colfax Avenue

John Calderazzo

Walking to the Tattered Cover bookstore past the lacy battlements of Denver East High and Pete's Greek restaurant, I hear a faint scrabbling of plastic on concrete. Not far down an empty side street I see a shaggy figure in an army surplus jacket waving a blind man's stick and turning uncertainly in the corner made by a locked warehouse and gray retaining wall. He takes a half step this way, then that, a green beetle trapped in a shoebox, one antenna gone.

He stops, letting his cane rest on the cracked sidewalk. I almost call out, then remind myself to give him time to work back through the bent geometry of his memory. Once, in a mangrove swamp in Florida, I lost myself in the late afternoon, paddling in circles in a canoe, snail-encrusted roots curving everywhere out of water, living walls too high to see over and too delicate to climb, threatening to crumble like branch coral under my weight. Ten thousand mirror-image islands darkened as the sky turned orange, then faded while mosquitoes closed in.

I willed myself to stop paddling. Then gravity began to show me the way, a ghost current I calmed myself enough to feel, following my breath out of myself, letting the flow tug me, finally, into the Nirvana of open water, where the line between silver sea and silver sky had disappeared. Like easeful death, I thought, not a place, but a state of mind I might float into the way this blind man cornered by concrete and his daily life might soon arrive at a calm center, as he stands in a garden waiting for flowers to break open, their fragrance laying a path of stones in whatever direction he needs to go. But now he waves the cane and turns again, and though I haven't moved or made a sound, he stops and faces me. He crooks an arm, lifts it, waits.

Befriending Barbie

Shari Caudron

Debbie Baker has extraordinary fingernails. They're long. Very long. And pink. Fantastically pink. So pink that if you weren't completely focused on your conversation with her, you'd be distracted by them. I'm trying not to be. I'm trying to learn why Debbie Baker has more than 3,000 Barbie dolls in her collection.

"So tell me," I ask, "what is it about Barbie that makes you so excited?"

Debbie straightens her right arm and gazes at her spread fingernails. "It's because Barbie is so beauuuutiful," she says. "She's hip. She keeps up with the trends. And she can do anything." Debbie falls silent for a moment as she thinks about all Barbie has accomplished. "I mean she can be a veterinarian. A stewardess. A secretary. *Anything.*"

I start to ask about Barbie's other careers when we're interrupted by a stout older woman with dull gray hair. "I need to put up the decorations for tonight's dinner and I can't get into the ballroom," she says. Debbie tells her to use the same entrance that was used for the fashion show. The woman stares at her, mystified.

"I'm with the design company," she says. "I didn't go to the fashion show."

"Oh!" Debbie apologizes. "You looked like a Barbie collector."

The woman widens her eyes and takes a step backward. She looks as if she's just been accused of being a racist, or wearing a thong. "I don't *think* so," she says, and huffs off.

Out of curiosity, I ask Debbie what a Barbie collector looks like.

"Those of us who love Barbie light up whenever we see anything to do with her. We love the dolls. We love the clothes. We love the Barbie '*B.*' And pink," she says, waving her lacquered nails. "We really, really love pink."

I've come to the 22nd annual National Barbie Doll Collectors Convention in an effort to understand the extraordinary attraction to the 11-1/2-inch plastic doll. A thousand men and women from all over the world have registered and converged on the Adam's Mark Hotel in downtown Denver for four days of doll shopping, workshops and social events.

According to people who study this sort of thing, doll collecting—especially Barbies—is second only to stamp collecting as the most popular collecting hobby in America. As an avowed non-collector, I want to know what the fuss is about. Years ago, I tried collecting antique Roseville pottery and actually managed to acquire five pieces before I lost three of them in a break-up. Of the two I have left, one is chipped and now worth maybe twelve dollars. I'm just not good at this sort of thing. I get bored easily. Plus, I think fanatics are a bit strange. I once attended a slide show given by an avid rock collector who described various pieces in her collection as "droolers" and "show-offs." After advancing to a slide of a rock with sparkling purple crystals, the rock collector slumped in her chair. "Ohhhh," she said. "This one could win a pageant." Afterward, I invited friends to stone me to death if I ever got like that. Because I'm not overly passionate by nature, I'm curious about people who are. A Barbie convention, the kind of place I'd normally not be caught dead at, seems the ideal place to understand where this kind of zeal comes from. Debbie Baker, the convention co-chair, is my first interview and she's giving me a crash course in all things Barbie.

"There are two kinds of collectors," she explains. First there are the people like her who keep their Barbies in the original boxes. To be of any value, the boxes must be clean with no razor cuts or dents. Debbie boasts that all of the 3,000 Barbies arranged around her small apartment are indeed fully boxed. The other group of collectors is known, somewhat disparagingly, as the "de-boxers." These are people who experience no remorse in removing Barbie from her cardboard casing even though the doll's value drops anywhere from forty to eighty percent upon exit. Debbie doesn't get these people.

"I can't watch anyone take Barbie out of her box," she says. "It hurts too much."

When pressed, Debbie confesses that when she first started collecting Barbies at age 18, she too was indiscriminate in her choice of dolls. In the box, out of the box—it didn't much matter. But she soon realized this lack of discipline would overwhelm her.

"If I bought every doll out there, I'd have no place to store them all," she says.

So Debbie decided early on to pursue only the most perfect and pristine specimens. Today, her collection is so valuable she's had to purchase additional insurance on her home.

"Do you collect anything else?" I ask.

"Oh definitely. I collect, let's see, Depression glass, elephants, butterflies, antiques. Oh, and chickens. I love chickens. My whole kitchen is filled with chickens. My convention co-chair also collects chickens and whenever we buy one for ourselves we have to buy one for each other."

"I see," I reply, although of course I don't see at all. I don't understand chickens. I don't understand Barbies. And while Debbie says that she would really like to spend more time with me, she has, you know, a convention to run. She stands and shakes my hand.

"Feel free to walk around," she says. "Barbie people are really friendly."

Debbie walks off to manage some co-chair mini-crisis and I walk into the convention sales area, which won't open for another fifteen minutes. Behind a pink cord, about 150 people wearing psychedelic clothing are standing in line. The theme of this year's conference is "Rocky Mountain Mod," which commemorates the Barbie era from 1968 to 1972, a time when Barbie wore bell-bottoms, hip-huggers and hot pants. To get into the spirit, conventioneers were encouraged to don their own mod-era clothing and every last one of them seems to have complied. In line are people wearing abstract geometric prints, Afro wigs and lime-green fringed vests. Two men at the front of the line are wearing matching striped bell-bottoms, white belts and platform shoes. Any moment now, I expect them to burst into a rendition of "I Got You Babe."

Taking advantage of my privileged position inside the pink cord, I walk around to get a good look at the sales items before the crowd converges. In the sales area, vendors are putting the final finishing touches on display booths and tables that are filled to overflowing with clothing, accessories, books, teeny-tiny jewelry, and more dolls than I've ever seen gathered in one place. The array of dolls is truly mind-boggling. There are I Love Lucy Barbies, Little Bo Peep Barbies, Erika Kane Barbies and Olympic Athlete Barbies. There are Barbies equipped for college, Barbies outfitted as medics in Desert Storm, and a presidential candidate Barbie who ran in both the 1992 and 2000 elections on a platform of animal rights, educational excellence and opportunity for girls. Obviously, Barbie is trying to repair her image. There's even a full military series of Barbies whose costumes, the boxes say, were approved by the Pentagon to ensure realism.

Turning a corner, I spot a boxed doll called the Big Boob Barbie. I stop to stare at it. Her. Whatever. How can there be a doll whose bust is bigger than the original Barbie whose figure, were she a real woman, would measure 39-18-33? I move to get a good look at Big Boob Barbie. She is lying on the sales table in a tight skirt and see-through blouse and appears identical to the standard-issue Barbie except that her breasts cover her entire torso and swell out spectacularly on either side of her body. Plus, she has large brown nipples. Something tells me this may not be an official issue from Mattel.

I stare at the doll with a kind of train-wreck fascination until Mattel's public relations representative, a thin young woman named Katie Caratelli, calls me from across the room.

"There you are!" she says.

I spin around in an effort to shield the well-endowed source of my enchantment. Either Katie hasn't noticed me staring at the doll, or she's too polite to mention it.

Katie grabs my elbow and steers me into an adjoining sales room, stopping along the way to point out the new 30th anniversary Malibu Barbie. "This is the official convention doll," she says, pointing to the dime-sized convention logo embroidered onto Malibu Barbie's tiny yellow beach towel. This particular Barbie has a turquoise one-piece bathing suit, surfboard-straight blond hair, and pink sunglasses just like the original Malibu Barbie thirty years ago. The only difference between that doll and this one is that this one comes equipped with sunscreen.

"See!" Katie says. "It's SPF 30!"

She picks up the box and holds it toward me with two hands as if she's presenting me with a bouquet of roses. I peer inside.

"Nice," I say, although in reality, I fail to come up with anything that resembles a reaction to the doll.

Katie puts the doll back on the shelf and we walk over to a large, well-stocked display booth in the center of the sales room. The booth features dolls from a company named Doll Attic, which is owned by Sandi Holder, a middle-aged woman from California with short reddish-brown hair. I chat with Sandi and learn that she started collecting Barbies when her two daughters were little. Her girls are now in high school and her collection has grown from a part-time family hobby into a 16-hour-a-day Barbie empire that does close to one million dollars in annual sales. She tells me her favorite Barbies are the Bubble Cuts.

"Which ones are those?" I ask.

Sandi leads me to a display table where rows of boxed dolls are stacked five high and arranged chronologically by year of issue. She tells me the Bubble Cuts were produced between 1961 and 1967 and were so named because of the lacquered bouffant-style hairdo. Picture Jackie Kennedy with reddish hair and you have some idea what a Bubble Cut is all about. As I admire the doll, my eyes catch sight of a vintage Barbie with a ponytail and black-and-white striped one-piece bathing suit.

Before I can stop myself, I tell Sandi, "That's the one my sisters played with!" Although I didn't play with Barbie, my older sisters had been fans and their old dolls—including the vintage Barbie on display here—were still around the house when I was a kid. Oddly, I find myself a little thrilled to recognize the doll. I confess this to Sandi.

She laughs. "That's what Barbie is all about," she says. "It's about reliving good memories and helping people get back a bit of their childhood." Sandi, who manages one of the largest Barbie auctions in the country, says the value of those childhood memories is going up each year. At her last auction, an in-the-box original Barbie issued in 1959 went for $15,750—a new auction record. The original price was three dollars. "But for me, money is secondary," she says. "What I like is bringing joy to people's lives."

I ask Sandi if she keeps her own dolls in their boxes. "No way!" she says. "It's like really anal to me to keep them in the box. Of course I respect people who want to do that. I mean, they're my customers. But when I see a Barbie who's been boxed for decades I feel like she's screaming: *Take me out! Take me out!*"

Sandi turns and introduces me to her assistant, George Marmolejo, a veterinarian from the San Francisco Bay Area who started collecting Barbies in the mid 1980s. He's short, wearing a tie-dyed T-shirt and a peace sign around his neck. At last count, he says, George had over 1,000 dolls in his collection, both in the box and out. Unlike other collectors, George swings both ways. But George's affection is not solely reserved for Barbie. He also collects children's books, old toys, vinyl records, and doll accessories.

"Some people collect fishing lures and duck decoys," he says. "That's not my thing, but I can understand why they do it. I mean I'm here, right?" George spreads his arms and looks around the sales room. "Where else can I be surrounded by 1,000 people who understand my passion and don't think I'm nuts when I spend $100 on doll clothes?"

I look around the room at zillions of dolls on display. Where else indeed?

George walks me through Barbie's various incarnations while pointing to dolls on the display table. I learn that Barbie #1 had an exotic face with white irises. Barbie #3 was less exotic, smelled like crayons, and had a tendency to fade. Barbie #5 was a red head with a hollow body. By the time she came around, the fading problem had been worked out.

We come to Sandi's favorite doll and in an effort to show off my new knowledge, I tell George: "Those are the Bubble Heads, right?"

He corrects me. "They're called Bubble *Cuts*."

George continues his historical tour and I learn about Talker Barbies, the American Girls, Twist 'n Turns—more commonly known as TNTs, and the Living Barbie, who was entirely posable and had flexible hands.

"Are there any other dolls still on your wish list?" I ask.

"Mostly, I'm satisfied with my collection."

"Really? There's nothing else you want?"

"Well," George admits. "I've been looking for a Glimmer Glamour Barbie, which was a Sears exclusive. She goes for between $1,700 and $1,800."

The 22nd Annual National Barbie Doll Collectors Convention is an especially poignant one for collectors because Ruth Handler, the Polish immigrant who created Barbie, recently passed away at the age of 85. After talking with George, I walk into the center of the convention area and see that a memorial to Handler has been set up on a card table. A vase with pink roses sits next to a journal where conference goers can record their thoughts. I scan the entries.

"Without Ruth Handler, all our lives would be emptier."

"Thank you for creating the most beautiful doll in the world that I love so much!!"

"I am 4-ever grateful."

Handler created Barbie, who was named after her daughter Barbara, to be a fashion show doll whose outfits could change with the season, and over the years Barbie's kept up her good fashion sense. According to a fact sheet by Mattel, the company Handler founded, Barbie has had more than a billion pairs of shoes. She receives over 100 additions to her wardrobe annually, including designs by Givenchy, Versace, Vera Wang and Gucci. Altogether, more than 105 million yards of fabric have gone into producing fashions for Barbie and her friends, making Mattel one of the largest apparel manufacturers in the world.

But to think Barbie is all about clothes would be to sell her short for she is, in fact, quite accomplished, having dabbled in more than 80 careers over the years.

She's also an animal lover who's cared for more than 43 pets, including 21 dogs, 14 horses, three ponies, a parrot and a panda. The unquenchable thirst for all things Barbie has swelled the Barbie line into a $2.5 billion-a-year industry. If placed head to toe, the number of Barbie dolls and her family members sold since 1959 would circle the earth more than seven times. That's assuming you could get all those dolls together, which is nigh on impossible. The craze in collecting means that countless Barbies have been taken out of circulation and put on display in the back bedrooms of suburban homes all across America.

All of which begs the question: *why?*

My understanding of Barbie still far from complete, I drive downtown and subject myself to a second day at Rocky Mountain Mod. Upon arriving at the hotel, I look at the convention program and try to decide what activity to attend. Unfortunately, I've already missed the Shagadelic Catwalk fashion show, and the competition room—where conventioneers have entered treasured pieces of their collections for prizes—won't be open until this afternoon. Reading the program, I learn that the rules of the competition are stiff. A doll dressed in "Sparkle Squares," for instance, will not be judged against "Jump Into Lace."

Looking at the schedule, I notice that the Fashion Doll Stole Workshop has just started. Deciding it's time for an up-close Barbie experience, I head to a small windowless conference room and sit down behind a long narrow table covered, naturally, in a pink tablecloth. Around me, about 30 people, mostly women, are hunched over their tables sewing and sticking straight pins into small rounds of fabric. There's a broad range of people here. Two older women in once-a-week beauty-parlor hairdos are reading the directions out loud to one another. A teenager with a black tattoo on her shoulder is breaking a strand of thread in her teeth. Next to me, two women who've just met are swapping stories about their doll clubs back home.

"We made pink, heart-shaped sandwiches at our last meeting."

"How *cute*," her new friend replies. "I'll have to remember that."

They stitch in silence for a few minutes until one asks the other, "Is your husband supportive of Barbie?".

"Oh, definitely. I have our club's Christmas party at my house and he helps me clean and cook and set up tables, and ten minutes before the guests arrive he disappears for the night."

"Sounds like the perfect husband."

As the workshop continues, the participants snip and sew and the room starts to buzz with activity and conversation. In front of me, two women are taking photos of one another holding up their newly made origami stoles. I see smiling teeth and popping flashbulbs and waving Barbies and for the first time since arriving yesterday, I'm feeling left out. Not that I want to sit down and make doll clothes but it would be nice to have a hobby where friends are so easily made and smiles so easy to come by.

After the workshop ends, I ride the hotel escalator upstairs to meet a woman named Judy Stegner, a 43-year-old collector and single mother from Fort Worth,

Texas. I've been told that Judy is a devoted collector and ardent advocate for all things Barbie. I notice a woman of medium build with straight-cut blond bangs looking around as if expecting to meet someone. I walk toward her and introduce myself.

"Hi, Shari!" she says, thrusting her hand toward mine. "I'm Judy! It's so nice to meet you! Howsabout we sit right here?"

Judy and I proceed to sit down on a leather bench underneath an enormous stone sculpture of a horse. As we are getting settled, Judy talks nonstop about the convention, and Denver, and the wonderful people she's met in Denver, and the wonderful people she's met at the convention. Her hands and her mouth and her bangs are moving constantly, and her frenetic, fuel-burning activity makes me like her instantly. When at last we are seated across from one another, Judy pushes her glasses, which have slipped down her nose, back into place. She takes a deep breath and begins to tell me, her voice a deep Texas twang, how she met her Barbie friends.

"Well . . . it was Thanksgivin' night in 1998 and my son Justin, who knew I loved Barbie, said to me, 'Mom, there's probably a chat room where you can talk with other Barbie people.' I looked at him like he was crazy. I mean, I didn't know anythin' about the Internet or chat rooms. Justin had to do everything. He found a site, logged me on, even gave me my screen name. I typed in some stupid sentence like 'Hi! I'm Judy. I collect Barbies and I've never done this before.' I was online that night talking to Barbie people until two in the mornin'." Judy laughs and rolls her eyes, as if she still can't *believe* that she of all people was able to figure out the complexities of online communication.

"But you know," she says, "the Barbie collectors I've met on the Internet are great people. I mean, I never could have made it without 'em."

I put down the bottle of water I've been holding. "What do you mean," I ask, "that you couldn't have made it without them?"

Judy exhales. "Well," she says, "maybe you heard about this. In September 1999, there was a shooting at Wedgewood Baptist Church in Fort Worth in which several kids were killed."

I tell her I vaguely recall the story about a man who entered the church during a youth rally and randomly started shooting.

"That's the one," she says. "He murdered seven people that day, including my son Justin." Judy's brown eyes grow pink with tears. "He was my only child."

I look at Judy, stunned by this information. The whir of noise and activity around us comes to an abrupt stop. I smell coffee from a nearby coffee cart. I notice the glossy deep green leaves of a potted plant. Through the window behind Judy, I see silent business people, their bodies bent forward, hurrying to work or meetings or other Very Important Places. How does this woman, how does anybody, go on with the routine of life after something like this?

Judy continues. "Well, my Texas friends gradually dropped out of sight after my son was killed. I mean, I don't blame 'em. They didn't know what to say. This kind of thing is hard for everybody. But my Barbie friends, you wouldn't believe what they did. They called or wrote to me every day. They sent me money. They sent care packages. They helped raise thousands of dollars for a tuition assistance fund in Justin's name. They also contacted Mattel. Can you believe that? They contacted Mattel and the company sent me a special collectible Barbie and a handwritten note the first Christmas after Justin died. My Barbie friends even had a special Angel doll made for me." Judy pauses to raise her glasses and wipe away tears. "I'm so blessed. This is the closest circle of friends I've ever had."

I swallow hard in an effort to hold back my own tears. I can't think of a single, comforting thing to say to Judy and feel deeply ashamed because of it.

Suddenly, Judy jumps to her feet. "Let me show you somethin'," she says.

I sense Judy Stegner is used to putting other people at ease over her grief. She grabs her convention tote bag, pulls out a quilt and unfolds it on the cushioned bench in front of us. The quilt, made to honor her son's life, features 18 hand-sewn panels created by her Internet Barbie friends in California, Texas, Oklahoma, Michigan, Virginia, New York and Australia. The back of the quilt is covered in a white flannel swath of vintage fabric covered with Barbie silhouettes.

Judy bends over and runs her hand along the soft material. "I can't imagine how much that cost," she says. "That's practically antique." As we stand there, admiring the fabric, two women with convention tote bags walk up to Judy and give her hugs.

"I wondered where you were," one of the women says to Judy. "Are you still meeting us for lunch?"

"Absolutely," she replies. "I'll be there as soon as I can."

The women leave and Judy returns her attention to the quilt. "You know, I used to have this hanging on a wall but then I thought that's silly. Quilts are meant to be used. Now I carry it with me everywhere—even here. At home, I curl up with it while watching television or reading a book. It makes me feel good. Makes me feel closer to Justin."

This finally pushes me over the edge, and my voice breaks. "That is so amazing," I say.

"Isn't it?" Judy asks, smiling. "You know, Barbie people everywhere are really giving. We're involved in lots of charities."

Judy then goes on to detail all the non-profit organizations she's been involved with, including Toys 4 Tots, doll auctions that raise money for children's charities, and an organization called Parents of Murdered Children. "Did you know this convention is also a fundraiser?" she asks. "The beneficiary is Angels Unaware, an organization that provides support for children living with HIV and AIDS. It was started in 1992 by a Barbie collector in Colorado."

"Why do you think Barbie collectors are so giving?" I ask.

"That's easy," she says. "It's because Barbie is about having fun, and when you're having fun you're not stressed and can naturally be more giving. We all have jobs and spouses and kids and things that make life hard. Anything that allows us to play is a good thing, and I don't know why people are so critical of Barbie sometimes. I mean, I can't believe it when people say Barbie is bad for a girl's self-image. That's ridiculous. It's a *doll*. Kids know that. It's adults that make Barbie a problem. In the 1960s, America was barely in space and there was already an astronaut Barbie. How can that be bad for kids?"

Feeling sheepish about my own past criticism of Barbie, I say nothing. Instead, I ask whether or not she plays with her dolls.

"It's total therapy for me to play," she says. "After my son died, I could lose myself for hours."

Across the lobby, another conventioneer calls to Judy and asks if she's ready for lunch.

Judy calls over to her. "I'll be there soon!"

I've never wanted to make sure someone meets up with her friends more than I want to make sure that Judy Stegner meets up with hers. I stand to thank Judy for her time, and she grabs my hand and shakes it vigorously, both of her hands encircling one of mine. It's the kind of handshake you might expect from someone who's just met you at the door and discovered she's won the Publisher's Clearinghouse Sweepstakes. It's not the handshake of a single mother whose only son was murdered in a church.

I leave Judy and walk back through the lobby to the main convention area. Along the way, I see three women seated at a table talking with similar sweepstakes-like enthusiasm. One of them has a blond Bubble Cut Barbie sticking out of the top of her purse. One of Barbie's arms is raised as if she's eager to answer a question. I look at the doll and its owner with something that feels, oddly enough, like admiration.

On the escalator back down to the convention hall, I think about my meeting with Judy and feel both sad and perplexed. I came here looking for an amusing human interest story, the kind of story I've written countless times before. The kind of story that beams a light on a bizarre little corner of the world and—wink, wink—invites readers to laugh with a sense of superiority. But instead of laughing, I'm filled with a vague yearning. I have friends, sure, but would they get together and craft a quilt for me? And I have interests, but do any of them offer "total therapy"?

The afternoon workshop on limb reattachment is just starting and several conventioneers are waiting at the door to see if they'll be admitted despite the fact they failed to pre-register. A young, slim man with dark hair turns to four women nearby.

"Do you think we'll get in?" he asks.

"I hope so," one of the women replies. "I've got two dolls I want to display but I can't get their legs to stay on."

"That's me too," he says, his eyes silently pleading with the door monitor to take pity.

After an anxious, ten-minute wait, the group is admitted and the workshop begins. There are about 35 people here and they're sporting an amazing array of pink. I see pink T-shirts, pink Barbie ball caps, pink hair bands, pink earrings and pink jeweled pins that spell out the name Barbie in fake gemstones. The attendees have laid out an assortment of naked and limbless Barbies on the pink tablecloths.

An instruction sheet listing a seven-step limb reattachment process is handed out. The first step reads: "Heat limb by dropping it into freshly boiled water for 2-3 minutes." To give people a hands-on reattachment experience, so to speak, there is a portable burner with a pot of boiling water set up at the front of the room. Starting with the first row and working backward, everyone will have a chance to dip their limbs and make their Barbies whole again.

While waiting for her turn, a large woman named Brenda Blanchard from Carson, California, begins speaking to me. Brenda is one of the few black people I've seen in this white-bread Barbie world and I'm curious how her interest began.

"I bought my first Barbie, a Holiday Barbie, for my daughter's high school graduation present," she explains.

Brenda speaks wistfully, like a war refugee describing her first taste of ice cream in the free world. "I liked that Holiday Barbie so much I took it back from my daughter. I now have 523 doll . . . no wait! Let's see, I've bought 12 dolls at the conference so far, add that to . . ." Brenda looks into her forehead and counts silently. "Yep! I've now got 523 dolls."

"Are you an in-the-box collector or a deboxer?" I ask.

"I do both," she confesses. "I buy duplicates of every doll so that I can play with one."

When I ask Brenda what she likes about Barbie, she has no trouble finding an answer. "I used to be a schoolteacher. I like Barbie because she doesn't talk back." Brenda also grew up in a poor family that couldn't afford toys. "I'm making up for lost time." And like Judy Stegner, one of the things Brenda Blanchard loves most about Barbie is that she can lose herself for hours each night dressing and redressing her dolls. "My kids just moved out and it gets kinda lonely," she says. "Oh! And one other thing. I like making clothes and creating dioramas that show dolls involved in different events. In fact, I won an award for a diorama earlier today. It was of the Black Panther Party."

Prior to coming to this workshop I'd stopped in the competition room and noticed Brenda's diorama. It was a small box with an open front, about the size of a toaster oven. Inside was a miniature kitchen, complete with 70's-era macramé curtains and a gold refrigerator. Three black male dolls stood talking to one another, while two black female dolls sat nearby, one trimming the other's hair. There were small black hair cuttings on the floor around them. The caption read:

"Black Panther Party leaders Eldrige Cleaver, Huey P. Newton and Stokely Carmichael prepare for a rally at Lake Merritt while the girls take a break from cooking to make sure they will look good."

Clearly, Brenda has found a way to creatively transform the white Barbie culture into something more directly meaningful for her own life. Instead of rebelling and rejecting the doll entirely—as I would have—Brenda has made it her own.

I tell Brenda that I saw the diorama and was impressed by its level of detail. She smiles and drops her eyes.

"Thank you," she says.

There's no way to neatly categorize Barbie collectors. When I arrived at the convention yesterday, I had narrowly typecast the group as nothing more than middle-aged Midwestern women. Since then, I've talked to a broad range of people, including Jim Faraone, who grew up in the Bronx and speaks like he's straight off the set of a Mafia movie. "I brought toity-seven dawls wit me," he says.

I've talked to men in flannel shirts who accompanied their wives and confess that they, too, enjoy the thrill of the hunt.

I've also learned that Barbie collectors tend to speak in exclamation points. I just witnessed a group of women in matching pink engineer caps approach one of their friends. "You won!" they squealed.

"I won?!" she squealed back.

"Yes! Your Barbie! She won second place! Isn't that great!"

Originally, cynically, I attributed the happy glaze on the conventioneers' faces to some mysterious narcotic effect resulting from prolonged exposure to molded plastic. Now, I'm smiling like the rest of them. And I'm not entirely sure what this means.

On my way out of the convention, I stop to thank the Mattel representative for her assistance, and she gives me a 30th anniversary Malibu Barbie as a memento. She presents it to me gently, with both hands outstretched.

I leave, place Malibu Barbie on the passenger seat of my car, and drive toward the exit of the parking garage. The cashier sees the doll riding shotgun.

"Oh! You have a Barbie!" she says, standing on her tiptoes to get a better look at the doll. "Which one is it?"

"It's the new Malibu Barbie," I say. And as I pick up the doll to show her, I'm astonished to find that I'm a teeny bit proud of my new acquisition.

"See!" I add. "She even has sunscreen."

Independence Day, Manley Hot Springs, Alaska

Lisa D. Chavez

Independence Day, 1975. I was twelve. A little more than a month before, my mother had withdrawn me from school early, loaded up our car—a flashy but impractical Camaro with dual side-pipes—and headed north for Alaska. She brought with her everything she thought essential: daughter; dog; photos of the family she was leaving behind; a haphazard scattering of household goods; and two army surplus sleeping bags, purchased especially for the trip. What she was traveling toward was uncertain but full of promise—a mysterious box, beguilingly wrapped.

What she was leaving behind was certain; perhaps that is why she was so eager to go. A narrow rented house in southern California; a steady, if boring, secretarial job; a marriage proposal from a man she didn't love. What she was leaving behind were her everyday fears: her route to work through Watts, a place blighted and dangerous even then. The muggings in the company parking lot. The fear of being a young woman alone with her child in a decaying neighborhood, a derelict factory looming across the street. The fear, perhaps, of succumbing to a loveless marriage for the security it offered.

I was too young to really understand my mother's concerns, but I felt her tension. My mother and her women friends wore their fears like perfume, like the lingering scent of smoke from the erupting fires of those violent days. I remember the things my mother's friends talked about: the Manson murders; the serial killer who left body parts scattered on the freeway in trash bags; the man in our own town who killed five people in a movie theater. And the more personal terrors, the ones they alluded to less directly: fear of the arm slipping around the neck from behind, fear of the window breaking in the house in the middle of the night. Fear for their children in a place gone crazy. Or just the fear of being alone. And while my world was a child's world, full of long imaginative games in the park near our house, or afternoons watching Disney movies at the mall, I also heard my mother and her friends talking about getting out, moving to someplace safe. My mother was looking for sanctuary, and for a new start. She picked Alaska, as far north as she could drive.

Independence Day, 1975. We've been in Alaska less than a month and are still exploring. Now we have driven as far north as the road will take us, landed here, on the banks of the Tanana River. Manley Hot Springs. A town with no function really, except for the raw springs: two pools of hot water bubbling up out of the ground. There's a lodge with a few desultory cabins ringing it. A combination gas station/store. That is all. Down the river a half a dozen miles lies Minto, an Athabascan Indian village. Fairbanks, the biggest city in the interior, swollen to a population of 60,000 by pipeline construction, lies less than a hundred miles south, far enough away—along these rough gravel roads—to be totally insignificant.

And I am twelve. Everything new astounds me, and everything is new. My mother parks near the river and goes to find a place to stay. Instantly I am occupied, walking our dog, wetting the toes of my canvas tennis shoes in the silty current, kicking sprays of gravel into the air. Under my breath a constant stream of conversation. I narrate the scene to myself, add it to the elaborate and constant story I whisper of my adventures in Alaska. Drunk on the stories of Jack London, the poems of Robert Service, I imagine myself a lone adventurer, a sled dog driver, a saloon girl. I do not see what is in front of me: a shabby small town where people stare openly at that frivolous car—bright orange and marked by its out-of-state plates—and the young woman in white, high-heeled sandals and her daughter that have emerged from it. I do not see the men swigging out of a bottle at the picnic table by the river. I do not see the people getting out of a banged up riverboat, or the beer cans they toss in the current. No. I am in my own Alaska, and it is beautiful. I erase the people, and I am alone in my fantasy of wilderness, only graceful paper birch and the sun turning the river to tinfoil. Even when two men pull a rifle out of the boat, aim it at the sky and shoot, I am unsurprised. Only when my mother hurries me into the car do I understand I should be afraid.

There is only one place to stay, in the hulking log building that serves as a lodge. And there is only one room left, above the bar. We take it, noting the sagging double bed and rust-stained sink. The bathroom is down the hall.

Manley holds few attractions. The hot springs itself—housed in another log structure, this one with steamy windows that gaze at the road like rheumy eyes—is booked out by the hour, and we discover it is rented for the entire evening. We go for a walk with our German shepherd, but we quickly run out of road to walk on. We circle the gas station yet again.

"When does it get dark?" I ask my mother; even though I already know that it does not get dark at night in Fairbanks, I cannot be sure the rules are not different here.

"In August," my mother replies, an answer she has learned from the locals. She looks nervous, walks fast. Finally, I manage to really see around me, to note the people drinking at picnic tables, the hairy-faced men entering the store with guns in holsters. She hustles us back to our little room.

And I continue to ponder the light. If it never gets dark, I wonder, when do kids get to shoot off their fireworks? This year I have no fireworks, no magical cones of cardboard with their heady black smell of powder, cones with names like "Showers of Falling Stars" and "Golden Peacock" that spray the summer night with shivering sparks of sheer delight. Fireworks are illegal here, my mother tells me, and I feel sorely cheated.

All through the sunlit night we hear voices shout and slur from the bar, and outside gunfire and laughter. Years later I will discover that Alaska is not the only place where people discharge guns on holidays, but then I knew only my mother's fear which passed to me like a virus. I lay still on the double bed beside her, pretending to sleep. At 5:00 A.M. a shot in the bar and a shuddering silence. From the car, distant and insistent, our dog's furious barking.

Time passes. I pretend to sleep. The dog barks. My mother nudges me. "Someone needs to walk the dog." That someone is me.

Years later I recount the story. People question me. Why did she send you, a child? What they are asking, what they are telling me, is that my mother was a bad mother. Perhaps. But maybe she thought it was safe; how could she know? And she was tired, and scared herself, and perhaps she thought my childishness would protect me in a way her youth and gender might not protect her.

Perhaps it was a mark of my mother's blind innocence. I like to think that she had some of the indomitable optimism of those who made the same trek before: the stampeders to the gold rush of '98, or the others that came, like we did, lured north by the pipeline boom of '74 and '75. She wanted to believe—like so many did—that Alaska was a land of golden opportunity. Think of what she had done: left a good-paying job and man who wanted to marry her to journey to a place where she knew no one, where she had no prospects at all. For her, I think Alaska represented the possibility of the undiscovered, while California was a territory already mapped with freeways and shopping malls, mile upon mile of housing developments, and the barbed wire threat of barrio and ghetto.

That summer, we were still caught up in the romance of Alaska. We sang Johnny Horton songs on the Alcan Highway: "North to Alaska," and "When It's Springtime in Alaska It's Forty Below." I wrote "Alaska or Bust" with my finger in the dust that caked the car, and my mother smiled and let it stay. She told me that we would have our own house in the country, and I believed her, even though when we got to Fairbanks we lived in a campground next to the fairgrounds, and I stayed there all day exploring muskeg woods behind the camp while my mother worked at Dairy Queen. There were none of the expected high-paying jobs, none of the dream houses that we could afford. We knew no one. But my mother, like me, was lost in her own dream of Alaska, and she refused to be discouraged. So now, when I think back to that time, I try not to judge her too harshly. Alaska was her sanctuary, and she could not imagine, then, that anything could go wrong.

I am a child; I do what she asks. Put on my worn jean jacket. Push my straight dark hair behind my ears, then tie it back with a blue bandana. This is the look I have adopted since I arrived, Indian chic. I do not know what it means, exactly, to dress like this, but I have seen young men and women outfitted in this way—people my mother told me were Indian—and I decide I will dress that way too, because Indians are cool, aren't they? And as I am a bit Indian—a mixture of Chicana and Southwestern Indian and Norwegian that I will much later learn to call Mestiza—I am determined to dress appropriately. My attire adjusted, I move toward the door. Look pleadingly at my mother's blanketed back. I really don't want to go out. Then, in imitation of my mother, I sigh loudly, pick up the keys. Step out into the hall.

Creep down the narrow stairs. Afraid, in my childish way, of strangers, of being where I think I am not supposed to be, up late in a room above a bar. And I see a man on the landing. His back to me. And he whips around and raises a shotgun and aims it at my face. "I told all you goddamn Indians to get the fuck out of my bar."

I am twelve, and I have never seen a gun before. I am twelve, and I come from California, where night follows day in an orderly fashion, where on the Fourth of July I whirl like a comet with sparklers clutched tight in two hands. Where I place black pellets on the pavement to watch them transform into sooty snakes. I am twelve, and I am frozen on the landing of a strange staircase, with a shotgun staring in my face with its one, unblinking eye.

I am usually a silent child, but my fear makes me speak. My mouth opens and out rush words, tumbling over one another like frightened animals. My mother. California. The dog in the car, maybe already peeing on the seat. The dog is like a ship I swim to, desperately. He lowers the gun and I skitter past, fly to the door. Which I cannot open; it is locked. The man raises the latch, shoves me outside.

I stand outside on the cool grass, the early morning bright and exotic around me. I close my eyes for a moment and wish hard for home. Then open them to see revelers sway aimlessly by, laughing, cursing, swigging from bottles. I move toward the safety of the car.

And I am twelve, and I don't know what to do, can't think about what happened to me in any coherent fashion. I do not understand. I know racism exists—though I do not know what it is called—but not like this. I thought it was something else, people who called black people bad names, people who snickered when they heard my last name. Mexican, they'd sneer. I knew that. Knew shame, about my last name, which I claimed was Spanish, not Mexican, knowing that to be less shameful, although I didn't know why. But nothing more. Not then. And Indian, what was that to me? An exotic people with feathers, that had some slight relation to my father, to me. But I was not Indian. Nor Mexican. Nor Norwegian. Not really. I am just myself, a quiet girl who liked to read, to write, a girl who had always loved the Fourth of July, the night's rich promise broken by the sizzle and spark of fire.

And now I have been shaken into a world I don't understand, a cold, foreign world, where men I don't know can hate me for the way I look. I don't know what to do, so I take the dog for a walk. She sniffs desultorily, squats on the lawn to pee. I look at the new grass stains on my jeans, souvenirs from the fall I took from the man's push. Two young men pass by, say hello. They have witnessed my ejection from the lodge.

"Did he hurt you?" one asks. They are both Indian; their glossy black hair is tied back with bandanas. They wear T-shirts, jean jackets.

I am afraid to answer, but I shake my head.

"He's an asshole," the other young man says. His words are slow and strangely accented; I will soon learn to recognize this as a village accent. "Fucking white man." He shakes a fist at the lodge.

I try to smile to show my gratefulness, and watch them with head bowed as they walk away. They are drunk; I know that even then, but their words redeem me nonetheless. Later I will understand those words as my introduction into a place I will dwell for all my time in Alaska, those words which delineate me as one of them, as a Native person. For in Alaska, as I would learn, the complexity of my ethnicity was irrelevant; I looked Native, therefore I was.

For a long time I crouch beside the car with my arms around the dog's neck. What will I do? I could sleep in the car, but my mother will be mad. But can I go back in? What if the man won't let me? What if he . . . my thoughts veer away from certain subjects. The dog pulls away, shakes herself. I must go back.

I stand at the door. Through the window I can see the man watching, see the slim shadow of the gun. I am afraid. My legs shake; my hand is weak, but I push the door open.

And the man grabs my shoulder hard. Twists me toward him. Peers down into my face. He is bearded and the hair on his face makes him as frightening as a fierce animal. "All right," he says, though I have no idea what he means. For me, nothing is right. He pushes me toward the stairs and I run up them, breathless, heart somersaulting. I imagine too clearly a sudden crack, a searing pain in my spine. In our room I collapse on the bed as if shot. Tears first, then the story.

My mother waits until the next morning to confront the lodge owner. She gets the story while I mop a pancake around my plate, too scared and shamed to eat. The bearded man is the man who owns the lodge, and he tells his side calmly, reasonably, as if there is nothing unusual about pointing shotguns at twelve-year-olds. Some Indians from Minto were partying in the bar, he tells us, and wouldn't leave at closing time. So he fired a shot of tear gas, cleared the place out. As for me, "she looks like a goddamn Native," he says, and shrugs. And the other guests eating breakfast look at me, nod. There is nothing more to say, no apologies necessary. And my mother's angry words are just irritations, like BBs fired at a grizzly bear.

We left soon after that, and my mother drove as fast as she dared on that gravel road, gripping the steering wheel tight, her hands like fists clenched. I was quiet. I didn't know I should be angry. Didn't know, really, why I felt so ashamed. Even my mother's anger couldn't take that shame away, for under her anger I sensed her own fear of this place she'd brought me to, of these people. Her confusion.

She repeated that the man had thought I was Indian, as if somehow that should explain it. But that confused me. Because I *was* Indian, though not Alaskan Indian, and not all Indian. Did that make what the man did excusable? My mother did not explain.

What did it mean to be Indian? Did I put it on with the clothes I wore? Why was my appearance read one way in California and another way in Alaska? In California, where everyone aimed for a tan, my skin color was something to be envied, when it could be separated from the stigma of my Mexican last name. I had grown vain of it, in a childish way. Proud that I often had the best "tan." I secretly looked down on lighter-skinned children, was sure their pink and white skin was ugly, undesirable. Otherwise why would my mother and so many others spend hours roasting themselves brown on the beach? I got it naturally; I must be superior. In Alaska, far from beaches, where the long dark winters bleached skin as pale as the long months of snow, brown skin did not mean beach and health, but it meant something else, something I would understand some people thought shameful. Native. That's what it meant, and I would discover how that word could be spit out with as much disgust as any racial slur.

Manley Hot Springs was a defining moment of my life in Alaska. It was the first time someone mistook me for an Alaskan Native—and one of the most frightening—but it would not be the last. My entire life in Alaska has been shaped by the fact that people—both white and Native—think I am Athabascan or Yupik, Tlingit or Inupiat. I reaped the benefits of that: smiles and conversation from old Yupik women on the bus, an unquestioned acceptance in villages and at Native cultural events. When I taught at the university, I connected easily with Native students. But I also reaped the pain.

When I tell this story to people, there is a coda I usually include. A few years after our trip up to Manley, a similar thing happened; again the lodge owner tried to throw some people out of the bar; again he waved a shotgun. But this time it was not at a child who looked Native. It was at a man—and while I don't know if he was white or Native, I do know he was armed, and he shot first and killed the lodge owner. As vengeful as it sounds, my mother and I were pleased by this, and when I retell it as the logical end to my own story, I smile. He infected me with his hatred, and I was—am—glad he is dead. I like this end because it is satisfying; it gives the story a sort of rough justice. It gives life—so messy and vague—an aesthetically pleasing shape, as neat as fiction. I also like the way I appear in this version: invulnerable, a tough person who can speak of death coolly. Perhaps my liking for this end is left over from my turbulent adolescence, a time so fraught with pain that my only tool of survival was the tough facade I adopted and my insistence that nothing could hurt me. Perhaps the story, ended this way, is proof of that.

The real end of the story is more complicated. Because of course I was not untouched. I learned to be afraid, learned that Alaska—as beloved as it would become—was not the sanctuary my mother had hoped for. My mother was able to close her eyes and keep hoping. For me, any possibility of sanctuary was shattered. On the drive back to Fairbanks, I had asked my mother if we could go home. She knew I didn't mean the campground. We live here now, was what she told me, and I remember crying when she said that. I think even then I wondered how I would survive.

In a few years, my mother would have what she dreamed of—the high-paying construction job, her own house. In a few years she would also slam into prejudice and violence on the job, but by then, Alaska was home, so she never seriously considered leaving.

In a few years, I would hear things and learn more: hear the smug tone of the high-school counselor as he tried to steer me into the vocational track—despite my good grades; hear, more than once, the anxiety in a white boyfriend's voice as he asked for assurance that I wasn't really Native; hear the nervous laughter at a party when a white man told how he raped "a squaw" in the back of a truck. Hear the silence that followed that laughter. I was spit at in small towns, refused service in bars. In just a few years, I could recite the litany of insults so many people of color know. But I would also learn to put a name to what was happening to me, and learn to be angry. I would learn that what happened to me was not my fault, nor was it unique to Alaska. Even later, I would learn to mold my anger into something I could use.

But I didn't know any of that then. I only knew fear, and shame.

I never wore the bandana or jean jacket again.

I'm Just Getting to the Disturbing Part

Steven Church

At this point in my story, this much I know for sure: I'm way too big for a pink plastic Barbie pool. At six foot four and 250 pounds, even if I sit cross-legged and squeeze my knees together with my elbows, I can only manage to get my ankles and rear end wet.

When I sit down, most of the water rises up and spills out, soaking into the brittle grass. I flop around in the pool and realize—vaguely at first, in the way that you realize your fly is open only by the way people are staring at your crotch—that to a passerby I probably look like a hairless wildebeest rolling around in a puddle on the hot savannah, a tanker ship in dry dock, a square peg in a round hole. I look like a jerk just wasting water. But I don't care how I appear, because even a little water can save you in this heat.

Rachel points at me and laughs—one of those big toothy wide-mouth laughs. "Oh my God," she says, "you're hilarious."

It seems cruel. But she has room to laugh. She's tiny, about half my size. She fits in the pool just fine. It's positively luxurious for her. She floats like a water bug on her back, paddling her little legs around and mocking me. "That's just wrong," I say when she shows off by submerging her entire body. She splashes me playfully as she climbs out, and the water feels so cold on my skin that it burns, leaving a smattering of wet fire across my legs and belly.

After a few failed attempts at cooling off, I finally figure out that the only way for me to soak my whole body is to fill the Barbie pool to the brim, squat down beside it, and then fall into the water, letting it splash over me and out onto the grass. My best friend, Rob, has to do the same thing, but he's three inches taller than me and skinny, and he looks like a giant gawky heron, flailing in a backyard birdbath.

We're out here because it's hot. And we need to be saved. This is what's important in the story.

Did I mention this: It's the middle of July, and all along the Front Range of Colorado we're suffering the sort of summer heat that burns when you inhale, singeing nose hair and scalding your sinus cavities; the particular brand of intense, abusive heat where your brain seems to expand inside your skull and you feel a little dumber, slower, and sleepier; the kind of heat that makes you see things funny—watery mirages, floating apparitions, ghosts of the everyday.

We have chosen this day, this hell-hot, broiling weekend, to make our final move down to the Front Range of Colorado from Breckenridge—high up in the Blue Valley at 9,000 feet, where the air is thin and cool, the kind of air they name deodorants after—Mountain Fresh, Cool Breeze, etc.

We loaded up the last loads of household junk and hauled it the 160 miles between apartments. We unpacked last night and sweated our way to sleep on the soft furnished mattress in our new apartment. We have no air conditioning. I tossed and turned all night, positioning and repositioning box fans to get the maximum whirlwind effect—all of it ultimately futile—and I finally rose at dawn, dug our coffee maker out of a box, and made a pot of dark French roast. I drank the whole thing and brewed another.

Rachel and I rented this one-bedroom place in Fort Collins, just half a block from the university where I will be attending graduate school for writing, and a short drive from another university where Rachel will begin her master's and certification in education. Rob, my best friend since high school, and his girlfriend, Jen, rented the apartment right next door to us. He's recovering from a botched hernia operation and volunteering with the Larimer County Wild Land Fire Crew, taking courses at the community college. Jen is clerking for a judge in the county court. We're all sort of in between things or just starting something new, definitely in a period of proverbial flux; and we're still getting used to the changes.

Heat is just one of the new challenges. Our apartments are poorly ventilated and stifling. So this morning, Rob and I drove out to Toys "R" Us and bought a pink plastic Barbie pool, the only model they had left. We brought it home, filled it up using a garden hose, and now we're all sitting around it in the backyard in green vinyl lawn chairs, half naked, our feet dipped in the water, taking turns soaking and refilling the pool.

We try not to think about the fact that it's 75 degrees in Breckenridge—sunny, but with a cool breeze and that mountain-crisp air—where we all recently lived and where we all, on some level, still wish we were living. We don't do the math. We don't think about the difference in comfort level that 30 degrees makes. The radio said it could get up to 110 today on the Front Range, and that's just not right. There's a drought, and Horsetooth Reservoir is drying up. There've been news reports about the retreat of water. The other day, it had receded so far they found a dead dog in the mud with cinder blocks tied to its feet. We told ourselves that someone must have tried to put a sick dog out of its misery. There wasn't much left of it—mostly bones and skin, hair and teeth.

It isn't fair, this oppressive heat. It does bad things to your head. Hot weather makes me grumpy. I feel swollen and bloated, oozing with sweat, like a fat sausage roasting on a grill. We try to distract ourselves with booze and food and small talk, but eventually we hit one of those awkward pauses in the conversation, a heat-induced lull that leaves each of us foul-faced and pissy, all thinking the same thing—we gotta get out of this heat before someone gets hurt.

Suddenly Rob's face brightens. "You guys want to take my kayak out to Horsetooth?"

A collective sigh releases from the group and smiles spread around the pink pool.

"Oh yeah, maybe do some swimming?" Rachel pipes in.

Three heads nod in unison.

But Jen the attorney says, "I'm pretty sure swimming is illegal there."

"No way," I protest. "Why?"

"It's dangerous, I guess," Jen says.

"But it's soooo hot," Rachel says.

"Let's just go," Rob says. "It's gotta be better than this." He gestures at the half-empty Barbie bath, bits of grass and dirt floating around, our feet lurking below the surface like pale fish, and in no time we are loading his fiberglass banana-colored kayak onto the roof of his jeep and emptying the pool water in the yard.

Let me tell you what I don't know at this point in my story: I will be afraid of water. It will happen a few years from now. This will be a new fear that develops unexpectedly, and it will be hard for me even to admit, difficult to reconcile with my childhood love of water. But one day I'll be walking along the Poudre River in Fort Collins with my three-year-old son (a boy who will be born and brought home to a house just two blocks away from this very apartment with the pink Barbie pool), and the water in the river will be moving fast, running as high as I've ever seen it, after two full days of rain rolling down from the mountains.

The boy will be the kind of child who likes to get down close and throw rocks in the water, his toes often dipped in at the edge, soaking his kiddie–Vans up to the Velcro straps. I will look at him down by the rushing river, and then up at the swirling brown force moving past, and I'll be seized with irrational gut-dropping panic. I know this now.

Like a brush fire, my imagination will flare up, burst, leap, and I'll picture him falling into the river, bobbing up a couple of times, and disappearing beneath the churn. I'll hear my own footsteps on the bank, running helplessly, and then watch myself dive into the water after him, swim down, deep, searching. I'll go with him. And before I know it, the fire of my thoughts will smolder, tamp, and I'll be back to the present future, nervously chewing my fingernails down to nothing and gripping his hand tight, pulling him back from the water, up to the path, away from my fears. He'll try to wiggle free from my grasp as he reaches for a rock. He'll always be wiggling away.

"I want to throw a rock in that wave, Daddy," he'll say plaintively, pointing at a cascade of foamy brown water pouring over a partially submerged tree.

"I know, buddy. But you have to hold my hand. It's like crossing the street. You always have to hold Daddy's hand when you're near the river."

"Why, Daddy?"

"Because it's dangerous. See how fast the river is moving? If you fell in, you could die."

This is true, but I should find a better way to say it. I don't want to plant fears in the loamy soil of his consciousness. I don't want him to think about dying.

"Because you could drown," I'll say, and pause, trying to shift the conversation away from this topic. "Because it's dangerous. Just trust me, OK?"

"OK, Daddy," he'll say, and I'll know that he means it.

We'll walk a little further along the river and I'll try to tell him about "eddy" currents and how they move backwards, against the flow of the main current, bits of flotsam and detritus swirling in the spin of story. We'll stop to watch several lines and tails spinning madly off of the main push, catching up twigs and debris, spawning tiny whirlpools; but he'll mostly just want to throw rocks at the surface of this scene, this image, this day. I'll still want him to be amazed and curious about water. I'll still want him to find things about rivers that aren't scary. But the fear will still be there, lurking beneath the surface of these casual interactions.

"Eddy," the boy will say. "That's silly."

"That's your Grandpa's name," I'll say.

"I know that, Daddy," he'll say impatiently, because he already knows how things come back again.

The boy will be naturally curious about the most dangerous things—waterfalls and ripples, noisy whitewater and submerged limbs, all the stuff beneath the surface of these days. I want to let him explore. I want to let go, let him learn to swim and survive and all that—but I will have developed this fear of water like I've never had before. It's just there, taking up space, weighing me down—and I don't want to give this burden to my son.

I think I always believed that as I grew older and matured, I'd shed phobias like old luggage or clothes—and I have lost a few along the way. But I never imagined that I'd get mossy green with new fears as the years progressed.

This one. This new fear of water. I can trace it back.

It starts at Horsetooth Reservoir on this miserable hot day in July.

Here is what should be clear by now: We are not alone in the water. Dozens of like-minded people have come to Horsetooth to escape the heat. But the lake is a place of sacrifice. What you gain in water, you lose in shade. What you gain in depth, you lose in vision.

There are few trees here, so people have set up large shade canopies, and bright blue Igloo coolers surround the perimeters like colorful sandbags. The dusty parking lot is crammed with cars. Boats and jet skis buzz up and down the lake, in and out of Satanka Cove, where the public dock is located, and many people have camped or squatted for the day along the banks of the cove, taking occasional illegal dips into the water. Some openly flout the posted warnings against swimming in the cove. We try to be subtle by sitting close to the edge and slipping in just to cool off. We take turns going out in Rob's boat, paddling out into the larger lake and splashing each other.

It's still hot, but it beats the Barbie pool.

The landscape around Satanka Cove is harsh and terra-cotta red, with slabs of uprooted sandstone rising all around like the plates of a buried stegosaurus. In the water, we paddle past striated shelves of crumbling shale. There is no beach, no sand. Just mud and rocks. But there is water and it is cool. We take a few turns, and Rob and I sit on the bank watching Rachel and Jen paddle back up to the edge. We are waiting our second turn out. They beach the boat and Rob straps on a life jacket. He climbs in and I'm helping Rachel out onto the bank, taking her life jacket, when we hear a voice calling to us, an anguished voice.

"Heeeelllp," she calls.

We turn and see an overweight woman in a tank top and jean shorts running toward us. She is screaming and waving her arms around. "Heelllp," she calls out again. I look behind her, expecting to see something or someone chasing her, but there's nothing.

She runs up to us. Rob sits in the boat. She is panting, trying to catch her breath. "He went under," she barks. "He went under and he's not coming up." She turns and points to a small inlet off the main cove, where I'd seen some boys diving from the rocks earlier. "He's not coming up," she repeats, then doubles over and puts her hands on her knees. We both seem to realize immediately what she is saying.

A boy is drowning. He needs our help.

Rob and I look at each other for a second and then take off in the direction from which she came—he in the boat, me running on the bank. Rob paddles like crazy, stirring up great roils of water. I run hard, my sandals slapping on the rock, and we both reach the inlet about the same time. We are the first ones there besides two other guys standing waist deep, breathing deeply, staring hopelessly at the water. They are dark-haired and deeply tanned, younger than us by a few years, and appear to be the drowning boy's swimming companions. Beer cans drift past in the water, and I get a sense of what they've been doing out here at the lake.

"My brother, man!" one of them says. "He went under."

"What happened?" Rob asks.

"We were swimming across and he started splashing and we thought he was joking," the boy says, staring at the water. "We thought he was joking," he says again.

"Where?" Rob asks, paddling his boat up close. I am standing on the opposite bank.

"Right fucking there, man!" the other boy says, pointing at a spot in the water.

Rob slips out of his life jacket and rolls out of his boat into the water. I climb down the bank and slip in over the edge. We both swim out to the area where the boy pointed. We look at each other, take a deep breath, and then dive. Again and again we dive down into the deep green water, surfacing only long enough to catch our breath.

I try to open my eyes underwater, but can't see a thing. I dive down as far as I can go, feeling pockets of cold water as I get closer to the bottom. I hit the mud and sweep my arms and legs out wildly, trying to feel his body, hoping to touch his slippery, cold flesh or maybe grab an arm. But my lungs will only let me stay down for a second or two before I have to swim hard for the surface. It's deep, 15 or 20 feet or more in spots.

As I break the surface and breach, gasping for air, Rob is quick behind me. We take a moment at the surface and then dive down again. I know how this works. I know that every second, every minute counts, and the quicker we can find him, the better chance he has to survive. We dive down repeatedly, finding and feeling nothing. Not a sign. Not a limb. Not a clump of hair or the brush of a swimsuit. Nothing but deep, cold water and slippery mud on the bottom. But we keep diving, dipping down below. Over and over again. There is nothing else to do but try.

I break the surface once and see Rachel swimming out to me. "Go back," I yell. "Please go back!" I can't bear the thought of losing her. By now there are other people in the water, seven or eight of us now, diving down and searching for him. Boats buzz past. I can hear a helicopter coming, rising up over the foothills. The sky looks wiped, skimmed, ironed like a blue shirt. Steep shale walls shade the cove, so it's cool in here. I dog-paddle, kicking my arms and legs out, knifing through the water, and try to breathe deeply, evenly.

A woman in a blue bikini stands on a fishing boat, screaming, "Does everyone have a buddy? You need to have a buddy!!"

I look at Rob. She means a swim buddy. But he's much more than that now.

We swim to the bank and pull ourselves up on the rocks. We've been diving for almost 20 minutes. We sit there, breathing hard, exhausted and weak. We look out at the crew of divers and a boat drifting slowly. Blue Bikini's husband has a sonar fish finder. Someone said we should use it, so now he's trolling back and forth across the inlet. *It's too late*, I think. The helicopter's blades go *thwop-thwop-thwop*, punctuating the air, echoing off the walls of the cove, and it lands lightly just above the boat ramp, kicking up a cloud of white dust.

Suddenly the guy in the boat stops. "Right there," he says, pointing down at his fish finder and then at the water. "There's something big, and it's not moving."

The gaggle of divers kicks and paddles furiously over to the spot, and one by one, each of them disappears under the water like a cormorant. Rob and I slip back in and swim out to the spot. We take deep breaths and dive under again, only to pop back up moments later without ever reaching the bottom. My dog paddle looks more like tired flailing than anything resembling a swim stroke.

"It's deep," I sputter. "I can't touch."

"Me neither," Rob says.

Just then a thin, wiry boy, maybe 17 or 18, breaches and hollers, "I touched him. I felt him lying down there, but I can't pull him up. It's too deep."

Another swimmer says, "Let's try again," and the two of them disappear.

Rob and I make another effort, but I can't get down that deep. I am exhausted, my lungs aching and my limbs all rubbery. We swim back to the bank. I look up and see Rachel and Jen sitting on the opposite bank. Rachel has her arms crossed over her knees and her head down.

"How long?" I ask, shivering from the cold water.

"I don't know," Rob says. "Must be close to a half hour."

"Too long," I say.

"He's gone," Rob says.

We hear the emergency vehicles approaching, their sirens rising and falling with the surrounding terrain until they come screaming down into Satanka Cove. They slip their rescue boat in the water and are upon us in seconds, plowing into the cove and pushing a wide white wake ahead of them. They order everyone out of the water, and a diver in a full wetsuit drops over the edge of the boat. We all wait on the bank for what seems like hours, but it's only a minute or so before the water bubbles, roils, and the diver pushes the boy up through the surface, breaking the thin skin of water that separates us from the deep.

His body thumps loudly against the fiberglass boat. He is fish-limp and heavy with full lungs. They work furiously on him from the minute he's in the boat, trying to revive him, but by the time they get back to the ramp and we have made our way over to the scene, the boy has been loaded into the helicopter and spirited away. He is dead. Everyone seems to know this, and there isn't much to be said about it.

The boy's brother is there, the one who was standing in the water when we first arrived. He looks dazed, confused. A wet towel drapes over his shoulders. Nobody asks us anything. No questions. No clarifications. I'm not sure what I expect, but I keep thinking that we'll need to give a statement or something.

I approach the brother. "I'm so sorry," I say. "I don't know what to say." And then I reach out and try to give him a hug, but it goes all wrong and we sort of half-embrace, each of us getting one arm up and around the other, then quickly separating. He doesn't speak a word. He doesn't seem to recognize me at all. I just stand there, watching him take the long walk up the grey concrete boat ramp, and I feel a cold chill rattle up and down my spine, knowing it's no comfort in the heat of this day.

Here is what I haven't told you up to this point in my story: My brother died when he was 18—killed in his car, slammed into a tree, head smashed in—a violent, noisy sort of death. Totally unlike a drowning. He was just a kid too.

This is how it all comes around again—moments and words caught up in the eddy current of backstory and memory.

They say that you experience euphoria as you are drowning, at least for a moment; but I've always wondered when this comes. At what point? Is it the euphoria of surrender, or something else that water does to the brain? And how exactly would they know? I suppose they interview people who have been pulled back to the surface and revived, given a chance to tell their story.

My brother never had a chance at euphoria. He couldn't have told any stories if he survived. His brain was too bruised, too battered and crushed. I imagine that he believed right up to the end that he could survive, that he would make it, and it hurts me to think he fought it. It hurts to know that I'm the only one who can tell his story.

When we're near the water—any water now—I'm completely paranoid and overprotective of my son. I'm afraid of the possibility, the subtle menace below the surface of a stream, crick, river, pond, or kiddie pool. He'll be four soon, and he still doesn't know how to swim. It helps me to think people can survive being underwater. They can be pulled back. There is a window there, between life and death, and it can last as long as 45 minutes in cold temperatures. I remind myself of this—those stories of kids being pulled from beneath the ice of a frozen lake and revived—and sometimes it works as a kind of psychological salve. Sometimes it helps tamp down the flare of this new fear.

On the rare occasions when we go swimming in a pool together, my son clings to my neck like a baby monkey and won't let go. When I try to get him to dog paddle on his own, his eyes lock onto me, his face is stricken with fear. I hold him out at arm's length, and he lifts his little chin desperately above the surface, squawking, "DADDY DADDY DADDY!" and it nearly breaks my heart every time. I know that we just need to spend more time in the water for him to get used to it and feel comfortable—but sometimes I wonder if I really want him to get comfortable in water.

I worry that I will pass my new fear on to him, that he will inherit it like a great and heavy piece of furniture that he must lug from house to house for the rest of his life. I don't want him to carry the weight of my fears, or he'll never learn to swim on his own, never shed the heft of my pathologies, and never experience the simple fun of gliding through the aqua-blue, weightless world of a swimming pool, skimming his body along the bottom and breaking the surface like a silver fish.

Here's the disturbing part: When that rescue diver pushed that drowned boy up through the skin of water, I couldn't be sure it wasn't my brother's body thumping on the fiberglass hull of the boat. I know it sounds strange, but I experienced some kind of transference in the water that day at Horsetooth. As the time dragged on and I knew the boy's life was slipping away, I felt as if I was slipping closer to my brother. I couldn't stop thinking about him. Every dive down was a dive closer to him. I felt his presence down there, in the dark and quiet green water, as if *he* was that boy on the bottom, waiting for me to pull him back up again.

Perhaps I felt something close to the other side, the chill of death in that deep green water; and I understood how quickly you can cross over, especially below the surface. I was afraid to open my eyes, afraid of what I might see—a smile, a wave, a tassel of hair, the bright neon of a swimsuit, or my brother's face. I was afraid part of me might want to stay down there, swimming in the euphoria of surrender, that I might just unhinge my jaw, swallow, and embrace it. And that's where this must have started, a big part of the reason I now lug around this new father-fear of water. It's hard to drop that day into the past, to just let it go in the wash of memory and watch it bob and roll and slip beneath the surface.

Silent Dancing

Judith Ortiz Cofer

We have a home movie of this party. Several times my mother and I have watched it together, and I have asked questions about the silent revelers coming in and out of focus. It is grainy and of short duration, but it's a great visual aid to my memory of life at that time. And it is in color—the only complete scene in color I can recall from those years.

We lived in Puerto Rico until my brother was born in 1954. Soon after, because of economic pressures on our growing family, my father joined the United States Navy. He was assigned to duty on a ship in Brooklyn Yard—a place of cement and steel that was to be his home base in the States until his retirement more than twenty years later. He left the Island first, alone, going to New York City and tracking down his uncle who lived with his family across the Hudson River in Paterson, New Jersey. There my father found a tiny apartment in a huge tenement that had once housed Jewish families but was just being taken over and transformed by Puerto Ricans, overflowing from New York City. In 1955 he sent for us. My mother was only twenty years old, I was not quite three, and my brother was a toddler when we arrived at El Building, as the place had been christened by its newest residents.

My memories of life in Paterson during those first few years are all in shades of gray. Maybe I was too young to absorb vivid colors and details, or to discriminate between the slate blue of the winter sky and the darker hues of the snow-bearing clouds, but that single color washes over the whole period. The building we lived in was gray, as were the streets, filled with slush the first few months of my life there. The coat my father had bought for me was similar in color and too big; it sat heavily on my thin frame.

I do remember the way the heater pipes banged and rattled, startling all of us out of sleep until we got so used to the sound that we automatically shut it out or raised our voices above the racket. The hiss from the valve punctuated my sleep (which has always been fitful) like a nonhuman presence in the room—a dragon sleeping at the entrance of my childhood. But the pipes were also a connection to all the other lives being lived around us. Having come from a house designed for a single family back in Puerto Rico—my mother's extended-family home—it was curious to know that strangers lived under our floor and above our heads, and that the heater pipe went through everyone's apartment. (My first spanking in Paterson came as a result of playing tunes on the pipes in my room to see if there would be an answer.) My mother was as new to this concept of bee-hive life as I was, but she had been given strict orders by my father to keep the doors locked, the noise down, ourselves to ourselves.

It seems that Father had learned some painful lessons about prejudice while searching for an apartment in Paterson. Not until years later did I hear how much resistance he had encountered with landlords who were panicking at the influx of Latinos into a neighborhood that had been Jewish for a couple of generations. It made no difference that it was the American phenomenon of ethnic turnover which was changing the urban core of Paterson, and that the human flood could not be held back with an accusing finger.

"You Cuban?" one man had asked my father, pointing at his name tag on the navy uniform—even though my father had the fair skin and light brown hair of his northern Spanish background, and the name Ortiz is as common in Puerto Rico as Johnson is in the United States.

"No," my father had answered, looking past the finger into his adversary's angry eyes. "I'm Puerto Rican."

"Same shit." And the door closed.

My father could have passed as European, but we couldn't. My brother and I both have our mother's black hair and olive skin, and so we lived in El Building and visited our great-uncle and his fair children on the next block. It was their private joke that they were the German branch of the family. Not many years later that area too would be mainly Puerto Rican. It was as if the heart of the city map were being gradually colored brown—*café con leche* brown. Our color.

The movie opens with a sweep of the living room. It is "typical" immigrant Puerto Rican decor for the time: the sofa and chairs are square and hard-looking, upholstered in bright colors (blue and yellow in this instance) and covered with the transparent plastic that furniture salesmen then were so adept at convincing women to buy. The linoleum on the floor is light blue; where it had been subjected to spike heels, as it was in most places, there were dime-size indentations all over it that cannot be seen in this movie. The room is full of people dressed up: dark suits for the men, red dresses for the women. When I have asked my mother why most of the women are in red that night, she has shrugged and said, "I don't remember. Just a coincidence." She doesn't have my obsession for assigning symbolism to everything.

The three women in red sitting on the couch are my mother, my eighteen-year-old cousin, and her brother's girlfriend. The novia *is just up from the Island, which is apparent in her body language. She sits up formally, her dress pulled over her knees. She is a pretty girl, but her posture makes her look insecure, lost in her full-skirted dress, which she has carefully tucked around her to make room for my gorgeous cousin, her future sister-in-law. My cousin has grown up in Paterson and is in her last year of high school.*

She doesn't have a trace of what Puerto Ricans call la mancha *(literally, the stain: the mark of the new immigrant—something about the posture, the voice, or the humble demeanor that makes it obvious to everyone the person has just arrived on the mainland). My cousin is wearing a light, sequined, cocktail dress. Her brown hair has been lightened with peroxide around the bangs, and she is holding a cigarette expertly between her fingers, bringing it up to her mouth in a sensuous arc of her arm as she talks animatedly. My mother, who has come up to sit between the two women, both only a few years younger than herself, is somewhere between the poles they represent in our culture.*

It became my father's obsession to get out of the barrio, and thus we were never permitted to form bonds with the place or with the people who lived there. Yet El Building was a comfort to my mother, who never got over yearning for *la isla*. She felt surrounded by her language: the walls were thin, and voices speaking and arguing in Spanish could be heard all day. *Salsas* blasted out of radios, turned on early in the morning and left on for company. Women seemed to cook rice and beans perpetually—the strong aroma of boiling red kidney beans permeated the hallways.

Though Father preferred that we do our grocery shopping at the supermarket when he came home on weekend leaves, my mother insisted that she could cook only with products whose labels she could read. Consequently, during the week I accompanied her and my little brother to La Bodega—a hole-in-the-wall grocery store across the street from El Building. There we squeezed down three narrow aisles jammed with various products. Goya and Libby's—those were the trademarks that were trusted by her *mamá*, so my mother bought many cans of Goya beans, soups, and condiments, as well as little cans of Libby's fruit juices for us. And she also bought Colgate toothpaste and Palmolive soap. (The final *e* is pronounced in both these products in Spanish, so for many years I believed that they were manufactured on the Island. I remember my surprise at first hearing a commercial on television in which "Colgate" rhymed with "ate.") We always lingered at La Bodega, for it was there that Mother breathed best, taking in the familiar aromas of the foods she knew from Mamá's kitchen. It was also there that she got to speak to the other women of El Building without violating outright Father's dictates against fraternizing with our neighbors.

Yet Father did his best to make our "assimilation" painless. I can still see him carrying a real Christmas tree up several flights of stairs to our apartment, leaving a trail of aromatic pine. He carried it formally, as if it were a flag in a parade. We were the only ones in El Building that I knew of who got presents on both Christmas and *día de Reyes*, the day when the Three Kings brought gifts to Christ and to Hispanic children.

Our supreme luxury in El Building was having our own television set. It must have been a result of Father's guilt feelings over the isolation he had imposed on us, but we were among the first in the barrio to have one. My brother quickly became an avid watcher of Captain Kangaroo and Jungle Jim, while I loved all the series showing families. By the time I started first grade, I could have drawn a map of Middle America as exemplified by the lives of characters in *Father*

Knows Best, The Donna Reed Show, Leave It to Beaver, My Three Sons, and (my favorite) *Bachelor Father,* where John Forsythe treated his adopted teenage daughter like a princess because he was rich and had a Chinese houseboy to do everything for him. In truth, compared to our neighbors in El Building, we were rich. My father's navy check provided us with financial security and a standard of living that the factory workers envied. The only thing his money could not buy us was a place to live away from the barrio—his greatest wish, Mother's greatest fear.

In the home movie the men are shown next, sitting around a card table set up in one corner of the living room, playing dominoes. The clack of the ivory pieces was a familiar sound. I heard it in many houses on the Island and in many apartments in Paterson. In Leave It to Beaver, *the Cleavers played bridge in every other episode; in my childhood, the men started every social occasion with a hotly debated round of dominoes. The women would sit around and watch, but they never participated in the games.*

Here and there you can see a small child. Children were always brought to parties and, whenever they got sleepy, were put to bed in the host's bedroom. Babysitting was a concept unrecognized by the Puerto Rican women I knew: a responsible mother did not leave her children with any stranger. And in a culture where children are not considered intrusive, there was no need to leave the children at home. We went where our mother went.

Of my preschool years I have only impressions: the sharp bite of the wind in December as we walked with our parents toward the brightly lit stores downtown; how I felt like a stuffed doll in my heavy coat, boots, and mittens; how good it was to walk into the five-and-dime and sit at the counter drinking hot chocolate. On Saturdays our whole family would walk downtown to shop at the big department stores on Broadway. Mother bought all our clothes at Penney's and Sears, and she liked to buy her dresses at the women's specialty shops like Lerner's and Diana's. At some point we'd go into Woolworth's and sit at the soda fountain to eat.

We never ran into other Latinos at these stores or when eating out, and it became clear to me only years later that the women from El Building shopped mainly in other places—stores owned by other Puerto Ricans or by Jewish merchants who had philosophically accepted our presence in the city and decided to make us their good customers, if not real neighbors and friends. These establishments were located not downtown but in the blocks around our street, and they were referred to generically as La Tienda, El Bazar, La Bodega, La Botánica. Everyone knew what was meant. These were the stores where your face did not turn a clerk to stone, where your money was as green as anyone else's.

One New Year's Eve we were dressed up like child models in the Sears catalogue: my brother in a miniature man's suit and bow tie, and I in black patent-leather shoes and a frilly dress with several layers of crinoline underneath. My mother wore a bright red dress that night, I remember, and spike heels; her long black hair hung to her waist. Father, who usually wore his navy uniform during his short visits home, had put on a dark civilian suit for the occasion: we had been invited to his uncle's house for a big celebration. Everyone was excited because my mother's brother Hernan—a bachelor who could indulge himself with luxuries—had bought a home movie camera, which he would be trying out that night.

Even the home movie cannot fill in the sensory details such a gathering left imprinted in a child's brain. The thick sweetness of women's perfumes mixing with the ever-present smells of food cooking in the kitchen: meat and plantain *pasteles,* as well as the ubiquitous rice dish made special with pigeon peas— *gandules*—and seasoned with precious *sofrito* sent up from the Island by some- body's mother or smuggled in by a recent traveler. *Sofrito* was one of the items that women hoarded, since it was hardly ever in stock at La Bodega. It was the fla- vor of Puerto Rico.

The men drank Palo Viejo rum, and some of the younger ones got weepy. The first time I saw a grown man cry was at a New Year's Eve party: he had been re- minded of his mother by the smells in the kitchen. But what I remember most were the boiled *pasteles,* plantain or yucca rectangles stuffed with corned beef or other meats, olives, and many other savory ingredients, all wrapped in banana leaves. Everybody had to fish one out with a fork. There was always a "trick" *pastel*—one without stuffing—and whoever got that one was the "New Year's Fool."

There was also the music. Long-playing albums were treated like precious china in these homes. Mexican recordings were popular, but the songs that brought tears to my mother's eyes were sung by the melancholy Daniel Santos, whose life as a drug addict was the stuff of legend. Felipe Rodríguez was a partic- ular favorite of couples, since he sang about faithless women and brokenhearted men. There is a snatch of one lyric that has stuck in my mind like a needle on a worn groove: *De piedra ha de ser mi cama, de piedra la cabezera . . . la mujer que a mi me quiera . . . ha de quererme de veras. Ay, Ay, Ay, corazón, porque no amas . . .* I must have heard it a thousand times since the idea of a bed made of stone, and its connection to love, first troubled me with its disturbing images.

The five-minute home movie ends with people dancing in a circle—the creative filmmaker must have set it up, so that all of them could file past him. It is both comical and sad to watch silent dancing. Since there is no justification for the ab- surd movements that music provides for some of us, people appear frantic, their faces embarrassingly intense. It's as if you were watching sex. Yet for years, I've had dreams in the form of this home movie. In a recurring scene, familiar faces push themselves forward into my mind's eye, plastering their features into dis- torted close-ups. And I'm asking them: "Who is *she?* Who is the old woman I don't recognize? Is she an aunt? Somebody's wife? Tell me who she is."

"See the beauty mark on her cheek as big as a hill on the lunar landscape of her face—well, that runs in the family. The women on your father's side of the family wrinkle early; it's the price they pay for that fair skin. The young girl with the green stain on her wedding dress is *la novia*—just up from the

Island. See, she lowers her eyes when she approaches the camera, as she's supposed to. Decent girls never look at you directly in the face. *Humilde,* humble, a girl should express humility in all her actions. She will make a good wife for your cousin. He should consider himself lucky to have met her only weeks after she arrived here. If he marries her quickly, she will make him a good Puerto Rican–style wife; but if he waits too long, she will be corrupted by the city, just like your cousin there."

"She means me. I do what I want. This is not some primitive island I live on. Do they expect me to wear a black mantilla on my head and go to mass every day? Not me. I'm an American woman, and I will do as I please. I can type faster than anyone in my senior class at Central High, and I'm going to be a secretary to a lawyer when I graduate. I can pass for an American girl anywhere—I've tried it. At least for Italian, anyway—I never speak Spanish in public. I hate these parties, but I wanted the dress. I look better than any of these *humildes* here. *My* life is going to be different. I have an American boyfriend. He is older and has a car. My parents don't know it, but I sneak out of the house late at night sometimes to be with him. If I marry him, even my name will be American. I hate rice and beans—that's what makes these women fat."

"Your *prima* is pregnant by that man she's been sneaking around with. Would I lie to you? I'm your *tía política,* your great-uncle's common-law wife— the one he abandoned on the Island to go marry your cousin's mother. *I* was not invited to this party, of course, but I came anyway. I came to tell you that story about your cousin that you've always wanted to hear. Do you remember the comment your mother made to a neighbor that has always haunted you? The only thing you heard was your cousin's name, and then you saw your mother pick up your doll from the couch and say: 'It was as big as this doll when they flushed it down the toilet.' This image has bothered you for years, hasn't it? You had nightmares about babies being flushed down the toilet, and you wondered why anyone would do such a horrible thing. You didn't dare ask your mother about it. She would only tell you that you had not heard her right, and yell at you for listening to adult conversations. But later, when you were old enough to know about abortions, you suspected.

"I am here to tell you that you were right. Your cousin was growing an *americanito* in her belly when this movie was made. Soon after, she put something long and pointy into her pretty self, thinking maybe she could get rid of the problem before breakfast and still make it to her first class at the high school. Well, *niña,* her screams could be heard downtown. Your aunt, her *mamá,* who had been a midwife on the Island, managed to pull the little thing out. Yes, they probably flushed it down the toilet. What else could they do with it—give it a Christian burial in a little white casket with blue bows and ribbons? Nobody wanted that baby—least of all the father, a teacher at her school with a house in West Paterson that he was filling with real children, and a wife who was a natural blonde.

"Girl, the scandal sent your uncle back to the bottle. And guess where your cousin ended up? Irony of ironies. She was sent to a village in Puerto Rico to live with a relative on her mother's side: a place so far away from civilization that you have to ride a mule to reach it. A real change in scenery. She found a man there—women like that cannot live without male company—but believe me, the men in Puerto Rico know how to put a saddle on a woman like her. *La gringa*, they call her. Ha, ha, ha. *La gringa* is what she always wanted to be. . . ."

The old woman's mouth becomes a cavernous black hole I fall into. And as I fall, I can feel the reverberations of her laughter. I hear the echoes of her last mocking words: *la gringa, la gringa!* And the conga line keeps moving silently past me. There is no music in my dream for the dancers.

When Odysseus visits Hades to see the spirit of his mother, he makes an offering of sacrificial blood, but since all the souls crave an audience with the living, he has to listen to many of them before he can ask questions. I, too, have to hear the dead and the forgotten speak in my dream. Those who are still part of my life remain silent, going around and around in their dance. The others keep pressing their faces forward to say things about the past.

My father's uncle is last in line. He is dying of alcoholism, shrunken and shriveled like a monkey, his face a mass of wrinkles and broken arteries. As he comes closer I realize that in his features I can see my whole family. If you were to stretch that rubbery flesh, you could find my father's face, and deep within *that* face—my own. I don't want to look into those eyes ringed in purple. In a few years he will retreat into silence, and take a long, long time to die. *Move back, Tío,* I tell him. *I don't want to hear what you have to say. Give the dancers room to move. Soon it will be midnight. Who is the New Year's Fool this time?*

On the Fringes of the Physical World

Meghan Daum

It started in cold weather; fall was drifting away into an intolerable chill. I was on the tail end of twenty-six, living in New York City, and trying to support myself as a writer. One morning I logged on to my America Online account to find a message under the heading "is this the real meghan daum?" It came from someone with the screen name PFSlider. The body of the message consisted of five sentences, written entirely in lowercase letters, of perfectly turned flattery, something about PFSlider's admiration of some newspaper and magazine articles I had published over the last year and a half, something else about his resulting infatuation with me, and something about his being a sportswriter in California.

I was charmed for a moment or so, engaged for the thirty seconds that it took me to read the message and fashion a reply. Though it felt strange to be in the position of confirming that I was indeed "the real meghan daum," I managed to say, "Yes, it's me. Thank you for writing." I clicked the "Send Now" icon and shot my words into the void, where I forgot about PFSlider until the next day when I received another message, this one entitled "eureka." "wow, it is you," he wrote, still in lowercase. He chronicled the various conditions under which he'd read my few and far between articles: a boardwalk in Laguna Beach, the spring training pressroom for the baseball team he covered for a Los Angeles newspaper. He confessed to having a "crazy crush" on me. He referred to me as "princess daum." He said he wanted to propose marriage or at least have lunch with me during one of his two annual trips to New York. He managed to do all of this without sounding like a schmuck. As I read the note, I smiled the kind of smile one tries to suppress, the kind of smile that arises during a sappy movie one never even admits to seeing. The letter was outrageous and endearingly pathetic, possibly the practical joke of a friend trying to rouse me out of a temporary writer's block. But the kindness pouring forth from my computer screen was unprecedented and bizarrely exhilarating. I logged off and thought about it for a few hours before writing back to express how flattered and touched—this was probably the first time I had ever used the word "touched" in earnest—I was by his message.

I had received e-mail messages from strangers before, most of them kind and friendly and courteous—all of those qualities that generally get checked with the coats at the cocktail parties that comprise what the information age has now forced us to call the "three-dimensional world." I am always warmed by an unsolicited gesture of admiration or encouragement, amazed that anyone would bother, shocked that communication from a stranger could be fueled by anything other than an attempt to get a job or make what the professional world has come to call "a connection."

I am not what most people would call a "computer person." I have utterly no interest in chat rooms, news groups, or most Web sites. I derive a palpable thrill from sticking an actual letter in the U.S. mail. But e-mail, though at that time I generally only sent and received a few messages a week, proves a useful forum for my particular communication anxieties. I have a constant, low-grade fear of the telephone. I often call people with the intention of getting their answering machines. There is something about the live voice that has become startling, unnervingly organic, as volatile as incendiary talk radio. PFSlider and I tossed a few innocuous, smart-assed notes back and forth over the week following his first message. His name was Pete. He was twenty-nine and single. I revealed very little about myself, relying instead on the ironic commentary and forced witticisms that are the conceit of most e-mail messages. But I quickly developed an oblique affection for PFSlider. I was excited when there was a message from him, mildly depressed when there wasn't. After a few weeks, he gave me his phone number. I did not give him mine but he looked me up anyway and called me one Friday night. I was home. I picked up the phone. His voice was jarring yet not unpleasant. He held up more than his end of the conversation for an hour and when he asked permission to call me again, I accepted as though we were in a previous century.

Pete, as I was forced to call him on the phone—I never could wrap my mind around his actual name, privately referring to him as PFSlider, "e-mail guy," or even "baseball boy"—began calling me two or three times a week. He asked if he could meet me in person and I said that would be okay. Christmas was a few weeks away and he would be returning east to see his family. From there, he would take the short flight to New York and have lunch with me. "It is my off-season mission to meet you," he said. "There will probably be a snowstorm," I said. "I'll take a team of sled dogs," he answered. We talked about our work and our families, about baseball and Bill Clinton and Howard Stern and sex, about his hatred for Los Angeles and how much he wanted a new job. Other times we would find each other logged on to America Online at the same time and type back and forth for hours. For me, this was far superior to the phone. Through typos and misspellings, he flirted maniacally. "I have an absurd crush on you," he said. "If I like you in person you must promise to marry me." I was coy and conceited, telling him to get a life, baiting him into complimenting me further, teasing him in a way I would never have dared in the real world or even on the phone. I would stay up until 3 A.M. typing with him, smiling at the screen, getting so giddy that I couldn't fall asleep. I was having difficulty recalling what I used to do at night. My phone was tied up for hours at a time. No one in the real world could reach me, and I didn't really care.

In off moments, I heard echoes of things I'd said just weeks earlier: "The Internet is destroying the world. Human communication will be rendered obsolete. We will all develop carpal tunnel syndrome and die." But curiously, the Internet, at least in the limited form in which I was using it, was having the opposite effect. My interaction with PFSlider was more human than much of what I experienced in the daylight realm of live beings. I was certainly putting more energy into the relationship than I had put into any before, giving him attention that was by definition undivided, relishing the safety of the distance by opting to be truthful rather than doling out the white lies that have become the staple of real life. The outside world—the place where I walked around on the concrete, avoiding people I didn't want to deal with, peppering the ground with half-truths, and applying my motto of "let the machine take it" to almost any scenario—was sliding into the periphery of my mind. I was a better person with PFSlider. I was someone I could live with.

This borrowed identity is, of course, the primary convention of Internet relationships. The false comfort of the cyberspace persona has been identified as one of the maladies of our time, another avenue for the remoteness that so famously plagues contemporary life. But the better person that I was to PFSlider was not a result of being a different person to him. It was simply that I was a desired person, the object of a blind man's gaze. I may not have known my suitor, but for the first time in my life, I knew the deal. I knew when I'd hear from him and how I'd hear from him. I knew he wanted me because he said he wanted me, because the distance and facelessness and lack of gravity of it all allowed him to be sweeter to me than most real-life people had ever managed. For the first time in my life, I was involved in a ritualized courtship. Never before had I realized how much that kind of structure was missing from my everyday life.

And so PFSlider became my everyday life. All the tangible stuff—the trees outside, my friends, the weather—fell away. I could physically feel my brain. My body did not exist. I had no skin, no hair, no bones; all desire had converted itself into a cerebral current that reached nothing but my frontal lobe. Lust was something not felt but thought. My brain was devouring all of my other organs and gaining speed with each swallow. There was no outdoors, the sky and wind were irrelevant. There was only the computer screen and the phone, my chair and maybe a glass of water. Pete started calling every day, sometimes twice, even three times. Most mornings I would wake up to find a message from PFSlider, composed in Pacific time while I slept in the wee hours. "I had a date last night," he wrote, "and I am not ashamed to say it was doomed from the start because I couldn't stop thinking about you." Then, a few days later, "If you stood before me now, I would plant the warmest kiss on your check that I could muster."

I fired back a message slapping this hand. "We must be careful where we tread," I said. This was true but not sincere. I wanted it, all of it. I wanted the deepest bow down before me. I wanted my ego not merely massaged but kneaded. I wanted unfettered affection, soul mating, true romance. In the weeks that had elapsed since I picked up "is this the real meghan daum?" the real me underwent some kind of meltdown, a systemic rejection of all the savvy and independence I had worn for years like a grown-up Girl Scout badge. Since graduating from college, I had spent three years in a serious relationship and two years in a state of neither looking for a boyfriend nor particularly avoiding one. I had had the requisite number of false starts and five-night stands, dates that I wasn't sure were dates, emphatically casual affairs that buckled under their own inertia even before dawn broke through the iron-guarded windows of stale, one-room city apartments. Even though I was heading into my late twenties, I was still a child, ignorant of dance steps or health insurance, a prisoner of credit-card debt and student loans and the nagging feeling that I didn't want anyone to find me until I had pulled myself into some semblance of an adult. I was true believer in the urban dream—in years of struggle succumbing to brilliant success, in getting a break, in making it. Like most of my friends, I was selfish by design. To want was more virtuous than to need. I wanted someone to love me but I certainly didn't need it. I didn't want to be alone, but as long as I was, I had no choice but to wear my solitude as though it were haute couture. The worst sin imaginable was not cruelty or bitchiness or even professional failure but vulnerability. To admit to loneliness was to slap the face of progress. It was to betray the times in which we lived.

But PFSlider derailed me. He gave me all of what I'd never realized I wanted. He called not only when he said he would, but unexpectedly, just to say hello. His guard was not merely down but nonexistent. He let his phone bill grow to towering proportions. He thought about me all the time and admitted it. He talked about me with his friends and admitted it. He arranged his holiday schedule around our impending date. He managed to charm me with sports analogies. He courted and wooed and romanced me. He didn't hesitate. He was unblinking and unapologetic, all nerviness and balls to the wall. He wasn't cheap. He went out of his way. I'd never seen anything like it.

Of all the troubling details of this story, the one that bothers me the most is the way I slurped up his attention like some kind of dying animal. My addiction to PFSlider's messages indicated a monstrous narcissism. But it also revealed a subtler desire that I didn't fully understand at the time. My need to experience an old-fashioned kind of courtship was stronger than I had ever imagined. The epistolary quality of our relationship put our communication closer to the eighteenth century than the uncertain millennium. For the first time in my life, I was not involved in a protracted "hang out" that would lead to a quasi-romance. I was involved in a well-defined structure, a neat little space in which we were both safe to express the panic and intrigue of our mutual affection. Our interaction was refreshingly orderly, noble in its vigor, dignified despite its shamelessness. It was far removed from the randomness of real-life relationships. We had an intimacy that seemed custom-made for our strange, lonely times. It seemed custom-made for me.

The day of our date was frigid and sunny. Pete was sitting at the bar of the restaurant when I arrived. We shook hands. For a split second he leaned toward me with his chin as if to kiss me. He was shorter than I had imagined, though he was not short. He registered to me as neither handsome nor un-handsome. He had very nice hands. He wore a very nice shirt. We were seated at a very nice table. I scanned the restaurant for people I knew, saw no one and couldn't decide how I felt about that.

He talked and I heard nothing he said. He talked and talked and talked. I stared at his profile and tried to figure out if I liked him. He seemed to be saying nothing in particular, though it went on forever. Later we went to the Museum of Natural History and watched a science film about the physics of storms. We walked around looking for the dinosaurs and he talked so much that I wanted to cry. Outside, walking along Central Park West at dusk, through the leaves, past the horse-drawn carriages and yellow cabs and splendid lights of Manhattan at Christmas, he grabbed my hand to kiss me and I didn't let him. I felt as if my brain had been stuffed with cotton. Then, for some reason, I invited him back to my apartment, gave him a few beers, and finally let him kiss me on the lumpy futon in my bedroom. The radiator clanked. The phone rang and the machine picked up. A car alarm blared outside. A key turned in the door as one of my roommates came home. I had no sensation at all, only the dull déjà vu of being back in some college dorm room, making out in a generic fashion on an Indian throw rug while Cat Stevens' *Greatest Hits* played on the portable stereo. I wanted Pete out of my apartment. I wanted to hand him his coat, close the door behind him, and fight the ensuing emptiness by turning on the computer and taking comfort in PFSlider.

When Pete finally did leave, I sulked. The ax had fallen. He'd talked way too much. He was hyper. He hadn't let me talk, although I hadn't tried very hard. I berated myself from every angle, for not kissing him on Central Park West, for letting him kiss me at all, for not liking him, for wanting to like him more than I had wanted anything in such a long time. I was horrified by the realization that I had invested so heavily in a made-up character, a character in whose creation I'd had a greater hand than even Pete himself. How could I, a person so self-congratulatingly reasonable, have gotten sucked into a scenario that was more akin to a television talk show than the relatively full and sophisticated life I was so convinced I led? How could I have received a fan letter and allowed it to go this far? Then a huge bouquet of FTD flowers arrived from him. No one had ever sent me flowers before. I was sick with sadness. I hated either the world or myself, and probably both.

No one had ever forced me to forgive them before. But for some reason, I forgave Pete. I cut him more slack than I ever had anyone. I granted him an official pardon, excused his failure for not living up to PFSlider. Instead of blaming him, I blamed the Earth itself, the invasion of tangible things into the immaculate communication PFSlider and I had created. With its roommates and ringing phones and subzero temperatures, the physical world came barreling in with all the obstreperousness of a major weather system, and I ignored it. As human beings with actual flesh and hand gestures and Gap clothing, Pete and I were utterly incompatible, but I pretended otherwise. In the weeks that followed I pictured him and saw the image of a plane lifting off over an overcast city. PFSlider was otherworldly, more a concept than a person. His romance lay in the notion of flight, the physics of gravity defiance. So when he offered to send me a plane ticket to spend the weekend with him in Los Angeles, I took it as an extension of our blissful remoteness, a three-dimensional e-mail message lasting an entire weekend. I pretended it was a good idea.

The temperature on the runway at JFK was seven degrees Fahrenheit. We sat for three hours waiting for de-icing. Finally we took off over the frozen city, the DC-10 hurling itself against the wind. The ground below shrank into a drawing of itself. Laptop computers were plopped onto tray tables. The air recirculated and dried out my contact lenses. I watched movies without the sound and thought to myself that they were probably better that way. Something about the plastic interior of the fuselage and the plastic forks and the din of the air and the engines was soothing and strangely sexy, as fabricated and seductive as PFSlider. I thought about Pete and wondered if I could ever turn him into an actual human being, if I could ever even want to. I knew so many people in real life, people to whom I spoke face-to-face, people who made me laugh or made me frustrated or happy or bored. But I'd never given any of them as much as I'd given PFSlider. I'd never forgiven their spasms and their speeches, never tied up my phone for hours in order to talk to them. I'd never bestowed such senseless tenderness on anyone.

We descended into LAX. We hit the tarmac and the seat belt signs blinked off. I hadn't moved my body in eight hours, and now, I was walking through the tunnel to the gate, my clothes wrinkled, my hair matted, my hands shaking. When I saw Pete in the terminal, his face registered to me as blank and impossible to process as the first time I'd met him. He kissed me chastely. On the way out to the parking lot, he told me that he was being seriously considered for a job in New York. He was flying back there next week. If he got the job he'd be moving within the month. I looked at him in astonishment. Something silent and invisible seemed to fall on us. Outside, the wind was warm and the Avis and Hertz buses ambled alongside the curb of Terminal 5. The palm trees shook and the air seemed as heavy and earthly as Pete's hand, which held mine for a few seconds before dropping it to get his car keys out of his pocket. The leaves on the trees were unmanageably real. He stood before me, all flesh and preoccupation. The physical world had invaded our space. For this I could not forgive him.

Everything now was for the touching. Everything was buildings and bushes, parking meters and screen doors and sofas. Gone was the computer; the erotic darkness of the telephone; the clean, single dimension of Pete's voice at 1 A.M. It was nighttime, yet the combination of sight and sound was blinding. We went to a restaurant and ate outside on the sidewalk. We were strained for conversation. I tried not to care. We drove to his apartment and stood under the ceiling light not really looking at each other. Something was happening that we needed to snap out of. Any moment now, I thought. Any moment and we'll be all right. These moments were crowded with elements, with carpet fibers and direct light and the smells of everything that had a smell. They left marks as they passed. It was all wrong. Gravity was all there was.

For three days, we crawled along the ground and tried to pull ourselves up. We talked about things that I can no longer remember. We read the *Los Angeles Times* over breakfast. We drove north past Santa Barbara to tour the wine country. I stomped around in my clunky shoes and black leather jacket, a killer of ants and earthworms and any hope in our abilities to speak and be understood. Not until studying myself in the bathroom mirror of a highway rest stop did I fully realize the preposterousness of my uniform. I felt like the shot in a human shot put, an object that could not be lifted, something that secretly weighed more than the world itself. We ate an expensive dinner. We checked into a hotel and watched television. Pete talked at me and through me and past me. I tried to listen. I tried to talk. But I bored myself and irritated him. Our conversation was a needle that could not be threaded. Still, we played nice. We tried to care and pretended to keep trying long after we had given up. In the car on the way home, he told me I was cynical, and I didn't have the presence of mind to ask him just how many cynics he had met who would travel three thousand miles to see someone they barely knew. Just for a chance. Just because the depths of my hope exceeded the thickness of my leather jacket and the thickness of my skin. And at that moment, I released myself into the sharp knowledge that communication had once again eliminated itself as a possibility.

Pete drove me to the airport at 7 A.M. so I could make my eight o'clock flight home. He kissed me goodbye, another chaste peck I recognized from countless dinner parties and dud dates from real life. He said he'd call me in a few days when he got to New York for his job interview, which he had discussed only in passing and with no reference to the fact that New York was where I happened to live. I returned home to the frozen January. A few days later, he came to New York and we didn't see each other. He called me from the plane back to Los Angeles to tell me, through the static, that he had gotten the job. He was moving to my city.

PFSlider was dead. Pete had killed him. I had killed him. I'd killed my own persona too, the girl on the phone and online, the character created by some writer who'd captured him one morning long ago as he read the newspaper. There would be no meeting him in distant hotel lobbies during the baseball season. There would be no more phone calls or e-mail messages. In a single moment, Pete had completed his journey out of our mating dance and officially stepped into the regular world, the world that gnawed at me daily, the world that fed those five-night stands, the world where romance could not be sustained because we simply did not know how to do it. Here, we were all chitchat and leather jackets, bold proclaimers of all that we did not need. But what struck me most about this affair was the unpredictable nature of our demise. Unlike most cyber romances, which seem to come fully equipped with the inevitable set of misrepresentations and false expectations, PFSlider and I had played it fairly straight. Neither of us had lied. We'd done the best we could. We were dead from natural causes rather than virtual ones.

Within a two-week period after I returned from Los Angeles, at least seven people confessed to me the vagaries of their own e-mail affairs. This topic arose, unprompted, over the course of normal conversation. Four of these people had gotten on planes and met their correspondents, traveling from New Haven to Baltimore, New York to Montana, Texas to Virginia, and New York to Johannesburg. These were normal people, writers and lawyers and scientists, whom I knew from the real world. They were all smart, attractive, and more than a little sheepish about admitting just how deep they had been sucked in. Very few had met in chat rooms. Instead, the messages had started after chance meetings at parties and on planes; some, like me, had received notes in response to things they'd written online or elsewhere. Two of these people had fallen in love, the others chalked it up to a strange, uniquely postmodern experience. They all did things they would never do in the real world: they sent flowers, they took chances, they forgave. I heard most of these stories in the close confines of smoky bars and crowded restaurants, and we would all shake our heads in bewilderment as we told our tales, our eyes focused on some distant point that could never be reigned in to the surface of the Earth. Mostly it was the courtship ritual that had drawn us in. We had finally wooed and been wooed, given an old-fashioned structure through which to attempt the process of romance. E-mail had become an electronic epistle, a yearned-for rule book. The black and white of the type, the welcome respite from the distractions of smells and weather and other people, had, in effect, allowed us to be vulnerable and passionate enough to actually care about something. It allowed us to do what was necessary to experience love. It was not the Internet that contributed to our remote, fragmented lives. The problem was life itself.

The story of PFSlider still makes me sad. Not so much because we no longer have anything to do with one another, but because it forces me to grapple with all three dimensions of daily life with greater awareness than I used to. After it became clear that our relationship would never transcend the screen and the phone, after the painful realization that our face-to-face knowledge of each other had in fact permanently contaminated the screen and the phone, I hit the pavement again, went through the motions of real life, said "hello" and "goodbye" to people in the regular way. In darker moments, I remain mortified by everything that happened with PFSlider. It terrifies me to admit to a firsthand understanding of the way the heart and the ego are entwined. Like diseased trees that have folded in on one another, our need to worship fuses with our need to be worshipped. Love eventually becomes only about how much mystique can be maintained. It upsets me even more to see how this entanglement is made so much more intense, so unhampered and intoxicating, by way of a remote access like e-mail. But I'm also thankful that I was forced to unpack the raw truth of my need and stare at it for a while. This was a dare I wouldn't have taken in three dimensions.

The last time I saw Pete he was in New York, thousands of miles away from what had been his home and a million miles away from PFSlider. In a final gesture of decency, in what I later realized was the most ordinary kind of closure, he took me out to dinner. We talked about nothing. He paid the bill. He drove me home in his rental car, the smell and sound of which was as arbitrary and impersonal as what we now were to each other. Then he disappeared forever. He became part of the muddy earth, as unmysterious as anything located next door. I stood on my stoop and felt that familiar rush of indifference. Pete had joined the angry and exhausted living. He drifted into my chaos, and joined me down in reality where, even if we met on the street, we'd never see each other again, our faces obscured by the branches and bodies and falling debris that make up the ether of the physical world.

Pool, A Love Story

J. D. Dolan

Maybe it all started when I got kicked out of the women's powder room at the Masonic Lodge. I was, I don't know, four or six—old enough to be lovestruck over my oldest sister's friends and young enough to be more or less invisible to them. I'd play quietly in the corner and sneak looks as these young women applied fresh lipstick, as they adjusted their bras just so and rolled pale stockings into the dark region between their pale legs. Sometimes, I wouldn't even have to look—I'd just close my eyes and breathe in their perfume, a scent as beautiful as their orchid corsages.

"Hey—what's *he* doing in here?" one woman I was in love with said, whereupon I was scooted out of the women's powder room forever.

The door shut behind me with a little whoosh of perfumed air, and I slowly scuffed my way downstairs to the poolroom, which right then happened to be empty. I was just above eye level with the huge mahogany pool table, and I rolled a few balls around the green baize—angrily at first and then with building interest. The solid weight of the table, the sea of green cloth, the click of the brightly colored balls, the soft thunk of the rails, the surprising angles—all of it was mesmerizing. This was, I realized, a beautiful game.

Or maybe it started about thirty years later, in Syracuse, New York. I moved there to go to graduate school, and I met a smart, beautiful woman, also in graduate school, and we fell in love fast. We were both passionate about our work, and that passion seemed to carry over into the time we spent together. She'd stop by my office between classes, and we'd lock the door and turn out the lights and kiss for a while in the dark. And we'd go cross-country skiing out at Green Lakes, then come back to my apartment and make love, and afterward we'd have cozy dinners and Belgian beers in front of my fireplace, right beside my pool table—my first—a beautiful 1920s model made of solid birch, with walnut rails and mother-of-pearl points.

And in Syracuse, I became friends with one of the great legends of pool, Arthur "Babe" Cranfield, the 1964 World Professional Pocket Billiard champion, who was seventy-nine when I met him at Cap's Cue Club for my first lesson.

Babe Cranfield is frail and slight, and in his checked polyester slacks and yellow polo shirt, he looks like an old duffer from a country club, except that the cuffs of his polyester slacks are rolled and his yellow shirt is faded. His right eye tears from a childhood baseball injury; his father had thought he was spending too much time in the poolroom, so Babe took up baseball and was nearly blinded by a line drive. He soon went back to pool, at which he was a prodigy.

Before we started the lesson, we both watched a shooter doing a tricky shot at a nearby table. The shooter did the same shot over and over, and he didn't miss.

"Wow!" I said.

Babe said, loud enough for the shooter to hear, "He's not shit."

The shooter ignored Babe, and Babe turned his back on the shooter.

"Look at him," Babe commanded.

I looked.

"What's he doing?"

"A hard shot?" I said, knowing already that my answer would be wrong.

"No, no, no!" Babe said. "He's just showing off. He's just practicing what he *knows*. Let me ask you something. You want to be a champion?"

My stomach clenched at this question. To answer it honestly—Yes, *of course* I want to be a champion—seemed, given my current abilities, absurd.

I said, hesitantly, yes.

There were tears coming from Babe's right eye, as if whatever he was about to say had come at great cost. Then he leaned close and whispered, "If you want to be a champion, practice your *weaknesses*."

A lot of guys seem to think that the ability to shoot pool is not something you learn but something you're born with. You simply are or are not a good pool player, and to not be a good pool player is to have been born deficient. And since most guys don't want to be deficient, they will play a game of pool—shooting too hard, missing horribly—and when they get lucky and pocket a ball, they'll think, *Hmm, pretty good.*

I was one of those guys. I actually fancied myself something of a pool shark when I first got to Syracuse. I could win beers in bars, relieve drunks of their money, hold court on a seven-foot coin-op.

All of which was not shit at Cap's Cue Club, a dingy poolroom filled with great players. I soon learned that I was no pool shark—I was no *player*. This knowledge came to me not through getting hustled or getting in any way beaten. It was worse than that. The players at Cap's Cue Club weren't just unimpressed with my game, they were *bored* with my game. For these players—skulking at the front counter, drinking coffee and smoking cigarettes, their hands blue with chalk dust—the prospect of playing me was more boring than, say, staring at Formica. I couldn't run a rack of balls, which, to a player, is the equivalent of crawling. I couldn't do a stop shot, a follow shot, a draw shot—or not with any consistency, and players are nothing if not consistent. I had no stroke, which meant that the cue ball would sometimes do as it was intended and sometimes, usually when a player was glancing my way, it would not.

In the Sunday-night handicapped tournaments at Cap's Cue Club, the ratings go from double-A all the way down to D. I was rated a D. There is nothing lower than a D, and several of the other D's could beat me.

Not long after we got together, my girlfriend told me she still had a lingering relationship with a man in Los Angeles, but it was a relationship mainly of inertia, she said. In truth, she made this man she once loved sound like an old dog she couldn't quite bring herself to shoot. But she didn't mention him often, and when she did, her voice took on a tone of bitterness at worst and pity at best.

One night, my girlfriend and I were snuggled in bed and talking about our future together, and we got onto the subject of names we might choose for a baby. We snuggled a little closer and talked some more, and as I was drifting off to sleep, she started crying into my shoulder. *"He* never even *talked* to me about our relationship," she said.

I was suddenly awake, but I didn't know how to react. How are you supposed to react when a woman sees you not for what you are but for what another man isn't? At that moment, though, it seemed convenient, and even noble, to be what he was not. Still, I didn't know what to tell her, so I told her the truth. "I love you," I said.

She held me tightly and said, "I love you, too." Then she said, "You're different."

The next morning, after she'd left, I found on my bathroom mirror a fresh, red lipstick kiss.

Every day at noon, I'd watch Babe shoot straight pool, and what I learned from watching him was cue-ball control. His days of three- and four-hundred-ball runs were long gone, but it wasn't unusual for him to run a hundred balls, shooting difficult shots when he had to—kisses, combinations, masses, banks—but usually positioning the cue ball so that his next shot was easy. His game had the logic and beauty and complexity of a chess match, and if you closed your eyes and just listened, it *sounded* like a chess match: *click, click, click.* . . . In practice, Babe once had a high run of 768. My high run stood at 16.

But my pool game was improving, and I got it into my head that I'd be an A-rated player by the time I left Syracuse. I was beginning to pocket balls consistently, and every now and then I'd even manage to run out in nine ball and shoot eighteen or twenty balls in straight pool. I wasn't a very good player yet, but I was less of a bad player.

My game improved dramatically, though, when I broke up with my girlfriend. She hadn't been able to end that other relationship, so eventually I had to end ours. Which, of course, left me wishing I'd ended it sooner, wishing I'd never gotten involved with her in the first place, and wishing more than anything that we could get back together. But our lives had become so intermingled that everything in my life reminded me of her, so I'd go down to Cap's Cue Club in an effort to get away from both of us.

And it worked. I developed a seriousness—a sudden dark concentration. Pool was still a beautiful, mysterious game, and I still loved to play it, but the beauty now was in understanding the mystery instead of just being amazed by it. The world was reduced to four and a half by nine feet. There were fifteen balls. Everything you needed was right there on the table. The rest was up to you.

By the time my girlfriend and I got back together, I was rated a C.

She'd ended that other relationship, she said, and we were for a while very happy, and I happily spent more time with her than I did at Cap's Cue Club. But even though I spent less time at it, my game continued to improve. My dark concentration had been replaced by a calm focus. And by the time we broke up again, when she told me she'd only *conditionally* ended that other relationship and I boxed up her nightgown, her toothbrush, her CDs, and all the rest of her stuff from my apartment and handed them to her with the sincere wish that she stay the fuck out of my life, I was rated a C-plus.

And this was when I got *very* serious about my game. Even the players at Cap's Cue Club noticed, and a few of them would play me once in a while. Sometimes, I'd come home from the poolroom and find pleading notes that my girlfriend—my ex-girlfriend—had left on my doorstep. One time, I found flowers. Another time, I found her. She assured me that the other relationship was over, it was done, it was dead. Common sense told me to run from her, but I couldn't shake the notion that the only roadblock in our relationship had come down—the road was open. I was rated a B.

My high run was now forty, which was respectable, if not stellar, pool. But my learning curve had gone flat. I'd become a B, and I stayed a B.

One day while I was watching him shoot, Babe started ranting to me about Minnesota Fats—one of Babe's favorite rants. "That bum couldn't run fifty balls," Babe said, and fired off a perfect wing shot. All serious pool players know that Minnesota Fats was little more than a middling player who happened to be a spectacular self-promoter. But if running fewer than fifty balls constituted a bum . . .

I was nearly done with graduate school. I had a teaching job lined up in the fall, and my girlfriend would be gone for a good part of the summer, finishing up her fieldwork. I knew that if there was ever a time to get my game up to A level, this was it.

Babe had just been inducted into the Billiard Congress of America Hall of Fame, and I thought about asking him to train me. I knew he'd probably agree to do it, but in pool, as in golf and tennis, the best players are not always the best teachers. Babe's stroke was unorthodox, and his teaching methods included whanging his ancient Herman Rambow cue against the rail and saying, "No, no, no!"

So I called a man whom many consider to be the best pool instructor in the country, former pro Jerry Briesath, a BCA Master Instructor who's trained hundreds of players, from beginners all the way up to top pros such as Danny Harriman and Jeff Carter. When five-time world champion Nick Varner wanted to give his father some pool lessons, he sent him to Jerry Briesath in Madison, Wisconsin.

Jerry said, "You say you're about a B-level player right now, huh? Well, what is it you want to do with your game?"

"Oh, not much," I said. "I'd just like to be able to beat Efren Reyes, Mike Sigel, and Earl Strickland."

Jerry got a good laugh at the idea of a B player suddenly able to beat three of the greatest pool players alive.

I was laughing, too, but secretly I was dead serious.

Jerry said, "Some people come for a day, some people come for as long as a week. . . ."

I thought about my upcoming summer alone and said, "A month. How good do you think I can get in a month?"

"Well," he said, still laughing a little, "you should definitely get better."

On the flight to Madison, I got myself worked up into something of a panic. Here I was with my thousand-dollar cue, a Mike Bender five-point made of ebony and bird's-eye maple with sterling-silver rings—a cue worthy of the player I wanted to become. But what if my best efforts were an utter flop? I was going to Madison with the assumption that I could get my game up to A level (which is, by the way, nowhere near good enough to beat a professional player, only good enough to *play one*). What if I practiced pool all day every day for a month with the best pool instructor in the country and I was still a B player, a B person—a man consigned to a B life?

Jerry didn't say I *would* definitely get better; he said I *should* definitely get better. And he was laughing when he said it.

I leaned back in my seat and thought about my girlfriend. Her flight had left a few hours before mine, and our goodbye at the airport—one of those clenched hugs and a swift, deep kiss—had been sad but also something of a relief. When I held her like that, I could smell her shampoo—a faint scent of clove and, I don't know, maybe cherry. I could almost smell it still, but not enough. This time apart, I figured, would be good for us. We'd gotten up that morning at 4:00 A.M. and made love like two people who have forever and who'll see each other in a month anyway.

A big sign at the airport read, WELCOME TO MADISON, WISCONSIN, THE NO.1 CITY IN AMERICA. All airports everywhere have signs like this, but as I rode in a taxi from the airport to the hotel, it seemed as if the sign had been right. Every yard seemed to be weedless; every flower seemed to be in perfect bloom. Everybody looked happy and healthy and well fed.

It was sort of creepy. "Is there a *bad* part of town?" I said to the cabdriver, and she looked at me in the rearview mirror and said, "Well, there are parts that aren't as *good*."

I kept seeing signs that read, MADISON, WISCONSIN, THE NO.1 CITY IN AMERICA, and when I asked the driver about it, she said, "*Money* magazine. *Last* year, they rated us number one."

"Oh, that's terrific," I said. I looked at the rearview mirror and noticed her eyes glaring at me.

Jerry Briesath has a camera pointed at me—a video camera—and he positions a few balls on the pool table and says, "Just shoot this shot the way you normally would." He says this the way a doctor might say, "Just breathe naturally" while checking you with a stethoscope for lung cancer.

But it's a simple shot, and I make it and most of the other shots that Jerry sets up—stop shots, draw shots, follow shots—and so I'm feeling pretty confident until we sit down to look at the video.

The Green Room is sort of a pool player's version of heaven. There are huge skylights overhead; there are twenty gorgeous new Brunswick Gold Crowns; there are two Verhoeven billiard tables with heated slates; and overlooking all of this is a big bar with lots of dark wood and polished brass and a good-looking waitress named Natalie.

None of which shows up on the video. What Jerry has chosen is a tight focus—not on the pool table or the pockets or the balls but on my arm. And what the video shows, again and again, is an impatient, spasmodic jab—the motion of a timid kid poking a frog with a stick.

The video seems endless, but Jerry finally stops the tape and says, "Do you *know* what a good stroke is?"

I've been shooting pool long enough to know that I'm supposed to know the answer to this. "Follow-through?" I say.

"Well, that's part of it," Jerry says, "but not all of it." He is sixty but looks ten years younger; he's tall and dark-haired, and with his thin, old-fashioned mustache, he reminds me of William Powell. It seems obvious that he likes the line he's about to deliver. "A good stroke," Jerry says, "is a beautiful throwing motion." He does a graceful golf swing with an imaginary club. "A beautiful throwing motion," he says. He winds up and pitches an imaginary baseball. "A beautiful throwing motion." Jerry pitches another imaginary baseball, but this time with the jerky urgency that's clearly an analogue to my pool stroke. "*Not* a beautiful throwing motion," he says, and lets out a high, cartoonish laugh. "Pool is one of those games where if you don't *look* good while you're doing it, you're *not* good."

This whole first week, I'm working on my system—that's what Jerry calls it, my *system*—which is everything I do from the time I look at the ball until it stops rolling, and it should CHIN LOCK be easy, learning what is, in essence, a simple swinging of the arm, but is ADDRESS THE BALL also a matter of *unlearning* something, unlearning SIGHT IN *everything*, and the mechanics have become complex, and in the complexity, I keep SLOW BACKSTROKE losing track of what I'm used to doing, namely pocketing balls, and so while STROKE TWICE I'm supposed to be here to improve my pool game, my pool game at present is worse than ever, it is, in fact, DON'T DROP THE ELBOW wretched, and my stroke does not resemble a beautiful PAUSE throwing motion, it is awkward and stiff and forced SIGHT IN and resembles the spasm of a broken robot, and what would have been a simple shot a week SMOOTH RHYTHM ago now seems impossible if I do everything else right, and there is a lot SLOW BACKSTROKE to do right, and I find myself mumbling Jerry's system like a mantra—his twangy, midwestern STROKE TWICE voice stuck in my head—and my first week of serious pool instruction has PAUSE my arm aching and my back aching, not from any difficulty SIGHT IN AGAIN of movement but from focusing so fucking LOOK AT THE OBJECT BALL much, and in the evenings, I walk away from the poolroom feeling SLOW BACKSTROKE regressive and whipped, sometimes skipping dinner SHOOT and sometimes going FOLLOW THROUGH for a sullen walk along beautiful Lake Mendota, and back at DON'T DROP THE ELBOW the hotel, I call my girlfriend to hear how she's doing and to take in the pure comfort KEEP THE TIP ON THE CLOTH of her voice, but we keep trading telephone messages, and we just can't seem to STAY DOWN connect.

By the second week, I've worked my way up to stop shots. Stop shots. I'd thought that by now I'd be working on three-rail kicks, pattern play, strategies for breaking up clusters. But no, I'm working on stop shots, and every now and then, I'll still hear Jerry's voice, sometimes real and sometimes imagined, telling me to slow down my backstroke and pause before I shoot—bad habits I can't seem to shake.

There are other people here like me, usually two or three every day, people who love pool and who've come here to have Jerry Briesath change their pool games and their lives, although almost nobody will admit it.

One young man from Michigan tells me he's come here to get better but not *too* much better—it would screw up his rating in the bar league back home. But later, he admits that he hasn't told anybody about coming here—not even his girlfriend. He doesn't want to look foolish if his game, as he puts it, "still sucks." An old guy on vacation stops in for a lesson. His Winnebago's out in the parking lot. He says he plays pool at about seventy senior centers around the country every year and wants to improve his game, but not *too* much, or else nobody at the senior centers will play him.

It makes me want to laugh—in fact, after I hear about the eighth guy say, "I don't want to get *too* much better," I do laugh. But it's safer, I guess, to believe that you actually *could* get too much better, that your capacity for transformation is boundless, and that your mediocre pool game is really the result of a shrewd and well-reasoned decision.

Jerry comes over to my table and studies me as I shoot a stop shot.

I shoot, the object ball drops in the pocket, and the cue ball stops as if it had hit glue. Perfect!

Jerry shakes his head gravely and says, "Pause! Pause before you shoot!" He's said this to me about a million times so far. It seems as if what he's really getting at is some kind of monstrous character flaw.

Maybe it's the payoff of endless repetition, or maybe it's the notion of enjoyment as a component of perfection. Whatever. By the end of the second week, my game, my *system*, is beginning to take shape.

My focus has shifted from what's happening out there on the table to what's happening right here with my arm, my stroke. Whether I'm shooting a draw shot or a shot with lots of English (and English, by the way, is sidespin), I take slow backstrokes, I pause, I follow through after I shoot, and I make sure that the tip of the cue is touching the cloth when I'm finished. Now when I do a follow shot, the cue ball hits the object ball, then rushes forward. When I do a draw shot, the cue ball hits the object ball, pauses for a second, then comes racing backward like a yo-yo on a string. What Jerry has been hammering into my head is beginning to make sense, and I'm beginning to feel it. My stroke is becoming a beautiful throwing motion.

I leave the poolroom feeling dizzy with accomplishment and walk along the State Street Mall—the number-one street in the number-one city in America. There are no cars allowed, only pedestrians and bicyclists and clean white buses that run on time. The bicyclists actually signal when they turn. The pedestrians stop at red lights. There are students and panhandlers and folk musicians and kids with blue hair and tattoos—and they all look so well scrubbed and cute! The State Street Mall, in its trendiness and diversity, reminds me of New York City's East Village, if the East Village had been built in Switzerland and run by Disney.

Madison seems to exude number-oneness, and I feel, with my new pool game, that I'm a part of it.

The next week. Jerry works with me on bank shots, rail-first shots, frozen-to-rail shots, pattern play, safeties, two- and three-rail kicks, and, by the end of the week, he says, "You should get into a low-stakes money game with somebody better than you and plan on losing twenty or thirty dollars. You need to practice under pressure."

So, as soon as I can, I get into a nine-ball game, with a guy named Gary, a fine player with a beautiful stroke. As he's putting together the flashy McDermott cue he won in a state tournament, he says, "What are you rated?"

I tell him I'm rated a B, and he offers to give me the eight ball, ten bucks a set, race to seven. I figure he'll make short work of my thirty dollars.

I'm a little nervous at first, but then I settle into my system—*sight in, slow backstrokes, pause before I shoot*—and soon I'm up a few games, and then I end up winning the set. This has to be some sort of fluke, I think, but we play another set, and I win that one, too.

"I'll play you the next set even," Gary says. "Otherwise, I'm done."

I feel this giddiness as I step up to the table—and miss my first shot, a simple one I should have made. So I concentrate on my system when I get to the table again—*sight in, slow backstrokes, pause before I shoot*—and I win the set seven games to four.

Gary says, "That's all for me." And as he's unscrewing his flashy McDermott cue, he says, curtly, "You are *not* a B."

When I call my girlfriend that night, the first thing I tell her is "I'm not a B anymore."

"What?" she says.

I start to tell her about the match, and about Gary, and about how we played the last set even, and she interrupts me and says, without enthusiasm, "That's great."

I ask her how things are going, and she says, "Fine."

I ask her how she's feeling, and she says, "Tired."

I ask her from what, and for a long time she doesn't say anything. Then she says, "I've just been feeling different lately." And when I ask her specifically *how* she feels different, she says, "Just different."

A few days later, I play in the weekly tournament at the Green Room. My first match is against a loudmouth from Kentucky who keeps snapping at Natalie the waitress and under his breath calls her a bitch. I have this urge to hit him upside the head with my pool cue, but my pool cue is too good for that. So I take extra-special pleasure when I win the match—easily. I win my next one easily, too, and the next, and the next, and it's not so much that the matches are easy as that I'm not making things difficult for myself.

My system, it seems, is working, because I end up winning the tournament. It's only forty dollars, but I'm still excited about it, and the first thing I do when I get back to the hotel is call my girlfriend and say, "What do you *mean*, 'different'?"

She seems moody and says she's tired and would rather not talk about it right now, and I say, "Talk about *what*?"

"I just feel different about *things*," she says

"Things," I say, and wait.

"Different about *us*," she says. There is pity in her voice, a pity edged with bitterness, and I get this sickening feeling not just that our relationship is ending but that it's already ended, and that she's ended it without bothering to include me in the process. And it's clear—I can hear it in her voice; it's a voice I know well—she's included someone else.

"No, sir," the desk clerk at the hotel says, "there *still* aren't any messages for you."

I hang up the pay phone and stalk back to my pool table, where I shoot another rack of balls too hard and too fast, and I really don't give a shit. In the last week, my game has abandoned me completely. Utterly. There is not a letter of the alphabet to categorize me now. It's my last day in town, thank God, since the Green Room and all of Madison have become sort of hellish. Even *Money* magazine seems to agree: Its new list has come out, and Madison has been demoted to the seventh-best city in America. I keep ordering coffees from Natalie just to catch the scent of her perfume. I've got so much caffeine in me, I'm vibrating. And I keep thinking, *different*, and shoot, *different*, and shoot—hard enough to send the balls to the moon.

At a nearby pool table, two hackers are narrating every shot they make, and the whole thing sounds disturbingly like a porno flick.

"Ooo, baby!"

"Stroke it!"

"Come, come, come!"

"Closer!"

"Oh, yeah! Oh, yeah!"

I try a long, difficult cut shot, and the ball is rolling toward the pocket, rolling *almost* in a perfect line, and I find myself standing up and leaning in the direction I want the ball to go. But the ball jaws in the pocket and doesn't drop.

Jerry materializes beside my table. "No," he says. "Do a mature miss." Jerry pronounces it "ma-toor."

"What's a *mature* miss?" I ask.

"A mature miss," he says, "is when you stay down and figure out what you did wrong. As long as you keep jumping up like that, you're just going to keep making the same mistake over and over." Jerry is just standing there, but he seems to be looming over me.

"Missing is part of the game," he says. "Learn from your misses."

Welcome to Afghanistan

Matt Farwell

It's three in the morning and I am falling hard into a five-foot-deep ditch. Like a cartoon character, legs splaying out in front of me, I land square on my back. The wind is knocked out of my chest. Luckily my body armor and helmet absorb most of the impact, and before the last profanity can even leave my mouth the machine gunner walking fifteen meters next to me is there, pulling me up. Under the weight of sixty-five pounds of weapons, ammunition, body armor, and gear, I stumble awkwardly to my feet and continue walking towards the mountain that we have to climb to look for Taliban activity. It's not even light out yet and I'm sweating my ass off, dirty and tired, hands and legs filled with tiny thorns. This day already sucks. Welcome to Afghanistan. As Drill Sergeant Berg would say, during rainy nights at Ft. Benning, "Welcome to the motherfuckin' infantry."

*

Before I was climbing mountains in full battle rattle and falling in ditches, I shared a dive apartment with a capricious college roommate. Dwayne was touched, slightly. He liked to break plates and scream randomly at passersby out of our second-story window. The apartment, in a rapidly gentrifying locale but still clinging to its shady, ghetto roots, was littered with the detritus of two overeducated children of privilege—books and papers stacked on every flat surface not already occupied with beer bottles; a sink overflowing with dishes; polo shirts and khakis strewn on the floor. Life was fun but filled with a certain amount of melancholy, the material maelstrom inside the apartment acting as a window into my conflicted brain. I'd never been particularly happy in college, and by the middle of my third year things were beginning to reach a boiling point. The apartment and what went on there were just the physical manifestations of that slow boil.

My living conditions are just a little different now. Instead of an apartment shared with just one whacked-out roommate, I now have nine crazy infantrymen all crammed into one room. It is thirty feet by fourteen feet, with dusty concrete floors and furniture roughly constructed out of unfinished plywood and two-by-fours. Spread about the room is the debris of nine men in constant flux and motion—white, cold-weather boots here; dirty socks next to them; a rolled up carpet there; half-drunk bottles of water and partially eaten bags of beef jerky and ramen noodles on the shelves and scattered around the floor. Except for the four sets of body armor, helmets, and front-load equipment carriers containing 210 rounds of 5.56 mm ball ammunition; Israeli tourniquets, canteens, and night vision goggles hung neatly off each bunk; and the assortment of M4 carbines, squad automatic weapons, grenade launchers, and shotguns around each bed, it might be familiar to any of my friends in college who live in similar dumps.

"Dude, I think I want to get a tattoo on my head when I go back to the States on leave . . . think I'd get in trouble for that? I want like a big fucking dagger right on the top or maybe some bullet holes or maybe just cracks, you know, like my head is cracked," Clit says.

Clit and I sit in the guard tower, staring emptily at the night below, panning the horizon to look for any movement. Clit speaks each sentence like it bears the utmost importance, but at least his sentences are always interesting.

"I always had a .38 and a TEK on me. The TEK fit perfectly under the seat. I wore gloves everywhere I went. We did a lot of illegal stuff. We used to go out on overpasses with bags of shit and piss and vinegar—like that's no joke, shit and piss and vinegar—and drop it on shit." He throws his cigarette butt over the sandbag barrier on the guard tower, stands up to stretch. He's one of the best guys in the platoon, a natural soldier and leader, smart and resourceful. He's got some great stories from before he joined the Army.

*

While I was growing up, my dad was in the Air Force. When I lived in Turkey and Germany, practically all my friends were military brats. My brother served as a grunt in Ranger Battalion and the 25th Infantry Division before he became an Army helicopter pilot. As a kid the thought of being in the Army had always been in the back of my mind. When it was time to start looking at colleges, I again thought about the military, applying for ROTC scholarships to cover the cost of Duke or Yale, and considered going to West Point. To figure out if I really wanted to become a cadet, I attended a weeklong recruiting session at the U.S. Military Academy. To put it in the most delicate way possible, it sucked. The potential cadets seemed stiff, wooden, and out of touch. The actual cadets were either bitter because they were stuck at the academy on their summer break, or they just seemed too uptight to hang out with. The only one who seemed to have any sort of sense about him was a prior service infantryman who spoke with a thick West Virginia accent around the thick wad of Copenhagen that was perpetually shoved into his lower lip. Most of my days there were spent with a New Hampshire skater whose mom had tricked him into attending, bugging the hell out of the straight-laced applicants and cadets by claiming to be a socialist or refusing to get out of bed in the morning because we were: "An Army of one. A tired Army of one."

West Point was out.

Then I was rejected by my top two college choices. Not getting into Yale was crushing because my girlfriend at the time was a freshman there and I had visions of happily ever after with an Ivy League degree. Not getting into Deep Springs, a bizarre all-male cattle ranch/college hidden in the middle of the California desert and populated by twenty brilliant misfits, was somewhat less of a disappointment, simply because it seemed so far out. So I went to the University of Virginia, or "the University," because it had accepted me into its honors program and I had in-state tuition. I decided to go to college in the first place because I was scared not to, because it seemed like the only thing for a smart kid graduating from an exclusive private boarding school to do. I really had no idea what I'd do once I got there.

Days here, whatever they are, are not filled with the same sort of uncertainty that occupied my college era. Between the normal humdrum of trying to survive in the heat, with the flies and bad food, there's the lingering knowledge that at any second one of my sergeants can come into the room and tell us to get our gear the fuck on, we've got to go. Our best time is three minutes—to throw on our body armor, load-carrying vest, and helmet, grab our weapons, and run out the door to our up-armored Humvees to respond to whatever crisis might erupt.

*

I remember sitting in UVA's Alderman Library stacks. I had twenty pages waiting to be filled with fleshed-out material from the couple of hundred note cards filled with citations, quotes, facts, and figures that all sat next to the computer. They sat there mockingly, a cluster of white paper bones waiting to be animated into a body. I had put an absurd amount of preparation into that paper—hours and hours in the library, on the phone, cruising databases, on the phone with sources, chewing through dusty old archives. All that work, all that preparation, for nothing. Twenty blank pages, all inconsequential pages. I remember thinking: *Why even bother?* All this preparation for something that will be read, halfheartedly, by a TA and then thrown away—another meaningless cluster of words carefully arranged and quickly forgotten. It seemed like a microcosm of my whole college career, a bunch of seemingly pointless preparations from grade school on up to receive a piece of parchment that signified nothing except that I can read, write, and show up to class on time. I was frustrated.

*

"Get your shit on and go to the trucks. Scouts got hit with an IED." The three guys from my platoon that I am eating with and I just look at each other for a second—then get up, leaving our trays, and run for the door. We run back to our barracks, half throw on our gear, and sprint out the front door to the truck still buckling and fastening straps.

"Radios on?" I ask, sliding into the back passenger seat, banging my M4 carbine and M203 grenade launcher against the seat's well.

"Yeah, they're good," our driver, Bautista, says as we pull out, while Burke is hopping into the turret behind the .50 caliber machine gun. "How's the FBCB2? Is it showing the screen?" I look up toward the computer monitor next to our lieutenant's seat, the glowing screen flickers to life and shows our map location as we move.

"Yeah, it's coming on."

"Fuck man."

"Yeah. Fuck."

*

Every Tuesday night on top of the dilapidated frat house was the same. James, Jon, me, and a case of Miller Light. James and Jon were both products of an exclusive Manhattan Jesuit high school, overeducated and neurotic. They half discussed, half debated Nietzsche and Heidegger every time we got together. I sat outside the conversation, gulped at my beer, looked at the stars, contributed comments here and there. I'd read those books, thought about them, written papers taking this position or that, but frankly, rants about the "thing unto itself" and the "übermensch" weren't interesting, not tangible at all.

As we got progressively drunker, the talk of continental philosophy drifted a bit. Jon usually started playing his guitar; James ranted about his father, his girlfriend, the normal bitching. Beer cans accumulated around our feet and were crushed. Then I would stumble down the stairs and begin the long walk back to my apartment.

*

"Who's going to get Rashid?" We pull up in front of the Tactical Operation Center and Burke climbs out of the turret, jumping awkwardly off the hood while we are still moving, then stumbling toward our interpreter's room. Rashid, a twenty-three year old Afghani who picked up English while a refugee in Peshawar, comes running out toward our truck. We pass him his body armor and Soviet-made pistol, and then wait to roll out of the gate. My hands are shaking slightly as I put on my gloves.

"Who's got batteries?" Burke asks. The sun will be going down in a couple of hours, and scouts are about that far from our location, so anything we do in the next twelve hours will have to be through the greenish glow of our night vision goggles.

"Um . . . I've got four, plus two in my camera if we're desperate," I tell him.

*

Sara was the beautiful, smart, vivacious Cuban-American senior I'd had a crush on for the better part of my junior year. One day, half-drunk, I slipped a note through her mail slot. It was a note a week in the making—revised over and over, a perfect profession of love and devotion. I received her reply two days later, two pages of beautiful red lettering. Each perfectly formed consonant and vowel was a knife to the heart, each overly precise sentence ripped chunks out of my ego. It was hard to look at the whole letter, so I read it in disjointed pieces, trying to amuse myself by putting the puzzle together. I already knew what it said in so many words.

I had called James's cell phone and told him, wirelessly tethering my burden to him.

"Fuckin' sucks, dude," he'd groaned. "She's a fuckin' bitch. Forget it. Me and Jon are smoking opium. Come over, it's pretty badass, feels like you're a couple of joints and a few Vicodin deep."

I hung up, drove back to my apartment, and demolished half a case of Heineken while watching overdue videos until I passed out. My pillow was wet when I woke up.

*

I'd been cramming my brain for this one particular exam—up all night, wired on Red Bull and nicotine, shoving public policy readings long neglected into my short-term memory. The exam sat on the desk in front of me, a neatly typed-up sheet next to an open blue book. The first question was easy, I recall knowing that one. But after that my mind went blank. I stared. For an hour I stared like that, while pens scratched on paper all around me. I got up, turned in the empty blue book, and walked straight to my dean's office.

"Sir, I fucked up my exam. I'm not sure I can do this anymore."

Within the day, the paperwork was filed, stamped, and put away. Officially I'd withdrawn for the semester and taken a leave of absence from the university. The hardest part was telling my parents. I was a college dropout.

*

"Dammit, I didn't grab any snivel gear."

In my rush to get out to the trucks I hadn't grabbed any raincoats or fleece, nothing to keep me warm during the cold Afghani night. We sit up at the Tactical Operations Center awaiting permission from the battalion commander to enter the fray. We wait for ten minutes, which seems like an eternity, then twenty, and then an hour. We never actually get permission to go tonight and so we return to our rooms, shedding our dusty gear as the adrenaline seeps from our bodies.

*

Still in Virginia, but no longer in school, I had taken a job at Lowe's, plotting my next move while hawking faucets and showerheads. That got old fast, naturally, but I really wasn't planning on going back to college for a while. The Army had always held a certain romantic appeal, even if I had decided West Point wasn't for me: Lowe's was going nowhere, college was boring, and shit . . . why not?

So one day, coming home from work, I walked into an Army recruiter's office and signed up for three years as an infantryman. It had seemed like a logical decision—I'd get some adventure, get out of my head, and get away from, at least for a little while, my privileged white-boy roots for a life in which I was no more special than the next guy with an identical haircut and identical camouflage clothing.

I couldn't see anything else in the Army I wanted to do but pull a trigger, couldn't see myself repairing helicopters or decoding messages or anything like that. I just had the itch to carry all my gear on my back, strap a weapon to my front, and train to "close with and destroy the enemy." Who knows, maybe that enemy was myself.

The Color of Monday

Hillary Frank

On May 9, 2002, a couple of hours before the first morning light, a man in Bremen, Maine, stepped into his yard, doused himself with gasoline, and lit a match. By the time the fire engine arrived, the sheriff's department had already extinguished the blaze and pronounced the man dead. The figure in the grass was badly burned but still clearly recognizable as a human being.

The following day, my dad received a Priority Mail package containing seventeen rolls of film and a suicide letter from Dan McClain, his friend and creative soul mate of twenty-eight years. The note, handwritten in angular, stretched-out script on Daniel J. McClain Design letterhead, explained that the pictures documented Dan's short time living in Maine, and that he'd planned on getting them developed when things got easier for him. But "things never got easier," he wrote, and "there is no one else in the world I trust more than you to see that this gets done." He told my dad to "take a close look" at the photos, then asked, "Can you see what I saw?"

This is a pretty charged question when you consider that it is one of the last things Dan asked of anyone before he died. My dad wasn't shocked when he got the call about Dan's death the previous day; Dan had a history of suicide attempts. But getting the letter, the package—that was a surprise. The profound sadness my dad felt over losing one of his closest friends was softened just a bit by the thought that he'd made it to Dan's checklist of things to do in the hours before he killed himself.

My dad is a photographer. He makes a living shooting portraits for annual reports and school view books. But his real passion is capturing the absurdity in everyday life. He almost always has a camera with him. He'll be walking down the street and suddenly he'll stop in his tracks and say, "Oh, *that's* a picture." I'll have no idea what he's talking about until I see him crouching and focusing his lens on a businessman scratching himself all over or a guy taking a nap under a truck fender.

One of my favorite photographs of my dad's is called "Man in Crowd." He took it at the Miss Nude America competition in 1974, a few years before I was born. While all the other photographers were snapping pictures of Miss Nude America, my dad chose to document a crowd of people as seen from behind. One pudgy man in the foreground stands out. That's because he's naked. Well, except for that Kangol cap. The Miss Nude America competition was held at a nudist colony but was open to the public, which meant there was a mix of nudists and non-nudists in the audience. My dad found an image that is funny and strange and makes you wonder, Could that *really* have happened? It's the kind of picture that makes most people laugh. But not many people can spot these moments in their own lives. Not many people get what my dad means when he says, "Oh, *that's* a picture." Dan was one of the few who did.

My dad met Dan in the halls at Time Inc., where Dan was an assistant art director for *People* magazine and my dad was a freelance photographer for *Money* and *Fortune*. My dad immediately admired Dan; here was a guy who'd moved from Kettering, Ohio, to Manhattan at eighteen and by his mid-twenties had made it pretty far up the graphic design ladder on no college education. The day Dan asked to see my dad's portfolio, my dad happened to be carrying around his personal work—his "Oh, *that's* a picture" pictures. My dad says he could tell that Dan latched on to those photos right away. Occasionally, he'd pass over an image that didn't grab him, but when he saw something he really liked he'd have this sweet, quiet way of looking absolutely delighted. Dan got that taking photos like these was not as simple as pushing a button. And it wasn't as simple as just spotting compelling moments, either. Photographers like my dad believe that the art of great photography is getting everything right while the film is still in the camera; that is, the exposure has to be spot on, the image must be in focus, and the composition must be perfectly framed in the viewfinder. No cropping allowed later on. And because Dan understood that all of these ingredients went into making pictures that were worth printing, my dad took Dan's understated delight as a huge compliment. My dad got into the habit of bringing new pictures to Dan whenever he went to Time Inc. And every time Dan smiled in his subtle but radiant way, my dad knew he'd really nailed a shot.

Eventually, Dan became art director at *Audubon* magazine. One day, on a whim, my dad called him up and said, "Hey, Dan, you all at *Audubon* take yourselves too seriously. You oughta cover the buzzards returning to Hinckley, Ohio, rather than the swallows returning to Capistrano." Dan hung up the phone and called my dad back in five minutes. "Pack your bags and get over there," he said. He wound up giving my dad a six-page black-and-white spread in the magazine. There was a shot of a few people buzzard-watching with opera glasses, one of a ranger holding a buzzard on a leash, one of locals and tourists enjoying the annual Buzzard Festival pancake breakfast. It was the first time *Audubon* had run pictures with a sense of humor. Before that my dad had done editorial work for magazines like *Car and Driver*, *Esquire*, and *The New York Times Magazine*, but at *Audubon*, and later on at *Oceans* magazine and *Field & Stream*, Dan's subsequent employers, Dan gave my dad a kind of creative freedom that he hadn't experienced at any other publication. For over a decade they collaborated on projects documenting naturalists. A couple of my dad's favorite pictures from that time include a mammalogist standing side by side with a stuffed buffalo in a natural history museum diorama, both staring straight into the camera, and a close-up portrait of an entomologist behind a screen watching brother and sister moths mate. These assignments, my dad says, were for him what photography was all about. Throughout their careers together Dan gave my dad little or no direction. My dad knew that meant Dan had faith in his ability to see. And to my dad, compliments don't come better than that.

I was sitting at my desk in my Chicago apartment when my parents called to tell me about Dan's suicide. I spent the rest of the afternoon staring into space, unable to comprehend how such a gentle guy could do something so violent to himself. Later that night I broke down crying and decided that it was very important to dig through some old boxes and find a painting Dan had given me when I was a kid. It's a watercolor, about the size of a tea bag, of a dog walking past a fence in the moonlight with a confused-looking cat perched on his back. I hung the picture by the door to my apartment, thinking it would be good to make myself remember Dan as much as possible.

The first thing I remembered was the time when I was six years old and my parents had dropped me off at Dan's office at Audubon for a meeting. They had recently asked me what I wanted to be when I grew up, and I'd told them I wanted to be a painter. They'd exchanged worried looks and said, "How about a graphic designer? They make more money." I didn't know what a graphic designer was, so they took me to Dan to find out. As soon as my parents left, Dan pulled out his book of color samples—page after page of every imaginable shade of the rainbow, each with its own ID number. He let me run my fingers over the chips and asked me to point out my favorites: the smoky blues, the zingy oranges. After that we sat at his desk to talk. Dan's voice was quiet, and he said so little that I felt like I had to listen hard. Like every word was important. I had this feeling that he wasn't only telling me how to be a graphic designer but how to be a grown-up. He asked questions in a way that made me think my answers really mattered. He wanted to know if I thought that each day of the week had a color. I stopped breathing for a second. "Who is this guy?" I thought. "How does this adult know that I assign colors to the days of the week?" I'd never talked about it with anyone before. Still reeling from his insight, I nodded, and he asked what color I thought Monday was. I said, "Red." He told me that he thought Monday was white. Silent, empty white. He said it peacefully, and his open hand gestured in the air, as if he were painting the emptiness. I knew this man was different from any other man I'd met; he was a man who understood the world of children. He understood there were things that children didn't talk about even with each other.

As I got older, I met with Dan a couple more times. Ostensibly, it was to discuss my future as an artist, but we would talk about other stuff, too. Once, when he lived by the beach, he told me that he took walks along the jetty to escape the torment of everyday life, and did I know what he meant? I told him I did. Of course I knew what he meant. I was sixteen. Again, I was impressed by his ability to read my innermost thoughts, but this time there was something a little dispiriting about it. I didn't want to believe that the desire to escape didn't go away when you grew up. I felt kind of sorry for him.

The last time I saw Dan, after I'd graduated from college, he told me about how he'd been driving home from Maine recently and came across an image so arresting he had to pull over to take a picture. He said that when he got out of the car he knew there was only one person in the world who'd understand why he'd stopped. That person was my father. When I got home I asked my dad to show me the print. It's a black-and-white image of the facade of a brick building with a sign that says James V. Smiley School. The school building itself looks fairly dreary, but in each window there's a paper smiley face, and each smiley face is wearing a Santa hat. Dan was right: my dad loved the whimsy of seeing smiley faces plastered all over the James V. Smiley School.

Looking at the photograph, taking in the oh-*that's*-a-pictureness of it all, I realized that Dan felt the same way about my dad as I had felt about Dan. He seemed to get me in this profound way—the assigning of colors to the days of the week, the wanting to escape. My dad was that for Dan. And I think what Dan was saying in his suicide note was that he hoped my dad saw him that way, too.

Thinking back on it now, it seems incongruous that the image I most associate with Dan is of a bunch of smiley faces. Though Dan never talked about his depression with my dad, my dad was painfully aware of it. As an adolescent, I learned the term *manic-depressive* because I heard my parents talking about an incident involving Dan. Something about him threatening to jump out of his office window. Before that there was an episode involving a knife. And in between there was a possibly non-accidental bike accident. As close as Dan and my dad were, Dan never talked about this part of his life with my dad. Dan's ex-wife once told my dad that Dan didn't want my dad to think of him "that way." But once a person actually does commit suicide it's impossible not to see his dark side. And my dad didn't like to think about Dan's dark side—he liked looking up to Dan, he liked seeing him as this flawless talent. So when he received Dan's undeveloped film, he hoped to get another glimpse of the brilliant man he knew. He couldn't help but think, "Portfolio!" He was like a pirate unearthing buried treasure; he just knew there would be golden pictures on those rolls, and he'd figure out exactly where to get them published. He was honored that Dan had known he was the right man for the job. My dad took the film to the photo lab and dropped off all seventeen rolls with these instructions: "Don't screw this up."

And then Dad got the contact sheets. He looked them over at the lab with his magnifying loupe, expecting to find gorgeous shots—pictures that made him smile, pictures worth pulling off the road for. Nothing jumped out at him right away, but still, he marked up a few frames with his grease pencil that seemed to have potential. When he got home he looked at the contact sheets again, this time realizing that the ones he'd marked up were out of focus and the wrong exposure. For the next couple of days he kept going back to the pictures, thinking there had to be at least five to ten strong ones in there somewhere. Finally, he showed the contacts to my mom and told her despondently, "I don't think there's anything here." Nothing that warranted being published in a book, or even a magazine.

Mostly, they're posed pictures of Dan's family. Then there are some abstracts of icy twigs on a dock, shadows on the side of a house from a ladder. My dad calls these "snapshots"—just regular old pictures, not "Oh, *that's* a picture" pictures. Now, not only was my dad devastated, he was pissed. He'd unlocked this treasure chest only to find foil-wrapped chocolate coins instead of gold. The bewildering thing is, my dad is certain that had he taken the images on those rolls of film and shown them to Dan, he would've politely passed. And my dad is convinced that if Dan had actually ever seen the film himself, he never would've sent it off.

I recently asked my dad how he would answer Dan's question, "Can you see what I saw?" He thought about it for a minute, then said, "I wanted to get it. I wanted to see what he saw." And then he quickly jumped back in and added with a twinge of anger, "Yeah, I saw what you saw, but, uh, I don't want to use the words, 'So what?' There were other things I know he could've seen on a better day that would've been profoundly more interesting." This was something new for my dad. He'd never been disappointed by any of Dan's work before. Connecting with Dan was never an effort. And now, when it seemed more important than ever to see things the way Dan did, he just couldn't.

At the end of Dan's letter he tells my dad, "Dick, the truth is the joy and wonder and mystery were too much for me to bear." It seems as if Dan was hoping his final photographs would reveal to my dad this joy and wonder and mystery, and that my dad would be so overwhelmed by the beauty he'd understand why Dan could not keep living. But instead, what Dan showed my dad in that film was his raw, unedited worldview. He showed my dad that what he saw was not always sophisticated or polished. It was sometimes blurry and grainy and dull. Maybe, without really meaning to, Dan actually let my dad in on how he saw Mondays. Silent, empty. White.

Northeast Direct

Dagoberto Gilb

I'm on board Amtrak's number 175 to Penn Station. I've traveled by train a couple of times in the past year, but last time I discovered that each car had one electrical outlet. Besides lots of room, besides that comforting, rolling motion, it's what I think about now when I think about the train. My Powerbook has a weak battery, and I can plug in and type as long as I want.

The car is empty. Maybe three of us new passengers, two previously seated. So I do feel a little awkward taking the seat right behind this guy who I saw hustle on several minutes before I did. He'd already reclined his aisle seat, thrown his day bag and warm coat on the one by the window. He was settled. I'm sure he was more than wondering why, with so many empty seats all around, I had to go and sit directly behind him. But I felt something too. Why did *he* have to pick a seat a row in front of the electrical outlet? And if he grumbled when I bumped the back of his seat to get by, I grumbled because I had to squeeze past to get over to the window seat behind him.

I'm over it quickly because I've got my machine on and I'm working. And he seems to be into his world too. He's taken a daily planner out, and he's checking a few things. I see this because, his seat reclined, I'm given a wedge view of his face looking forward and to the side. I see his left eye and the profile of his nose when he turns toward his window. When the conductor comes by for our tickets, he asks if there's a phone, then gets up to use it. I get immersed and barely notice him return.

I pause, and my eyes float up. He's holding a thick new book. I'm sort of looking it over with him. The way the cover feels, the way the chapters are set out. It seems like an attractively produced history book, and I bet he just bought it. He puts it down, then reaches over to the seat in front of me and brings up another.

The other book is the paperback of my novel! I *cannot* believe it! He stares at the cover for a moment, then he opens it. He's reading the acknowledgments page! When he's done he turns back to the title page for a moment, then puts the book down. He gets up and goes to a forward car, where the conductor said he'd find a phone.

How improbable is this? I mean, mine is definitely not a Danielle Steel, not a John Grisham. If it is this much shy of miraculous that I would be on a train with someone who had heard of my books at all, how much more miraculous that, because of an electrical outlet on a train, I'd be sitting inches from a person who just purchased the book and is opening it before my eyes? And look at it this way: of the possible combinations of seating arrangements in the train car, how many could give me this angle? And what if he hadn't put his seat back?

I know what you're thinking. That I should lean over and say, Hey man, you will *never* guess who's sitting behind you! No, that's not me. I don't want to do that. I won't. I want him to be my anonymous reader. How many opportunities does a writer have to learn a truthful reaction, really truthful, to his writing? How absorbed will he be? Will he smile at parts, groan at others? How about his facial expressions? Will his eyes light up or go dull?

As he's walking back, he's staring at me a little too strongly—but he can't know who I am. I'm feeling, naturally enough, self-conscious. He can't possibly know he's in the eyes of the author himself—to think it would be even *more* ridiculous than that it's true. It could be the bright yellow shirt I have on, which is a banner really, a United Farm Workers T-shirt celebrating Cesar Chávez. It reads *Cada trabajador es un organizador.* People are always looking at it and I practically can't wear it because they do. But he's not paying attention to my shirt. It's that I'm the dude sitting behind him, typing into his ear, breathing on his neck while we're on this empty train, with so much room, so many seats, with so much possible spacing. I think he probably doesn't like me. He's probably got names for me.

He sits down. He's picked up the book! He's gone to page one and he's *reading!* Somehow I just can't believe it, and I'm typing frantically about him and this phenomenon. He's a big guy, six-two. Wire glasses, blue, unplayful eyes. Grayish hair, indicating he's most likely not an undergrad, and beneath a Brown University cap, which, because he's wearing the cap, indicates he's probably not a professor. Grad student in English? Or he's into reading about the Southwest? Or maybe the cover has drawn him to the purchase. He's turned to page two! He's going! I have this huge smile as I'm typing. Bottom page two, and yes, his eyes shift to page three!

Suddenly he stops there. He gets up again. The phone is my bet. I'm taking the opportunity. I'm dying to know the name of the bookstore he's gone to, and I kind of arch upwards, over the back of the seat in front of me, to see a glossy store bag, when just as suddenly he's on his way back and he's eyeing me again. I squirm under the psychic weight of these circumstances, though now also from the guilty fact that I'm being so nosy. I pretend I am stretching, looking this way and that, rotating my neck—such uncomfortable seats, wouldn't you say?

He's reading the novel *again.* Page four, page five, page six! A woman walks by and he doesn't even glance up, isn't even curious whether she is attractive or not. He's so engrossed! He's *totally* reading now. No, wait. He stops, eyes to the window where it's New England, beautifully composed and framed by this snowy winter. Those tall, boxy two- and three-story board-and-batten houses painted colonial gray and colonial blue, two windows per floor, hip and gable roof, nubs of chimney poking up. Oh no, he's putting the book down. Closes it, mixes it into his other belongings on the seat next to him. It's because he's moving. He must hear my manic typing and he feels crowded and so he's picking up his stuff and going up an aisle. What an astute, serious, intelligent reader I have to feel so cramped! My reader wants to read in silence, be alone with his book and the thoughts generated by it and his reaction to it and he doesn't like some dude behind him jamming up his reading time and space with this muttering keyboard sound—it just makes me *smile* thinking how keen my reader's psychic synapses are to be responding to what his conscious mind cannot know is occurring. It must be a raging psychic heat, a dizzying psychic pheromone. When he has settled comfortably into his new seat, he pulls the novel back up. He's reading again! Reading and reading! When that young woman passes through on her return, no, again, he does not look up. He's dedicated, fully concentrating. He's really reading, one page after another.

New England: white snow, silver water, leafless branches and limbs. Lumber and boat and junk yards. The bare behind of industry, its dirty underwear, so beautifully disguised by winter.

My reader has fallen asleep. We haven't been on the train an hour and my writing has made him succumb to a nap? Nah, I don't find it a bad thing. Not in the slightest. It's really a compliment. How many books do you fall asleep with? The conductor wakes him up, though. He's sorry but he found that daily planner on the seat behind him and wanted to make sure it belonged to him. But my reader goes right back to sleep. He's dead asleep now. A goner. I pass him on my way to buy myself a drink, and he's got his left thumb locked inside the book, his index finger caressing the spine, pinching. You see, my reader does not want to lose his place.

We both wake up at New Haven. Probably getting a little carried away. I thought he might get off here—walking the book into Yale. He reopens it. He's at the beginning of chapter two. He does read slowly. He's lazy? I say he's thoughtful, a careful, considerate reader, complementing precisely the manner in which I wrote the novel. It's not meant to be read quickly. He's absolutely correct to read it the way he does.

Forty-five minutes outside Penn Station, many passengers have boarded, cutting my reader and me off. He is still up there reading, but with the passage of time, and our physical distance blunted more by a clutter of other minds sitting between and around us, the shock and mystery have lessened in me. I have adjusted, accepted it. By now I am behaving as though it were ordinary that a stranger two aisles above is reading my work. Like every other miracle that happens in life, I am taking the event for granted already, letting it fade into the everyday of people filling trains, going home from work, going. He is reading the novel, and I am certain, by the steady force and duration of his commitment, that he fully intends to read unto the end. He and I both can look around, inside the car and out the window, and then we go back, him to the book, me to the computer keyboard, no longer writing about this.

So when the moment comes, ask what, how? Tap him on the shoulder, say excuse me, but you know I couldn't help but notice that book you're reading, and it's such an amazing coincidence, it *really* is *so* amazing how this can happen, but I was just talking with a friend about that very novel this morning—change that—I was talking to two friends, and one thought it was just great, while the other—change that—and one thought it was just great, and I wondered what you felt about it, and how did you hear of it anyway?

After the conductor announces Penn Station, we stand and get our coats on, and, the train still swaying, move down the aisle and toward the door with our bags. I'm waiting right behind him. Can easily tap him on the shoulder. But nobody else is talking. No one, not a word. So I can't either, especially when I'd be making fake conversation. Train stops, door opens, people in front of him move forward, and a woman in an aisle steps in between me and him with her large, too-heavy-for-her suitcase. He's shot out quickly ahead of me now, up an escalator, several more people between us. When I reach the main floor of the station, get beneath the flapping electronic board that posts trains and times and departure tracks, I have caught up with him. He has stopped to get his bearings. Just as I am at his shoulder, he takes off in the same direction I'm going.

So we're walking briskly side by side in cold Penn Station. You know what? He doesn't want to talk. I am sure he has no desire to speak with me. Would definitely not want to have that conversation I'd planned. No time for me to fumble around and, maybe, eventually, tell him how I am the writer. This is New York City, no less. He's in a hurry. He'd grimace and shake his head, brush me off. He already thinks I am one of those irritating people you encounter on a trip, the one always at the edge of your sight, the one you can never seem to shake. And so as I begin a ride up the escalator toward the taxi lines, I watch him go straight ahead, both of us covered with anonymity like New England snow.

The People on the Bus

Adam Gopnik

Lately, I like to ride the bus. I don't mean the double-decker tourist buses that, half empty, warily circle the city, like dazed displaced troop carriers, or the long-distance buses that come sighing into the Port Authority Terminal, where it is eternally 3 A.M. and everyone looks exhausted before the journey starts, or even the yellow-and-blacks that still delicately deliver children from downtown to uptown at eight in the morning. I mean the ordinary city buses, those vaguely purposeless-looking, bulbous-faced, blue-and-bone M2s and 3s and 4s and 5s that chug up and down the avenues and along the cross streets, wheezing and whining, all day and night.

For twenty-odd years in New York, I never rode the bus at all—not, at least, after a single, traumatic bus experience. On the very first day I visited Manhattan, in the anxious (though, looking back, mostly unfrightened) summer of 1978—the summer when Jimmy Carter turned down the air-conditioning all over town—I got on a bus outside the Metropolitan Museum, saw that the fare was fifty cents, and, with the unquenchable cheerfulness of the visiting Canadian, proudly pulled out a dollar bill—an American dollar bill—folded it up neatly, stuffed the dollar in the fare box, two fares, and looked up, expecting the driver to beam at my efficiency. I will never forget his look of disbelief and disgust, mingled, I think, with a certain renewed awe at the enormities that out-of-towners were capable of.

From that day on, I don't think I ever rode another bus. I suppose I must have; transportational logic says that I must have—there must be a crosstown M86 or an uptown limited in there somewhere—but, if I did, I don't know when. Even if I had been on a bus, I don't think I would recall it. Bus-blindness is a standard New York illness; of all the regularities of life here, the bus is the least celebrated, the least inclined to tug at the heart, or be made into a symbol of our condition. The taxi has its checkered lore, the subway its legend, the limo a certain Michael Douglas-in-"Wall Street" icon quality—but if there is a memorable bus scene in literature, or an unforgettable moment in a movie that takes place on a New York City bus, I have not found it. (If you Google New York buses in movie scenes, you end up with a bus-enthusiasts' site and a shot of a New York City bus from a Sylvester Stallone movie called "Driven," and this bus turns out to be dressed up like a Chicago city bus, and filmed on location in Toronto.) There is nothing about buses that makes them intrinsically symbol-repellent: the London bus has a poetry as rich as the Tube's—there is Mary Poppins, there is Mrs. Dalloway. In Paris, Pascal rides the bus, Zazie rides the Métro, and that is, evenly, that. But as a symbolic repository the New York City bus does not exist. The only significant symbolic figure that the New York bus has had in Ralph Kramden, and what he symbolizes about the bus is that being stuck in one is in itself one more form of comic frustration and disappointment; the New York City bus might best be described by saying that it is exactly the kind of institution that would have Ralph Kramden as its significant symbolic figure.

If you had asked me why I avoided the bus, I suppose I would have said that the bus was for old people—or that taking the bus was one step short of not actually living in New York at all, and that if you stayed on the bus long enough it would take you right out of town. Riding the bus was one of those activities, like going to Radio City, that was in New York but not really of it. My mother-in-law rode the bus when she came to New York to visit, and that, I thought, said whom the bus was made for: elegant older women who didn't mind traveling forty-five minutes every morning to visit their grandchildren.

And then I didn't ride the bus because I loved the subway so. Compared with the vivid and evil and lurid subway, the bus seemed a drab bourgeois necessity—Shirley Booth to the subway's Tallulah Bankhead. When I began to ride the subway, particularly in the late seventies and early eighties, it was both grander and stranger than a newcomer can imagine now. The graffiti, for one thing, were both more sordid inside—all those "tags"—and more beautiful outside. When the wild-style cars came roaring into a station, they were as exciting and shimmering as Frank Stella birds. The air-conditioning was a lot spottier, too, and sometimes the windows were open, driving the stale and fetid air around in an illusion of cooling. When the air-conditioning worked, it was worse. You walked from steam bath to refrigerator, a change like a change of continents, and your perspiration seemed to freeze within your shirt, a phenomenon previously known only to Antarctic explorers.

Feral thugs and killer nerds rode the subway together, looking warily at one another. And yet there was something sublime about the subway. Although it was incidentally frightening, it was also systematically reassuring: it shouldn't have worked; it had stopped working; and yet it worked—vandalized, brutalized, a canvas and a pissoir, it reliably took you wherever you wanted to go. It was a rumbling, sleepless, snorting animal presence underfoot, more a god to be appeased and admired than a thing that had been mastered by its owners. If the stations seemed, as people said, Dantesque, that was not simply because the subway was belowground, and a punishment, but also because it offered an architectural order that seemed to be free from any interfering human hand, running by itself in its own grim circles. It was religious in the narrow sense as well: terror and transportation were joined together, fear propelled you to a higher plane. (The taxis, an alternative if you had the money, were alarming then, too—a silent or determined driver in a T-shirt resting on a mat of beads and demanding, fifty blocks before your destination, which side of the street you wanted—without being at all sublime.)

Coming home in 2000 after five years abroad, I took it for granted that I would return to the subway and the taxi, only to be stunned by the transformation in them both. The subway, now graffiti free, with dully gleaming metal cars (though obviously made to be as resistant to vandalism as a prison), had recorded announcements, and for a while a picture of the station manager at every stop. It seemed obviously improved but somehow degraded, grimly utilitarian, intended to suggest the receding future vision of "RoboCop": automatic voices encased in armor. The chaos was gone from inside the cabs, and held on only around them. After five years in Paris, where one phones for a cab or lines up in an orderly manner at a station, logically and fairly, I nearly wept tears of frustration at the anarchy of the street system—you waited for fifteen minutes and someone waltzed out into the middle of the block and stepped in front of you as a cab approached. (There is, of course, an implicit system of fair dealing in this—one block away is legitimate; the same corner is not—but I could no longer remember the rules, much less find the patience to practice them.)

And so the bus. Almost every day for the past year and a half, I've found myself taking a limited bus down an East Side avenue, and then, a few hours and frustrations later, taking it back uptown on the adjoining avenue. I stand or, in good hours, sit among the usual bus riders. The bus I find humane, in several ways. There is, first of all, the non-confrontational and yet collaborative nature of the seating. You look over people's shoulders, closely, and yet only rarely look directly at them, face to face, as you must on the subway. There is a hierarchy of seating on the bus, far more articulate than that of the subway. There are seats you must give up to handicapped people, seats you ought to give up to handicapped people if you have any decency at all, and seats—the bumpy, exhaust-scented row in the very back—that you never have to give up to anyone, if you're willing to sit there. (The reason for all those designated spaces is that law and propriety dictate that when someone in a wheelchair rolls up to a bus stop, the bus has to stop and let him on.) There is also on almost every New York bus a little single seat tucked in near the back door, which has the air of a dunce chair in a classroom. You can sit there, but you wouldn't want to. Late at night, there is even a policy of optional stops. You ask the driver to stop the bus where you're going and, if he can, he will.

The bus also has order, order as we know it from the fading patriarchal family, visible order kept by an irritable chief. The driver has not only control over his world but the delight of the exercise of arbitrary authority, like that of a French bureaucrat. Bus riders learn that, if your MetroCard turns out to be short fifty cents, the driver will look at you with distaste, tell you to find change from fellow-passengers (surprisingly, to a subway rider, people dig into their purses cheerfully), and, if this doesn't work, will wearily wave you on back. You are included, fool though you are, and this often at the moment when the driver is ignoring the pounded fists and half-audible pleas for admission of the last few people who, running for the bus, arrived a second too late. The driver's control of the back door is just as imperious. A red zone of acceptability exists around the bus stop, known only to the driver, who opens and closes the door as he senses the zone appearing and receding.

It is uniquely possible to overhear conversations on the bus. The other morning, for instance—a beautiful morning of our time, the sky blue, the alert orange, and the *Times* sports pages ominously upside down—a man behind me was trying to remember the names of popular Drake's snacks from his childhood.

"What are those things? There were Ring-Dings and Drake's cakes."

"You mean Twinkies," the man he was with said, with assurance. I couldn't see either face, but their voices had the peaceable quarrelsomeness of those who have just passed from middle-aged to elderly.

"No, I don't mean Twinkies," he said angrily. "I mean them other things."

Long pause. We couldn't resist. "Devil Dogs," someone said, "Devil Dogs."

"Yes, thanks, Devil Dogs. How come you don't ever see Devil Dogs these days?"

This is a typical bit of bus talk. (In a taxi you would stew on the issue all by yourself. The millionaire in his limo could ask the driver, I suppose, but he would be too embarrassed to answer. On the subway, no one would hear, in the first place; and if the words "Devil Dog" were said with enough emphasis to be heard, it would cause a panicked mass exodus.) On another morning, a man and a woman were riding together down Fifth Avenue and saw the new, comically twinned, comically misnamed AOL Time Warner Center—the Delusional States Building, as it will doubtless someday be known—come into view. (And those two towers rising, however plainly, have become a source of pride: *something's* rising.) "That Trump," the man said, chuckling. "He always does things in twos. Have you ever noticed how he always does things in twos?"

"I've noticed that. That's his thing, his signature, doing two of everything."

"Well, there he does it again. Two towers again."

Sage nods. The fact that, as it occurred to me later, the towers are not by Trump, and that, in any case, Trump, in his long career, has never done two of anything, should not diminish the glory of this exchange. If you were on the subway, there would be nothing to look at; if you were in a limo, you would actually be Trump, building things, gloriously, in nonexistent pairs.

When I first started riding the bus, I mentioned it to people sheepishly, almost apologetically, as one might mention having had a new dental plate put in, or the advantages of low-fat yogurt—as one might mention something that, though not downright shameful, might still seem mildly embarrassing. But, to my surprise, almost everyone I talked to (and women, I think, in particular) turned out to feel the same way I do about the bus. "The bus lets you feel that you're in control, or that someone's in control," one woman said to me, and another friend said flatly, "You can see what's coming." The bus feels safe. Of course, there is no reason for the bus to feel safe. (A friend from Jerusalem got on the bus with understandable watchfulness.) Yet we have decided to create in the city a kind of imaginary geography of fear and safety that will somehow make us safer from It—from the next attack, of course, from the Other Shoe, the Dreadful Thing that we all await.

I have thought about it a lot while I am riding the bus, and I have come to the conclusion that, while anxiety seeks out the company of excitement, fear seeks out the illusion of certainty. People tend to write these days about anxiety and fear as though they were equal, or anyway continuous, emotions, one blending into the other, but anyone who has felt them—and anyone who hasn't felt them, at least a little, hasn't been living in New York in the past year—knows that they are as distinct as a bus from a subway, as a Devil Dog from a Ring-Ding. Anxiety is the ordinary New York emotion. It is a form of energy, and clings, like ivy to a garden wall, to whatever is around to cling to, whether the object is nationalism or the Knicks or Lizzie Grubman, as readers of the *New York Post* recognize. At the height of the bubble, anxiety was all around us: the anxiety of keeping up, of not falling behind, of holding one's place.

Fear, well earned or not, is a different thing. People who live with the higher kinds of fear—the ill, soldiers—live with it mostly by making structures of delusional domesticity. They try to create an illusion of safety, and of home. At Waterloo, soldiers welcomed the little signs of farm-keeping evident around them; in the dugouts of the Somme, every rat-ridden alley had a designation and every rat itself a pet name. The last time New Yorkers were genuinely afraid, as opposed to merely anxious, during the great crime wave of the sixties and mid-seventies, they responded in the same way: by constructing an elaborate, learn-it-by-heart geography of safe and unsafe enclaves, a map of safe rooms. The knowledge that the map could not truly protect you from what you feared then, any more than riding the bus can save you from it now, did not alter the need to have a map. People say that twentysomethings have sex out of fear—it is called terror sex—but twentysomethings have sex out of sex, and the adjective of the decade is always attached to it. In the eighties, they had safe sex, and in the nineties boom sex, and they will have sex-among-the-ruins, if it comes to that.

What we have out of fear is not sex, or any other anxiety-energized activity, but stillness. It's said that people in the city are nicer now, or more cooperative, and I suppose this is true. But it is true for reasons that are not themselves entirely nice. The motivation of this niceness is less rectitude and reform than just plain old-fashioned fright. There are no atheists in foxholes, but there are no religious arguments in foxholes, either. The fear we feel isn't as immediate or as real as the fear soldiers feel. But our response is the same. These structures of delusional domesticity are the mainstay of the lives of many of us in New York now. The bus, a permanently running dinner party among friends, a fiction of family for a dollar-fifty, a Starbucks on wheels, is the rolling image of the thing we dream of now as much as we wanted the Broadband Pipe to wash away our sins three years ago, and that is the Safe Room. For the first time, the bus has something to symbolize.

On the bus the other morning, the worst regularly scheduled thing that can happen on the bus happened. A guy in a wheelchair held things up for three minutes—no time at all, really, but an eternity on television, or in the subway, or, usually, in the city. As bus riders know, buses are equipped to stop and, by lowering a clever elevator device, let a wheelchair-bound rider board the bus. This, though a civic mitzvah, involves a sequence where the driver locks the front door, works the elevator at the rear door, hoists up the wheelchair on the lift, and then folds up the designated seats to give the wheelchair man room (it is nearly always a man). There is something artisanal, handmade about it—the lock, the voyage, working the elevator—in which a municipal employee is reduced, or raised, to a valet.

"It's the lame and the halt on the bus," one woman said.

"What's the difference between the lame and the halt?"

"The lame are, like, lame, and the halt, halt."

"You mean the halt don't walk."

"I mean they halt. But they halt because they're lame."

It is the kind of conversation—discursive, word-sensitive—that is possible on the bus right now, and nowhere else. I keep meaning to look up the difference.

On The Bus

Vivian Gornick

For many years I taught one semester a year in graduate writing programs, nearly all of them far from home. Some time ago I was offered a position at a state university two hundred miles from New York and, calculating quickly that I could easily commute, I accepted the job. Sure enough, things worked out as I had hoped, and I came home every weekend. What I did not expect (or bargain for) was that I would be traveling to the school and back on a Greyhound bus. The university, as it turned out, was in the exact middle of nowhere. Like most New Yorkers, I don't own a car, and getting to it by train or plane was so roundabout and expensive a process that a four-an-a-half-hour bus ride proved to be the only realistic means of transportation.

The bus I took left the Port Authority terminal in Manhattan six times a day bound for Cleveland, Chicago, and either San Francisco or Salt Lake City. On Monday I'd board it at 5:00 in the afternoon and be dropped at 9:30 in the evening at a truck stop fifteen miles from the school, where I'd be picked up and driven into town. On Thursday nights, I'd be returned to the truck stop at 8:30, and be back at the Port Authority at 1:00 in the morning.

Often I was the only one to leave the bus at this truck stop. Most of the other passengers were headed for Cleveland or Chicago, although a significant number were setting out for either California or Utah, often looking as exhausted at the start as they undoubtedly would be at the finish. The bus was, in fact, a study in exhaustion—a thing I came to realize only slowly. Most of my traveling companions were working-class blacks or Latinos or Asians who didn't speak a word of English, and many of them were badly, even incoherently, put together. But it wasn't the ragged dress code, as I first thought, that gave the bus its derelict look. It was the exhaustion. Exhaustion is deracinating.

It began in New York in the bowels of the Port Authority terminal, where people started lining up at the lower-level gate more than an hour before the bus was due to leave, although almost no one was actually standing in line. People slumped against the wall, or sprawled across duffel bags, or sat cross-legged on the floor. As the line grew and began to snake ever farther out and away from the gate itself, the lassitude of the crowd grew apace. A kind of low-grade melancholy began to seep into the atmosphere. The Asians were almost entirely silent, the blacks looked asleep on their feet, the Latinos sad and murmurous. The line soon became a crowd of refugees: people with no rights, only obligations. By the time the driver pushed the door open and started taking tickets, everyone looked beaten.

It was always a surprise to me when I found one of the front seats empty. Although those seats were a special concern of mine—on a long trip it is my invariable hope to dream out the front window—by the time I arrived at the gate, there were always twenty-five people ahead of me in line. There go the front seats, I'd sigh inwardly, but when I climbed the steps of the bus, more often than not I'd find one of the four empty. Almost everyone ahead of me had made for the back. By the time we were loaded and ready to go, three out of five passengers were burrowed down in their seats, eyes closed, shoulders slumped, heads disappearing below the level of the backrests.

Sometimes, however, I would have to settle farther back in the bus, and quite often when I did—again to my surprise—the tired-looking person in the next seat would start talking at me: how long was it gonna take to get this show on the road; never can make these recliners work; the leg room here is pathetic. I did not welcome these harmless openers, since I knew that they almost always meant I'd soon be taken hostage. Because I am compulsively sociable, it is impossible for me to turn a deaf ear or an expressionless face to someone speaking to me. Even though I usually end up wishing the earth would open up and swallow the one inflicting tedium on me, on my face there remains an attentive expression and out of my mouth, every now and then, comes an unavoidable "Really!" or "I know what you mean." I have spent a fair amount of my life trapped by those who are boring me into a rage because once they start talking I am forced to listen. It was always remarkable to me on those Monday-Thursday Greyhound trips that those talking to me never seemed to notice that I hardly said a word.

One Thursday night in the late fall of my second year at this school, I climbed onto the bus at the truck stop and found a seat beside a woman sitting three rows back from the front. She was thin, with long blonde hair framing a narrow face, wearing a teenager's tank top, miniskirt, and high-heeled white boots. Her head was propped against the headrest, her eyes closed, her body limp. She seemed drained to the point of illness. But as I sank down beside her, she opened her eyes, turned, and asked if I lived around here. "No," I said. "I don't." "You from New York?" she asked. "Yes," I said. "Nothing like the city," she said. I smiled. "I'm from Cleveland," she said. I nodded. "Ever been in Cleveland?" I shook my head no. "Don't bother," she said. I smiled again. "I live in New York but my mother's sick, so I'm back and forth between Cleveland and New York these days."

Her name was Jewel. Twenty years ago, right after high school (make that twenty-five, I thought), she'd come to New York to become a stage actress. Things hadn't exactly worked out as she had planned, but she said she was one of the most sought-after extras for nearly every movie made in the city. She also worked as a bartender in midtown. Before we got to the Port Authority, Jewel told me that her mother was dying of cancer, her father was a sweet man who had a hard time making a decision, and her brother, a doctor, was keeping their mother alive by some pretty extraordinary artificial means.

A week later, I climbed onto the bus and there was Jewel again, sitting the same three rows back, with the same empty seat beside her. She waved to me, and I felt obliged to sit down next to her. She looked as worn out as she had the week before but, smiling warmly, she asked how my week had been, waited patiently for me to say okay, then launched herself. "I don't know," she began, "something doesn't feel right to me, it just doesn't feel right." I took a deep breath and said, "What do you mean?" "My brother," she said. "It's like he's *obsessed*." She talked steadily for the next two hours.

They'd been raised on a farm just outside Cleveland, her father had never made a living, her mother had been cold to her and devoted to her brother. The brother was married and a father himself, but he seemed never to have felt for anyone what he felt for their mother. Of course, Jewel was just guessing. Nobody ever *said* anything in that family. But her brother and her mother *did* speak to each other every morning, and clearly each preferred the other's company to that of anyone else. When she got sick, he cheerfully went to work to save her. There was no question of not finding a way. But she had not responded to any of the many treatments that had been tried. Now she was a bag of bones and kept saying she thought it was time for her to go. "No, Ma," Jewel's brother kept saying. "Not yet. I can't let you go yet."

Between late October and Christmas of that year, I sat on the bus every Thursday night listening to Jewel rehearse the latest episode in the family romance of the doomed mother and the entranced son. "You should see the two of them in the hospital room," she'd say. "They've got eyes for no one but each other. My father and I just sit there. We don't even look at each other. It's embarrassing. I keep thinking we've got no business watching them." Chekhov once said that people who travel lose all reserve; he must have had Jewel in mind.

I, meanwhile, said almost nothing. Week after week I sat beside Jewel, my body turned toward her, my elbow on the armrest between us, fingers ridging up into either my right or left temple, eyes trained on her face, nearly silent.

On the last Thursday of the semester, I settled into the seat beside Jewel, and we pulled out into a cold, clear night made magical by the colored lights outlining the vast eighteen-wheelers dancing up or down the highway on either side of the bus. I let myself be mesmerized. Hardly noticing that I wasn't really there, Jewel rattled on—he was pulling her back from the grave, the other doctors thought he'd gone over the edge, his wife was on the verge of divorce.

At one in the morning, the driver steered the bus into its Port Authority berth and turned on the inside lights. Everyone in front stood at once, picking up

packages, putting on coats. I stepped into the aisle just behind Jewel. As we approached the door, she turned, flung her arms around my neck, and said, "I don't
know what I would have done all these weeks without you talking to me."

"Jewel," I protested. "I didn't do anything. You did it all yourself."

For a few moments she looked startled. Then she put her mouth close to my
ear and in a voice of unforgettable dignity said, "You let me talk. That's the same
thing as talking to me."

I pulled back and looked at her. Her face seemed full of emotion. It was
strained but alert, slightly puzzled but oddly excited. One thing it was not was exhausted.

The Death of Personal Blogs

Emily Gould

This past December marked the tenth anniversary of the blog, or at least of the shortening of the phrase "Web log." By now your grandmother probably knows what a blog is. She probably has one, and it's probably good! No matter, though. In my mind, at least, blogs are done for.

I got sucked into the world of personal blogs around 2003, which, to borrow the parlance of people who have been following each other's online diaries since 1996, makes me a "noob." In the late 1990s, the people who were discovering the potential of the Internet were mostly hardcore nerds, so their personal websites had an insular kind of appeal. But come Y2K, these homespun sites were breaking news, humanizing political candidates, and making money. My favorites, though, were the dear-diary musings of strangers, people who were putting their sometimes deep, usually banal thoughts online for anyone to see. Just because they could.

And so could I. Shortly after moving in together in 2003, my roommate and best friend Bennett and I started a site called *The Universal Review*, and soon our deep/banal thoughts were joining everyone else's on the Internet. We reviewed and assigned letter grades not just to books and movies and TV shows and restaurants, but also to "types of people," "lifestyle choices," and "sundries." (The bums on our corner, for example, got an F.) When Bennett moved out and our blog broke up, I started a site of my own, which kept the judgmental attitude of *The Universal Review* but added more girly life-pondering.

We bloggers weren't motivated by profit, nor by the desire for any kind of attention besides that of our sometimes friendly, sometimes contentious communities of anonymous commentators. We just wanted to express ourselves and communicate with each other without the mediation of editorial approval or advertisers' agendas, man! At least, that's how it seemed to me then.

And then came the party crashers. Bloggers started getting book deals, and it seemed like agents and editors were just rushing to cash in on a trend without thinking about whether what was special about a blog would translate to the page. A handful of bloggers, like Wendy McClure and Julie Powell, became authors gracefully; a few others, like Dana Vachon and Jessica Cutler, sold their books for six figures. But what happened more often was bloggers getting small-ish deals for half-baked books that no one ever read.

Loads more bloggers succumbed to the allure of corporate blogging. They quit whatever boring jobs had once enabled them to spend hours of their days composing posts about what had happened on the subway that morning and started blogging for a living, recapping television shows for Bravo or enthusing about crap pop culture for VH1's *Best Week Ever* blog. I took a job as an editor at *Gawker*, the then-four-year-old site focused on New York and media-related news and gossip.

Churning out a bunch of blog posts for a biggish audience every day was exhilarating—hard, and scary, like performing in an improv comedy show for ten hours at a time. When not glued to my computer, I was sneaking into parties and interviewing people on the streets of my neighborhood about how they felt about celebrity couples' breakups—fun! And I loved getting up on my high horse about literary scandals and bad book deals. But soon the coworkers I respected left *Gawker*, there was a new emphasis on page views, and the tone of the site was shifting. The grind of having to know everything at all times and constantly think of clever ways to repackage information started to wear on me. And my personal blog had gone from infrequently updated to neglected to all but forgotten. It felt like there was too much Internet already. And it felt like I was becoming part of the problem.

I was burnt out, and not in a way that was fun to write about—or read about. On December 1, I quit.

Checking in on the sites I used to frequent five years ago during the golden age of the blog reveals an online graveyard. Many of my old virtual friends' last few posts follow the same sad pattern—the initial spate of "sorry I haven't posted in so long"s followed by the inevitable "it's over, but check out what I'm doing at [corporate blog]!" Of course, hundreds of thousands of new blogs have sprung up in their place—a cacophony of voices shouting into the void, jockeying for their places in the big time, whatever they think that might mean.

Noobs, I wish you the best of luck.

Red Sky at Morning

Patricia Hampl

Years ago, in another life, I woke to look out the smeared window of a Greyhound bus I had been riding all night, and in the still-dark morning of a small Missouri river town where the driver had made a scheduled stop at a grimy diner, I saw below me a stout middle-aged woman in a flowered housedress turn and kiss full on the mouth a godlike young man with golden curls. But I've got that wrong: *he* was kissing *her*. Passionately, without regard for the world and its incomprehension. He had abandoned himself to his love, and she, stolid, matronly, received this adoration with simple grandeur, like a socialist-realist statue of a woman taking up sheaves of wheat.

Their ages dictated that he must be her son, but I had just come out of the cramped, ruinous half sleep of a night on a Greyhound and I was clairvoyant: This was that thing called love. The morning light cracked blood red along the river.

Of course, when she lumbered onto the bus a moment later, lurching forward with her two bulging bags, she chose the empty aisle seat next to me as her own. She pitched one bag onto the overhead rack, and then heaved herself into the seat as if she were used to hoisting sacks of potatoes onto the flatbed of a pickup. She held the other bag on her lap, and leaned toward the window. The beautiful boy was blowing kisses. He couldn't see where she was in the dark interior, so he blew kisses up and down the side of the bus, gazing ardently at the blank windows. "Pardon me," the woman said without looking at me, and leaned over, bag and all, to rap the glass. Her beautiful boy ran back to our window and kissed and kissed, and finally hugged himself, shutting his eyes in an ecstatic pantomime of love-sweet-love. She smiled and waved back.

Then the bus was moving. She slumped back in her seat, and I turned to her. I suppose I looked transfixed. As our eyes met she said, "Everybody thinks he's my son. But he's not. He's my husband." She let that sink in. She was a farm woman with hands that could have been a man's; I was a university student, hair down to my waist. It was long ago, as I said, in another life. It was even another life for the country. The Vietnam War was the time we were living through, and I was traveling, as I did every three weeks, to visit my boyfriend who was in a federal prison. "Draft dodger," my brother said. "Draft resister," I piously retorted. I had never been kissed the way this woman had been kissed. I was living in a tattered corner of a romantic idyll, the one where the hero is willing to suffer for his beliefs. I was the girlfriend. I lived on pride, not love.

My neighbor patted her short cap of hair, and settled in for the long haul as we pulled onto the highway along the river, heading south. "We been married five years and we're happy," she said with a penetrating satisfaction, the satisfaction that passeth understanding. "Oh," she let out a profound sigh as if she mined her truths from the bountiful, bulky earth, "Oh, I could tell you stories." She put her arms snugly around her bag, gazed off for a moment, apparently made pensive by her remark. Then she closed her eyes and fell asleep.

I looked out the window smudged by my nose which had been pressed against it at the bus stop to see the face of true love reveal itself. Beyond the bus the sky, instead of becoming paler with the dawn, drew itself out of a black line along the Mississippi into an alarming red flare. It was very beautiful. The old caution— *Red sky in the morning, sailor take warning*—darted through my mind and fell away. Remember this, I remember telling myself, hang on to this. I could feel it all skittering away, whatever conjunction of beauty and improbability I had stumbled upon.

It is hard to describe the indelible bittersweetness of that moment. Which is why, no doubt, it had to be remembered. The very word—*Remember!*—spiraled up like a snake out of a basket, a magic catch in its sound, the doubling of the m— *re mem-memem*—setting up a low murmur full of inchoate associations as if a loved voice were speaking into my ear alone, occultly.

Whether it was the unguarded face of love, or the red gash down the middle of the warring country I was traveling through, or this exhausted farm woman's promise of untold tales that bewitched me, I couldn't say. Over it all rose and remains only the injunction to remember. This, the most impossible command we lay upon ourselves, claimed me and then perversely disappeared, trailing an illusive silken tissue of meaning, without giving a story, refusing to leave me in peace.

Because everyone "has" a memoir, we all have a stake in how such stories are told. For we do not, after all, simply *have* experience; we are entrusted with it. We must do something—make something—with it. A story, we sense, is the only possible habitation for the burden of our witnessing.

The tantalizing formula of my companion on the Greyhound—*oh, I could tell you stories*—is the memoirist's opening line, but it has none of the delicious promise of the storyteller's "Once upon a time . . ." In fact, it is a perverse statement. The woman on the bus told me nothing—she fell asleep and escaped to her dreams. For the little sentence inaugurates nothing, and leads nowhere after its *dot dot dot* of expectation. Whatever experience lies tangled within its seductive promise remains forever balled up in the woolly impossibility of telling the-truth-the-whole-truth of a life, any life.

Memoirists, unlike fiction writers, do not really want to "tell a story." They want to tell it *all*—the all of personal experience, of consciousness itself. That includes a story, but also the whole expanding universe of sensation and thought that flows beyond the confines of narrative and proves every life to be not only an isolated story line but a bit of the cosmos, spinning and streaming into the great, ungraspable pattern of existence. Memoirists wish to tell their mind, not their story.

The wistfulness implicit in that conditional verb—*I could tell*—conveys an urge more primitive than a storyteller's search for an audience. It betrays not a loneliness for someone who will listen but a hopelessness about language itself and a sad recognition of its limitations. How much reality can subject-verb-object bear on the frail shoulders of the sentence? The sigh within the statement is more like this: I could tell you stories—if only stories could tell what I have in me to tell.

For this reason, autobiographical writing is bedeviled. It is caught in a self which must become a world—and not, please, a narcissistic world. The memoir, once considered a marginal literary form, has emerged in the past decade as the signature genre of the age. "The triumph of memoir is now established fact," James Atlas trumpeted in a cover story on "The Age of the Literary Memoir" in the *New York Times Magazine*. "Fiction," he claimed, "isn't delivering the news. Memoir is."

With its "triumph," the memoir has, of course, not denied the truth and necessity of fiction. In fact, it leans heavily on novelistic assumptions. But the contemporary memoir has reaffirmed the primacy of the first person voice in American imaginative writing established by Whitman's "Song of Myself." Maybe a reader's love of memoir is less an intrusive lust for confession than a hankering for the intimacy of this first-person voice, the deeply satisfying sense of being spoken to privately. More than a story, we want a voice speaking softly, urgently, in our ear. Which is to say, to our heart. That voice carries its implacable command, the ancient murmur that called out to me in the middle of the country in the middle of a war—remember, remember (*I dare you, I tempt you*).

Looking out the Greyhound window that red morning all those years ago, I saw the improbable face of love. But even more puzzling was the cryptic remark of the beloved as she sat next to me. I think of her more often than makes sense. Though he was the beauty, she is the one who comes back. How faint his golden curls have become (he also had a smile, crooked and charming, but I can only remember the idea of it—the image is gone). It is she, stout and unbeautiful, wearing her flowery cotton housedress with a zipper down the middle, who has taken up residence with her canny eye and her acceptance of adoration. To be loved like that, loved improbably: of course, she had stories to tell. She took it for granted in some unapologetic way, like being born to wealth. Take the money and run.

But that moment before she fell asleep, when she looked pensive, the red morning rising over the Mississippi, was a wistful moment. *I could tell you stories*—but she could not. What she had to tell was too big, too much, too something, for her to place in the small shrine that a story is.

When we met—if what happened between us was a meeting—I felt nothing had ever happened to me and nothing ever would. I didn't understand that riding this filthy Greyhound down the middle of bloodied America in the middle of a mutinous war was itself a story and that something *was* happening to me. I thought if something was happening to anybody around me it was happening to people like my boyfriend: They were the heroes, according to the lights that shined for me then. I was just riding shotgun in my own life. I could not have imagined containing, as the farm woman slumped next to me did, the sheer narrative bulk to say, "I could tell you stories," and then drifting off with the secret heaviness of experience into the silence where stories live their real lives, crumbling into the loss we call remembrance.

The boastful little declaration, pathetically conditional (not "I'll tell you a story" but "I could") wavered wistfully for an instant between us. The stranger's remark, launched in the dark of the Greyhound, floated across the human landscape like the lingering tone of a struck bell from a village church, and joined all the silence that ever was, as I turned my face to the window where the world was rushing by along the slow river.

Neighbors

Richard Hoffman

The apparition of these faces in the crowd;

Petals on a wet, black bough.

—"In a Station of the Metro," Ezra Pound

Boston's MBTA Red Line used to end at Porter Square, until recently the town-gown divide in Cambridge, with working people living north of Porter and east into Somerville's Davis Square and Powderhouse neighborhoods. Now it continues through Davis to Alewife Station with its tiered parking garage for commuters from the suburbs. All this change, along with the repeal of rent control, has transformed the neighborhoods so that Cambridge now has the greatest number of homes worth over a million dollars of any city in the United States, and Somerville's Davis Square is going through the familiar transition from workers to artists to money.

Outside Porter Station a forty-six-foot tall red steel sculpture, "Gift of the Wind" by Susumu Shingu, makes its benefactor visible in a mesmerizing and graceful kinesis above the plaza. A remarkable work, it seems to allude to a weathervane and Ferris wheel and sail and horseshoe crab and lobster all at once while it swivels and dips and turns like a prayer wheel or thurible, its blessings quintessentially New England.

I love the Red Line's public art. Over at the Davis stop are life-size statues by James Tyler of people he recruited from the neighborhood, and people from out of town are always having their pictures taken with them. The sculptor's given them masks. Tourists pose with them to see if they can fool the folks back home, if only for a moment: *Who are those people with you? Why are they wearing masks? Oh.* Elsewhere the art is themed to the stop; at Kendall/MIT, for example, the walls chronicle the history of scientific and technological discovery, and a button on the wall activates a series of colliding chimes between the inbound and outbound tracks.

On this particular rainy day, just inside the door of Porter station, the flower vendor has her ephemeral inventory arranged in buckets on risers, but it seems futile: who buys flowers on their way *to* work? At the top of the escalator a man hands each commuter a Metro, a mere outline of a newspaper, little more than headlines and advertising. I take mine and step onto the moving stairs down.

The escalators plunge deep into the earth, the first long ride down bringing you from street level to a plaza with a snack bar, an ATM machine, and a vendor whose cart, depending upon the season, is loaded with baseball caps, sweaters, scarves, gloves, battery-operated fans, and of course incense and prepaid telephone cards. Both vendors, the man with the cart and the man at the snack bar, are clearly Arab, and I have wanted to ask each where he is from but worry the question would seem an affront, my sociable curiosity freighted as it is with history and politics and fear. Next to the vendor's cart a man is selling *Spare Change*, "The Newspaper By, For, And About The Homeless." He is always there lately, standing with his stack of papers under one arm, holding out a copy to us as we debark the stairs. His left eye might be glass; it stares up and to the left so that the one eye that is fixed on you seems ferocious and accusative. And why should he not be angry? Or his fierce gaze may be serving him as a disguise, a mask suggesting danger, covering his otherwise naked vulnerability. No doubt he is homeless himself, and he seems surrounded by unasked questions about how he came to be here glaring at us and importuning us to buy for a dollar what we wish not to know.

Just ahead of me on the escalator down, a woman is rummaging in a huge purse hanging from her shoulder while her child, a girl about four or five, holds onto the moving black handrail with both hands. This is the next chapter of the descent, an additional hundred and fifty feet or so to the inbound platform; there's still another level down after that, to the outbound trains. And here's more art: the bronzed gloves of the workers who dug and tunneled and blasted and laid track and tiled and otherwise carved this now taken-for-granted place out of earth and rock not so long ago; there are pairs of them at intervals along the aluminum console that separates the UP and DOWN escalators. The artist, Meg Harries, calls them "narrative sculpture," presumably because they allude to the story of the building of this station but also because one is led from one glove or pair of gloves to the next as one moves through the narrative of one's own journey. The little girl in front of me notices the first pair and cranes her neck to keep looking as the stairs take her away, and then another pair comes into her view; now she realizes there must be others, too, and she looks both up and down to see where they are. She pulls at her mother's sleeve to show her and her mother says, yes, yes, I see, I see, but she is deep in her bag and isn't looking. Watching this child, I think I understand something; I see that art, this art anyway, can serve to direct our gaze, to somehow help us manage our attention. Art gives us something to do with our voracious eyes; it occupies our thoughts, tempers our anxieties, soothes our discomforts. At least until we get to the platform itself, where commercial space begins, with ads for booze, for dating services, for Christian Fellowship and deodorant.

In some situations, public transit being one of them, it is important to "keep custody of the eyes," as the nuns used to teach my classmates and me in talking about temptations of the flesh. When we were in third or fourth grade we were curious to understand this phrase but still too young to grasp its meaning; later we weren't at all interested. I always figured it meant, sort of, "mind your own business." Once, not long ago, I heard a woman on the street yell at a man, "You keep your goddamned eyes to yourself!" and I couldn't decide whether she was crazy or if the man, who of course gave me an exaggerated innocent shocked look, had been leering at her.

Today the music is provided by a young woman playing the violin, a Bach Partita interrupted by a recorded announcement reminding us that for our safety we should report any unattended packages or suspicious persons to the station manager. Her music is on a stand before her, case open on the floor with a few coins and a couple of bills in it. A few other people have distributed themselves here and there on the platform, some students, an older Asian couple who are both wearing white surgical masks, two mothers with babies in strollers. One of the people looks remarkably like my brother Joe who lives in Pennsylvania and whom I see too seldom. I've been seeing this guy around the neighborhood for years; once when my daughter Veronica was small she grabbed my arm and pulled me down to her to ask, in a hot little whisper, cupping both hands around my ear, "Is that Uncle Joe?" and I had to look hard to assure myself he wasn't my brother. The guy's a dead ringer. Over the years Veronica would tell me now and then that she had seen "the Uncle Joe guy" again.

A few feet away from me on the platform, the woman with the heavy purse—now sliding down her arm—grabs the little girl by the wrist and yanks her arm and slaps at her bottom all at once, but the little girl, practiced, I guess, in these matters, goes limp and twists herself away from the blow. The mother yanks her back to her feet. "Stand up!" she says. Then she spits on a handkerchief and wipes the child's face with it. "I'm not going to tell you again. You hear me?" The little girl seems far from crying. She doesn't look like she's ever cried in her whole short life. I can see she is watching her mother's hands. Suddenly the mother is looking at me, a glaring challenge: What*chew* lookin' at? As I turn my gaze away I register for the briefest moment that the child is giving me the same look: I've witnessed her shame and now she hates me from behind her mother's leg.

You can feel the train approaching before you hear it or see its light in the tunnel because it pushes air ahead of it into the station. I take out my iPod, put in my earbuds, choose some Thelonious Monk for the ride, and as the train pulls into the station, I check my watch, which is always set ten minutes fast, a strategy that depends on my fooling myself all day long.

*   *   *

I generally look for that single seat in the corner of the car, and it was free, not many people on the train yet since Porter is only the third stop. Monk was laying down a deep melodic and harmonic framework, a starting point for his explorations, and I took out my paperback of *The Idiot*, settled my half-lenses on my nose, and looked forward to picking up the story of Prince Myshkin where I'd left off the day before. Of course as we entered the tunnel I checked myself out in the dark mirror of the window across from me, a ritual of self-consciousness I try to keep in check. And then, wearing the most unthreatening look I could muster, I looked around at the others. To my left was a young man, well dressed, with a leather briefcase flat on his lap. Across from me a man was sprawled across three or four seats, sleeping I supposed. Among the other thirty or forty people in the car there seemed to be four or five different uniforms, depending on race, class, and occupation. Though some people were dressed to call attention to themselves, to stand out, most people seemed dressed to blend in, to become invisible. In the middle of the car was a man impeccably outfitted and assiduously groomed but whose hair was clearly not his own; in fact, it didn't look much like hair at all. The way he was glaring at himself in the window, brushing at his coif with his hand, made him seem mercilessly impatient with himself, a miserable sort of narcissism I thought, as if his attempts to make himself blend in and become acceptably invisible had backfired and he wondered why it wasn't working, why everyone was still, well, giving him those *looks*. He caught me gazing at him, looked away, reached under the seat for a discarded newspaper to read.

Can a person *feel* a look? Of course he can. In situations like this, when we are together not by choice but by necessity, we get nervous, we get on one another's nerves, and our sense of personal boundaries becomes acute. Decorum requires nearly absolute self-containment, and the lack of privacy feels threatening. Both observer and observed are caught in a double bind. We're not supposed to stare; in fact, our stolen looks, like shots made with a secret camera, prove our implacable desire, our utter fascination with one another. Fortunately, there's art. What else could possibly aid us in averting our gaze, brimming with curiosity, judgment, desire, and fear, but art? What else is more interesting than other human beings except, perhaps, the things human beings make to look at, touch, read, hear? Thelonious Monk was just unraveling the melody like taking apart an elegant theorem while pleasurably demonstrating how the parts might be reconfigured to create a different mood, even a different set of premises from which to start over. Without entirely intending to, I looked at myself in the window again. I assessed what I saw there: not an unpleasant face, better from the left because my nose is crooked, beard needs a trim, hairline receded but in a way that seemed all right to me, forehead high and shiny, smart, mature. I was wearing my nobody's fool expression, and trying, I think, to avoid the image just behind the image of myself, the blackness roaring there. One thing is for certain, anyone who thinks his reflection in a piece of glass is what other people see when they look at him is even a bigger fool than he is a narcissist.

I tried to return to the story of Myshkin; I was just picking up at the part when Roghozin attempts to murder him, but we were slowing down and soon had pulled into Harvard Station. As people came through the door, they looked at the seats across from me where the man was sprawled and moved away to find seats elsewhere. I think this was what first got my attention, and I noticed that the man sprawled across from me seemed not to be merely sleeping. For one thing, his posture wasn't that of someone trying to make himself comfortable—one arm was hooked behind the seats at an angle that made me wince to see it, and his other arm was folded behind him. His head was lolled back, mouth open, the whites of his eyes visible under half-shut lids. His skin had the color and granular look of the inside of a baked potato, and his lips were chalky white. All in all there was an alarming rigidity about him. About a dozen people came into the car, people with shopping bags or newspapers folded just so to the articles they were reading, students with backpacks, a mother with a child in a stroller. I watched each register discomfort with the ghastly body angled across the seats as they moved away.

As the doors closed I looked to my left at the young man with the leather briefcase in his lap who had been watching me take in the scene, and now he gave me a conspiratorial smirk, a look that said "It takes all kinds—," a look that asked for reassurance that whatever kind we were, we were different from whatever kind he was over there across from us looking like a broken puppet. I looked from the young man to others around us. A smirk from a young woman, clearly a student, who went back to highlighting her spiral-bound text. A dark-skinned woman, her hair in cornrows and with enormous rings on several of her fingers, avoided eye contact with me and was moving her lips, perhaps praying, maybe in another language. I thought the unconscious man was breathing, that I could see his chest rise and fall. But then I wasn't sure if it wasn't simply the rocking of the train. A man in business attire except for a Red Sox cap caught my eye; he raised his eyebrows, gave me a tight-lipped smile, looked over at the sprawled man, back at me, and shook his head.

*   *   *

I have never been especially squeamish. Even in school, back in the first grade, I was the one—along with my friend Patrick McFadden—whom the nun would send to the janitor's closet for the bag of sawdust and the spaghetti mop and the wheeled pail with wooden rollers whenever one of my classmates threw up. And in college for a time I worked as an ambulance attendant in the Bronx, back in the days when the only certification you needed was a card from the Red Cross and a strong stomach. No, the force field around this man was an entirely different kind of fear.

Somehow, with more of us in the car, the looks that went around began to take on a multiplicity of meanings, shot through with distaste, disapproval, annoyance, and a little panic, as if to say, "Isn't there somebody here who can take care of this?" Monk by now had the melody in pieces spread out like an exploded diagram so that if you hadn't listened from the beginning it would be nothing but chaos, noise. We all wanted someone official, someone who worked for the transit authority, maybe a cop, to clear up the question of whether the broken man was alive or dead and to remove the offending item of his contorted body and slack-jawed awful face. The train continued on its way. I looked and looked. I turned off Monk, who was by then raging against the rules of harmony, asking if they were for real, and put the earbuds and my book in my bag. I was already in motion, I can see now, even though I didn't really know what I was going to do, or even that I was going to do anything at all. The situation was simply intolerable. An ad above the inanimate man read DO YOU SUFFER FROM DEPRESSION? with an 800 number to call, and on a larger placard beside him, next to the window, a school promised to change one's career prospects, but there were none of the paper tear-off applications left. The man did not appear drunk to me. I thought that he might be an addict overdosed on heroin. Or an Oxycontin casualty. He was dressed in clothing sensible for winter, with none of the signs of one who lives on the streets.

I got up and lurched the few steps across the car; holding onto the horizontal pole above him I leaned over. "Sir? Sir! Are you okay?" I chided myself, *Oh yeah, he's great. Never felt better.* I looked at his sallow skin and his slack jaw; his eyes rolled back in his head, little crescents of white visible where the lids were not quite shut. The last guy I saw who looked this bad was dead, I thought, and it was true. A woman in the Bronx had called for an ambulance after coming home from work to find her husband dead in his Barcalounger, evidently for several hours. He had stiffened in the shape of a shallow Z. We couldn't use the stretcher and had to take him down by making a seat of our clasped arms.

This close I was able to see that the man was breathing. I looked up and everyone was watching us. Now there was drama. The young man with the briefcase made a face at me that I took to mean, "Don't bother. He's a doper. Let him sleep it off." Others gave me that sneer and shake of the head that accompanies an attitude of superiority. A tall man came toward me, clearly a workman, with plaster-spattered, rust-colored clothing and molded knee pads now slipped down to his calves, his leather tool bag slung over one shoulder. "Is he breathing?"

"Barely. But I can't get any response from him. Sir!" I barked at him again.

"Let's try and sit him up. Hey buddy. Hey, come on now, let's try to sit you up." I managed to free the arm from behind the seat. The hand was cold and the arm was stiff. The workman was holding the man's head straight and tapped him, gently, on his clean-shaven cheek. His eyelids twitched just slightly. "Hey buddy, you with us? Can you hear me?" The man seemed to be trying unsuccessfully to regain consciousness.

At the next station, Central Square, I stepped out onto the platform; there's always a brakeman somewhere midway in the train who sticks his head out and looks up and down the platform before closing the doors, and when I was sure he saw me, I waved my arms and pointed into the car with both hands. I waved and waved at him, but I wasn't sure he was going to do anything; he pulled his head back into the car. The workman, still holding the other man upright, looked to me for information and I shrugged. I felt prissy in my sport jacket and topcoat, stupid and ineffectual. Then I noticed the callbox a few steps away, next to the door between cars: three louvered slots above a red button. I pressed it and heard a crackling sound. I wasn't sure it was working, and I also found myself wordless: I didn't want to say that someone was sick in our car; that would sound like somebody'd puked and I didn't think that would be taken very seriously. I said, "Excuse me. Someone is very ill here. We have a medical emergency in our car." There was no answer.

I sat next to the unconscious man to help prop him up. Although the man had not regained consciousness, the workman kept talking to him in a warm and soothing voice. "You just hang in there, buddy. It's gonna be all right. Just hang in there, okay?" The callbox crackled and a voice said, "Hello? Hello? Can I help you?" just as a uniformed man I recognized as the brakeman I'd been waving at entered the car. "What's the trouble here?"

I happened to see, behind him, a look of exasperated disgust on the face of a man who, exhaling loudly through his nose, made a big fuss of looking at his watch.

"I'm not sure," I said. "This man's not well."

The brakeman's face had a strangely skeptical look on it, as if we might all be playing a joke on him. Finally he spoke into his walkie-talkie: "Yes. This is seven nine. We have a situation here. Central Station. Caucasian male, unconscious. Requesting medical assistance."

The unconscious man seemed to stiffen and his head rolled back. The workman opened the man's jacket and loosened his collar. "No, no. Stay with us, buddy. Stay with us," the workman said, and he held the man's head upright, his face between his hands as if he meant to kiss him, his thumb moving on the man's cheek below his eye, for reassurance.

The callbox beside the door was crackling, "Hello? Did you call for assistance? Hello?" The brakeman ignored it, so I pressed the red button and said that help had arrived. In fact it was another ten minutes or so before three EMTs lugging boxes, oxygen, and a folding stretcher arrived. The leader of the group proceeded to take his futile turn at rousing the man, and he almost managed, too; there seemed something in his voice that was calling the man forth from wherever he was up there where his eyeballs had rolled. To me the man's voice made questions sound like commands, an assertive concern asking, in a deep baritone, for help in solving a problem he and the patient had in common, and I could see the man trying to open his eyes. Then, softly but clearly, he said, "Gerald," though his eyes remained closed.

"Is that your name, sir? Gerald? Gerald? Can you hear me? Do you take any medications, Gerald? Any medicine? Gerald?"

The man shook his head from side to side and said, "No," in what was somehow only half a syllable. One of the EMTs already had Gerald's coat off and sleeve rolled up, caressing his forearm as if to rub the circulation back into it. I thought he was looking for heroin tracks. "Gerald, we're going to start an IV. Gerald. Try and stay with us, Gerald." He called the brakeman over and they conferred. Then the brakeman turned to us, "Let's give these men the room they need to work, okay? Move back everyone. Give them room." A number of people, already impatient, hoping no doubt the EMTs would carry the man off the train so we could be on our way, groaned at the implication we would be stuck there for awhile, and the man I'd noticed looking at his watch harrumphed off the train, flashing me a glare and muttering that he would try to find a cab. Most of us moved away, to the other end of the car, including the tall workman with the kneepads. I only moved a step or two away myself. I felt a little proprietary; after all, I was the one who had set this all in motion. I thought that maybe the EMTs would have some questions for me. When the brakeman took a step toward me and said, "Sir, we need you to move away and give these men room to work," I felt insulted. How dare he talk to me as if I were an obstacle? Wasn't I the one who'd summoned him? Didn't I earn the right to learn the outcome of this situation?

As I moved away one of the EMTs was looking in Gerald's wallet. He pulled out a card, "There it is," he said, "diabetic."

"I'm already on it," said the man on one knee by the first-aid box. "Gerald, we've started an IV. Gerald, can you hear me? Hang on, pal. We're going to get you through this."

As I walked deeper into the car people looked at me and then away into newspapers, books, puzzles. Maybe three or four minutes later the brakeman instructed us to evacuate and move to one of the adjoining cars. I met eyes for a moment with the tall workman, and though I cannot explain it, his look managed to communicate to me what these new instructions must have meant: either there had been a sudden crisis, a heart attack or stroke, or Gerald was dead. Once again, we were momentarily coconspirators, savvy, in-the-know, and I wanted to cut through the crowd and talk to him, but the look he'd given me had also somehow put that off limits.

At Kendall the platform was quite full; the train was late and as it slowed to a stop I could see the impatience and anxiety in peoples' faces and postures. The car filled.

Soon we were rising into the light and over the Longfellow Bridge, its four stone towers giving it character beyond its function. An Anglo-American bridge, unlike the bridges of Paris, say, or Prague, it makes no promises of angelic protection. It was a gray day, but the rain turned the river to a beautiful infinity of intersecting rings. When the recorded voice intoned "Charles MGH. Mass. General Hospital" and we pulled alongside the crowded, elevated platform, I wondered if the EMTs would have taken Gerald off the train back at Central or continued until now, which seemed to me to be a faster, surer route to the hospital than an ambulance through city streets.

When you leave Charles MGH you accelerate past a brick apartment building very close to the tracks, and just when you are about to get a glimpse of somebody's kitchen, you're plunged into darkness and your own reflection again and the train descends on its way to Park Street. By the time our tightly packed train pulled into the crowded station, passengers were readying to debark in a hurry. The doors first open on one side and then the other, and I moved with the crowd onto the center platform, making our way through the reluctantly parting throng of passengers waiting to board. A man behind me bumped me, hard, as he went past, in a way that may well have been deliberate. I moved away from the train and turned to look back at the car still emptying like a burst pod, the new passengers beginning to surge forward, and I noticed that the next car back, the one on which I'd started my commute, was still closed to riders, and I wondered what that meant. Above the track a great bronze hand, one of a pair comprising Ralph Helmick's sculpture "Benedictions," in the unmistakable sign of blessing, bestowed its peace on every single one of us. I looked at my watch, but I knew the time was wrong.

Where Worlds Collide

Pico Iyer

They come out, blinking, into the bleached, forgetful sunshine, in Dodgers caps and Rodeo Drive T-shirts, with the maps their cousins have drawn for them and the images they've brought over from *Cops* and *Terminator 2*; they come out, dazed, disoriented, heads still partly in the clouds, bodies still several time zones—or centuries—away, and they step into the Promised Land.

In front of them is a Van Stop, a Bus Stop, a Courtesy Tram Stop, and a Shuttle Bus Stop (the shuttles themselves tracing circuits A, B, and C). At the Shuttle Bus Stop, they see the All American Shuttle, the Apollo Shuttle, Celebrity Airport Livery, the Great American Stageline, the Movie Shuttle, the Transport, Ride-4-You, and forty-two other magic buses waiting to whisk them everywhere from Bakersfield to Disneyland. They see Koreans piling into the Taeguk Airport Shuttle and the Seoul Shuttle, which will take them to Koreatown without their ever feeling they've left home; they see newcomers from the Middle East disappearing under the Arabic script of the Sahara Shuttle. They see fast-talking, finger-snapping, palm-slapping jive artists straight from their TV screens shouting incomprehensible slogans about deals, destinations, and drugs. Over there is a block-long white limo, a Lincoln Continental, and, over there, a black Chevy Blazer with Mexican stickers all over its windows, being towed. They have arrived in the Land of Opportunity, and the opportunities are swirling dizzily, promiscuously, around them.

They have already braved the ranks of Asian officials, the criminal-looking security men in jackets that say "Elsinore Airport Services," the men shaking tins that say "Helping America's Hopeless." They have already seen the tilting mugs that say "California: a new slant on life" and the portable fruit machines in the gift shop. They have already, perhaps, visited the rest room where someone has written, "Yes on Proposition 187. Mexicans go home," the snack bar where a slice of pizza costs $3.19 (18 quetzals, they think in horror, or 35,000 dong), and the sign that urges them to try the Cockatoo Inn Grand Hotel. The latest arrivals at Los Angeles International Airport are ready now to claim their new lives.

Above them in the terminal, voices are repeating, over and over, in Japanese, Spanish, and unintelligible English, "Maintain visual contact with your personal property at all times." Out on the sidewalk, a man's voice and a woman's voice are alternating an unending refrain: "The white zone is for loading and unloading of passengers only. No parking." There are "Do Not Cross" yellow lines cordoning off parts of the sidewalk and "Wells Fargo Alarm Services" stickers on the windows; there are "Aviation Safeguard" signs on the baggage carts and "Beware of Solicitors" signs on the columns; there are even special phones "To Report Trouble." More male and female voices are intoning, continuously, "Do not leave your car unattended" and "Unattended cars are subject to immediate towaway." There are no military planes on the tarmac here, the newcomers notice, no khaki soldiers in fatigues, no instructions not to take photographs, as at home; but there are civilian restrictions every bit as strict as in many a police state.

"This Terminal Is in a Medfly Quarantine Area," says the sign between the terminals. "Stop the Spread of Medfly!" If, by chance, the new Americans have to enter a parking lot on their way out, they will be faced with "Cars left over 30 days may be impounded at Owner's Expense" and "Do not enter without a ticket." It will cost them $16 if they lose their parking ticket, they read, and $56 if they park in the wrong zone. Around them is an unending cacophony of antitheft devices, sirens, beepers, and car-door openers; lights are flashing everywhere, and the man who fines them $16 for losing their parking ticket has the tribal scars of Tigre across his forehead.

The blue skies and palm trees they saw on TV are scarcely visible from here: just an undifferentiated smoggy haze, billboards advertising Nissan and Panasonic and Canon, and beyond those an endlessly receding mess of gray streets. Overhead, they can see the all-too-familiar signs of Hilton and Hyatt and Holiday Inn; in the distance, a sea of tract houses, mini-malls, and high-rises. The City of Angels awaits them.

It is a commonplace nowadays to say that cities look more and more like airports, cross-cultural spaces that are a gathering of tribes and races and variegated tongues; and it has always been true that airports are in many ways like miniature cities, whole, self-sufficient communities, with their own chapels and museums and gymnasiums. Not only have airports colored our speech (teaching us about being upgraded, bumped, and put on standby, coaching us in the ways of fly-by-night operations, holding patterns, and the Mile High Club); they have also taught us their own rules, their own codes, their own customs. We eat and sleep and shower in airports; we pray and weep and kiss there. Some people stay for days at a time in these perfectly convenient, hermetically sealed, climate-controlled duty-free zones, which offer a kind of caesura from the obligations of daily life.

Airports are also, of course, the new epicenters and paradigms of our dawning post-national age—not just the bus terminals of the global village but the prototypes, in some sense, for our polyglot, multicolored, user-friendly future. And in their very universality—like the mall, the motel, or the McDonald's outlet—they advance the notion of a future in which all the world's a multiculture. If you believe that more and more of the world is a kind of mongrel hybrid in which many cities (Sydney, Toronto, Singapore) are simply suburbs of a single universal order, then Los Angeles's LAX, London's Heathrow, and Hong Kong's Kai Tak are merely stages on some great global Circle Line, shuttling variations on a common global theme. Mass travel has made L.A. contiguous to Seoul and adjacent to São Paulo, and has made all of them now feel a little like bedroom communities for Tokyo.

And as with most social trends, especially the ones involving tomorrow, what is true of the world is doubly true of America, and what is doubly true of America is quadruply true of Los Angeles. L.A., legendarily, has more Thais than any city but Bangkok, more Koreans than any city but Seoul, more El Salvadorans than any city outside of San Salvador, more Druze than anywhere but Beirut; it is, at the very least, the easternmost outpost of Asia and the northernmost province of Mexico. When I stopped at a Traveler's Aid desk at LAX recently, I was told I could request help in Khamu, Mien, Tigrinya, Tajiki, Pashto, Dari, Pangasinan, Pampangan, Waray-Waray, Bambara, Twi, and Bicolano (as well, of course, as French, German, and eleven languages from India). LAX is as clear an image as exists today of the world we are about to enter, and of the world that's entering us.

For me, though, LAX has always had a more personal resonance: it was in LAX that I arrived myself as a new immigrant, in 1966; and from the time I was in the fourth grade, it was to LAX that I would go three times a year, as an "unaccompanied minor," to fly to school in London—and to LAX that I returned three times a year for my holidays. Sometimes it seems as if I have spent half my life in LAX. For me, it is the site of my liberation (from school, from the Old World, from home) and the place where I came to design my own new future.

Often when I have set off from L.A. to some distant place—Havana, say, or Hanoi, or Pyongyang—I have felt that the multicultural drama on display in LAX, the interaction of exoticism and familiarity, was just as bizarre as anything I would find when I arrived at my foreign destination. The airport is an Amy Tan novel, a short story by Bharati Mukherjee, a Henry James sketch set to an MTV beat; it is a cross-generational saga about Chang Hsieng meeting his daughter Cindy and finding that she's wearing a nose ring now and is shacked up with a surfer from Berlin. The very best kind of airport reading to be found in LAX these days is the triple-decker melodrama being played out all around one—a complex tragicomedy of love and war and exile, about people fleeing centuries-old rivalries and thirteenth-century mullahs and stepping out into a fresh, forgetful, born-again city that is rewriting its script every moment.

Not long ago I went to spend a week in LAX. I haunted the airport by day and by night, I joined the gloomy drinkers listening to air-control-tower instructions on earphones at the Proud Bird bar. I listened each morning to Airport Radio (530 AM), and I slept each night at the Airport Sheraton or the Airport Hilton. I lived off cellophaned crackers and Styrofoam cups of tea, browsed for hours among Best Actor statuettes and Beverly Hills magnets, and tried to see what kinds of America the city presents to the new Americans, who are remaking America each day.

It is almost too easy to say that LAX is a perfect metaphor for L.A., a flat, spaced-out desert kind of place, highly automotive, not deeply hospitable, with little reading matter and no organizing principle. (There are eight satellites without a center here, many international arrivals are shunted out into the bleak basement of Terminal 2, and there is no airline that serves to dominate LAX as Pan Am once did JFK.) Whereas "SIN" is a famously ironical airline code for Singapore, cathedral of puritanical rectitude, "LAX" has always seemed perilously well chosen for a city whose main industries were traditionally thought to be laxity and relaxation. LAX is at once a vacuum waiting to be colonized and a joyless theme park—Tomorrowland, Adventureland, and Fantasyland all at once.

The postcards on sale here (made in Korea) dutifully call the airport "one of the busiest and most beautiful air facilities in the world," and it is certainly true that LAX, with thirty thousand international arrivals each day—roughly the same number of tourists that have visited the Himalayan country of Bhutan in its entire history—is not uncrowded. But bigger is less and less related to better: in a recent survey of travel facilities, *Business Traveller* placed LAX among the five worst airports in the world for customs, luggage retrieval, and passport processing.

LAX is, in fact, a surprisingly shabby and hollowed-out kind of place, certainly not adorned with the amenities one might expect of the world's strongest and richest power. When you come out into the Arrivals area in the International Terminal, you will find exactly one tiny snack bar, which serves nine items; of them, five are identified as Cheese Dog, Chili Dog, Chili Cheese Dog, Nachos with Cheese, and Chili Cheese Nachos. There is a large panel on the wall offering rental-car services and hotels, and the newly deplaned American dreamer can choose between the Cadillac Hotel, the Banana Bungalow (which offers a Basketball Court, "Free Toast," "Free Bed Sheets," and "Free Movies and Parties"), and the Backpacker's Paradise (with "Free Afternoon Tea and Crumpets" and "Free Evening Party Including Food and Champagne").

Around one in the terminal is a swirl of priests rattling cans, Iranians in suits brandishing pictures of torture victims, and Japanese girls in Goofy hats. "I'm looking for something called Clearasil," a distinguished-looking Indian man diffidently tells a cashier. "Clearasil?" shouts the girl. "For your face?"

Upstairs, in the Terrace Restaurant, passengers are gulping down "Dutch Chocolate" and "Japanese Coffee" while students translate back and forth between English and American, explaining that "soliciting" loses something of its cachet when you go across the Atlantic. A fat man is nuzzling the neck of his outrageously pretty Filipina companion, and a few Brits are staring doubtfully at the sign that assures them that seafood is "cheerfully served at your table!" Only in America, they are doubtless thinking. A man goes from table to table, plunking down on each one a key chain attached to a globe. As soon as an unsuspecting customer picks one up, touched by the largesse of the New World and convinced now that there is such a thing as a free lunch in America, the man appears again, flashes a sign that says "I Am a Deaf," and requests a dollar for the gift.

At a bank of phones, a saffron-robed monk gingerly inserts a credit card, while schoolkids page Jesse Jackson at the nearest "white courtesy telephone."

One notable feature of the modern airport is that it is wired, with a vengeance: even in a tiny, two-urinal men's room, I found two telephones on offer; LAX bars rent out cellular phones; and in the Arrivals area, as you come out into the land of plenty, you face a bank of forty-six phones of every kind, with screens and buttons and translations, from which newcomers are calling direct to Bangalore or Baghdad. Airports are places for connections of all kinds and *loci classici*, perhaps, for a world ruled by IDD and MCI, DOS and JAL.

Yet for all these grounding reminders of the world outside, everywhere I went in the airport I felt myself in an odd kind of twilight zone of consciousness, that weightless limbo of a world in which people are between lives and between selves, almost sleepwalking, not really sure of who or where they are. Light-headed from the trips they've taken, ears popping and eyes about to do so, under a potent foreign influence, people are at the far edge of themselves in airports, ready to break down or through. You see strangers pouring out their life stories to strangers here, or making new life stories with other strangers. Everything is at once intensified and slightly unreal. One L.A. psychiatrist advises shy women to practice their flirting here, and religious groups circle in the hope of catching un-attached souls.

Airports, which often have a kind of perpetual morning-after feeling (the end of the holiday, the end of the affair), are places where everyone is ruled by the clock, but all the clocks show different times. These days, after all, we fly not only into yesterday or this morning when we go across the world but into different decades, often, of the world's life and our own: in ten or fifteen hours, we are taken back into the twelfth century or into worlds we haven't seen since child-hood. And in the process we are subjected to transitions more jolting than any imagined by Oscar Wilde or Sigmund Freud: if the average individual today sees as many images in a day as a Victorian saw in a lifetime, the average person today also has to negotiate switches between continents inconceivable only fifty years ago. Frequent fliers like Ted Turner have actually become ill from touching down and taking off so often; but, in less diagnosable ways, all of us are being asked to handle difficult suspensions of the laws of Nature and Society when moving be-tween competing worlds.

This helps to compound the strange statelessness of airports, where all bets are off and all laws are annulled—modern equivalents, perhaps, to the hundred yards of no-man's-land between two frontier crossings. In airports we are often in dreamy, floating, out-of-body states, as ready to be claimed as that suitcase on Carousel C. Even I, not traveling, didn't know sometimes if I was awake or asleep in LAX, as I heard an announcer intone, "John Cheever, John Cheever, please con-tact a Northwest representative in the Baggage Claim area. John Cheever, please contact a service representative at the Northwest Baggage Claim area."

As I started to sink into this odd, amphibious, bipolar state, I could begin to see why a place like LAX is a particular zone of fear, more terrifying to many peo-ple than anywhere but the dentist's office. Though dying in a plane is, notori-ously, twenty times less likely than dying in a car, every single airline crash is front-page news and so dramatic—not a single death but three hundred—that airports are for many people killing grounds. Their runways are associated in the mind's (televisual) eye with hostages and hijackings; with bodies on the tarmac or antiterrorist squads storming the plane.

That general sense of unsettledness is doubtless intensified by all the people in uniform in LAX. There are ten different security agencies working the Tom Bradley Terminal alone, and the streets outside are jam-packed with Airport Police cars, FBI men, and black-clad airport policemen on bicycles. All of them do as much, I suspect, to instill fear as to still it. "People are scared here," a gloomy Pakistani security guard told me, "because undercover are working. Police are working. You could be undercover, I could be undercover. Who knows?"

And just as L.A. is a province of the future in part because so many people take it to be the future, so it is a danger zone precisely because it is imagined to be dangerous. In Osaka's new $16 billion airport recently, I cross-examined the Skynet computer (in the Departures area) about what to expect when arriving at LAX or any other foreign airport. "Guard against theft in the arrival hall," it told me (and, presumably, even warier Japanese). "A thief is waiting for a chance to take advantage of you." Elsewhere it added, "Do not dress too touristy," and, "Be on your guard when approached by a group of suspicious-looking children, such as girls wearing bright-colored shirts and scarves." True to such dark prognostications, the side doors of the Airport Sheraton at LAX are locked every day from 8:00 P.M. to 6:00 A.M., and you cannot even activate the elevators without a room key. "Be extra careful in parking garages and stairwells," the hotel advises visitors. "Always try to use the main entrance to your hotel, particularly late in the evening. Never answer your hotel room door without verifying who is there."

One reason airports enjoy such central status in our imaginations is that they play such a large part in forming our first (which is sometimes our last) impression of a place; this is the reason that poor countries often throw all their resources into making their airports sleek, with beautifully landscaped roads leading out of them into town. L.A., by contrast, has the bareness of arrogance, or simple inhospitability. Usually what you see as you approach the city is a grim penitential haze through which is visible nothing but rows of gray buildings, a few dun-hued warehouses, and ribbons of dirty freeway: a no-colored blur without even the comforting lapis ornaments of the swimming pools that dot New York or Johannesburg. (Ideally, in fact, one should enter L.A. by night, when the whole city pulses like an electric grid of lights—or the back of a transistor radio, in Thomas Pynchon's inspired metaphor. While I was staying in LAX, Jackie Collins actually told *Los Angeles* magazine that "Flying in [to LAX] at night is just an orgasmic thrill.") You land, with a bump, on a mess of gray runways with no signs of welcome, a hangar that says "T ans W rld Airlines," another broken sign that announces "Tom Bradl y International Ai port," and an air-control tower under scaffolding.

The first thing that greeted me on a recent arrival was a row of Asians sitting on the floor of the terminal, under a sign that told them of a $25,000 fine for bringing in the wrong kinds of food. As I passed through endless corridors, I was faced with almost nothing except long escalators (a surprisingly high percentage of the accidents recorded at airports comes from escalators, bewildering to new-comers) and bare hallways. The other surprise, for many of my fellow travelers, no doubt, was that almost no one we saw looked like Robert Redford or Julia Roberts or, indeed, like anyone belonging to the race we'd been celebrating in our in-flight movies. As we passed into the huge, bare assembly hall that is the Customs and Immigration Center here, I was directed into one of the chaotic lines by a Noriko and formally admitted to the country by a C. Chen. The man waiting to transfer my baggage (as a beagle sniffed around us in a coat that said "Agriculture's Beagle Brigade" on one side and "Protecting American Agricul-ture" on the other) was named Yoji Yosaka. And the first sign I saw, when I stepped into America, was a big board being waved by the "Executive Sedan Service" for one "Mr. T. Ego."

For many immigrants, in fact, LAX is quietly offering them a view of their own near futures: the woman at the Host Coffee Shop is themselves, in a sense, two years from now, and the man sweeping up the refuse is the American dream in practice. The staff at the airport seems to be made up almost entirely of recent immigrants: on my very first afternoon there, I was served by a Hoa, an Ephraim, and a Glinda; the waitpeople at a coffee shop in Terminal 5 were called Ignacio, Ever, Aura, and Erick. Even at the Airport Sheraton (where the employees all wear nameplates), I was checked in by Viera (from "Bratislavia") and ran into Hasmik and Yovik (from Ethiopia), Faye (from Vietnam), Ingrid (from Guatemala City), Khrystyne (from Long Beach, by way of Phnom Penh, I think), and Moe (from West L.A., she said). Many of the bright-eyed dreamers who arrive at LAX so full of hope never actually leave the place.

The deeper drama of any airport is that it features a kind of interaction almost unique in our lives, wherein many of us do not know whom we are going to meet or whom others are going to meet in us. You see people standing at the barriers outside the Customs area looking into their pasts, while wide-open newcomers drift out, searching for their futures. Lovers do not know if they will see the same person who kissed them good-bye a month ago; grandparents wonder what the baby they last saw twenty years ago will look like now.

In L.A. all of this has an added charge, because unlike many cities, it is not a hub but a terminus: a place where people come to arrive. Thus many of the meet-ings you witness are between the haves and the hope-to-haves, between those who are affecting a new ease in their new home and those who are here in search of that ease. Both parties, especially if they are un-American by birth, are eager to stress their Americanness or their fitness for America; and both, as they look at each other's made-up self, see themselves either before or after a stay in L.A.'s theater of transformation. And so they stream in, wearing running shoes or cow-boy hats or 49ers jackets, anxious to make a good first impression; and the people who wait for them, under a halfhearted mural of Desertland, are often American enough not to try to look the part. Juan and Esperanza both have ponytails now, and Kimmie is wearing a Harley-Davidson cap backward and necking with a Japanese guy; the uncle from Delhi arrives to find that Rajiv not only has grown darker but has lost weight, so that he looks more like a peasant from back home than ever.

And the newcomers pour in in astonishing numbers. A typical Sunday evening, in a single hour, sees flights arriving from England, Taiwan, the Philippines, Indonesia, Mexico, Austria, Germany, Spain, Costa Rica, and Guatemala; and each new group colors and transforms the airport: an explosion of tropical shades from Hawaiian Air, a rash of blue blazers and white shirts around the early flight from Tokyo. Red-haired Thais bearing pirated Schwarzenegger videos, lonely Africans in Aerial Assault sneakers, farmers from changeless Confucian cultures peering into the smiles of a Prozac city, children whose parents can't pronounce their names. Many of them are returning, like Odysseus, with the spoils of war: young brides from Luzon, business cards from Shanghai, boxes of macadamia nuts from Oahu. And for many of them the whole wild carnival will feature sights they have never seen before: Japanese look anxiously at the first El Salvadorans they've ever seen, and El Salvadorans ogle sleek girls from Bangkok in thigh-high boots. All of them, moreover, may not be pleased to realize that the America they've dreamed of is, in fact, a land of tacos and pita and pad thai—full, indeed, of the very Third World cultures that other Third Worlders look down upon.

One day over lunch I asked my Ethiopian waitress about her life here. She liked it well enough, she said, but still she missed her home. And yet, she added, she couldn't go back. "Why not?" I asked, still smiling. "Because they killed my family," she said. "Two years back. They killed my father. They killed my brother." "They," I realized, referred to the Tigreans—many of them working just down the corridor in other parts of the hotel. So, too, Tibetans who have finally managed to flee their Chinese-occupied homeland arrive at LAX to find Chinese faces everywhere; those who fled the Sandinistas find themselves standing next to Sandinistas fleeing their successors. And all these people from ancient cultures find themselves in a country as amnesiac as the morning, where World War II is just a rumor and the Gulf War a distant memory. Their pasts are escaped, yes, but by the same token they are unlikely to be honored.

It is dangerously tempting to start formulating socioeconomic principles in the midst of LAX: people from rich countries (Germany and Japan, say) travel light, if only because they are sure that they can return any time; those from poor countries come with their whole lives in cardboard boxes imperfectly tied with string. People from poor countries are often met by huge crowds—for them each arrival is a special occasion—and stagger through customs with string bags and Gold Digger apple crates, their addresses handwritten on them in pencil; the Okinawan honeymooners, by contrast, in the color-coordinated outfits they will change every day, somehow have packed all their needs into a tiny case.

If airports have some of the excitement of bars, because so many people are composing (and decomposing) selves there, they also have some of the sadness of bars, the poignancy of people sitting unclaimed while everyone around them has paired off. A pretty girl dressed in next to nothing sits alone in an empty Baggage

Claim area, waiting for a date who never comes; a Vietnamese man, lost, tells an official that he has friends in Orange County who can help him, but when the friends are contacted, they say they know no one from Vietnam. I hear of a woman who got off and asked for "San Mateo," only to learn that she was meant to disembark in San Francisco; and a woman from Nigeria who came out expecting to see her husband in Monroe, Louisiana, only to learn that someone in Lagos had mistaken "La." on her itinerary for "L.A."

The greetings I saw in the Arrivals area were much more tentative than I had expected, less passionate—as ritualized in their way as the kisses placed on Bob Barker's cheek—and much of that may be because so many people are meeting strangers, even if they are meeting people they once knew. Places like LAX—places like L.A.—perpetuate the sense that everyone is a stranger in our new floating world. I spent one afternoon in the airport with a Californian blonde, and I saw her complimented on her English by a sweet Korean woman and asked by an Iranian if she was Indian. Airports have some of the unsteady brashness of singles bars, where no one knows quite what is expected of them. "Mike, is that you?" "Oh, I didn't recognize you." "I'd have known you anywhere." "It's so kind of you to come and pick me up." And already at a loss, a young Japanese girl and a broad, lonely-looking man head off toward the parking lot, not knowing, in any sense, who is going to be in the driver's seat.

The driving takes place, of course, in what many of the newcomers, primed by video screenings of *L.A. Law* and *Speed,* regard as the ultimate heart of darkness, a place at least as forbidding and dangerous as Africa must have seemed to the Victorians. They have heard about how America is the murder capital of the world; they have seen Rodney King get pummeled by L.A.'s finest; they know of the city as the site of drive-by shootings and freeway snipers, of riots and celebrity murders. The "homeless" and the "tempest-tost" that the Statue of Liberty invites are arriving, increasingly, in a city that is itself famous for its homeless population and its fires, floods, and earthquakes.

In that context, the ideal symbol of LAX is, perhaps, the great object that for thirty years has been the distinctive image of the place: the ugly white quadruped that sits in the middle of the airport like a beached white whale or a jet-age beetle, featuring a 360-degree circular restaurant that does not revolve and an observation deck from which the main view is of twenty-three thousand parking places. The Theme Building, at 201 World Way, is a sad image of a future that never arrived, a monument to Kennedy-era idealism and the thrusting modernity of the American empire when it was in its prime; it now has the poignancy of an abandoned present with its price tag stuck to it. When you go there (and almost nobody does) you are greeted by photos of Saturn's rings and Jupiter and its moons, by a plaque laid down by L.B.J. and a whole set of symbols from the time when NASA was shooting for the heavens. Now the "landmark" building, with its "gourmet-type restaurant," looks like a relic from a time long past, when it must have looked like the face of the future.

Upstairs, a few desperately merry waiters are serving nonalcoholic drinks and cheeseburgers to sallow diners who look as if they've arrived at the end of the world; on the tarmac outside, speedbirds inch ahead like cars in a traffic jam. "Hello All the New People of LAX—Welcome," says the graffiti on the elevator.

The Theme Restaurant comes to us from an era when L.A. was leading the world. Nowadays, of course, L.A. is being formed and reformed and led by the world around it. And as I got ready to leave LAX, I could not help but feel that the Theme Building stands, more and more, for a city left behind by our accelerating planet. LAX, I was coming to realize, was a good deal scruffier than the airports even of Bangkok or Jakarta, more chaotic, more suggestive of Third World lawlessness. And the city around it is no more golden than Seoul, no more sunny than Taipei, and no more laid-back than Moscow. Beverly Hills, after all, is largely speaking Farsi now. Hollywood Boulevard is sleazier than 42nd Street. And Malibu is falling into the sea.

Yet just as I was about to give up on L.A. as yesterday's piece of modernity, I got on the shuttle bus that moves between the terminals in a never-ending loop. The seats next to me were taken by two tough-looking dudes from nearby South Central, who were riding the free buses and helping people on and off with their cases (acting, I presumed, on the safe assumption that the Japanese, say, new to the country and bewildered, had been warned beforehand to tip often and handsomely for every service they received). In between terminals, as a terrified-looking Miss Kudo and her friend guarded their luggage, en route from Nagoya to Las Vegas, the two gold-plated sharks talked about the Raiders' last game and the Lakers' next season. Then one of them, without warning, announced, "The bottom line is the spirit is with you. When you work out, you chill out and, like, you meditate in your spirit. You know what I mean? Meditation is recreation. Learn math, follow your path. That's all I do, man, that's all I live for: learnin' about God, learnin' about Jesus. I am *possessed* by that spirit. You know, I used to have all these problems, with the flute and all, but when I heard about God, I learned about the body, the mind, and the flesh. People forget, they don't know, that the Bible isn't talkin' about the flesh, it's talkin' about the spirit. And I was reborn again in the spirit."

His friend nodded. "When you recreate, you meditate. Recreation is a spiritually uplifting experience."

"Yeah. When you do that, you allow the spirit to breathe."

"Because you're gettin' into the physical world. You're lettin' the spirit flow. You're helpin' the secretion of the endorphins in the brain."

Nearby, the Soldiers of the Cross of Christ Church stood by the escalators, taking donations, and a man in a dog collar approached another stranger.

I watched the hustlers allowing the spirit to breathe, I heard the Hare Krishna devotees plying their wares, I spotted some Farrakhan flunkies collecting a dollar for a copy of their newspaper, *The Final Call*—redemption and corruption all around us in the air—and I thought: welcome to America, Miss Kudo, welcome to L.A.

Stripped for Parts

Jennifer Kahn

The television in the dead man's room stays on all night. Right now the program is *Shipmates*, a reality-dating drama that's barely audible over the hiss of the ventilator. It's 4 A.M., and I've been here for six hours, sitting in the corner while three nurses fuss intermittently over a set of intravenous drips. They're worried about the dead man's health.

To me, he looks fine. His face is slack but flush, he breathes steadily, and his heart beats like a clock, despite the fact that his lungs have recently begun to leak fluid. The nurses roll the body from side to side periodically so that the liquid doesn't pool. At one point, a white plastic vest designed to clear the lungs inflates and begins to vibrate violently—as if some invisible person has seized the dead man by the shoulders and is trying to shake him awake. The rest of the time, the nurses consult monitors and watch for signs of cardiac arrest. When someone scratches the bottom of the dead man's foot, it twitches.

None of this is what I expected from an organ transplant. When I arrived last night at this Northern California hospital I was prepared to see a fast-paced surgery culminating in renewal: the mortally ill patient restored to glorious health. In all my preliminary research on transplants, the dead man was rarely mentioned. Even doctors I spoke with avoided the subject, and popular accounts I came across ducked the matter of provenance altogether. In the movies, for instance, surgeons tended to say it would take time to "find" a heart—as though one had been hidden behind a tree or misplaced along with the car keys. Insofar as corpses came up, it was only in anxious reference to the would-be recipient whose time was running out.

In the dead man's room, a different calculus is unfolding. Here the organ is the patient, and the patient a mere container, the safest place to store body parts until surgeons are ready to use them. It can be more than a day from the time a donor dies until his organs are harvested—the surgery alone takes hours, not to mention the time needed to do blood tests, match tissue, and fly in special surgical teams for the evisceration. And yet, a heart lasts at most six hours outside the body, even after it has been kneaded, flushed with preservatives, and packed in a cooler. Organs left on ice too long tend to perform poorly in their new environment, and doctors are picky about which viscera they're willing to work with. Even an ailing cadaver is a better container than a cooler.

These conditions create a strange medical specialty. Rather than extracting this man's vitals right away, the hospital contacts the California Transplant Donor Network, which dispatches a procurement team to begin "donor maintenance": the process of artificially supporting a dead body until recipients are ready. When the parathyroid gland stops regulating calcium, key to keeping the heart pumping, the team sends the proper amount down an intravenous drip. When blood pressure drops, they add vasoconstrictors, which contract the blood vessels. Normally the brain would compensate for a decrease in blood pressure, but with it out of commission, the three-nurse procurement team must take over.

In this case, the eroding balance will have to be sustained for almost 24 hours. The goal is to fool the body into believing that it's alive and well, even as everything is falling apart. As one crew member concedes, "It's unbelievable that all this stuff is being done to a dead person."

Unbelievable and, to me, somehow barbaric. Sustaining a dead body until its organs can be harvested is a tricky process requiring the latest in medical technology. But it's also a distinct anachronism in an era when medicine is becoming less and less invasive. Fixing blocked coronary arteries, which not long ago required prying a patient's chest open with a saw and spreader, can now be accomplished with a tiny stent delivered to the heart on a slender wire threaded up the leg. Exploratory surgery has given way to robot cameras and high-resolution imaging. Already, we are eyeing the tantalizing summit of gene therapy, where diseases are cured even before they do damage. Compared with such microscale cures, transplants—which consist of salvaging entire organs from a heart-beating cadaver and sewing them into a different body—seem crudely mechanical, even medieval.

"To let an organ reach a state where the only solution is to cut it out is not progress; it's a failure of medicine," says pathologist Neil Theise of NYU. Theise, who was the first researcher to demonstrate that stem cells can become liver cells in humans, argues that the future of transplantation lies in regeneration. Within five years, he estimates, we'll be able to instruct the body to send stem cells to the liver from the store that exists in bone marrow, hopefully countering the effects of a disease like hepatitis A or B and letting the body heal itself. And numerous researchers are forging similar paths. One outspoken surgeon, Richard Satava from the University of Washington, says that medicine is only now catching on to the fundamental lesson of modern industry, which is that when our car alternator breaks, we get a brand new one. Transplantation, he argues, is a dying art.

Few researchers predict that human-harvested organs will become obsolete anytime soon, however; one cardiovascular pathologist, Charles Murry, says we'll still be using them a century from now. But it's reasonable to expect—and hope for—an alternative. "I don't think anybody enjoys recovering organs," Murry says frankly. "You tell yourself it's for a good cause, which it is, a very good cause, but you're still butchering a human."

Intensive care is not a good place to spend the evening. Tonight, the ward has perhaps 12 patients, including a woman who moans constantly and a deathly pale man who reportedly jumped out the window of a moving Greyhound bus. The absence of clocks and the always-on lights create a casino-like timelessness. In the staff lounge, which smells of stale pizza, a lone nurse corners me and describes watching a man bleed to death ("He was conscious. He knew what was happening"), and announces, sotto voce, that she knows of South American organ brokers who charge $60,000 for a heart, then swap it for a baboon's.

Although I don't admit it to the procurement team, I've grown attached to the dead man. There's something vulnerable about his rumpled hair and middle-aged body, naked save a waist-high sheet. Under the hospital lights, everything is exposed: the muscular arms gone flabby above the elbow; the legs, wiry and lean, foreshortened under a powerful torso. It's the body of a man in his fifties, simultaneously bullish and elfin. One foot, the right, peeps out from the sheet, and for a brief moment I want to hold it and rub the toes that must be cold—a hopeless gesture of consolation.

Organ support is about staving off entropy. In the moments after death, a cascade of changes sweeps over the body. Potassium diminishes and salt accumulates, drawing fluid into cells. Sugar builds up in the blood. With the pituitary system offline, the heart fills with lactic acid like the muscles of an exhausted runner. Free radicals circulate unchecked and disrupt other cells, in effect causing the body to rust. The process quickly becomes irreversible. As cell membranes grow porous, a "death gene" is activated and damaged cells begin to self-destruct. All this happens in minutes.

When transplant activists talk about an organ shortage, it's usually to lament how few people are willing to donate. This is a valid worry, but it eclipses an important point, which is that the window for retrieving a viable organ is staggeringly small. Because of how fast the body degrades once the heart stops, there's no way to recover an organ from someone who dies at home, in a car, in an ambulance, or even while on the operating table. In fact, the only situation that really lends itself to harvest is brain death, which means finding an otherwise healthy patient whose brain activity has ceased but whose heart continues to beat—right up until the moment it's taken out. In short, victims of stroke or severe head injury. These cases are so rare (approximately 0.5 percent of all deaths in the US) that even if everybody in America were to become a donor, they wouldn't clear the organ wait lists.

This is partly a scientific problem. Cell death remains poorly understood, and for years now, cadaveric transplants have lingered on a research plateau. While immunosuppressants have improved incrementally, transplants proceed much as they did 20 years ago. Compared with a field like psychopharmacology, the procedure has come to a near-standstill.

But there are cultural factors as well. Medicine has always reserved its glory for the living. Even among transplant surgeons, a hierarchy exists: Those who put organs into living patients have a higher status than those who extract them from the dead. One anesthesiologist confesses that his peers don't like to work on cadaveric organ recoveries. (Even brain-dead bodies require sedation, since spinal reflexes can make a corpse "buck" in surgery.) "You spend all this time monitoring the heartbeat, the blood pressure," the anesthesiologist explains. "To just turn everything off when you're done and walk out. It's bizarre."

Although the procurement team will stay up all night, I break at 4:30 A.M. for a two-hour nap on an empty bed in the ICU. The nurse removes a wrinkled top sheet but leaves the bottom one. Doctors sleep like this all the time, I know, catnapping on gurneys, but I can't shake the feeling of climbing onto my deathbed. The room is identical to the one I've been sitting in for the past eight hours, and I'd prefer to sleep almost anywhere else—in the nurses' lounge or even on the small outside balcony. Instead, I lie down in my clothes and pull the sheet up under my arms.

For a while I read a magazine, then finally close my eyes, hoping I won't dream.

By morning, little seems to have changed, except that the commotion of chest X-rays and ultrasounds has left the dead man's hair more mussed. On both sides of his bed, vital stats scroll across screens: oxygen ratios, pulse, blood volumes.

All of this vigilance is good, of course: After all, transplants save lives. Every year, thousands of people who would otherwise die survive with organs from brain-dead donors; sometimes, doctors say, a patient's color will visibly change on the operating table once a newly attached liver begins to work. Still—and with the possible exception of kidneys—transplants have never quite lived up to their initial promise. In the early 1970s, few who received new organs lasted even a year, and most died within weeks. Even today, 22 percent of heart recipients die in less than four years, and 12 percent reject a new heart within the first few months. Those who survive are usually consigned to a lifetime regime of costly immunosuppressive drugs, some with debilitating side effects. Recipients of artificial hearts traditionally fare the worst, alongside those who receive transplants from animals. Under the circumstances, it took a weird kind of perseverance for doctors operating in 1984 to suggest sewing a walnut-sized baboon heart into a human baby. And there was grief, if not surprise, when the patient died of a morbid immune reaction just 21 days later.

By the time we head into surgery, the patient has been dead for more than 24 hours, but he still looks pink and healthy. In the operating room, all the intravenous drips are still flowing, convincing the body that everything's fine even as it's cleaved in half.

Although multiorgan transfer can involve as many as five teams in the OR at once, this time there is only one: a four-man surgical unit from Southern California. They've flown in to retrieve the liver, but because teams sometimes swap favors, they'll also remove the kidneys for a group of doctors elsewhere—saving them a last-minute, late-night flight. One of the doctors has brought a footstool for me to stand on at the head of the operating table, so that I can see over the sheet that hangs between the patient's head and body. I've been warned that the room will smell bad during the "opening," like flesh and burning bone—an odor that has something in common with a dentist's drill. Behind me, the anesthesiologist checks the dead man's mask and confirms that he's sedated. The surgery will take four hours, and the doctors have arranged for the score of Game Five of the World Series to be phoned in at intervals.

I've heard that transplant doctors are the endurance athletes of medicine, and the longer I stand on the stool, the better I understand the comparison. Below me, the rib cage has been split, and I can see the heart, strangely yellow, beating inside a cave of red muscle. It doesn't beat forward, as I expect, but knocks anxiously back and forth like a small animal trapped in a cage. Farther down, the doctors rummage under the slough of intestines as though through a poorly organized toolbox. When I tell the anesthesiologist that the heart is beautiful, he says that livers are the transplants to watch. "Hearts are slash and burn," he shrugs, adjusting a dial. "No finesse."

Two hours pass, and the surgeons make progress. Despite the procurement team's best efforts, however, most of the organs have already been lost. The pancreas was deemed too old before surgery. One lung was bad at the outset, and the other turned out to be too big for the only matching recipients—a short list given the donor's rare blood type. At 7 this morning, the heart went bust after someone at the receiving hospital suggested a shot of thyroid hormone, shown in some studies to stimulate contractions—but even before then, the surgeon had had second thoughts. A 54-year-old heart can't travel far—and this one was already questionable—but the hospital may have thought this would improve its chances. Instead, the dead man's pulse shot to 140, and his blood began circulating so fast it nearly ruptured his arteries. Now the heart will go to Cryolife, a biosupply company that irradiates and freeze-dries the valves, then packages them for sale to hospitals in screw-top jars. The kidneys have remained healthy enough to be passed on—one to a man who will soon be in line for a pancreas, the other to a 42-year-old woman.

Both kidneys have been packed off in quart-sized plastic jars. Originally, the liver was going to a nearby hospital, but an ultrasound suggested it was hyperechoic, or probably fatty. On the second pass, it was accepted by a doctor in Southern California and ensconced in a bag of icy slurry.

The liver is enormous—it looks like a polished stone, flat and purplish—and with it gone, the body seems eerily empty, although the heart continues to beat. Watching this pumping vessel makes me oddly anxious. It's sped up slightly, as though sensing what will happen next. Below me, the man's face is still flushed. He's the one I wish would survive, I realize, even though there was never any chance of that. Meanwhile, the head surgeon has walked away. He's busy examining the liver and relaying a description over the phone to the doctor who will perform the attachment. Almost unnoticed, an aide clamps the arteries above and below the heart, and cuts. The patient's face doesn't move, but its pinkness drains to a waxy yellow. After 24 hours, the dead man finally looks dead.

Once all the organs are out, the tempo picks up in the operating room. The heart is packed in a cardboard box also loaded with the kidneys, which are traveling by Learjet to a city a few hundred miles away. Someday, I'm convinced, transporting organs in coolers will seem as strange and outdated as putting a patient in an iron lung. In the meantime, transplants will survive: a vehicle, like the dead man, to get us to a better place. As an assistant closes, sewing up the body so that it will be ready for its funeral, I get on the plane with the heart and the kidneys. They've become a strange, unhealthy orange in their little jars. But no one else seems worried. "A kidney almost always perks up," someone tells me, "once we get it in a happier environment."

Life in Motion

Nicole Lamy

1

There years ago I took pictures of all the houses I've lived in. The houses impress not in beauty but in number—twelve houses before I turned thirteen. For me the moves had always resisted coherent explanation—no military reassignments or evasion of the law. I wanted to gather the photos as charms against fallible memory, like the list of lost things I used to keep: a plastic purse filled with silver dollars, a mole-colored beret, a strip of negatives from my brother's first day of kindergarten. I planned to bind the photos in an album and give them to my mother. Maybe then, I thought, we could read our lives like straightforward narratives. Wise readers know that all stories follow one of two paths: The Stranger Comes to Town or The Journey. My life in motion suggested both.

2

When idea turned to plan, I asked my father for a list of the addresses I couldn't remember. Instead, as I had hoped, he offered to drive me through Maine, New Hampshire, and Massachusetts himself. My father, too, took photographs, and I wanted to draw him into my life a little, remind him of the times during car trips when, as dusk deepened, he would switch on the light inside the car, without prompting, so that I could continue to read.

3

I photographed the houses and the apartments and the surprising number of duplexes (so often did we live in the left half of a house that I wonder if I've developed a right-hemisphere problem—I imagine the right side of my brain paler and more shriveled than its better half, as atrophied and bleached as an arm that has been in a cast all summer), though I never asked to be let inside. I remembered the flow of rooms in most houses and I could imagine walking through them in a sort of Ciceronian memory system for childhood.

4

The photographs pretend no artistic merit. I centered most of the houses in my viewfinder as I stood on opposite sidewalks. Occasionally a branch or a piece of the neighboring house appears at the edge of the frame. Otherwise the book is a collection of residential mug shots. I wasn't accustomed to snapping pictures of whole buildings without people cluttering the frames, and as I focused before each shot I thought of the pictures my father had taken during his early twenties: ducks and snowdrifts and weathered cottages. Looking through my father's pictures, my mother would squint with mock earnestness at yet another image of a dilapidated barn and ask, "Where were we, behind the barn?"

5

At the first house—125 Wood Street, a gray three-family at the edge of the campus where my father had been a sophomore—I toyed with perspective. I held my camera at my hip; I crouched by the mailboxes, trying to imagine a toddler's vantage point. No pre-school impressions came flooding back; I gained nothing but stares from the neighbors. I thought of the family lore about the short time we lived on Wood Street. By 1972, the sixties still hadn't retreated from Lewiston, Maine. The perennial students who shared our building kept the house reeking pleasantly of weed, and our downstairs neighbor wandered up to our apartment now and again to shower, since her bathtub was occupied by her pet duck. Her thesis, my mother insisted, had something to do with roller skates, and she decorated her apartment with black lights and mini-marshmallows, dipped in fluorescent paint, which she stuck to branches that hung from her ceiling. At night, when the lights came on, visitors were treated to an electrifying set of unlikely constellations.

6

From Maine we moved south to New Hampshire. Rooting out the apartments in the freshly overdeveloped landscape of New Hampshire was a trickier prospect; some of the photos of these houses show unfamiliar additions, self-installed skylights. Some had new, paved-over driveways, others aluminum siding. One apartment complex in southern New Hampshire remained intact, though the surrounding woods had been leveled to receive three new strip malls. When we wandered closer to the Massachusetts border, images reversed themselves and I found myself remembering the houses' odd absences: an oval of yellowed grass showed where an above-ground pool had sat; a chimney stopped abruptly with no fireplace attached.

During each move, after the boxes had been unpacked, my father would turn their openings to the ground and use a pocketknife to cut windows and doors. The refrigerator boxes were best, skyscrapers with grass floors. In my cardboard house I would read cross-legged into the evening, ignoring my parents' invitations to take-out dinners in our new yard until my father lifted the box off me and walked away, bearing my cardboard home, leaving me blinking in the dusk.

7

Now when I leave my apartment for vacation, no matter how anticipated the trip, I experience numbing panic—will I ever see home again? I'm sympathetic to Rilke's Eurydice: What did she care about Orpheus and his willpower? Sure, she had her reasons: hell living had filled her with death and isolated her from human touch. No doubt she could have grown accustomed to the rocks and rivers of Hades. Who among us can get our mind around a move that drastic? From one side of the eternal duplex to the other. Each time I return home from vacation, rooms don't appear the same as I left them. Walls seem to meet floors at subtly altered angles. Careful inspections—heel-toe, heel-toe around each of the rooms— reveal no evidence of the perceived.

8

After my parents split, I kept most of my assorted five-year-old's treasures at the white three-family where I lived with my mother, watched over by a grim, disapproving landlady. My father's wall-to-wall-carpeted bachelor apartment always smelled faintly of hops; he and his two roommates all owned water beds and motorcycles. My personal inventory at my father's new home was limited to a Holly Hobbie nightgown, *The Little Princess*, and Milton Bradley's Sorry!, a game that requires players to apologize without sincerity after forcing their competitors to start again.

9

I found the post-divorce houses on my own. At one address, the brown-stained house I had known in early grade school wasn't there at all. Developers had knocked it down, then paved over the spot to provide parking for the neighboring convenience store and candy shop. On the winter afternoon when I visited, I snapped a photo of a stray shopping cart that had rolled away from the convenience store to the spot where the kitchen had been. The shot, of the lonely shopping cart illuminated by a hazy beam of light, has a Hallmark devotional-card quality. I have no sentimental feelings about the house, though. I even felt satisfaction when I saw the smoothly paved parking lot; it was as though I had willed the destruction of the site of many childhood disappointments (new stepfather! mid-first-grade school switch! dog runs away from home!).

The edges of the photograph give more away. At the top of the frame I can spot a sliver of the foundation of the house that backed up to ours. My friend Annette lived there, an only child whose mother cut women's hair in the pink room adjacent to their dining room and whose father cured meat, hung in strips—dark and pale, meat and fat—in their cellar.

At the left edge of the frame, the tail of an *a* is visible, part of a glowing sign advertising "Gina—Psychic," the fortune-teller who set up shop next door.

10

In a decorative gesture, I planned to hand-color the photographs as if they were pre-Kodachrome portraits of children with blossom-pink cheeks and lips. Armed with the oils and pencils, however, I only touched up a piece of every home—a chimney, a storm door, a front gate. If stacked, they'd make a flip-book composite of a home.

Red shutters and verdant bushes decorate the house after the last fold in the book. There, the three of us—mother, sister, and new brother, aged three—began living alone together for the first time. The stepfather had come and gone, leaving the three of us to find balance in our uneasy triumvirate. Neighbors and shop-keepers looked at us, curious. I could tell that the age gaps perplexed them—too few years between a mother and daughter who chatted like girlfriends and too many between a sister and brother who looked almost like mother and son. Their confusion was compounded by my mother's youth and beauty and by the way at age thirteen I seemed to have passed directly to thirty-five.

The red-shuttered house was home the longest, and it is the only house my brother remembers. When I handed the coloring pencils over to him to spruce up the image of the old house, he colored the whole thing. He and my mother still live in that duplex, formerly the parish house for the Congregational church across the street. We haven't been the only ones comfortable there. Pets and pests flourish: a dog, rabbits, guinea pigs, escaped reptiles, moths and silverfish, hollow shells of worms in macaroni boxes, squirrels in the attic.

The parish house has walls that slant toward the middle and floorboards that creak too frequently and too loudly to be creepy. During the first year, while discovering the rules and limits of our new family, we cleared the dining room table each night after dinner and began to play.

The three of us played games from my mother's childhood—tiddledywinks, pick-up-sticks, PIT. And after my brother fell asleep, my mother and I drank tea and played Password, Boggle, and Scrabble, stopping only when the board was almost filled and our wooden racks held two or three impossible consonants. A few years ago, chasing a marble that had slipped through a wrought iron heating grate, my brother lifted the panel by one of its iron curls and found, caught in the black cloth, game pieces of all kinds: dice, tiddledywinks, cribbage pegs, smooth wooden squares with black letters—pieces we had barely missed from games we had continued to play.

11

When the photo project was complete, I felt a historian's satisfaction. I had gathered the proof of my life and given it a shape. To create the album I cut a long strip of black paper and folded and flipped it as if to cut paper dolls. I printed the images small and pasted them in the accordion book. Held from the top, the book tumbles open to reveal twelve homes logically connected.

My mother saw the book as evidence of a life hastily lived. When she unknotted the ribbon around the tidy package and allowed it to unfold, I watched her face seize up.

"Ha, ha," she pushed the sounds out with effort. "All my failures," she said as she held the book away from her in an exaggerated gesture. I had tried to piece a story out of a life that I saw as largely unplanned. For my mother, this life led by reaction had eventually settled into a kind of choice. I was ashamed I thought it was mine to figure out.

12

One night, a few weeks before I moved out of the parish house duplex into my own apartment, I returned home and wheeled my bike around to the back of the house. Glancing up at the brightly lit windows, I was afforded an unusual glimpse of the daily theater of my family. From my spot in the yard I saw a woman in the kitchen chopping vegetables and talking on the phone, while a couple of rooms over, a gangly teenage boy sat in a chair by the television. Startled to be given a chance to see the house as a stranger might, I watched for a few moments and tried to imagine the lives of those inside.

13, 1977, 21

Jonathan Lethem

1. In the summer of 1977 I saw *Star Wars*—the original, which is all I want to discuss here—twenty-one times. Better to blurt this at the start so I'm less tempted to retreat from what still seems to me a sort of raw, howling confession, one I've long hidden in shame. Again, to pin myself like a Nabokovian butterfly (no high-lit reference is going to bail me out here, I know) to my page in geek history: I watched *Star Wars* twenty-one times in the space of four months. I was that kid alone in the ticket line, slipping past ushers who'd begun to recognize me, muttering in impatience at a urinal before finding my favorite seat. That was me, occult as a porn customer, yes, though I've sometimes denied it. Now, a quarter of a century later, I'm ready for my close-up. Sort of.

2. That year I was thirteen, and likely as ideal an audience member as any mogul could have drooled for. Say every kid in the United States with even the passingest fondness for comic books or adventure fiction, *any kid with a television, even,* had bought a ticket for the same film in a single summer: blah, blah, right, that's what happened. So figure that for every hundred kids who traveled an ordinary path (*Cool movie. Wouldn't mind seeing it again with my friends*) there might be one who'd make himself ill returning to the cookie jar five or six times (*It's really still good the fourth time, I swear!*) before copping to a tummy ache. Next figure that for each *five* hundred, one or two would slip into some brain-warped identificatory obsession (*I am Star Wars. Star Wars am me, goo goo ga joob*) and return to the primal site often enough to push into the realm of trance and memorization. That's me, with my gaudy *twenty-one*, like DiMaggio's *fifty-six*. But what actually occurred within the secret brackets of that experience? What emotions lurk within that ludicrous temple of hours? *What the fuck was I thinking?*

3. Every one of those twenty-one viewings took place at the Loew's Astor Plaza on Forty-fourth Street, just off Times Square. I'd never seen a movie there before (and unless you count *The Empire Strikes Back*, I didn't again until 1999—*The Matrix*). And I've still never seen *Star Wars* anywhere else. The Astor Plaza was a low, deep-stretched hall with a massive screen and state-of-the-art sound, and newly enough renovated to be free of too much soda-rotted carpet, a plague among New York theaters those days. Though architecturally undistinguished, it was a superior place to see anything. I suppose. But for me it was a shrine meant for just one purpose—I took it as weirdly significant that "Astor: could be rearranged into "astro"—and in a very *New Yorker*-coverish way I believed it to be the only real and right place to see *Star Wars*, the very ground zero of the phenomenon. I felt a definite but not at all urgent pity for any benighted fools stuck watching it elsewhere. I think I associated the Astor Plaza with the Death Star, in a way. Getting in always felt like an accomplishment, both elevating and slightly dangerous.

4. Along those lines I should say it was vaguely unnerving to be a white kid in spectacles routinely visiting Times Square by subway in the middle of the 1970s. Nobody ever said anything clearly about what was wrong or fascinating about that part of the city we lived in—the information was absorbed in hints and mutterings from a polyphony of sources. In fact, though I was conscious of a certain seamy energy in those acres of sex shows and drug dealers and their furtive sidewalk customers, I was never once hassled (and this was a time when my home neighborhood, in Brooklyn, was a minefield for me personally). But the zone's reputation ensured I'd always plan my visits to fall wholly within summer's long daylight hours.

5. Problem: it doesn't seem at all likely that I went to the movie alone the first time, but I can't remember who I was with. I've polled a few of my likeliest friends from that period, but they're unable to help. In truth I can't recall a "first time" in any real sense, though I do retain a flash memory of the moment the prologue first began to crawl in tilted perspective up the screen, an Alice-in-Wonderland doorway to dream. I'd been so primed, so attuned and ready to love it (I remember mocking my friend Evan for his thinking that the title meant it was going to be some kind of all-star cavalcade of a comedy, like *It's a Mad Mad Mad Mad World* or *Smokey and the Bandit*) that my first time was gulped impatiently, then covered quickly in the memory of return visits. From the first I was "seeing it again." I think this memory glitch is significant. I associate it with my practice of bluffing familiarity with various drug experiences, later (not much later). My refusal to recall or admit to a first time was an assertion of maturity: I was *always already* a *Star Wars* fanatic.

6. I didn't buy twenty-one tickets. My count was amassed by seeing the movie twice in a day over and over again. And one famous day (famous to myself) I sat

through it three times. That practice of seeing a film twice through originated earlier. Somebody—my mother?—had floated the idea that it wasn't important to be on time for a movie, or even to check the screening times before going. Instead, moviegoing in Brooklyn Heights or on Fulton Street with my brother or with friends, we'd pop in at any point in the story, watch to the end, then sit through the break and watch the beginning. Which led naturally, if the film was any good, to staying past the original point of entry to see the end twice. Which itself led to routinely twice-watching a movie we liked, even if we hadn't been late. This was encouraged, partly according to a general *Steal This Book*-ish anticapitalist imperative for taking freebies in my parents' circle in the seventies. Of course somebody—my mother?—had also figured out a convenient way to get the kids out of the house for long stretches.

7. I hate arriving late for movies now and would never watch one in this broken fashion. (It seems to me, though, that I probably learned something about the construction of narratives from the practice.) The life-long moviegoing habit which does originate for me with *Star Wars* is that of sitting in movie theaters alone. I probably only had company in the Loew's Astor Plaza four or five times. The rest of my visits were solitary, which is certainly central to any guesses I'd make about the emotional meaning of the ritual viewings.

8. I still go to the movies alone, all the time. In the absenting of self which results—so different from the quality of solitude at my writing desk—this seems to me as near as I come in my life to any reverent or worshipful or meditational practice. That's not to say it isn't also indulgent, with a frisson of guilt, of stolen privilege, every time. I'm acutely conscious of this joyous guilt in the fact that when as a solitary moviegoer I take a break to go to the bathroom *I can return to another part of the theater and watch from a different seat.* I first discovered this thrill during my *Star Wars* summer, and it's one which never diminishes. The rupture of the spectator's contract with perspective feels as transgressive as wife-swapping.

9. The function or dysfunction of my *Star Wars* obsession was paradoxical. I was using the movie as a place to hide, sure. That's obvious. At the same time, this activity of hiding inside the Loew's Astor Plaza, and inside my private, *deeper-than-yours, deeper-than-anyone's* communion with the film itself, was something I boasted widely about. By building my lamebrain World Record for screenings (fat chance, I learned later) I was teaching myself to package my own craving for solitude, and my own obsessive tendencies, as something to be admired. *You can't join me inside this box where I hide,* I was saying, *but you sure can praise the box. You're permitted to marvel at me for going inside.*

10. What I was hiding from is easy, though. My parents had separated a couple of years earlier. Then my mother had begun having seizures, been diagnosed with a brain tumor, and had had the first of two surgeries. The summer of *Star Wars* she

was five or six months from the second, unsuccessful surgery, and a year from dying.

11. I took my brother, and he stayed through it twice. We may have done that together more than once—neither of us clearly remembers. I took a girl, on a quasi-date: Alissa, the sister of my best friend, Joel. I took my mother. I tried to take my grandmother.

12. That same summer I once followed Alissa to a ballet class at Carnegie Hall and hung around the studio, expressing a polite curiosity which was cover for another, less polite curiosity. The instructor was misled or chose to misunderstand—a thirteen-year-old boy willing to set foot inside a ballet studio was a commodity, a raw material. I was offered free classes, and the teacher called my house and strong-armed my parents. I remember vividly my mother's pleasure in refusing on my behalf—I was too much of a coward—and how strongly she fastened on the fact that my visit had had nothing to do with any interest in ballet. For years this seemed to me an inexplicable cruelty in my mother toward the ballet teacher. Later I understood that in those first years of adolescence I was giving off a lot of signals to my parents that I might be gay. I was a delicate, obedient, and bookish kid, a constant teacher's pet. Earlier that year my father had questioned me regarding a series of distended cartoon noses I'd drawn in ballpoint on my loose-leaf binder—they had come out looking a lot like penises. And my proclaimed favorite *Star Wars* character was the tweaking English robot, C-3PO.

13. I did and do find C-3PO sexy. It's as if a strand of DNA from Fritz Lang's fetishized girl robot in *Metropolis* has carried forward to the bland world of *Star Wars*. Also, whereas Carrie Fisher's robes went to her ankles, C-3PO is obviously naked, and ashamed of it.

14. Alissa thought the movie was okay (my overstated claims generally cued a compensating shrug in others) and that was our last date, if it was a date. We're friends now.

15. I don't know how much of an effort it was for my mother to travel by subway to a movie theater in Manhattan by the summer of '77, but I do know it was unusual, and that she was certainly doing it to oblige me. It might have been one of our last ventures out together, before it was impossible for her. I remember fussing over rituals inside the theater, showing her my favorite seat, and straining not to watch her watch it throughout, not to hang on her every reaction. Afterward she too found the movie just okay. It wasn't her kind of thing, but she could understand why I liked it so much. Those were pretty close to her exact words. Maybe with her characteristic Queens hard-boiled tone: *I see why you like it, kiddo.* Then, in a turn I find painful to relate, she left me there to watch it a second time, and took the subway home alone. What a heartbreaking rehearsal! I was saying, in effect: *Come and see my future, post-mom self. Enact with me your*

parting from it. Here's the world of cinema and stories and obsessive identification I'm using to survive your going—now go. How generous of her to play in this masquerade, if she knew.

16. I spent a certain amount of time that year trying hopelessly to distract my grandmother from the coming loss of her only child—it would mostly wreck her—by pushing my new enthusiasms at her. For instance she and I had a recurrent argument about rock and roll, one which it now strikes me was probably a faint echo, for her, of struggles over my mother's dropping out of Queens College in favor of a Greenwich Village beatnik-folk lifestyle. I worked to find a hit song she couldn't quibble with, and thought I'd found one in Wings' "Mull of Kintyre," which is really just a strummy faux-Irish folk song. I played it for her at top volume and she grimaced, her displeasure not at the music but at the apparent trump card I'd played. Then, on the fade, Paul McCartney gave out a kind of *whoop-whoop* holler and my grandmother seized on this, with relish: "You hear that? He had to go and scream. It wasn't good enough just to sing, he had to scream like an animal!" Her will was too much for me. So when she resisted being dragged to *Star Wars* I probably didn't mind, being uninterested in having her trample on my secret sand castle. She and I were ultimately in a kind of argument about whether or not our family was a site of tragedy, and I probably sensed I was on the losing end of that one.

17. My father lived in a commune for part of that summer, though my mother's illness sometimes drew him back into the house. There was a man in the commune—call him George Lucas—whose married life, which included two young children, was coming apart. George Lucas was the person I knew who'd seen *Star Wars* the most times, apart from me, and we had a ritualized bond over it. He'd ask me how many times I'd seen the film and I'd report, like an emissary with good news from the front. George Lucas had a copy of the soundtrack and we'd sit in the commune's living room and play it on the stereo, which I seem to remember being somewhat unpopular with the commune's larger membership. George Lucas, who played piano and had some classical training, would always proclaim that the score was *really pretty good symphonic composition*—he'd also play me Gustav Holst's *Planets Suite* as a kind of primer, and to show me how the Death Star theme came from Holst's Jupiter—I would dutifully parrot this for my friends, with great severity: John Williams's score was *really pretty good symphonic composition.*

18. The movie itself, right: of course, I must have enjoyed it immensely the first few times. That's what I least recall. Instead I recall now how as I memorized scenes I fought my impatience, and yet fought not to know I was fighting impatience—all that mattered were the winnowed satisfactions of crucial moments occurring once again, like stations of the cross: "Help me, Obi-Wan Kenobi, you're my only hope," "These aren't the droids you're looking for," "If you strike me down, I'll become more powerful than you can possibly imagine,"

and the dunk shot of Luke's missiles entering the Death Star's duct. I hated, absolutely, the scene in the Death Star's sewers. I hated Han Solo and Princess Leia's flirtation, after a while, feeling I was being manipulated, that it was too mannered and rote: of course they're grumbling now, that's how it *always* goes. I hated the triumphalist ceremony at the end, though the spiffing-up of the robots was a consolation, a necessary relief. I think I came to hate a lot of the film, but I couldn't permit myself to know it. I even came, within a year or so, to hate the fact that I'd seen the movie twenty-one times.

19. Why that number? Probably I thought it was safely ridiculous and extreme to get my record into the twenties, yet stopping at only twenty seemed too mechanically round. Adding one more felt plausibly arbitrary, more *realistic*. That was likely all I could stand. Perhaps at twenty-one I'd also attained the symbolic number of adulthood, of maturity. By bringing together *thirteen* and *twenty-one* I'd made *Star Wars* my Bar Mitzvah, a ritual I didn't have and probably could have used that year. Now I was a man.

20. By the time I was fifteen, not only had I long since quit boasting about my love of *Star Wars* but it had become privately crucial to have another favorite movie inscribed in its place. I decided Kubrick's *2001: A Space Odyssey* was a suitably noble and alienated choice, but that in order to make it official I'd have to see it more times than *Star Wars*. An exhausting proposition, but I went right at it. One day at the Thalia on West Ninety-fifth Street I sat alone through *2001* three times in a row in a nearly empty theater, a commitment of some nine hours. That day I brought along a tape recorder in order to whisper notes on this immersion experience to my friend Eliot—I also taped *Also sprach Zarathustra* all six times. If *Star Wars* was my Bar Mitzvah then *2001* was getting laid, an experience requiring a more persuasive maturity, and one which I more honestly enjoyed, especially fifteen or twenty showings in. Oddly enough, though, I never did completely overwrite *Star Wars* with *2001*. Instead I stuck at precisely twenty-one viewings of the second movie as well, leaving the two in a dead heat. Even that number was only attained years later, at the University Theater in Berkeley, California, two days after the 1989 Loma Prieta earthquake. There was a mild aftershock which rumbled the old theater during the Star Gate sequence, a nice touch.

21. I'll never see another film so many times, though I still count. I've seen *The Searchers* twelve times—a cheat, since it was partly research. Otherwise, I usually peak out at six or seven viewings, as with *Bringing Up Baby* and *Three Women* and *Love Streams* and *Vertigo*, all films I believe I love more than either *Star Wars* or *2001*. But that kid who still can't decide which of the two futuristic epics to let win the struggle for his mortal soul, the kid who left the question hanging, the kid who partly invented himself in the vacuum collision of *Star Wars*—and real loss—that kid is me.

Portrait of My Body

Phillip Lopate

I am a man who tilts. When I am sitting, my head slants to the right; when walking, the upper part of my body reaches forward to catch a sneak preview of the street. One way or another, I seem to be off-center—or "uncentered," to use the jargon of holism. My lousy posture, a tendency to slump or put myself into lazy, contorted misalignments, undoubtedly contributes to lower back pain. For a while I correct my bad habits, do morning exercises, sit straight, breathe deeply, but always an inner demon that insists on approaching the world askew resists perpendicularity.

I think if I had broader shoulders I would be more squarely anchored. But my shoulders are narrow, barely wider than my hips. This has always made shopping for suits an embarrassing business. (Françoise Gilot's *Life with Picasso* tells how Picasso was so touchy about his disproportionate body—in his case all shoulders, no legs—that he insisted the tailor fit him at home.)

When I was growing up in Brooklyn, my hero was Sandy Koufax, the Dodgers' Jewish pitcher. In the doldrums of Hebrew choir practice at Feigenbaum's Mansion & Catering Hall, I would fantasize striking out the side, even whiffing twenty-seven batters in a row. Lack of shoulder development put an end to this identification; I became a writer instead of a Koufax.

It occurs to me that the restless angling of my head is an attempt to distract viewers' attention from its paltry base. I want people to look at my head, partly because I live in my head most of the time. My sister, a trained masseuse, often warns me of the penalties, like neck tension, that may arise from failing to integrate body and mind. Once, about ten years ago, she and I were at the beach and she was scrutinizing my body with a sister's critical eye. "You're getting flabby," she said. "You should exercise every day. I do—look at me, not an ounce of fat." She pulled at her midriff, celebrating (as is her wont) her physical attributes with the third-person enthusiasm of a carnival barker.

"But"—she threw me a bone—"you do have a powerful head. There's an intensity. . . ." A graduate student of mine (who was slightly loony) told someone that she regularly saw an aura around my head in class. One reason I like to teach is that it focuses fifteen or so dependent gazes on me with such paranoiac intensity as cannot help but generate an aura in my behalf.

I also have a commanding stare, large sad brown eyes that can be read as either gentle or severe. Once I watched several hours of myself on videotape. I discovered to my horror that my face moved at different rates: sometimes my mouth would be laughing, eyebrows circumflexed in mirth, while my eyes coolly gauged the interviewer to see what effect I was making. I am something of an actor. And, as with many performers, the mood I sense most in myself is that of energy-conserving watchfulness; but this expression is often mistaken (perhaps because of the way brown eyes are read in our culture) for sympathy. I see myself as determined to the point of stubbornness, selfish, even a bit cruel—in any case, I am all too aware of the limits of my compassion, so that it puzzles me when people report a first impression of me as gentle, kind, solicitous. In my youth I felt obliged to come across as dynamic, arrogant, intimidating, the life of the party; now, surer of myself, I hold back some energy, thereby winning time to gather information and make better judgments. This results sometimes in a misimpression of my being mildly depressed. Of course, the simple truth is that I have less energy than I once did, and that accumulated experiences have made me, almost against my will, kinder and sadder.

Sometimes I can feel my mouth arching downward in an ironic smile, which, at its best, reassures others that we need not take everything so seriously—because we are all in the same comedy together—and, at its worst, expresses a superior skepticism. This smile, which can be charming when not supercilious, has elements of the bashful that mesh with the worldly—the shyness, let us say, of a cultivated man who is often embarrassed for others by their willful shallowness or self-deception. Many times, however, my ironic smile is nothing more than a neutral stall among people who do not seem to appreciate my "contribution." I hate that pain-in-the-ass half-smile of mine; I want to jump in, participate, be loud, thoughtless, vulgar.

Often I give off a sort of psychic stench to myself, I do not like myself at all, but out of stubborn pride I act like a man who does. I appear for all the world poised, contented, sanguine when inside I may be feeling self-revulsion bordering on the suicidal. What a wonder to be so misread! Of course, if in the beginning I had thought I was coming across accurately, I never would have bothered to become a writer. And the truth is I am not misread, because another part of me is never less than fully contented with myself.

I am vain about these parts of my body: my eyes, my fingers, my legs. It is true that my legs are long and not unshapely, but my vanity about them has less to do with their comeliness than with their contribution to my height. Montaigne, a man who was himself on the short side, wrote that "the beauty of stature is the only beauty of men." But even if Montaigne had never said it, I would continue to attribute a good deal of my self-worth and benevolent liberalism to being tall. When I go out into the street, I feel well-disposed toward the (mostly shorter) swarms of humanity; crowds not only do not dismay, they enliven me; and I am tempted to think that my passion for urbanism is linked to my height. By no means am I suggesting that only tall people love cities; merely that, in my case, part of the pleasure I derive from walking in crowded streets issues from a confidence that I can see above the heads of others, and cut a fairly impressive, elevated figure as I saunter along the sidewalk.

Some of my best friends have been—short. Brilliant men, brimming with poetic and worldly ideas, they deserved all of my and the world's respect. Yet at times I have had to master an impulse to rumple their heads; and I suspect they have developed manners of a more formal, *noli me tangere* nature, largely in response to this petting impulse of taller others.

The accident of my tallness has inclined me to both a seemingly egalitarian informality and a desire to lead. Had I not been a writer, I would surely have become a politician; I was even headed in that direction in my teens. Ever since I shot up to a little over six feet, I have had at my command what feels like a natural, Gregory Peck authority when addressing an audience. Far from experiencing stage fright, I have actually sought out situations in which I could make speeches, give readings, sit on panel discussions, and generally tower over everyone else onstage. To be tall is to look down on the world and meet its eyes on your terms. But this topic, the noblesse oblige of tall men, is a dangerously provoking one, and so let us say no more about it.

The mental image of one's body changes slower than one's body. Mine was for a long while arrested in my early twenties, when I was tall and thin (165 pounds) and gobbled down whatever I felt like. I ate food that was cheap and filling, cheeseburgers, pizza, without any thought to putting on weight. But a young person's metabolism is more dietetically forgiving. To compound the problem, the older you get, the more cultivated your palate grows—and the more life's setbacks make you inclined to fill the hollowness of disappointment with the pleasures of the table.

Between the age of thirty and forty I put on ten pounds, mostly around the midsection. Since then my gut has suffered another expansion, and I tip the scales at over 180. That I took a while to notice the change may be shown by my continuing to purchase clothes at my primordial adult size (33 waist, 15½ collar), until a girlfriend started pointing out that all my clothes were too tight. I rationalized this circumstance as the result of changing fashions (thinking myself still subconsciously loyal to the sixties' penchant for skintight fits) and laundry shrinkage rather than anything to do with my own body. She began buying me larger replacements for birthdays or holidays, and I found I enjoyed this "baggier" style, which allowed me to button my trousers comfortably, or to wear a tie and, for the first time in years, close my top shirt button. But it took even longer before I was able to enter a clothing store myself and give the salesman realistically enlarged size numbers.

Clothes can disguise the defects of one's body, up to a point. I get dressed with great optimism, adding one color to another, mixing my favorite Japanese and Italian designers, matching the patterns and textures, selecting ties, then proceed to the bathroom mirror to judge the result. There is an ideal in my mind of the effect I am essaying by wearing a particular choice of garments, based, no doubt, on male models in fashion ads—and I fall so far short of this insouciant gigolo handsomeness that I cannot help but be a little disappointed when I turn up so depressingly myself, narrow-shouldered, Talmudic, that grim, set mouth, that long, narrow face, those appraising eyes, the Semitic hooked nose, all of which express both the strain of intellectual overachieving and the tabula rasa of immaturity . . . for it is still, underneath, a boy in the mirror. A boy with a rapidly receding hairline.

How is it that I've remained a boy all this time, into my late forties? I remember, at seventeen, drawing a self-portrait of myself as I looked in the mirror. I was so appalled at the weak chin and pleading eyes that I ended up focusing on the neckline of the cotton T-shirt. Ever since then I have tried to toughen myself up, but I still encounter in the glass that haunted uncertainty—shielded by a bluffing shell of cynicism, perhaps, but untouched by wisdom. So I approach the mirror warily, without lighting up as much as I would for the least of my acquaintances; I go one-on-one with that frowning schmuck.

And yet, it would be insulting to those who labor under the burden of true ugliness to palm myself off as an unattractive man. I'm at times almost handsome, if you squinted your eyes and rounded me off to the nearest *beau idéal*. I lack even a shred of cowboy virility, true, but I believe I fall into a category of adorable nerd or absentminded professor that awakens the amorous curiosity of some women. "Cute" is a word often applied to me by those I've been fortunate enough to attract. Then again, I attract only women of a certain lopsided prettiness: the head-turning, professional beauties never fall for me. They seem to look right through me, in fact. Their utter lack of interest in my appeal has always fascinated me. Can it be so simple an explanation as that beauty calls to beauty, as wealth to wealth?

I think of poor (though not in his writing gifts) Cesare Pavese, who kept chasing after starlets, models, and ballerinas—exquisite lovelies who couldn't appreciate his morose coffeehouse charm. Before he killed himself, he wrote a poem addressed to one of them, "Death Will Come Bearing Your Eyes"—thereby unfairly promoting her from rejecting lover to unwitting executioner. Perhaps he believed that only beautiful women (not literary critics, who kept awarding him prestigious prizes) saw him clearly, with twenty-twenty vision, and had the right to judge him. Had I been more headstrong, if masochistic, I might have followed his path and chased some beauty until she was forced to tell me, like an oracle, what it was about me, physically, that so failed to excite her. Then I might know something crucial about my body, before I passed into my next reincarnation.

Jung says somewhere that we pay dearly over many years to learn about ourselves what a stranger can see at a glance. This is the way I feel about my back. Fitting rooms aside, we none of us know what we look like from the back. It is the area of ourselves whose presentation we can least control, and which therefore may be the most honest part of us.

I divide backs into two kinds: my own and everyone else's. The others' backs are often mysterious, exquisite, and uncannily sympathetic. I have always loved backs. To walk behind a pretty woman in a backless dress and savor how a good pair of shoulder blades, heightened by shadow, has the same power to pierce the heart as chiseled cheekbones! . . . I wonder what it says about me that I worship a part of the body that signals a turning away. Does it mean I'm a glutton for being abandoned, or a timid voyeur who prefers a surreptitious gaze that will not be met and challenged? I only know I have often felt the deepest love at just that moment when the beloved turns her back to me to get some sleep.

I have no autoerotic feelings about my own back. I cannot even picture it; visually it is a stranger to me. I know it only as an annoyance, which came into my consciousness twenty years ago, when I started getting lower back pain. Yes, we all know that homo sapiens is constructed incorrectly; our erect posture puts too much pressure on the base of the spine; more workdays are lost because of lower back pain than any other cause. Being a writer, I sit all day, compounding the problem. My back is the enemy of my writing life: if I don't do exercises daily, I immediately ache; and if I do, I am still not spared. I could say more, but there is nothing duller than lower back pain. So common, mundane an ailment brings no credit to the sufferer. One has to dramatize it somehow, as in the phrase "I threw my back out."

Here is a gossip column about my body: My eyebrows grow quite bushy across my forehead, and whenever I get my hair cut, the barber asks me diplomatically if I want them trimmed or not. (I generally say no, associating bushy eyebrows with Balzackian virility, *élan vital*; but sometimes I acquiesce, to soothe his fastidiousness.) . . . My belly button is a modest, embedded slit, not a jaunty swirl like my father's. Still, I like to sniff the odor that comes from jabbing my finger in it: a very ripe, underground smell, impossible to describe, but let us say a combination of old gym socks and stuffed derma (the Yiddish word for this oniony dish of ground intestines is, fittingly, *kish-kas*). . . . I have a scar on my tongue from childhood, which I can only surmise I received by landing it on a sharp object, somehow. Or perhaps I bit it hard. I have the habit of sticking my tongue out like a dog when exerting myself physically, as though to urge my muscles on; and maybe I accidentally chomped into it at such a moment. . . . I gnash my teeth, sleeping or waking. Awake, the sensation makes me feel alert and in contact with the world when I start to drift off in a daydream. Another way of grounding myself is to pinch my cheek—drawing a pocket of flesh downward and squeezing it—as I once saw JFK do in a filmed motorcade. I do this cheek-pinching especially when I am trying to keep mentally focused during teaching or other public situations. I also scratch the nape of my neck under public stress, so much so that I raise welts or sores which then eventually grow scabs; and I take great delight in secretly picking the scabs off. . . . My nose itches whenever I think about it, and I scratch it often, especially lying in bed trying to fall asleep (maybe because I am conscious of my breathing then). I also pick my nose with formidable thoroughness when no one, I hope, is looking. . . . There is a white scar about the size of a quarter on the juicy part of my knee; I got it as a boy running into a car fender, and I can still remember staring with detached calm at the blood that gushed from it like a pretty, half-eaten peach. Otherwise, the sight of my own blood makes me awfully nervous. I used to faint dead away when a blood sample was taken, and now I can control the impulse to do so only by biting the insides of my cheeks while steadfastly looking away from the needle's action. . . . I like to clean out my ear wax as often as possible (the smell is curiously sulfurous; I associate it with the bodies of dead insects). I refuse to listen to warnings that it is dangerous to stick cleaning objects into your ears. I love Q-Tips immoderately; I buy them in huge quantities and store them the way a former refugee will stock canned foodstuffs. . . . My toes are long and apelike; I have very little fellow feeling for them; they are so far away, they may as well belong to someone else. . . . My flattish buttocks are not offensively large, but neither do they have the "dream" configuration one sees in jeans ads. Perhaps for this reason, it disturbed me puritanically when asses started to be treated by Madison Avenue, around the seventies, as crucial sexual equipment, and I began to receive compositions from teenage girl students declaring that they liked some boy because he had "a cute butt." It confused me; I had thought the action was elsewhere.

About my penis there is nothing, I think, unusual. It has a brown stem, and a pink mushroom head where the foreskin is pulled back. Like most heterosexual males, I have little comparative knowledge to go by, so that I always feel like an outsider when I am around women or gay men who talk zestfully about differences in penises. I am afraid that they might judge me harshly, ridicule me like the boys who stripped me of my bathing suit in summer camp when I was ten. But perhaps they would simply declare it an ordinary penis, which changes size with the stimulus or weather or time of day. Actually, my penis does have a peculiarity: it has two peeing holes. They are very close to each other, so that usually only one stream of urine issues, but sometimes a hair gets caught across them, or some such contretemps, and they squirt out in two directions at once.

This part of me, which is so synecdochically identified with the male body (as the term "male member" indicates), has given me both too little, and too much, information about what it means to be a man. It has a personality like a cat's. I have prayed to it to behave better, to be less frisky, or more; I have followed its nose in matters of love, ignoring good sense, and paid the price; but I have also come to appreciate that it has its own specialized form of intelligence which must be listened to, or another price will be extracted.

Even to say the word "impotence" aloud makes me nervous. I used to tremble when I saw it in print, and its close relation, "importance," if hastily scanned, had the same effect, as if they were publishing a secret about me. But why should it be *my* secret, when my penis has regularly given me erections lo these many years—except for about a dozen times, mostly when I was younger? Because, even if it has not been that big a problem for me, it has dominated my thinking as an adult male. I've no sooner to go to bed with a woman than I'm in suspense. The power of the flaccid penis's statement, "I don't want you," is so stark, so cruelly direct, that it continues to exert a fascination out of all proportion to its actual incidence. Those few times when I was unable to function were like a wall forcing me to take another path—just as, after I tried to kill myself at seventeen, I was obliged to give up pessimism for a time. Each had instructed me by its too painful manner that I could not handle the world as I had previously construed it, that my confusion and rage were being found out. I would have to get more wily or else grow up.

Yet for the very reason that I was compelled to leave them behind, these two options of my youth, impotence and suicide, continue to command an underground loyalty, as though they were more "honest" than the devious strategies of potency and survival which I adopted. Put it this way: sometimes we encounter a person who has had a nervous breakdown years before and who seems cemented over sloppily, his vulnerability ruthlessly guarded against as dangerous; we sense he left a crucial part of himself back in the chaos of breakdown, and has since grown rigidly jovial. So suicide and impotence became for me "the roads not taken," the paths I had repressed.

Whenever I hear an anecdote about impotence—a woman who successfully coaxed an ex-priest who had been celibate and unable to make love, first by lying next to him for six months without any touching, then by cuddling for six more months, then by easing him slowly into a sexual embrace—I think they are talking about me. I identify completely: this, in spite of the fact, which I promise not to repeat again, that I have generally been able to do it whenever called upon. Believe it or not, I am not boasting when I say that: a part of me is contemptuous of this virility, as though it were merely a mechanical trick that violated my true nature, that of an impotent man absolutely frightened of women, absolutely secluded, cut off.

I now see the way I have idealized impotence: I've connected it with pushing the world away, as a kind of integrity, as in Molière's *The Misanthrope*—connected it with that part of me which, gregarious socializer that I am, continues to insist that I am a recluse, too good for this life. Of course, it is not true that I am terrified of women. I exaggerate my terror of them for dramatic effect, or for the purposes of a good scare.

My final word about impotence: Once, in a period when I was going out with many women, as though purposely trying to ignore my hypersensitive side and force it to grow callous by thrusting myself into foreign situations (not only sexual) and seeing if I was able to "rise to the occasion," I dated a woman who was attractive, tall and blond, named Susan. She had something to do with the pop music business, was a follower of the visionary religious futurist Teilhard de Chardin, and considered herself a religious pacifist. In fact, she told me her telephone number in the form of the anagram, N-O-T-O-W-A-R. I thought she was joking and laughed aloud, but she gave me a solemn look. In passing, I should say that all the women with whom I was impotent or close to it had solemn natures. The sex act has always seemed to me in many ways ridiculous, and I am most comfortable when a woman who enters the sheets with me shares that sense of the comic pomposity behind such a grandiloquently rhetorical use of the flesh. It is as though the prose of the body were being drastically squeezed into metrical verse. I would not have known how to stop guffawing had I been D.H. Lawrence's lover, and I am sure he would have been pretty annoyed at me. But a smile saying "All this will pass" has an erotic effect on me like nothing else.

They claim that men who have long, long fingers also have lengthy penises. I can tell you with a surety that my fingers are long and sensitive, the most perfect, elegant, handsome part of my anatomy. They are not entirely perfect—the last knuckle of my right middle finger is twisted permanently, broken in a softball game when I was trying to block the plate—but even this slight disfigurement, harbinger of mortality, adds to the pleasure I take in my hands' rugged beauty. My penis does not excite in me nearly the same contemplative delight when I look at it as do my fingers. Pianists' hands, I have been told often; and though I do not play the piano, I derive an aesthetic satisfaction from them that is as pure and Apollonian as any I am capable of. I can stare at my fingers for hours. No wonder I have them so often in my mouth, biting my fingernails to bring them closer. When I write, I almost feel that they, and not my intellect, are the clever progenitors of the text. Whatever narcissism, fetishism, and proud sense of masculinity I possess about my body must begin and end with my fingers.

I Met a Man Who Has Seen the Ivory-billed Woodpecker, and This Is What He Told Me

Nancy Lord

The Woods

The swamp forest is only a corridor between rice fields, but the ancient cypress tower there. Winds the week before had bared the trees, laying a carpet of tupelo golds, sweetgum reds, the rusty cypress needles. It was possible to walk dry-footed among the fluted trunks and spreading knees, the wet-season watermarks waist-high on a man.

Woodpeckers

The usual woodpeckers were all there: their bouncing flight, the sounds of rapping, scrabbling on bark. They called *keer-uck* and *querrr-querrr, pik* and *peek, yucka, yucka yucka*. The downy and the hairy were there, the red-bellied, the yellow-bellied sapsucker. The pileated was there, the largest of them, the red crest, drumming like the pounding of mallets, loud. It was a birdy place: the wildness of trees in every aspect of life and death, with pecked-out cavities, with beetles, with peeling bark.

Woodpecker!

This is the word he let out as he grabbed for his wife's arm. He knew what he was seeing, and he could not believe that he was, in fact, seeing it. If for 60 years something has been missing, it takes more than the sight of a large, utterly distinct flying bird to convince a man of what is possible.

Eight Seconds

One for the bird flying toward him from deep forest. Two for the bird landing 12 feet up a cypress trunk and clinging there in profile. Three for the bird sliding around to the back of the tree, hiding itself. Two for the bird flashing back the way it came, a single whomping wingbeat and all that white.

Color

The colossal male crest, of course—the brilliant flame so inescapably, unignorably red and pointedly tall. The white was more the surprise, down the neck and across the shoulders like a saddle, and the two large wedges shaped by folded wings. And the black, the black that was not charcoal, not ebony, only the absolutest of all blacks, and blacker still beside white.

Sound

He never heard the bird, not the *henk, henk* of its call, not its tooting, staccato song, not the double rap that distinguishes its tree knocking from any other woodpecker's. The early naturalists described ivory-bills as social and raucous, but whatever birds have survived have had to be shy and wary, as quiet as bark. They live by stealth.

What He Missed

Not the bill, not the length, which he showed me, holding his fingers apart— "Three inches." Not the thickness of the bill—this time, making a fat circle of forefinger and thumb. What he forgot to notice was the pale color of the bill, the look of ivory. In the blitz of recognition, he missed that, as he missed the very yellow eye.

The Quote

No puny pileated but a whacking big bird, he said, quoting Roger Tory Peterson, who witnessed the ivory-bill in 1941 and called that occasion the greatest birding moment of his long birding career. Peterson kept a page for the bird in his guidebooks, hope against hope, for years after others had shifted it to the extinct category. But a decade ago, even Peterson concluded that the bird had reached its end, like the woodlands it had inhabited, and no longer existed except in memory.

After

For a long time, he had to sit on a log and not say anything. He played the image of the bird over and over and over in his mind. It was too great a thing to comprehend—that he was there, and the bird was there, and he and the bird were breathing the same air. After the descriptions and illustrations by Catesby, Audubon, and Wilson; and after the photos and films from the Louisiana swamps in the 1940s; and after the late but extensive Tanner scholarship about life history and habitat; and after Peterson's passion and despair; and after the fleeting white of new video and all the talk about the ghost bird and the grail bird and the Lord God bird; and after his dead father's lifetime of desire and his own matching but far-fetched desire and all the desire of the world; after all that, the ivory-billed woodpecker was still more than a person could imagine. It was as beautiful and as perfect as only it itself, its living being, could be.

Brothers

Bret Lott

This much is fact: There is a home movie of the two of us sitting on the edge of the swimming pool at our grandma and grandpa's old apartment building in Culver City. The movie, taken sometime in early 1960, is in color, though the color has faded, leaving my brother Brad and me milk white and harmless children, me a year and a half old, Brad almost four, our brown hair faded to only the thought of brown hair. Our mother, impossibly young, sits next to me on the right of the screen. Her hair, for all the fading of the film, is coal black, shoulder length, and parted in the middle, curled up on the sides. She has on a bathing suit covered in purple and blue flowers, the color in them nearly gone. Next to me on the left of the screen is Brad, in his white swimming trunks. I am in the center, my fat arms up, bent at the elbows, fingers curled into fists, my legs kicking away at the water, splashing and splashing. I am smiling, the baby of the family, the center of the world at that very instant, though my little brother, Tim, is only some six or seven months off, and my little sister, Leslie, the last child, just three years distant. The pool water before us is only a thin sky blue, the bushes behind us a dull and lifeless light green. There is no sound.

My mother speaks to me, points at the water, then looks up. She lifts a hand to block the sun, says something to the camera. Her skin is the same white as ours, but her lips are red, a sharp cut of lipstick moving as she speaks. I am still kicking. Brad is looking to his right, off the screen, his feet in the water, too, but moving slowly. His hands are on the edge of the pool, and he leans forward a little, looks down into the water. My mother still speaks to the camera, and I give an extra-hard kick, splash up shards of white water.

Brad flinches at the water, squints his eyes, while my mother laughs, puts a hand to her face. She looks back to the camera, keeps talking, a hand low to the water to keep more from hitting her. I still kick hard, still send up bits of water, and I am laughing a baby's laugh, mouth open and eyes nearly closed, arms still up, fingers still curled into fists.

More water splashes at Brad, who leans over to me, says something. Nothing about me changes: I only kick, laugh. He says something again, his face leans a little closer to mine. Still I kick.

This is when he lifts his left hand from the edge of the pool, places it on my right thigh, and pinches hard. It's not a simple pinch, not two fingers on a fraction of skin, but his whole hand, all his fingers grabbing the flesh just above my knee and squeezing down hard. He grimaces, his eyes on his hand, on my leg.

My expression changes, of course: In an instant I go from a laughing baby to a shocked one, my mouth a perfect O, my body shivering so that my legs kick even harder, even quicker, but just this one last time. They stop, and I cry, my mouth open even more, my eyes all the way closed. My hands are still in fists.

Then Brad's hand is away, and my mother turns from speaking to the camera to me. She leans in close, asking, I am certain, what's wrong. The movie cuts then to my grandma, white skin and silver hair, seated on a patio chair by the pool, above her a green-and-white-striped umbrella. She has a cigarette in one hand, waves off the camera with the other. Though she died eight years ago, and though she, too, loses color with each viewing, she is still alive up there, still waves, annoyed, at my grandpa and his camera, the moment my brother pinched hell out of me already gone.

This much is fact, too: Thumbtacked to the wall of my office is a photograph of Brad and me taken by my wife in November 1980, the date printed on the border. In it we stand together, me a good six inches taller than him, my arm around his shoulder. The photograph is black and white, as though the home movie and its sinking colors were a prophecy pointing to this day twenty years later: We are at the tidepools at Portuguese Bend, out on the Palos Verdes Peninsula; in the background are the stone-gray bluffs, to the left of us the beginning of the black rocks of the pools, above us the perfect white of an overcast sky.

Brad has on a white Panama hat, a collarless shirt beneath a gray hooded sweatshirt. His face is smooth shaven, and he is grinning, lips together, eyes squinted nearly shut beneath the brim of the hat. It is a goofy smile, but a real one.

I have on a cardigan with an alpine design around the shoulders, the rest of it white, the shawl collar on it black here, though I know it to have been navy blue. I have on a buttondown Oxford shirt, sideburns almost to my earlobes. I have a mustache, a pair of glasses too large for my face; and I am smiling, my mouth open to reveal my big teeth. It isn't my goofy smile, but it's a real one too.

These are the facts of my brother: the four-year-old pinching me, the twenty-four-year-old leaning into me, grinning.

But between the fact of these two images lie twenty years of the play of memory, the dark and bright pictures my mind has retained, embroidered upon, made into things they are and things they are not. There are twenty years of things that happened between my brother and me, from the fistfight we had in high school over who got the honey bun for breakfast, to his phone call to me from a tattoo parlor in Hong Kong where he'd just gotten a Chinese junk stitched beneath the skin of his right shoulder blade; from his showing me one summer day how to do a death drop from the jungle gym at Elizabeth Dickerson Elementary, to him watching while his best friend and our next-door neighbor, Lynn Tinton, beat me up on the driveway of our home in a fight over whether I'd fouled Lynn or not at basketball. I remember—no true picture, necessarily, but what I have made the truth by holding tight to it, playing it back in my head at will and in the direction I wish it to go—I remember lying on my back, Lynn's knees pinning my shoulders to the driveway while he hit my chest, and looking up at Brad, the basketball there at his hip, him watching.

I have two children now. Both boys, born two and a half years apart. I showed the older one, Zeb—almost eight—the photograph, asked him who those two people were. He held it in his hands a long while.

We were in the kitchen. The bus comes at seven-twenty each morning, and I have to have lunches made and breakfasts set out—all before that bus comes and before Melanie takes off for work, Jacob in tow, to be dropped off at the Montessori school on her way in to her office.

I waited, and waited, finally turned from him to get going on his lunch.

"It's you," he said. "You have a lot of hair," he said.

"Who's the other guy?" I said. I looked back at him, saw the concentration on his face, the way he brought the photograph close, my son's eyes taking in his uncle as best he could.

He said, "I don't know."

"That's your uncle Brad," I said. "Your mom took that picture ten years ago, long before you were ever born."

He still looked at the picture. He said, "He has a beard now."

I turned from him, finished with the peanut butter, and spread jelly on the other piece of bread. This is the only kind of sandwich he will eat at school. He said from behind me, "Only three years before I was born. That's not a long time." I stopped, turned again to him. He touched the picture with a finger. He said, "Three years isn't a long time, Dad."

But I was thinking of my question: *Who's the other guy?* and of the truth of his answer: *I don't know.*

Zeb and Jake fight. Melanie and I were upstairs wrapping Christmas presents in my office, a room kept locked the entire month of December for the gifts piled up in there. We heard Jake wailing, dropped the bucket of Legos and the red-and-green HO! HO! HO! paper, ran for the hall and down the stairs.

There in the kitchen stood my two sons, Jacob's eyes wet, him whimpering now, a hand to his bottom lip. I made it first, yelled, "What happened?"

"I didn't do it," Zeb said, and backed away from me, there with my hand to Jacob's jaw.

Melanie stroked Jacob's hair, whispered, "What's wrong?"

Jacob opened his mouth then, showed us the thick wash of blood between his bottom lip and his tongue, a single tooth, horribly white, swimming up from it. "We were playing Karate Kid," Zeb said, and now he was crying. "I didn't do it," he said, and backed away even farther.

One late afternoon a month or so ago, Melanie backed the van into the driveway to make it easier to unload all the plastic bags of groceries. When we'd finished we let the boys play outside, glad for them to be out of the kitchen while we sorted through the bags heaped on the counter, put everything away. Melanie's last words to the two of them, her leaning out the front door into the near-dark: "Don't play in the van!"

Not ten minutes later Jacob came into the house, slammed shut the front door like he always does. He walked into the kitchen, his hands behind him. He said, "Zeb's locked in the van." His face takes on the cast of the guilty when he knows he's done something wrong: His mouth gets pursed, his eyebrows go up, his eyes look right into mine. He doesn't know enough yet to look away. "He told me to come get you." He turned, headed for the door, and I followed him out onto the porch, where, before I could even see the van in the dark, I heard Zeb screaming.

I went to the van, tried one of the doors. It was locked, and Zeb was still screaming.

"Get the keys!" he was saying. "Get the keys!" I pressed my face to the glass of the back window, saw Zeb inside jumping up and down. "My hand's caught," he cried.

I ran into the house, got the keys from the hook beneath the cupboard, only enough time for me to say to Melanie, "Zeb's hand's closed in the back door," and turn, run back out. I made it to the van, unlocked the big back door, and pushed it up as quick as I could, Melanie already beside me.

Zeb stood holding the hand that'd been closed in the door. Melanie and I both took his hand, gently examined the skin, wiggled the fingers, and in the dull glow of the dome light we saw that nothing'd been broken, no skin torn. The black foam lining the door had cushioned his fingers, so that they'd only been smashed a little, but a little enough to scare him, and to make blue bruises there the next day. Beneath the dome light there was the sound of his weeping, then the choked words, "Jacob pulled the door down on me."

From the darkness just past the line of light from inside the van came my second son's voice: "I didn't do it."

I have no memory of the pinch Brad gave me on the edge of that apartment-complex pool, no memory of my mother's black hair—now it's a sort of brown—nor even any memory of the pool itself. There is only that bit of film.

But I can remember putting my arm around his shoulder in 1980, leaning into him, the awkward and alien comfort of that touch. In the photograph we are both smiling, me a newlywed with a full head of hair, him only a month or so back from working a drilling platform in the Gulf of Mexico. He'd missed my wedding six months before, stranded on the rig, he'd told us, because of a storm.

What I believe is this: That pinch was entry into our childhood; my arm around him, our smiling, is the proof of us two surfacing, alive but not unscathed.

And here are my own two boys, already embarked.

Listen to the Sounds of the House

Jared Jacang Maher

When my father was young, one of his many chores was to spend a week shoveling three feet of livestock manure and hay that had built up on the barn floor during the freezing Indiana winter. It was responsibilities like this that had also built up the muscles in his massive shoulders and back, which today remain as one of the few physical indicators left of his rural tractors-and-church roots. Looking back, it was also probably one of the reasons why my dad would make me and my brother accompany him on semi-annual poop patrols through the neighborhood to recoup all that our dog had laid down over the seasons and reclaim it as our own. As boys we would follow him along the sidewalk armed with small shovels and plastic buckets lined with trash bags, scooping turds of all shapes and sizes, the petrifieds and the fresh-uns, from the manicured greenbelts and paths around our home. Inevitably, we would return with four times the crap that our Brittany Spaniel mutt could produce in a year. For my father, the bags of other people's dog shit sitting at the bottom of our driveway at the end of the day symbolized a job well done. And that, in a small way, was social progress.

Of course, one man's utopian vision is another man's institutional oppression. My brother and I protested little during the years of fence-post-hole digging, tree-stump hacking, rock shoveling, sod laying, and the never-ending list of yard labor. At twenty-four, though, I liked to pretend that I was a grown man under no obligation for father-forced scutwork, especially those tasks of a stinky nature. But when back living with my parents, the past and future felt somehow locked in an unnatural embrace. It was like my new adult-self was on the couch making out with my old kid-self and had everyone at the welcome home party feeling very, very uncomfortable.

One morning my dad came in from the garage wearing his leather work gloves and tattered weekend T-shirt, which had a minefield of little holes that pockmarked his torso. I was at the kitchen table, sitting in the same seat, in the exact same position as I held when I was twelve. The only difference was that I had traded Cap'n Crunch and the comics section for a mug of fair-trade Sumatran and *The New York Times*. My mother was out at various supermarkets, as per her customary five-hour routine of coupon-guided power shopping. I scratched at my stubble, reading an article on tort reform or something, while my dad consulted his to-do list on the dry-erase board mounted to the refrigerator. Today the list said: "mow lawn, put winter tires in attic, move cabinet, marinate chicken," and so on. Then, at the end was written, "show boys sprinkler drain." He asked me what my plans were for the day.

"Ahh," I drew out like I was in the middle of a really engrossing paragraph. "Ahh, I've got to, well, you know . . ." My voice trailed off. "Things like . . ."

My daughter, still in her Hello Kitty nightgown, poked her head up from the couch-cushion fort she had constructed in the living room. "Like what things?" she asked.

"Like important adult things," I answered. "Like giving-little-girls-showers things and brushing-the-tangles-out-of-their-hair things." Her head disappeared with a yelp. She knew that the longer I was left undisturbed with my coffee and newspaper, the longer she would remain immersed in a sea of warm, glorious Saturday morning cartoons. The program she was watching was about a group of grade schoolers who had discovered one of those little folded paper, fortune-teller contraptions, which they dubbed the "Cootie Catcher."

"Pick a color," one kid said.

"Red."

"Pick a number." Once the numeral was chosen, he worked his hands like little crab claws. "One, two, three, four."

"Will I get a new bike this summer?"

The little triangle flap was lifted. They gasped. "Yes, definitely."

The whole story was about how the kids began to consult the Cootie Catcher on everything—if they should study for the next geography test, if they should swing at baseballs, if they should watch certain television shows—and how their reliance on its powers began to dominate their lives. Since they felt the future was pre-determined, or at least being shaped by some unseen force, they had no option but to hand over every decision to the judgment of the pocket oracle. But when the Cootie Catcher accidentally got put through the wash, the kids were left helpless, unable to function in a world of unrelenting choices and grand expectations. Were I to write an analytical English essay on the cartoon, I would conclude the Cootie Catcher was an indictment about the postmodern condition. Although I think my daughter thought it was just funny.

But I didn't need a Cootie Catcher to predict what my father had in mind for me that day. After I got Gianni showered and dressed, I followed him out around the side of the house where the manifolds for the sprinklers met the main water line. Eventually my brother crawled out from his bed in the pitch-black basement and emerged for the tutorial, only slightly more bleary-eyed and indifferent than usual. We stared into the hole while my father explained the system in wrenching detail. To drain the line between this and that, the uppermost valve here would have to be turned counterclockwise, etc. I nodded reflexively and concentrated on a very tan woman speed walking a stroller that contained a very terrified looking toddler. Both my brother and I knew full well that the process of draining the sprinkler system would be described to us verbatim again and again until the time came to actually drain the sprinkler system. That's when my dad would most likely fax us a meticulously written course of action and then talk us through the steps via a long-distance phone call.

In a month, my parents were moving to the island of Oahu in Hawaii. It was where my mom was born and raised, working in the pineapple canneries, and where my dad had fled for college as a way to escape the oppressively grey Midwestern sky. They were returning to Hawaii to work for the public school system—my mom as a special-ed teacher, my dad as a school social worker—while I presumably would hold down the house in Colorado until it could be put on the market and sold. I was unsure how I felt about the plan. My hope to get my own apartment somewhere downtown by the end of the summer would now be postponed for at least another year. The distance was only about ten miles, but to me it constituted a world of disparity. Even when we first moved into the house in my sixth-grade year, I had never felt quite at home in "The Ranch," a suburban hamlet named for the once pristine dry-grass prairie it plowed over for thirty-five acres of cookie-cutter suburban housing. No one in my family had golfed in their entire lives, a fact that would not change despite the eighteen-hole course that stretched through the development. For a time, we belonged to the country club at the top of the hill, which had a tennis bubble and pool. But somehow it didn't feel the same as the more modest, family-oriented swim and tennis club we had left behind.

As I grew into my late teens, the distaste that I harbored for the place fit neatly into my budding political attitude. I scoffed at the preening elitism of the country-club members and their children, all dressed in cream-colored polo shirts, tooting toward the driving range in their electric golf carts. Every day around 10 a.m., just after the last SUV had rolled out toward the office or the mall, I would take note of the migration of lawn-care crews sputtering their battered Chevy trucks into the neighborhood, armed with weed whackers and leaf blowers. Despite passing two years of Spanish, I could string together nary a single sentence in *Espanola*. But as I trimmed the front-yard hedges in the blazing sun, I felt that somehow I shared a common language with my fellow landscapers. *Never give up, compadres, one day we will overcome*, I would think, brushing the grass clippings from my brow. *But for now, we must work . . . Viva la John Deere!*

The summer before my last year in high school, some buddies and I hijacked a high-powered golf cart from the clubhouse in the middle of the night and took it on a drunken joyride down the course. We declared ourselves revolutionaries and gleefully plowed through sand traps, small trees, and wetland bogs, stopping only to "plant" beer bottles into the green and urinate in the ball washers. When the police finally trapped our cart in a cul-de-sac, I was the only one who managed to escape arrest because of my thorough knowledge of the neighborhood's many escape routes, and my ability to climb fifty feet into a cottonwood tree and hide there until daybreak.

Four years of college and five years of parenthood had managed to tamper my tendency for beer-fueled vandalism and redirect it toward a penchant for wine-induced philosophizing. For me, suburbia represented the worst excesses of American-style consumerism. The endless sprawl pattern of soulless chain stores and outsized McMansions was a showcase of everything that was homogeneous, unsustainable, and wrong with the world. I had skateboarded through the multi-layered neighborhoods of New York and San Francisco. I had ridden the El train around every corner of Chicago. I had spent six months traversing Vancouver's bridges by bike. And now I was back to where I started, Westminster, Colorado, where my only choices for a bike destination was the Starbucks one mile to the east, or the Starbucks one mile to the west.

But more than the standardized scenery, I was increasingly agitated by the idea of living back at home. I had read the statistics about how more and more twentysomethings were residing with their parents, heard the varying explanations from social scientists who described the phenomenon as a kind of elongated childhood. Was it that young people had been pampered, they fretted, not taught the true value of a dollar and hard work? Yes, yes, that *must* be it. I wasn't as upset by this supposed generational occurrence as I was about the idea that I was a part of it. I hated the fact that I could be identified as a delegate in some pathetic cultural trend of leeches unable to survive in the real world, a cliché that has become fodder for sitcoms and local news telecasts. I had tried my whole life to choose a path of creativity rather than conformity, and here I was struggling to fit my identity into my old bedroom where I could hear my parents snore at night.

"Yeah, I'm staying out at my parents' house right now," I would reveal to friends and vague acquaintances. "But I'm, you know, just helping them out right now with some stuff. Yup, it is totally temporary." They would smile wanly and then change the subject. Because the truth of the matter was that with my random freelance writing gigs, there was no way I could afford to live on my own, at least not any kind of place where I could house my daughter during the three days a week she was in my care. In a practical sense, living at home was the best option for everybody. My parents loved having their sons and their grandkid in the house, and I needed a place to live.

But after more than a year at my parents' house, I began to ask myself, "Is any of this really temporary?"

One, two, three, four.

The answer is unclear. Try again later.

My dad was showing us how to replace a broken sprinkler head when an Audi with personalized plates that read "FLUFFI" pulled up to the stop sign.

"Hey, I see you still got those boys working for you!" yelled Jim, who lived down the street with his wife Cathy.

"Well, you know," my father ambled up to the car with the usual neighborly banter, "the only job they're really good at is cleaning out the refrigerator." Though he can be short and to-the-point when there's a task at hand, my father is not a harsh man. He laughs often and with great enthusiasm. It begins as a pained wheeze, with the growing hilarity stuck somewhere in his windpipe, building pressure like a Mount St. Helens of merriment. When it finally does escape, the laughter explodes in a series of high-pitched shrieks. If seated at a dinner table, he will slap at the table with his open palm as if it has been bad. As kids, my brother and I would glance at each other wondering who this deranged man was, and how we were supposed to get him back to the shelter. Lacking a flat surface, he smacks his leg until the redness leaves his face, at which point he exhales and tries to recall what was so funny in the first place. He laughs the hardest at his own jokes. "That's just *toooo* much," he sighs.

"Well, we'll be sure to keep an eye on the boys when you're gone," Cathy beamed, and then called out to me and Adam, "No kegger parties now, alright you guys?" She laughed. "I have binoculars!"

I mustered a few ha-has and waved slightly. Adam didn't bother. For the rest of the sprinkler lesson, I made it a point to retain as little information as possible. After my brother left to go to work, my dad started telling me about how there was always the possibility that a winter cold snap could freeze a pipe, which could then break, flooding the basement.

"If you're upstairs, all you'll hear is water running," he said. "You know what that sounds like, right?"

"Are you asking me if I know what running water sounds like?"

"It's like a *wwssshhhh*."

"Yes, Dad, I know."

He said he knows I know, but then he took me inside the house and had me stand in the front hallway. He turned off the radio and told Gianni to go play outside. "Listen," he said, pointing his finger into the air.

I listened. I heard a semi go by on the road. I heard a dog bark down the street. For a second I thought I heard an ice-cream truck, but it was just the neighbor's wind chimes.

"Do you hear that?" he said.

"Yes!" I said. "No. Hear what?"

"The house," he nodded. He explained that when one has been a homeowner for three decades like him, they become attuned to the noises their house makes. It's kind of like a residential mind-meld that creates a sixth sense for leaky faucets and dirty furnace filters. When my parents moved out of state, he said it was going to fall on me, this task of house therapy.

"I don't know," I said, half expecting him to pull a pebble from his pocket and order me to grab it from his upturned palm, "I mean, this house is so big. Do you really think I'm ready? Maybe I should start by listening to the coat closet."

I chuckled and waited for a reaction, but my father seemed lost in thought. He cocked his head and pointed his finger toward the ceiling. "That goddamn toilet upstairs is running again," he said, rushing into the garage for his tools.

In the first month after my parents had left for Hawaii, I felt like a new man. I began spending more time at home, amazed by its sudden emptiness. The pantry slowly emptied of the stockpile of Little Debbie snacks and cheese puffs that my mom would buy on sale, replaced with small plastic bags of dried fruits and wheat crackers that I would get from the health-food store. For my birthday that fall, my friends came over and we made fondue with a seventies-era melting pot that I discovered in the basement. Soon it was past midnight and we started taking shots of Jagermeister and dancing wildly in the living room to my mom's Hawaiian music CDs. I awoke at the break of dawn with a raging hangover and decided to climb through an upstairs window and onto the roof. The morning air was cold and there was a thin layer of frost on the wooden shingles. I watched the sun creep into the east, illuminating the long wisps of clouds that wrapped around the sky. Red, orange, yellow, blue. If someone asked me to pick a color, I don't think I would have been able to choose. The future seemed so distant and beautiful, but it was terrifying how all of it sat down on top of you, like a bully on your chest squishing your whole body until you couldn't breath. It was like the kind of freedom that's also confining in a way, the immensity of it all.

I stood and began making my way woozily back toward the window when I slipped on a patch of ice and started sliding on my ass sideways toward the edge of the roof. Propping my arm forward, I managed to wedge my arm against a skylight and halt my descent. When I got back inside, I took a shower, pulled the splinters out of my butt, and laughed, vowing never to die in such a pitiful manner. A jet-ski crash or a moped accident maybe, but never would my last memory be how the aluminum gutters needed to be dredged before I broke my neck in a bush that had become overgrown and required trimming.

I scored a job as a reporter for the local alternative newsweekly, and through the winter months found myself working excessively long hours in front of the computer and slogging through rush-hour traffic like all the other suckers in the 9-to-5 world. When springtime came I actually began taking pleasure in being able to be outside in the sun, away from my keyboard, doing something physical for a change. The first thing I did was water the garden, checking to see how the tomato and zucchini plants were coming in. I got the sprinkler system turned on again, but for some reason the water pressure was way too low and much of the lawn wasn't getting the proper moisture. For two weeks, the grass got hit with an intense heat spell and began to look brown and withered. Scared that the whole lawn was going to die and require re-sodding, I rechecked the manifolds and all the valves, kicking myself for not paying attention to the sprinkler lecture. Finally, I called Hawaii and my dad immediately identified the problem and all the steps to fix it. Soon the lawn was flourishing along with the shrubs and flowers.

After putting the mower away and hauling the bags of grass clippings to the end of the driveway, I cracked a beer and sat on my front porch. I admired how the lines ran parallel across the lawn, but rose and bended with the contours of the land, how the setting sun fell upon the straightness, the order of it all. Neighbors drove by and I waved cheerfully. I thought about my parents sitting in the middle of the vast Pacific Ocean. I wondered if they felt the same way as I did, returning to a place they lived when they were young—young, in their mid-twenties, like me now—and having to reconfigure psychology with geography. The first house they bought together in the late seventies was a small postwar unit not too far from here. They both had full-time jobs and promising careers with health insurance and 401Ks. Eventually they saved up enough money to get a mortgage for a bigger house nearby. On weekends, my father built a huge back porch where we would have birthday parties and make homemade ice cream with neighbors. Where my father grew up, there was no backyard or golf course, just a huge cornfield and a long list of chores that had to be done if the family was to survive. When my parents decided to upgrade to the house in The Ranch, they did it for all the reasons anybody else did it—more square footage, better schools, the feeling of movement, change. If I were ever to buy property, this home probably wouldn't be my choice for a place to live. But while, for me, the house symbolized snobbery and conformity, for my father it represented hard work. And that, in a way, is progress.

One night I heard a car passing outside and I jumped out of bed to peek through a crack in the Venetian blinds. A car full of teenagers had stopped at a house down the street. A week earlier someone had driven through my lawn and left tire-track scars deep in the Kentucky Bluegrass. I'd had fantasies of catching the punks in the act. Sometimes I smashed their windshield with a brick, other times I used the metal baseball bat that I'd begun to keep in the coat closet. But that night, the teenagers drove off and the night was once again silent. I checked on my daughter and pulled the sheets back over her slumbering body. I went downstairs and got a glass of water. I moved through the house wearing only my boxers. My bare feet felt good on the cold, hardwood floor. One, two, three, four, five, six. Is it possible to predict the future? *No, definitely not.* Instead there are only sounds. I listened to the refrigerator humming. I listened to the furnace clicking on and heat blowing through the basement ducts into different sections of the house, rattling the vent covers. But other than that, the house was quiet, and that meant everything was going to be okay.

Some Things About That Day

Debra Marquart

The placards I walked through. The wet raincoat on a hook. The questionnaire on a clipboard placed before me. Couples sat around me in the waiting room. They were young. What am I saying? I was only thirty-two.

But I remember, the men seemed the more bereft. Facing forward, their elbows resting on knees, their faces covered with hands. Or pushed back hard in the seats, gazing at a spot on the floor, legs stretched out in the aisles.

Difficult to remember the order in which things happened. The clipboard taken away, my name was called—our names were all called, the waiting room emptying and filling. Small orange pill in a tiny plastic cup. Water for washing it down. I was led to another room.

The gown that tied at the back, the bright fluorescent light, the posters with diagrams on the walls. Plenty of time to look around. The sound of vacuuming in another room.

The doctor arrives, hurried and unfriendly. Her one day in this clinic, she's flown in from another state. Death threats follow her. She asks me if I want to proceed. I tell her, yes. I lie back in the stirrups. The apparatus arrives—a silver canister on wheels with gauges and hoses attached to a long, cylindrical tube, thin like a spout. The sound of vacuuming close now. The nurse by my side, holding my shoulder. The doctor working away behind the thin film of my gown.

A blank space surrounds this moment. Sleepy from the sedative, yes, and numb. But let me not gloss over it. A feeling of tugging, mild discomfort. When the vacuum stops, the doctor asks if I want to know the sex. I tell her, *no*.

When I informed my husband I was pregnant, he said, *Is it mine?* Not the best beginning. We'd been married for a month. Married on Leap Day. Who else's could it be? He had an important meeting at work that day, some critical task. I had driven myself.

Sleep, after the procedure. (My friend tried to soften it for me afterwards. *Just say you had a procedure, dear.*) Nothing about it was procedural. I woke in a room of sleeping beauties. Afterwards, cramping, nausea. Faint, when I woke up, dizzy.

Orange juice and back down for twenty minutes. And then the odd assemblage of street clothes smoothed onto my limbs, the parting advice from the nurse, the script for a prescription pushed into my hand. Strange to walk out the door. The protesters gone. My car started just fine, slipped right into gear. I backed out, went forward. Drove light-headed to the drug store.

At the pharmacy, the man in the white coat looked at me when I handed him the script. Could he see from the prescription where I'd been? A softness dawned on his face. *Go home*, he said. They would deliver it.

Only then, in the car, did I start to cry. So stupid. Over the kindness of the pharmacist. When I got home, my husband was on the couch, watching the NBA playoffs. Even before the drugs arrived—even after—he couldn't stop telling me what a brave girl I had been.

The Search for Marvin Gardens

John McPhee

Go. I roll the dice—a six and a two. Through the air I move my token, the flat-iron, to Vermont Avenue, where dog packs range.

The dogs are moving (some are limping) through ruins, rubble, fire damage, open garbage. Doorways are gone. Lath is visible in the crumbling walls of the buildings. The street sparkles with shattered glass. I have never seen, anywhere, so many broken windows. A sign—"Slow, Children at Play"—has been bent backward by an automobile. At the lighthouse, the dogs turn up Pacific and disappear. George Meade, Army engineer, built the lighthouse—brick upon brick, six hundred thousand bricks, to reach up high enough to throw a beam twenty miles over the sea. Meade, seven years later, saved the Union at Gettysburg.

I buy Vermont Avenue for $100. My opponent is a tall, shadowy figure, across from me, but I know him well, and I know his game like a favorite tune. If he can, he will always go for the quick kill. And when it is foolish to go for the quick kill he will be foolish. On the whole, though, he is a master assessor of percentages. It is a mistake to underestimate him. His eleven carries his top hat to St. Charles Place, which he buys for $140.

The sidewalks of St. Charles Place have been cracked to shards by through-growing weeds. There are no buildings. Mansions, hotels once stood here. A few street lamps now drop cones of light on broken glass and vacant space behind a chain-link fence that some great machine has in places bent to the ground. Five plane trees—in full summer leaf, flecking the light—are all that live on St. Charles Place.

Block upon block, gradually, we are cancelling each other out—in the blues, the lavenders, the oranges, the greens. My opponent follows a plan of his own devising. I use the Hornblower & Weeks opening and the Zuricher defense. The first game draws tight, will soon finish. In 1971, a group of people in Racine, Wisconsin, played for seven hundred and sixty-eight hours. A game begun a month later in Danville, California, lasted eight hundred and twenty hours. These are official records, and they stun us. We have been playing for eight minutes. It amazes us that Monopoly is thought of as a long game. It is possible to play to a complete, absolute, and final conclusion in less than fifteen minutes, all within the rules as written. My opponent and I have done so thousands of times. No wonder we are sitting across from each other now in this best-of-seven series for the international singles championship of the world.

On Illinois Avenue, three men lean out from second-story windows. A girl is coming down the street. She wears dungarees and a bright-red shirt, has ample breasts and a Hadendoan Afro, a black halo, two feet in diameter. Ice rattles in the glasses in the hands of the men.

"Hey, sister!"

"Come on up!"

She looks up, looks from one to another to the other, looks them flat in the eye.

"What for?" she says, and she walks on.

I buy Illinois for $240. It solidifies my chances, for I already own Kentucky and Indiana. My opponent pales. If he had landed first on Illinois, the game would have been over then and there, for he has houses built on Boardwalk and Park Place, we share the railroads equally, and we have cancelled each other everywhere else. We never trade.

In 1852, R. B. Osborne, an immigrant Englishman, civil engineer, surveyed the route of a railroad line that would run from Camden to Absecon Island, in New Jersey, traversing the state from the Delaware River to the barrier beaches of the sea. He then sketched in the plan of a "bathing village" that would surround the eastern terminus of the line. His pen flew glibly, framing and naming spacious avenues parallel to the shore—Mediterranean, Baltic, Oriental, Ventnor—and narrower transsecting avenues: North Carolina, Pennsylvania, Vermont, Connecticut, States, Virginia, Tennessee, New York, Kentucky, Indiana, Illinois. The place as a whole had no name, so when he had completed the plan Osborne wrote in large letters over the ocean, "Atlantic City." No one ever challenged the name, or the names of Osborne's streets. Monopoly was invented in the early nineteen-thirties by Charles B. Darrow, but Darrow was only transliterating what Osborne had created. The railroads, crucial to any player, were the making of Atlantic City. After the rails were down, houses and hotels burgeoned from Mediterranean and Baltic to New York and Kentucky. Properties—building lots—sold for as little as six dollars apiece and as much as a thousand dollars. The original investors in the railroads and the real estate called themselves the Camden & Atlantic Land Company. Reverently, I repeat their names: Dwight Bell, William Coffin, John DaCosta, Daniel Deal, William Fleming, Andrew Hay, Joseph Porter, Jonathan Pitney, Samuel Richards—founders, fathers, forerunners, archetypical masters of the quick kill.

My opponent and I are now in a deep situation of classical Monopoly. The torsion is almost perfect—Boardwalk and Park Place versus the brilliant reds. His cash position is weak, though, and if I escape him now he may fade. I land on Luxury Tax, contiguous to but in sanctuary from his power. I have four houses on Indiana. He lands there. He concedes.

Indiana Avenue was the address of the Brighton Hotel, gone now. The Brighton was exclusive—a word that no longer has retail value in the city. If you arrived by automobile and tried to register at the Brighton, you were sent away. Brighton-class people came in private railroad cars. Brighton-class people had other private railroad cars for their horses—dawn rides on the firm sand at water's edge, skirts flying. Colonel Anthony J. Drexel Biddle—the sort of name that would constrict throats in Philadelphia—lived, much of the year, in the Brighton.

Colonel Sanders' fried chicken is on Kentucky Avenue. So is Clifton's Club Harlem, with the Sepia Revue and the Sepia Follies, featuring the Honey Bees, the Fashions, and the Lords.

My opponent and I, many years ago, played 2,428 games of Monopoly in a single season. He was then a recent graduate of the Harvard Law School, and he was working for a downtown firm, looking up law. Two people we knew—one from Chase Manhattan, the other from Morgan, Stanley—tried to get into the game, but after a few rounds we found that they were not in the conversation and we sent them home. Monopoly should always be *mano a mano* anyway. My opponent won 1,199 games, and so did I. Thirty were ties. He was called into the Army, and we stopped just there. Now, in Game 2 of the series, I go immediately to jail, and again to jail while my opponent seines property. He is dumbfoundingly lucky. He wins in twelve minutes.

Visiting hours are daily, eleven to two; Sunday, eleven to one; evenings, six to nine. "NO MINORS, NO FOOD, Immediate Family Only Allowed in Jail." All this above a blue steel door in a blue cement wall in the windowless interior of the basement of the city hall. The desk sergeant sits opposite the door to the jail. In a cigar box in front of him are pills in every color, a banquet of fruit salad an inch and a half deep—leapers, co-pilots, footballs, truck drivers, peanuts, blue angels, yellow jackets, redbirds, rainbows. Near the desk are two soldiers, waiting to go through the blue door. They are about eighteen years old. One of them is trying hard to light a cigarette. His wrists are in steel cuffs. A military policeman waits, too. He is a year or so older than the soldiers, taller, studious in appearance, gentle, fat. On a bench against a wall sits a good-looking girl in slacks. The blue door rattles, swings heavily open. A turnkey stands in the doorway. "Don't you guys kill yourselves back there now," says the sergeant to the soldiers.

"One kid, he overdosed himself about ten and a half hours ago," says the M.P.

The M.P., the soldiers, the turnkey, and the girl on the bench are white. The sergeant is black. "If you take off the handcuffs, take off the belts," says the sergeant to the M.P. "I don't want them hanging themselves back there." The door shuts and its tumblers move. When it opens again, five minutes later, a young white man in sandals and dungarees and a blue polo shirt emerges. His hair is in a ponytail. He has no beard. He grins at the good-looking girl. She rises, joins him. The sergeant hands him a manila envelope. From it he removes his belt and a small notebook. He borrows a pencil, makes an entry in the notebook. He is out of jail, free. What did he do? He offended Atlantic City in some way. He spent a night in the jail. In the nineteen-thirties, men visiting Atlantic City went to jail, directly to jail, did not pass Go, for appearing in topless bathing suits on the beach. A city statute requiring all men to wear full-length bathing suits was not seriously challenged until 1937, and the first year in which a man could legally go bare-chested on the beach was 1940.

Game 3. After seventeen minutes, I am ready to begin construction on overpriced and sluggish Pacific, North Carolina, and Pennsylvania. Nothing else being open, opponent concedes.

The physical profile of streets perpendicular to the shore is something like a playground slide. It begins in the high skyline of Boardwalk hotels, plummets into warrens of "side-avenue" motels, crosses Pacific, slopes through church missions, convalescent homes, burlesque houses, rooming houses, and liquor stores, crosses Atlantic, and runs level through the bombed-out ghetto as far—Baltic, Mediterranean—as the eye can see. North Carolina Avenue, for example, is flanked at its beach end by the Chalfonte and the Haddon Hall (908 rooms, air-conditioned), where, according to one biographer, John Philip Sousa (1854–1932) first played when he was twenty-two, insisting, even then, that everyone call him by his entire name. Behind these big hotels, motels—Barbizon, Catalina—crouch. Between Pacific and Atlantic is an occasional house from 1910—wooden porch, wooden mullions, old yellow paint—and two churches, a package store, a strip show, a dealer in fruits and vegetables. Then, beyond Atlantic Avenue, North Carolina moves on into the vast ghetto, the bulk of the city, and it looks like Metz in 1919, Cologne in 1944. Nothing has actually exploded. It is not bomb damage. It is deep and complex decay. Roofs are off. Bricks are scattered in the street. People sit on porches, six deep, at nine on a Monday morning. When they go off to wait in unemployment lines, they wait sometimes two hours. Between Mediterranean and Baltic runs a chain-link fence, enclosing rubble. A patrol car sits idling by the curb. In the back seat is a German shepherd. A sign on the fence says, "Beware of Bad Dogs."

Mediterranean and Baltic are the principal avenues of the ghetto. Dogs are everywhere. A pack of seven passes me. Block after block, there are three-story brick row houses. Whole segments of them are abandoned, a thousand broken windows. Some parts are intact, occupied. A mattress lies in the street, soaking in a pool of water. Wet stuffing is coming out of the mattress. A postman is having a rye and a beer in the Plantation Bar at nine-fifteen in the morning. I ask him idly if he knows where Marvin Gardens is. He does not. "HOOKED AND NEED HELP? CONTACT N.A.R.C.O." "REVIVAL NOW GOING ON, CONDUCTED BY REVEREND H. HENDERSON OF TEXAS." These are signboards on Mediterranean and Baltic. The second one is upside down and leans against a boarded-up window of the Faith Temple Church of God in Christ. There is an old peeling poster on a warehouse wall showing a figure in an electric chair. "The Black Panther Manifesto" is the title of the poster, and its message is, or was, that "the fascists have already decided in advance to murder Chairman Bobby Seale in the electric chair." I pass an old woman who carries a bucket. She wears blue sneakers, worn through. Her feet spill out. She wears red socks, rolled at the knees. A white handkerchief, spread over her head, is knotted at the corners. Does she know where Marvin Gardens is? "I sure don't know," she says, setting down the bucket. "I sure don't know. I've heard of it somewhere, but I just can't say where." I walk on, through a block of shattered glass. The glass crunches underfoot like coarse sand. I remember when I first came here—a long train ride from Trenton, long ago, games of poker in the train—to play basketball against Atlantic City. We were half black, they were all black. We scored forty points, they scored eighty, or something like it. What I remember most is that they had glass backboards—glittering, pendent, expensive glass backboards, a rarity then in high schools, even in colleges, the only ones we played on all year.

I turn on Pennsylvania, and start back toward the sea. The windows of the Hotel Astoria, on Pennsylvania near Baltic, are boarded up. A sheet of unpainted plywood is the door, and in it is a triangular peephole that now frames an eye. The plywood door opens. A man answers my question. Rooms there are six, seven, and ten dollars a week. I thank him for the information and move on, emerging from the ghetto at the Catholic Daughters of America Women's Guest House, between Atlantic and Pacific. Between Pacific and the Boardwalk are the blinking vacancy signs of the Aristocrat and Colton Manor motels. Pennsylvania terminates at the Sheraton-Seaside—thirty-two dollars a day, ocean corner. I take a walk on the Boardwalk and into the Holiday Inn (twenty-three stories). A guest is registering. "You reserved for Wednesday, and this is Monday," the clerk tells him. "But that's all right. We have *plenty* of rooms." The clerk is very young, female, and has soft brown hair that hangs below her waist. Her superior kicks her.

He is a middle-aged man with red spiderwebs in his face. He is jacketed and tied. He takes her aside. "Don't say 'plenty,'" he says. "Say 'You are fortunate, sir. We have rooms available.'"

The face of the young woman turns sour. "We have all the rooms you need," she says to the customer, and, to her superior, "How's that?"

Game 4. My opponent's luck has become abrasive. He has Boardwalk and Park Place, and has sealed the board.

Darrow was a plumber. He was, specifically, a radiator repairman who lived in Germantown, Pennsylvania. His first Monopoly board was a sheet of linoleum. On it he placed houses and hotels that he had carved from blocks of wood. The game he thus invented was brilliantly conceived, for it was an uncannily exact reflection of the business milieu at large. In its depth, range, and subtlety, in its luck-skill ratio, in its sense of infrastructure and socio-economic parameters, in its philosophical characteristics, it reached to the profundity of the financial community. It was as scientific as the stock market. It suggested the manner and means through which an underdeveloped world had been developed. It was chess at Wall Street level. "Advance token to the nearest Railroad and pay owner twice the rental to which he is otherwise entitled. If Railroad is unowned, you may buy it from the Bank. Get out of Jail, free. Advance token to nearest Utility. If unowned, you may buy it from Bank. If owned, throw dice and pay owner a total ten times the amount thrown. You are assessed for street repairs: $40 per house, $115 per hotel. Pay poor tax of $15. Go to Jail. Go directly to Jail. Do not pass Go. Do not collect $200."

The turnkey opens the blue door. The turnkey is known to the inmates as Sidney K. Above his desk are ten closed-circuit-TV screens—assorted viewpoints of the jail. There are three cellblocks—men, women, juvenile boys. Six days is the average stay. Showers twice a week. The steel doors and the equipment that operates them were made in San Antonio. The prisoners sleep on bunks of butcher block. There are no mattresses. There are three prisoners to a cell. In winter, it is cold in here. Prisoners burn newspapers to keep warm. Cell corners are black with smudge. The jail is three years old. The men's block echoes with chatter. The man in the cell nearest Sidney K. is pacing. His shirt is covered with broad stains of blood. The block for juvenile boys is, by contrast, utterly silent—empty corridor, empty cells. There is only one prisoner. He is small and black and appears to be thirteen. He says he is sixteen and that he has been alone in here for three days.
    "Why are you here? What did you do?"
    "I hit a jitney driver."

The series stands at three all. We have split the fifth and sixth games. We are scrambling for property. Around the board we fairly fly. We move so fast because we do our own banking and search our own deeds. My opponent grows tense.

Ventnor Avenue, a street of delicatessens and doctors' offices, is leafy with plane trees and hydrangeas, the city flower. Water Works is on the mainland. The water comes over in submarine pipes. Electric Company gets power from across the state, on the Delaware River, in Deepwater. States Avenue, now a wasteland like St. Charles, once had gardens running down the middle of the street, a horse-drawn trolley, private homes. States Avenue was as exclusive as the Brighton. Only an apartment house, a small motel, and the All Wars Memorial Building—monadnocks spaced widely apart—stand along States Avenue now. Pawnshops, convalescent homes, and the Paradise Soul Saving Station are on Virginia Avenue.

The soul-saving station is pink, orange, and yellow. In the windows flanking the door of the Virginia Money Loan Office are Nikons, Polaroids, Yashicas, Sony TVs, Underwood typewriters, Singer sewing machines, and pictures of Christ. On the far side of town, beside a single track and locked up most of the time, is the new railroad station, a small hut made of glazed firebrick, all that is left of the lines that built the city. An authentic phrenologist works on New York Avenue close to Frank's Extra Dry Bar and a church where the sermon today is "Death in the Pot." The church is of pink brick, has blue and amber windows and two red doors. St. James Place, narrow and twisting, is lined with boarding houses that have wooden porches on each of three stories, suggesting a New Orleans made of salt-bleached pine. In a vacant lot on Tennessee is a white Ford station wagon stripped to the chassis. The windows are smashed. A plastic Clorox bottle sits on the driver's seat. The wind has pressed newspaper against the chain-link fence around the lot. Atlantic Avenue, the city's principal thoroughfare, could be seventeen American Main Streets placed end to end—discount vitamins and Vienna Corset shops, movie theatres, shoe stores, and funeral homes. The Boardwalk is made of yellow pine and Douglas fir, soaked in pentachlorophenol. Downbeach, it reaches far beyond the city. Signs everywhere—on windows, lampposts, trash baskets—proclaim "Bienvenue Canadiens!" The salt air is full of Canadian French. In the Claridge Hotel, on Park Place, I ask a clerk if she knows where Marvin Gardens is. She says, "Is it a floral shop?" I ask a cabdriver, parked outside. He says, "Never heard of it." Park Place is one block long, Pacific to Boardwalk. On the roof of the Claridge is the Solarium, the highest point in town—panoramic view of the ocean, the bay, the salt-water ghetto. I look down at the rooftops of the side-avenue motels and into swimming pools. There are hundreds of people around the rooftop pools, sunbathing, reading—many more people than are on the beach. Walls, windows, and a block of sky are all that is visible from these pools—no sand, no sea. The pools are craters, and with the people around them they are countersunk into the motels.

The seventh, and final, game is ten minutes old and I have hotels on Oriental, Vermont, and Connecticut. I have Tennessee and St. James. I have North Carolina and Pacific. I have Boardwalk, Atlantic, Ventnor, Illinois, Indiana. My fingers are forming a "V." I have mortgaged most of these properties in order to pay for others, and I have mortgaged the others to pay for the hotels. I have seven dollars. I will pay off the mortgages and build my reserves with income from the three hotels. My cash position may be low, but I feel like a rocket in an underground silo. Meanwhile, if I could just go to jail for a time I could pause there, wait there, until my opponent, in his inescapable rounds, pays the rates of my hotels. Jail, at times, is the strategic place to be. I roll boxcars from the Reading and move the flatiron to Community Chest. "Go to Jail. Go directly to Jail."

The prisoners, of course, have no pens and no pencils. They take paper napkins, roll them tight as crayons, char the ends with matches, and write on the walls. The things they write are not entirely idiomatic; for example, "In God We Trust." All is in carbon. Time is required in the writing. "Only humanity could know of such pain." "God So Loved the World." "There is no greater pain than life itself." In the women's block now, there are six blacks, giggling, and a white asleep in red shoes. She is drunk. The others are pushers, prostitutes, an auto thief, a burglar caught with pistol in purse. A sixteen-year-old accused of murder was in here last week. These words are written on the wall of a now empty cell: "Laying here I see two bunks about six inches thick, not counting the one I'm laying on, which is hard as brick. No cushion for my back. No pillow for my head. Just a couple scratchy blankets which is best to use it's said. I wake up in the morning so shivery and cold, waiting and waiting till I am told the food is coming. It's on its way. It's not worth waiting for, but I eat it anyway. I know one thing when they set me free I'm gonna be good if it kills me."

How many years must a game be played to produce an Anthony J. Drexel Biddle and chestnut geldings on the beach? About half a century was the original answer, from the first railroad to Biddle at his peak. Biddle, at his peak, hit an Atlantic City streetcar conductor with his fist, laid him out with one punch. This increased Biddle's legend. He did not go to jail. While John Philip Sousa led his band along the Boardwalk playing "The Stars and Stripes Forever" and Jack Dempsey ran up and down in training for his fight with Gene Tunney, the city crossed the high curve of its parabola. Al Capone held conventions here—upstairs with his sleeves rolled, apportioning among his lieutenant governors the states of the Eastern seaboard. The natural history of an American resort proceeds from Indians to French Canadians via Biddles and Capones. French Canadians, whatever they may be at home, are Visigoths here. Bienvenue Visigoths!

My opponent plods along incredibly well. He has got his fourth railroad, and patiently, unbelievably, he has picked up my potential winners until he has blocked me everywhere but Marvin Gardens. He has avoided, in the fifty-dollar zoning, my increasingly petty hotels. His cash flow swells. His railroads are costing me two hundred dollars a minute. He is building hotels on States, Virginia, and St. Charles. He has temporarily reversed the current. With the yellow monopolies and my blue monopolies, I could probably defeat his lavenders and his railroads. I have Atlantic and Ventnor. I need Marvin Gardens. My only hope is Marvin Gardens.

There is a plaque at Boardwalk and Park Place, and on it in relief is the leonine profile of a man who looks like an officer in a metropolitan bank—"Charles B. Darrow, 1889–1967, inventor of the game of Monopoly." "Darrow," I address him, aloud. "Where is Marvin Gardens?" There is, of course, no answer. Bronze, impassive, Darrow looks south down the Boardwalk. "Mr. Darrow, please, where is Marvin Gardens?" Nothing. Not a sign. He just looks south down the Boardwalk.

My opponent accepts the trophy with his natural ease, and I make, from notes, remarks that are even less graceful than his.

Marvin Gardens is the one color-block Monopoly property that is not in Atlantic City. It is a suburb within a suburb, secluded. It is a planned compound of seventy-two handsome houses set on curvilinear private streets under yews and cedars, poplars and willows. The compound was built around 1920, in Margate, New Jersey, and consists of solid buildings of stucco, brick, and wood, with slate roofs, tile roofs, multimullioned porches, Giraldic towers, and Spanish grilles. Marvin Gardens, the ultimate outwash of Monopoly, is a citadel and sanctuary of the middle class. "We're heavily patrolled by police here. We don't take no chances. Me? I'm living here nine years. I paid seventeen thousand dollars and I've been offered thirty. Number one, I don't want to move. Number two, I don't need the money. I have four bedrooms, two and a half baths, front den, back den. No basement. The Atlantic is down there. Six feet down and you float. A lot of people have a hard time finding this place. People that lived in Atlantic City all their life don't know how to find it. They don't know where the hell they're going. They just know it's south, down the Boardwalk."

In Plain Sight

Tom Montgomery-Fate

No method or discipline can supersede the necessity of being forever on the alert. What is a course of history or philosophy, or poetry, no matter how well selected, or the best society, or the most admirable routine of life, compared with the discipline of looking always at what is to be seen? Will you be a reader, a student merely, or a seer?

Henry David Thoreau, *Walden*

A great blue heron pumps slowly across the empty sky. It is headed toward the small river that is the eastern boundary of our land. Last month, five pairs of herons flapped back to our farm, as they have for the last four years, to repair their great prickly bowls of sticks and lay their eggs. The nests are about three feet across and set 90 feet off the ground near the top of a huge sycamore tree. The tree drapes over the Galien River—which is 25 miles long and sprouts tiny branches all over southwest Michigan before draining into the lake. Thirty years ago, the Galien was loaded with fish and was a favorite swimming hole for those who didn't live on the lake. But today it is very sick. Last year the Department of Environmental Equality declared it unsafe for even partial bodily contact. A sample taken at a bridge just down the road contained 40 times the acceptable level of *E. coli* bacteria.

Though herons are not endangered, and rookeries with dozens of nests and hundreds of birds are common, the return of these birds to this 50-acre patch of woods and meadow gives me hope. And the hope is deeper this year, as there are seven new nests in an even taller sycamore tree on the other side of the river. These birds may be the offspring of the first year's hatching, as they often return to their parents' nesting site two or three years later. I'm not sure if the herons' thriving here is due to a new conservation program to clean up the river and control soil erosion, or simply their own adaptation. Either way, if they can find enough fish and frogs to feed themselves and their offspring, it is a good sign.

Our land, like much of the central Midwest, has been wrecked by agriculture, unfettered industry, and new development (half-million-dollar vacation homes have started popping up just down the road). Thus, the animals that live here are the tough kind—raccoons and possums and coyotes; starlings and grackles and turkey vultures—species that could quickly adapt to the ravaged habitat, to erosion and fertilizers and pesticides and herbicides, and to a river that has absorbed them. Their abundance, and the rapid extinction of a myriad of other species, is primarily due to my—to the human's—inability to belong to the ecosystem, to imagine *enough* of anything.

The *E. coli* level in our river exemplifies this human "never-enoughness." Feeding cattle people food (corn) rather than cow food (grass) plays havoc with their digestive tracts (too much starch) and creates the dangerous strain of bacteria. The justification for grain-feeding is economic: grain-fed cattle reach slaughter weight in a little over a year, rather than the four to five years required for grass-fed cattle. The process is also accelerated with growth hormones. And antibiotics are needed to offset the traumatic effects of corn on the cows' intestines. All of this finds its way back into the woodland stream and the human bloodstream.

This afternoon I walk along the river carrying both the reality of the human role in its slow destruction, and the hope of the returning herons. I don't think a writer can ever resolve such conflicts, though it is worth considering *how* one writes about nature. Broadly speaking, it seems some writers seek to discover the unspoiled, the exotic and wild, which they fly to in jets and bush planes. Other writers may seek to recover the spoiled, the non-wilderness. They observe and analyze and reflect on their own towns and cities and suburbs and backyards. Certainly there is value in both approaches, and they sometimes blur or overlap, but I most identify with those writers who stay put, who know their own ground. And it's worth mentioning here that I don't really have a choice. No magazine has offered to fly me to the highlands of Guatemala to count *quetzales*, or to the Philippines to describe the last "healthy" coral reef, or to the Aleutian Islands to observe whale migration.

Yet, clearly the reason the "untouched" wilderness has become increasingly less wild is because it has been touched too many times. Exploration—of the Arctic, of coral reefs, of rain forests—has invariably led to exploitation. Thus, our children and their children will one day understand all that touching and exploring as a kind of violence, as rape. Instead of attempting to get to some new or "pure" bit of the natural world, they will need to learn to find the wild in the recovery of the ravaged, in the return of fish and fowl and wildflowers to the decimated woodlands and rivers of the Midwest.

That is what I seek here—not the marvel of the untouched, but of learning how to be touched by the commonplace. The miracle here is "revision"—learning to see again. I am looking less and less for a pure subject, and more and more for moments of pure sight, for a glimpse of the wild in the mundane, of rapture in the ordinary. Wildness, after all—as Thoreau and others have written—is not an undiscovered insect or island, but a quality of awareness, a way of seeing. And seeing the world always precedes saving it.

Last week I read a little piece of this article to my 12-year-old daughter, Tessa. I was preparing an excerpt for a radio essay about the herons and wanted to see what she thought. She stopped me when I said the word "polluted," because it didn't align with what she had seen. "The river's polluted?" she asked. "But I think it's pretty." "I do too," I said. "It's just that there's a lot we can't see: chemical runoff and livestock excrement, leaking septic tanks, small factories dumping sewage. That kills a lot of plants and fish." "Oh," she said, in a tone that means, "That's enough of an answer for now."

Like Tessa, my eyes are not scientifically trained to see very far past the Galien's façade of health. But on my frequent walks, I notice that minnows and pan fish are very rare. I've seen no crawdads backing out of their muddy holes along the riverbank, and no turtles sunning themselves on deadfalls. Tadpoles and frogs should still be more abundant. And I know all the algae growth diminishes oxygen levels. Yet, a recent paper by the Department of Natural Resources reports the presence of trout and walleye in a part of the river that is less polluted and closer to the lake. As I watch the slow-moving water, I wonder if those fish will ever live here, in this neck of the Galien. I would be happy just to see a sucker or a carp—the bottom feeders that I loved to catch as a kid.

It hasn't rained for a week, so the river is only three feet deep and quite clear. When I reach the next bend and look south, I see the beauty Tessa does: the gurgling riffles around rocks and deadfalls and an abandoned tractor tire. A timeless current runs over the yellow sandy bottom, making a sad music that the wind carries to the blooming wildflowers. These delicate yellow wheels and purple cups and white-petaled tubes—spring beauties, phlox, trillium, jack-in-the-pulpit—dot the green explosion of returning foliage. The trees have already turned the sunlight into a half-formed canopy, which will keep closing for a couple of more weeks until it blocks most of the light and wind from the woods. By then the herons will no longer be visible, and the mosquitoes will be breeding and rising in swarms off the river into the humming, blood-seeking clouds that drift through the stillness and shadow, looking for me.

The other blood seekers I know best—the deer and dog ticks—are already out, though not in full force. They sit waiting for our warm mammalian blood—in trees and on vines, on the tips of thistles and goldenrod and tall grasses, always ready to attack, or I mean to *attach*, to whatever deer or dog or raccoon or person they can find. This behavior, this perching on the leaves and stems with forelegs extended, is called "questing." When something brushes them, they climb on and plunge a beak-like projection into the warm flesh, drawing in a quantity of blood that is a hundred times their "empty" weight. It is mostly the dog ticks that find me—the bigger ones. They crawl out of my socks, or I feel them creeping on my ankles or down my back. I end their quest as quickly as I can, not wanting to find an embedded blood bloat in the morning.

I keep walking along the river. Fifty yards ahead of me, a four-foot-high gray-feathered bird is a statue in the river's swampy oxbow. The curve of its thin neck, head, and beak, and the straight of its body form a ruffled question mark. Presuming he is fishing, I also freeze. This is only the second time I've seen a heron on the ground and not scared it away. Because of the sentinel warning system they use around the rookery, it is hard to get close. I watch him for several minutes, but he soon lifts off in a wild *thwapping*, unfolding eight feet of wing.

Though I've never seen a heron catch a fish on the Galien, I have watched them eat small sunfish at a nearby lake, tilting back their heads to gurgle-swallow them whole. Sometimes they spear perch, to wound or kill them before eating them. Audubon once wrote about watching a heron try to spear a fish in Florida that was so big that the heron got stuck. The fish pulled the impaled heron out and under the water, and nearly drowned it before the bird could unhook itself and escape from its "prey."

I keep tramping along the river, through the wild-rose brambles and reeds. Soon I can hear the herons' funny low grumbling in their nests in the distance. They sound like my Uncle Carl—rough, low voices—like they're trying to both clear their throat and tease me with a question. "*Whaht, Whaht, Whaht, Whaht* are you doing here?" is what I hear. I only visit the birds every three or four weeks, as I don't want to disturb them. Sometimes heron fledglings become so flustered by predators or other distractions that they fall out of the nest to their deaths only days before learning to fly.

When I arrive at the old sycamore tree, I lie flat on my back underneath it with my binoculars aimed at the nests. I watch for perhaps a half hour—until I feel a warm, sticky dripping on my arm, and then on my neck. Could it be . . . ? Yes, guano rain. The birds are crapping on me. I take the hint. But just before I leave, one bird gets anxious. She peers over the rim of the nest at me with a haunting yellow-ringed eye, makes her decision, nervously stumbles around in the sticks for a second, unfolds that great prehistoric *S* of a body, and tumbles into the air with an awkward beauty—quickly drop-gliding to the river bank. Surprised she has flown down rather than up, I remain still and watch the odd stalk of bone and feather and beak take three slow, methodical steps along the sandy bank before swiveling her head to look at me. Then a chemical charge fires: "danger" surges from brain to wings. She is harried, but not a sparrow or wren, so not equipped for quick, fluid movements. The gawky lifting of her body out of the river reminds me of one of the Wright Brothers' early flying machines, which you were never quite sure would make it through takeoff. But unlike those early planes, the heron becomes more graceful as she rises. Once aloft, she is easy in the air. She flies across the canvas of the day as herons have for thousands of years, stroking the empty sky with the wild brush of her gray-blue body. I watch her circle our land and wonder what she sees, what she knows of the quivering strands of life that still connect us.

Grammar Lessons: The Subjunctive Mood

Michele Morano

Think of it this way: Learning to use the subjunctive mood is like learning to drive a stick shift. It's like falling in love with a car that isn't new or sporty but has a tilt steering wheel and a price you can afford. It's like being so in love with the possibilities, with the places you might go and the experiences you might have, that you pick up your new used car without quite knowing how to drive it, sputtering and stalling and rolling backward at every light. Then you drive the car each day for months, until the stalling stops and you figure out how to downshift, until you can hear the engine's registers and move through them with grace. And later, after you've gained control over the driving and lost control over so much else, you sell the car and most of your possessions and move yourself to Spain, to a place where language and circumstance will help you understand the subjunctive.

Remember that the subjunctive is a mood, not a tense. Verb tenses tell *when* something happens; moods tell *how true*. It's easy to skim over moods in a new language, to translate the words and think you've understood, which is why your first months in Spain will lack nuance. But eventually, after enough conversations have passed, enough hours of talking with your students at the University of Oviedo and your housemate, Lola, and the friends you make when you wander the streets looking like a foreigner, you'll discover that you need the subjunctive in order to finish a question, or an answer, or a thought you couldn't have had without it.

In language, as in life, moods are complicated, but at least in language there are only two. The indicative mood is for knowledge, facts, absolutes, for describing what's real or definite. You'd use the indicative to say, for example:

I was in love.

Or, *The man I loved tried to kill himself.*
Or, *I moved to Spain because the man I loved, the man who tried to kill himself, was driving me insane.*

The indicative helps you tell what happened or is happening or will happen in the future (when you believe you know for sure what the future will bring).

The subjunctive mood, on the other hand, is uncertain. It helps you tell what could have been or might be or what you want but may not get. You'd use the subjunctive to say:

I thought he'd improve without me.
Or, *I left so that he'd begin to take care of himself.*

Or later, after your perspective has been altered, by time and distance and a couple of *cervezas* in a brightly lit bar, you might say:

I deserted him (indicative).
I left him alone with his crazy self for a year (indicative).
Because I hoped (after which begins the subjunctive) *that being apart might allow us to come together again.*

English is losing the subjunctive mood. It lingers in some constructions ("If he *were* dead," for example), but it's no longer pervasive. That's the beauty and also the danger of English—that the definite and the might-be often look so much alike. And it's the reason why, during a period in your life when everything feels hypothetical, Spain will be a very seductive place to live.

In Spanish, verbs change to accommodate the subjunctive in every tense, and the rules, which are many and varied, have exceptions. In the beginning you may feel defeated by this, even hopeless and angry sometimes. But eventually, in spite of your frustration with trying to explain, you'll know in the part of your mind that holds your stories, the part where grammar is felt before it's understood, that the uses of the subjunctive matter.

1. with *Ojalá*

Ojalá means I hope or, more literally, "that Allah is willing!" It's one of the many words left over from the Moorish occupation of Spain, one that's followed by the subjunctive mood because, of course, you never know for sure what Allah has in mind.

During the first months in Spain, you'll use the word by itself, a kind of dangling wish. "It's supposed to rain," Lola will say, and you'll respond "*Ojalá.*" You'll know you're confusing her, leaving her to figure out whether you want the rain or not, but sometimes the mistakes are too hard to bear. "That Allah is willing it wouldn't have raining," you might accidentally say. And besides, so early into this year of living freely, you're not quite sure what to hope for.

Each time you say *Ojalá*, it will feel like a prayer, the "ja" and "la" like breaths, like faith woven right into the language. It will remind you of La Mezquita, the enormous, graceful mosque in Córdoba. Of being eighteen years old and visiting Spain for the first time, how you stood in the courtyard filled with orange trees, trying to admire the building before you. You had a fever then, a summer virus you hadn't yet recognized because it was so hot outside. Too hot to lift a hand to fan your face. Too hot to wonder why your head throbbed and the world spun slowly around you.

Inside, the darkness felt like cool water covering your eyes, such contrast, such relief. And then the pillars began to emerge, rows and rows of pillars supporting red and white brick arches, a massive stone ceiling balanced above them like a thought. You swam behind the guide, not even trying to understand his words but soothed by the vastness, by the shadows. Each time you felt dizzy you looked up toward the arches, the floating stone. Toward something that felt, you realized uncomfortably, like God. Or Allah. Or whatever force inspired people to defy gravity this way.

Later, after ten years have passed, after you've moved to Oviedo and become fascinated with the contours of language, the man you left behind in New York will come to visit. You'll travel south with him, returning to La Mezquita on a January afternoon when the air is mild and the orange trees wave tiny green fruit. He'll carry the guidebook, checking it periodically to get the history straight, while you try to reconcile the place before you with the place in your memory, comparing the shadows of this low sun with the light of another season.

You'll be here because you want this man to see La Mezquita. You want him to feel the mystery of a darkness that amazes and consoles, that makes you feel the presence in empty spaces of something you can't explain. Approaching the shadow of the door, you'll each untie the sweaters from around your waists, slipping your arms into them and then into each other's. He will squint and you will hold your breath. *Ojalá*, you'll think, glimpsing in the shadows the subjunctive mood at work.

2. after words of suasion and negation

In Oviedo, you'll become a swimmer. Can you imagine? Two or three times a week you'll pack a bag and walk for thirty-five minutes to the university pool, where you'll place clothes and contact lenses in a locker, then sink into a crowded lane. The pool is a mass of blurry heads and arms, some of which know what they're doing and most of which, like you, are flailing. You keep bumping into people as you make your way from one end of the pool to the other, but no one gets upset, and you reason that any form of motion equals exercise.

Then one day a miracle happens. You notice the guy in the next lane swimming like a pro, his long arms cutting ahead as he glides, rhythmically, stroke-stroke-breath. You see and hear and feel the rhythm, and before long you're following him, stroking when he strokes, breathing when he breathes. He keeps getting away, swimming three laps to your one, so you wait at the edge of the pool for him to come back, then follow again, practicing. At the end of an hour, you realize that this man you don't know, a man you wouldn't recognize clothed, has taught you to swim. To breathe. To use the water instead of fighting against it. For this alone, you'll later say, it was worth moving to Spain.

Stroke-stroke-breath becomes the rhythm of your days, the rhythm of your life in Oviedo. All through the fall months, missing him the way you'd miss a limb, your muscles strain to create distance. Shallow end to deep end and back, you're swimming away. From memories of abrupt mood shifts. From the way a question, a comment, a person walking past a restaurant window could transform him into a hunched-over man wearing anger like a shawl. From the echo of your own voice trying to be patient and calm, saying, *Listen to me. I want you to call the doctor.* In English you said *listen* and *call*, and they were the same words you'd use to relate a fact instead of make a plea. But in Spanish, in the language that fills your mind as you swim continually away, the moment you try to persuade someone, or dissuade, you enter the realm of the subjunctive. The verb ends differently so there can be no mistake: requesting is not at all the same as getting.

3. with *"si"* or *"como si"*

Si means *if. Como si* means *as if.* A clause that begins with *si* or *como si* is followed by the subjunctive when the meaning is hypothetical or contrary to fact. For example:

> *If I'd known he would harm himself, I wouldn't have left him alone.*

But here we have to think about whether the if-clause really is contrary to fact. Two days before, you'd asked him what he felt like doing that night and he'd responded, "I feel like jumping off the Mid-Hudson Bridge." He'd looked serious when he said it, and even so you'd replied, "Really? Would you like me to drive you there?" *As if* it were a joke.

If you knew he were serious, that he were thinking of taking his life, would you have replied with such sarcasm? In retrospect it seems impossible not to have known—the classic signs were there. For weeks he'd been sad, self-pitying. He'd been sleeping too much, getting up to teach his Freshman Composition class in the morning, then going home some days and staying in bed until evening. His sense of humor had waned. He'd begun asking the people around him to cheer him up, make him feel better, please.

And yet he'd been funny. Ironic, self-deprecating, hyperbolic. So no one's saying you should have known, just that maybe you felt a hint of threat in his statement about the river. And maybe that angered you because it meant you were failing to be enough for him. Maybe you were tired, too, in need of cheering up yourself because suddenly your perfect guy had turned inside out. Or maybe that realization came later, after you'd had the time and space to develop theories.

The truth is, only you know what you know. And what you know takes the indicative, remember?

For example: You knew he was hurting himself. The moment you saw the note on his office door, in the campus building where you were supposed to meet him on a Sunday afternoon, you knew. The note said, "I'm not feeling well. I'm going home. I guess I'll see you tomorrow." He didn't use your name.

You tried calling him several times but there was no answer, so you drove to the apartment he shared with another graduate student. The front door was unlocked, but his bedroom door wouldn't budge. You knocked steadily but not too loud, because his housemate's bedroom door was also closed, and you assumed he was inside taking a nap. *If* you'd known that his housemate was not actually home, you would have broken down the door. That scenario is hypothetical, so it takes the subjunctive—even though you're quite sure.

The human mind can reason its way around anything. On the drive to your own apartment, you told yourself, he's angry with me. That's why the door was locked, why he wouldn't answer the phone. You thought: If he weren't so close to his family, I'd really be worried. If today weren't Mother's Day. If he didn't talk so affectionately about his parents. About his brother and sisters. About our future. If, if, if.

When the phone rang and there was silence on the other end, you began to shout, "What have you done?"

In Spain, late at night over *chupitos* of bourbon or brandy, you and Lola will trade stories. Early on you won't understand a lot of what she says, and she'll understand what you say but not what you mean. You won't know how to say what you mean in Spanish; sometimes you won't even know how to say it in English. But as time goes on, the stories you tell will become more complicated. More subtle. More grammatically daring. You'll begin to feel more at ease in the unreal.

For example: *If* you hadn't gone straight home from his apartment. *If* you hadn't answered the phone. *If* you hadn't jumped back into your car to drive nine miles in record time, hoping the whole way to be stopped by the police. *If* you hadn't met him on the porch where he had staggered in blood-soaked clothes. *If* you hadn't rushed upstairs for a towel and discovered a flooded bedroom floor, the blood separating into water and rust-colored clumps. *If* you hadn't been available for this emergency.

As the months pass in Spain, you'll begin to risk the *then*. His housemate would have come home and found him the way you found him: deep gashes in his arm, but the wounds clotting enough to keep him alive, enough to narrowly avoid a transfusion. His housemate would have called the paramedics, ridden to the hospital in the ambulance, notified his parents from the emergency room, greeted them after their three-hour drive. His housemate would have done all the things you did, and he would have cleaned the mess by himself instead of with your help, the two of you borrowing a neighbor's wet-vac and working diligently until you—or he—or both of you—burst into hysterical laughter. Later this housemate would have moved to a new apartment, just as he has done, and would probably be no worse off than he is right now.

You, on the other hand, would have felt ashamed, guilty, remiss for not being available in a time of crisis. But you wouldn't have found yourself leaning over a stretcher in the emergency room, a promise slipping from your mouth before you could think it through: "I won't leave you. Don't worry, I won't leave you." *As if* it were true.

4. after impersonal expressions

Such as *it is possible, it is a shame, it is absurd.*

"*It's possible* that I'm making things worse in some ways," you told the counselor you saw on Thursday afternoons. He'd been out of the hospital for a few months by then and had a habit of missing his therapy appointments, to which you could only respond by signing up for your own.

She asked how you were making things worse, and you explained that when you told him you needed to be alone for a night and he showed up anyway at 11:00 PM, pleading to stay over, you couldn't turn him away. She said, "*It's a shame* he won't honor your request," and you pressed your fingernails into the flesh of your palm to keep your eyes from filling. She asked why you didn't want him to stay over, and you said that sometimes you just wanted to sleep, without waking up when he went to the bathroom and listening to make sure he came back to bed instead of taking all the Tylenol in the medicine cabinet. Or sticking his head in the gas oven. Or diving from the balcony onto the hillside three stories below. There is nothing, you told her, nothing I haven't thought of.

She said, "Do you think he's manipulating you?" and you answered in the mood of certainty, "Yes. Absolutely." Then you asked, "*Isn't it absurd* that I let him manipulate me?" and what you wanted, of course, was some reassurance that it wasn't absurd. That you were a normal person, reacting in a normal way, to a crazy situation.

Instead she said, "Let's talk about why you let him. Let's talk about what's in this for you."

5. after verbs of doubt or emotion

You didn't think he was much of a prospect at first. Because he seemed arrogant. Because in the initial meetings for new instructors, he talked as if he were doing it the right way and the rest of you were pushovers. Because he looked at you with one eye squinted, as if he couldn't quite decide.

You liked that he was funny, a little theatrical and a great fan of supermarkets. At 10:00 PM, after evening classes ended, he'd say, "Are you going home?" Sometimes you'd offer to drop him off at his place. Sometimes you'd agree to go out for a beer. And sometimes you'd say, "Yeah, but I have to go to the store first," and his eyes would light up. In the supermarket he'd push the cart and you'd pick items off the shelf. Maybe you'd turn around and there would be a whole rack of frozen ribs in your cart, or after you put them back, three boxes of Lucky Charms. Maybe he'd be holding a package of pfeffernusse and telling a story about his German grandmother. Maybe it would take two hours to run your errand because he was courting you in ShopRite.

You doubted that you'd sleep with him a second time. After the first time, you both lay very still for a while, flat on your backs, not touching. He seemed to be asleep. You watched the digital clock hit 2:30 AM and thought about finding your turtleneck and sweater and wool socks, lacing up your boots, and heading out into the snow. And then out of the blue he rolled toward you, pulled the blanket up around your shoulders, and said, "Is there anything I can get you? A cup of tea? A sandwich?"

You were thrilled at the breaks in his depression, breaks that felt like new beginnings, every time. Days, sometimes even weeks, when he seemed more like himself than ever before. Friends would ask how he was doing, and he'd offer a genuine smile. "Much better," he'd say, putting his arm around you, "She's pulling me through the death-wish phase." Everyone would laugh with relief, and at those moments you'd feel luckier than ever before, because of the contrast.

Do you see the pattern?

6. to express good wishes

Que tengas muy bien viaje, Lola will say, kissing each of your cheeks before leaving you off at the bus station. *May you have a good trip*. A hope, a wish, a prayer of sorts, even without the *Ojalá*.

The bus ride from Oviedo to Madrid is nearly six hours, so you have a lot of time for imagining. It's two days after Christmas, and you know he spent the holiday at his parents' house, that he's there right now, maybe eating breakfast, maybe packing. Tonight his father will drive him to Kennedy Airport, and tomorrow morning, very early, you'll meet him at Barajas in Madrid. You try to envision what he'll look like, the expression on his face when he sees you, but you're having trouble recalling what it's like to be in his presence.

You try not to hope too much, although now, four months into your life in Spain, you want to move toward, instead of away. Toward long drives on winding, mountain roads, toward the cathedral of Toledo, the mosque at Córdoba, the Alhambra in Granada. Toward romantic dinners along the Mediterranean. Toward a new place from which to view the increasingly distant past. You want this trip to create a separation, in your mind and in his, between your first relationship and your real relationship, the one that will be so wonderful, so stable, you'll never leave him again.

Once you've reached Madrid and found the *pensión* where you've reserved a room, you'll get the innkeeper to help you make an international call. His father will say, "My God, he can't sit still today," and then there will be his voice, asking how your bus ride was, where you are, how far from the airport. You'll say, "I'll see you in the morning." He'll reply, "In seventeen hours."

The next morning, the taxi driver is chatty. He wants to know why you're going to the airport without luggage, and your voice is happy and excited when you explain. He asks whether this boyfriend writes you letters, and you smile and nod at the reflection in the rearview mirror. "Many letters?" he continues, "Do you enjoy receiving the letters?" In Spain you're always having odd conversations with strangers, so you hesitate only a moment, wondering why he cares, and then you say, "Yes. Very much." He nods emphatically. "*Muy bien.*" At the terminal he drops you off with a broad smile. "*Que lo pases bien con tu novio,*" he says. *Have a good time with your boyfriend.* In his words you hear the requisite subjunctive mood.

7. in adverbial clauses denoting purpose, provision, exception

How different to walk down the street in Madrid, Toledo, Córdoba, to notice an elaborate fountain or a tiny car parked half on the sidewalk, and comment aloud. You've loved being alone in Spain and now, even more, you love being paired.

On the fifth day you reach Granada, find lodging in someone's home. Down the hallway you can hear the family watching TV, cooking, preparing to celebrate New Year's Eve. In the afternoon you climb the long, slow hill leading to the Alhambra and spend hours touring the complex. You marvel at the elaborate irrigation system, the indoor baths with running water, the stunning mosaic tiles and views of the Sierra Nevada. Here is the room where Boabdil signed the city's surrender to Ferdinand and Isabella; here is where Washington Irving lived while writing *Tales of the Alhambra.* Occasionally you separate, as he inspects a mural and you follow a hallway into a lush courtyard, each of your imaginations working to restore this place to its original splendor. When you come together again, every time, there's a thrill.

He looks rested, relaxed, strolling through the gardens with his hands tucked into the front pockets of his pants. When you enter the Patio of the Lions—the famous courtyard where a circle of marble lions project water into a reflecting pool—he turns to you, wide-eyed, his face as open as a boy's.

"Isn't it pretty?" you keep asking, feeling shy because what you mean is: "Are you glad to be here?"

"*So* pretty," he responds, taking hold of your arm, touching his lips to your hair. The day is perfect, you think. The trip is perfect. You allow yourself a moment of triumph: I left him *so that* he would get better without me, and he did. I worked hard and saved money and invited him on this trip *in case* there's still hope for us. And there is.

Unless. In language, as in experience, we have purpose, provision, exception. None of which necessarily matches reality, and all of which take the subjunctive.

On the long walk back down the hill toward your room, he turns quiet. You find yourself talking more than usual, trying to fill the empty space with cheerful commentary, but it doesn't help. The shape of his face begins to change until there it is again, that landscape of furrows and crags. The jaw thrusts slightly, lips pucker, eyebrows arch as if to say, "I don't care. About anything."

Back in the room, you ask him what's wrong, plead with him to tell you. You can talk about anything, you assure him, anything at all. And yet you're stunned when his brooding turns accusatory. He says it isn't fair. You don't understand how difficult it is to be him. Your life is easy, so easy that even moving to a new country, taking up a new language, is effortless. While every day is a struggle for him. Don't you see that? Every day is a struggle.

He lowers the window shade and gets into bed, his back turned toward you.

What to do? You want to go back outside into the mild air and sunshine, walk until you remember what it feels like to be completely alone. But you're afraid to leave him. For the duration of his ninety-minute nap, you sit paralyzed. Everything feels unreal, the darkened room, the squeals of children in another part of the house, the burning sensation in your stomach. You tremble, first with sadness and fear, then with anger. Part of you wants to wake him, tell him to collect his things, then drive him back to the airport in Madrid. You want to send him home again, away from your new country, the place where you live unencumbered—but with a good deal of effort, thank you. The other part of you wants to wail, to beat your fists against the wall and howl, *Give him back to me.*

Remember: purpose, provision, exception. The subjunctive runs parallel to reality.

8. after certain indications of time, if the action has not occurred

While is a subjunctive state of mind. So are *until, as soon as, before,* and *after.* By now you understand why, right? Because until something *has happened*, you can't be sure.

In Tarifa, the wind blows and blows. You learn this even before arriving, as you drive down Route 15 past Gibraltar. You're heading toward the southernmost point in Spain, toward warm sea breezes and a small town off the beaten path. You drive confidently, shifting quickly through the gears to keep pace with the traffic around you. He reclines in the passenger's seat, one foot propped against the dashboard, reading from the *Real Guide* open against his thigh. "Spreading out beyond its Moorish walls, Tarifa is known in Spain for its abnormally high suicide rate—a result of the unremitting winds that blow across the town and its environs."

You say, "Tell me you're joking." He says, "How's that for luck?"

Three days before, you'd stood in Granada's crowded city square at midnight, each eating a grape for every stroke of the New Year. If you eat all twelve grapes in time, tradition says, you'll have plenty of luck in the coming year. It sounds wonderful—such an easy way to secure good fortune—until you start eating and time gets ahead, so far ahead that no matter how fast you chew and swallow, midnight sounds with three grapes left.

In Tarifa, you come down with the flu. It hits hard and fast—one minute you're strolling through a white-washed coastal town, and the next you're huddled in bed in a stupor. He goes to the pharmacy and, with a handful of Spanish words and many gestures, procures the right medicine. You sleep all day, through the midday meal, through the time of siesta, past sundown, and into the evening. When you wake the room is fuzzy and you're alone, with a vague memory of him rubbing your back, saying something about a movie.

Carefully you rise and make your way to the bathroom—holding onto the bed, the doorway, the sink—then stand on your toes and look out the window into the blackness. By day there's a thin line of blue mountains across the strait, and you imagine catching the ferry at dawn and watching that sliver of Morocco rise up from the shadows to become a whole continent. You imagine standing on the other side and looking back toward the tip of Spain, this tiny town where the winds blow and blow. That's how easy it is to keep traveling once you start, putting distance between the various parts of your life, imagining yourself over and over again into entirely new places.

Chilly and sweating, you make your way back to bed, your stomach fluttering nervously. You think back to Granada, how he'd woken from a nap on that dark afternoon and apologized. "I don't know what got into me today," he'd said. "This hasn't been happening." You believe it's true, it hasn't been happening. But you don't know *how true*.

You think: He's fine now. There's no need to worry. He's been fine for days, happy and calm. I'm overreacting. But overreaction is a slippery slope. With the wind howling continuously outside, the room feels small and isolated. You don't know that he's happy and calm right now, do you? You don't know how he is today at all, because you've slept and slept and barely talked to him.

You think: If the movie started on time—but movies never start on time in Spain, so you add, subtract, try to play it safe, and determine that by 10:45 PM your fretting will be justified. At 11:00 PM you'll get dressed and go looking, and if you can't find him, what will you do? Wait until midnight for extra measure? And then call the police? And tell them what, that he isn't back yet, and you're afraid because you're sick and he's alone and the wind here blows and blows, enough to make people crazy, the book says, make them suicidal?

This is the *when*, the *while*, the *until*. The *before* and *after*. The real and the unreal in precarious balance. This is what you moved to Spain to escape from, and here it is again, following you.

The next time you wake, the room seems brighter, more familiar. You sit up and squint against the light. His cheeks are flushed, hair mussed from the wind. His eyes are clear as a morning sky. "Hi, sweetie," he says, putting a hand on your forehead. "You still have a fever. How do you feel?" He smells a little musty, like the inside of a community theater where not many people go on a Sunday night in early January. He says, "The movie was hilarious." You ask whether he understood it and he shrugs. Then he acts out a scene using random Spanish words as a voice-over, and you laugh and cough until he flops down on his stomach beside you.

Here it comes again, the contrast between what was, just a little while ago, and what is now. After all this time and all these miles, you're both here, in a Spanish town with a view of Africa. You feel amazed, dizzy, as if swimming outside yourself. You're talking with him, but you're also watching yourself talk with him. And then you're sleeping and watching yourself sleep, dreaming and thinking about the dreams. Throughout the night you move back and forth, here and there, between what is and what might be, tossed by language and possibility and the constantly shifting wind.

9. in certain independent clauses

There's something extraordinary—isn't there?—about learning to speak Spanish as an adult, about coming to see grammar as a set of guidelines not just for saying what you mean but for understanding the way you live. There's something extraordinary about thinking in a language that insists on marking the limited power of desire.

For example: At Barajas Airport in Madrid, you walk him to the boarding gate. He turns to face you, hands on your arms, eyes green as the sea. He says, "Only a few more months and we'll be together for good, right sweetie?" He watches your face, waiting for a response, but you know this isn't a decision, something you can say yes to. So you smile, eyes burning, and give a slight nod. What you mean is, *I hope so*. What you think is, *Ojalá*. And what you know is this: The subjunctive is the mood of mystery. Of luck. Of faith interwoven with doubt. It's a held breath, a hand reaching out, carefully touching wood. It's humility, deference, the opposite of hubris. And it's going to take a long time to master.

But at least the final rule of usage is simple, self-contained, one you can commit to memory: Certain independent clauses exist only in the subjunctive mood, lacing optimism with resignation, hope with heartache. *Be that as it may*, for example. Or the phrase one says at parting, eyes closed as if in prayer, *May all go well with you*.

Lifelike

Susan Orlean

As soon as the 2003 World Taxidermy Championships opened, the heads came rolling in the door. There were foxes and moose and freeze-dried wild turkeys; mallards and buffalo and chipmunks and wolves; weasels and buffleheads and bobcats and jackdaws; big fish and little fish and razor-backed boar. The deer came in herds, in carloads, and on pallets: dozens and dozens of whitetail and roe; half deer and whole deer and deer with deformities, sneezing and glowering and nuzzling and yawning; does chewing apples and bucks nibbling leaves. There were millions of eyes, boxes and bowls of them, some as small as a lentil and some as big as a poached egg. There were animal mannequins, blank faced and brooding, earless and eyeless and utterly bald: ghostly gray duikers and spectral pine martens and black-bellied tree ducks from some other world. An entire exhibit hall was filled with equipment, all the gear required to bring something dead back to life: replacement noses for grizzlies, false teeth for beavers, fish-fin cream, casting clay, upholstery nails.

The championships were held in April at the Springfield, Illinois, Crowne Plaza hotel, the sort of nicely appointed place that seems more suited to regional sales conferences and rehearsal dinners than to having wolves in the corridors and people crossing the lobby shouting, "Heads up! Buffalo coming through!" A thousand taxidermists converged on Springfield to have their best pieces judged and to attend such seminars as "Mounting Flying Waterfowl," "Whitetail Deer—From a Master!," and "Using a Fleshing Machine." In the Crowne Plaza lobby, across from the concierge desk, a grooming area had been set up. The taxidermists were bent over their animals, holding flashlights to check problem areas like tear ducts and nostrils and wielding toothbrushes to tidy flyaway fur. People milled around, greeting fellow taxidermists they hadn't seen since the last world championships, held in Springfield two years ago, and talking shop:

"Acetone rubbed on a squirrel tail will fluff it right back up."

"My feeling is that it's quite tough to do a good tongue."

"The toes on a real competitive piece are very important. I think Bondo works nicely, and so does Super Glue."

"I knew a fellow with cattle, and I told him, 'If you ever have one stillborn, I'd really like to have it.' I thought it would make a really nice mount."

That there is a taxidermy championship at all is something of an astonishment, not only to the people in the world who have no use for a Dan-D-Noser and Soft Touch Duck Degreaser, but also to taxidermists themselves. For a long time, taxidermists kept their own counsel. Taxidermy, the three-dimensional representation of animals for permanent display, has been around since the eighteenth century, but it was first brought into popular regard by the Victorians, who thrilled to all tokens of exotic travel and especially to any domesticated representations of wilderness—the glassed-in miniature rain forest on the tea table, the mounted antelope by the front door. The original taxidermists were upholsterers who tanned the hides of hunting trophies and then plumped them up with rags and cotton, so that they reassumed their original shape and size; those early poses were stiff and simple, the expressions fairly expressionless. The practice grew popular in this country, too: By 1882, there was a Society of American Taxidermists, which held annual meetings and published scholarly reports, especially on the matter of preparing animals for museum display. As long as taxidermy served to preserve wild animals and make them available for study, it was viewed as an honorable trade, but most people were still discomfited by it. How could you not be? It was the business of dealing with dead things, coupled with the questionable enterprise of making dead things look like live things. In spite of its scientific value, it was usually regarded as almost a black art, a wholly owned subsidiary of witchcraft and voodoo. By the early part of the twentieth century, taxidermists such as Carl E. Akeley, William T. Hornaday, and Leon Pray had refined techniques and begun emphasizing artistry. But the more the techniques of taxidermy improved, the more it discomfited: Instead of the lumpy moose head that was so artless that it looked fake, there were mounts of pouncing bobcats so immaculately and exactly preserved, they made you flinch.

For the next several decades, taxidermy existed in the margins—a few practitioners here and there, often self-taught and usually known only by word of mouth. Then, in the late 1960s, a sort of transformation began: The business started to seem cleaner and less creepy—or maybe, in that messy, morbid time, popular culture started to again appreciate the messy, morbid business of mounting animals for display. An ironic reinterpretation of cluttered, bourgeois Victoriana and its strained juxtapositions of the natural and the man-made was in full revival—what hippie outpost didn't have a stuffed owl or a moose head draped with a silk shawl?—so, once again, taxidermy found a place in the public eye. Supply houses concocted new solvents and better tanning compounds, came out with lightweight mannequins, produced modern formulations of resins and clays. Taxidermy schools opened; previously, any aspiring taxidermist could hope to learn the trade only by apprenticing or by taking one of a few correspondence courses available. In 1971, the National Taxidermy Association was formed (the old society had moldered long before). In 1974, a trade magazine called

Taxidermy Review began sponsoring national competitions. For the first time, most taxidermists had a chance to meet one another and share advice on how to glue tongues into jaw sets or accurately measure the carcass of a squirrel.

The competitions were also the first time that taxidermists could compare their skills and see who in the business could sculpt the best moose septum or could most perfectly capture the look on a prowling coyote's face. Taxidermic skill is a function of how deft you are at skinning an animal and then stretching its hide over a mannequin and sewing it into place. Top-of-the-line taxidermists sculpt their own mannequins; otherwise they will buy a ready-made polyurethane foam form and tailor the skin to fit. Body parts that can't be preserved (ears, eyes, noses, lips, tongues) can be either store-bought or handmade. How good the mount looks—that is, how alive it looks—is a function of how assiduously the taxidermist has studied reference material (photographs, drawings, and actual live animals) so that he or she knows the particular creature literally and figuratively inside out.

To be good at taxidermy, you have to be good at sewing, sculpting, painting, and hairdressing, and mostly you have to be a little bit of a zoology nerd. You have to love animals—love looking at them, taking photographs of them, hunting them, measuring them, casting them in plaster of Paris when they're dead so that you have a reference when you're, say, attaching ears or lips and want to get the angle and shape exactly right. Some taxidermists raise the animals they most often mount, so they can just step out in the backyard when they're trying to remember exactly how a deer looks when it's licking its nose, especially because modern taxidermy emphasizes mounts with interesting expressions, rather than the stunned-looking creations of the past. Taxidermists seem to make little distinction between loving animals that are alive and loving ones that are not. "I love deer," one of the champions in the Whitetail division said to me. "They're my babies."

Taxidermy is now estimated to be a five-hundred-and-seventy-million-dollar annual business, made up of small operators around the country who mount animals for museums, for decorators, and mostly for the thirteen million or so Americans who are recreational hunters and on occasion want to preserve and display something they killed and who are willing to shell out anywhere from two hundred dollars to mount a pheasant to several thousand for a kudu or a grizzly bear. There are state and regional taxidermy competitions throughout the year and the world championships, which are held every other year; two trade magazines; a score of taxidermy schools; and three thousand visits to Taxidermy.net every day, where taxidermists can trade information and goods with as little self-consciousness as you would find on a knitting website:

"I am in need of several pair of frozen goat feet!"

"Hi! I have up to 300 sets of goat feet and up to 1000 sets of sheep feet per month. Drop me an email at frozencritters.com . . . or give me a call and we can discuss your needs."

"I have a very nice small raccoon that is frozen whole. I forgot he was in the freezer. Without taking exact measurements I would guess he is about twelve inches or so—very cute little one. Will make a very nice mount."

"Can I rinse a boar hide good and freeze it?"

"Bob, if it's salted, don't worry about it!"

"Can someone please tell me the proper way to preserve turkey legs and spurs? Thanks!"

"Brian, I inject the feet with Preservz-It. . . . Enjoy!"

The word in the grooming area was that the piece to beat was Chris Krueger's happy-looking otters swimming in a perpetual circle around a leopard frog. A posting on Taxidermy.net earlier in the week declared, "EVERYTHING about this mount KICKS BUTT!!" Kicking butt, in this era of taxidermy, requires having a mount that is not just lifelike but also artistic. It used to be enough to do what taxidermists call "fish on a stick" displays; now a serious competitor worries about things like flow and negative space and originality. One of this year's contenders, for instance, Ken Walker's giant panda, had artistry and accuracy going for it, along with the element of surprise. The thing looked a hundred percent pure panda, but you can't go out and shoot a panda, and you aren't likely to get hold of a panda that has met a natural end, so everyone was dying to know how he had done it. The day the show opened, Walker was in the grooming area, gluing bamboo into place behind the animal's back paws, and a crowd had gathered around him. Walker works as a staff taxidermist for the Smithsonian. He is a breezy, shaggy-haired guy whose hands are always busy. One day, I saw him holding a piece of clay while waiting for a seminar to begin, and within thirty seconds or so, without actually paying much attention to it, he had molded the clay into a little minklike creature.

"The panda was actually pretty easy," he was saying. "I just took two black bears and bleached one of them—I think I used Clairol Basic. Then I sewed the two skins together into a panda pattern." He took out a toothbrush and fluffed the fur on the panda's face. "At the world championship two years ago, a guy came in with an extinct Labrador duck. I was in awe. I thought, What could beat that—an extinct duck? And I came up with this idea." He said he thought that the panda would get points for creativity alone. "You can score a ninety-eight with a squirrel, but it's still a squirrel," he said. "So that means I'm going with a panda."

"What did you do for toenails, Ken?" someone asked.

"I left the black bear's toenails in," he said. "They looked pretty good."

Another passerby stopped to admire the panda. He was carrying a grooming kit, which appeared to contain Elmer's glue, brown and black paint, a small tool set, and a bottle of Suave mousse. "I killed a blond bear once," he said to Ken. "A two-hundred-pound sow. Whew, she made a beautiful mount."

"I'll bet," Ken said. He stepped back to admire the panda. "I like doing re-creations of these endangered animals and extinct animals, since that's the only way anyone's going to have one. Two years ago, I did a saber-toothed cat. I got an old lioness from a zoo and bleached her."

The panda was entered in the Re-Creation (Mammal) division, one of the dozens of divisions and subdivisions and sub-subcategories, ranging from the superspecific (Whitetail Deer Long Hair, Open Mouth division) to the sweepingly colossal (Best in World), that would share in twenty-five thousand dollars' worth of prizes. (There is even a sub-sub-subspecialty known as "fish carving," which uses no natural fish parts at all; it is resin and wood sculpted into a fish form and then painted.) Nearly all the competitors are professionals, and they publicize their awards wherever possible. For instance, instead of ordering just any Boar Eye-Setting Reference Head out of a taxidermy catalog, you can order the Noonkester's #NRBERH head sculpted by Bones Johnson, which was, as the catalog notes, the 2000 National Taxidermy Association Champion Gamehead.

The taxidermists take the competition very seriously. During the time I was in Springfield, I heard conversations analyzing such arcane subjects as exactly how much a javelina's snout wrinkles when it snarls and which molars deer use to chew acorns as opposed to which ones they use to chew leaves. This is important because the ultimate goal of a taxidermist is to make the animal look exactly as if it had never died, as if it were still in the middle of doing ordinary animal things like plucking berries off a bush or taking a nap. When I walked around with the judges one morning, I heard discussions that were practically Talmudic, about whether the eyelids on a particular bison mount were overdetailed, and whether the nostrils on a springbok were too wide, and whether the placement of whiskers on an otter appeared too deliberate. "You do get compulsive," a taxidermist in the exhibit hall explained to me one afternoon. At the time, he was running a feather duster over his entry—a bobcat hanging off an icicle-covered rock—in the last moments before the judging would begin. "When you're working on a piece, you forget to eat, you forget to drink, you even forget to sleep. You get up in the middle of the night and go into the shop so you can keep working. You get completely caught up in it. You want it to be perfect. You're trying to make something come back to life."

I said that his bobcat was beautiful and that even the icicles on the piece looked completely real. "I made them myself," he said. "I used clear acrylic toilet plunger handles. The good Lord sent the idea to me while I was in a hardware store. I just took the handles and put them in the oven at four hundred degrees." He tapped the icicles and then added, "My wife was pretty worried, but I did it on a nonstick cookie sheet."

So who wants to be a taxidermist? "I was a meat cutter for fifteen years," a taxidermist from Kentucky said to me. "That whole time, no one ever said to me, 'Boy, that was a wonderful steak you cut me.' Now I get told all the time what a great job I've done." Steve Faechner, who is the president and chairman of the Academy of Realistic Taxidermy, in Havre, Montana, started mounting animals in 1989, after years spent working on the railroad. "I had gotten hurt and was looking for something to do," he said. "I was with a friend who did taxidermy and I thought to myself, I have got to get a life. And this was it." Larry Blomquist, who is the owner of the World Taxidermy Championships and of *Breakthrough*, the trade magazine that sponsors the competition, was a schoolteacher for three years before setting up his business. There are a number of women taxidermists (one was teaching this year's seminar, "Problem Areas in Mammal Taxidermy"), and there are budding junior taxidermists, who had their own competition division, for kids fourteen and younger, at the show.

The night the show opened, I went to dinner with three taxidermists who had driven in from Kentucky, Michigan, and Maryland. They were all married, and all had wives who complained when they found one too many antelope carcasses in the family freezer, and all worked full-time mounting animals—mostly deer for local hunters, but occasional safari work for people who had shot something in Africa. When I mentioned that I had no idea that a person could make a living as a taxidermist, they burst out laughing, and the guy from Kentucky pointed out that he lived in a little town and there were two other full-time taxidermists in business right down the road.

"What's the big buzz this year?" the man from Michigan asked.

"I don't know. Probably something new with eyes," the guy from Maryland answered. "That's where you see the big advances. Remember at the last championship, those Russian eyes?" These were glass animal eyes that had a reflective paint embedded in them, so that if you shone a light, they would shine back at you, sort of like the way real animals' eyes do. The men discussed those for a while, then talked about the new fish eyes being introduced this year, which have photographic transfers of actual fish eyes printed on plastic lenses. We happened to be in a restaurant with a sports theme, and there were about a hundred televisions on around the room, broadcasting dozens of different athletic events, but the men never glanced at them and never stopped talking about their trade. We had all ordered barbecued ribs. When dinner was over, all three of them were fiddling around with the bones before the waitress came to clear our plates.

"Look at these," the man from Kentucky said, holding up a rib. "You could take these home and use them to make a skeleton."

In the seminars, the atmosphere was as sober and exacting as a tax law colloquium. "Whiskers," one of the instructors said to the group, giving them a stern look. "I pull them out. I label them. There are left whiskers and there are right whiskers. If you want to get those top awards, you're going to have to think about whiskers." Everyone took notes. In the next room: "Folks, remember, your carcass is your key. The best thing you can do is to keep your carcass in the freezer. Freeze the head, cast it in plaster. It's going to really help if your head is perfect." During the breaks, the group made jokes about a T-shirt that had been seen at one of the regional competitions. The shirt said PETA in big letters, but when you got up close you saw that PETA didn't spell out People for the Ethical Treatment of Animals, the bane of all hunters and, by extension, all taxidermists; it spelled out "People Eating Tasty Animals." Chuckles all around, then back to the solemn business of mounting flying waterfowl: "People, follow what the bird is telling you. Study it, do your homework. When you've got it ready, fluff the head, shake it, and then get your eyes. There are a lot of good eyes out there on the market today. Do your legwork, and you can have a beautiful mount."

It was brisk and misty outside—the antler vendors in the parking lot looked chilled and miserable—and the modest charms of Springfield, with its mall and the Oliver P. Parks Telephone Museum and Abraham Lincoln's tomb, couldn't compete with the strange and wondrous sights inside the hotel. The mere experience of waiting for the elevator—knowing that the doors would peel back to reveal maybe a man and a moose, or a bush pig, or a cougar—was much more exciting than the usual elevator wait in the usual Crowne Plaza hotel. The trade show was a sort of mad tea party of body parts and taxidermy supplies, things for pulling flesh off a carcass, for rinsing blood out of fur—a surreal carnality, but all conveyed with the usual trade show earnestness and hucksterism, with no irony and no acknowledgment that having buckets of bear noses for sale was anything out of the ordinary. "Come take a look at our beautiful synthetic fur! We're the hair club for lions! If you happen to shoot a lion who is out of season or bald, we can provide you with a gorgeous replacement mane!" "Too many squirrels? Are they driving you nuts? Let us mount them for you!" "Divide and Conquer animal forms—an amazing advance in small-mammal mannequins, patent pending!"

The big winner at the show turned out to be a tiny thing—a mount of two tree sparrows, submitted by a strapping German named Uwe Bauch, who had grown up in the former East Germany dreaming of competing in an American taxidermy show. The piece was precise and lovely, almost haunting, since the more you looked at it, the more certain you were that the birds would just stop building their nest, spread their wings, and fly away. Early one morning, before I left Springfield, I took a last walk around the competition hall. It was quiet and uncanny, with hundreds of mounts arranged on long tables throughout the room; the deer heads clustered together, each in a slightly different pose and angle, looked like a kind of animal Roman forum caught in mid-debate. A few of the mounts were a little gruesome—a deer with a mailbox impaled on an antler, another festooned with barbed wire, and one with an arrow stuck in its brisket— and one display, a coyote whose torso was split open to reveal a miniature scene of the destruction of the World Trade Center, complete with little firemen and rubble piles, was surpassingly weird. Otherwise, the room was biblically tranquil, the lion at last lying down with the Corsican lamb, the family of jackdaws in everlasting, unrequited pursuit of a big green beetle, and the stillborn Bengal tiger cub magically revived, its face in an eternal snarl, alive looking, although it had never lived.

Quinto Sol

Michelle Otero

"All grants of land made by the Mexican government . . . shall be respected as valid . . ." —ARTICLE X, Treaty of Guadalupe Hidalgo, signed by representatives of Mexican and U.S. governments in February 1848; stricken from treaty ratified by U.S. Congress in May 1848

"Our people were kings," your father would whisper after handing over the day's corn and *chile verde* to El Lagartijo, a man with one polished star to hold up his pants and another to cover his heart. A man whose boots were never dusty, even when he sat at a table in the fields, a scale beside him, the harvest stacked in burlap behind him, a ledger opened before him, the *curandera* holding an umbrella over him. A man with thick hands and skin so clear you could almost see his blood run. It made him seem more real, more alive somehow, than you, your father or any of the Mexicans on the new border.

Now you must ask permission to pull *chile verde* or tomatoes from the vines. So many for them. Sometimes there is enough for you.

El Lagartijo's doctor opens your father's mouth, tapping his teeth with a silver spike, the way your father once inspected horses. "This one can work," he says.

One day the *curandera* is gone. Before Lagartijo and his doctor, the people paid her to heal. She was the first to hold you as the afterbirth and too much blood gushed from between your mother's legs. Your father gave her the calf he'd smoked in a desert pit, eggs to cleanse your blood and spirit, rosemary to sweep away *el susto. Susto.* A fright so great it sends the soul into hiding. Now the calves belong to the company—a mine, a railroad, a ranch. The eggs and even the herbs belong to the town, which is just another name for mine or railroad or ranch.

You imagine the *curandera* becomes wind.

El Lagartijo will take you one night. His boys will take your daughters. You are property here. This one can work.

They make your father sign a parchment littered with a language he can't read, and the next day they come to collect. You learn a new phrase that day. Water rights. You never knew a man could own what so clearly belongs to the earth.

You will sign with an X, the only letter you write, the same in either language, on either side.

Now there are sides. Us. Them. (And you don't know which you are.) Up. Down. Here. There. They will come up here from down there. They won't stop. No matter how many fences, how many Rangers tracking them through crosshairs, how hot the sun that spirits of dead mothers blow across the sky. No matter how strong *la migra*, how many signs on this side reading "No dogs or Mexicans allowed."

They will come.

You bury your father on the plot set aside for "you people," mark his grave with an agate you place face-down and lift only in those silent moments when you whisper to him, squatting on what must be his feet. Tracing your dark finger along concentric bands of color, you imagine a heart cracked open must look the same way.

Our people were kings.

You will forget that your people built Paquimé and Tenochtitlán. You will never climb the steps leading to the moon at Teotihuacán. Your children will learn half of two languages and that will never equal one. This new country will hand them uniforms—soldier, miner, waitress, mechanic. Their names stitched in red over their hearts, your children will wander across these lands, thirsting beneath the Fifth Sun.

A Few Things I Know about Softball

Carol Paik

I learned to play softball when I was in sixth grade, from a man named Mr. Robbins. I have had far too much education in my lifetime, and far too many teachers, principals, music teachers, conductors, professors, bosses, senior colleagues—but of all those potential positive influences and mentors, only Mr. Robbins stands out in my mind as someone who gave me advice I still remember, believe, and occasionally find useful. Tall, skinny Mr. Robbins, with his thin hair hanging over his eyes and his little mustache. I didn't know much about the rest of his life, the part that took place away from the softball field. I don't think I ever knew, for example, what he did for a living. I looked to him for one thing only—how to play softball. For all I know, that was his only talent—I can't really say. But why should I care what else he knew, what else he did, to what he aspired, of what he dreamed? He taught a group of girls how to play softball. And I'm so grateful to Mr. Robbins for the knowledge he imparted that I feel some obligation to spread his teachings around.

So here, briefly, is what I know.

Lesson 1: Put your body in front of the ball.

My town—a small one with lots of trees, situated about a 45-minute drive west of Boston—had the usual Little League and Bantam Hockey League for the boys, but we also had something unusual for that time and place: the Sudbury Girls' Softball League. This was the mid-1970s, an era in which girls were required to take Home Ec while boys were required to take Shop. But nearly every girl in town played SGS.

The first year I played, I was placed on an expansion team in the Junior Division. All the teams in the junior Division (fifth to eighth grades) had bird names, and we were the Flickers. We were issued dark green short-sleeved T-shirts that said "Sudbury Girls Softball," with no apostrophe. We were small, and so were the shirts. I joined the league primarily because my best friend, Debbie Kutenplon, played in the Junior Division and said I should. Up until that point I had not shown much interest in sports, and my parents were somewhat taken aback to find me suddenly demanding to be driven to games and practices. My two older brothers played both Little League baseball and Bantam League hockey, as well as regular pick-up games of all sorts in the neighborhood. My father would frequently take them across the street and through the woods to the elementary school to play basketball, and if I expressed an interest in joining them, he would tell me I could stand on the side and cheer. He meant no harm, no negative judgment—it just was how he saw the world. I thought this unfair but I didn't push it, since I knew that on the bright side of my father's attitude lay the compensatory fact that he would never make me mow the lawn or shovel the driveway. My mother, meanwhile, boasted frequently about her own athletic abilities and took a lot of genetic credit for my brothers' accomplishments—told me because she was born left-handed she batted lefty, although she had been taught to catch righty— but not once do I recall ever seeing her hit, throw, or catch a ball.

So I was on my own. Usually, I needed only to stay between the high walls of parental expectation and keep up the brisk pace set by my brothers—I didn't really need to pay much attention to where I was going. But softball was a whole new open field upon which neither brother had ever set a cleated foot.

The first year I played, it was actually *Mrs.* Robbins who signed up to take the team. Mrs. Robbins was blonde and pretty—in the way that, say, professional female skiers are. We all liked her at first, because she was so pretty. I don't know why she was interested in girls' softball, since she had two little boys. She brought them with her to our games and practices, where they predictably enough misbehaved in ways designed to get her full and immediate attention. Between trying to coach us and trying to instill some discipline in them, she had her hands full, resulting in an overall ineffectiveness. Mr. Robbins started coming along to practices to help her out.

Neither Mrs. nor Mr. Robbins knew my brothers, and so didn't have any idea of what to expect from me. It may have been the first time in my life I made my own first impression on someone. In this case, however, the first impression I made all by myself probably weighed against me—a scrawny Asian American ten-year-old, wearing thick, blue-rimmed glasses.

Most of us, the Flickers being an expansion team, were not very good at catching the ball. I had one advantage—my brother Dick's old glove. Dick had taken obsessively good care of this glove. He had rubbed it all over with a rag dipped in cooking oil every night for years, and it was soft and supple as Wonder Bread. When he got a new glove, he bequeathed the old one to me. The first time Mr. Robbins saw it—it actually caught his eye—he put it on his own hand, punched the pocket a few times, opened and closed it, and gave it back to me. "That's a great glove," he said. "That's the best glove I've ever seen." And I could tell the glove had given him something to weigh against scrawny, slanty-eyed, and bespectacled.

But even with this consecrated equipment, catching the ball was a challenge. A softball, after all, really is not "soft," although admittedly it lacks the intimidating skull-like hardness of a baseball, and doesn't make quite the same purposeful whistling sound that a baseball makes when it's tunneling through the air. But even so, it can leave you with a painful fluorescent purple-green bruise if it hits you, and if you were to see one hurtling in your direction, your fundamental instinct really might not be to place yourself in front of it. The instinct, particularly among fifth- and sixth-grade girls who were new to the sport, was to avert the face and cower.

I had even more reason than most to be wary. Too vividly in my mind's eye, I saw the ball's straight path ending abruptly in the middle of Dick's face during the father-son game at the church picnic. Too clearly I heard and heard again the *crunch!* All too well I remembered my father (it was he who had hit the ball) running over to where Dick lay on the ground with gore pouring from his nose. Also I recalled the ensuing weeks during which Dick had to wear a maroon plastic cast over the broken feature, and every time he called Mom, it came out *Bob*.

Mrs. Robbins seemed to think that repetition was the road to enlightenment, and so she had us practice throwing and catching in two parallel lines that, in her dreams, moved further and further apart in direct proportion to the growth of our abilities. We practiced a lot, but what seemed like a bucketful of progress during practice quickly revealed its emptiness in the game situation. Catching a ball tossed directly, by a friendly teammate, into your glove from a few feet away was quite different from staying calm in the face of an unpredictable ball in a hostile context. It was easy to get flustered, to take the easy, safe way out. Those were the times you told yourself, "It's only a dumb game."

It wasn't long before Mr. Robbins started making suggestions. "Dana," he'd say to Mrs. Robbins helpfully, "why dontcha try. . ." And she'd flash him the look of death. But it was he who really taught us—taught us, rather than expected us to teach ourselves. He understood that it was our instincts, not just our shoulders, elbows, and wrists, that had to be trained. He assured us that our gloves would protect us—it was merely a matter of positioning. We were in the habit of holding our gloves out and as far away from our bodies as possible, heels of our hands facing up in a hopeful, supplicating way. "Hold the gloves up!" he exhorted. "UP! In front of yuh faces!" So we learned to hold our gloves up—first as a shield, then, tentatively, more and more as a receptacle.

But more importantly, he told us over and over that we had to be *standing in the right place*. It did no good to stand to the side out of harm's way and sort of stick out your arm in a well-meaning gesture. If you harbored any genuine intention of catching the ball, you had to be smack in front of it. That way, even if you didn't catch it with your glove, you still had a chance of stopping it in some other creative and spontaneous manner. Since we so frequently had to resort to the creative and spontaneous stopping methods, this lesson was critically important. It was, at any rate, a start.

We lost every game but one—the last one—that year. At every game at least one girl cried, usually several. But that final game gave us a tiny glimpse—far,

far in the distance—of an alternate future, and the following year we all came back.

Lesson 2: Catch with both hands.

The second year, Mr. and Mrs. Robbins took the team as co-coaches. I suppose we ought to have known this was not a felicitous plan. I wonder, now, how they could rationally have come to that decision. Anyway, it did not work out well. Mrs. Robbins grew more touchy and defensive. Mr. Robbins seethed and steamed. The two boys grew more boisterous and unruly, and both of their parents yelled at them a lot.

But we girls were noticeably less afraid of the ball. We were ready for the next lesson.

"Use both hands!"

Sometimes, with a great cry of triumph, one of us would hold the ball aloft, netted serendipitously in the web of our glove. But Mr. Robbins knew dumb luck when he saw it. He knew we could not be counted on to do it again. He knew we had closed our eyes and stuck out our hand, and the ball had fallen in. He would not congratulate us for unearned good fortune.

"Use both hands!"

Worse, there were the times when the ball would be there, it would be there, and then it would be gone. Bounced out. Then Mr. Robbins would smack his fore-head with his bony hand.

"Both hands for God's sake! Trap that ball! Get both hands up theah!"

I should mention that on the softball field we all spoke with strong New England accents, even those of us who normally didn't. It wasn't an effort to be someone we weren't. It wasn't some kind of affectation. It just came with the terri-tory. In my town, you never heard anyone pronounce the "r" in "batter" in "She's no batter." You might just as well call out, "She is not any batter," that's how stu-pid it would have sounded. The word was "battah," and any other pronunciation would have led to misunderstanding.

Madeline Berdy, who was a great friend on the field but would never speak to me in school, was our team's beauty-to-be. Woven silver rings covered every finger. She had long wavy brown hair that she would never tie back in a ponytail, bright silver braces, and silver earrings. She gave off a great glinty, silvery impres-sion on sunny days, and she didn't like to use both hands. It looked too effortful.

"Berdy," Mr. Robbins would say. "Yuh drop even one ball because yuh didn't use both hands, I'll deck yuh."

And even after we were able to catch the ball solidly, competently, convinc-ingly, he'd still frown at us until we had quickly, quickly brought up our right hands to cover what we held—firmly it seemed, but who knew, perhaps not firmly enough—in our left.

That year we went 6-6.

Lesson 3: Throw the ball ahead of the runner.

By the third year, Mrs. Robbins and Mr. Robbins were getting a divorce, and Mr. Robbins took the team on his own. No one was surprised. The parents, sort of nervously joking among themselves, would say, "It was the team that did it," and since all we girls knew about Mr. and Mrs. Robbins was what we saw on the field, we sort of thought that was true. We kind of felt bad about it, but not really. People were getting divorced all over the place at that time, and Mr. and Mrs. Robbins seemed fairly amicable. Sometimes she would still come to games with the boys.

"When he moved out, the only thing he took with him was his clothes and the Flickers team picture," she told everybody, laughing.

By this time, having taught us to use our bodies, Mr. Robbins was trying to teach us to use our heads. It was slow going.

"If yuh runnuh is headed to first base, wheah do you throw the ball?"

Silence.

"Wheah do you throw the ball?"

"Uh . . . first base?"

"NO! The runnah's practically theah. If yunna hurry to throw her out, yuh gonna make a bad throw. Yuh throw it ovuh the first baseman's head, and now wheah's yuh runnuh? Headed for SECOND! Then whaddayuh do, first baseman?"

"Um . . . throw it to second?"

"NO! She's theah! Throw it to third, or hold on to it and run it into the pitchuh. Don't staht throwing that ball around!"

Mr. Robbins stood at the plate and hit balls to us in the field. "Runnuh on third!" Crack! "Wheah do you throw the ball? Stop the runnuh yuh know yuh can stop."

That was hard to learn, because it was counterintuitive. When you saw that girl running, you wanted to stop her, even if you knew it was too late. It was hard to ignore that front runner and focus on the one sneaking up on you from behind. It was hard to think in terms of damage control. But Mr. Robbins, I guess, knew all about that.

That year, we went undefeated and won the championship. If this were fiction, I probably would have to change that in the interests of verisimilitude. It strains credibility for any team to go from 1-11 to 12-0 and the championship in three seasons—that kind of thing only happens in bad movies starring adorable child actresses who grow up to be substance abusers. But I'm not making this up, so there it is.

Lesson 4: Make them throw you out.

By the fourth year, some of us were ninth graders and had graduated into the Senior Division. Mr. Robbins stayed with the depleted Flickers that year, and those of us in ninth grade had to suffer through a year with Mr. Marino, Lauren

Marino's father. I began to understand that the fact that Mr. Robbins didn't have a daughter made him a much better coach. Lauren—naturally curly dirty-blond hair—got to play whatever position she wanted. Mr. Marino made me play catcher one game, and I actually swore at him. This was something I wouldn't have done in my ordinary life, swear at an adult, but my softball life was different. I swore at Mr. Marino and threw the catcher's mask and got thrown out of the game. Mr. Robbins used to say he would retire from coaching once all the Flickers graduated to the senior division. But then he came to see Mr. Marino coach a game. After that, we were able to talk him into moving up to Seniors instead.

In the Senior Division, the teams were given cat names. We were the Jaguars now. Our shirts had three stripes on the sleeves, and there was now enough room on the front of the shirts for the apostrophe.

Softball had become indistinguishable from springtime for me. The season started when the weather was still cold, the grass brown and breath white. We played softball through dim evenings, April rains and resulting mud, first bird-songs, discarded windbreakers in a pile. It ended in late June, when the outfield wore a humming, low-lying cover of bugs and we in the green outfield wore jeans to protect our legs against them, even when the rest of the team wore shorts.

By the time we were in the Senior Division, most of the girls possessed basic catching, throwing, and hitting skills, and our lessons became more complex.

"People will make mistakes if yuh give them enough chance," said Mr. Robbins. "So give them as much chance as possible."

He was teaching us how to run bases. When you're running to first base, you have a choice to make. You can veer to the inside of the first base line as you run, so that the curve of your path naturally takes you into foul territory after you touch first and you cannot be thrown out, so the other team won't try. Or, you can veer to the outside and then you'll run fair, towards second. When you do that, whoever has the ball will throw it to first. You run a risk, of course, that they will succeed. But there's always the possibility that they'll screw up. So you create that opportunity as often as you can by heading for second.

At the other bases, there's never any question. You keep running for the next base and make them throw the ball. If you force them to throw the ball, chances are they will miss, because two people are involved—the thrower and the catcher. Where two people are involved, the possibility of error is very high. Other teams did not know what to make of girls who would not stop at the next base but instead kept on going. Other teams had not been taught as well as we had been to hold onto the ball, and would start throwing it around with increasing frustration in an effort to catch us. Every time they threw the ball, more people became involved. With more than two people involved, a mistake is almost inevitable. So the idea was, as long as you could run you ran, and kept running, and didn't stop until they made you.

Of course, this general rule required some fine-tuning. Overrunning third base, for example, became an issue because of Nanette Doiron, who couldn't seem to learn that it wasn't enough simply to keep running, she had to run *towards home*. Nanette had lank, shoulder-length brown hair, and a turned-up nose that seemed perpetually sunburned. She wore a shell necklace tight around her neck. Nanette was a solid hitter. If she was up, you could pretty much count on her to advance the runners. But even senior year I remember her overrunning third base—not towards home, and not by some discreet, correctable amount, but straight into the bleachers while the other team calmly threw her out. Mr. Robbins clutched at his by now quite thin hair, but no one could get angry at Nanette. It simply did no good. The third-base coach could hold up both her hands and screech "Nanette! STOP!"—to no avail. Nothing could stop Nanette; she was determined to run into the bleachers. Who can explain it?

But generally, for everyone other than the Nanettes of the world, the advice is sound. The other team may be able to stop you eventually, but you should never, ever, make it easy for them by being the obstacle in your own path.

Lesson 5: Run and look over your shoulder.

By sophomore year in high school, I had become established in left field. The outfield: where they stick the kids who can't catch. Left field was not quite as ignominious as right field. The Junior Division had been able to claim only a handful of hitters strong enough to reach the outfield, and none of them batted lefty, so right field might as well have been left protected by the weeds. In left field, at least some modicum of attention was required. Back in the Juniors, I wanted so badly to play second base—not first base (too much responsibility), and not third base (too far to throw to first), but second. I wanted to be up front, close to what was going on, part of the inner circle.

But by the time we reached the Seniors, several things had changed. Most noticeably, the body shape of the average SGS player. Several girls who just the year before were skinny and pink-cheeked, their physical futures still hidden in their bones, had suddenly grown large breasts and thick legs. In spite of new women's bodies, though, these girls still wore pigtails, which made their heads seem quite small. These girl-women hit to the outfield on a regular basis, and it got busy out there.

The other thing that changed, I guess, was me. I had become accustomed to left field. I found that I far preferred standing on the grass to the clumpy, yellowish dirt, and I liked being alone out there. I didn't like how fast you had to react in the infield—I enjoyed the luxury of seeing the ball rise off the bat, knowing I didn't have any responsibility towards it until it had begun its descent. And how often in a suburban life do you get to stand by yourself in a field? How often are you sufficiently far away from anything else that there's nothing to measure yourself against, and you can no longer tell how big or small you are? How often do you get to see how the world is circular and you're in the exact center? I realize that to spectators, infielders, to everyone else, it looked as if I was the one far away on the periphery—but that's a misperception. The truth is, when I played left field, *I* was in the middle, while the rest of the game was taking place in a distant corner.

Left field was mine in a way that no part of the infield could belong to any-body, with all those people running through, across, and around it. Nothing came into my personal domain without my permission. By the time I was in high school, I knew how to place myself in front of the ball, how to take control of it, how to hit my cut-off person—Lisa Brasington, our sweet-natured shortstop, who had acne and ended up in ROTC—in a clean motion. But suddenly, just as quickly as they had started hitting balls to me, the big girls gained another 20 pounds and started hitting them *past me*.

"Yuh can't back up on those," said Mr. Robbins. "Yuh run backwards, yuh gunna fall. When yuh know wheah that ball's goin', *turn around and run!* Look ovah yuh left shouldah, keep your eye on it, and reach for it! Reach!" The days of standing and waiting were over.

The first time I made use of this lesson, the batter was a very big girl. Mighty. The word "Sudbury" strained and stretched across the expanse of her chest. I watched her on deck as she swung her bat and surveyed the outfield with her small, buried eyes. She was a righty, and therefore her ball would likely be mine. She stepped up to the plate, surveyed, and pointed the bat in my general direction. I could tell that she had registered the fact that I was the smallest of the outfielders. There was no question now that it was between her and me. Our pitcher, Donna Somers, let fly. The big girl whacked the ball soundlessly, and a moment later I heard the report—the crack always made it out to left field after a short delay. Up went the ball. There was a lot of sky, and a speck of ball. It hung suspended. Then gradually less sky, more ball. More and more ball—and by now I could tell it was headed past me. I turned around and ran. I was running, and looking back. Right—no, left shoulder. Running, looking back. I wasn't going to get to it, but—"*reach!*"—I dove and fell. I hadn't felt any impact or heard any reassuring noise, but I opened my glove . . . there it was! and I rolled over and held it up. From the vast distance I saw the big girl, who was just rounding third, throw down her cap, and Mr. Robbins leap in the air. Third out. I casually threw the ball to Lisa and trotted in while the rest of my teammates came out to jump on me and hit me with their gloves.

I heard the other coach consoling the disappointed girl. "It was a great hit. That kid just made an *unbelievable* catch. You were *robbed*."

Great hit! She'll never remember that "great hit," since it got her exactly nowhere. Lay it on top of the great garbage barge of memory and let it drift away, honey, along with all the other beautiful might-have-beens, almost-weres. But I'll remember that catch until I die.

That year my teammates picked me for the All-Stars.

I never would grow up to be an athlete. In college, I played softball for one season, but it was a fast-pitch league and I couldn't adjust my sluggish swing. I think some of those girls got into college on the strength of their softball abilities, and I was outclassed by a long shot. The girl who beat me out for left field, a true and graceful athlete who could catch anything as well as hit anything, *had only one arm*. Practices were at 5:30 AM starting in the winter months: the smell of the inside of the cage was of last year's sweat and bore no resemblance to Sudbury's warm fields. We were expected to do unacceptable things like lifting weights and Indian running. This was not the game I knew, and I didn't love it any more. So as it turns out, the first impression of me—that I was not an athlete—was pretty much correct.

It was a little sad, the first spring that I did not play softball. That spring, when I smelled the sharp grassy smell and felt the first kinder breeze lift my hair, I felt there was someplace I was supposed to be. And I still feel that way sometimes, some two decades later—even in the middle of the city where I can't smell the grass at all, I only imagine I do.

But there will always be the year I made All-Stars.

Now, I'm talking about softball, I'm not talking about Life. Although, when I think about it, the things I learned from Mr. Robbins *could* be life lessons. There are many activities people do with one hand that could benefit from the use of both—driving, for instance. And not running backwards is a good rule in any context. But all I really want to say is that Mr. Robbins knew something about something, and because of him, now I know something about something too. Life seems so swampy sometimes. Statements with subtexts, people who aren't who they seem to be, social conventions that mask despair—all these leave me floundering. But I know, if you place me on a softball field, in that very particular situation I will know what I ought to do, even if I couldn't in reality execute it. For that certainty I thank Mr. Robbins, and I think of him often.

To All Those Who Say Write What You Know

Kate Petersen

I will just say this. I know a river or two, the easy ones—the Thames, the Danube and Seine—quick to give their beauty to everyone who nears their banks. I know others who keep more to themselves—the Hudson and Snake, the Elwha—content to take and carry your secrets with their own, they leave you for the sea, though you keep watching the eddies for some answer that is not quite love, staying past hope, the way you stay every Sunday for the singer's last song in the bar on Fourth and Lafayette because that voice, you think, will finally give her away.

I know the silver ready of takeoff and the unearned divinity of cruising altitude. I know, too, the melancholy rush of final approach, of returning, as we knew we must, to earth. I know the allure of always going somewhere else.

I know the winter hush of a cathedral, the effect of prayer on stone, light through stained glass some sort of proof, and the dare of my own footfalls in the nave, how they become a sudden hallelujah. I look up, the echoed nowhere, *Sanctus*.

I know girls who still love their bodies, who let their hips draw commas in the air before them, paving the way. I know women who used to, whose hands and teeth and shoes are asking always: *how do I get back there.*

I know noise: car alarms, steamed milk, sex, baseball crowds, last call, the drone of mortar fire on an unwatched TV, a train abiding its rails.

I know sounds, too: the crystal wink of a champagne toast, a bedsheet lifting at lights out, a dead piano key, a breath held, the surprise of insects on summer screens, the quick applause of embers from flame, snow underfoot, a flicker of birds in the cemetery trees.

I know the smell of juniper, the bright gin and tree of it, and of unbathed bodies, street-heavy and ripe with someone else's shame. I know in these streets our sadness.

I know something of desire. I know the blue spell of afternoon on his skin, the way a minute's kiss can absolve one hundred wasted days. The plain chance of bodies I've been willing to mistake for fate, like playing cards found facedown on the sidewalk. I know the words—the yes and the sorry and gone—that stand in for other things we can't say. The constellation of freckles on my left arm I am waiting for someone to read me like tarot. I know the aftermath of want.

And past the cemetery fence on the hill above Southstoke, I know a gray horse, his nose in grass, mud to his fetlocks, dappled with the threat of rain. I was there four years ago now, every afternoon in that cemetery deep with strangers, because I did not know any more to write. And now I find myself there more nights than not, dreamwalking over the bone soil, the gray horse standing between me and another profane morning in the world.

Sensing me he lifts his neck, a movement slow and improbable as marble, and nickers a welcome, the kind that says he knows I will not stay, for I am just passing by. And yet in his voice there is the recognition that we've met some-where before, and we have—I swear I know him, though from where I couldn't say. I stop for a moment, though I do not reach out. Touch is too easy an answer.

In the town below, certain windows have been left open, letting in the sky. Rain nears. The streetlamps stand at ease, waiting for night to come again and bring them purpose. I can feel the light inside the churches shifting its weight. Breath between us, little else. Across the vale in Landsdowne, all the greens confuse themselves, bleed willingly into storm.

With no warning, a lark lifts itself out of the boughs, rising against the rain, which is coming now, still weightless. The headstones grow dark with water. Aloft, the bird waits, buoyed by an updraft off the hillside or by some other unlikelihood, maybe the one that has kept me here, too, past sundown all those evenings ago and now, years later, still tethered by some sweet reluctance to this field of stones, to the memory of this lone bird in the green transept of my unmade cathedral, waiting for the *Ave,* for the first winging chords of a song I want so badly to know.

Virtually Romance
A Discourse on Love in the Information Age

Wendy Rawlings

In the Atharvaveda *time is regarded as the generator of all things, including Brahman, and will be the source of their destruction.*

> —Dictionary of Philosophy and Religion

The key points of Netiquette serve a useful purpose: they keep the information flow efficient, civil, and comprehensible.

> —Navigating the Internet with your Macintosh

Women take a haptic, holistic view of men.

> —John Updike

In a computer store, out-of-season greeting cards tilting in their rickety racks, in a depressed Utah town east of Salt Lake City, I observe my companion, a writer visiting the university here for a week. I know him about as well as I know this depressed town. And yet already to look at him is as unbearable as it is to look away. The hands jammed in jeans pockets. Quizzical tilt of the head, this almost constant, the way dogs' heads cock when receiving sounds far out of human range. Listening, lips pressed together, a smile barely suppressed. Not "good features." Not "handsome." Only gesture, a premonition of touch.

It's no longer bearable. I look up at the ceiling. I can still hear him gently barraging the man behind the counter: "What's the economy like in this place?" "How do Anglos and Native Americans get along?" "What do people around here do for work?"

The ceiling. Quite unexpectedly in a shop so rundown that generations of black flies are living and dying in the front window, the ceiling is magnificent, ornate as an antebellum ballroom's. There should be a chandelier hanging from it. "Look," I tell him. Up his head tilts.

At Marion's Five and Dime Luncheonette we both order grilled cheese on white as everything else on the menu starts with Spam. Spam and beans. Spam and mashed potatoes. Spam on toast. It is at once understood that neither of us trusts meat byproduct shaped like the can it's packaged in, though as a child of a dual-career couple Spam and Mary Kitchen Hash were my dual-career dinner, a marriage made in aluminum. Looking elsewhere so as to observe something other than my companion sitting across the Formica-topped table from me, my eyes catch Elvis clocks, hips swinging with each tick: spam-spam-spam.

At the Protestant church on the Indian Reservation more generations of black flies live by stained glass and die on the carpet. "This time of day is the worst, with the sun," says the pastor, a man with denim shorts and braids to his waist. Cheapie pictures on the walls depict Jesus lugging the cross all over the place.

My companion, head cocked, is pointing out the window. "What's with that little model of the church?"

Out behind the church is a child-size facsimile of a church, ramshackle and littered with trash. The pastor shrugs. "We built that a few years ago for the kids. I keep meaning to repair it." Later, in the Indian burying ground, my companion tells me, "That's how they are about time." I find an unexpired state identification card on the ground. He shows me relics left at the gravestones: a Budweiser can, dirty one-eared porcelain bunnies, a tiny pile of fading green M&M's, a hank of hair tied to a stick.

"You looked up. That's great. I never look up," he says.

I've knocked him a little sideways. I too am out of my groove. Bad had been brewing between my live-in boyfriend and me, but now I've upped the ante. We are driving back from the Reservation to the city and I'm two hours later than I told my boyfriend I would be.

"When you're forty I'll be sixty. When you're fifty I'll be seventy. When you're seventy-five I'll be ninety-five." All this math and we haven't even touched each other yet. He of the gloomy algebra and moss growing on his antlers thinks he knows the kind of woman I am. The kind of woman he thinks I am: observant. Indeed I am observant; in fact, I am a deeply distracted and by the standards of late-twentieth-century capitalism shamefully unproductive woman. I have no husband or children to take care of, no yard to weed; I'm a dismal cook whose culinary forays are restricted to boiling freeze-dried Indian meals. By my own shaky algebra I spend sixty-five to seventy percent of an average day observing. And yet I looked up not because I was particularly curious about the ceiling but because I was worried he might catch me in an act of naked observation: staring. At what? At him.

He loves my hair, he confesses. My hair? He has been looking at me all day. I punctuate our kisses with little sighs out of range of human hearing. When I take off my glasses I don't hear as acutely. "I'm glad you can't see without your glasses," he says. He feels he's fat. Oh, Jesus. Vanity the cross we all lug. He might be fat but what would I care? I only care if I'm fat. This is the way women's lust works. On the counter in his hotel room sit two bags, up close I see without my glasses are Doritos and Twizzlers. "When you're seventy I'll be in an urn," he says. I think of Jack Nicholson and Helen Hunt, Warren Beatty and Annette Bening, Anthony Hopkins and any number of starlets. "I don't even think about your age," I say. The sort of thing young women are supposed to tell men worried about moss and math.

He's in town a week, and then he has to go back where he came from.

Cyberspace

From: Tully@aol.com
To: Wendy@aol.com
Subject: Re: Romance

In a message dated XX/XX/XX 02:18:31 EST, you write:
<< I knew I never should have allowed you to take off my underwear . . .>>

Sweetie, I don't mean to be critical, but you DO seem to have a slightly irrational attachment to your underwear, and a slightly exaggerated sense of your underwear's magical ability to ward off evil (or me). We'll have to work on this, perhaps get you a therapist . . .

Tempus Fugit

Virtual romance is a freeze-dried package of Saag Paneer. It is Saag Paneer, yes: by American standards an adventurous meal. It is not, say, chicken-flavored ramen noodles. It is not a can of Spam. And yet, when you slit the silver package open and pour its contents on a bed of basmati rice, there is the infinitely disappointing trace odor of whatever chemicals are used to preserve this food in freeze-dried form. A food facsimile. You feel you are eating a meal poured out of a Mylar balloon. If you keep a jar of chutney in the refrigerator you have, nonetheless, in a hundred and twenty shifts of Elvis's hips, a virtual Indian meal.

Cyberspace

From: Tully@aol.com
To: Wendy@aol.com
Subject: Re: Romance

It's amazing that we'll see each other so soon (given the distance) and it'll be nice to be together around Christmas. And then it won't be so long before it's your birthday.

Shit—I really have to get off and get to work. But I wanted to tell you that everything's okay for December, that I am incredibly in love with you, that you will have to use a crowbar to get my arms off you when I see you (do you REALLY have to pee alone? do you really like being apart from me that much?).

Mostly Incommunicado, Tortola, British Virgin Islands

"Tortola" is a word that feels like food. "Tor-tolla!" my father exhorts in a bad Italian accent. My father, he of the moss rapidly accumulating on at least one antler, is recovering from an earlier fiasco alfresco with a cocktail at the Moorings boat charter clubhouse. He and my sister compete to see who will be the first to tie a maraschino cherry stem with their tongues. At four-thirty that morning, he warned my sister and me about not forgetting things, then misplaced the plane tickets and made us miss the flight. The tickets were in the car trunk the whole time, so we can make jokes about senility. *You'll be in an urn.* We are chartering a sailboat for five days, a Christmas trip my father has talked about for years.

At the dock he examines the boat's steering mechanism and finds a penny going green as the Statue of Liberty. "The wire's snapped," he says, spinning the steering wheel in futile circles. "They don't maintain these." *A marriage made in aluminum.* He and my mother have been divorced just over a year, my mother in menopause too high maintenance. Maraschino cherries prick in me a bright nostalgia for before divorce, the four of us at restaurants for seafood, "Shirley Temples for the girls."

My sister's popping Bonine to ward off even the idea of sickness. I keep thinking *home* instead of *sea.* It's my computer I miss out here. Black women have provisioned our boat, named *Karen Anne* as if it's a girlfriend you climb on. Over Triscuits and Cheez Wiz I feel guilty. I'm white and sailing, they're not and not. "Is there any Spam down there?" I call to my sister in the galley. No, she says, but nine cans of Coco Lopez. It takes three sips of a Painkiller before I taste it's rancid and spit.

At the topmost island, The Bitter End, as I am lovesick and hungerless, I can't abide the all-you-can-eat buffet ($32.50 per person). Instead I order drinks, three Painkillers at $6.25 each.

We return to our boat in the dinghy, me holding the hurricane lamp out in front. Up fish jump in the path the light casts. I shout for my father and sister to look.

Tully calls on our ship-to-shore phone from a blizzard in New York: Subzero. Ice storms. Power lines down. And me? Snorkeling. Rancid Coco Lopez. Too many Painkillers. My guide to Caribbean marine life says the brown fish I saw today, with prominent lips and what look like thick eyebrows, are called Jewfish. Racial slur? Trying to describe snorkeling to someone who has never snorkeled is like trying to describe making love to someone who has never loved.

Underneath the boat a barracuda spooks my sister, transfixed by swarms of white fish. "That's some sick rush hour," she says as she climbs up *Karen Anne's* ladder. For dinner the next night we have the special, trigger fish.

Synchronous, Manhattan

Tully is vexed at the sight of my suntanned torso. At fifty, his flesh next to mine makes him think of death. At the hotel he unpacks not Doritos and Twizzlers but economy-sized bottles of Listerine and conditioner. Will we co-gargle? We'll only be here for two days, never mind that he of the mossy antlers might have more in the way of moss than hair. Why condition?

He gives me a Maxfield Parrish pop-up book, a naked nymphette bending on the cover. Can he imagine me at thirty an old Lolita? "You're not supposed to *read* it," he says. Chastened, I look and pull the pop-up tabs.

In bed he talks about the 1850s in England and the concept of the individual. As he speaks I'm already counting the hours until I'll have to be back on the plane to Utah: 32.5. *That's how they are about time.* I like the middle of the night because I can't guess the hour. "You're not supposed to *laugh* during sex," he says, chagrined beneath me. But always in the middle of it I think of a word like "spatula."

My sister works in pharmaceuticals. For Monday lunch we take a subway to meet her. I show Tully my T-shirt declared *The Zoloft Smile*. "You have to get me one of those," he says. A shirt or a smile? It is the late twentieth century; it is America. Maybe even a smile can be purchased. At the pharmaceutical company the wall in the reception area has water running down it, like nature. I say it's like nature the way smiling on Zoloft is like being happy. We are clearly out of place here. Water on a wall. He in a wool hat pulled to his eyebrows like a terrorist, me in a thrift store plaid man's winter jacket. All around us swirl people done up in suits and hair gel, including my sister. "Everyone says it's very feng-shui," she says of the water-on-wall.

At a sushi place we talk divorce. Not very feng-shui. He's been divorced a year and thinks in the end the ones who might be worse fucked up than him are his kids. My gelled sister of divorced parents soothes him, trades some of her California rolls for his kappa maki. The Zoloft Smile. Maybe he will fall for her and dump ungelled me, Spam in jeans. *I too am out of groove.*

Naked, I am peeing in the hotel bathroom. Two and a half hours before I have to catch a shuttle to La Guardia. In my stomach is the start of a little sickness, not home not sea. I might cry. *Spatula. Spatula.* In the bedroom he's combing through newspaper advertisements for computers, as his hard drive is growing moss. *When you're forty I'll be sixty.* I'm on the toilet and in he walks with the newspaper, slips one hand between my legs and tastes his wet palm. Later, in a deli near Grand Central: "Did that shock you?" I admit it did. Across the table he is blinking at me, his eyes sea. *Up fish jump.*

And then I have to go back where I came from.

Tempus Fugit

Virtual romance is the runway at La Guardia airport. Planes more often than they should during takeoff career into the water surrounding the airport: the runway is too short. In the beginning you have every intention of taking off. Back in Utah, I think not of him but of his e-mails: *You will have to use a crowbar to get my arms off you when I see you again. Right now, any part of you I touched would burn me.*

Interim, Utah

I return to the apartment where my boyfriend and I still live with each other. *Spins the steering wheel in futile circles.* We'll get through Christmas together and I'll move out New Year's Day. We're splitting for good in a social season, everyone decking halls and coming all ye faithful except me, he the cuckolded. Will I go with him to his company Christmas party anyway? All around us swirl people done up in hair gel and holiday attire. "Are they all Mormon?" I ask, already woozy on wine. Of four conversations I have, two concern fertility issues. Of two men in couples concerned with fertility issues two are named Bryce, one with an "I." I want to say, "We have futility issues."

My boyfriend gets an award for on-time delivery: fifty bucks and a toy FedEx truck as big as my leg. He's on time, I'm thinking about moss and math. Several people comment on what a great couple we make. Does no one else see our futility issues? After the party we sit in our holiday attire on the kitchen floor and drink Painkillers made with rum I got from Cane Garden Bay. Grating the nutmeg I cut my finger.

"So you and grandpa really dig each other?" he asks. Is it possible for a heart to go rancid? "Do me a favor and don't go running in to check your e-mail in your underwear," he says. We walk together with our drinks from one end of the apartment to another. Feeble box elder bugs, refugees from summer, make cameo appearances on the windowsills. He smears them with his hand.

"I waited eight years to live together, then two more after you moved in. You never talked," I say. He shrugs, nonplussed by my calculations. "Irish people don't talk." We're standing on the balcony, me shivering in velvet, him with his ubiquitous pack of smokes. It's my computer I miss.

Cyberspace

From: Tully@aol.com
To: Wendy@aol.com
Subject: Re: Romance

In a message dated XX/XX/XX 13:53:44 EST, you write:
<<You know, to me it's just an organ that for the most part all I do is WIPE.>>

You know, sweetie, there are ways of writing about this that can imbue it with epic romance—and you choose these words? For example, I prefer to think of it/you as the humid scabbard into which I will thrust my fiery sword! :)

Tempus Fugit

In what ways does a romance in cyberspace collapse the opposition between silence and speech? Between being there in person and not being there at all? Between saying and feeling? Online, we send and receive messages so quickly and so often that my typing (hurried, harried) and reading (hurried, harried) of messages feels like feeling itself, like ink spreading on cloth.

Cyberspace

From: Tully@aol.com
To: Wendy@aol.com
Subject: Re: Romance

You know I'm kidding, right? About the scabbard and the fiery sword?

Remote, Utah

Our landlord has promised me an apartment four blocks from our apartment. It's New Year's Eve, two hours until the year is new, eleven until I make my move. The two of us, each on our own sections of the sectional sofa, are watching Dick Clark's Rockin' Eve and drinking Painkillers. In between the bands people have volunteered to do what the host calls "the world's most dangerous stunts." *You will have to use a crowbar.* The evening's pièce de résistance will be a man in a truck dropped from a crane an absurd yet calculated number of feet. He's going to escape the truck before impact.

"A cat lives in the boiler room of that apartment," my landlord calls to tell me. (It's 10:37 P.M. on New Year's Eve.) "It's forced heat. Are you that allergic to cats?"

I'm that allergic. Cats give me a necklace of hives, just for starters. The landlord has an apartment I can rent in the building next door.

"Next door?"

My ex says he'll help me move my things across the courtyard. *The runway is too short.* On e-mail, Tully will want to know how far from the ex-boyfriend's door to mine. How far can I stretch sixty feet?

Cyberspace

From: Tully@aol.com
To: Wendy@aol.com
Subject: Re: pining

Anyway I am writing this in haste so you have something to read when you get up in the morning.

Adjacent, Utah

My ex has overnight guests. I have my computer. In my underwear I trip straight from sleep each morning, a beeline to online. *This time of day is the worst.* Sometimes there are no messages; sometimes the modem buzzes and halts like a dying fly. Sometimes in my underwear I hit my computer with the heel of my hand: virtual domestic violence.

The overnight guest's name is LaHoma. "What fucking kind of name is that?" I ask. He says Indian. "Indian Indian or Indian Native American?" "American Indian." I think of the pastor with braids to his waist. "So where did you meet this person?" "On my pick-up route." Pick-up route! "How old is she?" She's twenty-three.

Cyberspace

From: Tully@aol.com
To: Wendy@aol.com
Subject: Re: pining

In a message dated XX/XX/XX 14:50:02 EST, you write:

<< It's okay that you've abandoned me; I have a call in to my therapist and she says the Zoloft prescription will be ready this afternoon. Meanwhile, I'm testing my shower rod to see if it can hold a 120 lb. woman>>

Okay okay I am trying to race out of here but I got all your messages just now finally and want to let you know I haven't abandoned you . . .

Tempus Fugit

Virtual romance, the heart's bulimia. You fill and fill and fill on words, and yet it is the necessary silences that absent themselves. "When I look down, I miss all the good stuff," a woman on the radio sings, "when I look up, I just trip over things." *The ceiling is magnificent.*

Cyberspace

From: Tully@aol.com
To: Wendy@aol.com
Subject: Re: lonely online

Sweetheart:
What was I doing? I was trying to catch up with my life. I was going to write you last night but I couldn't get online (AOL is sometimes packed). I think of you about every three minutes.

Abiding, Utah

"What if we get married?" my ex says. We are sitting on his kitchen floor with an almost empty magnum of cheapie Chardonnay. "Is that a proposal?" I ask. *A marriage made.* "What if it is?" On his bulletin board, postcards depicting the British Virgin Islands and Palm Springs. "Who went to Palm Springs?" I ask. "LaHoma." "Why are you asking me to get married?" I ask. "I'm not asking you to get married, I'm saying what if we get married." *The Irish don't talk.* Drunk, I climb back into our old bed with him and go to sleep. In the middle of the night we wake together, groggy and hellbent for water. "That whole proposal thing probably wasn't a good idea," he says. We're in the dark kitchen, trading swigs out of his bottled water. *A virtual proposal.* "No," I say. "Even though you still love me in some sad and belated way," he says. *Me pricked bright.* I recognize his words. "That's from my e-mails."

"I know," he says. "I read them all."

Retreat, Utah

In my economy-sized box of Q-Tips, I find a plastic calling card worth ten free minutes of long distance phone conversation: an excuse to call Tully midday, a break with protocol. But bending the rules isn't always welcome: "He *read* them all?" (Emphasis on *read.*) "He read them *all*?" (Emphasis on *all.*) He's been violated, he says.

Cyberspace

From: Tully@aol.com
To: Wendy@aol.com
Subject: Re: hello (again)

For whatever reason I've been drifting farther and farther out of that zone of passion that drove us at first.

How to Purchase a Personal Computer

Midtown, Computerland—Used computers are cheap, but also a risk. They have the marks of other people's labor: a faded shift key, scuffmarks, some other small but intolerable shoddiness. We wandered through the store in our frayed wool coats, him in his terrorist hat, our noses cold, neither of us able to pay proper attention. *I just trip over things.* He, the potential computer buyer, was making an attempt to put aside our romance for a moment so he could make his purchase. The sales clerks, all men, seemed to have the same disinterested and elite-sounding accent. *Indian Indian or Indian Native American?* Tully got one man to set up some laptops so he could try them. THIS IS A NICE LITTLE MACHINE. I CAN TYPE VERY QUICKLY, he typed very quickly. I stood beside him, hands jammed in my pockets. Secretly I was watching his face. I LOVE YOU WENDY, he typed. Secretly I was watching his face.

A Guide to Snorkeling in the British Virgin Islands

Common sense will serve you as well in the Caribbean as it does on Nantucket or Catalina. The classic rule around water remains: Don't go alone. Diving with someone of equal ability makes it more fun.

—Adventuring in the Caribbean

Snorkelers are advised to wear long-sleeved shirts and drawstring pants while in the water in order to protect their skin from sunburn and coral scrapes: "Remember that if you get hurt on coral, you have also injured the coral's own delicate protoplasm." And yet I cannot bring myself to empty my mailbox of the one hundred and sixty-seven messages he sent. *There is the infinitely disappointing trace odor.* If they were letters at least I could build a fire and, as lovers have for centuries, burn them. *I'll be in an urn.* The messages scroll up each time I log onto my account. *Right now, any part of you I touched would burn me.*

Would I like them better if they were a thousand white fish? A thousand bits of shredded paper? I see myself drifting still in bright water, my arms loose and weightless, surrounded by white swarms. Thousands of them. We never touch.

Celebrating Creation

Chet Raymo

Even the sparrow finds a home, and the swallow a nest, where she rears her brood beside thy altars.

—Psalm 84:3

Late last summer, in the west of Ireland, I spent a night in the Gallarus Oratory, a tiny seventh-century church of unmortared stone. It is the oldest intact building in Ireland, and one of the oldest in Europe. The oratory is about the size of a one-car garage, in the shape of an overturned boat. It has a narrow entrance at the front and a single tiny window at the rear, both open to the elements. Even during the day one needs a flashlight to explore the interior.

I can't say exactly why I was there, or why I intended to sit up all night, sleeplessly, in that dark space. I had been thinking about skepticism and prayer, and I wanted to experience something of whatever it was that inspired Irish monks to seek out these rough hermitages perched on the edge of Europe, or—as they imagined—the edge of eternity. They were pilgrims of the Absolute, seeking their God in a raw, ecstatic encounter with stone, wind, sea, and sky.

The Gallarus Oratory is something of a tourist mecca, but at night the place is isolated and dark, far from human habitation. From the door of the oratory, one looks down a sloping mile of fields to the twinkling lights of the village of Bally-david on Smerwick Harbor.

The sun had long set when I arrived, although at that latitude in summer the twilight never quite fades from the northern horizon. It was a moonless night, ablaze with stars, Jupiter brightest of all. Meteors occasionally streaked the sky, and satellites cruised more stately orbits. Inside, I snuggled into a back corner of the oratory, tucked my knees under my chin, and waited. I could see nothing but the starlit outline of the door, not even my hand in front of my face. The silence was broken only by the low swish of my own breath.

As the hours passed, I began to feel a presence, a powerful sensation of something or someone sharing that empty darkness. I am not a mystical person, but I knew that I was not alone, and I could imagine those hermit monks of the seventh century sharing the same intense conviction of "someone in the room." At last, I was spooked to the point that I abandoned my interior corner and went outside.

A night of exceptional clarity! Stars spilling into the sea. And in the north, as if as a reward for my lonely vigil, the aurora borealis danced toward the zenith. How can I describe what I saw? Rays of silver light streaming up from the sea, as if from some enchanted Oz just over the horizon, shimmering columns of fairy radiance. As I watched from the doorway of oratory, I remembered something the nineteenth-century explorer Charles Francis Hall wrote about watching the aurora from the Arctic: "My first thought was, 'Among the gods there is none like unto Thee, O Lord; neither are there any works like unto thy works!' . . . We looked, we SAW, we TREMBLED."

Hall knew he was watching a natural physical phenomenon, not a miracle, but his reaction suggests the power of the aurora even on a mind trained in the methods of science. What then did the monks of Gallarus think of the aurora, 1,300 years ago, at a time when the supernatural was the explanation of choice for exceptional phenomena? Stepping out from the inky darkness of their stone chapel, they must surely have felt that the shimmering columns of light were somehow meant for them alone, a sign or a revelation, an answer to their prayers.

We have left the age of miracles behind, but not, I trust, our sense of wonder. Our quest for encounter with the Absolute goes arm in arm with our search for answers. We are pilgrim scientists, perched on the edge of eternity, curious and attentive. The Gallarus Oratory was built for prayer, at a time when the world was universally thought to be charged with the active spirit of a personal God: Every stone might be moved by incantation, every zephyr blew good or ill; springs flowed or dried up at the deity's whim; lights danced in a predawn sky as a blessing or portent. Today, we know the lights are caused by electrons crashing down from the sun, igniting luminescence. But our response to the lights might still be one of prayerful attention, and they lead us, if we let them, into encounters with the Absolute.

Traditional religious faiths have three components: a shared cosmology (a story of the universe and our place in it), spirituality (personal response to the numinous), and liturgy (public expressions of celebration and gratitude, including rites of passage). The apparent antagonism of science and religion centers almost entirely on cosmology: What is the universe? Where did it come from? How does it work? What is the human self? What is our fate? Humans have always had answers to these questions. The answers have been embodied in stories—tribal myths, scriptures, church traditions. All of these stories derived from a raw experience of the creation, such as my experiences inside and outside of the Gallarus Oratory. All of them contain enduring wisdom. But as a reliable cosmological component of religious faith they have been superseded by what cultural historian and Roman Catholic priest Thomas Berry calls the New Story—the scientific story of the world.

The New Story is the product of thousands of years of human curiosity, observation, experimentation, and creativity. It is an evolving story, not yet finished. Perhaps it will never be finished. It is a story that begins with an explosion from a seed of infinite energy. The seed expands and cools. Particles form, then atoms of hydrogen and helium. Stars and galaxies coalesce from swirling gas. Stars burn and explode, forging heavy elements—carbon, nitrogen, oxygen—and hurl them into space. New stars are born, with planets made of heavy elements. On one planet near a typical star in a typical galaxy life appears in the form of microscopic self-replicating ensembles of atoms. Life evolves, over billions of years, resulting in ever more complex organisms. Continents move. Seas rise and fall. The atmosphere changes. Millions of species of life appear and become extinct. Others adapt, survive, and spill out progeny. At last, human consciousness appears. One species experiences the ineffable and wonders what it means, and makes up stories—of invisible spirits who harbor in darkness, of gods who light up the sky in answer to our prayers—eventually making up the New Story.

The New Story has important advantages over all the stories that have gone before:

It works. It works so well that it has become the irreplaceable basis of technological civilization. We test the New Story in every way we can, in its particulars and in its totality. We build giant particle accelerating machines to see what happened in the first hot moments of the Big Bang. We put telescopes into space to look for the radiation of the primeval explosion. With spectroscopes and radiation detectors we analyze the composition of stars and galaxies and compare them to our theories for the origin of the world. Always and in every way we try to prove the story wrong. When the story fails, we change it.

It is a universal story. Although originally a product of Western culture, it has become the story of all educated peoples throughout the world; scientists of all cultures, religions, and political persuasions exchange ideas freely and apply the same criteria of verification and falsification. Like most children, I was taught that my story—Adam and Eve, angels, miracles, incarnation, heaven, hell, and all the rest—was the "true story," and that all others were false. Sometimes our so-called "true" stories gave us permission to hurt those who lived by other stories. The New Story, by its universality, helps put the old animosities behind us.

It is a story that emphasizes the connectedness of all people and all things. Some of the old stories, such as the one I was taught as a child, placed humankind outside of space and time, gifted us with unworldly spirit, and gave us dominion over the millions of Earth's other creatures. The New Story places us squarely in a cosmic unfolding of space and time, and teaches our biological affinity to all humanity. We are ephemeral beings, inextricably related to all of life, to the planet itself, and even to the lives of stars.

It is a story that asserts our responsibility for our own lives and the future of the planet. In the New Story, no omniscient deity intervenes at will in the creation, answers prayers, or leads all things to a predetermined end. We are on our own, in the immensity of creation, with an awesome responsibility to use our talents wisely.

It is a story that reveals a universe of unanticipated complexity, beauty, and dimension. The God revealed by the New Story is not the paltry personal projection of ourselves who attracted and bedeviled our ancestors. It is, in the words of the Jesuit theologian David Toolan, "the Unnamable One/Ancient of the Days of the mystics, of whom we can only speak negatively (not this, not that), a 'wholly other' hidden God of Glory," or in the felicitous phrase of novelist Nikos Kazantzakis, "the dread essence beyond logic."

We should treasure the ancient stories for the wisdom and values they contain. We should celebrate the creation in whatever poetic languages and rituals our traditional cultures have taught us. But only the New Story has the global authority to help us navigate the future. It is not the "true" story, but it is certainly the truest. Of all the stories that might provide the cosmological basis of contemporary religious feeling, it is the only one that has had its feet held to the fire of exacting experience.

The New Story informed my response to the dancing lights in the night sky at Gallarus. What I saw was not a portent or miracle, but rather nature's exquisite signature of the magnetic and material entanglement of Earth and sun.

As the sun brightened the eastern horizon and the last shreds of aurora faded, I was suddenly startled by a pair of swallows that began to dart in and out of the Gallarus Oratory, hunting insects on the wing. I followed them inside and discovered a nest with three chicks perched on a protruding stone just above the place I had been sitting. The mysterious presence I had felt so strongly in the darkness was not a god, nor spirit, nor succubus, nor demon, but the respirations and featherings of swallows.

Disappointment

Richard Rodriguez

Though John Steinbeck was not, in my opinion, the best California writer of the last century, *The Grapes of Wrath* remains California's greatest novel. The native son imagined California from the outside, as a foreigner might; imagined wanting California desperately; imagined California as a remedy for the trial of the nation.

Otherwise, I might think of John Milton when I think of California and the writer's task. Milton devised that, after the Fall, the temperature in San Diego would remain at 75 degrees, but Adam and Eve's relationship to a perfect winter day would be changed to one of goose bumps.

The traditional task of the writer in California has been to write about what it means to be human in a place advertised as paradise. Not the Buckeye or the Empire, not the Can-do or the Show-me, California is the Postlapsarian State. Disappointment has always been the theme of California.

For example, my own.

I cannot afford to live here. I mean I do live here—I rent two large rooms, two stories above California Street. My light comes from the south. But if I had to move, I could not afford to live here anymore.

In San Francisco, small Victorians, small rooms, steep stairs, are selling for three or four million and are repainted to resemble Bavarian cuckoo clocks—browns and creams and the mute greens tending to blue. That is my mood. If I owned one of the Victorians, I would no doubt choose another comparison. It is like living on a street of cuckoo clocks—and all the cuckoos are on cell phones—I won't say striking thirteen; nevertheless a version of postmodernity I had not anticipated. Only well-to-do futurists and stuffed T-shirts can afford to live in this 19th-century neighborhood.

My complaint with my city is that I am middle-aged.

The sidewalks in my neighborhood are uncannily empty save for Mexican laborers and Mexican nannies and Mexican caregivers, and women wearing baseball hats who walk with the exaggerated vigor of wounded pride (as do I). The streets are in disrepair; the city has no money; really, the streets have never been worse. And the city can no longer afford to maintain the park across the street. The park has never looked worse—the hedges are falling to ruin; are not trimmed; the grass is not watered. Can you imagine Adam and Eve grousing about run-down Eden?

California has been the occasion for disappointment since the 1850s, since men wrote home from the gold fields, from Auburn, from Tulare or Sonora, from tree stumps and tent-hotels.

I have no doubt I will prevail here, but you may not think my thicker skin is the proper reformation of an Ohio son. The men here are rough, they grunt and growl and guard their plates with their arms. Now I reach past my neighbor, and grunt, too, and shove, too, and I would cuss just for the pleasure of saying something out loud. I don't believe I have said more than ten words since I came to this place. I realize any oath I might devise would pale next to the colorful flannel they run up here . . .

And yet the streets are clogged with pickups and delivery vans, cable vans, and the vans of construction workers—certain evidence of prosperity. Crews of men, recently from old countries, work to reconstruct the houses of futurists—houses that were reconstructed not two years ago. One cannot drive down any street without having to go around the pickups and the vans, without muttering under one's breath at the temporary No Parking signs that paper every street, because everyone knows the only reason for the No Parking permits is to enable construction workers to drive to work.

Men from every corner of the world converged on the gold fields in the 1850s, prompting Karl Marx to proclaim the creation of a global society in California, a society unprecedented in the world up to that time. The gold parliament was an achievement of necessity as much as of greed.

Kevin Starr, the preeminent historian of California from the 1850s to the end of the 20th century, has described California as a chronology of proper names: Stanford. Atherton. Giannini. Disney.

Disappointment was arrival. Letters went out to the world, diaries, newspaper reports, warnings, laments, together with personal effects—eyeglasses, pen nibs, broken-backed Bibles—wrapped in soiled canvas. The stolen claim. Or the fortune squandered. (*Lottie, dear, I have wasted our dream . . .*) The trusting disposition. The false friend. The fog-shrouded wharf. The Spaniard Marquis, etc. The ring, the brooch, the opium den, etc.

Narratives of disappointment flowed eastward, like an auguring smoke, or bumped back over rutted trails, as coffins bump or buckboards slow, to meet the stories of the desolations of the prairie life, rolled over those, flowed back to the Atlantic shore, where the raw line separating the North and South was beginning to fester.

Nineteenth-century California rewarded only a few of its brotherhood, but it rewarded them as deliriously as an ancient king in an ancient myth would reward. The dream of a lucky chance encouraged a mass migration, toward "el norte" or "gold mountain," or from across the plains of America.

For, as much as California's story was a story of proper names or of luck or election, California was also a story of mass—mass migrations, unmarked graves, missing persons, accident. By the time he reaches the 1990s in his great work, Kevin Starr seems to sense an influential shift: The list of singular makers of California gives way to forces of unmaking—to gangs, earthquakes, riots, floods, propositions, stalled traffic.

Disappointment is a fine literary theme—"universal"—as the young high school English teacher, himself disappointed, was fond to say, and it wears like leather.

Disappointment continued to be mined in California's literature throughout the 20th century. Joan Didion gave us domestic broken dreamers, not so much driven as driving. In the great Didion essays of the sixties, the dystopian mother abandons her daughter on the median of the San Bernardino freeway; dirty dishes pile up in the sink; the hot wind blows from the desert.

Mike Davis gives us the California Club version of the broken dream— paper evidence that a deal was cut. The water, the electricity, the coastline— everything can be bought or sold in the Promised Land, and has been.

California's most influential prose has turned out to be that of mystery writers, more in line with John Milton, who regard Eden as only an occasion for temptation and fall. For example, the eighteen-year-old cheerleader from Sioux City returns her engagement ring, a poor-grade sapphire she got from a boy named Herbert (not after the president); cashes in her scholarship to the teacher's college; buys a ticket to L.A., enjoins herself to become the new, the next—*Whaddaya think?*—Jean Harlow. But she ends up a manicurist in Van Nuys; she ends up the blue, blonde Jane Doe-of-the-month in the North Hollywood morgue. It requires a private investigator who is broke, dyspeptic, alcoholic, but also something of a Puritan, to want to incriminate California. The golden.

One of my favorite California essays is a disappointment essay—F. Scott Fitzgerald's "The Crack-Up"—an incautious memoir, meticulous, snide.

What an unenviable prospect, though, to be forced to listen to the same lament—the Hollywood screenwriter's lament—at one o'clock in the morning in the Polo Lounge. I once suffered a very long evening thus, listening to a young man complain, in breath that smelled of boiled eggs for lunch, about the difficulty of being a "serious" writer in a town that idolized Spielberg. It was Spielberg that year; I imagine it still is Spielberg.

Francis Scott Fitzgerald at one o'clock in the morning: "I saw that the novel, which at my maturity was the strongest and supplest medium for conveying thought and emotion from one human being to another, was becoming subordinated to a mechanical and communal art that, whether in the hands of Hollywood merchants or Russian idealists, was capable of reflecting only the tritest thought, the most obvious emotion."

Many decades after Fitzgerald cracked up, I saw with my own eyes a still orbiting fragment of his legend. I saw Sheila Graham, a tarnished blond in a black cocktail dress. She floated from table to table at Mr. Chow's restaurant, myopic, bending at the waist to kiss the air behind the ears of revelers. As a public sinner, she was something of a disappointment.

What Fitzgerald was too aureate to imagine was that unfastidious merchants of Hollywood—the ham-fisted, the thickfingered, the steak-minded— nevertheless could pay somebody (scale) to develop the screenwriter's complaint into a script—a picture about a pretty-boy screenwriter who ends up floating facedown in a swimming pool on Sunset Boulevard.

The question is: Does California have anything left to say to America, or to the world, or even to itself, beyond disappointment? True, a vast literature is forming upon the Dewey-decimal coast. Vietnamese-Californian, Japanese-Californian, Pakistani-Californian, Hispanics, all sorts, including my own. The question many people legitimately ask about this literature is whether our voices describe more than a hyphenated state.

My first literary recognition of California came from reading William Saroyan, because Saroyan described the world I recognized. It was as simple as that. Armenian Fresno was related to my Sacramento. It was as simple as that—the extreme Valley heat (outlanders swore they never could stand it, or the flatness either, or the alfalfa green); also the taste of water from a garden hose—the realization that California, that any life, that my life, therefore, was potentially the stuff of literature.

Here is the quote from Saroyan that I typed and pasted on the inside of my bedroom door, a manifesto:

> *Try to learn to breathe deeply, really to taste food when you eat, and when you sleep, really to sleep. Try as much as possible to be wholly alive, with all your might, and when you laugh, laugh like hell, and when you get angry, get good and angry. Try to be alive. You will be dead soon enough.*

That was Saroyan's "advice to a young writer." I took the advice at a time when I had no expectation of being a writer or any desire or sense of obligation. (It comes to me only now, as I type this, that Saroyan's advice has nothing to do with writing; it is advice for any mortal, sentient being.)

It would be another two decades before I came upon the words that made me think I had a story to tell—the opening words of Maxine Hong Kingston's *The Woman Warrior*:

> *"You must not tell anyone," my mother said, "what I am about to tell you."*

The mother's prohibition to her daughter reminded me of my own mother's warning about spreading "family secrets." In the face of all California's fame for blatancy—in the face of pervasive light, ingenuousness, glass and aluminum housing, bikinis, billboards—Mrs. Hong recommended concealment. Her shrine is a published book.

About this time, Aram Saroyan, William Saroyan's son, published a bitter memoir of his father's last years.

William Saroyan was not on any syllabus I ever saw at Stanford or Berkeley, nor, incidentally, was Steinbeck. Stanford, Berkeley—these were schools established in the 19th century by professors from the Ivy League who had come west, like Peace Corps volunteers, to evangelize California for the Atlantic Enlightenment. So perhaps it was not surprising that, even in the 1960s and 1970s, very little attention was paid to California in any university course, despite the fact that California in those years was at the center of the national imagination. The only California novel assigned in any course I took, either in college or graduate school, was Nathaniel West's *The Day of the Locust*, probably because it fulfilled some East Coast expectation that California would come to doom.

And speaking of doom, the editor from *Time* magazine wanted an essay on California because it was a season (this was ten years ago) when the national newsweeklies were hitting the stands with titles like "Is the Golden State Tarnished?"

The *Time* editor wanted 750 words worth of tarnish: "It would be nice if you could give us a Joan Didion essay."

"What's that?" I said.

"You know," she said. "Sardonic."

I unfold and refold that fraying *Time* story whenever I go to lunch with a California writer, handy to pull out if the conversation turns to New York. When the conversation inevitably turns to New York.

It is not sardonicism, sardony; it is the flat Valley pitch. And it is precision.

Anyway, California is getting too old to play the unhappy child or even the sardonic—too rich, too glued, too Angelica Huston walking substantially down some steps into the garden, to play the exuberant, the naïf. And California has grown children of her own. Two of the most interesting cities in North America are California daughters. Las Vegas, the open-throttled city, mimics California's youth, when land was cheap and cities were built in opposition to nature. Tijuana wants so little, she terrifies us for needing so much.

And: New York, truly, I am sorry to say, is not New York anymore. I say this having once been the boy who strained—the antenna on our roof raked through the starlight—to catch any shred of conversation from New York. I watched James Baldwin interviewed by David Susskind. I watched Norman Mailer chafing at America on *The Dick Cavett Show*. New York was a conversation. I guess I am stuck there. Buckley and Galbraith, Yale and Harvard, W. H. Auden, and Hermione Gingold.

Unread copies of *The New Yorker* slip and slide on the opposite end of my couch—damn slippery things—opposite to the end of the couch where I read. Still, every once in a while there's an essential article. I stopped my subscription to the *New York Review of Books* some years ago. When I was in college, in graduate school, and for many years after, the *NYRB* fed my ravenous appetite for Oxbridge-Manhattan conversation. But then—what? I got too old; the conversation got too old. And surely the world must be larger than New York and London. Even now, I could pick up right where I left off: *SWM seeks SWF, for argument's sake.*

On an April day in 1970, I saw Dwight MacDonald. We both were stranded on a concrete island in the middle of Broadway. He was an old man in a raincoat in the rain. I was a student. The rain was glorious, tall, immoderate. Everything was glorious. Broadway. No, I did not dare congratulate MacDonald for his bravery as a public intellectual, the best of his kind, and for whom the rain, that day, at least from the look of him, was just one more goddamned thing. Then the light changed.

Because Irving Kristol correctly predicted the light would change; that the intellectual center of America would shift from the shores of the Hudson to the Potomac.

For the writer, the problem of the absence of New York is the problem of the absence of a critical center, where opinion can be trusted to support talent or call down the falsely reasoned text. Washington think tanks are too far gone in the thrall to political power to provide that center. In the absence of critical structures, where does the young writer from California, or any writer, present himself for review; to what city does he apply for notice and contest? Nowadays, it is not Norman Mailer or James Baldwin who converse on television, it is Dr. Bill Frist or Harry Reid, and it is poor.

I was once interviewed on C-SPAN during the Los Angeles Times Book Festival. Five minutes max, the producer promised. Put this in your ear. Look over there. 5 . . . 4 . . . 3 . . . 2 . . . I was standing on a crowded plaza at UCLA between two stalls, one for African-American books, another for Latino books. I said to my interviewer, who was in Washington, D.C., which was inside an electronic button, which was inside my ear, that I regretted these two neighboring book booths represented so little understanding of what California is becoming.

The earphone remained as neutral as a can opener.

. . . *I mean California's destiny is marriage. All the races of the world* . . .

Two-second delay. Obviously I have wasted . . . the earphone asked if I was going to attend the Great Debate.

I'm sorry?

"Our viewers are going to watch a debate between California and New York," the earphone enthused (a brightening of tone).

(California would be "represented" by Ms. Ariana Huffington, New York by Mr. Pete Hamill.)

You'd do better to stage a conversation between Duluth and El Paso.

The earphone paused for an awful moment (c.f. Bishop Proudie's wife, *Barchester Towers*, suspecting sarcasm) before leaping from my ear.

Americans have been promised—by God, by the Constitution of the United States, by Edna Ferber—that we shall enjoy liberty to pursue happiness. The pursuit constitutes what we have come to call the American Dream.

Americans feel disappointment so keenly because our optimism is so large and is so often insisted upon by historians. And so often justified by history. The stock market measures optimism. If you don't feel optimistic there must be something wrong with you. There are pills for disappointment.

The California Dream was a codicil to the American Dream, an opening. Internal immigrants sought from California at least a softer winter, a wider sky, at least a thousand miles' distance between themselves and whatever dissatisfaction they felt with "home."

Midwestern California, the California of internal immigrants, was everywhere apparent when I was growing up, in the nervous impulse to build and to live in a house that had never been lived in or died in; where the old lady never spilled milk, the dog never bit, the bully never lurked behind the elm tree; where widows and discomfited children never stared at the moon through runny glass, or listened to the wind at night. This California was created by newcomers from Illinois and Nebraska, and it shaped my life. This was California as America's America.

Simultaneous with Midwestern California was the California of Maxine Hong Kingston and William Saroyan, and my Mexican mother and father and my Indian relatives, a California of private family secrets, yes, unorthodox ingredients, turmeric, cilantro, Santa Maria Purisima, but also some surpassing relief at having found in California a blind from tragedy. The relief California offered immigrants from other countries was comparable to the imagined restoration of the Joads. Ours was a California far removed from the drama of Midwestern disappointment, from the all-new, and why-am-I-not happy?, though we lived next door to it, to Nebraska and Illinois.

Thus, in my lifetime, I experienced two Californias concurrently. I discovered (because I was attuned to) a sort of hybrid of these two Californias in the writings of John Muir. Muir was born in Scotland; he moved with his family to Wisconsin when he was 11. Muir saw California with a Midwesterner's delight in the refulgence of it—he called California "the grand side of the mountain." Yet I recognized in John Muir as well the quiet, grateful voice of the immigrant from overseas. Muir sailed into California. He first saw the coastline as if through Pacific eyes; he saw immediately the implication of the coastline: California (and America) is finite.

When I grew up in the 1950s, freeways offered freedom from implication. California was neurotically rebuilding itself as an ever rangier-house in a further-flung subdivision. As a loyal son of California, I believed in all this, in the "new" and the other "e-z" adjectives real estate agents employed to lure Midwesterners. And though the advertisement the real estate developer placed in the Midwestern newspaper was not a bluff, too many people believed, too many people came. The traffic on the freeway has slowed from Jetsons to "Now what?" to Sig-alert.

What is obsolete now in California is the future. For a century and a half Americans spoke of California as the future when they wanted to escape inevitability. Now the future attaches consequences and promises constriction. Technocrats in Sacramento warn of a future that is overwhelmed by students, pollution, immigrants, cars, fluorocarbons, old people. Or the future is diminished—water quality, soil quality, air quality, education quality, highway quality, life quality. There are not enough doctors for the state's emergency rooms, not enough blue parking spaces outside, not enough oil, not enough natural gas, not enough electricity. More blackouts, more brownouts, too many air-conditioners, too few houses, frogs on the verge of extinction, a fugitive middle class. A state without a white center. To the rest of the nation California now represents what the nation fears to become.

The brilliance of Midwestern California, the California that is founded upon discontent (and the reason why so much technological innovation springs from the West Coast), is that having confronted the finitude of the coastline, technologists in Silicon Valley have shrunk the needed commodity—the future (thousands of miles of Zen pathway)—to the size of a fleck of gold dust, to a microchip.

A few months ago, I went to have dinner in Menlo Park, where I met a young man who wore a linen jacket of the very blackest label and the scent of the winner's circle. He owns, very firmly owns, I imagine, on sheaves of legal-sized hardcopy, electronic portals (virtual) through which the most ephemeral chatter and the finest thoughts of humankind pass as undifferentiated "content." (I imagine Ensor's painting of *Christ's Entry Into Brussels* at the Getty.)

When I answered the young man's uninterested inquiry by identifying myself as a writer, his only response was to recommend I consign every published sentence I now guard with copyright onto the Web and give it away. No one owns an idea in this age, was his advice (and all of a sudden he sounded like someone one would have met on a riverboat). Except his idea, of course.

The young man's fortune comes, not from the "content" his technology conveys or conveys a quester toward, but rather from the means of conveyance—or, no, not even that. A sort of dock, is it? For swan boats. He will make more money by, at intervals, changing some aspect of conveyance or by padlocking the old portal (I imagine the Suez Canal) so that people have to pay to modify their means of access. He is set on weaning the minds of youth from the snares of merchandisers ("middlemen" he quaintly calls them). Young people are conveyed to the belief they should obtain intellectual property without paying for it, and without packaging. Packaging is sentimentality.

The young man is content to disassemble, by making "free," all intellectual property and factories of intellectual properties (recording studios, for example, or publishing houses), and all clearinghouses of intellectual properties (such as New York, such as Los Angeles), in order that he can charge more for his arch or his gondola or his Victorian bathing machine.

The technologist now publishes to the world that place is over. California used to be the summation of the expansionist dream; now we foretell constriction. The future has been condensed to the head of a pin. Not Go West, not even Go Home. Rather, stay at home. Run in place. You are still connected, whether you are in the air or on a train or never leave Wisconsin. The great invention—rather, the refinement—of Silicon Valley is portability.

For a long season, California was the most important purveyor of narrative to the world. Hollywood was filled with stories in the last century, stories bought and sold— more stories than anyone could listen to or use. When other lures to California were exhausted or quieted down, Hollywood became its own narrative, became the golden dream; people wanted, literally, "to get into the pictures."

Toward the end of dinner, the optimistic young man from Silicon Valley, having imbibed a liter or so of Napa Valley pish-posh '69, got around to his detestation of the congestion of California. In the end, it would appear, he has to live in a real body, in real space and in real time, and buckled into his hundred-thousand-dollar funk: "Traffic is a bitch every fucking morning."

. . . *When you get angry, get good and angry. Try to be alive. You will be dead soon enough.*

I, too, was an optimist. Well, I took Saroyan's pronouncement for optimism. Like many children of immigrant parents, Saroyan and I grew up among shadows, grotesque shadows thrown from a grandmother's stories, stories that might show us up as foreigners if they ever saw the light of day. How could the Saroyan boy not be beguiled in the direction of games and sunlight. And then limelight. And then Paris.

I saw him once, in a bookstore in San Francisco, a bookstore made of wood, now long gone. He dressed like a stage bohemian; he wore a walrus moustache, and a fedora hat, and his cashmere coat rested upon his shoulders. He threw back his head to bellow, by which gesture he represented mirth. He was entirely admirable and theatrical. Saroyan's literary persona remained that of a carefree bon vivant, at ease with the world and delighted by it, tasting, breathing, laughing like hell. He'd never be a Princeton man—but so what?

The legend: William Saroyan of Fresno, California, and Paris, France, was haunted by the early promise of himself. Critics withheld from the middle-aged man the praise they had once lavished on the youth. He was the same man. What gives? He became dark-minded and spiteful and stingy and mistrustful of friends and family and agents and stockbrokers and the IRS. The world smelled spoiled to him. He felt passed over by the world that mattered, the small, glittering, passing world.

The last time I was in Fresno, about a year ago, I gave a luncheon address at the African-American Cultural Center to a roomful of journalists from ethnic newspapers and radio and television stations, called, altogether, "New California Media." (The Pakistani radio station in San Diego. The Iranian television station in L.A. *The Oaxacan. The Mandarin.*) Everyone in the room spoke interestedly of a California that was crowded with voices, most of which they could not translate but they knew implicated them. No one knew what I was asking, when I asked where Saroyan had lived.

The question for the night is the question of content, I think, not conveyance. A new generation of writers in California will not speak of separate neighborhoods, certainly not of brown hills and dairy cows, or the taste of water from a hose, or the sound of train whistles at night. Nor will they dote on New York, as I doted on New York. Oh, maybe they will, why deny them that? Perhaps New York will be Shanghai.

In the time of your life, live, was Saroyan's advice. I believe the difference between the literature of California's past and the literature to come will be the difference of expectation. There are children growing up in California today who take it as a given that the 101 North, the 405 South, and the 10 East are unavailable after two in the afternoon.

Knowing Where You've Been

Robert L. Root, Jr.

The first afternoon. We head for the Blodgett Creek Trail. Our environmental writing workshop at the Teller Refuge takes up the mornings but leaves us the afternoons free, and the three of us are eager to get out into the Montana wilderness. We are midwestern flatlanders, all raised not far inland from the shores of the Great Lakes, though Ron has been a Montanan for nine years now. Waiting after lunch for someone who never shows up, we start out an hour later than we hoped. I drive the Refuge minivan and Linda navigates, directing me from Corvallis across the valley floor to Hamilton and into the foothills of the Bitterroot Mountains. Dirt roads take us gradually up out of pasture land into steep forest. We round a bend, cross Blodgett Creek, and park at the trailhead.

Blodgett Creek is swollen and foaming, a roar and blur of tumbling white water just beyond the trees along the trail. In mid-May western Montana is just beginning its second week of summer-like temperatures, and rapid snow melt generates swift, turbulent run-off. Farmers and ranchers in the Bitterroot Valley worry whether the supply of water will last the growing season.

We strangers, however, eagerly immerse ourselves in new terrain. We set off briskly from the trailhead and, in very little time, see canyon walls, sheer granite facing with jagged rims, emerge above the trees. The trail roughly parallels the creek, passing through narrow bands of ponderosa pine and larch that line its banks. Here the forest is hemmed in by the canyon's narrowness, its inhospitable granite walls, and thick layers of talus piled on the sides of the canyon floor. At a couple of places on the trail we skirt the limits of talus, looking up a forty-five degree angle across a vast slope of dark boulders that ends a third of the way up toward a sheer precipice. The canyon wall here is so solid and impervious that a channel-less white stream of snow melt merely slides down the stone face like hose water down a sidewalk.

We dawdle along the trail. Linda identifies the birds, Ron the flowers, trees, and shrubs; I can only nod appreciatively at each of their pronouncements, finding no rhetorical forms to point out in return. We stroll rather than hike, looking around us as we move. We pause to search for a winter wren or a varied thrush singing in the trees, to examine a ring of blue clematis or some alum root sax-ifrage rising from the mossy ground, to gaze at a bend in the creek where the overflow has created a calm backwater and the dark shape of a trout drifts through dapples of sunlight. At times we dance up the trail, straddling runoff, leaping from stone to stone, dry spot to damp spot, following the worn path of horses and hikers.

An hour into the walk conversation ebbs and we begin to hike more rapidly. The canyon floor widens and the trail veers away from the creek bed, still tracing the talus wall. Where the forest opens temporarily at a recent burn, Linda drops behind to write in her journal and return more slowly down the slope; Ron and I quicken our pace through the charred trees and flourishing ground cover. The rocky terrain demands more of our attention as we move. Ahead of us, some three miles up from the trailhead, a packbridge crosses the creek, and we set that milestone as our destination. We hike with uncertain urgency, knowing that soon we will have to start back to the workshop for evening events.

Sunday hikers coming down the trail greet us. We overtake a slow-moving family who tell us they have seen a moose three hundred yards back, close to the trail. The pack bridge is still perhaps half a mile ahead, but we turn back, search-ing the brush for the moose we had overlooked in our rush upward. When we find her, she is lying down behind a log, her long dark head raised just into our view, her large ears scanning the sounds around her. The trail is still on rocky ground, but the moose is twenty yards away amidst a floor of rich green grass spreading among widely-spaced Douglas firs from the slope to the creek. For a few minutes we stand silently, watching her ostentatiously ignore us. Turning back to find her has inadvertently been decisive. By unspoken agreement we hurry back down the trail.

Returning toward the trailhead, I see only the forest ahead of me and occa-sionally the craggy rim of the canyon emerging on either side. Soon we are in the trees again. I wonder how close we came to the pack bridge, what we might have seen of Blodgett Canyon as we looked back at the Bitterroot Valley crossing the creek, and I find my appetite for the mountains sharpened, not sated, by the hike.

"When you look back at where you have been," Norman Maclean writes, "it often seems as if you have never been there or even as if there were no such place." In his story "USFS 1919: The Logger, the Cook, and the Hole in the Sky," the narra-tor has paused at the top of a divide, reflecting on where he has been and where he is going. Where he has been is Idaho, at a U.S. Forest Service camp, and more particularly at a lookout tower on Grave Peak; where he is going is Hamilton, in Montana, on the other side of the Bitterroot Mountains, his summer job ended. The distance is thirty-four miles, "fourteen miles up and fourteen miles down with five or six miles still left to go." He intends to walk it in a single day.

Beginning in a mountain meadow he climbs toward gray cliffs that eventu-ally will place him higher than the mountain goats he spots in the distance; along the way he spooks a bull moose on the trail. On the divide, after marking his own version of the state line in urine, he locates Grave Peak. "From the divide the mountain I had lived on was bronze sculpture. It was all shape with nothing on it, just nothing. It was just color and shape and sky." He muses, "So perhaps at a certain perspective what we leave behind is often wonderland, always different from what it was and generally more beautiful."

From the top of the divide, looking into Blodgett Canyon, he recognizes its glacial orgins. "Coming at me from almost straight below was a Jacob's ladder of switchbacks, rising out of what I later discovered geologists call a cirque but what to me looked like the original nest of a green coiled glacier." He plunges down the Montana side of the divide, cutting straight across the switchbacks, little avalanches following his path. From the bottom of the basin he follows Blodgett Creek to the mouth of the canyon and trudges the remaining five or six miles to Hamilton.

When I told a friend from Montana that I would be spending a week in the Bitterroot Valley, he referred me immediately to Maclean's story and urged me to hike in the canyon. On the flight west I read the story. Disappointed in its lack of detail about the canyon (it really isn't a hiking story, after all) and immediately aware that I wouldn't have time to trek the fourteen miles to Blodgett Pass, I nonetheless checked the trail in a Bitterroots guide and, before the plane had reached Montanan airspace, set myself that goal of reaching the pack bridge.

Now, as I came away from the canyon, pleased with my companions and energized by the experience of the trail, I realized that I was disappointed, and I struggled to figure out why. Perhaps it had to do with not reaching the pack bridge,—with failing to achieve a relatively simple destination—but I wasn't certain why that mattered. Perhaps I hoped to have looked around me and somehow recognized the canyon, discovered the distant switchbacks and the rim of the pass. Perhaps I had hoped that standing on the pack bridge would have placed me so I could see where I had been, where I could be going. While Linda and Ron talked in the van, I tried to remember the words to the children's song about the bear going over the mountain, "to see what he could see." I identified with that bear. As far as I had gone, I still hadn't come away with a sense of knowing where I had been.

The second afternoon. We mill around after the morning workshop, plans shifting, destinations uncertain, finally resolving to go back into the mountains, to another trail. Though eight of us are going, we are all "environmental writers" (by official designation of the Institute) and tend to go to wilderness for solitude, not companionship. At the trailhead, people plan to drop out or stay behind, and the progress up the Mill Creek Trail spreads us out and separates us. Some start out slowly and fall to the rear; others keep on far enough to separate themselves from those behind, then slow down to let those ahead go on without them.

Mill Creek is only a few miles north of Blodgett Creek, descending at the easternmost point of the promontory between Blodgett Canyon and the next canyon north. After a short stretch in open forest, the terrain is often rocky. The forest is dense and broad on either side of the stream, unrestrained by canyon walls. A mile or so along the trail we cross to the north side of the creek on a solid double-log bridge and find ourselves moving parallel to the creek but often away from its banks, intermittently but persistently climbing. Not far beyond the bridge the group is reduced to Ron, Jeff, and me. We begin to push ourselves to reach the falls a couple more miles ahead, making it harder on ourselves by talking about writing most of the way without slackening our pace.

For a little while we parallel sheer canyon walls but soon we are deep into the forest. The walking is easier than in Blodgett Canyon, the terrain more varied, the forest seemingly older, denser. Within a couple miles of the log bridge, past a large boulder and a big wooden sign, we enter the Selway-Bitterroot National Wilderness. Soon the trail steepens and repeatedly winds away from the creek until a final loop brings it closer again. The creek's continuous rumble becomes a roar. Through the trees we can see the foaming waters of the falls and follow the trail up to an opening in the forest near the top.

Beyond the clearing the ground rises sharply again and ahead of us the trail disappears back into forest, but this rounded hump of basalt is covered shallowly with only lichens, wildflowers, and low grasses. Near the creek nothing grows except for a few stunted pines; most of the rock is naked and exposed, shaved clean by plummeting snow melt. Upstream the forest closes in tightly on the creek bed; below the falls the creek is all foamy billows of whitewater slicing through towering forests of ponderosa pine and Douglas fir; across the stream, on the south bank, the trees are thick, impenetrable. Only on the north bank of the falls is the rock swept clean and the surface open to the sun.

We take our time surveying the falls, moving slowly up and down its rock face to consider it from above and below, all the while inundated by the sound of mountain water. As falls go this one is neither majestic nor exceptional, angling down sixty to eighty feet or so rather than plunging vertically from the lip of a precipice. Swollen with snow melt, its foam as white as the snowpack that feeds it, the creek plummets over rugged terraces and outcroppings. We feel its wild power and stand smiling in the spray and the sound, respectful of its reckless turbulence.

The roar makes conversation difficult but Jeff and Ron survey the plant life away from the brink and we each independently declare a desire to camp on the level ground across the clearing. Someone wonders where the trail goes, and I look longingly at the point where it reenters the forest and disappears. The wall of trees prevents us from knowing where we might have gone and, aware that we have overstayed, we turn back toward where we have been to head down the mountainside toward the trailhead and the rest of our party. Our retreat is so swift that I don't notice when I can no longer hear the thunder of the falls and our pace allows me no time to look back.

When I asked my friend from Montana about places to hike in the Bitterroot Valley, he looked thoughtful for a moment, shook his head, and said, "Well, as early as you're going, there'll be too much snow to bag a peak." I laughed and assured him that "bagging a peak" wasn't a priority with me. But the term tended to stay with me on the trip, especially as I trudged along the flat farm roads of the Teller Refuge where the snow-capped peaks of the Bitterroot Range punctuated the horizon. After our return from the Mill Creek Trail, when someone asked me later in the day if I had been "one of the *men* who had gone for distance" on the trail, I thought again about the concept of bagging a peak.

We'd come back to the Mill Creek Trailhead to find the van gone and a note promising that someone would return for us. No doubt we'd delayed people eager to get back to the Refuge, and those who'd stopped along the way had returned to the trailhead with a sense of accomplishment and completion far sooner than we had. If they had been waiting for us, we owed them apologies. But I really couldn't accept the implicit gender explanation for our approach to the hike—after all, I knew from reading their essays that some of the women in the Environmental Writing Institute had had far more arduous adventures than I was ever likely to attempt. The only peaks I've "bagged" not only have not been hard to reach but also were ascended for the view rather than for distance or height.

But the Mill Creek Falls hadn't been a peak, after all, and its distance had only been a few miles. Though I knew what *hadn't* moved me to reach the falls, I wasn't certain what *had*, or why it felt so good to have been there.

The final afternoon. The morning workshop over, the group disperses for various tours and activities. Ron, Valerie, and I meet Janine Benyus and her father, Doug, who both live in the Bitterroot Valley. Janine, whose *Northwoods Wildlife Guide* I value, has volunteered to take workshoppers hiking. Somehow I expect a leisurely excursion and don't bother to change out of sneakers. Although her plan had been to take us to either Blodgett or Mill Creek, when she learns that Ron and I have been to both, she opts for the Bear Creek Overlook Trail instead, a change from creek-bed habitat, a promise of a vista.

Janine drives the minivan to the trailhead, pointing out from the highway the shoulder of the mountain where the Bear Creek Overlook is located. We climb the foothills on back roads threading through pasture lands, then swing onto a twisting, narrow, shoulderless dirt road, an eighty-degree grade sloping away from it. In the front passenger seat my attention is divided between Janine's conversation and the slope we lean toward with every other lurch of the vehicle. Doug Benyus recounts hitting a patch of ice on otherwise dry road a few weeks earlier and plunging over the edge in a Toyota Four-Runner; luckily he had hit a tree a little ways past the edge and was able to back up the slope and continue down the road. Father and daughter tell of other switchback terrors as we ride, but Janine doesn't slow down. I tell myself she knows how to drive these roads better than I, and remind myself to sit in the back on the way down.

The trailhead is an open area on the side of the mountain, with the valley floor a couple thousand feet below, spread out in a gray haze not thick enough to obscure the distant outline of the Sapphire Mountains across the valley. We set out hiking easily through open forest. Lodgepole pines tower above us; the forest floor is carpeted with needles. The wide trail follows a series of switchbacks that take us rapidly up the mountainside with little need for the attentive footing that the creek trails demanded. The day is warm, the mountain breezes refreshing, and our progress consistent. We pause from time to time when Janine draws our attention to some element of the habitat—dwarf mistletoe sprouting from a limb of lodgepole pine, its seeds released by an inner "spring" that fires it fifty feet into the forest, to stick to another tree or be transported on the feathers of the bird that triggered its release; the activity of pitch beetles that bore into pines and, through a symbiotic relationship with bacteria in their mouths and their own excavating, girdle a tree and plug its channels of sap until the tree dies; a blue grouse spooked by Doug Benyus's hound, Barney, fluttering out of reach into a spruce and perching, immobile, waiting for us to lose sight of her. The Benyuses instruct us through a genial symbiosis, feeding each other questions, volunteering each other's information.

Less than halfway up the trail we discover patches of snow across the path. The trees change to spruce and Douglas fir. We look for blazed tree trunks more frequently now, as the trail disappears beneath the snow for longer and longer stretches. Finally, an hour or so into the trail, we reach a turn of a switchback and see an unbroken field of snow stretching through the trees. Janine tells us that it will be mostly snow the rest of the way, and gives us the option of struggling up the slope or turning back and looking for a creekbed. Valerie votes for turning back. Ron and I make noises about not caring either way until the possibility of turning back becomes too real; then we admit to wanting to continue to the overlook. We have seen creek beds, we say, and Valerie urges us to go on while she meanders back.

We are all in tee-shirts, Janine and Ron in shorts, but are kept warm by exertion as we cross the snow. We slip with every step as it gives way beneath us. Often we find ourselves postholing across the snow, sinking in past our ankles, sometimes up to our knees. On separate occasions Janine and I each strike a pocket of air beneath the snow, where it has covered a fallen tree, and plunge in up to our crotches with one leg while the other slips across firmer footing. The icy granules of snow soak through my sneakers and socks and I grumble to myself about my lack of planning until I realize that my hiking boots too would have eventually succumbed to wetness.

It takes us longer than we hoped to reach the crest. The terrain opens up, the trees more stunted and sparse than at lower levels, the snow ranging in ever larger fields. Suddenly we emerge onto the base of a rocky ridge. The timbers of a collapsed line cabin or watch tower poke through a deep covering of empacked snow. Rising above the ridge is a barren crag with contorted shapes of scrub around its base; through the trees on the top of the ridge I look across at a snowy peak dotted with scruffy trees, extending another thousand feet or more above us. The way to the top of the crag is rough and tricky, along precipices and across barren, lichen-free basalt. The west side of our mountain is almost vertical, nearly devoid of plant life except for occasional pioneers jutting from scanty toe-holds in the cliff face. But from that exposed peninsula of rock the three valleys of Bear Creek open out to us.

Directly to the west the South Fork of Bear Creek runs down the center of the valley, lush and green and thickly carpeted with conifers. From where we stand we can see the mountains beyond the valley, the distant sources of Bear Creek's water. To the northwest is another valley, another fork of the creek, that we can trace glinting through the trees until it divides into two more streams, the Middle and North Forks, each descending its own valley. The trees thin out along the slopes of these valleys, turn darker the higher up they go, until they are only random silhouettes against ever-broadening snowfields. All the peaks around us are snow-covered, as must be the peak of the mountain upon whose shoulder we stand.

We are viewing classic glacial terrain. Empty white basins of snow identify cirques, the glacial bowls that will become Bryan Lake and Bear Lake by the end of summer. Above and around them are weathered horns and aretes, the peaks that formed them and the ridges that hold them in place; the valleys extending from the cirques take the wide U-shape of the glaciers that carved them. Directly below us the merged forks of Bear Creek produce a wide foaming cataract rushing snow melt and glacial debris toward the outwash plains that form part of the foothills.

Janine tells us that, when the Pacific plate pushed under the North American plate, it raised the mountains of the Idaho Batholith to a point where the mountaintops became unstable and slid off to the east, creating the broad level plain that would become the Bitterroot Valley (itself later scoured by glaciers) and ending up as the Sapphire Mountains. From this crag we can see beyond the Sapphires to spires of the Garnet Range and the Continental Divide near Anaconda. We can also see a long way toward the beginning of time.

I slowly scan it all with my binoculars. I know that I could sit for hours minutely surveying those valleys and still not feel I had taken them in. Nonetheless I feel myself smiling all the while, feel myself stirred and moved by everything around me. It isn't just the beauty, though it is transcendently beautiful, and it certainly isn't the distance, because everything around us reminds us of how much further we could go. It isn't how far at all but how deep.

That's it. That's the epiphany that dispells my uncertainty about my motives on these hikes. That's what I've been pursuing after all. I simply need to go as deeply into wilderness as it takes before the wilderness comes into me. Sometimes you need to go as deeply as possible where you've never been to reach a place you recognize at once, recognize entirely. That's where I find myself in the Bitterroots.

We stand there a while longer, reveling in arrival. When we finally, reluctantly, turn to descend, I don't need to look back to know where I've been.

Cloud Crossing

Scott Russell Sanders

Clouds are temporary creatures. So is the Milky Way, for that matter, if you take the long entropic view of things. I awake on a Saturday in mid-October with the ache of nightmares in my brain, as if I have strained a muscle in my head. Just a week before I turn thirty-three, just a month before my son turns one, I do not need physics or nightmares to remind me that we also are temporary creatures.

Baby Jesse is changing cloud-fast before my eyes. His perky voice begins pinning labels on dogs and bathtubs and sun. When I say, "Want to go for a walk?" on this morning that began with nightmares of entropy, he does not crawl towards me as he would have done only a few days ago. He tugs himself upright with the help of a chair, then staggers toward me like a refugee crossing the border, arms outstretched, crowing, "Wa! Wa!"

So I pack baby and water and graham crackers into the car, and drive thirty miles southeast of Eugene, Oregon, to a trailhead on Hardesty Mountain. There are several hiking paths to the top, ranging in length from one mile to six. I choose the shortest, because I will be carrying Jesse's twenty-two pounds on my back. I have not come here to labor, to be reminded of my hustling heart. I have come to watch clouds.

Markers on the logging road tell us when we drive up past 2,500 feet, then 2,750 and 3,000. Around 3,250 the Fiat noses through the first vapors, great wrinkled slabs of clouds that thicken on the windshield. In the back seat Jesse strains against his safety harness, his hands fisted on the window, hungry to get out there into that white stuff. I drive the last few hundred yards to the trailhead with lights on, in case we meet a car groping its way down the mountain.

Beside a wooden sign carved to announce HARDESTY MOUNTAIN TRAIL, I park the Fiat with its muzzle downhill, so we can coast back to the highway after our walk in case the weary machine refuses to start. I lean the backpack against the bumper and guide Jesse's excited feet through the leg-holes, one of his calves in each of my hands. "Wa! Wa!" he cries, and almost tips the pack over into

254

the sorrel dust of the logging road. Shouldering the pack requires acrobatic balancing, to keep him from tumbling out while I snake my arms through the straps. Once safely aloft, assured of a ride, he jounces so hard in the seat that I stagger a few paces with the same drunken uncertainty he shows in his own walking.

Clouds embrace us. Far overhead, between the fretted crowns of the Douglas fir, I see hints of blue. Down here among the roots and matted needles, the air is mist. My beard soon grows damp; beads glisten on my eyelashes. A few yards along the trail a Forest Service board, with miniature roof to protect its messages, informs us we are at 3,600 feet and must hike to 4,237 in order to reach the top of Hardesty. Since I came to see the clouds, not to swim in them, I hope we are able to climb above them into that tantalizing blue.

On my back Jesse carries on a fierce indecipherable oration concerning the wonders of this ghostly forest. Giddy with being outside and aloft, he drums on my head, yanks fistfuls of my hair. Every trunk we pass tempts him more strongly than the apple tree could ever have tempted Eve and Adam. He lurches from side to side, outstretched fingers desperate to feel the bark. I pause at a mammoth stump to let him touch. Viewed up close, the bark looks like a contour map of the Badlands, an eroded landscape where you might expect to uncover fossils. While Jesse traces the awesome ridges and fissures, I squint to read another Forest Service sign. No motorized vehicles, it warns, and no pack animals.

I surely qualify as a pack animal. For long spells in my adult life, while moving house or humping rucksacks onto trains or hauling firewood, I have felt more like a donkey than anything else. I have felt most like a beast of burden when hauling my two children, first Eva and now Jesse. My neck and shoulders never forget their weight from one portage to another. And I realize that carrying Jesse up the mountain to see clouds is a penance as well as a pleasure—penance for the hours I have sat glaring at my typewriter while he scrabbled mewing outside my door, penance for the thousands of things my wife has not been able to do on account of my word mania, penance for all the countless times I have told daughter Eva "no, I can't; I am writing." I know the rangers did not have human beasts in mind when they posted their sign, yet I am content to be a pack animal, saddled with my crowing son.

As I resume walking, I feel a tug. Jesse snaps a chunk of bark from the stump and carries it with him, to examine at leisure. Beneath one of the rare cottonwoods I pick up a leathery golden leaf, which I hand over my shoulder to the baby, who clutches it by the stem and turns it slowly around, tickling his nose with the starpoints. The leaf is a wonder to him, and therefore also to me. Everything he notices, every pebble, every layered slab of bark, is renewed for me. Once I carried Eva outside, in the first spring of her life, and a gust of wind caught her full in the face. She blinked, and then gazed at the invisible breath as if it were a flight of angels streaming past. Holding her in the crook of my arm that day, I rediscovered wind.

Fascinated by his leaf, Jesse snuggles down in the pack and rides quietly. My heart begins to dance faster as the trail zigzags up the mountain through a series of switchbacks. Autumn has been dry in Oregon, so the dirt underfoot is powdery. Someone has been along here inspecting mushrooms. The discarded ones litter the trail like blackening pancakes. Except for the path, worn raw by deer and hikers, the floor of the woods is covered with moss. Fallen wood is soon hidden by the creeping emerald carpet, the land burying its own dead. Limegreen moss clings fuzzily to the upright trunks and dangles in fluffy hanks from limbs, like freshly dyed wool hung out to dry. A wad of it caught in the fist squeezes down to nothing.

A lurch from the backpack tells me that Jesse has spied some new temptation in the forest. Craning around, I see his spidery little hands reaching for the sky. Then I also look up, and notice the shafts of light slanting down through the treetops. The light seems substantial, as if made of glass, like the rays of searchlights that carve up the night sky to celebrate a store's opening or a war's end. "Light," I say to Jesse. "Sunlight. We're almost above the clouds." Wherever the beams strike, they turn cobwebs into jeweled diagrams, bracelet limbs with rhinestones of dew. Cloud vapors turn to smoke.

The blue glimpsed between trees gradually thickens, turns solid, and we emerge onto a treeless stony ridge. Clear sky above, flotillas of clouds below, mountains humping their dark green backs as far as I can see. The sight of so many slick backs arching above the clouds reminds me of watching porpoises from a ship in the Gulf of Mexico. Vapors spiral up and down between cloud layers as if on escalators. Entire continents and hemispheres and galaxies of mist drift by. I sit on the trail with backpack propped against a stone ledge, to watch this migration.

No peace for meditation with an eleven-month-old on your back. An ache in my shoulders signals that Jesse, so near the ground, is leaning out of the pack to capture something. A pebble or beetle to swallow? A stick to gnaw? Moss, it turns out, an emerald hunk of it ripped from the rockface. "Moss," I tell him, as he rotates this treasure about three inches in front of his eyes. "Here, feel," and I stroke one of his palms across the velvety clump. He tugs the hand free and resumes his private exploration. This independence grows on him these days faster than his hair.

"Clouds," I tell him, pointing out into the gulf of air. Jesse glances up, sees only vagueness where I see a ballet of shapes, and so he resumes his scrutiny of the moss. "Not to eat," I warn him. When I check on him again half a minute later, the moss is half its former size and his lips are powdered with green. Nothing to do but hoist him out of the pack, dig what I can from his mouth, then plop him back in, meanwhile risking spilling both of us down the mountainside. A glance down the dizzying slope reminds me of my wife's warning, that I have no business climbing this mountain alone with a baby. She's right, of course. But guilt, like the grace of God, works in strange ways, and guilt drives me up here among the skittery rocks to watch clouds with my son.

"Let Daddy have it," I say, teasing the hunk of moss from his hand. "Have a stick, pretty stick." While he imprints the stick with the marks of his teeth, four above and two below, I spit on the underside of the moss and glue it back down to the rock. Grow, I urge it. Looking more closely at the rockface, I see that it is crumbling beneath roots and weather, sloughing away like old skin. The entire mountain is migrating, not so swiftly as the clouds, but just as surely, heading grain by grain to the sea.

Jesse seems to have acquired some of the mountain's mass as I stand upright again and hoist his full weight. With the stick he idly swats me on the ear.

The trail carries us through woods again, then up along a ridge to the clearing at the top of Hardesty Mountain. There is no dramatic feeling of expansiveness, as there is on some peaks, because here the view is divvied up into modest sweeps by Douglas firs, cottonwoods, great gangling heaps of briars. The forest has laid siege to the rocky crest, and will abolish the view altogether before Jesse is old enough to carry his own baby up here. For now, by moving from spot to spot on the summit, I can see in all directions. What I see mostly are a few thousand square miles of humpbacked mountains looming through the clouds. Once in Ohio I lived in a valley which the Army Corps of Engineers thought would make a convenient bed for a reservoir. So the Mahoning River was dammed, and as the waters backed up in that valley, covering everything but the highest ridges, drowning my childhood, they looked very much like these clouds poured among the mountains.

"Ba! Ba!" Jesse suddenly bellows, leaping in his saddle like a bronco rider.

Bath, I wonder? Bed? Bottle? Ball? He has been prolific of B-words lately, and their tail-ends are hard to tell apart. Ball, I finally decide, for there at the end of the arrow made by his arm is the moon, a chalky peachpit hanging down near the horizon. "Moon," I say.

"Ba! Ba!" he insists.

Let it stay a ball for a while, something to play catch with, roll across the linoleum. His sister's first sentence was, "There's the moon." Her second was, "Want it, Daddy." So began her astronomical yearnings, my astronomical failures. She has the itch for space flight in her, my daughter does. Jesse is still too much of a pup for me to say whether he has caught it.

We explore the mountaintop while the ocean of cloud gradually rises. There are charred rings from old campfires. In a sandy patch, red-painted bricks are laid in the shape of a letter A. Not large enough to be visible from airplanes. If Hardesty Mountain were in a story by Hawthorne, of course, I could use the scarlet A to accuse it of some vast geological harlotry. If this were a folklore mountain, I could explain the letter as an alphabetical inscription left by giants. But since this is no literary landscape, I decide that the bricks formed the foundation for some telescope or radio transmitter or other gizmo back in the days when this summit had a lookout tower.

Nearby is another remnant from those days, a square plank cover for a cistern. The boards are weathered to a silvery sheen, with rows of rustblackened nailheads marking the joints. Through a square opening at the center of the planks I catch a glint. Water? Still gathering here after all these years? Leaning over the hole, one boot on the brittle planks, I see that the glint is from a tin can. The cistern is choked with trash.

At the very peak, amid a jumble of rocks, we find nine concrete piers that once supported the fire tower. By squatting down beside one of those piers I can rest Jesse's weight on the concrete, and relieve the throb in my neck. I imagine the effort of hauling enough materials up this mountain to build a tower. Surely they used horses, or mules. Not men with backpacks. So what became of the tower when the Forest Service, graduated to spotter planes, no longer needed it? Did they pry out every nail and carry the boards back down again? A glance at the ground between my feet supplies the answer. Wedged among the rocks, where rains cannot wash them away, are chunks of glass, some of them an inch thick. I pick up one that resembles a tongue, about the size for a cocker spaniel. Another one, a wad of convolutions, might be a crystalline brain. Peering up through it at the sun, I see fracture lines and tiny bubbles. Frozen in the seams where one molten layer lapped onto another there are ashes. Of course they didn't dismantle the tower and lug its skeleton down the mountain. They waited for a windless day after a drenching rain and they burned it.

The spectacle fills me: the mountain peak like a great torch, a volcano, the tower heaving on its nine legs, the windows bursting from the heat, tumbling among the rocks, fusing into molten blobs, the glass taking on whatever shape it cooled against.

There should be nails. Looking closer I find them among the shards of glass, sixteen-penny nails mostly, what we called spikes when I was building houses. Each one is somber with rust, but perfectly straight, never having been pried from wood. I think of the men who drove those nails—the way sweat stung in their eyes, the way their forearms clenched with every stroke of the hammer—and I wonder if any of them were still around when the tower burned. The Geological Survey marker, a round lead disk driven into a rock beside one of the piers, is dated 1916. Most likely the tower already stood atop the mountain in that year. Most likely the builders are all dead by now.

So on its last day the Hardesty fire tower became a fire tower in earnest. Yesterday I read that two American physicists shared the Nobel Prize for discovering the background radiation left over from the Big Bang, which set our universe in motion some fifteen billion years ago. Some things last—not forever, of course, but for a long time—things like radiation, like bits of glass. I gather a few of the nails, some lumps of glass, a screw. Stuffing these shreds of evidence in my pocket, I discover the graham cracker in its wrapping of cellophane, and I realize I have not thought of Jesse for some minutes, have forgotten that he is riding me. That can mean only one thing. Sure enough, he is asleep, head scrunched down into the pack. Even while I peek at him over my shoulder he is changing, neurons hooking up secret connections in his brain, calcium swelling his bones as mud gathers in river deltas.

Smell warns me that the clouds have reached us. Looking out, the only peaks I can see are the Three Sisters, each of them a shade over 10,000 feet. Except for those peaks and the rocks where I stand, everything is cotton. There are no more clouds to watch, only Cloud, unanimous whiteness, an utter absence of shape. A panic seizes me—the same panic I used to feel as a child crossing the street when approaching cars seemed to have my name written on their grills. Suddenly the morning's nightmare comes back to me: everything I know is chalked upon a blackboard, and, while I watch, a hand erases every last mark.

Terror drives me down the Hardesty trail, down through vapors that leach color from the ferns, past trees that are dissolving. Stumps and downed logs lose their shape, merge into the clouds. The last hundred yards of the trail I jog. Yet Jesse never wakes until I haul him out of the pack and wrestle him into the car harness. His bellowing defies the clouds, the creeping emptiness. I bribe him with sips of water, a graham cracker, a song. But nothing comforts him, or comforts me, as we drive down the seven graveled miles of logging road to the highway. There we sink into open space again. The clouds are a featureless gray overhead.

As soon as the wheels are ringing beneath us on the blacktop, Jesse's internal weather shifts, and he begins one of his calm babbling orations, contentedly munching his cracker. The thread of his voice slowly draws me out of the annihilating ocean of whiteness. "Moon," he is piping from the back seat, "moon, moon!"

My Father Always Said

Mimi Schwartz

For years I heard the same line: "In Rindheim,[1] you didn't do such things!" It was repeated whenever the American world of his daughters took my father by surprise. Sometimes it came out softly, in amusement, as when I was a Pilgrim turkey in the P.S. 3 Thanksgiving play. But usually, it was a red-faced, high-blood-pressure shout—especially when my sister, Ruth, became "pinned" to Mel from Brooklyn or I wanted to go with friends whose families he didn't know.

"But they're Jewish," I'd say, since much of our side of Forest Hills was. The eight lanes of Queens Boulevard divided the Jews, Irish, and Italians pushing out of Brooklyn, the Bronx, and Manhattan from the old guard WASPs of Forest Hills Gardens. No Jews or Catholics over there—except for a few blocks near the Forest Hills Tennis Stadium where, from fifth grade on, we kids all went to watch what is now the U.S. Tennis Open, our end-of-summer ritual before school.

"You're not going," my father would announce before all such rituals.

"But everybody's going."

It was the wrong argument to make to a man who fled Hitler's Germany because of everybody. But I couldn't know that because he rarely talked about *that* Germany, only about his idyllic Rindheim where everybody (as opposed to the everybody I knew) did everything right. If my friends didn't have an aunt, grandmother, or great grandfather originally from Rindheim or vicinity, they were suspect. They could be anybody, which is exactly why I liked them—not like the Weil kids whose mother was "a born Tannhauser," as if that were a plus.

"I don't care about everybody!" my father would shout (that was his second favorite line); but it was a losing battle for him. My sister smoked at fifteen, I wore lipstick at twelve; we hung out at Penn Drug after Friday night basketball games

---

[1] I've changed the name, but all else is true.

with friends who were third-generation Brooklyn and Rumania—and didn't give a hoot that "In Rindheim, you didn't do such things!"

The irony of those words was inchoate—even to him, I realize now—until we went back to his village to visit the family graves. I was thirteen; it was eight years after World War II ended, and my father wanted to show me where his family had lived for generations, trading cattle. He wanted me, the first American-born in the family, to understand that "Forest Hills, Queens is not the world" (his third favorite line). A hard task to tackle, but my father was tough, a survivor who had led his whole clan, like Moses, out of Nazi Germany and into Queens, New York. He was ready for an American teen-age me.

"So Mimi-a-la, this is Rindheim!" my father boomed as the forest opened upon a cluster of fifty or so red-peaked houses set into the hillside of a tiny, green valley. We had driven for hours through what looked like Hansel and Gretel country, filled with foreboding evergreens that leaned over the narrow, winding roads of the *Schwarzwald*. Even the name, *Schwarzwald*, which meant Black Forest, gave me the creeps after being weaned on Nazi movies at the Midway Theater on 71st Avenue; but I was optimistic. Life here did look prettier than in Queens.

We drove up a rutted main street and stopped before a crumbling stone house with cow dung in the yard. "This was *our* house!" my father announced, as I watched horse flies attacking the dung, not just in *our* yard but in every yard on Eelinger Weg. And there were cows and chickens walking in front of our rented car. What a bust! My mother at least came from a place with sidewalks (we had driven by her old house in Stuttgart, sixty kilometers north, before coming here). My father, I decided at once, was a hick. All his country hero adventures about herding cows with a book hidden in one pocket and his mother's home-baked raspberry *linzertorte* in the other were discounted by two cows chewing away in stalls where I expected a car to be.

A stooped, old man with thick jowls and a feathered leather cap came out of the house with a big smile and a vigorous handshake for my dad who, looking squeezed in his pin-striped suit, nodded now and then and looked polite, but did not smile back.

"*Sind Sie nicht ein Loewengart, vielleicht Julius oder Artur?*" The man jabbered on, and my mother translated. He was Herr Schmidt, the blacksmith, and recognized my dad at once. "Aren't you a Loewengart, maybe Julius or Arthur?" This man had bought the family house in 1935 from Uncle Julius, the last of my family to leave Rindheim, and was remembering how my father and his brothers, Sol and Julius, used to play in his shop—with all his tools. "*Eine nette Familie, sehr nette,*" ("A fine family, very fine") he kept saying.

I understood nothing because I had learned no German in our house in Queens. When my father reached Ellis Island, he announced that our family would not speak the language of those who drove them out of Germany. Which was fine with me. It was embarrassing enough in those days to have parents who, for all my coaching, couldn't stop saying '*fader*' and '*moder*' to my American-born friends.

The man beckoned us towards my dad's old house, but my father shook his head, *"Nein, Danke!"* and backed us quickly away. I wanted to go in and see his old room; but my father did not. It would be forty years before I'd follow Frau Hummel, the blacksmith's daughter, up the narrow, dark stairs to a loft with two windows like cannon holes and search the heavy low beams for my dad's initials—A. L.—carved in the worn, smooth wood.

"And here's my downtown! No Penn Drugstore to hang around here!" my Dad said cheerfully, as we drove past four buildings leaning together like town drunks. "And here's where Grunwald had his kosher butcher shop and Zundorfer, his dry goods. And here's the *Gasthaus Kaiser*! We Jews had wonderful *Purim* and *Shuvuott* dances here—with green branches and ferns and pink flowers, like marbles in the candlelight. . . ." I could picture Mr. Grundwald—he sold sausages in Queens—but I couldn't picture my big-bellied, bald-headed Dad dancing, a kid like me.

We turned into an alley and stopped next to a gray building with stone columns in the doorway and corners decorated with what looked like railroad ties set into stone. I wouldn't have noticed it tucked among the houses.

"Here's where we spent every Friday night," my father said, getting us out of the car to look at the old synagogue. He pointed to a Hebrew inscription carved onto a stone plaque above the doorway: "How great is God's house and the doorway to Heaven," he translated haltingly in his rusty Hebrew. Right below the stone plaque was a wooden beam with another inscription, this one in German. It said the same thing, my father said, but it was new. He'd never seen it before.

I found out later that the German inscription had been added in 1952, the year before we came. That's when the Jewish synagogue was converted into the Protestant Evangelical Church to accommodate Eastern Germans who, fleeing the Russian troops late in World War II, resettled into the empty Jewish houses of this Catholics/Jewish village. Keeping the same words on the doorway inscription was meant as a tribute of respect: that this building was still God's house. But the 250 Rindheim Jews who had fled to America and Israel were never grateful. Their beautiful synagogue was no more; that's what counted.

"Well, at least it didn't become a gymnasium or a horse stable, like in other villages," the mayor's wife told me huffily in 1993 when I returned to Rindheim on my own. Two other villagers nodded vigorously, but a lively woman, who said she used to live next door to my great uncle, said, *"Na Ja,* I wouldn't be so happy if our Catholic church became a mosque—and believe me, we have plenty of Turks here . . ."

" . . . They are our new Jews," someone interjected.

" . . . *Na Ja,*" the lively woman shrugged and continued, "and I wouldn't feel good just because the Moslems said our church was still God's house."

They pointed out "the Moslems," four men squatting around a table and sipping Turkish coffee in a terraced yard below the synagogue. Many came, according to the lively woman, in the the 1960s as guest workers from Turkey and Afghanistan and now made up twenty percent of Rindheim. These men lived in the old *Gasthaus Kaiser*, where my father danced at *Purim* Festivals and where my Aunt Hilda and family once lived above the restaurant. This village is more like Forest Hills than you thought, Dad, I told myself, wishing he were around to discuss these ironies of migration. (The Forest Hills Gardens of my childhood is now owned by wealthy Asians and our block on 110th Street is now filled with Iranians.)

My father loosened his tie and wiped beads of sweat from his forehead with a checkered handkerchief. "And if you weren't in your synagogue by sundown on Friday, and not a minute later, *and* all day on Saturday, you were fined, a disgrace to your family. Three stars had to shine in the evening sky before *Shabbat* (the Sabbath) was over and you could go home."

I thought of his fury whenever I wanted to go bowling on Saturday at Foxy's Alley where all the boys hung out. Not that my father went to synagogue in Queens. The most religious he got, as far as I could see, was to play his record of Jan Pierce singing the *Kol Nidre* on *Yom Kippur*, the day of repentance. And he fasted—which I tried once or twice but got hungry when my mother ate a bagel. She never fasted.

The sun was high, the car seat sticky on my thighs, so I happily sat in the shade of four tall, arched windows which someone had been fixing. But my mother was heading for the car, saying she didn't like standing in the open where everyone could see us. We should go. In fact, she would have skipped Germany altogether and stayed in Belgium with my sister who had married a Belgian Jew (instead of Mel from Brooklyn); but my father insisted that we make this pilgrimage.

"Aren't we going inside?" I asked when my father started to follow my mother. He was usually the leader on everything, the man who, in 1933, as soon as Hitler came to power, convinced his brothers, sister, cousins, and parents-in-law, forty people in all, to leave Germany as quickly as possible; the man who figured out schemes for smuggling money taped to toilets on night trains to Switzerland—it took two years—so that they'd have enough cash for America to let them in. (Jews without a bank account or sponsor had no country willing to take them from Hitler's Germany.)

"No reason to go in. The building is just a shell. Everything was gutted by fire during *Kristallnacht*."

"What's that?"

I imagined some Jewish festival with candles out of control. In 1953 there was no *Schindler's List*, no Holocaust Museum, so I never heard about one night in 1938, when the Nazis systematically burned all the synagogues in Germany to destroy the Jewish life. All I knew was good Americans, who looked like Jimmy Stewart and Gregory Peck, fighting mean-looking men in black uniforms who clicked their heels a lot and shouted, "Heil Hitler." And we won.

"*Kristallnacht* was when the Jews finally realized they had to leave—and fast—even from Rindheim where it wasn't so bad. Jews felt safe here, too safe—until the synagogue was torched, everything in flames."

He stopped talking. "Go on!" I urged, but he held back, tentative. Not at all like him.

"My cousin Fritz . . . Do you remember him?" I shook my head, no. "He lived over there once," my father pointed down the alley, "and when he smelled smoke, he raced over. He was part of the Fire Brigade and began shouting to others in the Brigade, 'Why don't we do something? Get the hoses!' Men he knew all his life were standing around, silent. 'Against orders!' snapped a Nazi brownshirt, a stranger. 'Except if Christian houses start to burn!' He pointed his rifle at Fritz. So everything inside was lost—the Torah, the Ark. . . ."

I thought about the old blacksmith who lived in our house. Was he there? Was he one of those firemen? Why was he so friendly if he hated the Jews?

"But these people weren't from Rindheim," my father said quickly. "They were thugs from outside, brought in trucks by the Nazis to do their dirty work."

My father, already in America by then, had heard this from many Rindheim Jews who, like Fritz, left as soon after *Kristallnacht* as they could get exit visas. "The Rindheimers we grew up with didn't take part. They wouldn't do such a thing!" my father had been assured by those who resettled in America.

He opened the car door. "In fact many Non-Jews helped the Jews fix the store and house windows that were also smashed that night. But for that the Non-Jews got in trouble. Everyone who helped was sent to the Front as cannon fodder."

"What's that?" I asked.

"It's what you feed into big guns so they will shoot."

I imagined a young man being stuffed into a cannon, like at the circus, and aimed at American guns, his mother in the red doorway of the house we just passed, getting a telegram, crying like in the movies. But I wasn't going to feel sorry, not when they let the synagogue burn.

Later I would hear this term, cannon fodder, used again and again by Rindheim Jews—and always with the same "broken window" story. It was as if they had decided collectively on this tale and how it illustrated that their Non-Jewish neighbors meant well. "It wasn't their fault. They were afraid, too," they'd say with more sympathy than anger. But, like my parents, the Jews who returned to Rindheim to visit the family graves did so quickly, never wanting to stand and talk in the open or re-enter old rooms of memory.

I was hungry, but my father stopped again, this time in front of a shabby building with three tiers of windows. This was his school, he said, and it looked like mine, but P.S. 3 had a paved playground and good swings. This just had dirt.

"We Jews had the first floor and one teacher, Herr Spatz, who taught everybody, in all eight grades, everything. The Christians had the other two floors."

"How come?" I asked, for I'd never heard of dividing kids by anything but age.

My father looked surprised. "That's how it was done. We learned Torah and they didn't. They went to school on Saturdays and we didn't. But to high school, we went together, six kilometers to Horb, those who went."

"And did you talk to each other—and play games?" I thought of Tommy Molloy in the schoolyard, saying that I killed Christ, but then he asked me to play stickball on his team, and I said okay.

"Of course. We all got along. Rindheim was not so big."

I wouldn't argue about that! The schoolyard was deserted and, looking for movement in a meadow on the far hill, I saw a giant white cross ringed by menacing forest that kept its distance, like dark green bodyguards. The cross was also new, my father said. It wasn't even there when he was a child or even when he came home for a *Shabbat*, after moving to the city of Frankfurt in 1921 to work and later to marry.

"Remember how we had to park the car two kilometers away and walk to my father's?" He nudged my mother. "No Jew dared to drive here on *Shabbat*! Am I right?"

"Absolutely not. You'd be run out of town." My mother laughed for the first time all day and turned to tell me about how she, a big city girl from Stuttgart, first came to this village for her cousin Max's wedding. She wore a red, lace dress. "Very shocking!" she said with delight. "Everyone was whispering but your father. He came up and asked for every dance!" Her shoulders eased with nostalgia, wisps of black hair loosened from her chignon, and I leaned forward, close to her neck that always smelled of almond soap, to hear more about my parents having fun.

My father made a sharp left turn up a dirt road that zigzagged up a hill and stopped in front of a run-down stone farmhouse with half a roof. We needed a key for the Jewish cemetery and it was hanging on the peg "where it has always been," my father said. This was the Brenner family house; they were the gravediggers, who had been burying the Rindheim Jews for generations. Before Hitler, of course. A quarter of a mile farther, a giant stone portal emerged from nowhere—the kind that led to castles—and the fat key opened the heavy gate that led us deep into woods.

I still remember the sunlight on that day, how it streamed on the gravestones, a thousand of them tipped but all standing, in an enchanted forest light. It was a place to whisper and walk on tiptoe, even if you were an American thirteen. I remember the softness of the ground, a carpet of moss and leaves, and the stillness, as if the trees were holding their breath until we found everyone: my grandmother, Anna, born Tannhauser (1872–1915), and my grandfather, Rubin (1866–1925), both marked by sleek, dark marble gravestones that looked new despite the underbrush. And Rubin's father, Raphael (1821–1889), and his father, Rubin Feit (1787–1861), their pale sandstone gravestones carved with elaborate vines and scrolls eroded by time.

I tried to imagine faces: a grandfather who enforced strict rules about work, manners, and Torah; a grandmother who, in the faded photo over my parents' bed, laughed with my father's twinkle, when life pleased him. She had died when my father was not much older than I was, of infection, not Hitler, my father said. So had his dad, who refused to go to the hospital two hours away.

But all I could picture were the grandparents I knew: the *Omi* and *Opa* who lived three blocks away in Queens and "babysat," against my loudest objections that I was too old for that. This grandfather walked my dog so I didn't have to and wove yards of intricately patterned shawls and slipcovers on his loom in our attic. This grandmother made delicious, heart-shaped butter cookies and told stories of how they escaped in a little boat from Denmark to Sweden, and then to a chicken farm on Long Island where she, a city woman from Stuttgart, sang to her hens every morning—until my grandfather's heart attack made them move three blocks from us.

"Do you want to put down stones?" my father asked, placing small ones on his father's grave, his lips moving as in prayer, and then on his mother's grave—and on the others. He had found the stones under the wet leaves, and my mother, wobbling in high heels, was searching for more, enough for both of us.

"What for?" I asked, not wanting to take what she was offering. I would find my own.

"It's how you pay tribute to the dead," my father said, looking strangely gaunt despite his bulk. "The dead souls need the weight of remembrance, and then they rise up to God more easily . . . If we lived nearby, there'd be many stones," he said softly to his father's grave.

In later years, there would be more stones, as more Rindheim Jews came to visit the graves of their ancestors, but eight years after the war there were no others. I placed a smooth, speckled white with mica on Anna's grave and rougher grey ones on the men's. My father nodded. Some connection had been made, he knew, the one he had run from and returned to, the one I resisted even as I lay stones.

There were Loewengarts all over the place, mixed in with Pressburgers and Froehlichs and Grunwalds and Landauers, the same names again and again for they all married each other—or someone Jewish from a nearby village. There were four or five with Jews. My father said he had been daring to marry a woman from so far away—sixty kilometers! But when my mother found a gravestone that might be her second cousin on her mother's side, I thought: not so daring!

We were next to a wire fence in the far end of the cemetery where the weeds were high. My mother had disappeared, so it was just my father and I among rows of tiny graves no higher than my kneecaps, their writing almost rubbed off.

We were among the children's graves, my father said, slipping on wet leaves, but catching himself as I reached for his hand. I wanted him standing, especially with my mother gone. Above me, I heard the warble of a single bird and shivered. My father pointed out a headstone carved like a tree trunk but with its limbs cut off. It meant the person died young, in the prime of life, he said, and I thought of my sister Hannah who died soon after they arrived in America—before I was born. I didn't know the details then—how their doctor, also a German refugee, didn't know about the new antibiotics on the market—only that the sweet face with green eyes who hung over my parents' bed was buried in New Jersey somewhere.

I was glad to move back among the larger stones, worn and substantial like adults. I saw one dated 1703. You could tell the older stones, my father said, because all the writing—what little was left—was in Hebrew. The newer gravestones were mostly in German because by 1900, Jews no longer had to pay extra taxes as Jews, so they had started to feel very German, as if they really belonged.

"Did all the Rindheim Jews move to New York?" I was thinking about how many came to our house in Queens and pinched my cheeks over the years.

"Many, yes," he lectured, "but some moved to Palestine as a group. Others went to Chicago, Paris, even Buenos Aires . . ." We were now before a headstone carved with a broken flower, its stem snapped in two. He touched it. "And some stayed," he said quietly. "There were many, especially old people, who were like my *Tante* Rosa and thought no one would bother her. 'I'll be fine,' she kept saying. Later . . . we tried to send her money, but then . . ." His voice trailed off.

"Is she buried here?"

He shook his head. "She was deported." I asked no more, for I knew what deported meant, had seen the pictures of Auschwitz in *Life* magazine. I'd always been relieved that my Dad was smart and had gotten the whole family out in time—except for this *Tante* Rosa. I imagined a handful of old people getting into a wagon, but no one I knew, so it didn't seem so bad.

The sun rays had faded, the forest turned gray and dank, and we were near the entrance again, standing before a large monument in black stone, with the inscription, "Erected to honor the victims of the persecution of the Jews— 1933–1945." No individual names were listed, so I kept imagining only a handful of old people and walked on, stopping at a memorial that had a face: Joseph Zundorfer, his features carved in bronze above his name. He had been a Jewish fighter pilot in World War I with many medals. "Shot down," my father said, placing a stone on the grave, and I pictured a hero like Gregory Peck.

Eighty-seven Jews, not a handful, were deported from my father's village during 1941 and 1942, I found out forty years later. They died in the concentration camps of Lublin, Riga, Theresienstadt; but with no names engraved in stone and no faces to admire, they remained anonymous to me that day. What registered to an American teenager who lost no one she really knew was the sunlight on my family's graves, and how a thousand Jews, related to me, were buried, safe and secure for centuries in these high woods.

"In Rindheim, we didn't do such things!" suddenly carried more weight, giving me a history and legitimacy that would have made me not mind, as much, if my father continued to say that line. But he didn't. When we came home from that trip, he took up golf and played every weekend with American friends who never heard of Rindheim. Their world of congeniality became ours and I was expected to enter its promise. "Smile, smile! You are a lucky girl to be here!" is what I remember after that as my father's favorite line. His magical village of memory had disappeared among the graves that weren't there and the weightless souls with no stones of remembrance.

Chin Music

Michael Steinberg

I was wrapping up a discussion of *Huck Finn*, and as I began to recite the assignments, my students were already shuffling their feet, packing up books, and grabbing for their coats—the usual cues that it's time for the teacher to quit talking. In the past, I'd often take the hint and end the hour quickly. But lately, I noticed, I'd become less and less patient.

I paused for a second to look at my notes. That's when I spotted Drew—a student I'd already targeted as a trouble maker—moving toward the door. Just as he was about to open it, I said in a tone that was sharper than intended. "Excuse me, but class isn't over yet."

"I thought you were done," he said. Then he murmured under his breath, "You've been lecturing at us for over an hour." Whether it was deliberate or not, he said it loud enough for everyone to hear.

I knew I should let it go, or make light of it somehow. But before I could catch myself, it slipped out. "Drew, you're a fucking piss ant," I said. "Sit your god damned ass down 'til I dismiss the class."

Everyone, including me, was stunned. His eyes blazing, Drew shuffled back to his seat, deliberately kicking the trash can on his way. "Keep it up, pal," I whispered to myself. His coat buttoned to the throat, Drew sat down very slowly and turned his head toward the window.

This wasn't the first time we'd done this little dance. In the first week of the semester, Drew had written an exercise that I liked so much I read it to the class. When I praised the authenticity of the writing, he intervened. "None of that crap was true," he said. "I made the whole thing up."

Students had challenged me before, but never quite this aggressively, and certainly not without some provocation. So, I approached this kid a little more cautiously than I normally do.

"Why did you make it up?" I asked, making certain to keep my tone as neutral as possible.

"Because it was such a Mickey Mouse assignment," he said. So much for being tactful, I thought.

There were some "oohs," followed by a round of nervous giggles. I wanted to lash back, say something nasty or sarcastic. But instead, I took the high ground again. "Fiction or nonfiction," I said, "it's still a good piece of writing." And I left it at that.

Not so tonight, though. Visibly flustered, I stumbled through the litany of assignments. And when the class had filed out, I called Drew up to my desk.

"Look, Drew," I began. "I think you should know why I said wha . . ."

He cut me off in mid-sentence. "You showed me up in front of the whole class," he said. "You owe me an apology."

Then he waited a few seconds while I searched for a reply. Did this kid really believe that he'd done nothing wrong? Just as I was about to respond, he pivoted and headed for the door.

By the time I got home, I was furious—at him, of course—and at myself, for taking the bait. I took a walk around the block to try and calm down. But all I could think about was the anger and resentment that had been building inside me for such a long time.

Even before the eye surgeries, my patience with freshmen was wearing thin. When students said goofy things like "This sucks. Why can't we read happier books?" my comments were becoming more defensive. I even tossed a few guys out of class when they showed up unprepared or without books. Also a first for me.

The eye surgeries had given me a chance to step back from teaching for almost two years. Sometimes an enforced absence is just what you need to reinvigorate yourself. But when I got back in the classroom, I could see right away that things had changed.

Or maybe it was it me who'd changed. By mid-semester, I felt like a space invader in my own classroom. Some of my freshmen glided mindlessly into class on skateboards or roller blades. Some wore headphones and others ate snacks and drank soda while I talked. A few even had the chutzpah to take calls on their cell phones.

Conditions outside of class had also changed. For one, I was receiving frequent reports from the counseling center, bureaucratic memos informing me about students who were in alcohol or drug rehab, or who had eating disorders and histories of family abuse. And then there was the student who sent me an email apologizing for not doing her essay on time. She said, without a trace of irony, that she missed the deadline because she'd attempted suicide that weekend. She hoped I'd understand and that I'd give her an extension. Coupled with the effects of over two decades of student papers, mind-numbing faculty meetings, and obligatory committee work, this latest confrontation left me wondering if maybe it wasn't time to move on.

The next day, I was having lunch with a colleague from the Physiology department—someone who I meet with regularly to talk about teaching. She was telling me about two of her colleagues, one of whom she referred to as "an educator," and the other whom she called "a coach."

The word "coach" hit a nerve, and for a moment I drifted away from the conversation. In a sudden flashback, I saw myself at fifteen, standing next to Tom Sullivan, my old V.F.W. baseball coach. My God, I hadn't thought about this guy in almost forty years. Why now?

Just before I fell asleep that night, it all came rushing back. In my second year on Sullivan's team, I'd had a run-in with him, a skirmish that made me think seriously about quitting the game. A game I loved more than anything else in my adolescent world.

The episode came about on a bone-chilling Saturday morning in early March. It was the last day of tryouts and we were down to the final cut. I was on the mound and my best friend, Mike Rubin, was at bat. Last year we'd both made it to the final tryouts. But for some reason, Sullivan cut Rubin and kept me.

I only got to pitch in a few games that summer, so I was apprehensive when right before this year's tryouts began, Sullivan called me into his office. The room was a steam-heated cubbyhole above the St. Francis De Sales gym. Amidst the banging and hissing of the old pipes he told me in no uncertain terms that if I wanted to pitch this season I'd have to convince him that a Belle Harbor "sugar baby" had what it took to play ball for him.

And now, here I was on the mound of the church field staring down at Mike Rubin, who stood sixty feet six inches away nervously taking his practice cuts. Last year's team almost made it to the state finals at Cooperstown. We got eliminated in Westchester County—the final game of the regionals. I'd been thinking about it all winter, and I didn't want to blow my shot at playing summer league ball. But what about Mike? Since we were eight years old, we'd played on every team from Little League through P.A.L. This was his last chance to make the V.F.W. team. Next year we'd move up to American Legion, a tougher, more competitive league.

I knew Rubin couldn't hit the curve ball. If I threw him low breaking balls, my stock-in-trade, he was finished. Kaput. But if I pitched him too fat, Big Tom would know it. Then I'd be history too. While I was trying to figure out what to throw, Sullivan yelled, "Game situation," and ordered Andy Ortiz to be the runner at third. This was not a good sign. Ortiz was a football player from the Arverne projects. And he could hurt you. That's when Sullivan called for a suicide squeeze. It's a risky play, and it's meant to work like this: as soon as I go into my wind-up, Ortiz will head for home and Rubin will square around to bunt. My job is to make certain he doesn't bunt the ball in fair territory.

Instead of tossing me the ball, Sullivan swaggered out to the mound. As he slapped the grass-stained baseball into my glove, he deliberately sprayed black, bitter tobacco juice across the bridge of my nose. Then he motioned Danny Whalen, another football goon, to the mound.

Sullivan and I were inches apart. I could feel his breath on my right cheek. His nose was red and swollen, and slanted to the right. Broken three times in his college football days. Just as Whalen arrived, Coach rasped, "Steinberg, when Ortiz breaks from third, throw it at his head."

He meant the batter, Rubin. Why would I want to throw a baseball at my best friend's head? It wasn't the right strategy. It was another one of Big Tom's stupid tests of courage. I knew that sooner or later he'd be testing me. I just hadn't expected it to happen now.

"At his head, Coach?" I said, stalling for time.

Sullivan gave me his "that's-the-way-it's-done-around-here" look. It wasn't like I didn't know what he was doing. Everyone on the team understood that if you wanted to play ball for Big Tom you did what you were told and you kept your mouth shut. Why was I being such a smart-ass? It wasn't like me. Why was I so willing to risk it all here?

I tried to calm myself down, remind myself what the costs were. I kept telling myself to cool it. Just try and think it through. Pretend to go along with Big Tom's program. The whole time, though, I could feel the knot in my stomach twist and tighten.

Sullivan glared at the third base bleachers where the final eight guys fidgeted nervously, waiting for their chance to bat. Then he looked back at me. With his cap pulled low, the coach's steel-blue pig eyes seemed all the more penetrating. He smiled, but because part of his mouth was distorted from taking too many football hits without a face mask, it came off looking like a mocking leer. The gesture unnerved me even more. I could feel my palms getting clammy and my armpits were drenched with perspiration.

He said loudly for everyone to hear, "Steinberg, you've been with me for two years; let's show this wet-nosed bunch of rookies how we play this game."

Then he grabbed his crotch with his left hand. It was the old comrade routine. He was giving his second-year pitcher a chance to look like a leader by pretending we were buddies. But we weren't. Big Tom and I didn't operate in the same universe. He was a bull-yock Irishman from Hell's Kitchen, a high school stud who learned to fight in the streets. His platoon had fought in the Pacific, and the pride still showed in his eyes. To him, guys like Rubin and me were too privileged. And he resented us for it.

I turned to glance at Rubin. He looked like a Thanksgiving turkey on the block. I was embarrassed for him. Maybe the wind was just blowing at his sweatpants, the stiff ocean breeze we get on the Long Island south shore in early spring. Then again, maybe his knees really were shaking.

"Let's get the god-damned show on the road," Sullivan muttered. I thought about quitting, but our team was good. I had visions of Linda Foreman, our head cheerleader, walking around school wearing my V.F.W. jacket. And there was another incentive. We all knew that our high school coach, Jack Kerchman, scouted his players in the summer—looking to see who was getting better and who was dogging it.

Whalen trotted back behind the plate and Sullivan turned to leave. To him this kind of stuff was routine. I wanted to refuse, but this was my only chance to make it to Cooperstown, to see my dad sitting in the stands watching me pitch at Doubleday Field. I was red-in-the-face pissed, hoping it looked like windburn.

I tried to buy some time, hoping I could reason with Sullivan. Convince him there was another way to do this.

"You want me to stop the bunt, right?" I said meekly.

He turned. What the hell was I saying? Nobody second-guesses the Coach. Sullivan walked back to the mound and spat another wad of chew on the ground, making sure to splatter some on my new spikes. He looked at Whalen, then at Ortiz. Then he turned to me and shook his head from side to side.

"That's right, Steinberg. You stop the bunt. Now, let's please execute the fucking play, shall we?" He muttered to himself through clenched teeth as he trotted back toward the dugout.

It was out of my mouth before I knew it. "Suppose I hit him in the head?" Sullivan's own head swung around like a tetherball making the last tight twist at the top of the pole.

"Don't worry, it's not a vital organ. Pitch."

I think Big Tom knew that he was undermining his credibility by arguing with a piss-ant kid. So he turned and silenced everyone's murmurs with a long glare. As if rehearsed, the eight guys behind me started to grumble, distancing themselves from me and Sullivan's wrath.

"Pitch the fuckin' ball," yelled Whalen from behind the plate.

"Do what Coach tell you, man," spat Ortiz from third.

To those guys, Sullivan was George God. If he told them to take a dump at home plate, they'd get diarrhea. But me? I'm Gary Cooper in *High Noon*. Everyone's watching, no one's volunteering to help.

Then I noticed Mike Rubin, still frozen in his batter's crouch. He looked like a mannequin with bulging eyes. Poor Mike didn't have a prayer. But before I could think, the words slipped out.

"It's the wrong play, Coach."

It was my voice, all right, but it couldn't have been me who said it. I'd never have the guts to say anything like that to Sullivan's face.

Dead silence. You could hear the breeze whistling through the wire mesh of the backstop. At first, Sullivan was too surprised to even curse me out. But after a long moment, he turned and strode up to Rubin, who was still frozen in the box.

It was a considered ploy. I'd seen it before, in the streets. Coach was going to punish me by humiliating my best friend. Like all of us, Rubin was jack-rabbit scared of Sullivan. And just like a rabbit about to be prey, he stood riveted to the ground.

"God damn it," Sullivan ripped off his cap, exposing a jet black crewcut and sunburned forehead. He spoke like rolling thunder, enunciating every word.

"WHAT DID HE SAY, RUBIN?"

My stomach turned over watching Sullivan humiliate my best friend just for the amusement of the guys in the bleachers. And Big Tom knew it. Knew it oh so well.

Rubin managed weakly; "Uh, wrong—wrong play, Coach?"

Louder then, like a Marine D.I.: "NOBODY IN THE STANDS CAN HEAR YOU, RUBIN."

"WRONG PLAY, COACH."

Still advancing, Sullivan took it to the grandstand.

"ALL YOU LADIES, SAY IT!"

The accusing chorus rained down.

"WRONG PLAY, COACH."

"AGAIN."

"WRONG PLAY, COACH."

Then he ran out to the mound yelling, "YOU TOO, STEINBERG, YOU SAY IT."

He was hopping up and down like someone had pranked him with a hot foot. Adrenaline overcame me then, and before Sullivan could order another round, I let the words tumble out in a single breath. "If I throw a pitch-out chest high in the left hand batter's box, all Danny has to do is take two steps to his right and he has a clear shot at Ortiz." I was parroting what Joe Bleutrich, my P.A.L. coach, had taught me two years ago.

By now, my stomach was in knots, Rubin's eyes looked like marbles, and the whole team was hungry to see what would happen next. Sullivan squared himself and casually put his cap back on. He was trying to regain his composure. He'd let a snot-nosed high school kid get to him and now he had to regain control.

Softly now: "That's enough, Steinberg."

Then to Rubin: "Get back in the box. Let's do the play."

And to be sure there was no misunderstanding, he took it right back to me: "My play," he said deliberately. "My play, my way."

He was giving me a second chance. Why didn't I just fake it? I had good control. I'd brushed off plenty of hitters before. Maybe deep down I believed that Sullivan was right about me. Maybe I didn't have what it took to play for him.

I wanted to give in, get it over with. So I said, "I can't do it."

Sullivan slammed his cap to the ground, and in one honest, reckless moment, it came out:

"You Belle Harbor Jews are all alike. No god-damn guts. You're a disgrace to your own people."

Nobody moved. The wind whipped a funnel of dust through the hard clay infield.

So that's what this was all about. Some of the guys, I'm sure, had thought the same thing. But we were teammates and they'd never say it to my face. We all knew that Big Tom didn't favor Jews. But even in my worst moments I believed that this stuff was for the anti-Semites from the sticks, the ones who say "Jew York."

There was no chance Sullivan would apologize. He'd used tactics like this before—to get us mad, to fire us up. If I wanted to be a real putz, I could report him to the league's advisory board. My dad knew most of the officers. But I knew I wouldn't do it. Because if I turned him in, it would confirm what he already thought of me. And I didn't want to give him the satisfaction. Besides, I needed him. And in some odd way, I must have sensed that he needed me. Why else would he be testing me like this? For the moment we were yoked to each other, like Sidney Poitier and Tony Curtis in that movie *The Defiant Ones*.

I think Sullivan believed that somehow I had made him say what he said. He was angry at me for making him look bad. So to cover himself he had to make it seem like it was my fault.

"Get out of my sight, Steinberg," he snapped. "You make me wanna puke."

He motioned toward the bullpen. "Levy, get your butt in here and pitch."

Why Levy? Bert was also a Belle Harbor Jew. And to my mind, he was more timid than anyone else in the neighborhood. On second thought, maybe that was part of Big Tom's design.

Sullivan grunted, the cords of his muscular neck wound tight. He reached to take the ball. Just as he grabbed for it, something snapped inside me; I snatched the baseball back. Then an eerie calm began to wash over me. My stomach stopped churning, my chest didn't feel as if it was about to burst, and my neck wasn't burning. I could tell that Sullivan sensed something was going on, but he wasn't sure what it was. Neither was I. Not yet, anyway.

"I'm not leaving, Coach," I said.

Yeah, he sensed it all right. But he misread it. He waved Levy away. Maybe this was Sullivan's obtuse way of atoning for the Jew remark, by allowing me to stay on *his* pitcher's mound.

"Get back in the box, Rubin," he snapped.

"No, Coach," I said.

"What?"

"You grab a bat, Coach."

A frozen moment. Was I really doing this? I recalled the day at football practice when Stuie Scheneider had knocked Coach Kerchman right on his ass. Kerchman goaded him into it, and Stuie took the bait. Is this what was happening here?

Sullivan looked at me, then he looked at the guys in the bleachers and laughed out loud. We all knew he was going to do it. He ripped off his windbreaker and took a couple of practice cuts, biceps rippling. Sullivan didn't seem to mind when muffled cheers rose up from the third base side. He was wearing that crooked-ass grin of his. The players in the bleachers spilled into foul territory, inching closer to the backstop.

"Okay, Coach," I'm thinking. "You're gonna get just what you asked for."

I was ready to play me some chin music. Chin music, where the ball whistles as it passes under the batter's throat. Before I went into my windup, Whalen took two steps up the first base line. He was sure I was going to throw the pitch-out. Can't blame him. It's what he would have done. It's what anyone in his right mind would have done. Sullivan must have thought so too, that's why he was grinning.

It was the smirk that did it. "Screw chin music, I'll take his goddamn head off."

Then I saw Ortiz streaking from third toward home. In that split second I realized, maybe for the first time, that this really was happening. As Big Tom squared to bunt, I zeroed in on the black line that runs along the inside corner of the plate. "Calm down," I told myself. "Brush him back. Just let him know you're here."

That's what my head was saying, but when I started my motion I lifted my eyes away from the plate and locked them on the bill of Sullivan's cap. Then I pushed hard off the rubber and cut loose. I watched the ball tailing in, in, in, right toward Sullivan's head. But he didn't back off, not even an inch. That shit-eating grin was still on his face. I yelled, "HEADS UP," tucked my chin into my chest and shut my eyes. Then I heard a dull thud. I opened my eyes and watched his cap fly off his head. And as I saw him crumble, feet splayed in the dirt, I felt nauseous.

Stunned players surrounded the fallen Sullivan, not knowing what to do. With leaden strides, I joined them, growing a little more lucid. Rubin shot me a "Man, you are dead meat" look, and I thought about suspension from school. Jail even. But the coach sat up. Jesus, was he lucky. Was I lucky. I must have clipped him right on the bill of the cap. Why was I so surprised? It was the target I was aiming at.

Sighs escaped as one breath. Legs and arms unraveled. Players backed away. Slowly, Big Tom lifted himself up and brushed the dirt off the seat of his pants. He shook his head like a wet cocker spaniel who'd just taken a dip in the ocean. Then he wobbled to the bleachers, looking like a young girl testing out her mother's high-heeled shoes.

Before I could collect my thoughts, Sullivan's voice boomed out: "All right, here we go again. Ortiz, hustle back to third, Rubin, up to bat, Steinberg, get your butt back on the hill. Suicide squeeze, same play as before. This time I know we will get it right, won't we, ladies?"

He'd caught me by surprise again. I should have known that he'd have the last word. But this time I couldn't—wouldn't—jump through his hoops again. So, I took a deep breath, bowed my head, and slowly walked toward the mound—all the time knowing exactly where I was headed. When I got to the rubber, I kept going. At second base, I pushed off the bag with my right foot and began to sprint. I began unbuttoning my shirt, and as I passed our center fielder, Ducky Warshauer, I tossed my cap and uniform jersey right at him. Ducky stared at me like I'd just gone Section Eight. When I stepped onto the walkway outside the locker room, I heard the metallic clack, clack, clack of my spikes on the concrete floor. I opened the door and inhaled the familiar perfume of chlorine, Oil of Wintergreen, and stale sweat socks. For a moment I thought about going back out there; instead I headed straight for the shower and pushed the lever as far to the right as it would go. As the needle spray bit into my shoulders, I watched the steam rise up to surround me.

On the bus ride home, I was thinking about what I'd just done. I did it, I told myself, because he provoked me. It wasn't a conscious decision; it was a knee-jerk response.

All weekend, I thought about the incident. Should I take what was left of my uniform to his office right before the next practice? Nope, all that would do is let him know he'd won. Ok, I'll wait for him to ask for it. But what if he doesn't? Will I lose my nerve and give in?

Sunday night, seven-thirty, he called me at home. Ten minutes later I was back in that stifling office, the steam pipes hissing and banging away. Sullivan was sitting at his desk, head down, shuffling papers. He made me wait for about two minutes. Didn't even look up. When he knew I couldn't take the tension any longer, he said matter-of-factly—as if nothing had ever happened—"I'll see you at practice on Saturday."

Without taking his eyes off his papers, he handed me my cap and jersey and said, "Get your butt out of here, kid. I got work to do."

Of course I went back. That's what you do when you're fifteen and your identity is wrapped up in playing baseball. I had a pretty good season too. And though we didn't win the state title, we did make it to Cooperstown.

While I was on the mound that summer I'd hear Sullivan razzing us from the bench. I always listened closely, curious to see how far he'd push me. But whatever else he yelled, I never heard him shout "sugar baby." And I later found out that Sullivan did indeed invite Coach Kerchman to scout me. He just never took the trouble to tell me about it.

The "incident" happened over four decades ago, and I still couldn't decide whether I won or lost that confrontation. Sometimes I think I got the best of him, and sometimes I think I misread him—that he deliberately goaded me into throwing the ball at his head.

But wondering who won or lost, I told myself, is really to miss the point. Like me, Sullivan was in his early fifties when this happened. Could it be that now in my fifties, I was turning into a version of my old coach?

In the past few years, I noticed that many of my colleagues had turned cynical in the latter stages of their careers. But they stayed on anyway—out of a kind of inertia or fear, perhaps. Or because they needed to put more time in before they could take their benefits or pensions. It was certainly not the way I wanted to end my teaching career.

When I first began to teach, I promised myself I'd never use fear or intimidation to motivate or punish my students. And for the most part, I'd kept that promise. But in the past decade, I'd noticed that there were more and more students like Drew, who, for one reason or another, could push my hot buttons. They could provoke me in the same way that Sullivan had done four decades ago. And the impulsive severity of my retaliation surprised me as much now as it did then. Having crossed that line with Drew, I wanted to make sure it didn't happen again.

The first order of business was to talk privately with him. Yes, he was a mean-spirited kid. But he was also one of the best writers in the class. And despite our run-in, or maybe even because of it, I knew he would expect a high grade— probably a 4.0. I also knew that if he didn't get it, it was within his rights to file a grievance against me.

You walk a fine line with students like that. You don't want to let their insolence pass. Nor do you want to reward them for it. I thought again about the incident with Sullivan. As bigoted as Big Tom was, and as much as I hold him responsible for the Jew remark, I was still the one that hit him in the head with a baseball. And he was the one that put me back on the team. In his own misguided way then, Sullivan had allowed us both to save face and move on. It wasn't pretty, but it was precisely the outcome I wanted to affect with my belligerent student.

Three days later, I called Drew into my office and calmly explained my side of the story—including the earlier scenario that had triggered my outburst. I waited for him to respond, and when it was clear that he was going to hold his ground, I simply apologized.

Naturally, I was disappointed. But, there were two more issues left to resolve. The next night, I apologized to the class for what I'd said to Drew. But I made it clear that I didn't condone or approve of what either of us had done.

For the final month of the semester, Drew and I did not bait one another again. Nor did I single his work out for praise or censure. As if nothing had ever happened, he continued to write with the same insight and imagination—and defiance—as he had before. And when it came time to give the final grade, it was a 3.5, not the 4.0 I knew he was expecting.

Two weeks after the spring semester ended, I applied for early retirement.

How I Became a Bed-Maker

Kate Torgovnick

I realized a very scary thing this morning: I've become the kind of person who makes her bed every day. I woke up to the evil buzzing of my alarm clock, like always. And as I came out of that two minutes of post-sleep daze, I found myself at the end of my bed, wrestling to get the lines of my comforter parallel to the edge of my mattress.

I, Kate Torgovnick, make my bed every morning. *Every* morning. Not just days when friends might be coming over or days when I've done the laundry and need to change my sheets—we're talking every weekday, weekend, and holiday. It doesn't matter if I'm running late for work or if I have a hangover from too many gin and tonics the night before. No matter what, I make my bed.

And I'm not just talking about the throwing of covers over everything and thinking, *The bed is done, man, the bed is done*, like that kid with the long hair in *Don't Tell Mom the Babysitter's Dead* would say. I make my bed in a way that would please any drill sergeant. First, I fluff each sham (I don't even know where I picked up this term) and prop it up against my headboard, making sure no edges are flopping over. Then I shake out both of my pillows. I tuck three sides of the top sheet—yes, there's a *top sheet*—between the mattress and box spring and pull the loose end over my pillows. Next, I attack the comforter. I pull it over the whole kit and caboodle and take at least a minute to straighten it out (this was the point I was at when I came to this awful, dizzying realization this morning). Oh, but we're not done yet. Next, at the head of the bed, I fold the top sheet and comforter down about four inches, the way maids in hotels are taught to do. Finally, from the right side of the bed where I've neatly stacked my toss pillows, I grab each one individually and arrange them big ones in the back, small ones in the front. I've developed a meticulous process that takes approximately four minutes to complete—yet until today, I never even realized that I do any of it at all.

How could this have happened? Trust me, I am *not* a bed-maker. Or, at least, I wasn't a bed-maker? I like to think of myself as laid back, cool, smart, funny, and not nearly compulsive enough to attend to the details listed above. I'm hardly someone you would call organized—I've barely touched the day planner I bought years ago and instead jot my appointments down on paper scraps that become a jumbled mess at the bottom of my purse. I pay my bills late and they're often stained with jelly. As a teenager, my room was messy with the requisite piles of clothing, mix tapes, and the occasional abandoned cupcake. I actually remember making fun of my parents for their always-made bed. My freshman dorm room was a respectable pigsty—the floor a sea of crumpled jeans, half-written papers, and trash I couldn't be bothered to bring to a trashcan. Nowhere in my life has bed-making ever entered into the equation. So when did this happen?

First step, I must figure out how long this bed-making has been going on. It's 8:30 a.m., but I panic and call my boyfriend, Chuck. After three long rings, he finally picks up.

"Hey," he says, his voice betraying that I'm calling well before his alarm clock. "Everything okay?"

I try to think of the best way to phrase this. "Have you noticed that I make my bed?" I ask.

I hear a relieved sigh on the other end of the line. He seems thankful that the serious note in my voice is not anything bad. "Um . . . yeah."

"How long have I been doing this?" I delve. "Do you remember when it started?"

He pauses for a minute. "You've always made your bed. At least since we've been together."

Wow. That's three years. How can someone make their bed every day for three years and not even notice? I snap back into the conversation. "Did you ever think that's a little strange?"

"Not really," he says. "I mean, that's pretty normal. Lots of people do it."

"Well, have there been any days when I haven't made my bed?" I ask in a last-ditch effort.

He thinks. "Not that I can remember. You even make my bed when you're over here." Crap. My bed-making's practically turning me into a fifties housewife.

I say goodbye and do the math in my head. It must have been sometime pre-2004 when the bed-making began. That narrows it down, but doesn't answer the question. I guess I'm going to have to dig back further.

I try calling Christina, my post-college roommate who I lived with for three years before moving into my own studio, but she's not picking up her phone. So I instant message Dana, my college roommate. Maybe she saw the first symptoms. "Hey there," I say. "Do you ever remember me making my bed?"

"No way," she messages back. "I don't think so."

"So I was a slob? On a scale of 1 to 10, how messy was my side of the room?"

"If 1 is a monk's cell and 10 is Britney Spears' career, it was an 8.5. But by senior year, maybe a 6," she offers. Bless her for her bluntness. "But it still looked like you had artfully planned to make sure no horizontal surface was exposed, be it floor, chair, bed, or desk." Maybe she is exaggerating (this is someone who would get annoyed if the toilet paper roll was placed on the holder with the end coming out underneath instead of over the top). But she's narrowed down the time frame considerably. Somewhere between graduating from college in 2002 and getting together with Chuck in 2004, the bed-making began.

Christina is the missing link. Thankfully, she calls back a few hours later. "Do you remember when I started making my bed?" I ask, completely forgetting the normal pleasantries.

She laughs. "Not really."

"Did I ever mention making my bed or anything like that?"

"Hmm . . . not that I can remember," she says.

"Sorry, I realized today that I make my bed every day, and I'm trying to figure out when that started," I say, suddenly aware that I'm sounding like a psycho.

"That's funny," she says. "I've started making my bed, too. In our old apartment I didn't care about it. But in my new apartment, my bed's in the middle of the room. If I don't make it in the morning, I come home and feel like my life is a mess."

This is inconceivable. Christina's now a bed-maker, too? Her room was always twice as messy as mine—mountains of clothes on the floor, books strewn every which way, the works. Is what I'm going though completely normal?

"Really?" I say, feeling calmed that she's going through this, too. "Well, do you ever remember me going on any cleaning spurts or anything like that?"

"When we were both looking for jobs, you'd go on cleaning kicks or resolve to organize the closet or something. Maybe it was then?" she offers.

And all of a sudden, I remember. I started making my bed in the fall of 2002. It makes sense now that I think about it—I was unemployed for months and probably would have slept all day had I not forced myself out of bed. Christina was in the unemployed trenches with me, but our third roommate, Susannah, was two years older than us and had a steady job. In the morning, she would always make her bed before leaving the apartment for work. In the evening, she'd casually tell us about the things she did at the office, and I'd feel embarrassed that the only thing I had to report on was whether Joey and Dawson hooked up in the day's episode of *Dawson's Creek*. So maybe I was copying Susannah, imitating what productive members of society do.

Or maybe I was trying to establish some sort of routine. I remember giving myself a schedule so I didn't fall too out of practice with having things to do. 10 a.m.: the aforementioned *Creek*. 11 a.m.: take a shower and get dressed. Noon: look for a job for an hour. 1 p.m.: Go to the grocery store and make lunch. 2 p.m.: five hours of *Law and Order* reruns. 7 p.m.: Call friends and come up with a plan for the night that didn't involve spending money. I remember one day during this period when the building across the street caught on fire. I noticed the smoke through our bay window just as the fire trucks came into view. I stood there for hours, watching as flames engulfed the building and it burned down to the ground. It never even crossed my mind to go see if anyone needed my help. No one was injured, so it's not as creepy as it sounds—but still, I consider this a low point. The fire seemed metaphorical for how powerless I was feeling at the time.

Four years at a highly ranked liberal arts college making Phi Beta Kappa and Summa Cum Laude, and I felt completely ineffectual in shaping my life. Just like the firefighters' hoses did nothing to calm the flames. Looking back, I think maybe my bed-making was my way of taking control of something. I couldn't find a job, not to mention a boyfriend, and my savings account had dwindled to nothing. But if I made my bed, I was the master of my universe, right?

But why do I continue this obscene behavior now that life has settled down—I've found my dream job, I'm halfway through writing my first book, and all and all I'm very pleased with my life? I can think of all sorts of logical reasons. I could say that it helps me wake up, explicitly defining that the night is over and that, as much as I might want to, I can't go back to bed. I could say that coming home to a neat bed after work makes me feel mentally in order. I could say, "Cleanliness is godliness," or some such quote that doesn't really make much sense. And while there might be an ounce of truth in these things, I think that there is more to it than that: I think that my unconscious bed-making means I'm truly an adult.

I've heard friends and coworkers utter the phrase, "pretending to be an adult," and until now I've completely understood the sentiment. This state of perpetual responsibility feels foreign to all of us. We all feel like we're acting out a part—playing dress-up and doing things we're supposed to do, like going to work and setting up 40lKs, but that these things never seem completely natural. In this way of thinking, being an adult is measured in firsts you never quite imagined you'd get to—your first apartment, your first job, the first time someone calls you "Ma'am," the first paycheck that reflects a salary and not an hourly rate, the first time you say "I'll pencil you in," the first property you own, the first birthday cake with number candles rather than individual ones, the first time you think about getting married and having children and it doesn't seem completely far-fetched. But I've been through every one of these milestones, and, while they sound big on paper, the truth is that I felt no different on the day before any of these things happened than I did on the day after.

But today, the day I realized that I am a bed-maker, I feel very, very different. See, I've come to realize that adulthood is a diffuse thing. It creeps up in the subtlest ways possible. It's making to-do lists on a regular basis instead of just doing things. It's getting annoyed at shows when people bump into you when you use to think that was big fun. It's no longer telling your friends to just come on over, but giving them a specific time to arrive so that you can clean up and make a cheese plate (preferably with grapes). Adultness seeps into the tiniest crevices of your everyday life, to the point where you don't even recognize it. It seems so natural that you can't pin it down. It's when stability and routine become the things you really want. When having the wildest-night-ever pales in comparison to the simple pleasure of untucking the comforter, crawling inside, pulling the sheet all the way up to your neck, and drifting off to sleep.

I know I have friends who'd be willing to stage an intervention to try to shake me free from making my bed. Maybe there's even a twelve-step program. But the truth is, I don't want to stop. I like the way this ritual feels—easy, small, and comforting. Sure, I don't ever want to be grown up to the point where the phrase "bed-maker" seems like a fitting way to describe myself. But I can accept this. I can accept that I make my bed every day, that I'm an adult, that my priorities are shifting, that there is no Never, Never Land.

I have to go now. Toss pillows to rearrange.

Going to the Movies

Susan Allen Toth

I

Aaron takes me only to art films. That's what I call them, anyway: strange movies with vague poetic images I don't understand, long dreamy movies about a distant Technicolor past, even longer black-and-white movies about the general meaninglessness of life. We do not go unless at least one reputable critic has found the cinematography superb. We went to *The Devil's Eye*, and Aaron turned to me in the middle and said, "My God, this is *funny*." I do not think he was pleased.

When Aaron and I go to the movies, we drive our cars separately and meet by the box office. Inside the theater he sits tentatively in his seat, ready to move if he can't see well, poised to leave if the film is disappointing. He leans away from me, careful not to touch the bare flesh of his arm against the bare flesh of mine. Sometimes he leans so far I am afraid he may be touching the woman on his other side instead. If the movie is very good, he leans forward too, peering between the heads of the couple in front of us. The light from the screen bounces off his glasses; he gleams with intensity, sitting there on the edge of his seat, watching the screen. Once I tapped him on the arm so I could whisper a comment in his ear. He jumped.

After *Belle de Jour*, Aaron said he wanted to ask me if he could stay overnight. "But I can't," he shook his head mournfully before I had a chance to answer, "because I know I never sleep well in strange beds." Then he apologized for asking. "It's just that after a film like that," he said, "I feel the need to assert myself."

II

Bob takes me only to movies that he thinks have a redeeming social conscience. He doesn't call them films. They tend to be about poverty, war, injustice, political corruption, struggling unions in the 1930s, and the military-industrial complex.

Bob doesn't like propaganda movies, though, and he doesn't like to be too depressed either. We stayed away from *The Sorrow and the Pity*; it would be, he said, too much. Besides, he assured me, things are never that hopeless. So most of the movies we see are made in Hollywood. Because they are always very topical, these movies offer what Bob calls "food for thought." When we saw *Coming Home*, Bob's jaw set so firmly with the first half that I knew we would end up at Poppin' Fresh Pies afterward.

When Bob and I go to the movies, we take turns driving so no one owes anyone else anything. We park far away from the theater so we don't have to pay for a space. If it's raining or snowing, Bob offers to let me off at the door, but I can tell he'll feel better if I go with him while he parks, so we share the walk too. Inside the theater Bob will hold my hand when I get scared if I ask him. He puts my hand firmly on his knee and covers it completely with his own hand. His knee never twitches. After a while, when the scary part is past, he loosens his hand slightly and I know that is a signal to take mine away. He sits companionably close, letting his jacket just touch my sweater, but he does not infringe. He thinks I ought to know he is there if I need him.

One night after *The China Syndrome* I asked Bob if he wouldn't like to stay for a second drink, even though it was past midnight. He thought awhile about that, considering my offer from all possible angles, but finally he said no. Relationships today, he said, have a tendency to move too quickly.

III

Sam likes movies that are entertaining. By that he means movies that Will Jones of the *Minneapolis Tribune* loved and either *Time* or *Newsweek* rather liked; also movies that do not have sappy love stories, are not musicals, do not have subtitles, and will not force him to think. He does not go to movies to think. He liked *California Suite* and *The Seduction of Joe Tynan*, though the plots, he said, could have been zippier. He saw it all coming too far in advance, and that took the fun out. He doesn't like to know what is going to happen. "I just want my brain to be tickled," he says. It is very hard for me to pick out movies for Sam.

When Sam takes me to the movies, he pays for everything. He thinks that's what a man ought to do. But I buy my own popcorn, because he doesn't approve of it; the grease might smear his flannel slacks. Inside the theater, Sam makes himself comfortable. He takes off his jacket, puts one arm around me, and all during the movie he plays with my hand, stroking my palm, beating a small tattoo on my wrist. Although he watches the movie intently, his body operates on instinct. Once I inclined my head and kissed him lightly just behind his ear. He beat a faster tattoo on my wrist, quick and musical, but he didn't look away from the screen.

When Sam takes me home from the movies, he stands outside my door and kisses me long and hard. He would like to come in, he says regretfully, but his steady girlfriend in Duluth wouldn't like it. When the *Tribune* gives a movie four stars, he has to save it to see with her. Otherwise her feelings might be hurt.

IV

I go to some movies by myself. On rainy Sunday afternoons I often sneak into a revival house or a college auditorium for old Technicolor musicals, *Kiss Me Kate, Seven Brides for Seven Brothers, Calamity Jane,* even, once, *The Sound of Music.* Wearing saggy jeans so I can prop my feet on the seat in front, I sit toward the rear where no one will see me. I eat large handfuls of popcorn with double butter. Once the movie starts, I feel completely at home. Howard Keel and I are old friends; I grin back at him on the screen, admiring all his teeth. I know the sound tracks by heart. Sometimes when I get really carried away I hum along with Kathryn Grayson, remembering how I once thought I would fill out a formal like that. Skirts whirl, feet tap, acrobatic young men perform impossible feats, and then the camera dissolves into a dream sequence I know I can comfortably follow. It is not, thank God, Bergman.

If I can't find an old musical, I settle for Hepburn and Tracy, vintage Grant or Gable, on adventurous days Claudette Colbert or James Stewart. Before I buy my ticket I make sure it will all end happily. If necessary, I ask the girl at the box office. I have never seen *Stella Dallas* or *Intermezzo.* Over the years I have developed other peccadilloes: I will, for example, see anything that is redeemed by Thelma Ritter. At the end of *Daddy Long Legs* I wait happily for the scene where Fred Clark, no longer angry, at last pours Thelma a convivial drink. They smile at each other, I smile at them, I feel they are smiling at me. In the movies I go to by myself, the men and women always like each other.

Undressing Victoria

Erika Vidal

It's a good thing I'm not at a bar with my friends right now, otherwise Blondie in black—the Guess model over by the cotton panties—would be toast. Today I have to be polite, because I am desperate for a job. I walk up to the register where a woman with long, streaked blonde hair almost down to her waist is standing. She's tall, probably close to six feet, and thin. Her cheekbones are high, sharp, and blushed with a pinkish hue to give her pale skin a flushed glow. She looks like Barbie, a doll I didn't really let into my play circles as a little girl. The ends of her hair look as if they've been carefully curled. "Hi," I say in my sweetest I'm-looking-for-a-job-voice, "I was wondering if you guys are hiring?"

"Yeah, actually," she says and hands me an application and tells me I can fill it out right here. "Most of my girls are getting ready to go back to school," she says while I fill in my name, social security number, past work experience, "which is a shame because some of them are really good. Have you worked retail before?"

She speaks in a low, breathy voice, almost a whisper, and edges forward to lean her elbow on the glass countertop. Her lips are small and thin, her eyes blue beneath lashes that have been recently curled and traced over with black mascara. Everything about her face seems small except her eyes, yet it is all strangely proportionate. If I were a man, I might start drooling.

I tell her I worked at Bath & Body Works for two years.

"Oh, did you like it there?" she asks.

"Yeah, it was pretty easy," I say. She mentions that Bath & Body Works, like Victoria's Secret, has a really high rate of employee turnover. I ask why and she hesitates, but then replies that she's not sure. When I finish filling out the short application, she tells me her name is Kirsten, and invites me to a group interview that is taking place the next morning.

"Oh," she adds, handing me a pink pamphlet, "they want you in dress code." She doesn't even really look at my application, so I'm somewhat surprised.

I take out my beat up cell phone and call my mom as soon as I leave the store to tell her about my interview.

"Alright," she says, "that's my girl." She wasn't expecting me to get two interviews in one day, but I guess that with summer ending and everyone going back to school, these places are pretty anxious to hire people fast. Today is my first day out looking for a job. In fact, it's my first day off the couch in a few days. My mom has been trying to console me since I moved back home. I've been in a post-college funk, mostly exploding into rants on my life, and how it sucks and I have hardly any friends left here, plus no experience that qualifies me for any type of English major related job, and what kind of jobs do English majors get, anyway? My mom's advice is to just go out and get any kind of job for now, take it easy, think about things, and focus on school.

"I want you to be happy," she says. She can't stand to see me start crying at random moments when I'm missing sitting on the green couch with my roommates watching *Elimidate*, or cooking dinner with my boyfriend. Always optimistic, she is confident that everything will work out for me.

I tell her they want me to be in dress code for the interview, and I read to her from my pink pamphlet. My outfit has to be mostly black with a blazer, which I don't have. I'm hoping she can take care of that for me.

"Since when do they wear blazers?" she wants to know.

"I don't know, but they do."

"I don't remember them wearing blazers, are you sure you need a blazer?" she insists.

"Well, that's what it says on the sheet and the lady I talked to was wearing one," I tell her, not sure why she is being so adamant about it when I'm reading to her straight from my pamphlet.

"Okay, but I don't remember them wearing blazers."

I assure her that I do in fact need a blazer. The only reason she's never noticed is because she refuses to pay full price for bras and underwear. She only shops at Victoria's Secret while their semi-annual sale is going on, during which they don't wear blazers.

"Can it be pinstriped?" she asks. I flip through the pamphlet quickly and it doesn't say anything about pinstripes, although it does say that our outfits have to be 90 percent black. Do pinstripes make up more than 10 percent of an outfit? If I wear pinstripes, do I have to wear a black shirt underneath the blazer, and most importantly, how and why have they arrived at that percentage? We are puzzled by this, but figure that I should just buy a suit since we're both hoping I'll eventually need one anyway.

I spent all of my money on a three-week backpacking trip to Europe after graduation. Of course it was worth every single penny I worked so hard for, but my bank account is pretty much empty, and I am forced to borrow shoes from my mother, almost always a scary ordeal, and ask her to buy me a suit for work. She tells me to go look for a cheap blazer and pants at the mall.

I call my boyfriend, Jonathan, to tell him the good news.

"I have an interview at Victoria's Secret tomorrow."

"Victoria's Secret, huh? Sweet," he says. "Do you get free underwear?"

"I don't know," I say. "I doubt it." I am convinced he is more fascinated by the idea of me surrounded by women's underwear and what I might bring home than he is happy for me about possibly getting a job. Just like all of my friends are more interested in my discount than my newfound income.

"Ooh la la," my friend Hazel will say when I tell her. "By the way, just so you know, I'm a 36C."

I walk upstairs to The Limited in search of a professional, but cute, outfit. At $75 a dress and $195 a blazer, The Limited clearly does not fall under the "cheap" guidelines I have been threatened to follow, and neither does its younger sister Express. When my mom gets here I need to have found a price-appropriate option. I fall in love with two different black dresses (the pamphlet says we are allowed to wear dresses as long as the tips of our fingers don't go past them while standing up straight—and you'll see when you try this at home that this is still pretty short), but I reluctantly realize that there is no way I can afford either of them, so I mope on over to Forever 21. Besides, the sales associate at The Limited keeps harassing me to open a credit card, and it's ruining my fitting room experience. At Forever 21, though, I find a fitted pair of black pants and a fitted black blazer, all for less than fifty dollars. My mom is happy with the price, she says when she arrives at the mall, and when I try it on and model for her, she tells me it looks very nice but she's worried that the pants might be too tight on the, as she likes to call it, big butt that I got from my mama. So when I get an interview for a *real* job—which we hope will be soon—I'll have to buy different pants.

Next on the pink pamphlet: no open-toe or open-heel shoes, no excessive jewelry, no visible tattoos, and we have to wear matching hosiery. My mother can supply the hosiery and the shoes. The butterfly tattoo is well hidden on my lower back, although I figure that if it does happen to pop out, there's pink inside the wings so at least it'll match the store.

Over dinner and a few glasses of wine, we wonder what questions they're going to ask me. I'm sure they'll ask why I want to work there, and I think about what I'll say.

"Why do they ask that?" my mother wonders aloud. "It's such a stupid question. You want to work there because you want to make money, duh." She could understand the question if, for instance, it were an interview for a job with a place where she works, a Charter School that is dedicated to teaching English as a Second Language to immigrants and then helping them find jobs. Whoever works there had better be dedicated to the cause. But it seems a little strange to ask, "Why are you dying to work as a sales associate at Victoria's Secret?" A retail job is a retail job. But, I think to myself, it *sounds* better than a lot of other retail jobs. I certainly don't want to make a career out of it, but it's a nice, clean, pretty place to work and the eventual 30 percent off will be a big plus. I guess my answer will revolve around the atmosphere of the store and respect for the product. I'll say that Victoria's Secret is the only lingerie I wear, which is so not true. I can't afford Victoria's Secret. I currently own three bras from there and some cotton underwear, all purchased for me by my mother. Besides, until recently, I was a fan of the no-bra look.

I think it's the name, the brand itself that makes it more attractive to me than another retail store. I figure that if I'm going to work in the low-paying retail world, I might as well make it Victoria's Secret. It sounds classier, or maybe just sexier than telling people I work at Contempo Casuals or J. C. Penny. I picture pink and white striped shopping bags stuffed with pink and white striped tissue wrapped around some intimate detail. I see myself waltzing around on the red carpet, shopping while I work and figuring in my 30 percent off. It sounds sexy, pink, and feminine. I can't help but think of beauty; the layout and decor of the store exude sensuality. The models Victoria's Secret uses are beautiful, but not at all attainable. While some could argue that the poses the half-naked models strike in the catalogues objectify women, it isn't actually an accessible image. They're too damn beautiful. And this makes them unattainable, which somehow makes them powerful—someone that every woman wants to be and every man wants to have.

I find it funny that at different times in the world's history, men have viewed women as powerful for reasons other than sex. During the Stone Age, for instance, women were treated like goddesses—a lot like actresses and models are today—only the respect stemmed from their ability to procreate (okay, so it still had a little to do with sex). Men built shrines to women, sculpting them as obese creatures, because in a time where food was hard to find, big was beautiful. Archaeologists have found countless artifacts that affirm the different power a woman's body—especially the breast—once represented. Women were primarily viewed as mothers and nurturers, idolized for the capacity to give birth and to feed. Instead of having a picture of a half-naked Giselle on the wall, a man might have had a statue of a woman with a protruding belly, holding up her breasts in non-sexual gesture. He would have worshipped her as a goddess.

Now, the majority of female representations are sexual in nature. When we flip through the pages of a Victoria's Secret catalogue, I doubt any of us is thinking, "My, what a wonderful mother she would make." And I'm not so sure that all women want to be viewed in that light anymore—or at least we've become accustomed to being seen, first and foremost, as sexual beings. Some of us even strive for it. So I guess in a way, that automatic correlation between these powerful women and me—you think Victoria's Secret, you think hot models—no matter how far-fetched, is appealing.

The next day, I get to the interview five minutes early. There's already a girl standing outside the store, staring in shyly like a child not knowing whether to cross the line. She is blonde with blue eyes and a peachy skin tone. Her eyeliner is electric blue, and long earrings dangle from her ears.

"Are you here for the interview?" one of us asks.

"Yeah," the other says. We walk in together cautiously, as if the bras hanging from the walls might crumple if we walk too carelessly.

"Are you two here for the group interview?" a manager asks. We both nod. It's not the same manager I spoke to yesterday. A few minutes later, a tall brunette who looks like a younger Salma Hayek walks in, her breasts hurtling through the air as she makes her way towards us. And then here we are—the blonde, the breasts, the legs, and the oversized ass—wearing black suits and smiling. The manager walks us to the back.

This manager, the one who is interviewing us, has shoulder-length curly brown hair and a pretty face; her skin is smooth, her features symmetrical. First, she tells us that she isn't going to be our manager because this is her last week working for Victoria's Secret. She seems relieved, happy, tells us it's been a rough few months. This store is going through a lot of changes right now, and it's been stressful. She gets back to business by reiterating the dress code and adds that they don't place too much emphasis on what's worn underneath the blazer. "As you can see," she says, motioning to her chest. I, being the observant person that I am, have already noticed the cleavage, mostly because I've been wishing that somehow it would jump from her chest to mine. Plus, let's face it: it's hard not to look.

She wants to know if any of us have retail experience. Not surprisingly, we all have at one point worked retail, although none of us have ever worked opening credit cards before but we're willing to try it out. We all feel we are right for this position because we are outgoing and reliable. When it comes to the last question, the dreaded, "Why do you want to work at Victoria's Secret?" we all choose atmosphere and discounts. At this point, they usually have interviewees go out onto the floor and practice greeting customers, just so management can get a feel for how we interact with the customers. Suddenly, I start feeling a little hot inside my black blazer, suffocated by the thought of going out there so utterly unprepared. It seems to be a ridiculous idea considering we knew nothing about anything. Thankfully, it's slow today, so she tells us the experiment would be pointless. I guess we've all been hired, because she tells us there is an orientation scheduled for Tuesday afternoon, and if we could all make it "that would be great."

The first Victoria's Secret opened its brass knobbed door in 1977 just outside of San Francisco, California. The idea arose in Roy Larson Raymond's mind after an embarrassing day of slip shopping for his wife. He felt uncomfortable beneath the glare of the librarian-like saleswomen who were giving him questioning glances, wondering if he was shopping or getting a cheap thrill, surrounding himself by women's intimate apparel. He thought there should exist a place where men could walk in and buy not too frilly, but not too bland lingerie without being perceived as some pervert lurking around women's underwear.

Raymond had received his MBA from Stanford University in 1969. He'd been in marketing ever since, but starting his own business had been a long time dream of his. Using a $40,000 loan from the bank and another $40,000 from his parents, Roy Larson Raymond initiated a more sensual and open approach to the buying and selling of lingerie. Using antique furniture and oriental rugs, he created a sort of Victorian boudoir out of his small boutique. Within its first year, sales were up to $500,000, and more stores soon opened as a result of its success. However, according to an article in *The New York Times*, Gary Pike, a public relations consultant for Victoria's Secret, said that Raymond had difficulties keeping up with the financial aspect of the business. On July 30, 1982 he was forced to sell his stores (there are conflicting reports on how many stores Raymond had opened, ranging from three to six) and thriving 42-page mail order catalogue to The Limited Inc., owned by Leslie H. Wexner, for a reported $4 million.

Leslie H. Wexner is described as a born entrepreneur by several business sources. In 1963, he adopted the quickly expanding notion of specialization and opened Leslie's Limited in Columbus, Ohio, selling only women's sportswear separates at moderate prices. He made only $435 on opening day, but by the end of the year sales were up to $160,000—double what he'd hoped for. The next year sales tripled. The Limited went public in 1969, and by the time it came into the possession of Victoria's Secret in 1982, it was operating more than 300 stores including The Limited, Express, and Lane Bryant, plus it had acquired Mast Industries, an international apparel purchasing and importing company.

Wexner added to the already Victorian mood of the store by strategically placing plush furniture throughout the store and playing classical music ranging from Beethoven to Vivaldi. (By 1995, Victoria's Secret had sold more than ten million tapes and CDs recorded by the London Symphony Orchestra especially for their label. In 1993, the December issue of *Forbes* magazine noted that of the ten classical albums to reach platinum status, Victoria's Secret has sold five.) He took a more aesthetic approach to the display of lingerie: instead of the traditional department store method of designating a hidden corner to intimate apparel and keeping merchandise in boxes, Victoria's Secret hung their satin nightgowns from the walls and laid panties out on tables according to color and style. Black, beige, and white were reduced to basics, while more vibrant colors and a choice of fabrics became a part of the lingerie shopping experience. Walking onto the soft rouge carpet of the store was a lot like walking into a romantically decorated bedroom complete with background music.

By 1986, Victoria's Secret was making $75 million a year in sales and had over 100 stores, a substantial growth in comparison to the nine that existed by the end of 1982. Through Victoria's Secret, The Limited Inc. transformed lingerie into a fashion business rather than a commodity.

The angels are barely dressed and smiling. They laugh and pout from within their black and white world while their slim bodies twist and stretch and strut to the beat of some sexy song, their skin spilling across the screen.

Each is wearing a bra and its matching underwear, and from their backs sprout soft white wings. Beautiful, half-naked supermodels disguised as angels.

I've seen this television commercial before. I shift around and try to get comfortable in the chipped metal chair they've folded out for me. But suddenly they aren't angels anymore, just stunningly beautiful women in lingerie—as if sculpted from the most graceful and the most delicate of bones—still sweeping across the screen in one fluid motion. Their long hair is everywhere: streaming behind them, whipping at their faces, caught between their lips, twirled around their fingers.

Suddenly the music stops: "Welcome to Team Victoria."

The nakedness seems unnecessary. I'm sitting in the stock room of Victoria's Secret, where they're trying to get the brand image across to us right away, trying from the very beginning of training to make us one with the image they want to convey to their customers. Along with three other women, I am here to become familiar with my duties as a Sales Support Specialist. Neither of the two girls that I interviewed with is here.

My mom was right about these black pants being a little too tight. It feels like they're sticking to the bottom of my thighs. I am an anxious person—the kind who can't eat before an interview because she may throw up on her interviewer—so I try to tell myself that it's not because I'm too fat for the pants, it's just because I'm so nervous and sweaty palmed. I've been secretly picking at my fingernails since we began. It's a bad habit I can't seem to break, and I'm hoping no one will notice their short, ragged edges. They're not like anything you'd ever see in a hand lotion commercial. *Cosmopolitan Magazine*'s advice to me was to paint over them with a clear polish, that way they'd look so pretty that it'll make me think twice about peeling away at them. But I've found that it doesn't work. I don't exactly look at my nails before attacking them; I usually just feel for a long juicy one and go at it.

A girl named Ashley is sitting to the right of me with her thick, dirty blond hair pulled back in a bun-slash-ponytail thing. She is wearing a tight red shirt, and it looks like someone very strategically took a knife to it—it is slit a few times at the chest to reveal a pair of kitten paws tattooed on the top of one of her pale breasts. It's something I might wear to a nightclub, but not to an interview. I wonder if our new manager, Nina, will have anything to say about this little insight Ashley's giving us, since the pink dress-code pamphlet we were given clearly states that visible tattoos are unacceptable. Nina has been prancing in and out of the room since we started filling out the paperwork and watching the videos, sometimes for so long that one of us—usually Ashley, who wants to get this over with—takes out the tapes when they're done and pops in a new one.

Ashley's eyes are big and blue and wide open in eternal surprise mode above her bubbled cheeks. She's not a small girl. She's not a particularly big girl either. Ashley is not at all bothered by this; her boyfriend loves it, and after her first few paychecks she's going to buy herself that sheer, hot-pink baby doll out on the sales floor, the one slit down the middle with the matching thong.

On the other side of Ashley sits a southern blonde with perfectly curled hair and carefully applied makeup. Lori looks like she popped right out of one of those old Oglivie home perm kit commercials. She has a Home Shopping Network smile. She appears to be in her early to mid 30's and she sits up straight with her legs crossed. She smiles and nods along to everything Nina says, and Nina smiles and nods along to everything Lori says. They are each other's silent, bobbing cheerleaders. This makes Ashley mad. "They're like best friends already," she whispers to me, giving Lori the evil eye.

Lori isn't shy about exploiting her past retail experiences. She knows all about customer service, and if a man walks in and wants her to model lingerie so he can see if it will fit his wife, she says she'll do it. I'm not sure if Nina heard that last part, although I have a feeling from her talk about God being the number one priority in her life that this type of behavior won't go over too well. She's a Christian, goes to church every Sunday, belts out those gospel songs like it's nobody's business. "Mhm, girl, I'm a Christian," she tells us, nodding her enthusiastic nod.

Ana is sitting to the left of me. She's 18 years old and in her last year of high school. Half Columbian and half Bolivian with dark brown hair and dark eyes, her skin is naturally tan, although she complains that in the winter she gets yellow.

"No, seriously," she says, "it's, like, so gross how yellow I get." She pauses dramatically, sighs lightly, brings her hands to her cheeks, and whimpers a quick, "Oh my God." Her black clothes cling tastefully to her small, straight frame. The tips of her black shoes are pointed, the heels tall and thin. I ask her how she can walk.

"I'm used to them," she says. I haven't yet adapted to the popularity of pointy-toed "witchy shoes."

My shoes, well, actually my mom's shoes, are almost flat with a thicker platform heel, and I'm slightly embarrassed to be in them while sitting here among all these trend-conscious women in the stock room of this trend-setting company. They're some kind of fake suede and they resemble penny loafers. They're simply not the right material for summer.

The four of us pay more attention to the merchandise around us than we do to the actual videos, and with Nina out of the room it's easy to get away with. "Oh, look how cute," one of us periodically points and says. The walls are interrupted by white shelves that hold cardboard boxes labeled in thick black marker: *BBV bras* or *dressy panties,* and on the floor below them are stacks of open boxes overflowing with bras and underwear that I don't yet recognize but that will soon be overflowing the top drawer of my own dresser. Closer to the back of the room, silver racks are lined with sleepwear according to style, size, and color. Headless mannequins, naked and pearl colored, lean against the walls in the comer behind us.

Every so often, the click of Nina's heels tapping rapidly towards us along the cream tiles turns our attention back to the nineteen-inch television screen. In one of the tapes we observe a sales associate in action. She's with a woman who is pretending to be a customer. We'll call our model associate Suzie. The video goes something like this: Suzie is illustrating the proper use of the Best at Bras Cycle-IOUE: Introduce the product, Offer bra fitting and personal testimony, Utilize the Bra Wardrobing Center, and, finally, Expand the sale. Suzie smiles real big and says, "Let's get you measured so we can find your perfect fit." The fake customer responds with an excited "Okay!" "Great," Suzie chirps after measuring her overly eager client. "Now that we know your perfect fit, let's get you into our most popular styles." Another overzealous "okay" escapes the mouth of our wannabe customer and next thing you know she's at the register buying a whole new drawer's worth of bras and panties.

Ashley scoffs at how easy they make it look. Now, Ashley's no retail rookie. She used to work at Gadzooks, where the stock room was a mess and the sensors (those plastic tabs that set off the security alarm if they aren't removed from garments) used to prick her fingers. So when it's time for the all-important safety video, she already knows all the tips and techniques—how to bend your knees when lifting a heavy box or how to avoid stabbing your fellow associate with a box cutter, and she doesn't get why she has to watch all this again because, hello, she's pretty much already seen it.

Now, I admit that I can't bring myself to pay too much attention to the videos either. The acting is comparable to one of those mind-numbingly bad, unconvincing after-school specials. Plus, I saw most of these videos when I trained for work at Bath & Body works. I'm still wondering how much they're going to pay me, since many of these retail jobs trick you into attending orientation without telling you how much you'll make. I was making $8.10 an hour at Bath & Body Works, not too bad for a retail job in the mall, although I got lucky there because my manager liked me and offered me the higher salary in exchange for working a lot of hours during Christmas. I'm 21 years old with a bachelor's degree, so this rate, barely above minimum wage, is not sounding especially tempting right now, but I guess I should have thought about this before I decided to major in English and become a writer.

If I had listened to my dad, I'd be an accountant, a flight attendant, or a nurse—never mind the fact that I failed and had to retake just about every math class I ever took, and never mind that I'm afraid of flying, and that I can't stand the sight of blood. To my father, all these things are small obstacles. Now this job isn't exactly what I had in mind for myself either, but I remind myself that this will be temporary.

The woman who interviewed me told me that I'd probably be making what I was making at Bath & Body Works, since they're both in "The Limited family." I keep hearing the words "real job" from my family, these words that do nothing but evoke fear in my recently graduated mind, and truthfully, I'm in no immediate rush to find one of these supposed "real jobs." I just graduated in May, and I keep telling myself that was only three months ago, it's okay to take this job, even though it has nothing to do with my major and it pays next to nothing. Right now, it's my master's degree I should be focusing on. Anyway, this job seems easy enough. We were told that the hardest part is getting the underwear to stay on the hangers, and I think I can handle that. Besides, I'm not even completely sure what I want to be doing. So while I search for those supposed "real jobs," why not take it easy for a while and get 30 percent off on some of the most coveted lingerie in the country?

After the videos, Nina click-clacks into the room on her heels. Her stomach is almost flat and when she walks the muscles in her calves flex to form a slightly curved line that is visible through her sable hose. I imagine that she was a cheerleader in high school because she's way too upbeat and hyper. She practically runs from one of us to the other exclaiming, "Woo-hoo!" usually after we've finished with a section of the orientation and she's handing out a different set of papers. "Here you go, hmm hmm," she smiles.

Her skin is the color of lightly creamed coffee, and she wears a deep brown lip liner that's darker than the rest of her full lips. Her face appears to be wrinkle free. Her eyes are large and brown, the cheekbones beneath them round and accentuated.

I like her. The company just transferred her to this store, but she's been part of Team Victoria for eight years and she takes her job seriously.

"Alrighty, hmm hmm," she begins, "how many of you have sold credit before?" None of us have, but Lori is confident that she's going to be great at it. Nina hands us each a little pamphlet listing the benefits of opening an Angels Account. This is a crucial part of the job, and we each have to enter two per shift. I have to admit that at this point I consider standing up, thanking Nina for this opportunity, and walking out. But here we are, about to become those girls who ask a million times a day if you want to open an Angels Account. Are you sure? Because now is a great time to open one. You get $75 in discounts and savings and there's no annual fee. We're supposed to ask three times before we're allowed to give up on a customer.

"It's so easy," she says. "You just have to talk to them like they're your friend. I usually get them on the floor and I'll just say, 'Do you have an Angels account with us?' or 'Let's put this purchase on your Angels account. Oh, you don't have one? Oh girl, we need to get you one, did you know that next month you get that bra half off?' See, it's so easy man," she says, scrunching up her face.

After we review all the benefits and she quizzes us by pretending to be a customer inquiring about the card, she hands us a big, thick book that lists all the collections of bras and underwear. I hadn't realized how many different bras there were. The Body by Victoria Shaping Demi, for example, provides support and a lined cup for shape, plus it's seamless, so "all you see is curves." The Very Sexy Push-up offers the same seamless look with double straps for a sexier look, plus some kind of liquid gel sewn into the fabric so your figure is enhanced by one full cup size. There are three main collections: Angels, Body by Victoria, and Very Sexy. Angels has nine different style bras, Body by Victoria (BBV) has ten, and Very Sexy has nine. And I might not even be adding them up right. Plus, the catalogue has things that have been discontinued in the stores, so I'm sure I'm missing some. Each collection can be most easily identified by how it feels to the touch. That adds up to twenty-eight styles—not including the specialty bras in the Such a Flirt and Glamour, and the upcoming Pink collection.

I find it strange that each bra feels so different, but they're all made from the same material. The BBV collection feels almost like cotton, it's a clothier feel than the satin touch Very Sexy has. In the Angels collection, some have a cup that feels like satin, while others have cups that feel like almost foamy. Almost every Angels bra has a touch of lace. All Victoria's Secret bras are made with Lycra® Spandex and Nylon. A lot of time and research was put into finding the perfect material for bras, and it wasn't until the 1980's that it was discovered:

> . . . dyeing the polyesters at extremely high temperatures destroyed the spandex, swimming pool chlorine damaged the fibers, and white spots appeared on the polyamide as soon as its stitches were stretched. . . . Lycra, a magic fiber, could be invisibly incorporated into the finest and most fluid materials, including silk, crepe, tulle, and lace. A natural or synthetic fiber blended with 2 to 4 percent Lycra will make a garment that will cling to every curve of the body.

The fiber can be stretched to four or five times its own length and recover instantly. Fine, soft, and ultra stretchy, it feels like a second skin, arousing new sensations in the women wearing it. Here finally was the dream fabric for making underwear.

In order to master the Bra Cycle, we need the proper tools. Nina presents us each with a pale pink tape measure, so we can learn how to properly fit women for bras. This is a crucial part of the Bra Cycle because, according to Nina, it almost always leads to a sale. If we do ten bra fittings an hour, we should make our bra goal. I am unsure as to whether that means ten bra fittings per person, or ten bra fittings in all. But they are constantly saying, "and remember: ten-to-win." She grabs one of us and shows us how to do a bra fitting: measure around her rib cage, directly beneath the breasts and add five. That's her band size. Now measure directly around the breasts and subtract the number you get from the band size. One means she's an A, two means a B, and so forth.

I'm confused. We're all confused. She shows us again.

A 31 around her rib cage plus 5 equals 36. This is the band size. The measurement around the actual breasts comes to 39, so you subtract three because the prior measurement was 36, which is a C. So that's a 36C. It doesn't seem to work out in even numbers for me, but maybe it's because I'm trying not to actually touch anyone's breast, which is hard. I always get a 33 or a 35, so I assume I'm supposed to round up.

Now Nina tells us we usually try to get her into a fitting room and down to her bra before measuring her, so she'll already be in the perfect position to try on a bunch of bras in her size. I feel kind of sleazy urging a poor unsuspecting woman into a fitting room—one of the most dreaded rooms ever invented. I feel like a man luring a woman into a room where she can get naked.

Nina measures me. I lift my arms out to the side and try to relax, looking away so that our faces aren't so close together. When you measure a woman, you're up close and personal, foreheads only inches away, noses threatening to touch. "34A," she says.

"That's not right," I tell her. "I'm a 34B."

She looks at my chest skeptically.

"You're a 34A, girl," she says, measuring me again.

I'm crushed. Have I been in denial all these years, wearing a 34B and wondering why there's a slight gap in some of my bras?

"75 percent of women are wearing the wrong size," Nina continues as though this fact might make me feel better. Ana measures at a 34A, and I look at her chest, and then I look at mine, and I know I'm bigger than her, and this only assures me that the tape measure is a liar.

"I'm a 34A, too," Nina says, trying to reassure us, but I really don't care what size she is. Plus from the looks of things I'm pretty sure she's lying.

I want my 34Bs back.

Ashley is over there with her shoulders back, her 36Cs jutting out. "Sometimes I wear a D," she says with her eyes open wide. I tell her that we should go into the operating room together so she could have a reduction and then they give me whatever they take out of her.

The company is in the beginning stages of launching a new bra called the Angels Lined Demi, which has a revolutionary seamless lace. We'll be getting one for free today. Well, I could get used to a free bra every once in a while, especially when I look at the light pink price tag and see that it's $36. Even with thirty percent off, it's still $20 more expensive than my $5 bra from Marshall's. We are to wear this Angels bra as often as possible in the coming weeks, so we can give our personal testimony. They are out of my size, so I grab a 36A and clip it closed on the tightest clasp.

I stare into the mirror for a while, feeling the laced back and how it doesn't itch or irritate, how the padded straps don't cut my skin, and how the lined cups, coupled with the lift the straps gives, allow for this shape I never knew I had to emerge. I might have to start shopping here a little more often.

When greeting customers we're not allowed to ask, "Can I help you?" We are instead supposed to ask open-ended questions: "What brings you in today?" or "Who are you shopping for?" Nina wants us to practice and try to get a credit card opened by the time we leave, so she hands each of us a sample of the coupon book that clients get when they're approved for the credit card.

How, I wonder, are we supposed to sell products we don't know about yet? We all gather around the underwear tables because at this point in our training, looking for a size small, medium, or large is much easier than finding exactly the type of bra a customer is looking for. Lori marches right up to the center of the store and begins talking to customers, repeating what we heard on the video.

"Hi, welcome to Victoria's Secret, how are you doing today? What can I help you out with? It's beautiful outside, isn't it? Did you know 75 percent of women are wearing the wrong size bra?"

There are mirrors everywhere, tall thin ones, their frames painted gold and chipping slightly. I'd gotten into a fight with my hair earlier, as I so often do, and I notice that it still isn't cooperating. I hadn't had time to blow dry it straight so the curls are now frizz-filled waves. At least I'm tan, having just arrived from Florida and Puerto Rico.

I stop staring in the mirror long enough to spot a customer flipping through the rows of underwear. I know that from now on I'll be conducting a lot of searches for extra smalls, extra larges, and everything in between. I've worked retail before. I know how to talk to customers, how not to bother them too much but just enough so that they feel comfortable asking for your help. But still, all those bras and all that credit are making me nervous.

I move a little closer to the woman who will be my first customer ever at Victoria's Secret. I get my sales voice ready. It comes out a little more high pitched than normal when I finally ask, "Can I help you find a size?"

Reflection Rag: Uncle Joe, Roberto Clemente, and I

Christine White

So much happened so quickly after Uncle Joe died. The tempo changed. This new rhythm blew aside the curtain and there it was, this other order of things that lies beneath or beyond: a hidden stage where we play out our lives and strange bedfellows mingle and the orchestra plays ragtime and spirits stand in the wings, feeding us our lines, leading us home.

Exit Uncle Joe

The year is 1999. the month is July. The day is 9. Uncle Joe dies after just a few days in the hospital. The obituary tells part of his story.

. . . born July 23, 1917, in Pittsburgh, Penn. . . . He lived nearly all his life in the Pittsburgh area before moving to Estes Park two years ago after Dorothy, his wife of fifty-three years, died. He received a degree in Petroleum Engineering. . . . Joe served as a Lt. Commander in the navy during World War II on Midway Island . . . Most of his career was spent as a white hat foreman for U.S. Steel. Joe enjoyed piloting his Cessna 150. . . . He was twice decorated and a recognized elite member of the Transcendental Explorers Club International. He is survived by his son Jimmy and his wife, with whom Joe lived in Estes Park, and four grandchildren.

At the top of the obituary is an old picture of Uncle Joe in his cowboy hat, white beard, and plaid shirt. Uncle Joe dressed that way a lot after his son Michael died. He looks like Gabby Hayes, like a real cowboy. He once was asked to be an extra in a Western movie. He looks like the real thing, Uncle Joe in that hat.

I know about Joe's years in the navy and his work with U.S. Steel, know how he loved to fly. But I don't know about the Transcendental Explorers Club

International and the decorations. I thought I knew Joe pretty well but I don't know about that.

I think about Uncle Joe a lot after he dies. I wonder where he is. Just a few months before his death, Uncle Joe was with me in Illinois, and just two weeks before he died, he had driven his van back to Pittsburgh. Eighty-one years old and still driving from Colorado to Pittsburgh all by himself. Even Joe said it was probably the last time. When he couldn't drive back home any more, I guess Uncle Joe decided it was time to die.

Cousin Jimmy was sitting on the bed next to Uncle Joe when my daughter Gia walked into Joe's room at the hospice in Estes Park. Jimmy looked tired and scraggly. "Pappy has passed. Just a couple minutes ago," Jimmy told her.

Gia sat down in a chair at the foot of the bed. Jimmy left to give the undertaker information for Joe's obituary, so Gia remained alone in the room with her dead great uncle. She watched as an attendant removed an IV tube from Joe's limp arm. Then Gia called me.

"Mom," came her little voice, calling Illinois all the way from Colorado. "Uncle Joe died, right before I got here."

I didn't realize at first that she was still in the room with Uncle Joe's body. "Where is Uncle Joe now?" I asked.

"Right here. I'm with him now," she said.

I suggested she wait someplace else but Gia said being in the room with Joe was a good feeling, that the late-afternoon light coming in the window made the room seem warm and soft, and that Joe, lying alone on the bed with the white sheet drawn up to his white chin, his white hair and white beard and mustache in place, looked peaceful. "Like all the sadness has seeped away," she said. "It's not bad to be where Uncle Joe is."

"When is the funeral?" I asked. Ever since Jimmy had called me two days ago, saying that Joe was dying, I had planned to go to the funeral.

"There is no funeral," Gia said. "Jimmy's having a memorial barbecue and then he's going to scatter Joe's ashes."

The thought of a barbecue in lieu of a funeral didn't strike her as odd.

ENTER ROBERTO CLEMENTE

The year is 1999. The month is July. The day is 16. I am inside the Unity Church in Boulder, Colorado. Uncle Joe, or at least his ashes, will be scattered tomorrow in Estes Park. I am at a performance of the Rocky Mountain Ragtime Festival. Gia and a friend have brought me here. The friend's uncle is a ragtime pianist who will perform as part of the concert this evening. The uncle gave us free tickets.

A pianist named Scott Kirby walks onto the small church stage. Kirby is handsome, dark and bearded. He bows, elegant in a flowing white silk shirt and dark trousers.

"I am going to play 'Roberto Clemente.'" That's all he says as he settles himself on the piano bench. "I am going to play 'Roberto Clemente.'"

This juxtaposition of baseball icon and piano rag jars me. I hear Clemente's name and I am back in Pittsburgh all over again. Back where I spent the first twenty years of my life. Back where Uncle Joe came from until he left Pittsburgh two years ago to live with Jimmy. Moving didn't change anything for Uncle Joe. Until he died last week, but maybe even still, Uncle Joe is always from Pittsburgh.

Kirby plays "Roberto Clemente." The music comes in gently syncopated waves, lapping at my consciousness. Lovely, happy waves. Waves that cut to my heart and steal my breath. Haunting and laughing at the same time. Joyful, really. Joyful and never taking itself too seriously. "I am going to play 'Roberto Clemente,'" he said. Not flamboyant and racing like some ragtime, but thoughtful and elegant, this Roberto Clemente. The repeats bring new waves, each telling the same story, but reinvented. The melodies keep returning, first soft, then strutting, now brassy, now defiant, now poignant. And still joyful.

Oh, I wish you could hear it!

I am entranced, mesmerized by "Roberto Clemente." At intermission, I buy a CD with the piece on it. The next day, as I drive to Estes Park to scatter Uncle Joe, I play "Roberto Clemente." Over and over in my car, driving U.S. 36, climbing into the Rocky Mountains, I listen and, as if for the first time, I introduce myself to Clemente just as he had made his presence known to me, last night, at a ragtime festival in Colorado. The notes flow in my mind, run through my blood, the way the Fall River rushes downhill alongside my car.

Ever since that night in Boulder when I heard the piece called "Roberto Clemente," I've been governed by this music. Music I hear and music I sense. It's become a pulse inside me. I'm not sure why I feel this bond to Roberto Clemente but I know better than to ignore the pull of this music because I believe the universe works this way. Uncle Joe and Roberto Clemente and I, we were destined to interact with each other. It doesn't matter that Joe died last week and Clemente died over twenty-five years ago and I'm still around. That's how time works sometimes.

And, I am to find out, that's how writing is sometimes. I start out chasing one story and then another story starts to chase me. I want to write about Uncle Joe but Roberto Clemente jumps in. And then other forces become involved. You see how it is. Sometimes a writer has no choice.

Uncle Joe's story is still warm; Roberto Clemente's trail is cold. As I write about them both, as I turn and chase them both, I re-enter the past and play games with time. I tell you, it's the best part of writing sometimes, to play hide and seek this way with the past, to live things again, and to write about ragtime.

ENTER SCOTT JOPLIN

The year is 1896. The place is Sedalia, Missouri, a gathering spot for ragtime musicians, a town still part of the American frontier. It is night. The East Main Street that by day is a collection of feed and hardware stores and harness shops is now the "District."

Sundown fills the wooden sidewalks with gamblers, dance-hall girls, sports, pimps, and just regular men out on the town. Honky tonks like the Williams brothers' Maple Leaf Club are wide open in this tenderloin district. Bets are placed. Liaisons arranged. In the bordellos and clubs, black and white customers hang around the Victorian-style bars, pool and gaming tables. The hanging gas chandeliers do not give off light so much as haze but, even so, clearly visible through the smoke in a far corner is an upright piano and on its lushly-covered stool sits a black man. The piano player. He plays all night. His music both describes and accompanies the melee around him. He plays ragtime.

The man at the upright that night in Sedalia may even have been Scott Joplin himself. Joplin, who would become the Ragtime King, the greatest ragtime composer ever, had just arrived in Sedalia in 1896 and it wasn't long before he was at the center of Sedalia's ragtime community.

It's a mystery how the fabric called ragtime came to be. A rag was originally a simple black folk melody. Early ragtime composers, men like Joplin, collected these rags, these scraps of melody they heard in the air around them, and sewed them into extended musical compositions called piano rags. They built their rags around folk melodies and strong rhythmic variations called syncopation. Ragtime, while not exclusively black, blended the gaiety of freedom with the underlying sadness of slavery.

Yes, it's possible. Joplin's music might have been what the piano man played that night in the tenderloin of Sedalia: lilting, contagious, ironic, spirited but somehow melancholy, gentle music filled with repetition and melody and rhythm.

THE CROWD GATHERS

The year is 1999. The month is July. The day is 17. Jimmy's already grilling the memorial meat when I arrive at his collection of condos along the Fall River. Once Jimmy told me he would piss on Joe's grave but he apparently has reconsidered.

I walk into the convention center where Jimmy is hosting the barbecue and Uncle Joe is everywhere. A long table, draped with a bright red Indian blanket, is covered with photographs and personal articles that belonged to Joe. The decades I had shared with Uncle Joe spread out before me.

I take it all in, this majestically pitiful sweep of a life, decades compressed and expanded, recalled by this collection of Joe's things: The keys to his van. A road atlas held open by a magnifying glass. A travel journal. Two hand saws next to a dusty hand drill. Reading glasses and Civil War books. Joe's hockey skates. A bowler hat and a walking cane with a rattlesnake head. I study the photographs on the wall. There's Joe as a young sailor, Joe close up in his Navy uniform, Joe and Dorothy at the altar of St. David's Church, Joe with his first son Michael, Joe with Michael and Jimmy, Joe alone in his old house with his last dog, his blind Airedale Quincy. But Jimmy's memorial is about more than Joe. As I walk along the wall, past the ink sketches of the Homestead steel mill, I pass pictures of my dead parents, of other long-departed aunts and uncles.

Jimmy has been following me along the wall. "Everyone's here," he says, in his husky drawn-out way, his sly voice that could mean almost anything.

Everyone *was* here, gathered from only God knows where, come to Estes Park for the barbecue. In the photos, Dorothy ages along with Joe, but even as she ages, she dazzles. Dorothy and Michael, both smiling, sit side by side on the living room sofa, shortly before Michael died. We were all happy then. Dorothy's blonde hair is pulled back, her black dress low-cut and elegant. Michael wears what appears to be a cutaway jacket, white shirt open at the neck, his red hair thinning, his red beard impeccable.

A large greeting card sits in the middle of the table, next to Joe's ice skates. Dorothy had once sent this card to Joe. Joe had saved it and now the card belongs to Jimmy. The front of the card shows a rabbit and a donkey, apparently a married couple, sitting back to back, each one secretly fuming about the other. The donkey is thinking, "You dumb bunny." The rabbit is thinking, "You jackass." The sentiment inside the card captures Dorothy's wit and sarcasm and bitterness about her marriage: "It's so nice having these conversations with you." Yet, as if to show that one reality is never the whole story, in her flowing graceful script, my aunt had signed the card, "Love, Dot."

RAGTIME AGAIN

The year is still 1896. Ragtime music generates controversy when it first becomes popular in the 1890s. There is, first of all, the predictable moralizing about ragtime's low origins: prejudice, beer, and back rooms are undeniably linked to ragtime. Ragtime's syncopations, broken rhythms, and shifting accents also cause great uproar. "Who put the sin in syncopation?" critics want to know.

Syncopation, ragtime's most recognizable rhythmic characteristic, superimposes an irregular rhythm over a regular one and comes from the interrelationship of the right and left hands. The left hand on the piano plays the stride bass *or basso continuo,* keeping the pulse with the characteristic *oom pah* beat. The right hand plays the melodies and rhythmically works against the left hand, displacing the left hand's *oom pahs,* putting the beat on the off-beat.

Scott Joplin wants to make sure the ragtime players can take in all the rhythms, melodies, and counter melodies of a piano rag, and so his advice on tempo is categorical: "Play slowly until you catch the swing, and never play ragtime fast at any time." Play ragtime like a slow march, Joplin says. Joplin wants ragtime seen as a legitimate art form accepted by people of culture. Not that anyone calls ragtime illegitimate, but the implications are clear. It just isn't good enough for some folks.

COUSIN JIMMY PLAYS

The barbecue is underway and I hang on the fringes, watching Jimmy greet the arriving guests. He is gracious. A gracious host. I haven't seen Jimmy since last February when we had sat and talked, as we had many times before, over lunch at the Boulderado Hotel.

Jimmy, who in past years and for past lunches had sauntered into the Boulderado looking like Dirty Harry, rugged and sexy and slightly sinister in black leather jacket and orange sunglasses, this sunny day in February just looks weary. His thinning hair is no longer red, just dark blond and straggling, hanging to his shoulders, and his face has become his mother Dorothy's face: the same skin, the same dazzling teeth and crystal clear blue eyes.

I tell Jimmy he looks tired. He nods. Then I ask about Joe.

Jimmy tells me Joe is still drinking. Joe drinks in secret and thinks no one knows. Joe's knees are bad and he has a hard time walking but he still drives through Rocky Mountain National Park every day. Joe takes over Jimmy's kitchen each night, cooking food no one wants, ranting at Jimmy. Joe rants in the kitchen and Jimmy goes to Alcoholics Anonymous meetings. Sometimes Joe goes with him. Every day it's like this.

Jimmy grins his wide, almost demonic smile that is either very open or very closed, I'm never sure which, leans toward me across his plate, and says, "Christine, I don't need all this opportunity for personal growth."

We reminisce. "It's sad we're such a small family," I say. Cousin Jimmy smiles.

"We're small but we're getting bigger every day." He grins his grin.

"I have a daughter," he says.

"I know. Six-year-old Lila," I say.

"No, another daughter. Annie. She's twenty-one."

"Oh," I say.

Jimmy tells me about finding this daughter Annie. Since joining AA he's been trying to fix the broken places, smooth the ragged edges of his life. Jimmy's trying to make perfect time. Or make time perfect, I think. He answers my question before I ask.

"Annie's last name is Martinez," he tells me. His blue eyes are far away now. "That's why I couldn't marry her mother. I never could've taken a Mexican woman home to my dad. You know how it was back then, Christine. In Pittsburgh. Twenty years ago. You remember."

TIME TRAVELER

I used to think of time as something that flows like a river, a continuum that moved from the past, through the present, and into the future. "Roberto Clemente" has disrupted this linear view of time. How can I be floating down this time river, all nice and easy, and suddenly find myself upstream when I haven't walked along the bank to get there?

But it happened. Some tributary lost in time took me back to Pittsburgh that night I heard "Roberto Clemente" for the first time, back up the Ohio River, back to where the Ohio is formed from the waters of the Allegheny and the Mononge-hela Rivers, back to the placed called The Point where the Ohio is born and where my grandparents lived with the other immigrants a century ago and where one day Roberto Clemente would play baseball at Three Rivers Stadium.

"Roberto Clemente" makes my mind play tricks with time, scrolling through events backwards and forwards in strange ways. I tell you the brain can be a time machine and sometimes, like when you hear ragtime, you can become a time traveler. Like this.

It is 1955. Pittsburgh is a smoky city, a dirty, tough steel mill town, still deeply entrenched in its ethnic enclaves of Germans, Italians, Irish, Latvians, and Poles, and Roberto Clemente, a black man from Puerto Rico, is a rookie for the Pittsburgh Pirates. The Pirates still play at Forbes Field. When Clemente comes to Pittsburgh, the Pirates are spectacular losers. Clemente chooses 21 for his uniform number, it is said, because his full name, "Roberto Clemente Walker," has exactly twenty-one letters.

Clemente struggles to gain acceptance in his new home. Pittsburgh has fixed racial barriers. Clemente describes himself as a "double nigger," both black and Latin, unable to speak much English, isolated and subjected to racial slurs, even from his own teammates and especially from the press. It's hard to look back and see how we were and have to say this is true. Sports writers, none of whom can speak Spanish, use phonetics to make Clemente look stupid, quoting Clemente as saying be "heet the peeetch gut" and the weather was "veree hot." When his style seems flamboyant, Pittsburgh sports writers call him a "Puerto Rican hot dog." When he finishes eighth in the balloting for MVP in 1960, after the Pirates' dramatic World Series win over the Yankees, Clemente feels he was denied the award, or at least a higher ranking, because he is Latin American.

I tell some friends that an essay is hounding me that somehow has something to do with Roberto Clemente. They're skeptical. "You can't write about Clemente," one male friend, also a writer, says. "You don't know anything about baseball."

For a while, I agree with them but then I realize that I do know the most important thing about baseball: baseball is about running home. Here's what I mean.

No one but my grandfather ever took me to baseball games, and then only a few times, when I was in grade school, all the way out to Forbes Field near Schenley Park where we would sit on the bleachers in the hot afternoon sun and Grandpap would follow every play carefully and silently.

Grandpap loved the Pirates. He would sip from his silver flask and occasionally pass the program to me. He bought me Coke and hot dogs. I mostly remember how handsome Grandpap looked in his pearl gray suit trousers, his wide gray-and-white striped suspenders, and his starched white monogrammed shirt, his sleeves rolled up, his French cuffs disappearing for a few hours while we sat watching the Pirates play baseball.

I skim some biographies of Clemente. My interest picks back up. Clemente was wary of writers. He's a prickly, enigmatic character. Baseball transformed him. Some say he transformed baseball.

He also died on my birthday.

When I read that, or remember that, for I must have known it once, the headlines blared it so at the time, when I read again that Clemente died on my birthday, I know that, somewhere our paths have surely crossed. Roberto Clemente must be in this story about Uncle Joe's ashes.

CLEMENTE DIES

The year is 1972. The month is December. The day is 31. Clemente boards a plane in San Juan, Puerto Rico, to personally accompany relief aid to earthquake victims in Nicaragua. Clemente believes that the military will not siphon off the donated food and clothing if he, El Magnifico, is there to supervise. He is tired. In his last game of what would prove to be his last season, he made hit number 3,000. He had felt the need to hurry and make this hit because, he tells reporters, he suspects he won't live to be old.

There are other premonitions that Clemente doesn't heed. His son sees the plane crashing. Clemente tells his wife "when your time comes, it comes." His father asks him not to go but Clemente boards the plane anyway. The plane crashes into the ocean about one mile off the coast of Puerto Rico, killing everyone aboard.

Thousands gather for days after the crash, standing at the ocean's edge at a place called Puente Maldonado outside of San Juan, watching the waves that stole Clemente's life. Clemente's body is never found. Clemente's sock, and later his briefcase, drift ashore. Everyone wants to know where Clemente is but the rescuers can find no trace of his body. When Pittsburgh catcher Manny Sanguillen hears about the crash, he runs to the beach and tries to jump into the water, but some of the waves that night are twelve feet tall. For the next five days, Sanguillen searches, making futile attempts to dive for Clemente's body. Thousands stand on the beach, just looking for some sign of Clemente.

MORE BASEBALL AND MORE RAGTIME

Ed Kaizer is the best pianist I know. We sit in his studio at Bradley University and talk about ragtime music and "Roberto Clemente." Ed understands both subjects. He is a classical pianist who also plays ragtime. He has played ragtime around the world. Ed also is from Pittsburgh and used to play semiprofessional baseball there in the late 1950s, but Ed never knew Clemente personally. Ed remembers once pitching a game in Forbes Field, though, when he was in high school. I guess you don't forget things like that.

Ed talks about piano rags and rhythm, reminding me how ragtime's distinctive syncopation comes when the left hand keeps the rhythm, the *oom pah* beat, while the right hand works out the melodies and plays the themes. Ed plays "Roberto Clemente" several times. When Ed's initial play-through doesn't sound like my CD, I realize how possessive I've become of the image I have in my head of Clemente. In Ed's hands, a different Clemente plays right field.

Ed hears what I hear in the piece. He goes with me back to Pittsburgh. "We can couch our memories in ragtime," he says. "It's nostalgic. It takes you wherever you want to go."

EL MAGNIFICO

Clemente was called "El Magnifico." The Magnificent One. A true Baseball Man. In the Caribbean there are a few who are called Baseball Men. For Baseball Men, baseball is a calling, a deep passion.

Dodger scout Al Campanis noticed the young Clemente when Clemente was seventeen and playing baseball in Puerto Rico. Campanis recognized his ferocious talent, called him "the greatest natural athlete I ever saw as a free agent," but did he know that Clemente would one day rise to the level of myth?

For eighteen seasons, 1955–72, Clemente was the mainstay of the Pittsburgh Pirate outfield. He won four National League batting crowns. His lifetime batting average was .317. in his career he scored 240 home runs and had 1,350 RBIs. He hit safety in all seven games of the 1960 and 1971 World Series and won the Most Valuable Player Award for the 1971 Series against Baltimore, where he batted .414 and hit two home runs. Clemente was a twelve-time All Star and twelve-time Gold Glove Award winner. He was the League's Most Valuable Player in 1966. He became only the eleventh player in major league history to record 3,000 hits. After his death in 1972, Clemente became the first Hispanic player elected to the National Baseball Hall of Frame. The Pirates then permanently retired Number 21.

ARRIBA! ARRIBA!

So skilled and alive and purposeful was Clemente when he played baseball that those who watched him have never forgotten. For Clemente, life was always about the right way to play the game, like when, in a game against the Astros, he ran flat-out into a wall, risking injury on a relatively meaningless play. "A catch for the ages," the *Houston Chronicle* called it, but some were dismayed.

Why did you *do* this? Why risk injury on a nothing play?

Genuinely puzzled because the answer was so obvious, Clemente answered simply. "I wanted to catch the ball."

Clemente put right field on the map. Throwing on the run from center field, Clemente let the ball loose at up to 110 miles per hour, it is said. He ran almost in desperation, as if chased by a beast, so furious was his speed. He slid with skill and at times hung suspended in air, parallel to the field, flat and fleeting as a shadow.

Clemente would swing at anything. He was a pitcher's nightmare. Someone once said he could hit .299 in an iron lung. And when Clemente hit, when his bat really connected with the ball, it would rise on a silent trajectory, kind of like time's arrow, flying away through space as if blasted from a shotgun. No wonder sports writer Roger Angell said Clemente played "a kind of baseball that none of us had ever seen before."

I'm surprised by how many people have a Clemente story. All this time there was a world of Clemente memories out there that I didn't know existed until now. Cousin Jimmy tells me this story about Roberto Clemente.

When he was in seventh grade, Jimmy and his friends liked to go to Forbes Field to watch the Pirates and they always sat in right field. He said they were drawn there. They tried to sit near Clemente. "He had a *baseball* look to him," Jimmy remembers. "Clemente was very proud and he would hold his head very high and move his neck." Jimmy calls this Clemente's "peacock thing."

In one game, Hank Aaron, who was playing for the Braves, hit a ball out of the infield and it rolled up toward second base. Jimmy says the ball lay on the ground about fifteen feet away from Clemente. Clemente never moved toward the ball. He dared Aaron to try for second. Aaron took off. Clemente ran so fast he scooped up the ball and threw Aaron out by a few inches. "It was the *Superman* move! Only Clemente could do that. We screamed *'Arriba! Arriba!'* We didn't know what that meant but we screamed *'Arriba!'* We couldn't believe it!"

As Jimmy is yelling *"Arriba!"* into the phone, jolting the lines between Illinois and Colorado, I notice that on my desk is a brochure for a new musical playing in Pittsburgh about Clemente that's called *"¡Arriba! ¡Arriba!"* The Roberto Clemente Story."

No Simple Stories

I think it would be nice to write a simple story for once but there are no simple stories. Just simple ideas and little insights that take a long time in telling. All of this back and forth, the meshing of the pieces of this ragtime puzzle, is how I sort through the ideas that fill my head when I write.

So many lovely parts to this puzzle. I turn over all the little bits looking for the right fit: A rag, originally a black folk tune, grew to describe an instrumental syncopated march. To rag an existing melody is to shift the accents. "To rag" also means to tease, to incorporate surprises, to introduce an unexpected rhythm. The crowds cheer when a baseball player hits a home run. Ragtime or jazz musicians say the music is "coming home" when, in the last strain or next-to-last, the tempo changes and the rhythm increases.

There's more. Ragtime came to be a written music. That was important. And Joplin insisted that players play note-for-note from the written score. No one could change the parts he didn't like. "Play it as I wrote it." Joplin said. Joplin's first published work in 1899 is called "Original Rags" and the last, published after his death in 1917, is aptly titled "Reflection Rag—Syncopated Musings."

I told you before. We really don't choose our stories. When we're hot, our stories chase us until we catch them.

Coming Home

Intense syncopation produces music that ragtime lovers call "hot." Clemente was hot. So hot in the 1971 World Series that the organist at Three Rivers Stadium played "Jesus Christ Superstar" every time Clemente came to bat.

Although the initial racial tensions faded and Pittsburgh loved him long before 1971, Clemente had always wanted national recognition of his baseball ability. Clemente wanted to be seen at the best ballplayer in the world. "I play as good as anybody . . . but I am not loved," Clemente said once. "I don't need to be loved. I wish it would happen. Do you know what I mean?"

Clemente was loved in Puerto Rico and he loved his homeland in return. Clemente's wife returned to Puerto Rico for the birth of each of their children, at her husband's request, and Clemente spent his off seasons in Puerto Rico. Clemente was always going home.

There's lots of ways to go home. It's instinctive, this returning, this circling the bases. Like birds and turtles and salmon, like Uncle Joe in his van making his loops between Colorado and Pittsburgh and like Roberto Clemente playing baseball, and maybe even like dying, we find ways to make that trip back upstream. Show me someone who has no desire for a return ticket and I will show you someone who has never heard ragtime.

CLEMENTE: DREAMER AND POET

In the final analysis, I think, we matter for the qualities we embody in this life and for the depth of our dreams. Clemente's dream was a build *Ciudad Deportiva*, City of Sport, for the underprivileged children of Puerto Rico. Today Clemente's City of Sport sits on 240 acres, just a few miles from where El Magnifico died and where, since his death, over 100,000 children have learned about sports and about hope. My research turns up a poem that Clemente wrote one Father's Day during a game at Three Rivers Stadium. Here, I believe, I have tapped into Clemente's soul.

> Who am I?
> I am a small point in the light of the full moon.
> I only need one ray of the sun to warm my face.
> I only need one breeze from the Alisios to refresh my soul.
> What else can I ask if I know that my sons really love me?

I had never before thought of baseball players as wise men but Clemente is right. What do any of us need, after all, beyond the sun and the breeze and the love of our children?

LOVE AGAIN LOST

The year is 1999. The month is March. The day is 5. Joe sits in my kitchen and tells me about Annie.

"I have a new granddaughter. She's a nice girl. Her name is Annie Martinez." At eighty-one, with time running out, Joe doesn't seem bothered any more by the sound of last names and the boundaries of old ethnic neighborhoods.

"She's getting married in September and Jim is giving her away. I gave her $10,000 for a wedding present." He chews thoughtfully on a piece of Italian bread. I almost choke on my spaghetti. Joe has always been tight with his money.

Ten thousand, I repeat.

Joe pauses and his fork with the spaghetti dangling stops in mid-air.

"Dorothy would have loved to have had a granddaughter. She would have loved to buy her pretty clothes, Annie would have made Dorothy so happy. I wish I had known." His voice trails off and I figure he's thinking about Dorothy's sad life and her despair at the end. The fork continues on toward his mouth. And then Joe starts to talk about his airplane.

Joe always was a traveler. Sometimes in his car and sometimes in his plane, he would just disappear. One day Joe told Dorothy he was going to the store to get groceries and he didn't come back for a week. When he returned, he said he had driven to the Outer Banks of North Carolina, just to look at it. Joe did things like that all the time. He drove to the place where the roads end just so he could drive back home again.

When we live our lives in metaphor like this, we risk that people won't understand.

Joe often went along to the AA Fellowship meetings with Jimmy. Sometimes Joe had a few drinks before he went to the meeting and sometimes he left early so he could have a few more before he went home. Because Joe's knees were filled with arthritis, he needed a comfortable chair and Jimmy had Joe's old brown living room chair moved into the AA hall. The brown chair still sits in the meeting room. I guess some other old man sits in it now.

Jimmy says he initially took care of Joe because it was the right thing to do, not because he loved him. Perhaps Jimmy loved his dad and doesn't know it yet. I asked Jimmy why he didn't have a traditional funeral for Joe. He thought for a minute and then said, "There was nothing to say."

Maybe saying nothing is better than saying the wrong thing. Silence is easier to take back or to amend. Scott Joplin had asked his wife to have the Maple Leaf Rag, his most famous work, played at his funeral. When the time came, she said no.

"How many, many times since then, I've wished to my heart that I'd said yes."

The Fellowship

Most of the guests at the barbecue are Jimmy's friends from the AA Fellowship Hall. A man with tattoos on his arms and a bear claw around his neck arrives on a big black Harley. A pudgy man in brown trousers and flowered sport shirt says hello. Ladies carry plates of deviled eggs and fruit salads and bags of potato chips. While Jimmy cooks sausages, Annie sets out platters for the meat. Everyone is eating the sausages as fast as Jimmy can grill them.

Jimmy's friends take brief note of the pictures on the table. They never really knew the Joe who is in all these photographs. They just remember him as Jimmy's dad who used to go to some of the AA meetings with Jim and finally stood up one night and said, "My name is Joe and I am an alcoholic."

I only have Joe's version of what took place, Joe said he had been going with Jimmy to the AA meetings for months. He liked to hear the stories and needed some place to spend time, he said. He was lonely in Estes Park. He missed Pittsburgh.

Joe said everyone was happy when he finally stood up and said that yes, he, too, was an alcoholic and he said he told some pretty hair-raising stories of his own. But it wasn't because he had a drinking problem that he went to the meetings, he told me. It was because they had really good food afterwards and he liked having a place to go for dinner.

The last time Joe visited me, he signed our guest book, my family's way of keeping track of all the people who pass through our house. "AA Hall—Keep coming back!! Joe R., Estes Park Colorado, 3–5–99."

I remember Joe laughing as he wrote. "That's what they keep saying after those damn AA meetings, Chris. 'Keep coming back. Keep coming back.' Hell, I just like the food."

HYPERTIME

Time, modern physicists say, is really an extra dimension. Einstein understood this. He said that the distinction between past, present, and future is only an illusion, even if a stubborn one. Einstein also believed that the road on which we travel through time can curve and go backwards; it doesn't have to be the straight-as-an-arrow trajectory Newton envisioned.

I scan back and forth over my ideas and stories like a composer scans back and forth over a musical score. A musical score gives a solid shape to time, allowing the composer to hold past, present, and future in his hands all at once. Perhaps then composers live outside of time in what physicists call "hypertime."

David Thomas Roberts is the composer of "Roberto Clemente." He lives not in hypertime but in Moss Point, Mississippi. Roberts is also a writer, artist, and poet. He studies metaphysics. He is as deeply immersed in his musical compositions as he is in the landscape. The American landscape is his passion. "American Landscape" is also the title of his CD that I carry with me everywhere so I can listen to "Roberto Clemente."

Our conversation takes a seemingly odd tack in the beginning. Roberts tells me that a good friend of his had died the night before. I tell him I first heard "Roberto Clemente" the night before my uncle's memorial. Is it a coincidence, I then ask, that I sit talking to you about your composition the night after your friend's death?

"Synchronicity," he replies, "is built into our reality, and there may be no such thing as coincidence."

WHAT THE MUSIC MEANS

Roberts was moved to write "Roberto Clemente" after seeing a film about Clemente during the 1979 World Series, and he describes the piece as a "folk elegy" and a "country funeral." After viewing the film, Clemente became for Roberts "a myth to be recalled with affection." I wonder, but do not ask, if Clemente has become for Roberts a part of the American landscape he loves so much, just as Uncle Joe has become a myth to me, a myth I recall with affection, a key figure in my personal landscape.

As a musical composition, "Roberto Clemente" has four musical themes or melodies. These themes vary and repeat, vary and repeat, returning with nuances and interpretations determined by the composer and the performer.

To me this sounds a lot like life.

"Roberto Clemente" is not, Roberts says, a retelling of Clemente's life and career as a sound poem might be, but the music evokes "the man as I had viewed him via the documentary." Roberts tells his concert audiences that he heard elements of the first phrase of the second theme in his head as he watched the Clemente film and that he associates this theme most implicitly with Clemente the man. Even so, he cautions. "Don't say 'that's what the music means.' . . . The symbolism is more elusive. More fragile. You can't reduce the irreducible."

Roberts then tells me something he has never told anyone. The Clemente documentary used footage of waves washing up on the shore in Puerto Rico and footage of Clemente circling the bases. Roberts can't recall if the pictures were actually superimposed in the film or if he just remembered them in conjuncture. But it was these two images, the waves on the shore and Clemente circling the bases, running home, that he wanted to communicate in his composition.

Roberts has written about the "plaintiveness" and "gentle anguish" that is associated with ragtime, and I tell him I feel this gentle pain when I listen to "Roberto Clemente" and think about Clemente's life.

"I was touched by the mingling of tragedy and hope that is all around us," Roberts tells me. "And I was asking myself this question: *What is so meaningful in this tough school which is what I believe the earth is?*"

"Do you think Clemente's death was unfair?" I ask Roberts.

"I think we choose our births and deaths," he tells me. "We are unconsciously fulfilling what we've mapped or assented to have mapped. I don't believe in tragedy in the conventional sense any longer."

GRACE NOTES

A grace note is a musical term for a quick note frequently used in ragtime that is usually attached to another note and is out of time with the rest of the piece. Roberts describes the grace notes in "Roberto Clemente" as *lagniappe*, a Creole term for "a little something extra" or "a show of appreciation," and points out how the grace notes in "Roberto Clemente" add to the Latin feel of the piece. Ed Kaizer calls these extra notes "embellishments" but I prefer to say "grace notes."

To me, grace notes, in music or in life, are those unexpected blessings that pass by so quickly we take them for granted unless we listen very carefully to the music. Grace notes, like synchronicities, are really little miracles.

THE HOAX REVEALED

Jimmy says there really is no Transcendental Explorers Club International. He tells me he made it up when, after talking to the undertaker, he felt Joe's obituary was lacking in accomplishments.

I think Jimmy is mistaken about there not being a club for transcendental explorers. Why else would we wonder where we are and where we're going and what exactly we have to do to get home? Why else would life go round and round us like ragtime, defining itself by the off-beat, dangling the hope ahead of the tragedy and offering us the occasional grace note? Why else would Roberto Clemente speak to me in a song?

I think *Jimmy* is really the elite member of this club, twice decorated, as he said of Joe. Otherwise he would have set lower sights for Joe when he added the grace note to his father's obituary. After all, he could have said Joe was the Grand Pooh-bah of the Shriners.

DOROTHY'S ASHES

The month is July. The day is 17. The year is 1999. There's no formal announcement. Those of us who really knew Joe just sense that it's time and we gravitate to the river. Jimmy and his wife and son climb across some boulders that reach out into the Fall River. River is really too big a word today for the water that flows by Jimmy's resort, just a fast-moving mountain stream it is, dashing among rocks and leaving trails of white foam at every turn. Joe's ashes are going to be scattered in this stream, but because Jimmy's condo construction had caused a fish kill in this same river last spring and the Environmental Protection Agency had levied a substantial fine against him, Jimmy hasn't talked much about his plan. The ashes have been kept under wraps.

I walk down close to the river's edge, so I can say goodbye to Uncle Joe as his ashes pass. Jimmy opens the container that holds Joe's ashes and removes the plastic bag. As he hands the bag to his son, I see another small brown cardboard box cut on the rock. Jimmy opens that box and removes another plastic bag that he holds close to his heart for a moment. Dorothy's ashes. Jimmy still has his mother's ashes.

The year was 1996. The month was February. The day was 21. Dorothy's funeral. Gentle anguish, Roberts would call it. As the priest talked about the pain that had lived in Dorothy's heart for too many years, I heard the ragtime piano player in the bawdy house back in Sedalia. His *basso continuo* pumped out the rhythm, the relentless *oom pah*, of her life. In the end, the priest had nothing more than words for comfort. After all, he's not a piano man.

But I hoped Joe was listening. Roberts understood the question: What is so meaningful in this tough school which is what I believe the earth is? Did Joe hear the repeats and the themes returning? As he buried Dorothy, I wanted Joe to hear the grace notes.

After mass, Joe and I sat in the pew. Joe turned to me and in a loud annoyed voice complained about the sermon. He said his hearing aid wasn't working right.

"Will someone please tell me what that damn priest was talking about? All I could hear was every now and then he said 'Dorothy.' I couldn't make out any other damn thing he was saying."

Coming Home Again

That was three years ago, the last time I saw Dorothy's ashes. Today Jimmy holds his mother close to his heart and then, as he dumps her into the Fall River, his son pours Uncle Joe into the river alongside Dorothy. The current rushes past me. I listen to the water. The voices are clear as the ashes pass by.

"Dumb bunny," the donkey says.

"Jackass," the rabbit answers.

Swirling from eddy to eddy, they're after each other again. Alive and sad and angry and hopeful. Playful, the tumbling ashes are. Rolling over large stones, like the stride bass of a piano rag. In a hurry. Defying Joplin's advice about never playing ragtime fast. The music is coming home now.

I wanted to catch the ball, Clemente said. *I don't need to be loved but I wish it would happen. What more can we ask if we know our children love us?* The piano shakes as the rags roll out. The left hand plays *oom pah, oom pah* and won't quit. The right hand spins and re-spins the melody. *Ragtime takes us anywhere we want to go.*

Keep coming back, Uncle Joe wrote in my book. *Never say that's what the music means*, Roberts told me.

The time of our lives. Time torn in pieces. Time sewn back together. Little bits of melody plucked from the air. Jagged time. Ragged time.

"Dumb bunny."

"Jackass."

I close my eyes and remember all the ragged times and wonder if this damn ragtime will ever stop. I don't want a life played out like a piano rag anymore and I'm tired of the tragedy even if it carries along a little hope. Then I remember the grace note. I remember that Dorothy had signed her bittersweet card to Joe with "Love."

"Love, Dot."

The music softens and the notes dance around silence. The crowds are waiting, hoping for another home run. A Superman move. Clemente jerks his neck, unwinds his bat, and seeks another meaningful connection.

"Arriba! Arriba!" we yell as the ball disappears over the stadium wall.

Part 2

Talking About Creative Nonfiction

One reason we're so enthusiastic about this evolving genre is the role of writers and teachers of creative nonfiction in defining the terms of the conversation. As both teachers and writers we've benefited from that conversation ourselves, and so we believe that writers entering the genre can gain from hearing these writers talk about the making of their own work. After all, in the long tradition of the genre, essayist/critics from Montaigne through Addison, Steele, Lamb, and Hazlitt to E. B. White have not only written the most enduring examples of the essay but also provided the most valuable commentary on the form.

Therefore, in Part 2, Talking About Creative Nonfiction, we've chosen pieces—many of them written by authors in Part 1—that reflect these writers' thoughts, opinions, speculations, theories, and critiques of creative nonfiction. They provide a multivoiced discussion of the genre on a wide range of topics related to writing creative nonfiction—from definitions of the form and overviews of some of the subgenres to informal histories of the genre, personal accounts of writing, and hints about strategies and practices. Some, like Patricia Foster and Steven Harvey, discuss their personal reasons for writing or talk about their composing strategies. Others offer us insight into the particular forms of creative nonfiction in which they work: Mary Clearman Blew and Patricia Hampl give us different perspectives on the memoir, especially the ways imagination transforms and transposes memory; Phillip Lopate and Scott Russell Sanders talk about the history of the personal essay; Tracy Kidder discusses his views and his experiences in literary journalism.

Along with the writers whose work appears in Part 1, others offer us insight into the issues surrounding creative nonfiction. Robert Root explains and illustrates how and why he writes disjunctive essays; Peggy Shumaker examines the varieties of forms in which short nonfiction "capture[s] our attention via compression"; Jocelyn Bartkevicius and Michael Pearson examine attempts to define and identify creative nonfiction; and Judith Kitchen and Brenda Miller approach the lyric essay from two different perspectives.

As we've mentioned earlier, many of these pieces can be paired with writings in Part 1. Just a glance at the table of contents will show you which authors appear in both sections of the book. A cursory look at the titles will give you some sense of the specific concerns that are represented here. For example, if you were to look at Mimi Schwartz's Part 1 memoir, "My Father Always Said," you'd discover an evocative story of how a family trip to the German town where her parents lived before World War II affects her understanding of the stories her father told about that community. If you then read her Part 2 essay, "Memoir? Fiction? Where's the Line?" you would gain insight into the way such a narrative draws upon memory and flirts with the boundaries between memoir and fiction.

Conversely, let's suppose that you wanted to read some of the Part 2 essays to gain a sense of a particular writer's theory of creative nonfiction before you read his or her sample of it in Part 1. For example, in his Part 2 piece, "Whatever Happened to the Personal Essay?" Phillip Lopate discusses the history of the personal essay as well as reveals his own particular slant on the kinds of essays he writes. Given that context, Lopate's Part 1 essay, "Portrait of My Body," becomes a model for what he means by "interrogating the self." Similarly, if you were to read Scott Russell Sanders' essay on essays in this section first, you would read his personal essay, "Cloud Crossing," with an awareness of what he hopes to accomplish in his writing.

Several of the writers whose works are presented in Part 2 are also working teachers in whose courses students often study creative nonfiction. Some of them teach courses expressly focused on creative nonfiction as a subject in itself. As a result, their pieces are at least tangentially about the connections between writing and teaching writing, especially writing and teaching creative nonfiction. Like Donald Murray, who first modeled this sensibility in *A Writer Teaches Writing* decades ago, teacher/writers such as Robert Root and Michael Steinberg take a writerly approach to this genre.

Although some of these selections involve critical analysis, they do not present a detached theoretical approach. All of these essays are designed to offer a writerly perspective on the evolving dialogue about creative nonfiction. As a result, the works selected for Part 2 ground creative nonfiction in the behaviors and motives of working writers and teachers, reflecting back on the examples of the form in Part 1 and projecting ahead to essays on composing the fourth genre in Part 3.

The Landscape of Creative Nonfiction

Jocelyn Bartkevicius

[I]naccuracy is very often a superior form of truth.

—Virginia Woolf, "Incongruous Memories"

1. The Stranger

I was standing in a garden, tomato plants ripening, chickens dashing about, when I first learned I was a stranger. I was quite young, maybe six or seven, watching my grandmother pick tomatoes and tell stories about her life as a farm girl in Eastern Europe. She had just gotten to the part about hiding in the forest from waves of invading armies—Russians then Prussians then Russians again—when she stopped, stood up, looked me in the eye, and said: "But you are an American; you don't understand."

How can I convey the force of these words? Of course, as a school girl I was familiar with the idea of "being an American." I said the pledge of allegiance, hand on heart like all the other kids. I sang the "Star Spangled Banner" (except for those unreachable glaring red high notes). But this identity had never been pinned upon me so specifically, so singularly, or as an impediment. "Being an American" had never made me an outsider. Standing in my grandmother's garden, among plants and animals raised the old ways, I was the other.

In memory, when she speaks these words, my grandmother is looking me right in the eye. She was a small woman, possibly reaching five feet at her healthiest, before the osteoporosis formed a permanent stoop. And I was a gangly girl who got all her height early. But now that I look at the memory, examine it instead of experiencing it, I must admit that a five-foot-tall six year old is an unlikely creature. Something is wrong with the memory. It is incongruous.

And then there are holes in the memory: I can't remember whether my grandmother continued her story after she stood up and spoke to me. Or whether she returned to her gardening. Or why she began the story at all. It was hard to get her to talk about Lithuania, especially about the years when, as a very young woman, she had to bury food in the forest to survive, had to prepare constantly to flee soldiers and their various hungers, had to watch city people (who could not grow their own food) sicken and die. Perhaps my father stood off to the side prompting her. But he is not in the memory. Maybe I—normally a very shy child and fearful of misunderstanding her difficult Lithuanian accent—had a rare fit of boldness and asked her a question about Europe.

The scene is one that I return to often, for her words fixed the moment as indelibly as a brand. I used to think that the memory drew me in spite of its incongruities and holes. But I am beginning to realize that this memory compels me *because* of the incongruities and holes. The pitted, nearly invisible landscape of the past is a mysterious, inviting place. Each exploration reveals a different topography.

Looking back, I find that my grandmother bequeathed layers of strangeness that day. Her words taught me that I was a stranger in her world. And they taught that, while there had been some unevenness in my life—near poverty, my parents' divorce, and so on—I was nevertheless a stranger to profound suffering and struggle. And now, looking not just at the moment but at the memory itself, at the moment as incongruous memory, I find that my grandmother's words taught me that there is a stranger within. That is, certain moments will not survive unravaged, that going back in time and memory I will discover losses, unreachable territories. Some of the territories remain, buried beneath the surface of daily life and ordinary reminiscence, inaccessible but for accident or imaginative self-interrogation.

In the case of my grandmother's garden, incongruities and obvious gaps drew me back to the memory, signaled its importance. Other moments may disappear without a trace, leaving no path, and the act of writing may be the only way to unearth them.

A few years after I stood with my grandmother in her garden, my father bought a farm—or what I called a farm before I moved from Connecticut to Iowa and saw working farms, counted among my friends actual farmers, and learned that in relation to Iowa farms, my father's place had been not a farm at all but an acreage. There on his land I built a miniature version of my grandmother's garden using compost from the manure pile, sprinkling lime from a stocking to discourage bugs. I followed my father around, riding barely trained horses, acting the cowboy, zipping through forests, sleeping under the stars. And this is how I remember those years, as a little grandma, a little immigrant, a peasant girl in a store-bought peasant blouse (it was the sixties), bringing home-grown organic carrots to high school for lunch. I remember a peaceful Eden punctuated by moments of playing the stereo in my father's hand-built log cabin, Joni Mitchell singing about getting back to the garden, Neil Young loving his country girl.

But recently, I found buried in an old trunk a black and white snapshot of my father and me, pitchfork and all like the pair in Grant Wood's *American Gothic.* Our pitchfork, though, is angled; we both stare at it, and impaled upon one of the tongs is a small bat. In my memory, I am a Romantic peasant girl, gardening as it has been handed down by my Eastern European ancestors, embracing Wood-stock, barefoot to Joni and Neil. In the photograph I am a party to the slaughter of a benign and beneficial mammal. Writing about the photograph awakened darker memories from the farm: another child's pointing a loaded pistol at me, my aim-ing a loaded BB gun at a sleeping bat as it hung from the shed door, and leaving the cabin after an argument to disappear alone into the dark country night.

The self—at least *my* self—is composed of misremembered and unremem-bered scenes. The path back to that uneven landscape is the path of the mind. Stu-dents in my creative nonfiction workshops frequently ask me to define for them, concisely and with directions for construction, "the personal essay." Usually I try to do so by offering a variety of creative nonfiction pieces along with several writ-ers' working definitions of the form. But at times I ask them to define for me, con-cisely (but without directions for construction), "a person." The definition of "per-sonal essay" is as complicated and various as that of "person," and the personal essay is just one possible manifestation of creative nonfiction.

In writing creative nonfiction, in order to tell the truth, I must let the incon-gruities be. I was standing in the garden with my grandmother and we were eye to eye although we could not be the same height. I was six while also being ten—perhaps six with shyness and the language barrier and ten chronologically. Or ten in my boldness and six chronologically. Or I was somehow taller for being a stranger and my grandmother was somehow shorter for changing my world. And in order to tell the truth in creative nonfiction I must explore the gaps. I was an earth child on my father's farm and yet I was shooting bats. I focus on the un-remembered photograph and dig for more. Memory, the mind's path, enacts wonders, and the creative nonfiction writer's work is not to reason those wonders away with mathematical formulae, but to embrace them, to recreate layer after layer of incongruity.

2. The Terms

The first time I heard the term "nonfiction," I was sitting with twenty other third graders at a veneered table in a grammar school library. I watched the librarian walk from wall to wall tapping books and signs with her pointer. Each book had a hand-typed Dewey decimal system number taped to its spine. Each section had a hand-printed sign fixed above it. She paused at the section labeled "fiction," tapped a row of spines, tapped the sign above, and said: "These books are fiction. They're made up; they aren't true." She stepped to the left, swung her pointer at the next section, labeled "nonfiction," tapped the sign, and said: "These books are not fiction. They aren't made up; they are fact." While the librarian went on with her presentation, my mind went elsewhere. Fiction was not true and nonfiction was not fiction; therefore nonfiction was *not* not true. She was using the forbidden double negative. I sat at the table wondering what made fiction, the not-true, so central that the term "nonfiction" was formed from it.

I probably would have forgotten that moment in the library if similar moments had not recurred throughout my life. The string of assumptions goes like this: Fiction is "made up," and thus crafted, invented, "made." Fiction is art because its creator draws upon imagination. Nonfiction is "not made up," and thus recorded, reported, "unmade." Nonfiction makes itself, the writer is a mere tape recorder or camera. Or, in cases where the material of nonfiction needs some shaping, the writer draws upon reason and logic alone.

Such assumptions are in part an issue of terminology. "Fiction," the root word, comes from "fingere," to form, mold, devise. "Non" simply means "not." Thus we get the implication that nonfiction is not formed, molded, or devised. Although this "non" negates the term "fiction," it is not the strongest available negative prefix. "Dis," which implies expulsion, as in "disfrock" or "disbar," would give us disfiction, a genre deprived of fiction, even, perhaps, expelled from it. "Un," which means "against" or "anti," would give us unfiction, a genre opposed to fiction. Nonfiction, looked at in this context, is not deprived of fiction or opposed to fiction, but simply, like the librarian said, not fiction.

There remains, however, an unsettling nuance to "non." While calling someone non-American does not brand them an enemy (as calling that person un-American would), it still suggests that they are other. A non-American is a foreigner, or, as my grandmother was sometimes called, an alien. Nonfiction is to fiction as non-American is to American. Thus, nonfiction is the stranger, the foreigner (or alien) in the land of fiction. What's more, in both cases, the root word is the point of reference. Many writers and editors add "creative" to "nonfiction" to mollify this sense of being strange and other, and to remind readers that creative nonfiction writers are more than recorders or appliers of reason and objectivity. Certainly many readers and writers of creative nonfiction recognize that the genre can share some elements of fiction; dialogue, place, characters, and plot, for example, might occur in both. When a piece of creative nonfiction resembles fiction, the "non" might suggest not so much "not," as something like "kicking off from." Why else insist that it is not fiction unless it is in danger of being mistaken for fiction?

If "nonfiction" might mean a work that is related to but different from fiction, perhaps works in the genre that are more akin to poetry—sharing with it lyric and image or a structure built on association and repetition rather than on narrative—would benefit from another name. I read some of Virginia Woolf's nonfiction (her lyrical, personal pieces like "Evening Over Sussex," and "The Death of the Moth," for example) for its poetry. Other writers come to mind: Terry Tempest Williams's *Desert Quartet*, for example, a lyrical, concentrated work with gaps and craters, a book written not only from reason, but also from imagination, dreams, and the body. Such works, while not poems per se, use poetry as their inspiration, their model, their "kicking off point." For them, I suggest the term "nonpoetry."

To play with terms and search for definitions can be more than an academic exercise. I'm interested in the genre's possibility, a possibility not just theoretical but practical—that is, involving practice. Rather than map out territory (and thus limit it) I mean to expand it. Rather than build fences, knock them down.

3. The Stars

A few months ago, a formerly estranged cousin gave me a copy of an old home movie. Over antipasto made the old way, we watched ourselves together, children moving in and out of a series of silent, disjointed scenes in black and white. My cousin and I sat together as his father's last birthday party unfolded before us; we watched ourselves celebrate just a few yards from the spot where an accident would later kill his father, shattering our family for decades. But on that night preserved on film, we all sit together on the pool deck of the hotel and nightclub his father and my stepfather ran together, happy beneath the stars. We sit at a long table, laughing and talking silently. Suddenly, my stepfather rises up, grabs a torch-like candle, and begins dancing around our table. While he circles the rest of us, we watch my uncle cut his Italian rum cake from Romano's.

My cousin broke the silence of that old flickering movie. "There must have been bugs," he said, "that's got to be a bug torch and he's spreading the fog around our table." But that's not what I saw. Though I didn't at first remember the scene, I knew my stepfather. He was dancing out his joy, his exuberance, the energy that pored from each cell of his body. "I'd rip the stars out of the sky for you," he used to tell my half sister, the child of his middle age, and there he was, ripping the stars out of the sky, lighting the night for one of our last happy moments together.

The camera recorded the scene for perpetuity. And yet my cousin and I, with similar family experiences, with memories of that moment, and with objective evidence before us, saw it differently. If put alone in separate rooms and interrogated or given blank sheets of paper and told to write that scene, we would come up with different stories. We both sat at the family table that night, and so the party is in our memories, embedded in the very matter of our brains. And we both watched the tape, separately and together, several times in recent months. Nevertheless we tell different stories. Which one is true? Which one imagined? His story and mine, I believe, contain elements of fact and imagination. Both are true, for they are true to how we remember, how we see, they recreate the topographies of our minds. We can return to the film and we can return to our memories. Either way, each of us returns to a different place.

Recently, I attended another birthday party, for a friend who is a writer. After he blew out the candles, and everyone made the requisite jokes about aging, our conversation turned to writing and memory. "You could never write this scene as nonfiction," one friend, a fiction writer, said. "You couldn't remember the dialogue verbatim; you'd end up remembering words wrong and so you'd have to change them. You'd forget things and leave them out. That would make it fiction." Several others at the table agreed, assuming that without a tape recorder you'd be left with fallible memory and therefore be incapable of creating nonfiction. There were only two ways to write the scene with dialogue, they believed, to write it as fiction (and freely invent and recreate words), or to write it as nonfiction (and record, transcribe, and then report the words exactly as spoken).

One of the guests, a lawyer, objected. "You should read briefs," he said. "Recorded dialogue doesn't make any sense."

"You need the background," another friend, a nonfiction writer, added, "the color of the walls, the smell of the food. How can you understand the dialogue without the scene?"

"What if someone's words trigger a memory?" I asked. "Let's say that as you're speaking, I'm reminded of a scene from my past, like standing in my grandmother's garden. Even if we filmed and taped this party, that wouldn't show up, and yet it changes my experience of the party."

"I was wondering," the literary theorist said, "what I'd do with that moment when I became obsessed with the pattern on this plate, or when I concentrated on the taste of the red beans and rice."

If my birthday party companions read this dialogue, they would no doubt revise it according to their own memories and perceptions. In fact, that same night we suggested—as a joke or perhaps as a challenge—that each of us, two fiction writers, a poet, two creative nonfiction writers, a theorist, a lawyer, and a decorator—should go off immediately and write the scene. By the time we were well into the cake and coffee, we more or less agreed that if we were true to the events as we'd each experienced them, if we didn't write, for example, that the lawyer had stood up, reached across the table, and punched the guest of honor as he blew out his candles (since he had done nothing of the kind), we would be writing creative nonfiction.

We reached common ground in the end, I think, because we shifted both our working notion of genre and our view of "the person." When my friends claimed that nonfiction could work only with the aid of a tape recorder, their concept of the person was external, the person as captured by a machine. They had shared the assumption, arrived at by habit, that nonfiction was restricted to objectivity and reporting, that incongruity must be reasoned away. Fact, as Virginia Woolf points out, is not necessarily the same as truth, and as we talked that night, we explored what it means to be at a birthday party, what it means to participate in a conversation, how much more it is than the sounds we make, the words we speak. What we say and how we move—what machines can pick up—is only the surface of the scene. "Nonfiction" is not a synonym for "recorded surface." It has the range to sweep inward, follow the path of the mind, add layers of contemporaneous imagination, memory, and dream to the observable events of the present moment.

Patricia Hampl, who has said that memory is a place, has also said that the nonfiction writer is homeless.

One such occasion was an informal talk after her reading in the third floor lounge of a certain university's humanities' building. Graduate students used to joke about the symbolism of the building's design: Fiction and poetry were on the top floor. Freshman composition was in the basement. In the middle (just above philosophy) was nonfiction, tucked away in a corner of the literature department. Although Hampl's reading drew a large audience, only a small group of die-hard nonfictionists showed up for the talk.

In our small quarters, nearly invisible in a wing of the literature department, her discussion of the nonfiction writer's homelessness rang true. The department had just changed the name of our program from "expository writing" to "nonfiction writing" and would soon rename it "creative nonfiction." We could see that we were the new kids on the block, that to many, our genre was ill defined and invisible. But there we sat listening to a writer who had made a career of creative nonfiction, who had written two memoirs and many personal essays, and who spoke optimistically about the genre's range and possibility. Many of us felt at home for the first time—not in our lounge, but in her words.

The prospect of literary homelessness drives and limits certain writers to formulae, say, memoir in five parts (action scene followed by predictable summation followed by continuation of the action and so on, like a sitcom or a mini series). They find a "home" and hole up in the corner. And they pass along a favored formula to groups of beginner or intermediate writers, regardless of any particular student writer's emphasis, place of origin, gender, culture, aesthetic, or concept of the self. Handing over a prepackaged piece of creative nonfiction is, in essence, putting the writer into a cell. The bolder explorers, happy not to be enclosed, take advantage of the unsettled terrain of nonfiction, wandering and exploring, allowing themselves to be vulnerable, following the path of the mind even when they enter shadows, pressing on into the territory of the unknown, the mysterious, the incongruous.

Creative nonfiction is at once flourishing and invisible, set and contested. The genre that embraces the often paradoxical nature of the self is itself often paradoxical (in its position in the world of writing and letters). Patricia Hampl provides the metaphor of the creative nonfiction writer as homeless. And she also turns it around. We're lucky, she says, we get to be out under the stars.

The Art of Memoir

Mary Clearman Blew

One of the oldest and loveliest of quilt patterns is the Double Wedding Ring, in which bands of colors lock and interlock in endless circles. If you want to make a Double Wedding Ring quilt, be a saver of fabric. Treasure the smallest scraps, from the maternity dress you have just sewn for your oldest daughter or the Halloween costume you cobbled together for your youngest, from the unfaded inside hems of worn-out clothing or the cotton left over from other quilts. Keep a pair of sharp scissors on hand, and also a pattern, which I like to cut from fine sandpaper, and which will be about an inch wide by two inches long and slightly flared, like a flower petal that has been rounded off at both ends. Whenever you have a scrap of fabric, lay out your pattern on it and snip out a few more blocks.

Save your blocks in a three-pound coffee can. When the can is full, empty the blocks out on the floor and arrange them in the shape of rainbow arcs with a juxtaposition of colors and textures that pleases you. Seven pieces to an arc, seventy-two arcs to a quilt. You can sew the blocks together on a sewing machine, but I like the spell cast by hand sewing. I use a #11 needle, which is an inch-long sliver of steel with an eye so fine that it will barely take the quilter's thread, which measures time by growing infinitesimally shorter with each dip and draw of the needle, and I wear the hundred-year-old thimble of a woman named Amelia Bunn on my finger.

When you have pieced your seventy-two arcs, you must choose a fabric to join your arcs, in a process that is called "setting up" the quilt. Traditionally a Double Wedding Ring quilt is set up on white, but remember that you have all colors to choose from; and while choosing one color means forgoing others, remind yourself that your coffee can of pieces will fill again. There will be another quilt at the back of your mind while you are piecing, quilting, and binding this one, which perhaps you will give to one of your daughters, to trace her childhood through the pieces. Or perhaps you will give it to a friend, to speak the words the pattern spoke to you.

For years I thought of myself as a fiction writer, even during the years in northern Montana when I virtually stopped writing. But in 1987 I came to a divide. My father had died, and my husband was suffering a mental breakdown along with the progressive lung disease that eventually killed him. I was estranged from my older children. Then I lost my job. It was the job that mattered the most. I had a small child to support. And so I looked for another job and found one, teaching in a small college in Idaho, with the northern Rockies between me and the first half of my life.

Far from home and teaching again after years in higher-ed. administration, I felt a hollowness that writing fiction seemed to do nothing to fill. And so I started all over again, writing essays to retrieve the past—in my case, the Montana homestead frontier with its harsh ideals for men and women, its tests and its limitations. The conventions of fiction, its masks and metaphors, came to seem more and more boring to me, like an unnecessary barricade between me and the material I was writing about. But because fiction was what I knew about, I used the techniques of fiction in these essays: plot, characterization, dialogue. What I began to discover was a form that worked for my purpose.

I would select an event out of family legend and retell it in a voice that grew out of my own experience and perceptions. Often the events that beckoned to me the most urgently were the ones that had been preserved in the "secret stories" my grandmothers and my great-aunts told around their Sunday tables after the dishes had been washed, elliptical and pointless and mystifying, in hushed voices that dropped or stopped altogether at the approach of one of the men or an unwise question from an eavesdropping child. Eventually I was trusted with a few of the secret stories, myself. I remember how my aunt's voice fell and her sentences became sparing when she told me a story about her mother, my grandmother. The story was about a time when my grandmother had lived alone on the homestead north of Denton, Montana, for eighteen months without seeing another woman. She had two small children and another baby on the way—her husband was away for weeks on end, trying to sell life insurance to make ends meet—and she had to carry her water in a bucket from a spring a quarter of a mile from the homestead shack, which she did at twilight, when the heat of the sun was not so oppressive. She began to hallucinate. She saw the shapes of women on the other side of the spring, shapes that looked like her dead mother and her dead sister, beckoning to her. She decided she was going crazy. She had her little children to think about. They might not be found for weeks if she broke down. And so she began to go for her water in the heat of the day, when the sun scorched her trail and bleached the color out of the grass and rocks. She never saw the beckoning shapes again.

Unlike my grandmother, I have chosen to follow the beckoning shapes. I don't understand the significance of that story for my grandmother, or why she kept it a secret except for the one time she whispered it to her younger sister in, I presume, those same stark sentences in which her sister whispered it to her niece, my aunt, the same sentences in which my aunt whispered the story just one time to me. But then, I don't fully understand why I continue to wear Amelia Bunn's thimble—it is sterling silver and engraved AB in a fine script—any more than I know what my great-grandmother looked like in life or as she appeared in the dying heat waves of that long-ago Montana twilight.

But sometimes I think I can see the turning points in the lives of dead men and women. For example, my grandmother's decision to return to schoolteaching in 1922, even though it meant breaking up her family, boarding out her oldest daughter, taking the younger children to live with her in a teacherage, leaving her husband alone on the homestead. What did that decision mean to her? I know what it means to me. Or my aunt's mowing machine accident in June of 1942, when a runaway team of sorrel horses spilled her in the path of a sickle bar that nearly cut off her foot. The disaster forced her out of the path of teaching in rural schools that she had been following and into a new life on the Olympic Peninsula. Did she understand the opportunity in the teeth of the sickle bar?

I feel an uneasy balance between writing about my grandmother and my aunt as their lives "really" were and writing about them as a projection of my own experiences. I keep reminding myself that the times when they lived are not my times. Nor do the nuances of their stories necessarily reflect my assumptions about language. And yet I am who I am because of these women and the stories they told; and, as I write about them, they live and breathe again through the umbilical tangle between character and writer.

I've been fortunate in my family's being one of storytellers and private writers who have "documented" their past. Tales, diaries, notebooks, and letters—they saved every scrap. Of course their stories were fictions as much as mine are, told over and over again and given shape and significance. Their connection to literal truth is suspect.

For my part, I struggled for a long time with the conflicting claims of the exact truth of the story and its emotional truth as I perceived it. I restrict myself to what I "know" happened: the concrete details, the objects, the history. When I speculate, I say so.

But any story depends upon its shape. In arranging the scraps that have been passed down to me, which are to be selected, which discarded? The boundaries of creative nonfiction will always be as fluid as water.

Students often ask, what can you decently write about other people? Whose permission do you have to ask? What can you decently reveal about yourself?

I can only speak for myself. I own my past and my present. Only I can decide whether or how to write about it. Also, I know that once I write about the past, I will have changed the past, in a sense set it in concrete, and I will never remember it in quite the same way. The experience itself is lost; like the old Sunday storytellers who told and retold their stories until what they remembered was the tale itself, what I will remember is what I have written.

Certainly, something personal is being sacrificed, for when I write about myself, I transform myself just as I do the past. A side-effect is that while the writing process itself can be painful, I experience a detachment from the finished essay, because I have come to exist in it as a character as separate from myself as any fictional character. I find that I can read my essays to audiences with very little emotion, although once, reading Annick Smith's essay "Homestead" to a creative writing class, I began to cry and thought I would not be able to go on. Her nonfiction character moved me in a way my own could not.

Lately I have been reading my aunt's diaries, which she kept without fail for fifty years. I feel haunted by the parallels between her life and mine. She chose, perhaps with greater self-discipline, perhaps from being closer to the source of the old punishing pressures, to stay all her life on a straight and narrow path I had been perilously near to embarking on. Her diaries reveal her unhappiness, her gradual, unwilling resignation to her lot, and finally, in her old age, her reconciliation with the lone woman she had set out to be. Which has left me with an enormous determination to resist those pressures and to try a new direction: having written my past, I will write the present and transform myself, as she did, in the interstices between fragment and pattern, through the endless interlocking connections between storyteller and story.

We'll see, we'll see. Opportunity lies in the teeth of the sickle bar.

The Intelligent Heart

Patricia Foster

What's at issue is that the personal essay is dead, the "I" evicted from the fashionable venues of literary nonfiction. Or so I've been told.

"The world is just *sick* of people writing about their lives," a colleague complains to me behind the closed door of my office. He is clever, wry, visionary, and I feel myself shrink as his eyes make a panoramic sweep of my desk where pages of a memoir lie stacked in a disheveled mess. I think of what I've written there, how my family hacked our way out of poverty and nailed ourselves to the middle class, the spikes digging deep into the marrow of our skills. I think of my mother who saves string, my father who prefers to eat in the kitchen, my aunt who says, "Ain't that right, honey?" when she wants to assert that the world is a rough and perilous place.

"Think about it," my colleague says. "All that narcissism, all that unresolved emotion."

When he leaves, I briefly worry that my writing is irrelevant, old-fashioned, tied too fervently to fury, to self-obsession, to the complicated issues of class. Perhaps I have no right to material so close to me, stories that fester and clot inside me like the beginnings of a chronic disease. Perhaps it is passé to write about the struggle between temperaments, the duel of consciousness within a family. Perhaps the old way of storytelling in the essay is dead. Now it's time to be experimental, sexy, to jump on the bandwagon of the new, new thing, those essays that intimidate and confuse, essays that defy the rest of us to see them with uncritical awe.

"It's better if it's a little more obscure," a student responds in class to an essay about a young man's relationship to his father. "If it has gaps, you know."

"Yeah, we need to unpack it," another student agrees. "That's what we're supposed to do . . . figure it out, you know, like unpacking a box, not being sure what we've got, not being sure what's really there, only what we *think* is there."

I see myself yanking out conflicts, tossing out reliable narrators, letting them wobble and shudder to a stop.

"The more fragmented, the better," the first student says. "Then it's one discourse pitted against another."

Well, maybe, I think to myself. But these are merely the buzzwords of academia, and such words—so easily misunderstood—often have little to do with the success of an essay, the clarity of the thinking, the hills and furrows of a meditative form, the ability of the writer to engage the intelligent heart.

But what is the intelligent heart and who gives a fig about that anymore?

Sometimes I think I sit alone in my room, in a solemn universe of me and like-minded friends to whom I can point and say frankly, "We care. We believe in the intelligent heart!" We believe that personal stories matter, that whether autobiographical or cultural, the story must act as a catalyst for thinking and feeling, that it is the congruence of both that elevates the essay to the status of art. The intelligent heart is the heart that seeks revelation in dreams, then turns dreams into insight, and insight into wisdom. The intelligent heart is the balance beam, the quivering tightrope we walk when we dip perilously into our psyches and gather up the stray bits and pieces we patch together and call art. Perhaps, more often, the intelligent heart is a masquerade, a carnival, a devilish trickster we wrestle with constantly, fighting shadows and phantoms in our attempt to find its true shape. Not that its true shape will give us any peace. Its true shape merely defines for us the oppositions we can work with, the strands of ambivalence we hold up to soft morning light. When functioning properly, the intelligent heart knocks at our door, awakens us from dreams, shudders from the drafty places in our apartments, and demands a quick audience. *Write this,* it says. *And this. And this. And this.* Faithfully we write it down, trying to quiet the alarm that it will be embarrassing, stupid, irrelevant, or that most insulting of faults: already done. We listen because it is urgent, because it sneaked up behind us and blithely tongued our ear. We listen because it seemed hungry and furious, as alive as thunder before a late summer rain. We listen because we know that stories come from the mystery of knowable places, the slime coating the muscle of an oyster, the brine of a shrimp, the tough, thready strands of a tangerine. We know that everything we receive—*even this, this summons*—must be untangled and distilled, worked like the unraveling of rope, piece by piece, thread by thread, then put back together with the embrace of two broken thumbs. The intelligent heart is no mere bud of ornamentation. The intelligent heart is the source, the goods, the first principle from which everything else is made.

But this is not to say that the intelligent heart is all. Should anyone demand this, I would rise up in protest and draw my sword. "All" is something that can't be defended, dictated, enlisted, tabulated, or decreed. In every piece of good writing there is something suspect, a shadow lurking in the corner, a stray hair fluttering across the page, a drift of wind, a low banked fog that obscures the promise of understanding. In every piece of good writing there is trouble, the quirks of personality and temperament, the dizzying gradations of self-love. No, the intelligent heart, in the end, is something elusive and longed for, the thing that can't quite be attained. The real problem for most of us is that the intelligent heart often remains buried for years, letting us grind out bare, quixotic but emotionless forms, forms that please our cerebral betters, that thrill grant committees, that delight bored academics. These are forms that grow hairy with stylish weight, but that live, we secretly know, because of lack. And there is safety in lack. Safety in style. There is even, I admit, a kind of awe.

But when all the huff and puff of fashion slips away, the safe, stylish essay cooked in the safe, stylish brain, is nothing but a husk, a fancy dress, a decorative facade covering an unknowable story, a secret life.

"Nobody wants any more of those personal stories," my colleague says. "Who cares about the I? Who cares about the woman in the storm? The family drowning? The mother clawing her way out of filth and dreary disease? Who cares?" he asks.

But I don't bow my head. "I do," I say, gathering up the pages of my story. I refuse to be dead.

A Narrator Leaps Past Journalism

Vivian Gornick

I began my working life in the 1970's as a writer of what was then called personal journalism, a hybrid term meaning part personal essay, part social criticism. On the barricades for radical feminism, it had seemed natural to me from the minute I approached the typewriter to use myself—to use my own response to a circumstance or an event—as a means of making some larger sense of things.

At the time, of course, that was a shared instinct. Many other writers felt similarly compelled. The personal had become political, and the headlines metaphoric. Immediate experience signified. But from the beginning, I saw the dangers of this kind of writing—people rushing into print with no clear idea of the relation between narrator and subject, falling quickly into confessionalism or therapy on the page or naked self-absorption—and I resolved to work hard at avoiding its pitfalls. The reliable reporter, I vowed, would keep the narrator trustworthy.

One day a book editor approached me with an idea that struck a note of response. I had confided to her the tale of an intimate friendship I'd made with an Egyptian whose childhood in Cairo had strongly resembled my own in the Bronx, and now I was being invited to go to Egypt to write about middle-class Cairenes. I said yes with easy pleasure, assuming that I would do in Cairo what I had been doing in New York. That is, I'd put myself down in the middle of the city, meet the people, use my own fears and prejudices to let them become themselves, and then I'd write as I always wrote.

But Cairo was not New York, and personal journalism turned out not exactly the right job description. The city—dark, nervous, tender; intelligent, ignorant, fearful—invaded me, and I saw myself swamped by thoughts and feelings I couldn't bring into line. When I had been a working journalist, politics had provided me with a situation, and polemics had given me my story.

Now, in Egypt, I found myself confused by a writing impulse whose requirements I could not penetrate but whose power I felt jerked around by.

What, exactly, was the situation here? And where was the story? Above all, where was my familiar, polemical narrator? I seemed to have lost her without having found a suitable replacement. At the time I didn't understand that it wasn't personal journalism I was trying to write; it was personal narrative. It would be years before I sat down at the desk with sufficient command of the distinction to control the material, to serve the situation and tell the kind of story I now wanted to tell.

A dozen years after Egypt I set out to write a memoir about my mother, myself, and a woman who lived next door to us when I was a child. Here, for the first time, I struggled to isolate the story (the thing I had come to say) from the situation (the plot, the context, the circumstance) and to puzzle out a narrator who would serve.

I soon discovered that if I wanted to speak truthfully in this memoir—that is, without cynicism or sentiment—I had to find a tone of voice normally not mine. The one I habitually lived with wouldn't do at all: it whined, it grated, it accused; above all, it accused. Then there was the matter of syntax: my own ordinary, everyday sentence—fragmented, interjecting, overriding—also wouldn't do; it had to be altered, modified, brought under control.

And then I could see, as soon as I began writing, that I needed to pull back—way back—from these people and these events to find the place where the story could draw a deep breath and take its own measure. In short, a useful point of view, one that would permit greater freedom of association—for that of course is what I have been describing—had to be brought along. What I didn't see, and for a long while, was that this point of view could only emerge from a narrator who was me and at the same time not me.

I began to correct for myself. The process was slow, painful and riddled with self-doubt. But one day I had her. I had a narrator on the page who was telling the story that I alone, in my everyday person, would not have been able to tell. Devotion to this narrator—this persona—became, while I was writing the book, an absorption that in time went unequaled. I longed each day to meet again with her. It was not only that I admired her style, her generosity, her detachment (such a respite from the me that was me); she had become the instrument of my illumination. She could tell the truth as I alone could not.

I reread the greats in the personal essay, the ones we think of as open, honest, confiding—Montaigne, Hazlitt, Orwell, Didion—and now I saw that it wasn't their confessing voices I was responding to, it was their brilliantly created personae, their persuasive truth speakers: Orwell's obsessed democrat, Hazlitt's irascible neurotic, Didion's anxiety-ridden Californian.

Each delivers that wholeness of being in a narrator that the reader experiences as reliable; the one we can trust will take us on a journey, make the piece arrive, bring us out into a clearing where the sense of things is larger than it was before.

Living as I now did with the idea of the nonfiction persona, I began to think better than I had before about the commonplace need, alive in all of us, to make large sense of things in the very moment, even as experience is overtaking us. Everywhere I turned in those days, I found an excuse for the observation that we pull from ourselves the narrator who will shape better than we alone can the inchoate flow of events into which we are continually being plunged.

I remember I once went on a rafting trip down the Rio Grande with the man who was then my husband and a friend of ours. The river was hot and wild; sad, brilliant, remote; closed in by canyon walls, desert banks, snakes and flash floods; on one side Texas, the other Mexico. A week after we'd been there, snipers on the Mexico side killed two people also floating on a raft.

Later we each wrote about the trip. My husband focused brightly on the "river rats" who were our guides, our friend soberly on the misery of illegal immigrants, I morbidly on what strangers my husband and I had become. Reading these pieces side by side was in itself an experience. We had all used the river, the heat, the remoteness to frame our stories. Beyond that, how alone each of us had been, sitting there together on that raft, carving out of our separating anxieties the narrator who, in the midst of all that beauty and oppressiveness, would keep us company and tell us what we were living through.

It mimics one of the earliest of narrative impulses, this kind of writing: to pull from one's own boring, agitated self the one who will make large sense of things; the persona—possessed of a tone, a syntax, a perspective not wholly one's own—who will find the story riding the tide that we, in our unmediated state, otherwise drown in.

That is what it means to become interested in one's own existence as a means of transforming event into writing experience.

Memory and Imagination

Patricia Hampl

When I was seven, my father, who played the violin on Sundays with a nicely tortured flair which we considered artistic, led me by the hand down a long, unlit corridor in St. Luke's School basement, a sort of tunnel that ended in a room full of pianos. There many little girls and a single sad boy were playing truly tortured scales and arpeggios in a mash of troubled sound. My father gave me over to Sister Olive Marie, who did look remarkably like an olive.

Her oily face gleamed as if it had just been rolled out of a can and laid on the white plate of her broad, spotless wimple. She was a small, plump woman; her body and the small window of her face seemed to interpret the entire alphabet of olive: her face was a sallow green olive placed upon the jumbo ripe olive of her black habit. I trusted her instantly and smiled, glad to have my hand placed in the hand of a woman who made sense, who provided the satisfaction of being what she was: an Olive who looked like an olive.

My father left me to discover the piano with Sister Olive Marie so that one day I would join him in mutually tortured piano-violin duets for the edification of my mother and brother who sat at the table meditatively spooning in the last of their pineapple sherbet until their part was called for: they put down their spoons and clapped while we bowed, while the sweet ice in their bowls melted, while the music melted, and we all melted a little into each other for a moment.

But first Sister Olive must do her work. I was shown middle C, which Sister seemed to think terribly important. I stared at middle C and then glanced away for a second. When my eye returned, middle C was gone, its slim finger lost in the complicated grasp of the keyboard. Sister Olive struck it again, finding it with laughable ease. She emphasized the importance of middle C, its central position, a sort of North Star of sound. I remember thinking, "Middle C is the belly button of the piano," an insight whose originality and accuracy stunned me with pride. For the first time in my life I was astonished by metaphor. I hesitated to tell the kindly

Olive for some reason; apparently I understood a true metaphor is a risky business, revealing of the self. In fact, I have never, until this moment of writing it down, told my first metaphor to anyone.

Sunlight flooded the room; the pianos, all black, gleamed. Sister Olive, dressed in the colors of the keyboard, gleamed; middle C shimmered with meaning and I resolved never—never—to forget its location: it was the center of the world.

Then Sister Olive, who had had to show me middle C twice but who seemed to have drawn no bad conclusions about me anyway, got up and went to the windows on the opposite wall. She pulled the shades down, one after the other. The sun was too bright, she said. She sneezed as she stood at the windows with the sun shedding its glare over her. She sneezed and sneezed, crazy little convulsive sneezes, one after another, as helpless as if she had the hiccups.

"The sun makes me sneeze," she said when the fit was over and she was back at the piano. This was odd, too odd to grasp in the mind. I associated sneezing with colds, and colds with rain, fog, snow and bad weather. The sun, however, had caused Sister Olive to sneeze in this wild way, Sister Olive who gleamed benignly and who was so certain of the location of the center of the world. The universe wobbled a bit and became unreliable. Things were not, after all, necessarily what they seemed. Appearance deceived: here was the sun acting totally out of character, hurling this woman into sneezes, a woman so mild that she was named, so it seemed, for a bland object on a relish tray.

I was given a red book, the first Thompson book, and told to play the first piece over and over at one of the black pianos where the other children were crashing away. This, I was told, was called practicing. It sounded alluringly adult, practicing. The piece itself consisted mainly of middle C, and I excelled, thrilled by my savvy at being able to locate that central note amidst the cunning camouflage of all the other white keys before me. Thrilled too by the shiny red book that gleamed, as the pianos did, as Sister Olive did, as my eager eyes probably did. I sat at the formidable machine of the piano and got to know middle C intimately, preparing to be as tortured as I could manage one day soon with my father's violin at my side.

But at the moment Mary Katherine Reilly was at my side, playing something at least two or three lessons more sophisticated than my piece. I believe she even struck a chord. I glanced at her from the peasantry of single notes, shy, ready to pay homage. She turned toward me, stopped playing, and sized me up.

Sized me up and found a person ready to be dominated. Without introduction she said, "My grandfather invented the collapsible opera hat."

I nodded, I acquiesced, I was hers. With that little stroke it was decided between us—that she should be the leader, and I the sidekick. My job was admiration. Even when she added, "But he didn't make a penny from it. He didn't have a patent"—even then, I knew and she knew that this was not an admission of powerlessness, but the easy candor of a master, of one who can afford a weakness or two.

With the clairvoyance of all fated relationships based on dominance and submission, it was decided in advance: that when the time came for us to play duets, I should always play second piano, that I should spend my allowance to buy her the Twinkies she craved but was not allowed to have, that finally, I should let her copy from my test paper, and when confronted by our teacher, confess with convincing hysteria that it was I, I who had cheated, who had reached above myself to steal what clearly belonged to the rightful heir of the inventor of the collapsible opera hat. . . .

There must be a reason I remember that little story about my first piano lesson. In fact, it isn't a story, just a moment, the beginning of what could perhaps become a story. For the memoirist, more than for the fiction writer, the story seems already *there,* already accomplished and fully achieved in history ("in reality," as we naively say). For the memoirist, the writing of the story is a matter of transcription.

That, anyway, is the myth. But no memoirist writes for long without experiencing an unsettling disbelief about the reliability of memory, a hunch that memory is not, after all, *just* memory. I don't know why I remembered this fragment about my first piano lesson. I don't, for instance, have a single recollection of my first arithmetic lesson, the first time I studied Latin, the first time my grandmother tried to teach me to knit. Yet these things occurred too, and must have their stories.

It is the piano lesson that has trudged forward, clearing the haze of forgetfulness, showing itself bright with detail more than thirty years after the event. I did not choose to remember the piano lesson. It was simply there, like a book that has always been on the shelf, whether I ever read it or not, the binding and title showing as I skim across the contents of my life. On the day I wrote this fragment I happened to take that memory, not some other, from the shelf and paged through it. I found more detail, more event, perhaps a little more entertainment than I had expected, but the memory itself was there from the start. Waiting for me.

Or was it? When I reread what I had written just after I finished it, I realized that I had told a number of lies. I *think* it was my father who took me the first time for my piano lesson—but maybe he only took me to meet my teacher and there was no actual lesson that day. And did I even know then that he played the violin—didn't he take up his violin again much later, as a result of my piano playing, and not the reverse? And is it even remotely accurate to describe as "tortured" the musicianship of a man who began every day by belting out "Oh What a Beautiful Morning" as he shaved?

More: Sister Olive Marie did sneeze in the sun, but was her name Olive? As for her skin tone—I would have sworn it was olive-like; I would have been willing to spend the better part of an afternoon trying to write the exact description of imported Italian or Greek olive her face suggested: I wanted to get it right. But now, were I to write that passage over, it is her intense black eyebrows I would see, for suddenly they seem the central fact of that face, some indicative mark of her serious and patient nature. But the truth is, I don't remember the woman at all. She's a sneeze in the sun and a finger touching middle C. That, at least, is steady and clear.

Worse: I didn't have the Thompson book as my piano text. I'm sure of that because I remember envying children who did have this wonderful book with its pictures of children and animals printed on the pages of music.

As for Mary Katherine Reilly. She didn't even go to grade school with me (and her name isn't Mary Katherine Reilly—but I made that change on purpose). I met her in Girl Scouts and only went to school with her later, in high school. Our relationship was not really one of leader and follower; I played first piano most of the time in duets. She certainly never copied anything from a test paper of mine: she was a better student, and cheating just wasn't a possibility with her. Though her grandfather (or someone in her family) did invent the collapsible opera hat and I remember that she was proud of that fact, she didn't tell me this news as a deft move in a childish power play.

So, what was I doing in this brief memoir? Is it simply an example of the curious relation a fiction writer has to the material of her own life? Maybe. That may have some value in itself. But to tell the truth (if anyone still believes me capable of telling the truth), I wasn't writing fiction. I was writing memoir—or was trying to. My desire was to be accurate. I wished to embody the myth of memoir: to write as an act of dutiful transcription.

Yet clearly the work of writing narrative caused me to do something very different from transcription. I am forced to admit that memoir is not a matter of transcription, that memory itself is not a warehouse of finished stories, not a static gallery of framed pictures. I must admit that I invented. But why?

Two whys: why did I invent, and then, if a memoirist must inevitably invent rather than transcribe, why do I—why should anybody—write memoir at all?

I must respond to these impertinent questions because they, like the bumper sticker I saw the other day commanding all who read it to QUESTION AUTHORITY, challenge my authority as a memoirist and as a witness.

It still comes as a shock to realize that I don't write about what I know: I write in order to find out what I know. Is it possible to convey to a reader the enormous degree of blankness, confusion, hunch and uncertainty lurking in the act of writing? When I am the reader, not the writer, I too fall into the lovely illusion that the words before me (in a story by Mavis Gallant, an essay by Carol Bly, a memoir by M. F. K. Fisher), which *read* so inevitably, must also have been *written* exactly as they appear, rhythm and cadence, language and syntax, the powerful waves of the sentences laying themselves on the smooth beach of the page one after another faultlessly.

But here I sit before a yellow legal pad, and the long page of the preceding two paragraphs is a jumble of crossed-out lines, false starts, confused order. A mess. The mess of my mind trying to find out what it wants to say. This is a writer's frantic, grabby mind, not the poised mind of a reader ready to be edified or entertained.

I sometimes think of the reader as a cat, endlessly fastidious, capable, by turns, of mordant indifference and riveted attention, luxurious, recumbent, and ever poised. Whereas the writer is absolutely a dog, panting and moping, too eager for an affectionate scratch behind the ears, lunging frantically after any old stick thrown in the distance.

The blankness of a new page never fails to intrigue and terrify me. Sometimes, in fact, I think my habit of writing on long yellow sheets comes from an atavistic fear of the writer's stereotypic "blank white page." At least when I begin writing, my page isn't utterly blank; at least it has a wash of color on it, even if the absence of words must finally be faced on a yellow sheet as truly as on a blank white one. Well, we all have our ways of whistling in the dark.

If I approach writing from memory with the assumption that I know what I wish to say, I assume that intentionality is running the show. Things are not that simple. Or perhaps writing is even more profoundly simple, more telegraphic and immediate in its choices than the grating wheels and chugging engine of logic and rational intention. The heart, the guardian of intuition with its secret, often fearful intentions, is the boss, its commands are what a writer obeys—often without knowing it. Or, I do.

That's why I'm a strong adherent of the first draft. And why it's worth pausing for a moment to consider what a first draft really is. By my lights, the piano lesson memoir is a first draft. That doesn't mean it exists here exactly as I first wrote it. I like to think I've cleaned it up from the first time I put it down on paper. I've cut some adjectives here, toned down the hyperbole there, smoothed a transition, cut a repetition—that sort of housekeeperly tidying-up. But the piece remains a first draft because I haven't yet gotten to know it, haven't given it a chance to tell me anything. For me, writing a first draft is a little like meeting someone for the first time. I come away with a wary acquaintanceship, but the real friendship (if any) and genuine intimacy—that's all down the road. Intimacy with a piece of writing, as with a person, comes from paying attention to the revelations it is capable of giving, not by imposing my own preconceived notions, no matter how well-intentioned they might be.

I try to let pretty much anything happen in a first draft. A careful first draft is a failed first draft. That may be why there are so many inaccuracies in the piano lesson memoir: I didn't censor, I didn't judge. I kept moving. But I would not publish this piece as a memoir on its own in its present state. It isn't the "lies" in the piece that give me pause, though a reader has a right to expect a memoir to be as accurate as the writer's memory can make it. No, it isn't the lies themselves that makes the piano lesson memoir a first draft and therefore "unpublishable."

The real trouble: the piece hasn't yet found its subject; it isn't yet about what it wants to be about. Note: what *it* wants, not what I want. The difference has to do with the relation a memoirist—any writer, in fact—has to unconscious or half-known intentions and impulses in composition.

Now that I have the fragment down on paper, I can read this little piece as a mystery which drops clues to the riddle of my feelings, like a culprit who wishes to be apprehended. My narrative self (the culprit who has invented) wishes to be discovered by my reflective self, the self who wants to understand and make sense of a half-remembered story about a nun sneezing in the sun. . . .

We only store in memory images of value. The value may be lost over the passage of time (I was baffled about why I remembered that sneezing nun, for example), but that's the implacable judgment of feeling: *this*, we say somewhere deep within us, is something I'm hanging on to. And of course, often we cleave to things because they possess heavy negative charges. Pain likes to be vivid.

Over time, the value (the feeling) and the stored memory (the image) may become estranged. Memoir seeks a permanent home for feeling and image, a habitation where they can live together in harmony. Naturally, I've had a lot of experiences since I packed away that one from the basement of St. Luke's School; that piano lesson has been effaced by waves of feeling for other moments and episodes. I persist in believing the event has value—after all, I remember it—but in writing the memoir I did not simply relive the experience. Rather, I explored the mysterious relationship between all the images I could round up and the even more impacted feelings that caused me to store the images safely away in memory. Stalking the relationship, seeking the congruence between stored image and hidden emotion—that's the real job of memoir.

By writing about that first piano lesson, I've come to know things I could not know otherwise. But I only know these things as a result of reading this first draft. While I was writing, I was following the images, letting the details fill the room of the page and use the furniture as they wished. I was their dutiful servant—or thought I was. In fact, I was the faithful retainer of my hidden feelings which were giving the commands.

I really did feel, for instance, that Mary Katherine Reilly was far superior to me. She was smarter, funnier, more wonderful in every way—that's how I saw it. Our friendship (or she herself) did not require that I become her vassal, yet perhaps in my heart that was something I wanted; I wanted a way to express my feeling of admiration. I suppose I waited until this memoir to begin to find the way.

Just as, in the memoir, I finally possess that red Thompson book with the barking dogs and bleating lambs and winsome children. I couldn't (and still can't) remember what my own music book was, so I grabbed the name and image of the one book I could remember. It was only in reviewing the piece after writing it that I saw my inaccuracy. In pondering this "lie," I came to see what I was up to: I was getting what I wanted. At last.

The truth of many circumstances and episodes in the past emerges for the memoirist through details (the red music book, the fascination with a nun's name and gleaming face), but these details are not merely information, not flat facts. Such details are not allowed to lounge. They must work. Their work is the creation of symbol. But it's more accurate to call it the *recognition* of symbol. For meaning is not "attached" to the detail by the memoirist; meaning is revealed. That's why a first draft is important. Just as the first meeting (good or bad) with someone who later becomes the beloved is important and is often reviewed for signals, meanings, omens, and indications.

Now I can look at that music book and see it not only as "a detail," but for what it is, how it *acts*. See it as the small red door leading straight into the dark room of my childhood longing and disappointment. That red book *becomes* the palpable evidence of that longing. In other words, it becomes symbol. There is no symbol, no life-of-the-spirit in the general or the abstract. Yet a writer wishes—indeed all of us wish—to speak about profound matters that are, like it or not, general and abstract. We wish to talk to each other about life and death, about love, despair, loss, and innocence. We sense that in order to live together we must learn to speak of peace, of history, of meaning and values. Those are a few.

We seek a means of exchange, a language which will renew these ancient concerns and make them wholly and pulsingly ours. Instinctively, we go to our store of private images and associations for our authority to speak of these weighty issues. We find, in our details and broken and obscured images, the language of symbol. Here memory impulsively reaches out its arms and embraces imagination. That is the resort to invention. It isn't a lie, but an act of necessity, as the innate urge to locate personal truth always is.

All right. Invention is inevitable. But why write memoir? Why not call it fiction and be done with all the hashing about, wondering where memory stops and imagination begins? And if memoir seeks to talk about "the big issues," about history and peace, death and love—why not leave these reflections to those with expert and scholarly knowledge? Why let the common or garden variety memoirist into the club? I'm thinking again of that bumper sticker: why Question Authority?

My answer, of course, is a memoirist's answer. Memoir must be written because each of us must have a created version of the past. Created: that is, real, tangible, made of the stuff of a life lived in place and in history. And the down side of any created thing as well: we must live with a version that attaches us to our limitations, to the inevitable subjectivity, of our points of view. We must acquiesce to our experience and our gift to transform experience into meaning and value. You tell me your story, I'll tell you my story.

If we refuse to do the work of creating this personal version of the past, someone else will do it for us. That is a scary political fact. "The struggle of man against power," a character in Milan Kundera's novel *The Book of Laughter and Forgetting* says, "is the struggle of memory against forgetting." He refers to willful political forgetting, the habit of nations and those in power (Question Authority!) to deny the truth of memory in order to disarm moral and ethical power. It's an efficient way of controlling masses of people. It doesn't even require much bloodshed, as long as people are entirely willing to give over their personal memories. Whole histories can be rewritten. As Czeslaw Milosz said in his 1980 Nobel Prize lecture, the number of books published that seek to deny the existence of the Nazi death camps now exceeds one hundred.

What is remembered is what *becomes* reality. If we "forget" Auschwitz, if we "forget" My Lai, what then do we remember? And what is the purpose of our remembering? If we think of memory naively, as a simple story, logged like a documentary in the archive of the mind, we miss its beauty but also its function. The beauty of memory rests in its talent for rendering detail, for paying homage to the senses, its capacity to love the particles of life, the richness and idiosyncrasy of our existence. The function of memory, on the other hand, is intensely personal and surprisingly political.

Our capacity to move forward as developing beings rests on a healthy relation with the past. Psychotherapy, that widespread method of mental health, relies heavily on memory and on the ability to retrieve and organize images and events from the personal past. We carry our wounds and perhaps even worse, our capacity to wound, forward with us. If we learn not only to tell our stories but to listen to what our stories tell us—to write the first draft and then return for the second draft—we are doing the work of memoir.

Memoir is the intersection of narration and reflection, of story-telling and essay-writing. It can present its story *and* reflect and consider the meaning of the story. It is a peculiarly open form, inviting broken and incomplete images, half-recollected fragments, all the mass (and mess) of detail. It offers to shape this confusion—and in shaping, of course it necessarily creates a work of art, not a legal document. But then, even legal documents are only valiant attempts to consign the truth, the whole truth and nothing but the truth to paper. Even they remain versions.

Locating touchstones—the red music book, the olive Olive, my father's violin playing—is deeply satisfying. Who knows why? Perhaps we all sense that we can't grasp the whole truth and nothing but the truth of our experience. Just can't be done. What can be achieved, however, is a version of its swirling, changing wholeness. A memoirist must acquiesce to selectivity, like any artist. The version we dare to write is the only truth, the only relationship we can have with the past. Refuse to write your life and you have no life. At least, that is the stern view of the memoirist.

Personal history, logged in memory, is a sort of slide projector flashing images on the wall of the mind. And there's precious little order to the slides in the rotating carousel. Beyond that confusion, who knows who is running the projector? A memoirist steps into this darkened room of flashing, unorganized images and stands blinking for a while. Maybe for a long while. But eventually, as with any attempt to tell a story, it is necessary to put something first, then something else. And so on, to the end. That's a first draft. Not necessarily the truth, not even *a* truth sometimes, but the first attempt to create a shape.

The first thing I usually notice at this stage of composition is the appalling inaccuracy of the piece. Witness my first piano lesson draft. Invention is screamingly evident in what I intended to be transcription. But here's the further truth: I feel no shame. In fact, it's only now that my interest in the piece truly quickens. For I can see what isn't there, what is shyly hugging the walls, hoping not to be seen. I see the filmy shape of the next draft. I see a more acute version of the episode or—this is more likely—an entirely new piece rising from the ashes of the first attempt.

The next draft of the piece would have to be a true re-vision, a new seeing of the materials of the first draft. Nothing merely cosmetic will do—no rouge buffing up the opening sentence, no glossy adjective to lift a sagging line, nothing to attempt covering a patch of gray writing. None of that. I can't say for sure, but my hunch is the revision would lead me to more writing about my father (why was I so impressed by that ancestral inventor of the collapsible opera hat? Did I feel I had nothing as remarkable in my own background? Did this make me feel inadequate?). I begin to think perhaps Sister Olive is less central to this business than she is in this draft. She is meant to be a moment, not a character.

And so I might proceed, if I were to undertake a new draft of the memoir. I begin to feel a relationship developing between a former self and me.

And, even more compelling, a relationship between an old world and me. Some people think of autobiographical writing as the precious occupation of a particularly self-absorbed person. Maybe, but I don't buy that. True memoir is written in an attempt to find not only a self but a world.

The self-absorption that seems to be the impetus and embarrassment of autobiography turns into (or perhaps always was) a hunger for the world. Actually, it begins as hunger for *a* world, one gone or lost, effaced by time or a more sudden brutality. But in the act of remembering, the personal environment expands, resonates beyond itself, beyond its "subject," into the endless and tragic recollection that is history.

We look at old family photographs in which we stand next to black, boxy Fords and are wearing period costumes, and we do not gaze fascinated because there we are young again, or there we are standing, as we never will again in life, next to our mother. We stare and drift because there we are . . . historical. It is the dress, the black car that dazzle us now and draw us beyond our mother's bright arms which once caught us. We reach into the attractive impersonality of something more significant than ourselves. We write memoir, in other words. We accept the humble position of writing a version rather than "the whole truth."

I suppose I write memoir because of the radiance of the past—it draws me back and back to it. Not that the past is beautiful. In our communal memoir, in history, the death camps *are* back there. In intimate life too, the record is usually pretty mixed. "I could tell you stories . . ." people say and drift off, meaning terrible things have happened to them.

But the past is radiant. It has the light of lived life. A memoirist wishes to touch it. No one owns the past, though typically the first act of new political regimes, whether of the left or the right, is to attempt to re-write history, to grab the past and make it over so the end comes out right. So their power looks inevitable.

No one owns the past, but it is a grave error (another age would have said a grave sin) not to inhabit memory. Sometimes I think it is all we really have. But that may be a trifle melodramatic. At any rate, memory possesses authority for the fearful self in a world where it is necessary to have authority in order to Question Authority.

There may be no more pressing intellectual need in our culture than for people to become sophisticated about the function of memory. The political implications of the loss of memory are obvious. The authority of memory is a personal confirmation of selfhood. To write one's life is to live it twice, and the second living is both spiritual and historical, for a memoir reaches deep within the personality as it seeks its narrative form and also grasps the life-of-the-times as no political treatise can.

Our most ancient metaphor says life is a journey. Memoir is travel writing, then, notes taken along the way, telling how things looked and what thoughts occurred. But I cannot think of the memoirist as a tourist. This is the traveller who goes on foot, living the journey, taking on mountains, enduring deserts, marveling at the lush green places. Moving through it all faithfully, not so much a survivor with a harrowing tale to tell as a pilgrim, seeking, wondering.

The Art of Self

Steven Harvey

On a flight recently I met a fiction writer. Both of us were on our way to a writer's conference in Portland, Oregon, and when I told her that I wrote personal essays she laughed. "Oh, I love the form," she said. "It's so easy." I heard the ice in our drinks rattle in the silence that ensued. I had plenty of time, before we landed, to think about what she had said.

Confusion about the essay begins with a misconception: that art must be invented. To be creative—the argument goes—literature must be made up. Since the personal essay begins with a real life, it is less creative, less artistic, than fiction. Such a view, I think, is mistaken, based not only on confusions about writing, but on confusions about art as well. What makes writing—writing of any kind—an art is not invention, but shape. Shapeliness. The facts, the events, the invented flights of fancy do not make up a work of art. The shapeliness of the author's composition takes us to that level.

The urge to shape begins in loss. All of us are losers, of course, because we are human, but artists console themselves, redeem losses, with their creations. John Logan has written that the baby, weaned from its mother's breast, begins moving its mouth as if to shape words, language beginning with the first loss. For the writer, these mouthings never stop. Understood this way, art does not begin with ego, but with feelings of self-annihilation, the artist creating a surrogate self. So, the potter shapes a pot. The painter catches a scene. The musician holds a note.

And the essayist fashions a text. "My advice to memoir writers," Annie Dillard writes, "is to embark upon a memoir for the same reason you would embark on any book: to fashion a text." The result is that the text—even if taken from the writer's life—has a life of its own, separate from the author. "After I've written about my experience," Dillard adds, "my memories are gone; they've been replaced by the work. The work is a sort of changeling on the doorstep." Only the text, shed of ourselves and hammered into shape, can redeem us. The enemy of the text, then, is what happened, and this is true whether the work is fictional or not. What happened may matter to us, but it is lost on us if we do not transform it into art.

Writers fashion a text, giving shape to our joys and fears, but making choices on the page. Choice—not invention or reportage—gives direction and purpose to a work of literature and there are certainly many choices to be made: When to begin? When to end? Do I fess up or lie? Should I use a pencil or a computer, yellow legal pad or typing paper? To drink or not to drink—and when! In the course of sifting through these and a thousand other choices, writers make a series of essential decisions that give singular shape to the work.

First, they must, at some point, settle on beginnings and endings. Life has none. It goes on and on. My dog lives in a constant blur, a stream-of-consciousness from Purina to Purina. Only humans can choose beginnings and endings. Meaning starts the moment we say "in the beginning" and "here endeth." These are crucial shaping choices.

The essayist also must make choices involving proportion and pace. There is much art in what is relegated to background information, the essential but dull material in an essay. Any editor will tell you there is art, as well, in what is left out entirely. By the same token, the writer must decide what counts and when to bear down. In a memoir, this may be the penultimate moment—that brink when an event can go either way. Sometimes, for the essayist, the moment is given over to an idea as nuances and ambiguities are exploited and explored. Here the writer chooses to savor an event by giving it its due.

Most crucial of all in shaping a text are the choices an author makes about language. A memoir writer comes to terms with an experience, and the terms that the writer settles on tell all. Each of us has many voices—the voice for a friend, a colleague, a student, a lover—and each voice is different. Personal essayists do not need to have enormous vocabularies or—spare us—a gift for grandiloquence, but they must constantly adjudicate the voices in their heads and choose the right language.

These, then, are the essential shaping devices, the tools of the essayist's craft: beginnings and endings, proportion and pace, and language. They do not involve invention, but they are the way to art—and they are rarely easy.

Recognizing that art is in the shaping of language not in inventing or being true to life, can be liberating for students. They do not need to have exciting lives in order to write about themselves, nor do they need to resort to fanciful creativity. Instead they can find that any event, when fashioned in words, can have meaning. But all of us, whether we be students, teachers, writers, or—bless their souls!—readers, reap benefits from carefully shaped composition. "All that you love you lose," Yeats wrote. Our life slips through greedy fingers even as we live it. Works of art may not give us our lives back, but they are money in the spiritual bank. With these hard-earned things of beauty we redeem a lifetime of losses.

The Real Who, What, When, and Why of Journalism

Sonya Huber-Humes

During the 2005-6 academic year, I taught journalism at a large, public university, where I also served as the adviser for its large-circulation student newspaper. I wondered then and I wonder now whether we are equipping students to become the kind of thoughtful, creative reporters we need to help us make sense of an increasingly chaotic world.

My own hectic teaching life replicated the hectic daily news cycle at the paper. I went to work every day, got caffeinated, and accomplished tasks. I talked with my students about writing, reporting, editing, and media ethics. My e-mail in box filled with listserv postings about the changing media landscape, the need to podcast and blog and "converge," as journalists these days describe the task of delivering the news in multiple formats and media. I felt bad for my students because I was sending them out into this wired world that I couldn't begin to comprehend or summarize in a study guide.

Journalism programs across the country have rolled out new curricula and courses emphasizing complex social issues, in-depth reporting, and "new media" such as online news sites with streaming audio and video. Journalism education has rightly taken its cue from media outlets that find themselves not relevant enough for a new generation of readers, not hip enough, not appealing enough to keep the advertising and subscription revenues rolling in. Citizen journalism, such as reporting that is either created by bloggers or readers or guided by reader feedback; new narrative approaches; multimedia formats; and efforts at increased editorial transparency are only a few of the positive recent responses to a new low in the public's trust of the news media. As a result, journalism faculty members find themselves confronted with a dazzling array of dilemmas to teach and toys to play with. The biggest challenge seems to be how to cram it all into a syllabus.

The media culture abhors both uncertainty and a vacuum. For journalists facing the daily yawning 24-hour news hole, uncertainty—even in the form of a moment's hesitation—is the enemy. The story has to get filed. We have to make sense of the world on a deadline. But is our frantic avoidance of uncertainty undermining our ability to teach students the value of reflection?

When I started as faculty adviser to *The Lantern*, I believed I would help my students navigate the maze of media change by building the skills that good, skeptical, analytical reporters need. Every afternoon in the newsroom, I felt a rush of pride when I saw my students' jaws harden with determination as they picked through a Board of Trustees meeting agenda or a notebook full of quotes, eager to find the story in the soup of words and sound bites. Student reporters need to learn how to connect subjects and verbs, make judgments, and analyze everything from art exhibits to zoning laws. My first task was to encourage students to piece together meaning from the maddening chaos of reality, and my second job was to help them communicate that meaning clearly to their readers.

In the process of putting out a daily newspaper, students become reporters. Resistance from sources, comments from readers, and feedback from editors all play a role in thickening their skins. Gradually many of them develop the reporter growl-and-scowl heard and seen in so many movies, the same brusqueness I myself had heard in the newsrooms when I worked as a reporter. My fledgling student reporters had only two hours to pry a 15-inch story and a few quotes from messy, contradictory reality, and it made them grouchy.

Once when I was mulling over a revision to my syllabus, I overheard a student editor telling a writer that one of his ideas for an article was stupid. It would never work, he said, for some reason or another. In his voice, I could hear time pressure motivating his irritation: "That story is going to be huge and complicated. You're going to get lost in it, and while you're busy extracting yourself, who is going to help me fill Pages 1, 2, and 3?"

What got to me was that I heard my own reporter's voice in his tone. He made hard-nosed-reporter comments—like "That source is lying. That's crap. It's all about the money. She just wants good PR. He's a politician."—that shut off experimentation or multiple interpretations in the interest of getting the story out.

Such cynicism is often a necessary and painful adaptation to the pressures of an understaffed newsroom. But while I am heartened by journalism schools' new emphasis on subject-driven, in-depth reporting, I worry that the focus on advanced analysis encourages students to think they know everything. Yes, reporters must be able to wrestle with complex subjects, but too often the role of expert that reporters tend to adopt results in patronizing news coverage that distances itself from and even disparages the events and people being reported on.

Trends like citizen journalism have attempted to counteract the negative potential of the reporter as expert by enabling readers to both generate and evaluate news. But reporters are still taught to see their reporting as the guiding consciousness of the news, often without questioning either the personal or organizational biases that frame the news being presented or the effect that being "covered" by the media has on a community or source. The study of "media effects" in most journalism or communication departments is separated from media ethics, and it shouldn't be. In the crush of a student reporter's jam-packed schedule, media ethics often amounts to: "How do I avoid getting sued for libel?"

Sitting at my desk surrounded by a sickening stack of doomsday predictions on media change and readership polls, I found myself fantasizing about a classroom where my reporters and I could all just shut up for a few minutes and turn our backs to the 24-hour news tapeworm that beckoned and hissed from beyond graduation. Was it possible, I wondered, to release my students from deadlines long enough to stare at uncertainty, to reflect deeply on what they don't know and how those gaps in knowledge and perception might shape their production of news? Wouldn't such reflection give them more tools with which to craft stories that answer—or even just pose—the questions worth asking? I fantasized about a course that veered away from computer-assisted reporting to focus on a single article, teasing out biases, experimenting with alternate approaches, re-interviewing sources to get to the varied hearts of the matter.

We did manage to spend a few classes speculating about why these young reporters and their friends turned away from newspapers in favor of Jon Stewart's *Daily Show*. We studied how the 18 to 35 demographic is the holy grail for news-media marketers and how news outlets court those elusive media users with come-ons like snappy hardware and hairstyles. But maybe these young news consumers do not eschew traditional news because they are cynical or jaded; maybe they simply realize that the news media's clipped, confident, declarative statements of "truth" often turn out to be wrong and fail to capture reality.

In my fantasy journalism class, I would ask students to sit silently for 10 minutes and notice what they are worrying about, what they are obsessed with, and how those worries and obsessions might contain better seeds of articles than any news release. I would describe interviews as not just a means for harvesting good quotes, or a series of mind games designed to strip sources' defenses and trick them into divulging carefully guarded information. Rather, I would suggest that interviews could be encounters in which one human being might actually attempt to listen to another. (I cringe as I write that sentence, hearing my reporter friends jeer at my Pollyannaism.) I would have students examine the quotes they've gathered for a story from three sources and identify the ways in which those quotes barely scratch the surface of what the story is really about.

I would want students to be able to say out loud the words "I don't know." I would want them to imagine working in a newsroom where "I don't know" is the trigger for a story, not a sign that the reporter needs to be transferred to the home-and-garden section.

Looking back at my own time crunch to help students put out a newspaper and release our content in every format possible, I wish I had had the guts or the time to assign some silence—perhaps by asking them to drive around a neighborhood where they felt lost and afraid, and then ask themselves how their fears might shape their coverage of a news story emerging from that neighborhood. When they pitched stories about pollution, health insurance, or cheap eats on the campus, I should have asked them to put their hands in the dirt, to stand outside a health clinic, to wash dishes in a fast-food restaurant.

I might actually have the chance to put my syllabus where my mouth is. I am now teaching creative nonfiction in a writing program far removed from journalism. Truth can get loosey-goosey when nonfiction is "creative"; there are as many temptations for creative writers to steer away from complex truths as there are for reporters to reduce reality to simplistic facts. I am hoping to bring my students into the murky territory between those two poles. There, the roles of reporter, writer, thinker, and community member might blend so that journalism students could attempt to capture both what's true and what's unknown; there, they might have the chance to absorb, record, and probe life's big questions.

Courting the Approval of the Dead

Tracy Kidder

I have never written much about myself, but, like most writers I know, I am interested in the subject. We live in an era surfeited with memoirs. This is my contribution to the excess.

My writing career began at Harvard College about thirty-two years ago, shortly after I enrolled as an undergraduate. I planned to fix the world by becoming a diplomat. I began by studying political science. Thinking I should have a hobby, I also took a course in creative writing. I didn't invest a lot of ego in the enterprise and maybe for that reason the first short stories that I wrote were rather sprightly. I think they contained some dialogue that human beings might have uttered. Anyway, the teacher liked them and, more important, so did some of the young women in the class. My first strong impulse to become a writer sprang from this realization: that writing could be a means of meeting and impressing girls.

The next year I got into a class taught by the poet and great translator Robert Fitzgerald. He admitted only about a dozen students from among dozens of applicants, and I seem to remember that I was the youngest of the anointed group. This mattered to me. In high school I had been addicted to competitive sports, and I conceived of writing in sporting terms. I figured I had won part of the competition already, by being the youngest student admitted to the class. The yearning for distinction is common among writers, and in that sense I had begun to become a writer.

I want to try to summon Mr. Fitzgerald back from the dead. I remember him as a small, elegant man, then in his sixties, I believe. Occasionally during office hours he smoked a cigarette, and did so with great deliberation, making every puff count—I think he'd been warned off tobacco, and had put himself on short rations. He would enter the classroom with a green bookbag slung over his shoulder, and would greet us with a smile and a sigh as he heaved the bag onto the long seminar table. Mr. Fitzgerald's green bag contained our work, *my* work, with his comments upon it. I could not have been more interested in that object if Mr. Fitzgerald had been our adult provider, returning with food he'd found out in the world. But the way he sighed, as he heaved that sack onto the table, insinuated that what lay inside wasn't as valuable as food. Certainly it looked like a heavy load for one professor to carry.

I have always talked too much and listened too little. What is it about certain people that has made me pay attention to everything they say? Their confidence and wit, I guess, but most of all their interest in *me.* Mr. Fitzgerald paid his students the great compliment of taking us seriously. He flattered us, dauntingly. I remember the first day of that class. From his place at the head of the table Mr. Fitzgerald eyed us all. He had a pair of reading glasses, half-glasses, which he often used to great effect. He lowered them and looking at us over the top of them, said something like, "The only reason for writing is to produce something *classic.* And I expect that you will produce *classic* work during this term."

I recall thinking, "You do?"

Of course, none of us did, with the possible exception of one young woman who wrote a poem entitled "The Splendor and the Terror of the Universe as Revealed to Me on Brattle Street." I don't recall the poem, but I still like the title.

Having told us of his expectations, Mr. Fitzgerald offered his first advice for meeting them. He jabbed an index finger at the wastebasket beside him and said, "The greatest repository I know of for writers. And I do hope that it will *precede* me."

After a few weeks of Mr. Fitzgerald, I gave up on political science. I quit right in the middle of a lecture by the then-not-very-famous professor Henry Kissinger. The lecture bored me. Professor Kissinger was only partly to blame. I now described myself as a writer, and I thought a writer shouldn't be interested in politics. I had not yet realized that a writer ought to know about something besides writing, so as to have something to write about. When I left that lecture I went right to the English department office and signed up. I'd already begun to do a lot of reading on my own, mostly fiction, which I was consuming at a rate I've never equaled since. At the same time, I had suddenly acquired an assigned-reading disability and a sleep disorder. I had trouble reading books that appeared on formal course lists, and I often worked all night on stories for Mr. Fitzgerald, then went to sleep around the time when my other classes began.

During the first part of Mr. Fitzgerald's class, he would talk about writing and read aloud to us, very occasionally stuff that a student had written, and more often works by wonderful, famous writers he had known, such as his old friend Flannery O'Connor. He read us one of her stories, and when he finished, he said, "That story unwinds like a Rolex watch." Listening to him read such estimable work made me want to try my hand. I think he aimed for that effect, because in the second half of every class he had us write. He warmed us up, and then made us exercise. It is a testament to those warmups of his that I can't recall ever being unable to write *something* in that room for him. In his presence, even poetry seemed possible. Mr. Fitzgerald insisted I try my hand at a poem now and then. I struggled but complied. Finally, I got one off that he seemed to like. It came back from him with this comment at the bottom: "This is very like a poem."

I prefer other memories, especially this one: I had written a short story, which an undergraduate, literary friend of mine had read and disliked. This was the first and at the time the only literary friend I'd acquired, and I thought him very wise and perspicacious, because he had encouraged me. I guessed that my friend must be right about my story. Once he'd pointed out its flaws, I saw them clearly, too. But I decided to show the thing to Mr. Fitzgerald, just so he'd know that I was working. He opened the next class by saying that he was going to read a student's story, a story that he particularly liked, and I remember sitting there wishing that he would some day single out a story of mine in that way and I recall vividly the moment when I realized that it was my story he was reading. The mellifluous voice that had read to us from the likes of James Agee and Wallace Stevens and Flannery O'Connor was reading something of mine! I felt frightened. Then I felt confused. I don't think it had ever occurred to me that intelligent people could disagree about the quality of a piece of writing. If my literary friend thought the story was lousy, Mr. Fitzgerald surely would, too. I see myself sitting at that table with my mouth hanging open—and closing it fast when I remembered the young women in the room. At first I wanted to ask Mr. Fitzgerald to stop, and then I hoped he never would.

I hoped, indeed expected, to have that experience again. I remember that I had given Mr. Fitzgerald a story I knew to be marvelous, a story I knew he'd want to single out in class. When I came into his office for the private visit all of us periodically received, I said to him, in a voice already exulting at his answer, "How'd you like that story, Mr. Fitzgerald?"

He performed his ritual of the reading glasses, pulling them an inch down his nose and looking at me over the top of them. "Not much," he said.

And then, of course, he told me what was wrong with the story, and I saw at once that he was right. I still have this problem. My judgment of my own work sometimes seems so malleable as not to rate as judgment at all. Any critic, no matter how stupid in praise or transparently spiteful in blame, convinces me—at least for awhile. Generally, harsh criticism tends to make me fear that the critic has an intelligence far superior to mine, and has found out things about my writing that I've been too blind to see myself. A person as easily confused by criticism as I am might well have quit writing after a few rejection slips came in for stories that my girlfriend and my mother thought were really good. Perhaps inadvertently, Mr. Fitzgerald taught me the value of trusting the judgment of just one person above all others—and of getting that judgment as the work is in progress, and a lot of help besides. Which is the role I've inflicted on a single editor, Richard Todd, for more than two decades.

I took Mr. Fitzgerald's course again and again, right up until I graduated. After my first semester with him, I didn't perform very well. It wasn't for lack of trying or, God knows, desire. I had become self-conscious about writing. At one point I started a novel. I wrote twenty pages or so, but the most interesting parts were the comments and little drawings I made in the margins—and created with greater care than anything in the actual text—imagining, as I created these notes in the margins, my biographer's delight in finding them. During this period, almost all of the stories I wrote in my room late at night, and the pastiches I committed in class, came back with such brief comments as "O.K., but no flash," all written in an elegantly penned script, which I can still see in my mind's eye, my heart sinking all over again. Mr. Fitzgerald used to talk about something he called "the luck of the conception," an idea I still believe in, but no longer dream about. I used to have a dream in which I had come upon the perfect story. The dream did not contain the story itself, just the fact that I possessed it. It was a dream suffused with joy, and I'd awake from it with a kind of sorrow that I haven't felt since adolescence. As a reader I felt then as I feel now, that any number of faults in a piece of writing are forgivable if there is life on the page. And there was no life in anything I wrote. Oddly, as the small natural talent I'd had for making up stories began to wane, my ambitions grew immense. Or maybe it was the other way around, and ambition stood in my way.

I can't blame Mr. Fitzgerald. He had only suggested that writing could be a high calling. I alone invented my desire to write for posterity. I am embarrassed to admit to this, but what I really had in mind was immortality. Once as a very young boy at a lecture at the Hayden Planetarium in New York, I learned that the earth would be destroyed in some two and a half billion years, and in spite of all my mother said, I was inconsolable for weeks. Maybe I was born especially susceptible to the fears that attend the fact of human mortality. Maybe I was influenced by certain of the English poets, those whose poems declare that their poems will make them immortal. Or it may be, as my wife suggests, that once a young man has solved the problem of how to meet and impress girls, it just naturally occurs to him that his next job is to figure out how to become immortal.

After college I went to Vietnam as a soldier—not the most likely way of gaining immortality, though I was never in much danger there. I came home with my body and my vaunting literary ambitions still intact and wrote a whole novel about experiences I didn't have in Vietnam. I designed that book for immortality. I borrowed heavily from Conrad, Melville, and Dostoyevsky. About thirty-five editors refused to publish it, thank God. I went to the Iowa Writers Workshop, where it began to seem to me that the well from which I drew for fiction had gone completely dry. (I have written fiction since then, all of it published, but the sum total is three short stories.) I decided to try my hand at nonfiction. That term covers a lot of territory, of course, from weighty treatises on the great problems of the world to diet books—some diet books qualify as nonfiction don't they? I dove into something then labeled The New Journalism. As many people have pointed out, only the term was new. I believe that the form already had a distinguished lineage, which included work by George Orwell and Joseph Mitchell and Mark Twain and Lillian Ross and Edmund Wilson and, my particular favorite, A. J. Liebling. This kind of nonfiction writing, whatever it's called, relies on narrative.

Some people describe it by saying that it borrows techniques of fiction, but the fact is that it employs techniques of storytelling that never did belong exclusively to fiction. It is an honorable literary form, not always honorably used, but one can certainly say the same about fiction.

When I first started trying to write in this genre, there was an idea in the air, which for me had the force of a revelation: that all journalism is inevitably subjective. I was in my mid-twenties then, and although my behavior was somewhat worse than it has been recently, I was quite a moralist. I decided that writers of nonfiction had a moral obligation to write in the first person—really write in the first person, making themselves characters on the page. In this way, I would disclose my biases. I would not hide the truth from the reader. I would proclaim that what I wrote was just my own subjective version of events. In retrospect, it seems clear that this prescription for honesty often served instead as a license for self-absorption on the page. But I was still very young, too young and self-absorbed to realize what now seems obvious—that I was less likely to write honestly about myself than about anyone else on earth.

I wrote a book about a murder case, in a swashbuckling first person. It *was* published, I'm sorry to say. On the other hand, it disappeared without a trace; that is, it never got reviewed in the *New York Times.* And I began writing nonfiction articles for the *Atlantic Monthly,* under the tutelage of Richard Todd, then a young editor there. For about five years, during which I didn't dare attempt another book, I worked on creating what many writer friends of mine call "voice." I didn't do this consciously. If I had, I probably wouldn't have gotten anywhere. But gradually, I think, I cultivated a writing voice, the voice of a person who was well-informed, fair-minded, and temperate—the voice, not of the person I was, but of a person I sometimes wanted to be. Then I went back to writing books, and discovered other points of view besides the first person.

Choosing a point of view is a matter of finding the best place to stand from which to tell a story. It shouldn't be determined by theory, but by immersion in the material itself. The choice of point of view, I've come to think, has nothing to do with morality. It's a choice among tools. I think it's true, however, that the wrong choice can lead to dishonesty. Point of view is primary; it affects everything else, including voice. Writing my last four books, I made my choices by instinct sometimes and sometimes by experiment. Most of my memories of time spent writing have merged together in a blur, but I remember vividly my first attempts to find a way to write *Among Schoolchildren,* a book about an inner-city schoolteacher. I had spent a year inside her classroom. I intended, vaguely, to fold into my account of events I'd witnessed in that little place a great deal about the lives of particular schoolchildren and about the problems of education in America. I tried out every point of view that I'd used in previous books, and every page I wrote felt lifeless. Finally, I hit on a restricted third-person narration.

The approach seemed to work. The world of that classroom seemed to come alive when the view of it was restricted mainly to observations of the teacher and to accounts of what the teacher saw and heard and smelled and felt. This choice narrowed my options. I ended up writing something less comprehensive than I'd planned. The book became essentially an account of a year in the emotional life of a schoolteacher. My choice of the restricted third person also obliged me to write parts of the book as if from within the teacher's mind. I felt entitled to describe her thoughts and feelings because she had described them to me, both during class and afterward, and because her descriptions rarely seemed self-serving. Believing in them myself, I thought that I could make them believable on the page.

Belief is an offering that a reader makes to an author, what Coleridge famously called "That willing suspension of disbelief for the moment, which constitutes poetic faith." It is up to the writer to entertain and inform without disappointing the reader into a loss of that faith. In fiction or poetry, of course, believability may have nothing to do with realism or even plausibility. It has everything to do with those things in nonfiction, in my opinion. I think that the nonfiction writer's fundamental job is to make what is true believable. I'm not sure that everyone agrees. Lately the job seems to have been defined differently. Here are some of the ways that some people now seem to define the nonfiction writer's job: to make believable what the writer thinks is true, if the writer wants to be scrupulous; to make believable what the writer wishes were true, if the writer isn't interested in scrupulosity; or to make believable what the writer thinks might be true, if the writer couldn't get the story and had to make it up.

I figure that if I call a piece of my own writing nonfiction it ought to be about real people, with their real names attached whenever possible, who say and do in print nothing that they didn't actually say and do. On the cover page of my last book I put a note that reads, "This is a work of nonfiction," and listed the several names that I was obliged to change in the text. I thought a longer note would be intrusive. I was afraid that it would stand between the reader and the spell that I wanted to create, inviting the reader into the world of a nursing home. But the definition of "nonfiction" has become so slippery that I wonder if I shouldn't have written more. So now I'll take this opportunity to explain that for my last book I spent a year doing research, that the name of the place I wrote about is its real name, that I didn't change the names of any of the major characters, and that I didn't invent dialogue or put any thoughts in characters' minds that the characters themselves didn't confess to.

I no longer care what rules other writers set for themselves. If I don't like what someone has written, I can stop reading, which is, after all, the worst punishment a writer can suffer. (It ought to be the worst punishment. Some critics seem to feel that the creation of a book that displeases them amounts to a felony.) But the expanded definitions of nonfiction have created problems for those writers who define the term narrowly. Many readers now view with suspicion every narrative that claims to be nonfiction, and yet scores of very good nonfiction writers do not make up their stories or the details in them—writers such as John McPhee, Jane Kramer, J. Anthony Lucas. There are also special cases that confound categories and all attempts to lay down rules for writers of narrative. I have in mind Norman Mailer and in particular his *Executioner's Song*, a hybrid of fact and fiction, carefully labeled as such—a book I admire.

Most writers lack Mailer's powers of invention. Some nonfiction writers do not lack his willingness to invent, but the candor to admit it. Some writers proceed by trying to discover the truth about a situation, and then invent or distort the facts as necessary. Even in these suspicious times, writers can get away with this. Often no one will know, and the subjects of the story may not care. They may not notice. But the writer always knows. I believe in immersion in the events of a story. I take it on faith that the truth lies in the events somewhere, and that immersion in those real events will yield glimpses of that truth. I try to hew to what has begun to seem like a narrow definition of nonfiction partly in that faith, and partly out of fear. I'm afraid that if I started making up things in a story that purported to be about real events and people, I'd stop believing it myself. And I imagine that such a loss of conviction would infect every sentence and make each one unbelievable.

I don't mean to imply that all a person has to do to write good narrative nonfiction is to take accurate notes and reproduce them. The kind of nonfiction I like to read is at bottom storytelling, as gracefully accomplished as good fiction. I don't think any technique should be ruled out to achieve it well. For myself, I rule out only invention. But I don't think that honesty and artifice are contradictory. They work together in good writing of every sort. Artfulness and an author's justified belief in a story often combine to produce the most believable nonfiction.

If you write a nonfiction story in the third person and show your face in public afterward, someone is bound to ask, "How did your presence in the scenes you relate affect the people you were observing?" Some readers seem to feel that third-person narration, all by itself, makes a narrative incomplete. The other day I came upon a book about the writing of ethnography. It interested me initially because its bibliography cited a couple of my books and one of its footnotes mentioned me. The author spelled my first name wrong and gave one of my books a slightly different title from the one I chose. I swear I don't hold a grudge on account of that. My first name is a little weird, and the title in question is a long one. But those little mistakes did make me vigilant as I read the following passage:

> Writers of literary tales seldom remark on the significance of their presence on the scenes they represent, and this is in some instances a bothersome problem to field workers in addition to the common concerns for reactivity in any situation. It is, for example, very difficult to imagine that as famous and dandy a writer as Tom Wolfe was merely a fashionable but unobtrusive fly on the wall in the classic uptown parlor scene of *Radical Chic* (1970), or that Tracey [sic] Kidder did not in any way influence the raising of the Souweines' roofbeams in *House* (1985). Since writers of ethnographic tales have begun to break their silence on these matters, it is seemingly time for writers of literary tales to do so too—especially when their accounts so clearly rest on intimacy.

I believe it's possible to learn something from anyone, including ethnographers who have begun to break their silence. But I can't work out the mechanics for calculating the *reactivity* that occurs during *field work*. As I imagine it, field work that is mindful of reactivity would have to proceed in this way: I'd open my notebook in front of a person I planned to write about, and I'd ask, "How did you feel when I opened my notebook just now?" Then I would probably be bound to ask, "How did you feel when I asked you that question about opening my notebook?"

I don't know for sure how my presence has influenced the behavior of any of the people I've written about. I don't believe that I can know, because I wasn't there when I wasn't there. To do the research for a book, I usually hang around with my subjects for a year or more. After a while, most seem to take my presence for granted. Not all do. It worked the other way with one of the carpenters I wrote about in *House.* I remember his saying at one point that he and the other builders ought to put a bell around my neck, so they'd know where I was at all times.

Obviously some readers expect to hear about the story behind the story. But all writing is selective. I think that a narrative should be judged mainly on its own terms, not according to a reader's preexisting expectations. As a reader, I know that I won't always sit still for the story behind the story. As a writer, I have often decided that it isn't worth telling.

I wrote my most recent book, *Old Friends,* which is about some of the residents of a nursing home, in the third person. I hope that I put my own voice in it, but I chose not to write about how I did my research and how I was affected by what I encountered inside the nursing home—never mind how my presence might, arguably, possibly, have affected the inmates' behavior—mainly because what I did—asking questions, listening, taking notes—was much less interesting than what I observed. It is true, however, that my solution to the problem that the book presented did have something to do with my own experience of life inside that place. After writing for a while, I realized that I wanted to reproduce, in a limited sense, the most important part of my experience there.

I entered the nursing home in the late fall of 1990. The place, which is situated in western Massachusetts, is called the Linda Manor Extended Care Facility. I went there with a notebook—I filled ninety notebooks eventually—and prowled around inside almost every day, and many nights, for about a year. And then for another year or so I spent about three days a week there. I chose a decent nursing home, not one of the very best but a clean, well-lighted place where residents weren't tied up and were allowed some of the trappings of their former lives.

I had visited a nursing home only once before in my life, and since then had averted both my eyes and thoughts as I passed by. That was part of the attraction; nursing homes seemed to me like secret places in the landscape. I went to Linda Manor tentatively, though. I was afraid that I might find it dull. I thought I might find myself in a kind of waiting room, a vestibule to eternity, where everything had been resolved or set aside and residents simply lay waiting to die. But waiting was the least of what went on in many of those clean, motel-like rooms. Nearly everyone, it seemed, was working on a project. Some were absurd—one resident kept hounding the office of a U.S. senator to complain about his breakfast eggs. Some were poignant—many of the demented residents roamed the halls searching for exits, asking everyone for directions home. A lot of projects were Quixotic. There was, for instance, one indomitable, wheelchair-bound woman who had set herself the task of raising about $30,000 to buy the nursing home its own chairlift van. She intended to do so through raffles and teacup auctions and by getting other residents to remember the van in their wills. There was also an elderly actress who kept herself and the place somewhat invigorated by putting on plays. Staging those productions took great determination, because Linda Manor had no stage and most of the actors and actresses were confined to wheelchairs and walkers. In between plays, when things got dull, the old actress livened things up by starting fights. There were many residents working doggedly to come to terms with the remorse they felt for past mistakes and offenses. There was also a man in his nineties named Lou Freed who summoned up memories with what seemed like the force of necessity, re-inhabiting his former life with something that resembled joy. And there were, of course, a number who knew their deaths were imminent and struggled to find ways to live in the face of that knowledge.

Even in a decent nursing home, the old often get treated like children. And yet many of the residents refused to become like children. The roommates Lou and Joe, for instance. Let me try to prove this point with a short passage from my book.

Joe and Lou could not control most of the substance of their life in here, but they had imposed a style on it. The way for instance that Joe and Lou had come, in the past months, to deal with matters of the bathroom. Joe had to go there what seemed to him like a ridiculous number of times each day and night. He and Lou referred to the bathroom as "the library." The mock-daintiness of the term amused Joe. The point was to make a joke out of anything you could around here. Up in the room after breakfast, Joe would say to Lou, "I gotta go to the library. I have to do my, uh, uh, prune evacuation."

This room was now their home. As in any household, people entering were expected to follow local rules. The nursing staff was overwhelmingly female. Lou and Joe referred to all of them as girls, and indeed, next to them, even the middleaged did look like girls. The staff had all, of course, been quite willing to talk frankly about matters of Lou and Joe's biology. Too frankly for Lou. Too frankly for Joe, once Lou had made the point. The aides, "the girls," used to come to the doorway, cradling opened in their arms the large, ledger-like Forest View "BM Book," and they'd call loudly in, "Did either of you gentlemen have a bowel movement today?" It was Lou, some months ago now, who responded to this question by inviting in the girls who asked it, and then telling them gently, "All you have to say is, 'Did you or didn't you.'" The way Lou did that job impressed Joe, Lou did it so diplomatically, so much more diplomatically than Joe would have. Lou, as he liked to say, had trained all the girls by now. Joe took care of reinforcement.

It was a morning in December. Joe had the television news on. He and Lou were listening to the dispatches from the Middle East. Joe wasn't waiting for the aide with the BM Book, but he had a question ready for her. When the aide came to the door, she asked, "For my book. Did you?"

"Yes." Joe tilted his head toward Lou. "And so did he." Then, a little smile blossoming, Joe looked at the aide and asked, "And what about you?"

"None of your business!" The aide looked embarrassed. She laughed.

"Well, you ask me," Joe said.

"But I get paid for it."

"*Good*bye," Joe said pleasantly, and went back to watching the news.

Many residents insisted on preserving their dignity, in spite of the indignities imposed by failing health and institutional confinement. Many people in there were attempting in one way or another to invent new lives for themselves. In the context of that place and of debilitating illnesses, their quests seemed important.

So when I began to write *Old Friends*, I didn't lack for interesting characters or stories. I felt I had an overabundance. I told myself before I started writing that I couldn't fit in everything, and then for about a year I tried to do just that. In the end I had to jettison a lot of portraits and stories that I had written many times and polished up. Among other things, I wrote four or five times and finally discarded what in all modesty I believe to have been the most riveting account of a session of Bingo ever composed. But the plain fact was that about half of what I wrote and rewrote got in the way of the main story that I wanted to tell.

Hundreds of articles and books deal with the big issues that surround aging in late-twentieth-century America. I read some of them. But I didn't want to approach this subject in a general way. It is useful, maybe even necessary, to imagine that a definable group called "the elderly" exists. But all such conceptions inevitably fail. It is accurate only to say that there are many individuals who have lived longer than most of the rest of the population, and that they differ widely among themselves. For various reasons, some can no longer manage what are called the activities of daily living at home, and, for lack of a better solution, some of those people end up living in nursing homes. I chose to write about a few of those people partly because so much well-meaning commentary on old age depicts white-haired folks in tennis clothes—a tendency, it seems to me, that inadvertently denigrates the lives of the many people who haven't been as lucky.

About five percent of Americans over sixty-five—about 1.5 million people—live in nursing homes and, according to one estimate, nearly half of all the people who live past sixty-five will spend some time inside a nursing home. Obviously, they are important places, but nursing homes weren't really the subject I wanted to address. There were already plenty of published exposés of bad nursing homes. I decided to do my research inside a good nursing home on the theory that a good one would be bad enough, inevitably a house of grief and pain, and also because I didn't want to write about the kinds of policy and management issues that would have assumed primary importance in a story set in an evil place. I wanted to write from the inside about the experience of being old and sick and confined to an institution. I wanted to come at the subject of aging, not through statistics, but through elderly people themselves. I wanted to write an interesting, engaging book. The residents of even a decent nursing home are people in a difficult situation, and I think that stories about people in difficult situations are almost always interesting, and often dramatic.

In some ways, research in that place was easy work. In the course of every story I'd done before, I had run into people who hadn't wanted to talk to me. But people in a nursing home never have enough willing listeners. A nursing home like Linda Manor may be the only place on earth where a person with a notebook can hope to receive a universal welcome.

Various sights, smells, and sounds distressed me at first. But gradually, I got used to the externals of the place and people. Almost everyone who has spent some time inside a nursing home begins to look beyond the bodies of the residents. It just happens. But around the time when that happened to me, another problem arose. I remember leaving the room of a dying, despondent resident and stopping in my tracks in a Linda Manor corridor, and hearing myself say to myself, "This is amazing! *Everybody* dies." And, of course, my next thought was, "Including me." I know that sounds silly. One is supposed to have figured that out before pushing fifty. But I hadn't believed it, I think.

I arranged some other troubling moments for myself, during my research. At one point, I decided that I ought to check into Linda Manor for a couple of days and nights, as if I were myself a resident. I hate the kind of story in which a perfectly healthy person decides to ride around in a wheelchair for a day and then proclaims himself an expert in what being wheelchair-bound is like. But I believe in the possibility of imaginatively experiencing what others experience, and I thought I might learn something. With vast amusement, a nurse ushered me into a little room. My roommate, an ancient man who couldn't speak much, terrified me as soon as I climbed into bed. He kept clicking his light on and off. At one point I saw his hand through the filmy, so-called "privacy curtain." His hand reached toward the curtain, grasping at it. He was trying to pull the curtain back, so that he could get a better look at me, and I had to stifle the impulse to yell at him to stop. Then, a little later, I heard a couple of the nurses in the hall outside, saying loudly, speaking of me, "Shall we give him an enema?" An old source of amusement among nurses, the enema.

I didn't learn much that I could use in my book, from my two-night stand at Linda Manor. Except for the fact that a few minutes can seem like eternity in a nursing-home bed and the fact that, from such a perspective, cheerful, attractive, average-sized nurses and nurse's aides can look huge and menacing. Those two nights I kept getting up and looking out the window, to make sure my car was still in the parking lot. I had planned to stay longer, but went home early the third morning in order to get some sleep.

At Linda Manor I got to know a nurse's aide who, when one of her residents had died, insisted on opening up the windows of the room. Asked why she did this, she said she felt she had to let the spirit out. All but a few of the staff were religious, at least in the sense that most believed in an afterlife. I think belief was a great comfort to them. At least I imagined it would be for me. But I possessed only a vague agnosticism. And I couldn't simply manufacture something stronger for the situation.

What troubled me most during my time at Linda Manor wasn't unpleasant sights or smells or even the reawakening of my fears about mortality. It was the problem of apparent meaninglessness. I watched people dying long before life had lost its savor for them or they their usefulness to others. I couldn't imagine any purpose behind the torments that many residents suffered in their last days. Sometimes I'd leave a resident's room feeling that everything, really everything in every life, was pointless. I remember thinking that we all just live awhile and end up dying painfully, or, even worse, bored and inert. What meaning could life have, I'd find myself wondering, if the best of the last things people get to do on earth is to play Bingo? At such times, I'd usually find my way upstairs to the room of the two old men named Lou and Joe. Gradually, I began to notice that a number of the staff did the same thing, even giving up their coffee breaks to go and chat with Lou and Joe. I didn't usually plan to go to their room at these moments of vicarious despair. I'd just find myself wanting to go there. After about ten minutes in their room, I usually felt much better. Lou and Joe had been placed together in one of Linda Manor's little rooms, in what for both would likely be their last place on earth, and they had become great friends. Other residents had formed friendships inside Linda Manor, but none was durable or seemed to run very deep. Out in the wider, youthful world, this accomplishment of Lou and Joe's would have seemed unremarkable but in that place it was profound.

The main thing I wanted to portray was that friendship, surrounded by the nursing home and all its varying forms of claustrophobia. I wanted to infuse the story of that friendship with sentiment, but not in a sentimental way. The difference, as I see it, is the difference between portraying emotion and merely asserting its existence, between capturing the reflection of something real on the page and merely providing handy cues designed to elicit an emotional response. It is, I realize, harder to depict manifestations of human goodness than manifestations of venality and evil. I don't know why that is. I do know that some people think that kindness, for example, is always superficial. That view is the logical equivalent of sentimentality. It's an easy way to feel and it gives some people a lot of pleasure. It has nothing to do with a tragic vision of life. It has about as much to do with an accurate vision of life as a Hallmark card. Anyway, that's how it seems to me. The world seems various to me, and depicting some of the virtue in it seems like a project worth attempting. I do not say that I pulled it off, but that's part of what I had in mind.

After my book was published, I continued to visit Linda Manor about once a week. I went partly because doing so made me feel like a good guy. But I had other reasons. Growing old with dignity calls for many acts of routine heroism, and some of the people I knew at Linda Manor were inspiring, admirable characters. All of them have died now, except for Lou, who has achieved the ripe old age of ninety-six. Joe died last winter. I visit only Lou now, but I used to go mainly in order to visit the two men. I *liked* visiting them. Their room was one place where I knew I was always welcome. They gave me good advice, on such subjects as child-rearing. They were funny, both intentionally and otherwise. Most important, their room was one place in the world where I could count on finding that amity prevailed. That was unusual, in my experience of the world. The crucial thing about Lou and Joe was that they remained *very good* friends, better friends every time I visited. They presented an antidote to despair, which is connectedness, and for me, I learned, it is only the connectedness of the human tribe that can hold despair at bay. Connectedness can, of course, take many different forms. One can find it in religion, or in family, or, as in the case of Lou and Joe, in friendship. Or perhaps in work, maybe even in the act of writing.

Harold Brodkey, who recently died of AIDS, wrote in an essay a couple of years ago, "I think anyone who spends his life working to become eligible for literary immortality is a fool." I agree. But I also think that only a fool would write merely for money or contemporary fame. I imagine that most writers—good, bad and mediocre—write partly for the sake of the private act of writing and partly in order to throw themselves out into the world. Most, I imagine, *endeavor* for connectedness, to create the kind of work that touches other lives and, in that sense at least, leaves something behind. I don't dream of immortality or plant marginalia for my biographers anymore. But I do wonder what Mr. Fitzgerald would think of what I've written and, especially, of what I'm going to write.

A few days after I got back from Vietnam, in June 1969, I traveled to Cambridge and called Mr. Fitzgerald from a pay phone. He invited me to lunch at his house the next afternoon. Of course, I didn't tell him this, but I wanted something from him, something ineffable, like hope. He had prepared sandwiches. I'm not sure that he made them himself, but I like to think that he did, and that he was responsible for cutting the crusts off the bread. I'm not sure why I remember that. It seemed a sweet gesture, a way of making me feel that I was important to him. It also made him seem old, older than I'd remembered him.

I saw Mr. Fitzgerald a few times more over the next year or two, and then he moved away and I moved out west for a while. I fell under other influences. My dreams of writing something classic gave way to my little dreams of writing something publishable, of making a living as a writer, which seemed hard enough. But those early dreams were dormant, not dead. When, almost ten years later, a book of mine, *The Soul of a New Machine,* was awarded the Pulitzer Prize and the American Book Award, my megalomaniacal dreams of literary glory came out of storage. I could tell myself at moments that I'd achieved them all. But I hesitated for a while before sending my book to Mr. Fitzgerald. I was afraid. When I finally worked up the nerve, I wrote an inscription to the effect that I hoped this piece of writing began to approach his expectations. I soon received a letter from him, in which he thanked me, remarked upon the "modesty" of my inscription—no doubt he saw right through that—and apologized for his inability to read the book just now. I wrote right back, proposing that I visit him. He did not reply. I never heard from him again. I don't remember exactly when he died. I think it was a few years later.

His silence has bothered me for a long time, not immoderately but in the way of those embarrassing memories that suddenly appear when you're checking the oil in your car or putting a key in a door. Two summers ago I met one of Mr. Fitzgerald's sons and told him the story. He insisted that his father would never have failed to answer my last letter, if he'd been able to read and write by then. I believed him. And I believe that if Mr. Fitzgerald had been able to read my book, he would have told me what he really thought. It's probably just as well that he never did. I've written other and, I think, better books since then. I'd rather know what he thought of *them*. I've been courting his approval ever since my first day in his class, and I continue to court his approval now, when he's certain to withhold it. That makes me sad sometimes, but not in my better moments. I'll never know if he'd approve of what I've written and am going to write. But I'll never know if he'd disapprove either. He's left me room to go on trying.

Mending Wall

Judith Kitchen

My father sat with his feet on the desk, a cup of coffee still steaming in front of him. I had just walked in the door of his workplace—an old storefront in Corning, NY, where the physicists at Corning Glass Works had temporarily located themselves while a new lab was being built. So, for the first time in my young life, I could see where my father "worked." I put quotations around the word even then because it didn't look like work, sitting with his feet propped up, his chair tilted back, just thinking.

When I asked about his work, he tried to define it for me, but eventually he settled for something like "sometimes an idea just comes, and then you have to try to prove that what you think is true is actually true." My father's conversation was peppered with words like "hypothesis" and "theorem" and "proof" and "therefore," and so I did kind of understand what he was getting at. Later, after I had a degree in literature and talked about writing and books and movies, he vociferously resisted the phrase "metaphorical truth" as something impossibly silly. Stonewall: trochaic verb, something to obfuscate and override. Stone wall: the spondee of what we built between us, so we agreed to agree that we did not speak each other's language.

Here's what I remember about those days with scientists: my Uncle Willy, a mathematician, insisting that Robert Frost really meant "good fences make good neighbors."

"He said so, didn't he?"

"No," I replied, "he let someone else say so, so he could question it."

I was in seventh grade, and my Uncle Willy just turned away in disgust. I grew more insistent: "Don't you see what he called his neighbor—an 'old-stone savage'? You're a scientist. You ought to know what *that* means."

Uncle Willy did not back down, and suddenly it felt as though his ability to read was compromised by his science. "It's right there, on the page." Yes, it was, but so was tone, and nuance. If Frost circled back to reconsider that idea, it was not for want of trying on other ways of thinking—and he does not give away whether he eventually agreed to agree with his neighbor.

"Too bad," said my wonderful professor, "that you have so many good ideas, and no vehicle with which to express them." Well, I had a vehicle, but it just wasn't the one he recognized—the language of the scholarly article. It just didn't dot the i's or cross the t's or proceed logically on its way to its point. It circled and spiraled; it doubled back; it digressed and prodded; it spoke in tongues. And yet I knew I knew what I knew—knew it in ways that, if I thought to remember, sounded a bit like my father's way of knowing something that he then had to prove. But since there is no such thing as "proof" in literature, it seemed to me that all I had to do was find a way to show the direction of my thoughts. Demonstrate them. Point the reader toward my inconclusive conclusions.

That was 1962. It took more than a quarter of a century for me to discover that, yes, you could simply put your feet on the desk and think on the page. You could let your thoughts float out—in their incomplete sentences, their sinuous meanderings—and maybe, sometimes, they would find a way to coalesce and become a larger thought, a meaning. So that's what I'm doing here: thinking my way toward what I suspect a lyric essay is, or should be, can, or should do. Thinking my way into the lyric part of the definition, because the essay part is easier, more down-to-earth. Why the qualifier? Well, because there are Uncle Willies out there, waiting to pounce: *It doesn't say so, so how do you know? It doesn't flat-out say so*. No, it doesn't; however, like a poem, the lyric essay must not only mean, but be. It is a way of seeing the world. A hybrid—a cross between poetry and nonfiction— it must, as Rene Char said of the poet, "leave traces of [its] passage, not proof," letting mystery into the knowing. Or the knowing to incorporate its mystery. And part of that knowing is through sound—the whisper of soft consonants, the repetition of an elongated vowel that squeaks its way across the page, the chipping away of *k-k-k-k*, the assonance and consonance of thought attuned to language. The internal rhyme of the mind. Which is something my father would have resisted also.

How do I know that? How can I say that with such certainty? Because his method of reading was that of a scientist. There were too many books to read in one lifetime, he said, so he would wait until the critics concluded which was the best book by an author, then he'd read that book. Save himself the trouble of reading all the others.

Maybe, I thought even then, but look at what he would miss if, in reading *The Great Gatsby,* he would never see Dick and Nicole on the beach in France, would never have to watch the war itself become a character, something lit from within. If, in reading *Grapes of Wrath,* he might never see the soft underbelly of empathy for Lenny. And what of Hemingway, because at that time—as now— there was no consensus as to which was best? What, for heaven's sake, of Faulkner, whose whole county unfolded from book to book? At the time, I did not ask myself the question of poetry, but thinking about it now I wonder if reading a poet's "best" poem is any way to know the poet at all. Isn't poetry, in the end, a way of experiencing the world? Another way not of meaning, but being?

So that is what I hunger for in the lyric essay—the author's way of inhabiting his or her own mind. Of responding, in language, to my Uncle Willy. To my beloved professor. To the world at large.

This past year, I attended a reading of "lyric essays," and nothing I heard was, to my mind, lyric. My ears did not quicken. My heart did not skip. What I heard was philosophical meditation, truncated memoir, slipshod research, and just-plain-discursive opinion. A wall of words. But not a lyric essay among them. The term had been minted (brilliantly, it seems to me) by Deborah Tall, then almost immediately undermined. Not all essays are lyric. Repeat. Not all essays are lyric. Not even all short essays are lyric. Some are merely short. Or plainly truncated. Or purely meditative. Or simply speculative. Or. Or. Or. But not lyric. Because, to be lyric, there must be a lyre.

That said, I believe there must also be some allegiance to the nonfiction aspect of the essay. The run-of-the-mill, workaday nature of reality. Of fact. The job of the lyric essayist is to find the prosody of fact, finger the emotional instrument, play the intuitive and the intrinsic, but all in service to the music of the real. Even if it's an imagined actuality. The aim is to make *of*, not *up*. The lyre, not the liar.

First, let's deal with the difference between a lyrical essay and a lyric essay. Any essay may be lyrical, as long as it pays attention to the sound of its language, or the sweep of its cadences. But a lyrical essay is often using its lyrics to serve a different end. A lyric essay, however, functions as *a lyric.* Can be held in the mind—must, in fact, be held in the mind—intact. It means as an entity. It swallows you, the way a poem swallows you, until you reside inside it. Try to take it apart and you spin out of control. It is held together by the glue of absence, the mortar of melody, the threnody of unspent inspiration. Like a Latin declension: inspire, inspirit, inspiration. Inspire: breathe in, (formerly) breathe life into. Something there is that animates the lyric essay. Something that doesn't love a wall.

The music of the lyric essay?

Maybe it's a music of language: "And so I reached out and there was the great, wet fruit of his nose, the velvet bone of his enormous face"—Stephen Kuusisto, *Eavesdropping.*

Maybe it's a music of structure: "Brown made Americans mindful of tunnels inside their bodies, about which they did not speak; about their ties to nature, about which they did not speak; about their ties to one another, about which they did not speak"—Richard Rodriguez, *Brown.*

Maybe it's a music of silence, of what is not, or cannot be, said: "It can't be found outside, this green—not exactly, though it wants to be, in a way that haunts the edges of almost knowing. It is not the green of pear-tree leaves nor the green of rhododendron; not even the green-gray of certain aromatic sages that can make you weep for a smell lost from childhood; not even the triple-dark green of a trout stream under cloud cover"—Marjorie Sandor, *The Night Gardener.*

Maybe it's not melodious, but at least it knows its own temperament, its timbre: "When the kids had gone to school and her husband to work, she would sometimes sit in the living room holding tightly to the arms of the chair feeling afraid and think, Maybe it is the woodwork getting me down"—Abigail Thomas, *Safekeeping*.

Maybe it's the grace note of white space—a gap, or a suspension bridge.

Maybe it's the music of the spheres—the sense that even though we don't know everything down to the last quark, there is some scientifically magical design in the way things keep spinning and work together to make up our explosive, expanding universe. The knowledge that light from some dead star will reach our eyes sometime ten years from now. As Albert Goldbarth says, "Go know."

So, does any of this say anything about the lyric essay? Probably not, or not in any way that has a vehicle with which to say it. A rocketship. A cable car. A handcart. On the other hand, I want to read the words of those authors I've quoted. H. D. said she would like to dance with Ezra Pound just for what he might say—I'd read them not for what they might say, but for the way they would dance. The way their hand might rest confidently at my waist, and their words brush my ear, just a tickle of thought. The way they would hold me lightly and, with one sure touch, send me twirling out, then, just as lightly, draw me back in.

I'd read for that lyric moment when I could inhale their very way of occupying mindspace, for that time when, somewhere before words, science and art speak the same language and I can catch them both with their feet on the desk and the coffee offering up its distinct aroma of anticipation.

QED.

What Happened to the Personal Essay?

Phillip Lopate

The personal or familiar essay is a wonderfully tolerant form, able to accommodate rumination, memoir, anecdote, diatribe, scholarship, fantasy, and moral philosophy. It can follow a rigorously elegant design, or—held together by little more than the author's voice—assume an amoebic shapelessness. Working in it liberates a writer from the structure of the well-made, epiphanous short story and allows one to ramble in a way that more truly reflects the mind at work. At this historical moment the essayist has an added freedom: no one is looking over his or her shoulder. No one much cares. Commercially, essay volumes rank even lower than poetry.

I know; when my first essay collection, *Bachelorhood*, came out, booksellers had trouble figuring out where to stock it. Autobiography? Self-help? Short stories? I felt like saying, "Hey, this category has been around for a long time; what's the big deal?" Yet, realistically, they were right: what had once been a thriving popular tradition had ceased being so. Readers who enjoyed the book often told me so with some surprise, because they hadn't thought they would like "essays." For them, the word conjured up those dreaded weekly compositions they were forced to write on the gasoline tax or the draft.

Essays are usually taught all wrong: they are harnessed to rhetoric and composition, in a two-birds-with-one-stone approach designed to sharpen freshman students' skills at argumentation. While it is true that historically the essay is related to rhetoric, it in fact seeks to persuade more by the delights of literary style than anything else. Elizabeth Hardwick, one of our best essayists, makes this point tellingly when she says: "The mastery of expository prose, the rhythm of sentences, the pacing, the sudden flash of unexpected vocabulary, redeem polemic. . . . The essay . . . is a great meadow of style and personal manner, freed from the need for defense except that provided by an individual intelligence and sparkle. We consent to watch a mind at work, without agreement often, but only for pleasure."

Equally questionable in teaching essays is the anthology approach, which assigns an essay apiece by a dozen writers according to our latest notions of a de-mographically representative and content-relevant sampling. It would be more instructive to read six pieces each by two writers, since the essay (particularly the familiar essay) is so rich a vehicle for displaying personality in all its willfully changing aspects.

Essays go back at least to classical Greece and Rome, but it was Michel de Montaigne, generally considered the "father of the essay," who first matched the word to the form around 1580. Reading this contemporary of Shakespeare (thought to have influenced the Bard himself), we are reminded of the original, pristine meaning of the word, from the French verb *essayer*: to attempt, to try, to leap experimentally into the unknown. Montaigne understood that, in an essay, the track of a person's thoughts struggling to achieve some understanding of a problem *is* the plot. The essayist must be willing to contradict himself (for which reason an essay is not a legal brief), to digress, even to risk ending up in a terrain very different from the one he embarked on. Particularly in Montaigne's magnifi-cent late essays, free-falls that sometimes go on for a hundred pages or more, it is possible for the reader to lose all contact with the ostensible subject, bearings, top, bottom, until there is nothing to do but surrender to this companionable voice, thinking alone in the dark. Eventually, one begins to share Montaigne's confi-dence that "all subjects are linked to one another," which makes any topic, how-ever small or far from the center, equally fertile.

It was Montaigne's peculiar project, which he claimed rightly or wrongly was original, to write about the one subject he knew best: himself. As with all suc-ceeding literary self-portraits—or all succeeding stream-of-consciousness, for that matter—success depended on having an interesting consciousness, and Mon-taigne was blessed with an undulatingly supple, learned, skeptical, deep, sane, and candid one. In point of fact, he frequently strayed to worldly subjects, giving his opinion on everything from cannibals to coaches, but we do learn a large number of intimate and odd details about the man, down to his bowels and kid-ney stones. "Sometimes there comes to me a feeling that I should not betray the story of my life," he writes. On the other hand: "No pleasure has any meaning for me without communication."

A modern reader may come away thinking that the old fox still kept a good deal of himself to himself. This is partly because we have upped the ante on auto-biographical revelation, but also because Montaigne was writing essays, not con-fessional memoirs, and in an essay it is as permissible, as honest, to chase down a reflection to its source as to admit some past shame. In any case, having decided that "the most barbarous of our maladies is to despise our being," Montaigne did succeed, via the protopsychoanalytic method of the *Essais*, in making friends with his mind.

Having taken the essay form to its very limits at the outset, Montaigne's dauntingly generous example was followed by an inevitable specialization, which included the un-Montaignean split between formal and informal essays. The formal essay derived from Francis Bacon; it is said to be "dogmatic, impersonal, systematic, and expository," written in a "stately" language, while the informal essay is "personal, intimate, relaxed, conversational, and frequently humorous" (*New Columbia Encyclopedia*). Never mind that most of the great essayists were adept at both modes, including Bacon (see, for example, his wonderful "Of Friendship"); it remains a helpful distinction.

Informal, familiar essays tend to seize on the parade and minutiae of daily life: vanities, fashions, oddballs, seasonal rituals, love and disappointment, the pleasures of solitude, reading, going to plays, walking in the street. It is a very urban form, enjoying a spectacular vogue in eighteenth- and early nineteenth-century London, when it enlisted the talents of such stylists as Swift, Dr. Johnson, Addison and Steele, Charles Lamb, William Hazlitt, and a visiting American, Washington Irving. The familiar essay was given a boost by the phenomenal growth of newspapers and magazines, all of which needed smart copy (such as that found in the *Spectator*) to help instruct their largely middle-class, *parvenu* readership on the manners of the class to which it aspired.

Although most of the *feuilletonistes* of this period were cynical hacks, the journalistic situation was still fluid enough to allow original thinkers a platform. The British tolerance for eccentricity seemed to encourage commentators to develop idiosyncratic voices. No one was as cantankerously marginal in his way, or as willing to write against the grain of community feeling, as William Hazlitt. His energetic prose style registered a temperament that passionately, moodily swung between sympathy and scorn. Anyone capable of writing so bracingly frank an essay as "The Pleasures of Hating" could not—as W.C. Fields would say—be all bad. At the same time, Hazlitt's enthusiasms could transform the humblest topic, such as going on a country walk or seeing a prizefight, into a description of visionary wholeness.

What many of the best essayists have had—what Hazlitt had in abundance—was quick access to their blood reactions, so that the merest flash of a prejudice or opinion might be dragged into the open and defended. Hazlitt's readiness to entertain opinions, coupled with his openness to new impressions, made him a fine critic of painting and the theater, but in his contrariness he ended by antagonizing all of his friends, even the benign, forgiving Charles Lamb. Not that Lamb did not have *his* contrary side. He, too, was singled out for a "perverse habit of contradiction," which helped give his "Elia" essays, among the quirkiest and most charming in the English language, their peculiar bite.

How I envy readers of *London* magazine, who might have picked up an issue in 1820 and encountered a new, high-spirited essay by Hazlitt, Lamb, or both! After their deaths, the familiar essay continued to attract brilliant practitioners such as Stevenson, DeQuincey, and Emerson. But subsequently, a little of the vitality seeped out of it. "Though we are mighty fine fellows nowadays, we cannot write like Hazlitt," Stevenson confessed. And by the turn of the century, it seemed rather played out and toothless.

The modernist aesthetic was also not particularly kind to this type of writing, relegating it to a genteel, antiquated nook, *belles lettres*—a phrase increasingly spoken with a sneer, as though implying a sauce without the meat. If "meat" is taken to mean the atrocities of life, it is true that the familiar essay has something obstinately non-apocalyptic about it. The very act of composing such an essay seems to implicate the writer in humanist-individualist assumptions that have come to appear suspect under the modernist critique.

Still, it would be unfair to pin the rap on modernism, which Lord knows gets blamed for everything else. One might as well "blame" the decline of the conversational style of writing. Familiar essays were fundamentally, even self-consciously, conversational: it is no surprise that Swift wrote one of his best short pieces on "Hints Toward an Essay on Conversation"; that Montaigne tackled "Of the Art of Discussion"; that Addison and Steele extensively analyzed true and false wit; that Hazlitt titled his books *Table Talk*, *Plain Speaker*, and *The Round Table*, or that Oliver Wendell Holmes actually cast his familiar essays in the form of mealtime dialogues. Why would a book like Holmes's *The Autocrat of the Breakfast Table*, a celebration of good talk that was so popular in its time, be so unlikely today? I cannot go along with those who say "The art of conversation has died, television killed it," since conversation grows and changes as inevitably as language. No, what has departed is not conversation but conversation-flavored writing, which implies a speaking relationship between writer and reader. How many readers today would sit still for a direct address by the author? To be called "gentle reader" or "*hypocrite lecteur*," to have one's arm pinched while dozing off, to be called to attention, flattered, kidded like a real person instead of a privileged fly on the wall—wouldn't most readers today find such devices archaic, intrusive, even impudent? Oh, you wouldn't? Good, we can go back to the old style, which I much prefer.

Maybe what has collapsed is the very fiction of "the educated reader," whom the old essayists seemed to be addressing in their conversational remarks. From Montaigne onward, essayists until this century have invoked a shared literary culture: the Greek and Latin authors and the best of their national poetry. The whole modern essay tradition sprang from quotation. Montaigne's *Essais* and Burton's *Anatomy of Melancholy* were essentially outgrowths of the "commonplace book," a personal journal in which quotable passages, literary excerpts, and comments were written. Though the early essayists' habit of quotation may seem excessive to a modern taste, it was this display of learning that linked them to their educated reading public and ultimately gave them the authority to speak so personally about themselves. Such a universal literary culture no longer exists; we have only popular culture to fall back on. While it is true that the old high culture was never really "universal"—excluding as it did a good deal of humanity—it is also true that without it, personal discourse has become more hard-pressed. What many modern essayists have tried to do is to replace that shared literary culture with more and more personal experience. It is a brave effort and an intriguing supposition, this notion that individual experience alone can constitute the universal text that all may dip into with enlightenment. But there are pitfalls: on the one hand, it may lead to cannibalizing oneself and one's privacy; on the other hand, much more common (and to my mind, worse) is the assertion of an earnestly honest or "vulnerable" manner without really candid chunks of experience to back it up.

As for popular culture, the essayist's chronic invocation of its latest bandwagon fads, however satirically framed, comes off frequently as a pandering to the audience's short attention span—a kind of literary ambulance chasing. Take the "life-style" pages in today's periodicals, which carry commentaries that are a distant nephew of the familiar essay: there is something so depressing about this desperate mining of things in the air, such a fevered search for a generational *Zeitgeist*, such an unctuously smarmy tone of "we," which assumes that everyone shares the same consumerist-boutique sensibility, that one longs for a Hazlittean shadow of misanthropic mistrust to fall between reader and writer. One longs for any evidence of a distinct human voice—anything but this ubiquitous Everyman/woman pizzazzy drone, listing tips for how to get the most from your dry cleaner's, take care of your butcher block, or bounce back from an unhappy love affair.

The familiar essay has naturally suffered from its parasitic economic dependency on magazines and newspapers. The streamlined telegraphic syntax and homogenized-perky prose that contemporary periodicals have evolved make it all the more difficult for thoughtful, thorny voices to be tolerated within the house style. The average reader of periodicals becomes conditioned to digest pure information, up-to-date, with its ideological viewpoint disguised as objectivity, and is thus ill-equipped to follow the rambling, cat-and-mouse game of perverse contrariety played by the great essayists of the past.

In any event, very few American periodicals today support house essayists to the tune of letting them write regularly and at comfortable length on the topics of their choice. The nearest thing we have are talented columnists like Russell Baker, Ellen Goodman, Leon Hale, and Mike Royko, who are in a sense carrying on the Addison and Steele tradition; they are so good at their professional task of hit-and-run wisdom that I only wish they were sometimes given the space to try out their essayistic wings. The problem with the column format is that it becomes too tight and pat: one idea per piece. Fran Lebowitz, for instance, is a very clever writer, and not afraid of adopting a cranky persona; but her one-liners have a cumulative sameness of affect that inhibits a true essayistic movement. What most column writing does not seem to allow for is self-surprise, the sudden deepening or darkening of tone, so that the writer might say, with Lamb: "I do not know how, upon a subject which I began treating half-seriously, I should have fallen upon a recital so eminently painful. . . ."

From time to time I see hopeful panel discussions offered on "The Resurgence of the Essay." Yes, it would be very nice, and it may come about yet. The fact is, however, that very few American writers today are essayists primarily.

Many of the essay collections issued each year are essentially random compilations of book reviews, speeches, journalism, and prefaces by authors who have made a name for themselves in other genres. The existence of these collections attests more to the celebrated authors' desires to see all their words between hardcovers than it does to any real devotion to the essay form. A tired air of grudgingly gracious civic duty hovers over many of these performances.

One recent American writer who did devote himself passionately to the essay was E. B. White. No one has written more consistently graceful, thoughtful essays in twentieth-century American language than White; on the other hand, I can't quite forgive his sedating influence on the form. White's Yankee gentleman-farmer persona is a complex balancing act between Whitmanian democratic and patrician values, best suited for the expression of mildness and tenderness with a resolute tug of elegiac depression underneath. Perhaps this is an unfair comparison, but there is not a single E.B. White essay that compares with the gamy, pungent, dangerous Orwell of "Such, Such Were the Joys . . ." or "Shooting an Elephant." When White does speak out on major issues of the day, his man-in-the-street, folksy humility and studiously plain-Joe air ring false, at least to me. And you would never know that the cute little wife he describes listening to baseball games on the radio was the powerful *New Yorker* editor Katharine White. The suppression or muting of ego as something ungentlemanly has left its mark on *The New Yorker* since, with the result that this magazine, which rightly prides itself on its freedom to publish extended prose, has not been a particularly supportive milieu for the gravelly voice of the personal essayist. The preferred model seems to be the scrupulously fair, sporting, impersonal, fact-gathering style of a John McPhee, which reminds me of nothing so much as a colony of industrious termites capable of patiently reducing any subject matter to a sawdust of detail.

The personal, familiar essay lives on in America today in an interestingly fragmented proliferation of specialized subgenres. The form is very much with us, particularly if you count the many popular nonfiction books that are in fact nothing but groups of personal essays strung together, and whose compelling subject matter makes the reading public overlook its ordinary indifference to this type of writing. Personal essays have also appeared for years under the protective umbrella of New Journalism (Joan Didion being the most substantial and quirky practitioner to emerge from that subsidized training ground, now largely defunct); of autobiographical-political meditations (Richard Rodriguez, Adrienne Rich, Vivian Gornick, Marcelle Clements, Wilfrid Sheed, Alice Walker, Nancy Mairs, Norman Mailer); nature and ecological-regional writing (Wendell Berry, Noel Perrin, John Graves, Edward Hoagland, Gretel Ehrlich, Edward Abbey, Carol Bly, Barry Lopez, Annie Dillard); literary criticism (Susan Sontag, Elizabeth Hardwick, Seymour Krim, Cynthia Ozick, Leslie Fiedler, Joyce Carol Oates); travel writing and mores (Mary McCarthy, V. S. Naipaul, Joseph Epstein, Eleanor Clark, Paul Theroux); humorous pieces (Max Apple, Roy Blount, Jr., Calvin Trillin); food (M. F. K. Fisher). I include this random and unfairly incomplete list merely to indicate the diversity and persistence of the form in American letters today. Against all odds, it continues to attract newcomers.

In Europe, the essay stayed alive largely by taking a turn toward the speculative and philosophical, as practiced by writers like Walter Benjamin, Theodor Adorno, Simone Weil, E. M. Cioran, Albert Camus, Roland Barthes, Czeslaw Milosz, and Nicola Chiaromonte. All, in a sense, are offspring of the epigrammatic style of Nietzsche. This fragmented, aphoristic, critical type of essay-writing became used as a subversive tool of skeptical probing, a critique of ideology in a time when large, synthesizing theories and systems of philosophy are no longer trusted. Adorno saw the essay, in fact, as a valuable countermethod: "The essay does not strive for closed, deductive or inductive construction. It revolts above all against the doctrine—deeply rooted since Plato—that the changing and ephemeral is unworthy of philosophy; against that ancient injustice toward the transitory, by which it is once more anathematized, conceptually. The essay shies away from the violence of dogma. . . . The essay gently defies the ideals of [Descartes'] *clara et distincta perceptio* and of absolute certainty. . . . Discontinuity is essential to the essay . . . as characteristic of the form's groping intention. . . . The slightly yielding quality of the essayist's thought forces him to greater intensity than discursive thought can offer; for the essay, unlike discursive thought, does not proceed blindly, automatically, but at every moment it must reflect on itself. . . . Therefore the law of the innermost form of the essay is heresy. By transgressing the orthodoxy of thought, something becomes visible in the object which it is orthodoxy's secret purpose to keep invisible."

This continental tradition of the self-reflexive, aphoristically subversive essay is only now beginning to have an influence on contemporary American writers. One saw it first, curiously, cropping up in ironic experimental fiction—in Renata Adler, William Gass, Donald Barthelme, John Barth. Their fictive discourse, like Kundera's, often resembles a broken essay, a personal/philosophical essay intermixed with narrative elements. The tendency of many postmodernist storytellers to parody the pedantry of the essay voice speaks both to their intellectual reliance on it and to their uneasiness about adopting the patriarchal stance of the Knower. That difficulty with assumption of authority is one reason why the essay remains "broken" for the time being.

In a penetrating discussion of the essay form, Georg Lukács put it this way: "The essay is a judgment, but the essential, the value-determining thing about it is not the verdict (as is the case with the system), but the process of judging." Uncomfortable words for an age when "judgmental" is a pejorative term. The familiar essayists of the past may have been nonspecialists—indeed, this was part of their attraction—but they knew how to speak with a generalist's easy authority. That is precisely what contemporary essayists have a hard time doing: in our technical age we are too aware of the advantage specialists hold over us. (This may explain the current confidence the public has in the physician-scientist school of essayists like Lewis Thomas, Richard Selzer, Stephen Jay Gould, F. Gonzalez-Crussi, Oliver Sacks: their meditations are embedded in a body of technical information, so that readers are reassured they are "learning" something, not just wasting their time on *belles lettres*.) The last of the old-fashioned generalists, men of letters who seemed able to write comfortably, knowledgeably, opinionatedly on everything under the sun, were Edmund Wilson and Paul Goodman; we may not soon see their like again.

In *The Last Intellectuals*, Russell Jacoby has pointed out the reticence of writers of the so-called generation of the sixties—my generation—to play the role of the public intellectual, as did Lionel Trilling, Harold Rosenberg, C. Wright Mills, Irving Howe, Alfred Kazin, Daniel Bell, Dwight Macdonald, Lionel Abel, etc., who judged cultural and political matters for a large general readership, often diving into the melee with both arms swinging. While Jacoby blames academia for absorbing the energies of my contemporaries, and while others have cited the drying up of print outlets for formal polemical essays, my own feeling is that it is not such a terrible thing to want to be excused from the job of pontificating to the public. Ours was not so much a failure to become our elders as it was a conscious swerving to a different path. The Vietnam War, the central experience of my generation, had a great deal to do with that deflection. As a veteran of the sixties, fooled many times about world politics because I had no firsthand knowledge of circumstances thousands of miles away (the most shameful example that comes to mind was defending, at first, the Khmer Rouge regime in Cambodia), I have grown skeptical of taking righteous public positions based on nothing but simpatico media reports and party feeling. As for matters that I've definitely made up my mind about, it would embarrass me, frankly, to pen an opinion piece deploring the clearly deplorable, like apartheid or invading Central America, without being able to add any new insights to the discussion. One does not want to be reduced to scolding, or to abstract progressive platitudes, well founded as these may be. It isn't that my generation doesn't think politics are important, but our earlier experiences in that storm may have made us a little hesitant about mouthing off in print. We—or I should say I—have not yet been able to develop the proper voice to deal with these large social and political issues, which will at the same time remain true to personal experience and hard-earned doubt.

All this is a way of saying that the present moment offers a remarkable opportunity for emerging essayists who can somehow locate the moral authority, within or outside themselves, to speak to these issues in the grand manner. But there is also room, as ever, for the informal essayist to wrestle with intellectual confusion, to offer feelings, to set down ideas in a particularly direct and exposed format—more so than in fiction, say, where the author's opinions can always be disguised as belonging to characters. The increasing willingness of contemporary writers to try the form, if not necessarily commit themselves to it, augurs well for the survival of the personal essay. And if we do offend, we can always fall back on Papa Montaigne's *"Que sçay-je?"*: What do I know?

Advice to My Friend Beth's Undergraduate Creative Nonfiction Students

Dustin Michael

One thing I like about creative nonfiction is that it allows us to tell our weird, jacked-up stories without having to change little details and try to pass them off as made-up. After all, we've probably each read our peers' work in some English class during the short story unit and thought, *Wait a minute . . . this Tracy-with-a-conspicuous-rash character is actually Stacy from home room! Oh snap!*

In creative nonfiction, Stacy can play herself.

But aside from the fun that comes from committing shameless acts of libel against your family and acquaintances, creative nonfiction is great because it lets you tell your own stories, and through that, lets your reader get to know you—the whole you, from silly to serious. I think it's just about the best way of letting others know who you are, and one of the most lasting.

I also like that there's really nothing you can't talk about. Maybe there are things you shouldn't talk about; I don't know. In the essay that got me started doing creative nonfiction, I told the story about how I learned, at age 17, that girls' breasts don't always have milk in them. Most of my essays are kind of like that, leaning heavily on bodily misunderstandings and malfunctions, that is, which worried me, until I read one written centuries ago by the founder of the modern personal essay, Michel de Montaigne, which talked at length about erections and farts. After that, I was pretty much like, "game on."

To go back to that point about creative nonfiction serving as a way to document yourself for other people, I think you're going to discover that it's as much about what you don't say as it is about what you do. If you're a visual artist, think of chiaroscuro. If you're a musician, think of silence and rest. Case in point: If I write about how I tried—unsuccessfully—to playoff a momentary loss of bowel control during a conference I foolishly held with a student when I had the flu, what I'm hoping my reader gets is that those conferences can sometimes be horrible for everybody involved, instructors, too. If I write all kinds of dumb little details about the crummy office I shared with a friend who died, what I want my reader to get is that I ache—*ache*—because that's all of the world I'll get to share with her. In each essay, I want the reader to know that I'm a real person, that there are both things I can't get past and things I can't get over. I think you'll find that the trick is in the balance of what's said and what's not, which touches on something similar. What the reader sees on the page is you trying to make yourself understood, but what you hope the reader gets is that you're really trying to understand yourself. The point is, you write, then you look back at what stands out in relief, in the silence of what you didn't say, and that's usually where you find your insight, and, with luck, where your reader finds you.

"Brenda Miller Has a Cold," or: How the Lyric Essay Happens

Brenda Miller

It happens like this:

I have a cold. It's what might be termed "a perfect cold," for while my head is stuffed up and my throat tickles (making me cough exactly every six minutes), I'm actually in good spirits, the cotton batting in my head a fine insulation between me and those pesky thoughts that normally bat about in my brain. I can't walk for long without losing my breath, and my muscles ache just enough to make me gravitate toward whatever couch or chair or bed is handy. I can't think very clearly, and when I speak my words come out in a voice hoarse and disguised, echoing in my plugged ears. I may be speaking too loudly or too softly— I can't really know, and this person who speaks seems a separate self, one who is a simpleton, focused only on what is right in front of her: the cup of tea, the box of tissues, a blanket wrapped around her feet. She can see only what happens to flit across her mucoused line of vision.

It's a perfect cold, because it just so happens that for this particular week I don't have to do anything but watch the ailment make its way through my body, stopping to gather a bit of snot here, to drain a bit there. I'm on an island, and I'm with a friend who ferociously writes poetry for ten hours at a time in a room near the water. I can't do much else but sit with a cup of tea in hand, staring at the fake fire or out the window, where I see a mess of deer fence caging saplings already so nibbled by said deer it's difficult to tell what they're trying to become.

I have a cold, and this means I wake up at odd hours, the night wholly black, and snatches of language float through my brain and stick there, fluttering like any caught prey. In my ordinary body—my clear, un-mucoused, narrative life—such fragments glide through continually, but rarely do they sit down and stay, even for a few moments, and lately I bustle right past them even if they do.

378

Instead, my omnipresent, stalwart "to-do" list pulses like one of those massive black magnets you'd see in a sci-fi flick, bent on destroying the world.

What I'm trying to say is: *The lyric essay happens when I'm sticky.*

Or it happens like this:

My friend wakes a few minutes after I do, and we say few words to one another, as the day is still dark, and there's coffee to be drunk, and porridge to be shuttled into the mouth, and we're barely aware of one another until I hear her in the shower, and she emerges, fresh and clean and smelling of roses, her briefcase packed, and she wishes me *adieu* as she swings down the path to her studio. Me— I've barely moved from the couch, into which I keep sinking deeper and deeper, my pajamas warm like a second skin, my eyelids ratcheting back down by increments to the sleep position.

But all this time, the pen stays in my hand, the notebook on my knee, and something is happening; words I can't explain—can't direct, not yet—dump onto the page. I write something like: ". . . saplings already so nibbled by said deer it's difficult to tell what they're trying to become . . ."

What I'm trying to say is: *The lyric essay happens when I've forgotten to get dressed. When I'm disheveled. When I'm not wearing any shoes.*

Or maybe it happens like this:

I've just returned from Michigan, where I probably caught this cold from shaking so many hands in friendly and earnest greeting. And there, the women's NCAA basketball tournament was underway; many, *many* tall young women wandered the hallways of my hotel, crowding the elevators—stunning in their gray T-shirts and shorts, everything about them declaring *athlete:* their radiant good health, the muscles sleek and toned with practice. They seemed eerily calm in the face of the competition ahead, but then I had no idea who these teams were, or what place they held, or how confident they deserved to be. I couldn't ask, because their beauty made me mute. I pushed the elevator button and nodded at them, got off at my floor without a word.

And what skids through my brain at the sight of these beautiful women is the way I've always loved basketball—to watch it, mind you, not to play—ever since I was a kid and my brothers played on the backyard court. I love the way action—beautiful, controlled—darts out of what appears to be a chaos of frenzied motion on the court. Bodies seem to sprout limbs more muscled, more gleaming, just all around more flesh, and then from the morass comes the arc of a steady three-point shot (the shooter can feel it in his hands when he knows it's clean, he turns and trots nonchalantly back to the other side of the court, arms spread wide, palms up, shoulders raised in the barest shrug, as if to say: what else did you expect?) . . .

. . . Or the inside layup—the point guard ferreting out traces of a path through all those bodies that jostle for position under the net, slinking through for the soundless score.

. . . Or the clean block, all ball, the hand arriving in position at exactly the right moment, the force of it, the surprise . . .

I knew even then—as a little girl in the LA Forum, or shyly watching my brothers from the sidelines in our own backyard—I knew even before I knew the words I'm going to use now: the aesthetic power of instinct coupled with improvisation, of training hitched to transience, the clarity of a plan of action amid a sea of flesh doing its darnedest to make you fail. Of course, I know now that teams have carefully choreographed plays; they know the strengths and weaknesses of every player on the court. That point guard who just made the impossible layup? She knows the exact moves to make, the quick head-fake, the dribble between the legs, the two-and-one-half steps it would take to lay it up and in. The fall-away reverse jump shot? Practiced dozens of times. Piece of cake.

But even so: you never know. If all we saw were the practiced drills, the results completely predictable every time—the crowds gathered in the bleachers with their giant "We're Number One" foam fingers and huge plastic tumblers filled with beer—we'd soon grow restless, long before the beer became warm, unappetizing dreg at the bottom of the cup. For much as we love to watch the athletes perform, we don't really want the practiced drill with the predictable outcome. We want the thrill of the unknown, the possibility of utter failure, the exultation of the barest victory, the high-fives in the stands . . . the sense that the crowd (the ones who watch) are a part of it all, making it happen with their steadfast attention.

So. Look there, down below, illuminated: The court is a given. The ball, a given. The referees with their shrill whistles, their heavy-footed lumber from one end of the court to another to make sure there is *some* comportment after all—they, too, are a given, and we hardly note their presence as we shuffle in sideways to our seats. But when those athletes trot onto the floor, that's when it all begins. Expectations rise (literally lift us out of our seats, cheering) and the game begins. From the initial tip of the ball, that first whistle—who knows what will happen next?

What I'm trying to say? *The lyric essay is a three-point shot. It's a desperation thirty footer. It's a technical foul in the last two seconds of the game.*

*

I have a cold, which means that at first I get up frequently to fetch the things that surround me—the box of tissues ("specially soft," according to the soothing voice on the box, "made in a special way with soft fibers on the outside and strong fibers on the inside. This gives you the softness you want and the strength you need.") A cup of Breathe Easy tea. A glass of grape juice. A few Advil to stave off the sinus headache lurking in the wings. But in all these forays off the couch, I've never, not even once, looked at myself in the mirror. For someone who usually checks her reflection at any opportunity, this avoidance of my reflection seems peculiar, an aberration. It feels as though—because I have a cold, and because I'm writing so hard, with all I've got—I've become diaphanous. Transparent. There's nothing really left of me to see.

What this essay is trying to say (ignore for a moment, its author, sitting on the couch, blowing her nose—pay no attention to her, she's getting a little carried away): The lyric essay doesn't look too long at itself in the mirror. It is not "self-reflective," in that it does not really reflect the self who scribbles it down. Rather, it is the mirror, the silver film reflecting whatever passes its way. Brenda does not think to look at herself this morning—this morning of the perfect cold—not because she'd rather spare herself the sight of her ugly mug, but because for these few hours she really has no self to speak of. That self—it's battened away for the moment, put away for safekeeping. And that's how the lyric essay happens: When there's no bothersome self to get in the way. When the writing finds its own core. When it finds the language it needs on its own. The lyric essay is *made in a special way with soft fibers on the outside and strong fibers on the inside. This gives you the softness you want and the strength you need.*

*

So I tell my friend Lee (and I'm lying to her, I'm making it up as I go along): "It's kind of an homage to Gay Talese. To that essay 'Frank Sinatra Has a Cold.'" And she glances at me with that startled, wide-eyed look she gets when she's delighted. I know that "Frank Sinatra Has a Cold" is one of her favorite essays of all time, and that's another reason I've made up this half-truth, to give some pleasure, to have this fleeting connection.

"Really?" she says. "Do *you* at least show up?"

In the Gay Talese profile, made famous on its publication in *Esquire* in 1966, Frank Sinatra has a cold. Which changes everything. The narrative shifts. Expectations shuffle and scuttle and get out of the way. The interview Talese was after? Gone. Sinatra never even looks at him. Sinatra's in a bad mood. The songs now will be difficult to sing. Not as polished. Not as rehearsed. Sinatra can't stand it. It feels as though the cold will last forever, that his voice will never be the same.

Talese hangs around anyway. Takes notes on all the things surrounding Sinatra, his ostensible subject. The notebook from his research is a thing of beauty itself, a piece of art, with doodles and arrows and words spilling across the margins. Nothing stays in place, but even through the scribble we see a structure emerge, a sense of direction: SCENE TWO, he writes in big block letters, surrounded by asterisks. ACT ONE. He watches Sinatra's character emerge, gain complexity, through his interactions with others. Sees him blow up over a pair of boots that Harlan Ellison wears at a club. Sees him smile at a woman in the crosswalk, disarming her completely, and then disappear. Sinatra's at the center, but we can't access him directly. He shows up, but only in flashes, only in transit. We have to sit on a bar stool a few feet away, just watching to see what might be revealed.

Do I show up? Sometimes I do, and sometimes I don't.

You try to tell a simple story, walk a simple path. But you keep losing sight of your destination. The destination is no longer as interesting as the diversions. You hear a wren sing so loudly inside the deer fence, and she startles you, and then you see her, how easily she slips through that cage around *saplings so nibbled by said deer, you can't tell what they're trying to become*. You are just trying to become. No, not trying. Trying is too trying. You're just becoming.

Anyway, you have a cold, so you're not going to walk too far. You'll sit down for frequent rest stops, just to catch your breath. Your breath will fascinate you, become something you can no longer take for granted, the rhythm of it: in . . . pause . . . out, and then, without even trying, the body's insistence on keeping you alive.

What I'm trying to say is: *The lyric essay happens in the gaps. In the pause before the next breath demands to be taken.*

So here's the deal:

You have a cold, and then you don't. Gradually you get better. Or you get worse, and then you get better. Rarely does anyone die of a head cold.

Sometimes you notice you're getting better, and sometimes you don't. Sometimes you just wake up one day and realize you didn't cough all night, that you have not one crumpled, sticky tissue lying next to your bed. Your body has been returned, intact and clear.

And your self? You can, if you so desire, now go to Point B from Point A with a brisk, direct stride, hardly pausing, undistracted by the scenery. You can go to work, and be your workaday self; you can be productive as all get-out. When people ask how you are, you can say "I'm fine" without lying. You can tell the truth, the unvarnished truth, no half-truths, no need to make anything up just for the heck of it. Well, that's *good*, people will say, I'm glad you're feeling *better*, and you'll nod in agreement, but some part of you, some part that's not fit for civilized company, wonders if this self—this clear, narrative, undeterred self—really is *good*, really is *better*. Some part of you longs to be sick again—not *sick* sick, just enough so that you can be buffered a little while longer, not quite so direct and so clear.

The poet, Mark Doty, says it happens like this: "Grace might descend in its odd, circuitous routes. We are visited by joy, seem to be given a poem or a song, something we encounter fills us to the rim of the self. Those things point the way, but who lives in that heightened state of awareness?"

In Michigan—amid the basketball players and the spring rains—protestors clog the streets with signs, commemorating the fourth anniversary of the Iraq war. They only want us to notice. Just notice. And to remember, even before that, the bombing of Afghanistan.

So I oblige. I'm an obliging person. I remember a large hall, with red-planked floors. Candlelight. A scattering of people sitting on *zafus* and *zabutons*, waiting for a bell, a bell that sits in front of me, waiting to be struck. Then someone hands me a slip of paper, and I nod, like a judge when she's just been apprised of the verdict. I deliberately set the piece of paper aside on my cushion, all eyes now on me, expectant, and I know, fleetingly, what it means to age: to have a snippet of knowledge a split second before someone else, to have the power to impart this knowledge or not, and the passing of this knowledge through you, leaving its trace.

I don't know what voice to use, how to convey the information that the world we live in—this noisy, familiar, workaday world—has now changed. That piece of paper changes everything.

I nod and set the paper aside. In a low voice, neutral, I whisper this bit of information to the people gathered here in a circle, these people who had come to the hall on a Wednesday evening with no particular agenda in mind but to practice breathing in and breathing out, to observe how predictably the mind will wander from that simple task to more complicated things. "They have started dropping bombs in Afghanistan," I say, and a dozen heads nod, as if we know what is meant by *they*, as if we know what is meant by *bombs*, as if we know *Afghanistan*. As if we know what to do with such knowledge now that it has become ours.

But they are only words on a piece of paper. I set it aside. I ring a little bell. We sit and breathe in and out—some of us, I'm sure, thinking (trying not to think) of children, of what happens to a body when it's dismembered. We know something has happened. But we don't really know. All we can do is imagine. All we can do is try to put the pieces together again.

What I'm trying to say is: In the lyric essay, it all shows up. The good and the bad—they jostle one another, rub shoulders, emit sparks. The stuff we try to re-member, and the stuff that remembers itself.

The lyric essay . . . *it's happening.*

That's all I'm trying to say. It's *a* happening, like those hippie gatherings I dreamt of as a teenager, as I walked to Patrick Henry Junior High, the suburban streets so calm, so predictable. Somewhere to the north of us, students burned the star-spangled banner, singing anthems that bore no resemblance to the patriotic hymn we belted out on the playground. In the streets of San Francisco, young men and women danced in circles, smiling at one another, *loving the one you're with.* They dropped acid and smoked pot and heard the *doors of perception* clatter open in their brains.

But we—my classmates and I—we lived in the suburbs of Los Angeles where life proceeded in routines so smooth we barely noticed them. Our parents did not get divorced, our houses did not fall apart, even in the occasional earthquake that rocked the town.

And then I read *The Electric Kool-Aid Acid Test* three times in a row, and I wanted nothing more than to attend a *happening.* A *happening* would change me forever. I imagined a large warehouse filled with beautiful people dancing their hearts out, breathing hard, doing strange and wondrous things to one another. The great thing about *happenings* was the way they just happened. No one planned them. No one knew what to expect.

You bring together a few elements as givens: A big empty space, some musicians prone to improvisation, a few substances geared to short-circuit one's capacity to make logical, streamlined narratives. But that's it. The rest is up to you. Well, not *you*, exactly, because there is no longer a solid concept of you, a you that has any true agency or control.

And who knows what might be alchemized in this mix? Maybe someone will make balloon animals, his breath huffing to bring them to life, squeaking them into the shapes of deer and foxes and wrens that really take flight. Maybe two someones will make love in the dark; one of them might have a cold, and the kisses will make her wheeze, but this will not diminish the force of her desire. A basketball game might erupt on the floor, or a hula hoop contest, or Frisbees might float weightless, suspended in the air. Maybe Sinatra will show up, crooning love songs, beaming his bright blue eyes to make us swoon. Maybe two giant puppets will lurch toward the stage, cradling the war dead in their arms.

The poet Paisley Rekdal says: *I suppose it is an accident anything is beautiful.*

But whatever happens, certainly we'll dance. Heads bopping, arms swinging, sweat glazing our backs. A feral, impulsive dance—one that makes itself up as it goes along. That's the only thing we can know for sure.

The Other Creative Writing

Michael Pearson

Creative writing is the art of storytelling, an art as elemental as fire and the circle of civilization. Poetry goes back to our farthest dreams of the past, joining language to our very heartbeat. Writing fiction, or telling lies to find the truth, is as old as Scheherazade and Odysseus, and playwriting is an ancient and respected activity. Our most sacrosanct anthologies include poetry, fiction, and drama, but rarely, and only very recently, do any include nonfiction as literature. If we see a mention of Edward Gibbon or James Boswell, it is most often as historian and biographer, not as literary artists. The Norton anthologies appropriately include modern fiction writers like John Cheever, Joyce Carol Oates, and Ralph Ellison, but where are E. B. White, John Hersey, or Joseph Mitchell? Where are we to place Joseph Mitchell's *The Bottom of the Harbor*, Truman Capote's *In Cold Blood*, Tom Wolfe's *The Electric Kool-Aid Acid Test*, John McPhee's *Coming into the Country*, Joan Didion's *Slouching Toward Bethlehem*, Edward Abbey's *Desert Solitaire*, or Frank McCourt's recent bestseller *Angela's Ashes*? Where do we include *this* literature made not of imagined reality but of verifiable fact, this literature that holds fast to historical truth even as it pursues a truth beyond the facts. Where do we place this "other" creative writing?

The first question to ask might be: does it make a difference if we make our stories out of facts or fictions any more than it matters if a sculptor makes a statue out of marble or clay? One material is more malleable than the other, but either can be used to create a work of art. In the end, everyone who aspires to be a writer makes stories out of the same source—words, the best ones in the best possible order. The essence of language is metaphor, and all metaphor—as Walker Percy said—is a wonderful, illuminating mistake. It's the sort of mistake that lifts the curtain of cliché and dull habit that blinds us, and it permits us to see, to really see ourselves and the world for a moment. That's where language and stories lead us—fiction and nonfiction writers and readers—toward some re-creation of experience, actual or imagined, toward some making of art out of marble or clay. All creative writers work with language, with metaphor, crafting dialogue and description, building character and symbol, using narration and drama. Usually, the progress is crab-like, the writer slowly suggesting, allowing one thing to lead to another, word shaping word until a new world is created. In this respect, all writers—poets, novelists, and nonfiction artists—face the same challenge: how to build something memorable out of something as insubstantial and strangely enduring as language. Nonfiction writers engage in the same activity that all writers are engaged in, attempting to conjure images for the purblind wayfarer, to make stories that by their very nature are ethereal and fundamental, there and not there at the same time.

The best nonfiction bestows a range of pleasures: it offers both information and stories, the specific site and shape of experience and a glimpse of its mysterious soul. In certain circles, actual pleasure in reading is tantamount to an intellectual sin. As David Denby recently wrote, "In some quarters, pleasure in reading has itself become a political error, rather like sex in Orwell's *1984*." Over 30 years ago, Barbara Tuchman objected to the narrowing of the word literature, saying, "I see no reason why the word should always be confined to writers of fiction and poetry while the rest of us are lumped together under the despicable term 'Nonfiction'—as if we were some sort of remainder."

Literature, and that means fiction or nonfiction, is a dreamworld, containing, as Northrop Frye says, both the nightmare and the wish-fulfillment. Similar to dreams, literature has an hallucinatory vividness, a reality that is somehow unreal, what Frye calls a vertical perspective that puts us, alternately, into the darkness and the light. The uniqueness of nonfiction literature is that it also affords a horizontal perspective. It compels our attention outward, toward the Life that it swears to represent accurately. Of course, the obligation to adhere to the known, the reported, the verifiable fact, often limits the depths a piece of nonfiction can discover or the heights it can reach. But, despite the limitations of the form, nonfiction must honor the facts and attempt to get beyond them. Nonfiction writers can use words with the force of poets, they can shape characters syllable by syllable until we feel that we know them better than we know ourselves, they can carve landscapes out of blank space: artistic nonfiction can reach into us as deeply as any literature. And it has the added power of being about actual people and real events.

Literary nonfiction carries a genuine obligation to factual truths. It is a form that has one sacred principle: you can't make it up. Imaginative speculation, based upon the gathered information, is fine as long as the writer tells the reader what he is doing and why. Richard Preston, *The New Yorker* writer, did it fairly and to good effect in *The Hot Zone*; John Demos, the historian, did it in his narrative of early American life *The Unredeemed Captive*. But the nonfiction writer can't just imagine the color of a character's eyes or change the street names to suit the music of the sentence. The dialogue must be accurate, the dates exact, the events real. During the past few years some scholars and writers have put their minds to the task of defining this genre, although there is not yet even consensus on what to call it (creative nonfiction, literary nonfiction, new journalism, personal journalism . . .), and these critics and artists have described many of the characteristics of the form.

Tom Wolfe called it the "new journalism" and with his typical magnification said that it would oust the novel from importance. He felt that it was possible "to write journalism that would . . . read like a novel." It would require, he said, scenic telling, full dialogue, the use of symbolic details, and a point of view that allowed the reader inside characters' minds. Gay Talese talked about the necessity of immersion reporting, of going so deep into the observation of people and scene that the writer attained a semblance of omniscience. The scholar Norman Sims extended the ideas about immersion and accuracy and added to the discussion about the necessary complexity and contradiction that readers should find in such nonfiction narratives. He also focused on the unique voice and the double responsibility of the writer to subject and to truth. Susan Orlean referred to what she called the heart of this kind of nonfiction: a type of writing that chronicles "the dignity of ordinariness," a phrase that reminds me of James Joyce's definition of *epiphany*, "the moment in which the soul of the commonest object . . . seems to us radiant." Although most readers might not see a clear kinship between Joyce and modern writers of nonfiction literature, the relationship exists. Joyce's belief that the artist is charged to find epiphanal moments not among the gods but in the lives of men and women in ordinary, even unpleasant, circumstances could as well be a description of Joseph Mitchell's philosophy in his nonfiction stories about New York.

Classics in the genre like James Agee's *Let Us Now Praise Famous Men* or John Hersey's *Hiroshima* depict the experiences and emotions of common people, not movie stars or politicians or generals. In this respect, as Mark Kramer said, there is something inherently democratic about literary nonfiction. It is "pluralistic, pro-individual, anti-cant, and anti-elite." Such nonfiction achieves creativity not by imagining people or events but by discovering a vision of character or situation, by finding a structure in the facts that will permit the writer to find "truth in the details of real lives." Ultimately, writers of literary nonfiction look to create a story that will endure. "The point," Tracy Kidder once said, "is to write as well as George Eliot in *Middlemarch* and to find a way to do that in nonfiction." The nonfiction writer might be wise to remember Flannery O'Connor's admonition—"to be humble in the face of what-is." Writers, as she suggested, transcend their limitations by staying within them. And probably the surest path to "perdition and melancholy," as Walker Percy reminded us, is to go after the BIG TRUTH. It's always smarter to get all the small details right, and the larger ones will take care of themselves.

Writers of literary nonfiction have been tending to the details for a number of years now. Although many people believe that the genre sprang full grown onto the scene in 1965 with Capote's *In Cold Blood*, the roots of nonfiction literature reach far deeper and were entangled with fiction from the very beginning. Aphra Behn's 17th-century novella *Oronooko* might be considered a highly stylized work of nonfiction, a work of observation and research. Daniel Defoe's *A Journal of a Plague Year*, which appeared in 1722, is a precise description of the

Black Plague from the point of view of a person who experienced it. But the relationship between what is imagined and what is observed or reported is not always clear in either of these books. In 19th-century works by Melville or Twain such as *Typee* or *Roughing It*, the reader is left with the same questions about what is made up and what is verifiably accurate. Writers like Stephen Crane and Ernest Hemingway played with the possibilities of literary nonfiction, but it wasn't until the 1930s that Joseph Mitchell began to write a nonfiction that had the echoes and resonances of literature while at the same time demanding an adherence to the verifiable or observed fact. Mitchell wrote a brand of nonfiction that seemed vital and new. He wrote about the denizens of the Bowery, those who gathered in McSorley's Saloon, the people who spent their days along the wharves and in the fish markets of lower Manhattan. He wrote with great care and patience, a symbolist who looked more to James Joyce than to his fellow journalists for ways to develop his characters and themes. When Mitchell writes about the rats in New York City, their claws rasping on the sidewalks, he is Kafka in nonfiction, and as readers we are haunted by the story, an eerie vision of the facts. There were other writers during the 1930s and '40s who demonstrated the elasticity and power of nonfiction—George Orwell, A. J. Liebling, E.B. White, John Hersey, Lillian Ross— and they opened the doors to the explosion of nonfiction writers in the last 30 years—from Capote's poetic vision of horror to Annie Dillard's clear-eyed view of Tinker Creek. Writers like Bruce Chatwin, Ian Frazier, and William Least Heat-Moon followed paths marked for them by diarists and travel writers in the 16th- and 17th-centuries. Gay Talese and Tracy Kidder must have learned something about immersion reporting from James Boswell's 18th-century account of Samuel Johnson's life. John McPhee could be kin to both Henry David Thoreau and Joseph Mitchell, both artist and reporter.

Most of these writers find a way of making memorable, in stories, the ordinary lives that they encounter. McPhee's description of the inhabitants of New Jersey's Pine Barrens or Didion's depiction of the suburban malaise in the land of golden dreams lingers in our imaginations as all true literature does. Nonfiction literature can appear in many forms: a "comic strip" about the Holocaust by Art Spiegelman or a piece of surrealistic reporting about the Vietnam War by Michael Herr. It can be a memoir by Tobias Wolff or Mary Karr or a satire by Hunter S. Thompson or Terry Southern. It can be seen in the courtroom play and human drama of Jonathan Harr's *A Civil Action*. It can stay with us in the alliterative imagery of Truman Capote's last sentence in *In Cold Blood*: "Then, starting home, he walked toward the trees, and under them, leaving behind him the big sky, the whisper of wind voices in the wind-bent wheat." Or it can reverberate with the power of Joan Didion's opening line to "Slouching Towards Bethlehem"— "The center was not holding"—and her unforgettable chronicling of the drug scene in Haight-Ashbury during the late '60s.

This brings me back to my original question: where do we place this "other" creative writing? For me, the answer is in the work itself: we enjoy it as literature, we place it alongside any other literature, any writing that has found what George Orwell described as a language charged with meaning to the utmost possible degree, whether it is poetry or nonfiction or drama. In his monumental non-fiction narrative about the Civil War, Shelby Foote said that before he began writing about any campaign he had to learn everything he could from all the available sources and then digest it until it was clear in his own mind. Once he had done that he had to try to reproduce it with even more sharpness and clarity than he had seen it before. He described the finished product as "a great wide sea of words with a redoubled necessity for precision." Finally, this may be the best definition of literary nonfiction that we have, a form of writing that Mark Twain might have said sounds like poetry even though it's the petrified truth.

Collage, Montage, Mosaic, Vignette, Episode, Segment

Robert L. Root, Jr.

It's a common problem among student writers, starting too far back in the narrative or trying to encompass too much time or too much activity in a single chronology. A paper about high school begins at the moment the writer entered the building for the first time in ninth grade and moves inexorably toward the moment of graduation, growing more perfunctory year by year; a paper about making the team or the cheerleading squad presents a minute by minute account of decision, preparation, and competition that loses more and more energy the longer it goes on.

But it isn't just a novice writer's problem alone. Any writer runs up against the insidious demands of linear presentation of material whenever he or she selects chronology—from the beginning to the end, from the first step through each individual step to the final step, from the inception through the planning and execution to the result—as the organizing principle of an essay or article. Linear schemes of organization come easily to us. We all tell stories and chronology is the simplest system of organization ("We began by . . ., then we . . ., and finally . . ."); process is the most accessible scheme of exposition ("First you . . ., next you . . ., and you conclude by . . ."); linear movement structures description the most directly ("Her hair was the color . . . her feet spilling out of tattered sandals"; "On the east side of the building . . . in the middle was . . . on the west side we saw"). But linear schemes don't automatically help with issues of compression and focus, particularly in an age of increasingly shorter attention spans and little patience for leisurely development of plot and character and theme.

The more complex the story is, the more interwoven with other subjects, ideas, incidents, experiences, the harder it is to make it all connect in a linear way that doesn't extend the narrative or the development beyond the patience of writer and reader alike. Moreover, the connections and associations that come so readily in the memory and in the imagination often defy simple linearity, easy transition from one subtopic to the next, when the writer has to force them into words on a page.

Mike, now past fifty, has been cleaning his mental attic for the past several years, rummaging through his souvenirs and writing essays about a lifetime playing sports—the high school pitching, the conflicts with coaches, the visits to historic ballparks. Now he begins an essay about how he came to give up his annual summer stint as manager and player for a fastpitch softball team.

He starts an early draft with a brief scene set in the present which serves as the trigger for a flashback that gives him the opportunity to review his long career with the team. "It's a lazy summer evening and I'm driving home from campus," he begins, and then tells how his weariness momentarily vanishes when he notices a game in progress at the ball park where he used to play: "for a moment I want to jump out of the car, climb into my softball uniform, and trot out to my old position in left field." He describes gazing at the field and continuing home. After these two brief paragraphs of introduction, he introduces the past in the third paragraph: "That night while reading my mind wanders, and for a suspended moment it is 1969 again. That summer, I was . . ." From here he relies on the act of composing itself to help him rediscover the subject matter. Chronology decides the order. He traces the arc of his involvement from the moment he decided to join the team, and one memory provokes another until he reaches his last game and the end of the draft.

By then he has covered a lot of ground. His draft surfaces deep-seated feelings about playing ball, about giving it up, about the satisfactions of moving on to new places in his life and expending his energies elsewhere. But it takes a long time to get to the place where these important and powerful feelings get voiced, because so much detail has emerged in his review of the chronology—early days on the team, the change from player to manager, road trips, destinations, the interaction with players, the near-misses for spots in regional and state tournaments, the interests that distracted him from the game, the aging processes that slowed him down. In the associative links of memory every detail makes sense, makes connections, but on the page the slow linear march of the chronology dissipates all the emphatic force of the narrative—there's a reason no one is proposing to cash in on the natural disaster film genre ("Twister," "Volcano") with a movie called "Glacier!" These narrative elements establish not only theme but also tone and voice, and many of them need to stay in the next draft, but he knows that he needs to lift scenes out of this linear history and highlight them as well as give more emphasis to the final summer.

His revision starts almost at the end of the previous draft, placing him on the road to the final tournament. "It's three A.M. Friday Labor Day weekend 1985. I left Sutton's Bay at ten P.M. headed for Houghton, which is about as far as driving to Nashville. I'm wearing my softball uniform and my wife Carole is asleep in the back seat, cotton balls stuffed in each ear while the tape deck blasts out a medley of Beach Boys and Beatles tunes—my favorite road music." But the present-tense narrative of that summer experience has barely begun before Mike inserts a paragraph break, white space on the page signaling a shift of scene or time, and in the past tense recounts his initial involvement with the softball team years before. A page later he inserts another break and shifts back to the present tense and the immediate circumstance to establish that he and his wife have plane tickets for Paris that conflict with the tournament dates (a point of information barely mentioned in the earlier draft's conclusion) and that they have put off foreign travel in the past to be available for championships that never materialized. The dramatic tension in this conflict makes the reader wonder from the beginning which option they will take in the end. Telling this part of the essay in present tense heightens that tension and establishes a sense of immediacy about the experience, as if the outcome had not been decided long ago.

Throughout the remainder of the essay past tense vignettes of a softball life alternate with present tense scenes from the decisive summer. Paragraph breaks allow Mike to crosscut between the past and the present and to ignore connections and transitions in either chronology. When he has finished his revisions, he has avoided the linear chronology that bogged down his earlier draft and achieved a tight, dense essay with more dramatic and pointed individual segments. The overall effect of the essay is the same he had hoped to achieve in the earlier draft, but it is more focused and consequently more powerful.

The white spaces on the page—the page breaks or paragraph breaks—are part of the composition. They serve as fade outs/fade ins do in films, as visual cues that we have ended one sequence and gone on to another. Often, somewhere in the early part of each segment, a word or phrase serves as a marker indicating the change of time or place, very much as a superimposed title on a movie scene might inform the viewer: "Twelve years later. Northern Michigan," to suggest that a lot has happened since the screen went dark and a new image began to emerge.

In almost any contemporary collection of creative nonfiction, many selections are segmented, sectioned off by white spaces or rows of asterisks or subheadings in italics or boldface. A thematic issue of the travel narrative journal *Grand Tour* has no unsegmented essays. In a recent essay issue of *Ploughshares*, fourteen of the twenty-three essays are segmented by paragraph breaks or, occasionally, some more pronounced method of subdividing. In a similar issue of *American Literary Review*, fifteen out of nineteen essays are segmented, their segments separated by rows of diamonds or white spaces, divided by subheadings, or numbered; only four essays are completely unsegmented.

In some of the *ALR* essays the segmenting in the fifteen is barely noticeable, almost a printer's convention rather than an actual break in the flow of thought or language; in most, however, the segmenting is emphatic, crucial. William Holtz numbers his thirteen segments in "Brother's Keeper: An Elegy" and begins eleven of them with the same sentence, "My brother now is dead," usually as the main clause in sentences with varying subordinate or coordinate elements. The repetitions give the segments the power of incantation or prayer. Lynne Sharon Schwartz, writing about translating the book *Smoke Over Birkenau*, begins her essay with a series of English words she listed in an Italian edition of the book—the opening line reads: "Strenuous. Grim. Resolute. Blithe. Alluring. Cringe. Recoil. Admonish." Occasional excerpts from the list interrupt the essay from time to time in place of asterisks or numbers or subheadings between segments ("Haggard. Cantankerous. Imploring. Dreary. Plucky. Banter. Superb. Vivacious. Snarling. Prattled.") Frederick Smock's "Anonymous: A Brief Memoir" opens with a section of Gwendolyn Brooks's poem, "Jane Addams," and is divided into segments subtitled by locations in his anonymous subject's home: "The Great-Room," "The Landing," "The Dining Room," "The Grotto," and so on. Paul Gruchow's "Eight Variations on the Idea of Failure" has eight numbered sections with self-contained vignettes of varying length that thematically explore the subject of failure. These are essays that call attention to their segmentation; they announce very early on to the reader that progress through them will not be linear, although it may be sequential, and that the force of the segments will come from their juxtaposition with one another and the effect of their accumulation by the end.

These are not traditional essays, the kind that composition textbooks usually teach you to write, the kind that begin with some sort of thesis statement, then march through a linked, linear series of supporting, illustrative paragraphs to a predictable, forceful conclusion. Textbooks tend to teach either the unattainable and ideal or the undesirable but teachable. The segmented essay has been with us for quite some time and may well be the dominant mode of the contemporary essay, but we are only just beginning to recognize it and try to teach it.

Shaken by her son's death in the crash of his Air Force jet, Carol sets out to retrace the path of his life. She and her husband drive from Michigan across the country to California, and then come back by way of the southeastern United States, all the while trying to connect to the life he led in scattered places. Throughout the trip she keeps a journal of her travels and eventually decides to write an essay about the journey.

As she begins writing, she finds herself hampered by the amount of detail she has accumulated about the trip, about her son's life, about her reactions to each location. So much information seems relevant and interrelated that it is difficult for her to be inclusive and yet get to the end of both the essay and the trip, where the real significance of her pilgrimage comes home to her. It is a trip of several weeks and thousands of miles and, unless she is to make it booklength, which she doesn't want to do, she needs to find another way to come at this mass of strongly felt material.

Eventually she discovers the key to the composing in the materials on which she bases the essay: the narrative of the trip, the reflections in her private journal, the references to her son's life. Alternating among episodes of narration, reflection, and reference, she uses the separate strands of her materials to comment on one another and to justify her breaking off one segment to move to another. The essay begins with a passage of narration and description about the onset of the journey ("We need this trip like the desert needs rain. For months the dining area has looked like a war games planning room with maps everywhere."); it is followed by an excerpt from her journal remarking on how she feels a few days later, set in italics to identify it immediately as separate from the narrative (*"June 7. Badlands. Last night when we walked back to our campsite in true dark, stars in the sky notwithstanding, we became disoriented."*); this is followed by description of another location, further down the road ("In Wyoming, as we drive north toward Sheridan, we watch antelope standing far off . . ."); then another excerpt from the journal; then a section reflecting her son's experiences ("Kirk loved Wyoming. In 1976 his father and I took him and his brother and sister to Yellowstone . . ."), and so on throughout the essay. Paragraph breaks between segments and changes in font make it easy for the reader to follow the shifts and jumpcuts. It becomes a travel montage with "voiceover" commentary and an alternating strand of personal history. The juxtaposition of landscape, biography, and commentary move us more quickly through the essay than full linear chronology could do, and yet the chronology is there, a beginning, a middle, and an end, given an almost cinematic force by the accumulation of a series of concentrated segments.

The recognition of the segmented form, if not the form itself, is so new that we have not yet settled on a name for it. At present it is most often called a "collage" essay, a term coined by Peter Elbow, referring to the technique in visual art of assembling disparate images into an integrated whole which expresses a specific theme (like the "American Dream" collage) through the interrelationships of the parts. Some use the filmmaking term "montage," the editing technique that arranges a series of shots and images into an expressive sequence. Carl Klaus, who has mulled over the terminology and objected to both collage and montage, has suggested "disjunctive" (as opposed to the more unified and "conjunctive" linear form), which he admits may have negative connotations, or "paratactic" (a grammatical term for "segments of discourse" arranged without connections or transitions), which may be too obscure. Rebecca Blevins Faery has described the form as "fragmented" and "polyphonic." At times all these terms seem applicable to some essays and not to others, perhaps because segmented essays tend to invent their own forms, not merely imitate established forms.

Take, for example, "The Ideal Particle and the Great Unconformity" by Reg Saner. In this complex essay, Saner connects two terms from geology which identify two different concepts of scale. The ideal particle is the term for a grain of sand one tenth of a millimeter, "the size most easily airborne in wind, thus the likeliest to begin a surface effect known as saltation," where one grain strikes other grains with enough force to make them capable of becoming airborne (163); the Great Unconformity is a gigantic gap in the geological record, a place where, following the Grand Canyon walls down the deposits of millennia, you encounter a layer so much older than the layer above it that 1,200 million years of deposits must have been erased before the layers you have been following were laid down. The Great Unconformity was created by the erosive power of the ideal particle and the enormity of the span of time in the life of the planet.

But Saner is not simply explaining these two concepts as a geology textbook might readily do in a paragraph or two. Rather, he is attempting to give the reader some sense of the scale involved here as well as what it is like to experience the scale. Thus, while the essay discusses the history of geological studies and major markers for dating the planet, it also has a personal narrative running through it. Saner recounts a hike into the Grand Canyon, alternating speculations and observations about geological theory and evidence with vignettes of encounters with other hikers. In order to understand the subject of the essay as Saner understands it, the reader has to experience it with him, not simply have it explained to him.

> Slowly we accepted the curve of the earth. It dawned on us like a great change of mind, after which, earth's size came easy. Not its age. Evidence was every-where underfoot, unmistakable. We chose not to see it. (154)

This opening segment is a brief verbal fanfare that sounds the theme of the essay. The segments that follow alternate exposition and argument with narration and description, taking the reader deeper and deeper into both the subject matter and the experience. We dig down through the segments, like layers of sedimentary deposits, the white spaces between segments marking them like layers of geologic time. Perhaps this is a geologic essay, then, or a tectonic essay, where the segments are like plates moving and colliding and rearranging themselves on the crust of the essay.

The ability to arrange and rearrange segments frees writers to generate unique forms. Mark Rudman has created a series of essays he refers to as "mosaics," such as his "Mosaic on Walking." The mosaic metaphor suggests an essay composed of little sections, like mosaic tiles, which create a larger picture by the way they are cumulatively arranged. For example, the opening tiles are these segments separated from one another by the grouting of white space:

> In this season I am often sulky, sullen, restless, withdrawn. I feel trans-parent, as if inhabited by the weather.

> Only while walking am I relieved from distress, only then, released from the burden of self, am I free to think. I wanted to say walking brings relief from tension without sadness and then I think it is not so—these walks bring their own form of *tristesse*. There is discomfort when movement stops.

> Though not exceptionally tall (a shade under six feet), I am a rangy, ram-bly walker. I take up a lot of space! (138)

In "Mosaic on Walking" the sequentiality of the arrangement is difficult to per-ceive; it might well have been written simply by composing a random number of segments which in some way relate to the theme of walking and then either hap-hazardly or systematically arranging them in a disjunctive or non-sequential or-der on the page—the way you might copy a list of sentences about walking in the order you discovered them in *Bartlett's Familiar Quotations*. The mosaic, at least as Rudman uses it, seems lacking in design, capable of being read in any order, virtually devoid of transition or sequence; it uses an accumulation of associative segments to create mood or attitude. Maybe we should use the term "cumulative essays" or "associative essays."

But Nancy Willard, in "The Friendship Tarot," begins with the image of a tarot card arrangement on the page ("I lay out the cards of our friendship"). Each section of the essay which follows is named for a specific tarot card in that arrangement—The Child, The Journey, The Garden, The Book—and opens with a description of the picture on the card ("The card shows a child with chocolate on his face wandering through an art gallery in downtown Poughkeepsie devoted—for two weeks—to illustrations from children's books."). The segments lead us through the sequence of the tarot reading to get at issues of change and growth in a particular friendship. Perhaps it is a "tarot essay" but I don't know if the term applies to all segmented essays or, in all the history of essays, to her essay alone.

It isn't that collaging or segmenting abandons structure—it's that it builds essay structure in ways that may be organic with the subject, ways that may not be immediately recognizable but which incrementally explain themselves as the reader progresses through the essay. In the models of structure that composition textbooks traditionally provide, the ancient and venerable rhetorical topic of arrangement is handled by providing molds into which to pour the molten thought and language of the essay: comparison/contrast, thesis/support, process—all prefabricated shapes to be selected off the rack to fit the body of the topic—or the five-paragraph theme, the one-size-fits-all product of the rhetorical department store. The segmented essay, on the other hand, attempts a tailor-made design, a structure that may be appropriate only to itself.

I am at a writer's workshop in Montana, happy to be among a talented group of writers who have brought manuscripts on the outdoors and thrilled by my first experience in the Western mountains. In the mornings we workshop one another's manuscripts under Gretel Ehrlich's directions; in the afternoon we hike the foothills of the Bitterroot Range or raft the Bitterroot River or ramble the valley floor. Late at night or early in the morning I write in my journal about the workshop sessions and the hiking, particularly where I have gone and what I have seen. In the end I have records of three hiking expeditions, one that takes me only a little way up Blodgett Canyon, one that takes me to a falls a few miles up the Mill Creek Trail, and a third that brings me to the awesome Bear Creek overlook on the shoulder of a mountain. When I try to analyze my frustrations and satisfactions about those hikes, I begin to see the possibility of an essay coming out of the experience.

Back in Michigan after the workshop, tinkering sullenly with the critiqued manuscript, I drop everything and instead begin writing about my Montana hiking. I give the essay the working title "Bitterroot" but eventually call it "Knowing Where You've Been," a title inspired by a Normal Maclean story about Blodgett Canyon which had helped me set a hiking destination in the first place. Perhaps because the other essays in the workshop have so often been segmented, divided into brief episodes or scenes or vignettes, I don't consider for a moment constructing an argumentative essay built around conclusions reached and made up of rationales for reaching them. At once I understand that I have come to the conclusions I have by taking three separate hikes, each of which went successively further into the wilderness, all of which culminated at the end of the final hike with a blissful moment of triumph and contentment, with a sense of arrival I hadn't had in the earlier hikes. I wonder if I can come at this by taking my reader through the three hikes with me, taking her deeper on each hike, leading her to the same moment and the same site of discovery that I reached. In brief, I wonder if I can somehow get the reader to reach my conclusions for herself by experiencing through my prose the same things I experienced.

This is risky, I know. Gretel Ehrlich's off-hand crack about the "plodding mid-western prose" of my workshop manuscript still chafes my ego like a fresh wound I can't stop picking at long enough to let heal. If I am to make my readers hike, the hiking better be brisk, lively, and limited, and each hike better be distinctive, so that it becomes clear why they've had to do three of them. I write the hikes in present tense, to make them feel more immediate, and I start them off the same way: I chip away at narrative that fills in the gaps of time between the hikes and tighten the prose for strength and speed. I also insert reflective interludes between the hikes, past tense segments responding to the hike just completed and pointing towards the next hike.

In the end the essay has five tight segments: hike ("The first afternoon. We walk the Blodgett Creek Trail"); interlude ("'When you look back at where you've been,' Norman Maclean writes, 'it often seems as if you have never been there or even as if there were no such place.'"); hike ("The second afternoon. We mill around after the morning workshop, plans shifting, destinations uncertain, finally resolving to go back into the mountains, to another trail."); interlude ("When I asked my friend from Montana about places to hike in the Bitterroot Valley, he looked thoughtful for a moment, shook his head, and said, 'Well, as early as you're going, there'll be too much snow to bag a peak.'"); hike ("The final afternoon. The morning workshop over, the group disperses for various tours and activities."). Each hike takes the narrator (and the reader) deeper into wilderness; each interlude raises issues that only an additional hike can resolve; the physical experiences of moving deeper and higher are echoed by intellectual and spiritual experiences, so that the physical moment of final achievement coincides with the spiritual moment of arrival. The successive drafts make me better understand exactly what it is I was feeling at the end of that hiking and push me to prepare the reader for that epiphany on the mountain ("It isn't how far at all but how deep. I need to go as deeply into wilderness as it takes before the wilderness comes into me.") in a way that makes it unnecessary for me to explain it afterward or add an epilogue of explication that breaks the reader down both physically and emotionally. The essay has to end on the mountain and the segmented format invites me to end it there.

The segmented essay makes demands not only on the writer but on the reader as well. Carl Klaus has noted how segments can be read both as isolated units and as reverberating links to other segments; it is "a strange reading experience, unlike that produced by any other kind of prose" which produces in him "an irresolvable tension between two different ways of reading and responding." From reading each segment "as a discrete entity as well as . . . in connection with its immediate neighbor," he finds that his "accumulating sense of recurrent or contrastive words, phrases, images, metaphors, ideas, topics, or themes" forces him to "intuitively mak[e] connections or distinctions between and among the segments, almost as if I were experiencing some of the very same associative leaps that might have provoked the essayist to write a piece in disjunctive form" (48). These "associative leaps" may replicate the fragmentary nature of "recollection and reflection" but they also suggest a willingness to accept unresolved or undefined associations.

Such writing demands that the reader learn to read the structure of the essay as well as its thought. That is a task for which the twentieth century reader is well prepared, because the episodic or segmented or disjunctive sequence is a familiar design in many other genres:

- the interrelated collection of short stories, for example, a concept suggested by Hemingway with the interludes between stories in *In Our Time* or carried out in Ray Bradbury's *The Martian Chronicles*;
- the playing with chronology and the episodic structure of novels like Milan Kundera's *The Unbearable Lightness of Being* and Kurt Vonnegut's *Slaughterhouse-Five*;
- cycles of thematically linked poems, each poem separate and independent but enriched by juxtaposition with poems on similar subjects or with similar perspectives;
- the "concept" album of interlinked songs—the Beatles' *Sgt. Pepper's Lonely Hearts Club Band* or the "suite" on half of *Abbey Road*, Pink Floyd's *The Wall*, or the more loosely thematic *Nebraska* and *Born In the USA* albums of Bruce Springsteen;
- sequences of brief scenes in motion pictures—Quentin Tarantino's *Pulp Fiction*, Gus Van Sant's *To Die For*, the recent critical favorites *The English Patient* and *Shine* all present their stories out of chronological sequence. In none of these is it hard to reconstruct the chronology, but telling the story in strict chronological order would have changed the emphases of these films. But even in strictly chronological films, the film progresses by sequences of shots or scenes, each separated from one another by visual cues as definite as chapter headings or theatrical intermissions.

Examples abound. It might be argued that the modern reader/viewer is more accustomed to disjunctiveness than to strict continuity.

I write this essay in segments. How can I explain what the segmented essay is like, or how it comes about, in an unsegmented essay?

I get up early in the morning to write, a common writer's habit. I am following a vague outline in my head of alternating segments—a more or less narrative example of someone composing a segmented essay alternating with a more or less expository section discussing the form. Practice alternates with theory. I have a lot of examples in mind that I think I might be able to use, and sometimes I type a section break or white space and insert a line of reference to spur my memory when I get to that segment ("Sandra's essay is giving her lots of trouble"; "I write this essay in segments"). Sometimes, by the time I reach that line, I have decided not to use it or have already used the example and I delete the line.

Some days I complete the draft of a segment in a single session, partly because I know I will have to revise it—go back to Mike's drafts to compare them again and to dig out more material for illustration, reread Carol's essay to refresh my memory about specific references, ask somebody about tarot readings, work on the concreteness of the language and clarity of the explanations. At first I am interested chiefly in having a structure to work in, and I have already cut and pasted segments in this draft to juxtapose them in different sequences.

Other days I only get through a portion of a segment. Some are harder than others to write, some have more detail, more development, quotes to look up and copy. I don't mind leaving them undone, because I think that when I return to them the next day my subconscious will have worked on them a little bit and it will be easier to launch into the drafting again. Even in an essay that isn't segmented we still work from section to section; it really isn't much different here.

And finally one morning when I feel I've said enough and need to worry less about finding something more to say than about finding ways to say what I've said better, I run off the full draft and try to work with what I have. Sometimes whole segments disappear or merge with others, sometimes new segments announce their necessity and have to be drafted and revised, sometimes the order of the segments changes again and again. I work harder on the language now, when I'm certain the ideas will stay. I am always reassured by a quote whose source may or may not have been Oscar Wilde: "I always revise everything eleven times, ten times to get the words right, and the eleventh time to put in that touch of spontaneity that everyone likes about my writing."

I teach creative nonfiction and composition classes, talk to friends about their essays, work on essays of my own. Sometimes I bring work in progress to my students, like a draft on men's rooms I photocopied, cut up, and distributed in pieces to see how different people would reassemble them and why. Often I advise other writers stuck in linearity and chronology, "Why don't you try collaging this?" I like making a verb of the noun, outraging any grammarians who overhear me.

I insist that my nonfiction students write at least one segmented essay during the term and provide such ways into the segmented essay as these:

- *definitions:* Simply explaining the segmented essay form calls up a range of alternatives: collage, montage, mosaic, vignette, episode, segment—all ways of approaching the form that suggest alternatives at that same time that they define distinctive forms.
- *models:* Readers respond to a handful of segmented essays with immediate understanding—Nancy Willard's "The Friendship Tarot," Annie Dillard's

"Living Like Weasels," Susan Allen Toth's "Going to Movies," William Holtz's "Brother's Keeper," Naomi Shihab Nye's "Three Pokes of a Thistle," Reg Saner's "The Ideal Particle and the Great Unconformity."
- *strategies:* Segmented essays tend to go together in several different ways—

  - by juxtaposition, arranging one item alongside another item so that they comment back and forth on one another (Toth's "Going to Movies" is four vignettes, three dates with different men, the fourth a solitary trip to the theater);
  - by parallelism, alternating or intertwining one continuous strand with another (a present tense strand with a past tense strand, a domestic strand with a foreign strand, the alternate strands of a piece like "The Ideal Particle and the Great Unconformity");
  - by patterning, choosing an extra-literary design and arranging literary segments accordingly (as Willard does with tarot cards in "The Friendship Tarot" or Frederick Smock does with rooms in "Anonymous: A Brief Memoir");
  - by accumulation, arranging a series of segments or scenes or episodes so that they add or enrich or alter meaning with each addition, perhaps reinterpreting earlier segments in later ones, up to a final segment (as Holtz does in "Brother's Keeper");
  - by journaling, actually writing in episodes or reconstructing the journal experience in drafts (Sydney Lea asks students to write lyrical essays trying to connect disparate items in their journals; Gretel Ehrlich uses the journal form as a narrative device in many of her works, such as the recent "Cold Comfort").

In the classroom I make students cluster and list and map ideas, all of which encourage segmentation, separate items to work from. They produce partial or full rough drafts in whatever format they choose and then they help each other find ways of collaging or segmenting appropriate to the pieces they're working on. Once they're open to the possibility of the segmented essay, there's virtually no limit to the variations a roomful of imaginative young writers can bring to the form.

Collage, montage, mosaic, vignette, episode, segment—I've never found a descriptive term for anything that, if I pressed on it, wasn't somehow incapable of bearing the weight of definitive definition. I don't worry about the most accurate term for this kind of essay, because when one writer suggests to another, "Why don't you collage this?" the result may as much define the form as conform to it.

Works Cited

Best American Essays 1991. Ed. Joyce Carol Oates. Series Editor: Robert Atwan. Boston: Ticknor and Fields, 1991.
Dillard, Annie. "Living Like Weasels." *Teaching a Stone to Talk: Expeditions and Encounters.* New York: Harper, 1982. 29–34.

Ehrlich, Gretel. "Cold Comfort." *Harper's* 294:1762 (March 1997): 34–44.

Elbow, Peter. *Writing With Power*. New York: Oxford University Press, 1981.

Faery, Rebecca Blevins. "Text and Context: The Essay and the Politics of Disjunctive Form." *What Do I Know? Reading, Writing, and Teaching the Essay*. Ed. Janis Forman. Portsmouth, NH: Boynton/Cook, 1996. 55–68.

Grand Tour, "Virtues & Vices" 1:4 (Fall 1996).

Gruchow, Paul. "Eight Variations on the Idea of Failure." *Old Friends, New Neighbors: A Celebration of the American Essay, American Literary Review*. Ed. W. Scott Olsen. 5:2 (Fall 1994): 31–38.

Holtz, William. "Brother's Keeper: an Elegy." *Old Friends, New Neighbors: A Celebration of the American Essay, American Literary Review*. Ed. W. Scott Olsen. 5:2 (Fall 1994): 147–63.

Klaus, Carl H. "Excursions of the Mind: Toward a Poetics of Uncertainty in the Disjunctive Essay." *What Do I Know? Reading, Writing, and Teaching the Essay*. Ed. Janis Forman. Portsmouth, NH: Boynton/Cook, 1996. 39–53.

Nye, Naomi Shihab. "Three Pokes of a Thistle." *Never in a Hurry: Essay on People and Places*. Columbia: University of South Carolina Press, 1996. 26–31.

Old Friends, New Neighbors: A Celebration of the American Essay, American Literary Review. Ed. W. Scott Olsen. 5:2 (Fall 1994).

Ploughshares. Ed. Rosellen Brown. 20: 2–3 (Fall 1994).

Rudman, Mark. "Mosaic on Walking." *The Best American Essays 1991*. Ed. Joyce Carol Oates. Boston: Ticknor and Fields, 1991: 138–153.

Sanford, Carol. Unpublished essay ["Always Looking"].

Schwartz, Lynne Sharon. "Time Off to Translate." *Old Friends, New Neighbors: A Celebration of the American Essay, American Literary Review*. Ed. W. Scott Olsen. 5:2 (Fall 1994): 15–30.

Smock, Frederick. "Anonymous: A Brief Memoir." *Old Friends, New Neighbors: A Celebration of the American Essay, American Literary Review*. Ed. W. Scott Olsen. 5:2 (Fall 1994): 68–72.

Steinberg, Michael. Unpublished essay ["'I've Got It, No, You 'Take It': An Aging Ballplayer's Dilemma" and "On the Road Again: A Softball Gypsy's Last Go-Round"].

Toth, Susan Allen. "Going to the Movies." *How to Prepare for Your High-School Reunion and Other Midlife Musings*. New York: Ballantine Books, 1990. 108–112.

Willard, Nancy. "The Friendship Tarot." *Between Friends*. Ed. Mickey Pearlman. Boston: Houghton Mifflin, 1994. 195–203.

The Singular First Person

Scott Russell Sanders

The first soapbox orator I ever saw was haranguing a crowd beside the Greyhound Station in Providence, Rhode Island, about the evils of fluoridated water. What the man stood on was actually an upturned milk crate, all the genuine soapboxes presumably having been snapped up by antique dealers. He wore an orange plaid sports coat and matching bow tie and held aloft a bottle filled with mossy green liquid. I don't remember the details of his spiel, except his warning that fluoride was an invention of the Communists designed to weaken our bones and thereby make us pushovers for a Red invasion. What amazed me, as a tongue-tied kid of seventeen newly arrived in the city from the boondocks, was not his message but his courage in delivering it to a mob of strangers. I figured it would have been easier for me to jump straight over the Greyhound Station than to stand there on that milk crate and utter my thoughts.

To this day, when I read or when I compose one of those curious monologues we call the personal essay, I often think of that soapbox orator. Nobody had asked him for his two cents' worth, but there he was declaring it with all the eloquence he could muster. The essay, although enacted in private, is no less arrogant a performance. Unlike novelists and playwrights, who lurk behind the scenes while distracting our attention with the puppet show of imaginary characters, unlike scholars and journalists, who quote the opinions of others and shelter behind the hedges of neutrality, the essayist has nowhere to hide. While the poet can lean back on a several-thousand-year-old legacy of ecstatic speech, the essayist inherits a much briefer and skimpier tradition. The poet is allowed to quit after a few lines, but the essayist must hold our attention over pages and pages. It is a brash and foolhardy form, this one-man or one-woman circus, which relies on the tricks of anecdote, conjecture, memory, and wit to enthrall us.

Addressing a monologue to the world seems all the more brazen or preposterous an act when you consider what a tiny fraction of the human chorus any single voice is. At the Boston Museum of Science an electronic meter records with flashing lights the population of the United States. Figuring in the rate of births, deaths, emigrants leaving the country and immigrants arriving, the meter calculates that we add one fellow citizen every twenty-one seconds. When I looked at it recently, the count stood at 249,958,483. As I wrote that figure in my notebook, the final number jumped from three to four. Another mouth, another set of ears and eyes, another brain. A counter for the earth's population would stand somewhere past five billion at the moment, and would be rising in a blur of digits. Amid this avalanche of selves, it is a wonder that anyone finds the gumption to sit down and write one of those naked, lonely, quixotic letters-to-the-world.

A surprising number do find the gumption. In fact, I have the impression there are more essayists at work in America today, and more gifted ones, than at any time in recent decades. Whom do I have in mind? Here is a sampler: Wendell Berry, Carol Bly, Joan Didion, Annie Dillard, Stephen Jay Gould, Elizabeth Hardwick, Edward Hoagland, Phillip Lopate, Barry Lopez, Peter Matthiessen, John McPhee, Cynthia Ozick, Paul Theroux, Lewis Thomas, Tom Wolfe. No doubt you could make up a list of your own—with a greater ethnic range, perhaps, or fewer nature enthusiasts—a list that would provide equally convincing support for the view that we are blessed right now with an abundance of essayists. We do not have anyone to rival Emerson or Thoreau, but in sheer quantity of first-rate work our time stands comparison with any period since the heyday of the form in the mid-nineteenth century.

Why are so many writers taking up this risky form, and why are so many readers—to judge by the statistics of book and magazine publication—seeking it out? In this era of prepackaged thought, the essay is the closest thing we have, on paper, to a record of the individual mind at work and play. It is an amateur's raid in a world of specialists. Feeling overwhelmed by data, random information, the flotsam and jetsam of mass culture, we relish the spectacle of a single consciousness making sense of a portion of the chaos. We are grateful to Lewis Thomas for shining his light into the dark corners of biology, to John McPhee for laying bare the geology beneath our landscape, to Annie Dillard for showing us the universal fire blazing in the branches of a cedar, to Peter Matthiessen for chasing after snow leopards and mystical insights in the Himalayas. No matter if they are sketchy, these maps of meaning are still welcome. As Joan Didion observes in her own collection of essays, *The White Album*, "We live entirely, especially if we are writers, by the imposition of a narrative line upon disparate images, by the 'ideas' with which we have learned to freeze the shifting phantasmagoria which is our actual experience." Dizzy from a dance that seems to accelerate hour by hour, we cling to the narrative line, even though it may be as pure an invention as the shapes drawn by Greeks to identify the constellations.

The essay is a haven for the private, idiosyncratic voice in an era of anonymous babble. Like the bland-burgers served in their millions along our highways, most language served up in public these days is textureless, tasteless mush. On television, over the phone, in the newspaper, wherever humans bandy words about, we encounter more and more abstractions, more empty formulas. Think of the pablum ladled out by politicians. Think of the fluffy white bread of advertising. Think, lord help us, of committee reports. By contrast, the essay remains stubbornly concrete and particular: it confronts you with an oil-smeared toilet at the Sunoco station, a red vinyl purse shaped like a valentine heart, a bowlegged dentist hunting deer with an elephant gun. As Orwell forcefully argued, and as dictators seem to agree, such a bypassing of abstractions, such an insistence on the concrete, is a politically subversive act. Clinging to this door, that child, this grief, following the zigzag motions of an inquisitive mind, the essay renews language and clears trash from the springs of thought. A century and a half ago, in the rousing manifesto entitled *Nature*, Emerson called on a new generation of writers to cast off the hand-me-down rhetoric of the day, to "pierce this rotten diction and fasten words again to visible things." The essayist aspires to do just that.

As if all these virtues were not enough to account for a renaissance of this protean genre, the essay has also taken over some of the territory abdicated by contemporary fiction. Whittled down to the bare bones of plot, camouflaged with irony, muttering in brief sentences and grade-school vocabulary, peopled with characters who stumble like sleepwalkers through numb lives, today's fashionable fiction avoids disclosing where the author stands on anything. In the essay, you had better speak from a region pretty close to the heart or the reader will detect the wind of phoniness whistling through your hollow phrases. In the essay you may be caught with your pants down, your ignorance and sentimentality showing, while you trot recklessly about on one of your hobbyhorses. You cannot stand back from the action, as Joyce instructed us to do, and pare your fingernails. You cannot palm off your cockamamie notions on some hapless character.

To our list of the essay's contemporary attractions we should add the perennial ones of verbal play, mental adventure, and sheer anarchic high spirits. To see how the capricious mind can be led astray, consider the foregoing paragraph, which drags in metaphors from the realms of toys, clothing, weather, and biology, among others. That is bad enough; but it could have been worse. For example, I began to draft a sentence in that paragraph with the following words: "More than once, in sitting down to beaver away at a narrative, felling trees of memory and hauling brush to build a dam that might slow down the waters of time . . . ." I had set out to make some innocent remark, and here I was gnawing down trees and building dams, all because I had let that *beaver* slip in. On this occasion I had the good sense to throw out the unruly word. I don't always, as no doubt you will have noticed. Whatever its more visible subject, an essay is also about the way a mind moves, the links and leaps and jigs of thought. I might as well drag in another metaphor—and another unoffending animal—by saying that each doggy sentence, as it noses forward into the underbrush of thought, scatters a bunch of rabbits that go bounding off in all directions. The essayist can afford to chase more of those rabbits than the fiction writer can, but fewer than the poet. If you refuse to chase any of them, and keep plodding along in a straight line, you and your reader will have a dull outing. If you chase too many, you will soon wind up lost in a thicket of confusion with your tongue hanging out.

The pursuit of mental rabbits was strictly forbidden by the teachers who instructed me in English composition. For that matter, nearly all the qualities of the personal essay, as I have been sketching them, violate the rules that many of us were taught in school. You recall we were supposed to begin with an outline and stick by it faithfully, like a train riding its rails, avoiding sidetracks. Each paragraph was to have a topic sentence pasted near the front, and these orderly paragraphs were to be coupled end-to-end like so many boxcars. Every item in those boxcars was to bear the stamp of some external authority, preferably a footnote referring to a thick book, although appeals to magazines and newspapers would do in a pinch. Our diction was to be formal, dignified, shunning the vernacular. Polysyllabic words derived from Latin were preferable to the blunt lingo of the streets. Metaphors were to be used only in emergencies, and no two of them were to be mixed. And even in emergencies we could not speak in the first person singular.

Already as a schoolboy, I chafed against those rules. Now I break them shamelessly, in particular the taboo against using the lonely capital *I*. Just look at what I'm doing right now. My speculations about the state of the essay arise, needless to say, from my own practice as reader and writer, and they reflect my own tastes, no matter how I may pretend to gaze dispassionately down on the question from a hot-air balloon. As Thoreau declares in his cocky manner on the opening page of *Walden*: "In most books the *I*, or first person, is omitted; in this it will be retained; that, in respect to egotism, is the main difference. We commonly do not remember that it is, after all, always the first person that is speaking. I should not talk so much about myself if there were anybody else whom I knew as well." True for the personal essay, it is doubly true for an essay about the essay: one speaks always and inescapably in the first person singular.

We could sort out essays along a spectrum according to the degree to which the writer's ego is on display—with John McPhee, perhaps, at the extreme of self-effacement, and Norman Mailer at the opposite extreme of self-dramatization. Brassy or shy, center stage or hanging back in the wings, the author's persona commands our attention. For the length of an essay, or a book of essays, we respond to that persona as we would to a friend caught up in a rapturous monologue. When the monologue is finished, we may not be able to say precisely what it was about, any more than we can draw conclusions from a piece of music. "Essays don't usually boil down to a summary, as articles do," notes Edward Hoagland, one of the least summarizable of companions, "and the style of the writer has a 'nap' to it, a combination of personality and originality and energetic loose ends that stand up like the nap of a piece of wool and can't be brushed flat" ("What I Think, What I Am"). We make assumptions about that speaking voice, assumptions we cannot validly make about the narrators in fiction. Only a sophomore is permitted to ask if Huckleberry Finn ever had any children; but even literary sophisticates wonder in print about Thoreau's love life, Montaigne's domestic arrangements, De Quincey's opium habit, Virginia Woolf's depression.

Montaigne, who not only invented the form but nearly perfected it as well, announced from the start that his true subject was himself. In his note "To the Reader" at the beginning of the *Essays*, he slyly proclaimed:

> I want to be seen here in my simple, natural, ordinary fashion, without strain-
> ing or artifice; for it is myself that I portray. My defects will here be read to the
> life, and also my natural form, as far as respect for the public has allowed. Had
> I been placed among those nations which are said to live still in the sweet free-
> dom of nature's first laws, I assure you I should very gladly have portrayed
> myself here entire and wholly naked.

A few pages after this disarming introduction, we are told of the Emperor Maximilian, who was so prudish about exposing his private parts that he would not let a servant dress him or see him in the bath. The Emperor went so far as to give orders that he be buried in his underdrawers. Having let us in on this intimacy about Maximilian, Montaigne then confessed that he himself, although "bold-mouthed," was equally prudish, and that "except under great stress of necessity or voluptuousness," he never allowed anyone to see him naked. Such modesty, he feared, was unbecoming in a soldier. But such honesty is quite becoming in an essayist. The very confession of his prudery is a far more revealing gesture than any doffing of clothes.

A curious reader will soon find out that the word *essay*, as adapted by Montaigne, means a trial or attempt. The Latin root carries the more vivid sense of a weighing out. In the days when that root was alive and green, merchants discovered the value of goods and alchemists discovered the composition of un-known metals by the use of scales. Just so the essay, as Montaigne was the first to show, is a weighing out, an inquiry into the value, meaning, and true nature of experience; it is a private experiment carried out in public. In each of three successive editions, Montaigne inserted new material into his essays without re-vising the old material. Often the new statements contradicted the original ones, but Montaigne let them stand, since he believed that the only consistent fact about human beings is their inconsistency. In a celebration called "Why Mon-taigne Is Not a Bore," Lewis Thomas has remarked of him that "He [was] fond of his mind, and affectionately entertained by everything in his head." What-ever Montaigne wrote about—and he wrote about everything under the sun: fears, smells, growing old, the pleasures of scratching—he weighed on the scales of his own character.

It is the *singularity* of the first person—its warts and crotchets and turn of voice—that lures many of us into reading essays, and that lingers with us after we finish. Consider the lonely, melancholy persona of Loren Eiseley, forever wandering, forever brooding on our dim and bestial past, his lips frosty with the chill of the Ice Age. Consider the volatile, Dionysian persona of D. H. Lawrence, with his incandescent gaze, his habit of turning peasants into gods and trees into flames, his quick hatred and quicker love. Consider that philosophical farmer, Wendell Berry, who speaks with a countryman's knowledge and a deacon's severity. Consider E. B. White, with his cheery affection for brown eggs and dachshunds, his unflappable way of herding geese while the radio warns of an approaching hurricane.

E. B. White, that engaging master of the genre, a champion of idiosyncrasy, introduced his own volume of *Essays* by admitting the danger of narcissism:

> I think some people find the essay the last resort of the egoist, a much too self-conscious and self-serving form for their taste; they feel that it is presumptuous of a writer to assume that his little excursions or his small observations will interest the reader. There is some justice in their complaint. I have always been aware that I am by nature self-absorbed and egoistical; to write of myself to the extent I have done indicates a too great attention to my own life, not enough to the lives of others.

Yet the self-absorbed Mr. White was in fact a delighted observer of the world, and shared that delight with us. Thus, after describing memorably how a circus girl practiced her bareback riding in the leisure moments between shows ("The Ring of Time"), he confessed: "As a writing man, or secretary, I have always felt charged with the safekeeping of all unexpected items of worldly or unworldly enchantment, as though I might be held personally responsible if even a small one were to be lost." That may still be presumptuous, but it is a presumption turned outward on the creation.

This looking outward helps distinguish the essay from pure autobiography, which dwells more complacently on the self. Mass murderers, movie stars, sports heroes, Wall Street crooks, and defrocked politicians may blather on about whatever high jinks or low jinks made them temporarily famous, may chronicle their exploits, their diets, their hobbies, in perfect confidence that the public is eager to gobble up every least gossipy scrap. And the public, according to sales figures, generally is. On the other hand, I assume the public does not give a hoot about my private life. If I write of hiking up a mountain with my one-year-old boy riding like a papoose on my back, and of what he babbled to me while we gazed down from the summit onto the scudding clouds, it is not because I am deluded into believing that my baby, like the offspring of Prince Charles, matters to the great world. It is because I know the great world produces babies of its own and watches them change cloudfast before its doting eyes. To make that climb up the mountain vividly present for readers is harder work than the climb itself. I choose to write about my experience not because it is mine, but because it seems to me a door through which others might pass.

On that cocky first page of *Walden*, Thoreau justified his own seeming self-absorption by saying that he wrote the book for the sake of his fellow citizens, who kept asking him to account for his peculiar experiment by the pond. There is at least a sliver of truth to this, since Thoreau, a town character, had been invited more than once to speak his mind at the public lectern. Most of us, however, cannot honestly say the townspeople have been clamoring for our words. I suspect that all writers of the essay, even Norman Mailer and Gore Vidal, must occasionally wonder if they are egomaniacs. For the essayist, in other words, the problem of authority is inescapable. By what right does one speak? Why should anyone listen? The traditional sources of authority no longer serve. You cannot justify your words by appealing to the Bible or some other holy text, you cannot merely stitch together a patchwork of quotations from classical authors, you cannot lean on a podium at the Atheneum and deliver your wisdom to a rapt audience.

In searching for your own soapbox, a sturdy platform from which to deliver your opinionated monologues, it helps if you have already distinguished yourself at some other, less fishy form. When Yeats describes his longing for Maud Gonne or muses on Ireland's misty lore, everything he says is charged with the prior strength of his poetry. When Virginia Woolf, in *A Room of One's Own*, reflects on the status of women and the conditions necessary for making art, she speaks as the author of *Mrs. Dalloway* and *To the Lighthouse*. The essayist may also lay claim to our attention by having lived through events or traveled through terrains that already bear a richness of meaning. When James Baldwin writes his *Notes of a Native Son*, he does not have to convince us that racism is a troubling reality. When Barry Lopez takes us on a meditative tour of the far north in *Arctic Dreams*, he can rely on our curiosity about that fabled and forbidding place. When Paul Theroux climbs aboard a train and invites us on a journey to some exotic destination, he can count on the romance of railroads and the allure of remote cities to bear us along.

Most essayists, however, cannot draw on any source of authority from beyond the page to lend force to the page itself. They can only use language to put themselves on display and to gesture at the world. When Annie Dillard tells us in the opening lines of *Pilgrim at Tinker Creek* about the tomcat with bloody paws who jumps through the window onto her chest, why should we listen? Well, because of the voice that goes on to say: "And some mornings I'd wake in daylight to find my body covered with paw prints in blood; I looked as though I'd been painted with roses." Listen to her explaining a few pages later what she is up to in this book, this broody, zestful record of her stay in the Roanoke Valley: "I propose to keep here what Thoreau called 'a meteorological journal of the mind,' telling some tales and describing some of the sights of this rather tamed valley, and exploring, in fear and trembling, some of the unmapped dim reaches and unholy fastnesses to which those tales and sights so dizzyingly lead." The sentence not only describes the method of her literary search, but also exhibits the breathless, often giddy, always eloquent and spiritually hungry soul who will do the searching. If you enjoy her company, you will relish Annie Dillard's essays; if you don't, you won't.

Listen to another voice which readers tend to find either captivating or insufferable:

> That summer I began to see, however dimly, that one of my ambitions, perhaps my governing ambition, was to belong fully to this place, to belong as the thrushes and the herons and the muskrats belonged, to be altogether at home here. That is still my ambition. But now I have come to see that it proposes an

enormous labor. It is a spiritual ambition, like goodness. The wild creatures belong to the place by nature, but as a man I can belong to it only by understanding and by virtue. It is an ambition I cannot hope to succeed in wholly, but I have come to believe that it is the most worthy of all.

That is Wendell Berry in "The Long-Legged House" writing about his patch of Kentucky. Once you have heard that stately, moralizing, cherishing voice, laced through with references to the land, you will not mistake it for anyone else's. Berry's themes are profound and arresting ones. But it is his voice, more than anything he speaks about, that either seizes us or drives us away.

Even so distinct a persona as Wendell Berry's or Annie Dillard's is still only a literary fabrication, of course. The first person singular is too narrow a gate for the whole writer to squeeze through. What we meet on the page is not the flesh-and-blood author, but a simulacrum, a character who wears the label *I*. Introducing the lectures that became *A Room of One's Own*, Virginia Woolf reminded her listeners that "'I' is only a convenient term for somebody who has no real being. Lies will flow from my lips, but there may perhaps be some truth mixed up with them; it is for you to seek out this truth and to decide whether any part of it is worth keeping." Here is a part I consider worth keeping: "Women have served all these centuries as looking-glasses possessing the magic and delicious power of reflecting the figure of man at twice its natural size." It is from such elegant, revelatory sentences that we build up our notion of the "I" who speaks to us under the name of Virginia Woolf.

What the essay tells us may not be true in any sense that would satisfy a court of law. As an example, think of Orwell's brief narrative, "A Hanging," which describes an execution in Burma. Anyone who has read it remembers how the condemned man as he walked to the gallows stepped aside to avoid a puddle. That is the sort of haunting detail only an eyewitness should be able to report. Alas, biographers, those zealous debunkers, have recently claimed that Orwell never saw such a hanging, that he reconstructed it from hearsay. What then do we make of his essay? Or has it become the sort of barefaced lie we prefer to call a story?

Frankly, I don't much care what label we put on "A Hanging"—fiction or nonfiction, it is a powerful statement either way—but Orwell might have cared a great deal. I say this because not long ago I was bemused and then vexed to find one of my own essays treated in a scholarly article as a work of fiction. Here was my earnest report about growing up on a military base, my heartfelt rendering of indelible memories, being confused with the airy figments of novelists! To be sure, in writing the piece I had used dialogue, scenes, settings, character descriptions, the whole fictional bag of tricks; sure, I picked and chose among a thousand beckoning details; sure, I downplayed some facts and highlighted others; but I was writing about the actual, not the invented. I shaped the matter, but I did not make it up.

To explain my vexation, I must break another taboo, which is to speak of the author's intent. My teachers warned me strenuously to avoid the intentional fallacy. They told me to regard poems and plays and stories as objects washed up on the page from some unknown and unknowable shores. Now that I am on the other side of the page, so to speak, I think quite recklessly of intention all the time. I believe that if we allow the question of intent in the case of murder, we should allow it in literature. The essay is distinguished from the short story, not by the presence or absence of literary devices, not by tone or theme or subject, but by the writer's stance toward the material. In composing an essay about what it was like to grow up on that military base, I *meant* something quite different from what I mean when concocting a story. I meant to preserve and record and help give voice to a reality that existed independently of me. I meant to pay my respects to a minor passage of history in an out-of-the-way place. I felt responsible to the truth as known by other people. I wanted to speak directly out of my own life into the lives of others.

You can see I am teetering on the brink of metaphysics. One step farther and I will plunge into the void, wondering as I fall how to prove there is any external truth for the essayist to pay homage to. I draw back from the brink and simply de-clare that I believe one writes, in essays, with a regard for the actual world, with a respect for the shared substance of history, the autonomy of other lives, the being of nature, the mystery and majesty of a creation we have not made.

When it comes to speculating about the creation, I feel more at ease with physics than with metaphysics. According to certain bold and lyrical cosmolo-gists, there is at the center of black holes a geometrical point, the tiniest conceiv-able speck, where all the matter of a collapsed star has been concentrated, and where everyday notions of time, space, and force break down. That point is called a singularity. The boldest and most poetic theories suggest that anything sucked into a singularity might be flung back out again, utterly changed, somewhere else in the universe. The lonely first person, the essayist's microcosmic "I," may be thought of as a verbal singularity at the center of the mind's black hole. The raw matter of experience, torn away from the axes of time and space, falls in con-stantly from all sides, undergoes the mind's inscrutable alchemy, and reemerges in the quirky, unprecedented shape of an essay.

Now it is time for me to step down, before another metaphor seizes hold of me, before you notice that I am standing, not on a soapbox, but on the purest air.

Memoir? Fiction? Where's the Line?

Mimi Schwartz

"It was very cold the night my mother died . . ."

Anna Quindlen

I don't remember what my second grade teacher wore! How can I recall the dialogue when my Dad left 10 years ago? All my summers in Maine blur together. That's what my students will say tomorrow when I return their first efforts at turning memories into memoir. They are mostly 21- and 22-year-old college seniors, plus a few retirees and second careerists, all eager to explore their lives on paper for themselves, friends and the world. No one is famous, although one woman said she won the lottery.

The memory worries will come mainly from marine biologists, psychology and history majors who deal in term papers and lab reports, rarely from poets and fiction writers who have taken enough creative writing workshops to understand, as V.S. Pritchett once wrote about memoir, "It's all in the art. You get no credit for living."

Some of these "creative" writers assume such advice excludes their boring lives, and so I have written "Great detail!" in many margins of first essays only to find out that the date rape or house burning down didn't happen. No, no, you can't do that, I say. That's fiction, not memoir. You have to play by the rules; there's a line you can't cross. And where is that? they ask. I don't know, only that if you make up too much, you've crossed it. The murkiness makes writer Anna Quindlen choose fiction over memoir. In "How Dark? How Stormy? I Can't

Recall!" (*New York Times Book Review*), she says that the newspaper reporter in her made her check old weather charts before she could publish the line, "It was very cold the night my mother died." Like my fact-conscious students, she worries: "Was it very cold or was that just the trick memory played on a girl who was sick and shivering, at least metaphorically?" and this worry, combined with a lousy memory, makes Quindlen avoid memoir, "a terrain too murky for me to tread." She says she can't, like Frank McCourt in *Angela's Ashes*, "remember half a century later the raw, itching sore that erupted between his eyebrows when he was a boy." So she writes fiction, preferring to create a world "from the ground up, the imagined minutiae of the lives of characters I invent from my knowledge of characters."

"But what about your *true* stories?" I would ask, if Anna were in my class. Don't you tell your friends, family, especially your children, about who you were, who your family was once upon a time? And do you want those stories to last more than one minute? If we stick only to facts, our past is as skeletal as black-and-white line drawings in a coloring book. We must color it in.

I tell the Annas in my class what I tell myself as memoir writer: Go for the emotional truth, that's what matters. Yes, gather the facts by all means. Look at old photos, return to old places, ask family members what they remember, look up time-line books for the correct songs and fashion styles, read old newspapers, encyclopedias, whatever—and then use the imagination to fill in the remembered experience. You don't need a tape recording of what your parents said to "remember" what they said that day. You don't need a photo of your kindergarten teacher to describe her; the clothes you imagine will match your feeling about her. Maybe you see a red, mini-suited girl; maybe you see a woman in a thick, long black dress with white cuffs. Either way, we see the teacher as you saw her. And who knows? She might even have worn those white cuffs! The subconscious is remembering.

That's also what I told my mother last week when she called to tell me that an essay I'd sent her about my love affair with horses was wrong. "I picked you up that day you fell off that horse, Sultan."

"You did not. I still remember everyone staring because my pants were ripped, my knee all bloody on the bus ride home."

"You were crying in the Pontiac."

"I was not."

It was her memory against mine with no one else to ask, so I wasn't changing my story. It was true for me—the humiliation following my glory riding Sultan—and she could tell her version, I said. That's what Rosemary Wolff threatened when her two sons, Geoffrey and Tobias, wrote separate and conflicting memoirs of their youth. (Or so Geoffrey Wolff said once in a workshop I took in Aspen.)

How subjective can you be in memoir, accidentally or on purpose? That is a central question, and different writers have different solutions. I teach the possibilities. You might start with a disclaimer the way John Irving did in "Trying to Save Piggy Sneed." He warns readers up front to "Please remember that all memoir is fiction," and then tells a wonderful story about how a retarded garbage man started him on his career as a writer. You might hint a disclaimer in your title, as Mary Carr does in *The Liar's Club*, and leave the reader wondering. You might tip off the reader with phrases such as "I imagine her . . . " or "Perhaps he said . . . ", the way Jane Bernstein does in her retelling of her sister's murder 2,000 miles away and 20 years before. You might use exaggeration as Russell Baker does in *Growing Up*, so that the dialogue of his interview to become a paperboy sounds as if he were being interviewed to head up IBM.

You might even give a lament that you don't remember, as Bret Lott does in his book, *Fathers, Sons, and Brothers*, before he gives a rich description of the morning that his son stopped calling him Mommy:

> The sad thing, though, is that I can't recall the first day he called me Daddy when I went into his room. I could make up a story about it, here and now; I could tell you how it was on a Tuesday—Melanie's morning—and how there seemed something different in his voice as I came up from sleep. . . .

Whatever else, there's always Joan Didion's wonderful permission in "On Reading a Notebook"—that if you remember it, it's true. I use it often.

> Perhaps it never did snow that August in Vermont; perhaps there never were flurries in the night wind, and maybe no one else felt the ground hardening and summer already dead even as we pretended to bask in it, but that was how it felt to me, and it might as well have snowed, could have snowed, did snow.

How it felt to me! What a relief to memoir writers who want to explore the emotional truth of memory. It may be "murky terrain," you may cross the line into fiction and have to step back reluctantly into what really happened—the struggle creates the tension that makes memoir either powerfully true or hopelessly phony. The challenge of this genre is that it hands you characters, plot and setting, and says, "Go figure them out!"—using fact, memory and imagination to recreate the complexity of real moments, big and small, with no invented rapes or houses burning down. If the challenge intrigues you, imaginatively and emotionally, and you find the right voice—one savvy and appealing enough to make the reader say, "Yes. I've been there. I know what you mean!"—you have something good. But if the voice you adopt annoys, embarrasses or bores because of lack of insight, then beware. The reader will say, "So what? I don't care about you!" often in anger.[1]

It's that personal, the judgment. It's YOU, not some anonymous character they are talking about. Like a smile at a cocktail party, the voice of memoir—far more than in fiction—can evoke a quick response. Phony or real. I like this person. I hate this person. Nothing lukewarm or impersonal about it.

---

[1]James Woolcott's recent article, "Me, Myself and I," in *Vanity Fair* is a good example of that anger. He attacks Anne Roiphe as "the true queen of the daytime soaps," Creative Nonfiction as "civic journalism for the soul," and others like Laurie Stone as "navel gazers"— as if the person, genre and subject ("no detail is too mundane to share") and not the art sinks the "I" of true stories.

That vulnerability—more than a bad memory, I suspect—makes many agree with writer Pam Houston: "I write fiction to tell the truth." The seeming anonymity of fiction, even autobiographical fiction, can be creatively freeing, as Jamaica Kincaid shows in *Annie John*. She makes her real-life, older brothers disappear so that the emotional focus is on a girl and her mother, and she calls the story fiction—even though other basics are true. (Kincaid, like the main character, Annie, grew up on the island of Antigua and left at 17.) But if your story is really about Mom in Iowa, why turn her into a half-sister in New York—unless in the transformation, you, like Kincaid, tap into the real story you need to tell?

One essay, out of the 25 I just finished reading, does hook me with its savvy. This young woman of 22, Nicole Ross, already knows what it has taken me years to figure out: that the ambiguity of memoir, its shifting planes of truth and memory, can take you somewhere important:

> I want to remember a childhood brimming with sunlight, with just enough suffering to make it seem real. Each Christmas becomes bleaker than the last; it always seems as if there are fewer presents under the tree, and less laughter as my grandparents grow older. Ironically, the Christmases of my childhood have become lavish feasts of endless caroling because I don't remember them any more. I think that my collection of memories is nothing more than a soothing deception; many details have been supplied by a fertile imagination. It can't be all bad, though, because my parents still smile at me the way they do in my memories of those early Christmases.

Unlike Anna, Nicole is comfortable with how memory, fact and imagination mix up her Christmases; she trusts the process. I wrote "Great!" in every margin of her six pages. I believed every word, heard the caroling, saw her parents smile.

There *is* one reason not to write memoir, aside from worries about memory and the restraints on creative freedom: Mom may not speak to you again if you write her story, and you care. Frank McCourt waited to publish his memoir until after his mother died because he didn't want to hurt her. Others don't wait and call their story fiction, so they can tell Mom, family, friends, anyone real who appears on the page: "Of course that isn't you. I made that part up." No one is fooled, but you save face, maybe a lawsuit.

A writer does have some fictive leeway even in memoir, I believe—*if* you are cautious (and not too famous). Tomorrow I will tell the student who wrote about her bulimic roommate that her profile could be just as powerful and less hurtful if she moved the girl next door, changed her hair color and did not call her Kimmie.[2] I will tell the class that in a memoir about six months in my marriage, I made a few composite characters of minor characters and wrote this disclaimer in

---

[2]This anonymity is essential if, like me, you have students share their work in progress in class. Why should the roommate's problems become public knowledge?

my introduction: "The story is 90 percent factual; the rest is made up to protect those who didn't ask to be in this book." The problem was not my husband and my children (I was willing to take my chances with them); it was my friends, like the one who was leaving her husband just as I was deciding to stay with mine. In fact, I had three friends who were thinking about divorce, so in the book, I made a composite character and we met for cappuccino.

Depending on the story's focus, you sometimes collapse time and characters as well, I will tell my students, and still are "true" on my truth scale. Writer Jack Connor, in a personal essay about a weekend of watching eagles, collapsed three days into one morning and mentioned only two of the four students who accompanied him on that trip. He wanted to capture how young people reawakened in him the simple pleasure of birding even in a mid-January freeze, and the number of days, the number of people, didn't matter—although in a scientific field report they would. I will show my students how his original journal entry of facts and private observations evolved many drafts later into a published story ("A Lesson from Mott's Creek") with a voice and a point of view.

Journal Entry:

> 1/11/94   —eagle weekend—
> one of the best birding experiences of the last year this weekend—the eagle survey with Jerry Liguori, Brian Sullivan, two folks from Ocean City (mcdermotts?), and on Sunday with Joe Mangion and Bil Seng.
>   . . . both days cold—and windy. temp in teens, with wind chill, probably below 10, maybe even bordering on zero. but blue sky, growing cloudy on saturday around one and then mostly cloudy. Sunday, blue until 2 or so and only partly cloudy after that. . . .

Essay Opening:

> "Binoculars in my fingers, tears in my eyes from the January glare, face stiff from the hard wind, I am standing between Brian Sullivan and Jerry Liguori and wonder, "Why don't I come out here every single day?"

I will also tell my students about a friend who is writing about her aunt who had a lobotomy 50 years ago. My friend visited the mental institution where it happened, looked up records, talked to a nurse and doctor who remembered her aunt and tried writing what her aunt's life was like. But those "facts" weren't enough to recreate the story. She must take an imaginative leap, our writing group told her, imagine herself as her aunt and what would it feel like, maybe write in first person. Draft in hand, my friend can then check with a psychiatrist—"Does this ring true?"—and with relatives, before revising for more accuracy.

The Joan Didions and John Irvings in tomorrow's class will nod their heads in agreement. The Anna Quindlens will not. They want clear-cut boundaries and would side with my writer friend, Andrea Herrmann, who warns me: "If the writer can make a composite character, what prevents her from making up scenes, blending parts of places together, switching historical time frames?" Making up anything, for them, is crossing the line into fiction and should be called that. But I disagree. If the main plot, characters, and setting are true, if the intent is to make honest sense of "how it felt to me" and tell that true story well (with disclaimers as needed), it's memoir to me.

In "Why Memoir Now?" Vivian Gornick writes, "What happened to the writer is not what matters; what matters is the larger sense that the writer is able to make of what happened. For that the power of a writing imagination is required." Use that imagination in memoir, I tell myself and my students, to find the language and complexity of real lives, not imagined ones. It's OK to trust yourself (with a bit of Quindlen's and Herrmann's wariness)—even if you can't remember the temperature on the night Mom died.

Prose Poems, Paragraphs, Brief Lyric Nonfiction

Peggy Shumaker

Brief pieces of prose, meant to stand on their own, capture our attention via compression. In *Short Takes,* the entries range from a couple of hundred words to a couple of thousand—leaving little space for grand exposition or lengthy character development. And yet the pieces in this volume compel us with their intensity, sustain us with their impact.

Mark Spragg, a novelist and memoirist accustomed to the expanse of three hundred pages, becomes a lyric poet for the two and a half pages of "In Wyoming." His gritty prose becomes an ode to the unforgiving land and weather of this mostly wild place. "This place is violent, and it is raw," Spragg writes. "Wyoming is not a land that lends itself to nakedness, or leniency. There is an edge here, living is accomplished on that edge."

This hymn to harshness sings. Spragg says, "There are precious few song-birds. Raptors ride the updrafts. The hares, voles, mice, skunks, squirrels, rats, shrews, and rabbits exist squinting into sun and wind, their eyes water, their hearts spike in terror when swept by the inevitable shadow of predators. The meadowlark is the state's bird, but I think of them as hors d' oeuvres, their song a dinner bell."

An ode in prose, Spragg's piece ends like this, ". . . I remain alert. In Wyoming, the price of innocence is high. There is a big wind out there, on its way home to our high plains."

Spragg's few words scour us, our faces tight against the wind. We know we'll end up like the bison whose bones have fallen to earth, bleached rose then white, then fallen finally to dust. This brief piece takes on how it's possible to live in extremity, how it's possible to live, period. What's come before us, what will endure, and the certainty of mortality—all these ideas whip through this piece, cutting as stiff winds.

Naomi Shihab Nye takes on big questions by focusing in on matters of daily life—the only kind we live. In *Mint Snowball,* her book of paragraphs, Nye's author's note reads as follows: "I think of these pieces as simple paragraphs rather than 'prose poems,' though a few might sneak into the prose poem category, were they traveling on their own. The paragraph, standing by itself, has a lovely pocket-sized quality. It garnishes the page as mint might garnish a plate. Many people say (foolishly of course) that they 'don't like poetry' but I've never heard anyone say they don't like paragraphs. It would be like disliking five minute increments on the clock."

Her selection in *Short Takes,* "Someone I Love," begins as she gets up at dawn, jetlagged after a long trip, and goes out to water her garden, to feel rooted again to the earth. She's stunned to discover that someone has destroyed her carefully-cultivated patch of primroses, has marched through it with the handmower, slicing down all the buds about to open. "He must have pushed really hard to get it to go," Nye tells us. She's distraught, too stricken to speak of her loss. ". . . I will not mention this, I am too sad to mention it, this is the pain this year deserves." That quiet mention of the year, a year of war and upheaval and dehumanizing, throws the whole piece into context. Suddenly we're not talking about a son failing to notice what matters to a mother. Instead we're talking about what gets taken away, how we live with loss, how we live with those who hurt us or our loved ones. In the piece, Nye cannot contain her fury, and goes "a little strange." She confronts her bewildered son. He responds by saying, "I don't notice flower things like that."

Her piece ends this way: "And it was the season of blooming and understanding. It was the season of pulling weeds in other corners, hiding from the headlines, wondering what it would do if the whole house had been erased or just the books and paintings and what about the whole reckless garden or (and then it gets unthinkable but we make ourselves think it now and then to stay human) the child's arms and legs, what would I do? If I did not love him, who would I become?"

Nye, whose relatives have lived in a war zone all their lives, makes peace-making a matter of personal responsibility, a matter of conscience. Her piece asks us, how do we live with those who have taken possessions, land, languages, loved ones from us? Until we learn this, we will not know peace.

My own contribution to the *Short Takes* anthology mixes the lyrical language of poetry with the urgency of a narrative scene. All the poets in this volume give up line breaks. Without that tool so intricate for pacing and emphasis and word-play and rhythms, sentences swell. Watch how varied sentences work—fragments, bits of dialogue, quick exposition, complex rhythms, and the great gush of language flash flooding.

Moving Water, Tucson

Thunderclouds gathered every afternoon during the monsoons. Warm rain felt good on faces lifted to lick water from the sky. We played outside, having sense enough to go out and revel in the rain. We savored the first cool hours since summer hit.

The arroyo behind our house trickled with moving water. Kids gathered to see what it might bring. Tumbleweed, spears of ocotillo, creosote, a doll's arm, some kid's fort. Broken bottles, a red sweater. Whatever was nailed down, torn loose.

We stood on edges of sand, waiting for brown walls of water. We could hear it, massive water, not far off. The whole desert might come apart at once, might send horny toads and Gila monsters swirling, wet nightmares clawing both banks of the worst they could imagine and then some.

Under sheet lightning cracking the sky, somebody's teenaged brother decided to ride the flash flood. He stood on wood in the bottom of the ditch, straddling the puny stream. "Get out, it's coming," kids yelled. "GET OUT," we yelled. The kid bent his knees, held out his arms.

Land turned liquid that fast, water yanked our feet, stole our thongs, pulled in the edges of the arroyo, dragged whole trees root wads and all along, battering rams thrust downstream, anything you left there gone, anything you meant to go back and get, history, water so high you couldn't touch bottom, water so fast you couldn't get out of it, water so huge the earth couldn't take it, water. We couldn't step back. We had to be there, to see for ourselves. Water in a place where water's always holy. Water remaking the world.

That kid on plywood, that kid waiting for the flood. He stood and the water lifted him. He stood, his eyes not seeing us. For a moment, we all wanted to be him, to be part of something so wet, so fast, so powerful, so much bigger than ourselves. That kid rode the flash flood inside us, the flash flood outside us. Artist unglued on a scrap of glued wood. For a few drenched seconds, he rode. The water took him, faster than you can believe. He kept his head up. Water you couldn't see through, water half dirt, water whirling hard. Heavy rain weighed down our clothes. We stepped closer to the crumbling shore, saw him downstream smash against the footbridge at the end of the block. Water held him there, rushing on.

Every time I read this piece, someone in the audience asks, "Did he live?" That tells me that 400 words are enough to create a character people can care about, and to tell a story convincing enough so that they want the next piece. The language has drawn them in, as surely as kids standing on the bank of an arroyo spellbound by dangerous floods.

The compression of the brief form, completely familiar to poets and to those who read poetry, gains a fine elasticity in nonfiction. Tone can range from somber to whimsical, lament to praise. Anything writers can do with long forms has parallels in brief forms.

Finding the Inner Story in Memoirs and Personal Essays

Michael Steinberg

The comment I find myself making most frequently to my students and to many of the writers who submit personal narratives to *Fourth Genre* is, "The main thing that's missing in this piece is *your story*." You're probably thinking, here comes another endorsement of those confessional narratives—the ones that give creative nonfiction a bad name. Actually, one of the reasons why I think we're seeing too many of those pieces is because a lot of nonfiction writers are narrating *only* the literal story of their experience, and leaving out the "inner story"; that is, the story of their thinking.

Let me give you a personal example. A while ago, I wrote a memoir called "Trading Off." It was about a four-year struggle I had with a high school coach who might or might not have been anti-Semitic. While I was writing it, I was trying to recall the shame I felt and the humiliation I allowed myself to put up with—both of which, I discovered, were the price I paid for wanting to play baseball for this punitive coach. At readings, whenever I introduce the piece as a baseball memoir, I watch the expressions on the faces of several of the women in the audience. Some roll their eyes, some cross their arms, some even grimace. To them, it's another baseball story, about some poor kid's bad experience with a mean-spirited coach—the kind of jock story their boyfriends or husbands may have told them over and over again.

It doesn't always happen that way, but often enough by the time I've finished reading the piece, the audience's body language has changed. Some people, men and women alike, have figured out that the memoir isn't really about baseball. Baseball is the setting, the stage for the conflict between the young boy and the coach. The coach is the gatekeeper and the narrator wants more than anything else at 13 to pitch for the high school baseball team. But the more interesting and important story is what goes on in the mind of the narrator as he agonizes over how badly he wants this, at the same time as he's questioning his decision to put up with this coach's tactics.

What he repeatedly asks himself throughout the memoir is "Why am I doing this?" Indeed, why *is* he doing it? What makes him so determined, and so desperate? And how much humiliation is he willing to put up with in order to make the team? Quite a bit, it seems. That's why I titled the memoir "Trading Off."

Often, during the question-and-answer period, or after the reading, some of the same people who initially resisted the piece will tell me their own stories about humiliating experiences they've had with similar kinds of gatekeepers: punitive teachers, abusive parents, cruel childhood friends, and so on. A woman once volunteered that the memoir reminded her of her own teenage struggle with a harsh and demanding ballet teacher.

That's exactly the kind of response I hope for. I don't want the reader to come away from the memoir thinking that it's another "poor, poor, pitiful me" story. I want the reader to feel the humiliation and shame that I did, as well as to understand that I willingly chose to make this tradeoff in order to prove myself to this hard-nosed coach.

But, I doubt that readers—especially the skeptical ones—would have been able to make those personal connections had I written only the literal "here's what happened to me" story.

In her book *The Situation and the Story: The Art of Personal Narrative*, Vivian Gornick makes this same point when she writes, "Every work [of literature] has both a situation and a story. The situation is the context or circumstance, sometimes the plot; the story is the emotional experience that preoccupies the writer: the insight, the wisdom, the thing one has come to say" (13).

When I teach workshops in personal narrative, most students bring memoirs. At *Fourth Genre,* over 75 percent of our submissions are memoirs. There are as many different reasons or impulses for writing a memoir as there are memoirists; some write to tell their story; some write to preserve a family history; some simply want to reminisce.

When I teach the form, I'm always urging my students to go beyond or probe beneath the literal story. My own editor for the memoir I'm currently writing is always challenging me to "dig deeper," to write, as she describes it, "more vertically."

I nudge my students, as well as myself, to examine why they're telling this particular story, and why it matters enough to write about it. How, I ask them, did this experience shape you? How did it change you? What were the costs? What was at stake? What, in other words, is compelling you to write the piece? Hopefully, these will all be discovered in the process of writing.

I also advise writers to think about memoir as having two stories: the story of the actual experience—the surface subject, the facts, the sequence of remembered events (what Gornick calls "the situation"), and the story of their thinking—that is, what do those facts and events mean? What are you thinking and feeling as you write the specific scenes? What I'm really asking the writer is: How do *you* interpret the story of your own experience?

A memoir, then, can have more than one voice. Sometimes it must. There's the voice that tells the surface story, and another, more reflective voice that comments, digresses, analyzes, and speculates about the story's events—in other words, a voice or narrative persona that looks to find a human connection or larger meaning in his/her personal experience.

Everything I've said about finding the inner story in memoir comes from reading, writing, and reading about personal essays. Since one of the hallmarks of the personal essay is its intimacy, most personal essays are inner explorations that open a window to the writer's inner life.

Scott Russell Sanders says that the "essay is the closest thing we have, on paper, to a record of the individual mind at work and play . . . the spectacle of a single consciousness making sense of part of the chaos' of experience." (189–90). The essay works by "following the zigzag motions of the inquisitive mind. . . . The writing of an essay is like finding one's way through a forest, without being quite sure what game you are chasing, what landmark you are seeking."

Working in the essay form, according to Phillip Lopate, "allows you to ramble in a way that reflects the mind at work . . . [I]n an essay, the track of a person's thoughts struggling to achieve some kind of understanding of a problem is the plot, the adventure. The essayist must be willing to contradict himself . . . to digress, and even to end up in an opposite place from where he started. . . . The essay offers the chance to wrestle with one's own intellectual confusion" (qtd. in Heilker 93).

The late critic and memoirist Alfred Kazin says, "The genuine essayist . . . [i]s the writer who thinks his way through the essay—and so comes out where perhaps he did not wish to. . . . He uses the essay as an open form—as a way of thinking things out for himself, as a way of discovering what he thinks. . . . [A]n essay is not meant to be the 'whole truth'. . . . [I]t is an expression of the self thinking" (qtd. in Heilker 90). In an essay, it is not the thought that counts but the experience we get of the writer's thought; not the self, but the self thinking."

In "The End," an essay by Judith Kitchen, she suggests that Kazin's point is the purpose of writing creative nonfiction. "The building of a process of thought," Kitchen says, "is what interests the reader. In essays, we participate by paying attention to the attention that is paid. The intimacy of the essay is a sharing of thought. We look as much for how an author approaches a subject as for the subject itself" (228). Kitchen closes the essay with some useful teaching advice. She writes,

Here are five things my students deny themselves as their stories draw to a close:

1. Retrospection—a looking back, an assessment
2. Intrusion—a stepping in, a commentary
3. Meditation—a thinking through and around, finding a perspective

4. Introspection—a self-examination, honest appraisal and discovery
5. Imagination (as distinct from invention)—which allows for alternatives, projections, juxtapositions, whatever could provide a larger frame (228)

I agree with Kitchen when she says that these are things her students "deny themselves." It's a generous and, I think, accurate way to phrase it. I'll add these others:

- reflection: thinking things out, searching for meaning
- speculation: playing "what if"
- self-interrogation: asking the hard questions, the ones you don't always want to know the answers to
- digression: allowing the mind to wander away from the subject
- projection: trying to predict what might happen.

There are many other touchstones we could all add. But the point is that in any· human situation or encounter, we can't get through 30 seconds without utilizing most or all of these things. We're *always* reacting internally.

The mind never stops searching for connections and asking questions. And that's the thinking/feeling self I'd like to see more of in the personal narratives I read, both as a teacher and as an editor.

Works Cited

Gornick, Vivian. *The Situation and the Story: The Art of Personal Narrative.* New York: Farrar, Straus and Giroux, 2001.

Heilker, Paul. *The Essay: Theory and Pedagogy for an Active Form.* Urbana: NCTE, 1996: 90.

Kitchen, Judith. "The End." *Fourth Genre.* 3:2 (Fall 2001): 228–234.

Sanders, Scott Russell. "The Singular First Person,"*Secrets of the Universe: Scenes from the Journey Home.* Boston: Beacon, 1991. 187–204.

Experimental Critical Writing

Marianna Torgovnick

At the 1988 MLA Convention I gave a paper called "Malinowski's Body." Since I was afraid to give this paper, I had announced it in the program by the deliberately neutral title "Looking at Anthropologists" so that I could change my mind up to the last minute and substitute something else instead. I was afraid because "Malinowski's Body" does not resemble the usual MLA paper in style or content. I knew that the audience would listen to it and respond to it, and I knew that some members of the audience would not like it and might even walk out—and not because there was another talk they wanted to hear at the same hour.

"Malinowski's Body" did not begin its life in any of the ways I have been taught to consider legitimate. In fact, I wrote it, almost as a dare, after my writing group found the first material I wrote on Malinowski dull. To prove I could do better I went home and wrote several pages that begin this way:

> Malinowski's body looks like Lord Jim's. It's cased rigidly in white or beige trousers and shirt that sometimes becomes stained a muddy brown. When this happens, Malinowski summons his servants and has the clothes washed, immediately. For his clothes somehow seem to him an important part of his body, not just a covering for it.
>
> It's a small body, well fed but not kindly disposed enough toward itself to put on flesh. It has a narrow chest—pale, with just a few hairs and no nipples to speak of. It has thin legs yearning for massive thighs; in fact, if this man does put on weight in later life (and he may) it will show in his thighs first. The buttocks lie flat, unwelcoming, with maybe a stray pimple. The penis is a center of anxiety for him but is in fact no smaller—and no bigger—than anyone else's. It's one of the few points of identification he can settle on between his body and theirs.
>
> Their bodies—almost naked—unnerve him. His body needs its clothes; his head, its hat. He rarely looks at his body—except when washing it. But he has to look at theirs. The dislike he sometimes feels for the natives comes over

him especially when in the presence of their bodies. "Come in and bathe," the natives say from their ponds and rivers. "No, thanks," says Malinowski, retrieving the pith helmet and camera he momentarily laid aside on the grass. He looks at their bodies and takes notes about size, ornamentation, haircuts, and other ethnographic data. He takes photographs. He talks to them about customs, trade, housing, sex. He feels okay about the customs, trade, and housing, but the sex makes him uneasy.

The pages are based on an intuition and a hunch about what Malinowski looked like that were formed before I had found any pictures of him. They begin with an image rather than with the kind of concise generalization that had been my customary opening. And they were designed to loosen my prose by giving my imagination free play. Inevitably, I used what I had read by and about Malinowski—but in an almost unrecognizable way. My premise was that I would undress the ethnographer for study as Malinowski himself undresses subjects in his ethnographies and undresses, in his diary, the women he meets in daily life. When I wrote "Malinowski's Body" I did not intend to use it in the book I was writing. My goals were simply to limber up my style and to get in touch with what I wanted to say. But "Malinowski's Body" makes so many points about the ethnographer's scripting of himself according to conventional ideas of what is moral and manly that I decided to include it in my book. It is a creative piece, risky for the MLA. And yet my audience, or at least most of its members, seemed delighted. They asked questions about my "intentions" and "effects" that made me feel like a writer, not just a critic—a heady moment for me and a reception that gave David Laurence reason to invite me to present my thoughts on experimental critical writing. And it was a moment that had not come easily.

When I began to write my newest book—called *Gone Primitive* and published in the spring of 1990—I knew that I wanted to write something significantly different in tone and style from my first two books. I had recently been tenured and then promoted to full professor, and I felt that I was no longer writing for any committees—I was writing for myself. It was not that I would rewrite the books I had written; I am in fact proud of them. What I wanted was to reach a larger audience and to go somewhere new. What I discovered was that at first I did not know how.

The turning point came when I showed an early chapter to the members of my newly formed writing group. I was writing on an untraditional, uncanonical topic—Edgar Rice Burroughs' Tarzan novels—but my approach was conventional and scholarly. I began by surveying the critical literature on Tarzan and protesting (a little uneasily) that earlier critics either had overidentified with Burroughs or had not taken Tarzan seriously with regard to race and gender relations. I tried to pack lots of statistics and facts in the opening paragraphs to prove that Tarzan was important. In my eagerness to meet accepted standards of academic seriousness, I had succeeded (to borrow a phrase Wayne Booth once used to describe the freshman essay) in being "boring from within."

The members of my group, from whom I had asked no mercy that day, showed none. The chapter was sluggish, they said; the prose was lifeless and cold. It had no momentum, no narrative. Instinctively, I defended myself; I talked about all the interesting things that happened as I was researching and writing the chapter, telling them how I often found articles on the rebirth of the Tarzan phenomenon in issues of magazines that report the assassination of President Kennedy and reproduce those astonishing pictures we all remember of Jackie and little John-John and of Oswald. I had tried in the chapter to place the Tarzan series in the contexts of the twenties (the decade of its first great popularity) and the sixties (the decade of its rebirth). But I had used a style that censored my own experiences and visceral responses and that hid my writing's source of energy. One member of the group said, cannily, "You know, none of what you've just said comes out in this chapter. And there's a huge difference between the things you say and the things you write. You never write anything funny. You often say funny things." She was right. The other members of the group asked me to say more about La, a barbarian priestess in the Tarzan novels whom I had mentioned in passing. As I warmed to my description of La's importance and La's wrongs, my friend said, "When you start to get dull, pretend you are La—because you *are* La." And she was also right.

For me, "writing like La" became a metaphor for getting to a place where I was not afraid to write in a voice that had passion as well as information—a voice that wanted to be heard. "Writing like La" meant letting myself out of the protective cage of the style I had mastered—a style I now call the thus-and-therefore style because it naturally tends to include distancing words like those. Before I could change my thus-and-therefore style, I had to defamiliarize it; I had to know my cage so that I could open it at will. A fifteen-minute exercise I did with my writing group was a significant breakthrough. In this exercise, I parodied my own dullest style in a description of grocery stores in Durham, North Carolina. I began the description with just the kind of generalization that was one of my primary tics as a writer: "In Durham, one can shop at Food Lion for bargains, or Kroger's for selection. The most interesting shopping of all, however, is done at Harris Teeter." This exercise made me laugh at my own habits and made it impossible for me afterward to write unknowingly in my usual way. But there were still many low points, when I found myself unable to do anything *but* write in my dullest style. In fact, I wrote my excruciatingly bad beginning on Malinowski— the material I replaced with "Malinowski's Body"—roughly eighteen months after I vowed to leave my old style behind.

In preparing this presentation, I discovered in my files my first draft on Malinowski. I would like to share part of its beginning with you as an example of one sort of standard academic prose:

> Implicitly, I have been suggesting that "objectivity" is a delusory principle undergirding both important strands of social scientific and ethnographic thought and aesthetic and artistic-literary theories and methods. Rereading Malinowski, I think I've found a direct and interesting analogy.

Malinowski founded what is called functionalism in anthropology, the theory (and derived method) that explains all elements of a culture in terms of interlocking functions: the ethnographer explicitly "constructs" a model in which all the parts are presumed to contribute to a whole that is organic and unified (though quirkier than a machine). To make his construction, the ethnographer lives inside the culture, inhabits it as a text. He tries to replicate the native's point of view, which is the ground and touchstone of meaning and "accuracy." Functionalism leads, in anthropology, to what is called structural functionalism and then, later, to structuralism.

A point-by-point analogy with New Criticism and other formal approaches exists. Here too the "student" (critic) inhabits the text, assuming the unity of the parts as a whole and constructing an account of that whole in terms of the interlocking functions of its parts. The original ground of meaning is the author's intentions.

What I was doing in these paragraphs was the writerly equivalent of scratching at a scab. I had to say what was closest to the surface of my mind in order to get rid of that content, in order to discover whether it was useful or not, interesting or not. Sometimes, what I write first as a throwaway turns out to contain the intellectual core of my argument; sometimes, as in this real throwaway, it does not. The difference is usually whether I begin with material that I really care about or with material that I think I should care about. In this instance, I began with critical categories and genealogies of influence that I knew, by training, were considered important—and I trotted them out dutifully. Other critics had scratched these scabs; now it was my turn. The paragraphs include a lot of qualifications and distinctions, often inserted in parenthetical remarks, that would be unlikely to interest anyone but me. Sticky academic language coats the whole—"implicitly," "explicitly," "strand of thought." And I explain things in more detail than most people would want to read.

I would be too embarrassed to reproduce this rejected passage if I did not realize that it's representative of the prose that I—and I suspect many of you—habitually write. For this style typifies a great deal of academic writing. How did it come to be a norm? Largely, I think by establishing itself in an era when less criticism was published and the circle of critics was small enough to allow its members to believe they were contributing to the building of a common edifice. In this construction project all the names could and should be named, like those of contributors on a memorial plaque; Professor Z would build on what Professors X and Y had said in their essays; years later, Professors A and B would come along and add some decorative touches or do major renovations.

All of us who write criticism today wrote dissertations yesterday. And our teachers often tried, and succeeded in handing on what they perceived as the correct—that is, the careful, the judicious, the fair—way to write. But the styles we were taught can't work now in the same way as they worked fifty or even fifteen years ago. No one who gets around to writing a book, or even an essay, ever reads everything that has been written about its subject. Yet we cling to the fiction of completeness and coverage that the academic style preserves. This style protects us, we fondly believe, from being careless or subjective or unfair. It prescribes certain moves to ensure that the writer will stay within the boundaries that the academy has drawn.

Like many people who choose an academic life, I have a fundamental need for approval. I needed approval from my graduate advisers, tenure and promotion committees, and reviewers; I need it from my students and colleagues. It has been crucial for me in the last few years to have a writing group that approved of my new writing style: the group provided a different audience from the one I once imagined as my academic superiors, who judged the material I wrote according to more traditional standards. But I have also become aware that I am now not just someone in need of approval but also someone (like many of you) who gives or withholds approval. When we pass on the academic style to our graduate students or newest colleague, we train them to stay within the boundaries, both stylistically and conceptually. When we encourage experimental critical writing, we do not always know what we will get, but we stimulate the profession to grow and to change. We don't control the future of the profession only when we give grades or make hiring or tenure decisions; we control it at the level of the sentence.

At this point I need to back up a bit. It seems pretty clear to me that if all we want to do is to write for professional advancement, to write for a fairly narrow circle of critics who exist within the same disciplinary boundaries as we do, there is nothing really wrong with the traditional academic style. In fact, it's the right style, the inevitable style, because it says, in every superfluous detail and in every familiar move, You don't need to read me except to write your own project; I am the kind of writing that does not want to be heard.

But when critics want to be read, and especially when they want to be read by a large audience, they have to court their readers. And the courtship begins when the critic begins to think of himself or herself as a writer as well, a process that for me, as for some other critics of my generation, means writing as a person with feelings, histories, and desires—as well as information and knowledge. When writers want to be read they have to be more flexible and take more chances than the standard scholarly style allows: often, they have to be more direct and more personal. In a very real way (although my writing includes precious few autobiographical revelations), I could not think of myself as a writer until I risked exposing myself in my writing.

I am not talking here, necessarily, about full-scale autobiographical writing—though I am not ruling it out either. But I am saying that writerly writing is personal writing, whether or not it is autobiographical. Even if it offers no facts from the writer's life, or offers just a hint of them here and there, it makes the reader know some things about the writer—a fundamental condition, it seems to me, of any real act of communication. And real communication is exciting. For me, at any rate, the experience of this new kind of writing—which not only recognizes the pitfalls of the standard academic style but goes out of its way to avoid them—has been exhilarating.

Part 3

Composing Creative Nonfiction

In the earlier sections of the book you've had the chance to pair up what people write when they write creative nonfiction with what people talk about when they talk about creative nonfiction. Many of the writers whose work appears in Part 1 also talk about the genre in which they work in Part 2. They often also talk about the ways they typically create the work they do in creative nonfiction. In Part 3, we take the discussion a little farther by pairing three pieces that could have gone in the first part of the book with three pieces in which their authors describe how they wrote them.

Writers' descriptions of what they did and what they went through as they wrote a particular essay or article often suggest strategies that other writers can use. Even the most experienced writers occasionally find themselves stymied by a project they've been working on, but, because they *are* experienced, they have strategies to fall back on which help them to begin writing again. Often their strategies arise not from their own problem solving but by the example of another writer. For example, many writers in many different forms have subscribed to Horace's advice, "Never a day without a line." They try to write every day, even if only for a limited time, because they find there is a creative equivalent of the law of inertia—"A mind in motion tends to stay in motion; a pen at rest tends to stay at rest." To that perhaps they add Hemingway's advice to quit writing for the day before you've exhausted your energy and your ideas and to return to writing the next day knowing where you're going to start up again. There are many sound principles and practices in the creative life, and writers often have to rummage among them for the ones that work for them. They also have to be prepared to discard them if they aren't working or if they don't seem to be very useful for a different project. Writers have to be flexible and adaptable in order to be productive, and the best place to find useful strategies and techniques other than those you discover for yourself is in the discoveries that other writers have made for themselves.

Even when writers have been successful in the past and would appear to know a number of moves they might make in their writing, they sometimes need to be reminded of the things they already know about writing. Sometimes the

430 PART 3 COMPOSING CREATIVE NONFICTION

press of a work-in-progress makes it difficult to step back from it and apply alternative approaches, until the writer stumbles on something someone else did and remembers that he or she knew about that approach before. Some writers collect quotes about writing and, to help them remember, tape them to the wall or the word processor—some writers have *a lot* of stuff sticking to their wall, because there's *a lot* of relevant advice out there.

Consider this section, then, as a way to see what other writers have done as they wrote the kind of writing you've been reading in this book. Taken as a whole, the Composing Creative Nonfiction section presents three pairs of essays, arranged alphabetically by author. The first piece in each pair is the work that serves as the focus of the second piece, which explains the writer's composing processes on that particular work. Reading all six pieces together is like sitting in on a writing group where each member reads something she's written and then explains what she went through to get the final draft. The writing is different enough that the responses of the writers and the shifting demands of purpose and form offer a range of strategies and creative decisions. Emily Chase's "Warping Time with Montaigne" is a personal critical essay linking the practices of Montaigne, the original essayist, with those of contemporary writer Richard Rodriguez in his essay "Late Victorians"; her "Notes from a Journey toward 'Warping Time'" explains how this piece of what Marianna Torgovnick calls "experimental critical writing" came about. Mary Elizabeth Pope's "Teacher Training" is an essay running in two parallel strands, one about her first teaching experience, the other about her fourth-grade teacher; "Composing 'Teacher Training'" follows the development of the essay from inception to publication, including changes after the piece was accepted. Maureen Stanton writes a very personal memoir of her fiancé's illness in "Zion" and recounts how she composed the essay in "On Writing 'Zion'." Four very different essays, four very different composing processes.

The selections here also connect to pieces in other parts of the book, and they can be read separately, in conjunction with other examples and discussions. Emily Chase's work is related to other pieces employing personal voice in cultural criticism, such as those of Chet Raymo and Richard Rodriguez in Part 1 or Sonya Huber-Humes in Part 2. Mary Beth Pope's writing can handily supplement the segmented essays in the book, especially those that leap lightly across time and space, like that of Mary Clearman Blew and Christine White. Maureen Stanton's memoir is appropriate to read along with any of the other memory pieces in the book as well as the essay dwelling on the human body by Phillip Lopate. Already in trying to cite a few relevant examples we've begun to repeat references, but that's because the writing in Part 3 reverberates in so many other readings throughout the book.

The other connection these selections make is, of course, to your writing. The process pieces here, where the writers describe composing their essays, don't prescribe failsafe procedures to which you should conform—quite the contrary. As these examples show, writers don't follow a rigid set of universal rules for composing; instead, they rely on general approaches and alternative strategies that they can alter to fit the shape of their individual works-in-progress. The experiences of these writers suggest strategies that you might be able to adapt to your own projects. They would be valuable to consult when you find yourself beginning or developing similar writing projects.

Finally, as you compose your own essays and assignments, you might consider keeping a journal on your own composing processes, to get a handle on what you generally do when you write and what you've done especially for certain projects. Think of Composing Creative Nonfiction as sitting in on a writing group in session, and feel free to enter the conversation with your own writing about your own composing.

Warping Time with Montaigne

Emily D. Chase

I sit bent over the breast beam of my 38 inch LeClerc floor loom pulling individual threads of brilliant, durable yarn through the metal heddles of its six harnesses. The heddles that have already been threaded hang in orderly lines waiting for the command to raise and lower those threads of yarn in the process of creating fabric; the unthreaded heddles hang in unorganized clusters patiently waiting for their turn to take part. This threading process is called "warping the loom" because the yarn that is being threaded onto the loom will become the "warp"—or lengthwise threads—in the fabric that will be woven. This process of reaching through the heddle with the threading hook, catching a strand of yarn, and pulling it back through the heddle does not require a lot of thought, other than that required to make sure the right piece of yarn gets threaded through the right heddle. My mind is free to wander as it will while I prepare my loom. "My style and my mind alike go roaming," Montaigne said (761). Of course I think of Montaigne; I have just spent two weeks reading essays by Montaigne, about Montaigne, and about essayists who have written essays on Montaigne. I have Montaigne on the brain: What sort of essays would Montaigne write if he were still alive? What would he say about the essays being written today? In particular, what would he say about Richard Rodriguez's essay "Late Victorians"? I pull a strand of yarn through a heddle and think of Montaigne and Rodriguez.

Rodriguez's essay uses many of the elements of the genre that Montaigne created. If Montaigne had not spun the first ideas of the essay into a new genre of literature, Rodriguez would not have been able to write "Late Victorians" without first spinning the thread of the genre on his own. I see that Montaigne's thoughts and ideas have been pulled through time to be used as the warp of essays since Montaigne's book *Essais* was first published in 1580. Now I am the one sitting at the loom of time, pulling the thoughts and ideas of Montaigne through the heddles. The full body of Montaigne's essays lies rolled up upon itself on the warp beam of the loom, waiting to be used by anyone with the knowledge and patience to thread it through time and secure it to this side of the past.

I reach through the eyelet of a heddle for a piece of Montaigne and imagine Rodriguez doing the same thing as he created "Late Victorians." For, certainly, he pulled Montaigne's motto through time—"Que scais-je?" (What do I know?). Rodriguez explores this question in "Late Victorians" as he asks himself how he should live his life and how he should *have lived* his life. These are the central questions and themes of his essay. He asks himself if he should have pursued "an earthly paradise charming," like the gay men he has known who have since died of AIDS (131). He considers the possibility of having pursued a career in office buildings which "were hives where money was made, and damn all" (128). At the end of "Late Victorians," he questions his future: Should he remain shifting his "tailbone upon the cold, hard pew," or should he rise to join the volunteers of the local AIDS Support Group (134)?

The genre of the essay offers Rodriguez an opportunity to explore these issues by using Montaigne's question, "What do I know?" Montaigne says:

> This . . . happens to me: that I do not find myself in the place where I look; and I find myself more by chance encounter than by searching my judgment. I will have tossed off some subtle remark as I write. Later I have lost the point so thoroughly that I do not know what I meant; and sometimes a stranger has discovered it before I do. If I erased every passage where this happens to me, there would be nothing left of myself. (26–27)

The form of the essay as Montaigne conceived it allows Rodriguez the freedom to seek answers, or to appear to seek answers, *while* he writes rather than exclusively *before* he writes. For Montaigne, writing was an *essai*, a trial or attempt. The presence of self and the absence of conclusion create a sense of freedom within Montaigne's essays. As he says: "The surest thing, in my opinion, would be to trace our actions to the neighboring circumstances, without getting into any further research and without drawing from them any other conclusions" (241). Like Montaigne, Rodriguez comes to no irrefutable conclusions in "Late Victorians." Instead, his thoughts wander through memories and observations as he seeks an understanding of the world by examining the things which touch his life directly.

As I consider the themes of "Late Victorians," I think of the title of one of Montaigne's essays, "By diverse means we arrive at the same end" (3). It occurs to me that this title describes the realm in which Rodriguez's thoughts wander. For what is Rodriguez writing about but diverse lifestyles and inevitable death? Running across his essay are the threads of gay life and death from AIDS. The texture of the weave is enhanced by Rodriguez's use of details from his own experience; these details form the weft of his essay, the crosswise threads. This weft is beaten into the fabric of "Late Victorians," as the "beater" on a loom locks the warp and weft tightly together by pushing each strand of weft snugly against the preceding strand, creating a cohesive, durable piece of fabric. Rodriguez weaves the fourteen sections of "Late Victorians" in this way, choosing different yarns for the weft of each section to create different textures and density of prose.

The first section is brief and is composed of two conflicting quotes. The first, by St. Augustine, hints at our discontent on earth in our mortal form due to our intuition that we are destined for a better life after death. Life is something to be restlessly passed through. The second quote, by Elizabeth Taylor, speaks of "cerulean" days in this life being undermined by sadness in the knowledge that these days and this life must end. These quotes show that, like Proteus, we are able to change our shape (the shape of our thoughts) as we try to avoid being bound by life. We are free to choose which way we will view life, whether we will suffer life and rejoice the end or embrace life and mourn the end. In "Late Victorians," Rodriguez tries to decide which view is the better view. He weaves these two quotes into his text to prepare us for the creation which is to follow. What is life? What is death? Which one wears the mask covering reality?

Throughout the essay, Rodriguez portrays the paradox of homosexual life in San Francisco. He uses the image of the Victorian house to help him accomplish this. By noting that the "three- or four-story Victorian house, like the Victorian novel, was built to contain several generations and several classes under one roof, behind a single oaken door" (123), he reveals the irony of the housing market whereby "gay men found themselves living with the architectural metaphor for family" (122). From this image, Rodriguez goes exploring through the homosexual landscape of his life and discovers multiple conflicting images. Rodriguez says, "The age-old description of homosexuality is of a sin against nature," yet he observes that as the peaceful, domestic, homosexual community of the Castro district thrived, the perverted "assortment of leather bars . . . outlaw sexuality . . . eroticism of the dark" on heterosexual Folsom street also thrived (124–25). In the Castro district, thanks to gays, "where recently there had been loudmouthed kids, hole-in-the-wall bars, [and] pimps," there were now "tweeds and perambulators, matrons and nannies" (125). The gay men, who have chosen to embrace "the complacencies of the barren house," have made the streets safe once again for the family (127).

This depiction of peaceful homosexual life is strikingly linked to another paradox of gay life as Rodriguez describes two parades in which gay men with AIDS march for gay rights. Rodriguez depicts gay men in one Gay Freedom Day parade as "the blessed in Renaissance paintings," martyrs who cherish "the apparatus of [their] martyrdom" (119). This passage is followed immediately by a description of a parade five years later, which includes "plum-spotted young men." The juxtaposition of the two passages creates the disturbing impression that these people are fighting to choose the way they wish to die rather than the way they wish to live.

How is Rodriguez going to reconcile all of these conflicting images? I pull another strand of Montaigne through time and see that the essay, as a form, allows Rodriguez to go exploring without *having* to reconcile these images. Montaigne says in his essay "Of repentance":

> This is a record of various and changeable occurrences, and of irresolute and, when it so befalls, contradictory ideas: whether I am different myself, or whether I take hold of my subjects in different circumstances and aspects. So, all in all, I may indeed contradict myself now and then; but truth, as Demades said, I do not contradict. If my mind could gain a firm footing, I would not make essays; I would make decisions; but it is always in apprenticeship and on trial. (611)

Montaigne is speaking of his contradictory thoughts and ideas, and yet the passage is equally applicable to Rodriguez's treatment of the paradox of gay life.

Montaigne's passage makes me wonder, as I slowly and steadily thread my way across the loom, if ALL of Montaigne is present in the warp of Rodriguez's essay. Would all of Montaigne's writings have to be threaded through time as an inseparable skein of thought, in order to remain true as a body of writing? Or could a person be selective when choosing which parts she pulled through time? I think of the warp on my loom, and I know that it is not possible to thread just part of a warp through the heddles. ALL of the strands of warp must be threaded, or the warp becomes tangled and knotted on the loom. For this reason, I have to think that all of Montaigne's thoughts are present in the warp of an essay, even when an essay presents an opposing view of that held by Montaigne.

I ponder this question because of the way I have linked Montaigne's quote from his essay "Of repentance" to the image of the AIDS victims in the Gay Freedom Day parades. The quote is pertinent as it applies to the issue of contradictions and paradox, yet Montaigne and Rodriguez do not agree completely on the actual subject of repentance. Both Montaigne and Rodriguez recognize the value of youth and of what is often deemed youth's foolishness. Rodriguez says:

> Though I am alive now, I do not believe that an old man's pessimism is truer than a young man's optimism simply because it comes after. There are things a young man knows that are true and are not yet in the old man's power to recollect. (120)

This is similar to a passage of Montaigne's, in his essay "Of repentance" in which he says:

> I should be ashamed and resentful if the misery and misfortune of my decrepitude were to be thought better than my good, healthy, lively, vigorous years, and if people were to esteem me not for what I have been, but for ceasing to be that. (619)

On the issue of repentance itself, however, Montaigne and Rodriguez differ. While Montaigne declares, "If I had to live over again, I would live as I have lived" (620), Rodriguez says, "It was then I saw that the greater sin against heaven was my unwillingness to embrace life" (132). There is an edge of repentance in Rodriguez's text, which does not exist in Montaigne's writings.

We are never sure, however, of what it is that Rodriguez feels the need to repent. In boldly talking about the gay community in San Francisco, Rodriguez appears to be revealing himself as a gay man, yet Phillip Lopate says, "Richard Rodriguez, for instance, is a master of the confessional tone, yet he tells us that his family calls him 'Mr. Secrets,' and he plays a hide-and-seek game of revealing himself" (xxvii). This is the case in "Late Victorians." Rodriguez describes the gay community of San Francisco from the perspective of a person who has been a part of that community. He has marched in a Gay Freedom Day parade; he has many male friends who are gay; he lives in a Victorian house which has been reclaimed and redecorated by gay men and now contains "four apartments; four single men"; he says, "To grow up homosexual is to live with secrets and within secrets" (122). And yet, on his deathbed, a friend of Rodriguez's, Cesar, says with irony that Rodriguez "would be the only one spared," that he was "too circumspect" (131). Rodriguez never actually says that he is gay. What are we to think?

I continue the process of pulling strands of yarn and thought through the loom: Does it matter if Rodriguez is gay? Does it matter if he tells us he is or isn't gay? What do I, as a reader, think of the authority of voice in the piece if this information appears to be purposefully concealed? Essayist E. B. White declared, "There is one thing the essayist cannot do—he cannot indulge himself in deceit or in concealment, for he will be found out in no time" (xxvi). And yet Alexander Smith wrote of Montaigne, "If you wish to preserve your secret, wrap it up in frankness" (Lopate xxvii). Montaigne said, "We must remove the mask," but he also said that he has "painted [his] inward self with colors clearer than [his] original ones" (504). Clearly, the act of making one's private thoughts public is not as simple as just recording the observations of one's life or even of simply attempting to capture one's mind in the act of thinking, as Montaigne set out to do.

I look back across the loom at the threads I have pulled through the heddles and am reminded that essays consist of explorations, questions, and contradictions. In his essay "Late Victorians," Rodriguez questions his life and lifestyle. Should he embrace life and mourn death, as his gay friends do, or should he withhold himself from life and look forward to death, as he does in his role as a skeptic? "Skepticism became my demeanor toward them—I was the dinner-party skeptic, a firm believer in Original Sin and in the limits of possibility" (Rodriguez 131). Rodriguez does not find the answer to his question in "Late Victorians." In the essay, he remains shifting his "tailbone on the cold, hard pew" while he tries to decide which role to play—which mask to put on or, perhaps, which mask to take off.

It is the *quest* for answers rather than the answers themselves that distinguishes the Montaignian essay. In this respect, "Late Victorians" is a good example of a contemporary essay that has been woven on a warp of Montaigne. In other respects, such as the inclusion of quotations, the essay differs from those of Montaigne. (Montaigne's essays include numerous quotations, Rodriguez's few.) However, when I gaze across the warp threaded through my loom, I am reminded that even this difference is a tribute to Montaigne, for I see Montaigne's strand of thought that advocates rebellion against accepted forms of discourse, including his own.

It is likely that Montaigne's thoughts go warping through most literary non-fiction essays. This is very different from what Montaigne envisioned when he wrote the preface, "To the Reader," for his book *Essais:*

> I have had no thought of serving either you or my own glory. My powers are inadequate for such a purpose. I have dedicated it to the private convenience of my relatives and friends, so that when they have lost me (as soon they must), they may recover here some features of my habits and temperament, and by this means keep the knowledge they have had of me more complete and alive. (2)

I think of this quote as I pull the last strand of warp through its heddle and secure it to the cloth beam on my side of the loom. My loom is now ready to be used to create a piece of individuality. I wonder what I will create. Shall I weave in some of the texture of Rodriguez or of Reg Saner? Emerson or Ehrlich? The possibilities are endless. I step on a treddle to open the warp, throw my shuttle of weft across the threads, and allow "my style and my mind alike" to go roaming. I have warped my loom with Montaigne.

Works Cited

Lopate, Phillip, ed. *The Art of the Personal Essay.* New York: Anchor Books, 1994.

Montaigne, Michel de. *The Complete Works of Montaigne.* Trans. Donald M. Frame. Stanford: Stanford UP, 1957.

Rodriguez, Richard. "Late Victorians." *The Best American Essays 1991.* Ed. Joyce Carol Oates. New York: Ticknor & Fields, 1991. 119–34.

White, E.B. *Essays of E.B. White.* New York: HarperCollins, 1977.

Notes from a Journey toward "Warping Time"

Emily D. Chase

The path that I took to create the essay "Warping Time with Montaigne" was not a direct path through the writing process. I meandered through personal experiences and through unfamiliar research before I found a thread to connect the two and to help me reach some sort of meaningful understanding of Montaigne and of myself. Since writing that essay, I have noticed that my path through the writing process is almost always indirect and that quite often the meandering path is the most direct way for me to get to insight and understanding. What follows here is essentially a travelogue of my journey toward "Warping Time with Montaigne."

The first time that I heard of Michel de Montaigne was in a course in Graduate Composition. Before that time, the term "essay," to me, was a generic term used by English teachers to refer to short pieces of nonfiction writing. I had no sense of the history of the term or the genre; however, I immediately became interested in Montaigne's writings and therefore decided to write about him for the required research paper in the class. The research paper was written immediately prior to "Warping Time with Montaigne" (the essay included here) and provided me with enough background information to pique my interest and to make me want to have some fun with the information in another piece of writing.

As part of the in-class prewriting for the research paper, I did a cluster/web off of the central term "literary nonfiction." The freewriting that followed the cluster exercise reveals the general direction in which I was drawn:

> Having to research an area of, or a figure in, literary nonfiction, I might like to compare and contrast the original essays everyone quotes—Montaigne, Newman, Emerson, Thoreau—with the modern essayists (especially the nature writers)—Dillard, Ehrlich, Selzer, White—to see if the originals have affected

the moderns. I'd like to find the ties, if any, between personal interaction with nature, religion . . . and the desire to write LNF essays. Part of this study would be taking a look at how each essayist recorded his thoughts (i.e. Thoreau and his journals). Is each day a personal scrutiny of life? an appreciation of being alive? Part of LNF is taking a real daily event and personalizing it by recording your interaction w/it.

But where is this going in terms of research?—Study the masters, study the moderns, draw conclusions. What are people already saying about this link? Has anyone already taken this tack? Is this productive? Is this worthwhile?

I see in this freewrite the idea of not just the original research paper I did on Montaigne but perhaps also the germ of the idea behind "Warping." I never let go of this interest in the correlation between the early essayists and the current essayists.

In just ten days, I discovered a topic and pulled together a reasonable essay about Montaigne and his influence; I used the metaphor of building construction as I discussed the construction of the genre of literary nonfiction upon the foundation of Montaigne's writings. I think better and have more fun writing when I use metaphors to organize and present my thoughts. This fact, no doubt, played a major role in the process that I went through to create the "Warping" essay.

As I was finishing the research paper on Montaigne and just before I began the "Warping" essay, I read Gerald Early's essay "Life with Daughters: Watching the Miss America Pageant" and Jane Tompkins' essay "At the Buffalo Bill Museum." I was overwhelmed by the power of Early's piece, and my original reaction to this essay in my journal reflects this:

> Wow! What an essay! . . . Like a freight train, the fully loaded essay started slowly, exerting effort to overcome inertia, then slowly accumulated speed until it rushed, unstoppably, toward its destination. With Early's final sentence, "My knees had begun to hurt and I realized, painfully, that I was much too old, much too at peace with stiffness and inflexibility, for children's games," the train rushed off the end of the track into the great unknown void of the future. Wow!

By contrast, I did not like Tompkins' essay—or rather I did not understand her essay. My journal reaction to her essay is one long attempt to understand her point; I never do reach that understanding but come to the conclusion that "this is a disturbing piece because I can't see where the author is coming from. I'm not sure a rereading would help." It may seem irrelevant that I read these two essays between writing my two Montaigne essays, yet I think it was crucial that I read as powerful a creative commentary essay as Early's and that I read (and struggled with) Tompkins' essay just as I was directed to write an analysis paper of current literary nonfiction in which I would "explore an individual essay, a series of essays, or a particular author or authors." Both Early and Tompkins use objects and events that they see in their surroundings to launch themselves into realms of contemplation. I must have subconsciously hung onto this technique such that it resurfaced later as I tried to figure out what to do with the analysis assignment.

My initial plans for the analysis paper returned to my interest in the link between Montaigne and the essayists that are writing today. I was still too interested in Montaigne and too convinced of his importance as a crucial element in the genre of literary nonfiction to let go of him. However, we were instructed to comment upon (interpret/analyze) a more current essay. I began to play with possible ways to link Montaigne with current essayists.

On the day that we began working on the analysis paper, I wrote the following prewrite in class:

> Having the chance to write on one element or author in nonfiction, I think I'd like to pursue the elements of Montaigne's essays which can be found in the works of other essayists. Perhaps I could tackle Emerson's essay, "Montaigne," and show how that essay uses Montaignian practices in the process of praising Montaigne. This is a possibility. However, I'd also like to look at Montaigne versus Bacon in terms of voice in the essay and then apply that comparison to critical articles today—(i.e. tackle the 4-woman writers' group who are trying to write "readable" literary criticism [Tompkins, Kaplan, Torgovnik, Davidson]). I'd need to find out if there is much out there in terms of articles/essays on this debate. If *College English* is including these articles now but labeling them as opinion, is anyone reacting to this practice? Is Tompkins? Is Sommers? I think that this could be a much more interesting topic/issue than the piece on Emerson. It would also get me involved in a current intellectual discussion. Having had "Critical Theory" I feel that I have a fairly good base to stand on. Where would Dillard's book, *Living by Fiction,* fit in? or would it? Robert Coles? Who is arguing for Baconian essays in academia? Does Montaigne ever get mentioned in support of personal criticism?—Probably not. But a discussion of Montaigne vs Bacon could be fairly enlightening. I have lots of articles discussing this. I have the background material. I'd just have to dig into the contemporary information. Back to the MLA Bibliography. . . .

I find it interesting as I reread this entry and as I dig through various drafts of the "Warping" essay that one comment I received during a peer editing session of the paper says, "Personally, I think this is better than a lot of the jargon-filled stuff I've read in academic journals." Again, I must have internalized the idea of "readable" criticism such that it resurfaced on its own later in the process.

On the same day that I wrote the above journal entry, as I was beginning work on this final paper, I kept trying to find a way to bring Montaigne into a criticism of a current essay. Because I have watched innumerable episodes of "Star Trek," it did not seem inconceivable to me that one of those hypothetical warps in the space-time continuum could allow Montaigne to suddenly appear in person to comment on the essays being written today. In the preceding research paper, I had already looked at how essayists since Montaigne had used his ideas and examples to help them create their own essays, so it seemed only fair that Montaigne should now have his say about the current essays that are being written.

The word "warp" turned out to be the necessary spark that ignited an inspirational firestorm.

I remember the excitement that I felt when it struck me that the word warp carries a number of different meanings. I had been thinking of the term with a Star Trekian mentality of traveling through time and dimensions of reality, but I am also a weaver, and so as I thought of "warping time," I automatically thought of "warping a loom"—threading a warp onto a loom. After writing the journal entry about Montaigne and Bacon, I jotted down the following notes to myself:

> exciting
> Some ^ thoughts-   "Warping Time: Montaigne on _____"
> & ideas   sitting at loom, threading warp, thinking about
>   assignments/readings
>   critique article in my head by remembering
>   what Montaigne & critics of M.
> this   have said.
> could   get up to pursue details for more specifics
> be   tie in with images of: thread
> really   warp/weaving
> fun!   distorted/warped time
>   structure & patterns & variations of woven cloth
>   lay warp on loom, like laying _____ on M.
>   or like laying M on _____.

In one moment of inspiration, I made the connection between the elements and process of threading a loom and the elements and process of writing an essay. I couldn't wait to start writing; all I needed was a modern essay to interpret in order to fulfill the requirements of the paper assignment.

It is probably important to note here that I had only one week in which to select and interpret a current essay. The title of Richard Rodriguez's "Late Victorians" drew me to his essay, and then his mix of dry humor and deadly seriousness fascinated me. As I read his essay with the warping idea in mind, I began to see Rodriguez as a weaver of essays and the fourteen sections of "Late Victorians" as variations of weft on the same warp. His essay seemed to be the perfect one for me to work with, and I could barely contain myself as I told my editing group about the ideas for my paper. I can still picture my teacher leaning forward on his chair with keen interest as I explained what I envisioned for my paper.

The writing of both my Montaigne papers was aided in large part by exercises and peer editing that were conducted as part of coursework in the Graduate Composition class. The drafting of each paper was preceded by a number of prewriting exercises to generate and organize ideas, and then once the drafting had begun, several different drafts of each paper were shared with a group of fellow students. I was a part of a four person editing group that provided valuable feedback and suggestions for revisions at every step of the drafting and revising process. The interaction of the editing group also tended to nurture creativity and spontaneity that proved to be crucial in the creation of "Warping Time with Montaigne."

Once I had shared my ideas for the paper with my group and with just two days left before my paper was due in class, I wrote the following journal entries as a way of organizing my thoughts and figuring out what I wanted to do with them in my paper:

"Warping time" has the potential to be a really interesting essay. I need to list everything I want to be sure to say about Rodriguez's essay, those quotes of Montaigne's which directly apply to the points I want to make, and, then, the precise affiliations I want to assign to each metaphor of time and the loom. I wish I had more time to work on this.

What are the parts to my metaphor? If the loom = time, the warp = Montaigne, and the weft = Rodriguez, then what is the process of "warping the loom"? Is the threading of Montaigne through the hettles of time, the same as Montaigne's transcendence of time? His thoughts have to be durable enough to stand the strain put on the warp by the tension of the loom as well as the wear of the opening and closing of the shed and the friction of the beater as it swings along Montaigne and locks the weft of Rodriguez's ideas into the grasp of Montaigne's warp, while at the same time the interlocking of Rodriguez into Montaigne creates a brand new unique object formed by the interaction of the inter-working parts of time with the materials of Montaigne and Rodriguez.

The ideas of original thinkers get spun into yarn for warp. Rodriguez's end product is a piece of cloth which is available to the reader to use to make other things such as clothing, blankets, or?

If Montaigne is the warp, what do the 2 ends signify? The first end is the full body of Montaigne wound around itself in its full potential. The end I am threading is his ideas being taken through time to be used in the creation of new essays. 2 steps to trip through time—hettles and dent. What are they? hettles = individual thoughts and quotes (arranged to create potential of a pattern). dent = combining and spacing of ideas to assure a solid, even weave of the new fabric—literature vs nonliterature? Final step is to tie off Montaigne in the present on the cloth beam in order to hang onto his thoughts in the present to enable the creation of new essays.

My thoughts as I thread the loom consider the process Rodriguez went through in the creation of "Late Victorians." As I tie off the warp on my loom, I have secured Montaigne for use in my own creation and I have examined the creation of an accomplished weaver to glean ideas and techniques. I am ready to write—conceivably the result is essay in the reader's hands. How to do that?

Ending—my thoughts pull Montaigne into the present, now I am ready to weave my thoughts into an essay, I step on the treadles to raise the shed, throw the first pass of the shuttle and create, "I sit bent over the breast beam of my 38 inch LeClerc floor loom . . ."

This last journal entry was written after I had begun drafting my paper but before I had figured out how to conclude the essay. I have quoted the first line of the paper, yet my ideas are still just beginning to take form. I had originally planned to create a circular essay in which the ending leads back to the beginning in a never-ending retelling of this process; however, that idea got too confusing to be adequately developed in the limited amount of time that I had and therefore was changed in favor of the current ending.

I had a number of issues that needed to be sorted out as I tried to create a complete draft of the paper; therefore, as a way of figuring out what ideas I wanted to weave into the paper, I entered in my journal the following lists of what I believed were critical points to be dealt with in my paper:

Individual thoughts of Montaigne:

- Que scais-je?
- I want to be seen in simple, natural . . . it is myself I portray
- essai = trial or attempt
- self-portrait vs autobiography
- to be known not remembered
- to follow wanderings of his mind in process of thinking
- my mind & my thoughts . . .
- find self through writing
- loose disconnected structure—mirrors spontaneous thought
- portrait as friendly gesture
- familiar tone
- rebellion against rigid styles, formal language
- absence of dispositio
- sense of honesty

Points from Rodriguez:

- we choose our lifestyles
- sometimes we choose our deaths
- we all die
- wisdom in youth's foolishness
- R. focused on tragedy Cesar—you cannot forbid tragedy
- R. full-time skeptic (131)(121)
- jealousy of responsible of irresponsible
- Victorian house as symbol of family—gay reclaim neighborhood
- new residents, new vision of family (Yuppies—birth control)
- masks (123)(131)
- caustic language (124–5) shock value, coarse cloth
- flipping of normal perspectives
- gays vs feminists
- nakedness (129)
- self-questioning in text (129)
- flowing thoughts (131)
- regret, repentance? (132)(134)

I spent successive late nights in the final week of the class working on this paper, as well as on revisions of other papers from that class. On the day before the final draft of the warping essay was due, my eyes felt unnaturally wide open from too much coffee and too little sleep, and yet still every time I thought about my paper, I felt excited about its possibilities. Not only did I not want to sleep, I knew that I couldn't sleep as long as I had the potentials of the warping metaphor at play in my head. It was with enthusiasm and playfulness, not with fatigue or despair, that I wrote the following journal entry:

> I am making progress on my "Warping" essay, but I have so far to go in the 24 hours I have left before I have to hand in the paper. I realize that I cannot get it into a polished state of existence in that time, but I would like to at least have the skeleton of the complete essay put together with some of the shaping musculature before I hand it in to be graded. I can drape it with the appropriate clothing after that. At this point I have 8 1/2 pages written and I feel as if I am 3/4 of the way through the essay. The essay still seems extremely muddy to me, so I am unable to see clearly the points I am trying to make. I need to sort out *exactly* what I want to say about Rodriguez's essay in order to clarify my essay. From there I need to weave my metaphor of the loom more thoroughly and securely into the piece. The entire piece has the substance of gauze, when I want the density of linsey-woolsey. It is also patched together with scraps of yarn, when I want high quality materials. And so I work on it. It is still fun and exciting to play with this essay. The metaphor of the loom and the warp has *many* possibilities. Time. I need a bigger loom for this project.

The final push through those twenty-four hours produced the tenth draft of the essay "Warping Time with Montaigne."

As with the first Montaigne paper, the beginning of this paper appeared in the first draft and remained largely unchanged throughout the remaining drafts. The rest of the essay changed drastically from draft to draft, and it was not until the eighth draft that I found the conclusion to the paper. The middle of the essay continued to grow and take shape, but the ending remained loose and unfinished. I had a loose collection of quotes and comments at the end of the early drafts that I knew I wanted to fit into the paper somewhere. I tend to do this when I write: I cultivate a garden patch of interesting and related thoughts at the end of whatever I am working on as a way of feeding life into my essay (and as a way of keeping me from forgetting insights I may have along the way). There are wonderful passages in that collection that never made it to the final draft. If I were to revise this paper again, I might try harder to fit them into the essay. At the time I was drafting this paper, though, I didn't have time to fit them in, and so after the essay became complete in the eighth draft, I used the ninth and tenth drafts to polish the language and the metaphor. I was forced to be done polishing when the due date arrived and I needed to submit the paper for a grade.

Looking back upon the process I went through to create "Warping Time with Montaigne" makes me realize that I almost always contain a heightened sense of excitement when I am in the process of learning something new or when

I am playing with language. I love every stage of the writing process because I am at play throughout all of it. Even when I am struggling with a concept or with an adequate way to present a concept, I am excited by the infinite possibilities that present themselves to me. I may procrastinate before I start to write, but once I sit down to write, the rest of the world disappears, or becomes a resource at my beck and call. In this sense, the process I went through when I wrote "Warping Time with Montaigne" is not unlike my normal writing process. It was simply heightened by a metaphor that possessed particularly great potential. As part of my response to a journal prompt that was given at the end of the class asking me to "compare the Research and Analysis papers with the earlier papers in the course (my experience)," I wrote the following passage:

> It was very difficult to make the transition from personal essay to academic paper. I felt like I had just gotten the hang of the personal essay and was enjoying the freedom of the collage essay, when suddenly, I had to juggle references, documentation, and other people's arguments. It was not that the research paper was particularly difficult, as the *switch* was difficult. However, having made the switch, I then felt like I was on excellent footing for writing the analysis paper. I had felt the freedom of the personal essay and had plumbed my depths to discover the wealth of details I have within me to use for my writing; I had then felt the rigid demands of the research paper with all of its formality and tradition. Having gone through these two exercises, I was better able to appreciate what literary nonfiction essayists are trying to accomplish. I was able to appreciate Tompkins' "Buffalo Bill" essay in a way that I was incapable of at the beginning of the course. As a result, I felt tremendous excitement about writing the analysis paper. I understood the requirements expected of me in terms of scholasticism, yet I felt the freedom to assert my own voice and technique. What fun!

THIS is the process that led me to "Warping Time with Montaigne." It was a journey of discovery: first of myself and my knowledge, then of different forms of writing available for my use, and finally of the power of freedom, innovation, and inspiration. Fortunately for me, I am now able to start from here as I prepare future journeys through the writing process.

Teacher Training

Mary Elizabeth Pope

I stand at the drinking fountain in the hallway outside my classroom. It is the first day of classes, and it is my first day as a graduate teaching assistant. I have no teaching certification to prepare me for this position, and as my qualifications are limited to the grades I earned as an undergraduate in English, I have no idea how I will meet the challenge of teaching Freshman Composition. Earlier, as I passed the classroom, I glanced in to see a number of students sitting in their desks, waiting. I think of all those students now, and wonder about all their different needs—how can I address them collectively, and still address them as individuals? How can I know what they need from me when I have no training or experience with teaching? My watch reads 7:59 am, so I move reluctantly toward the door behind which my students sit. My hands are shaking, and the knot in my stomach is threatening to snap me in half. My heels click on the tiled floor as I enter the classroom and make my way to the podium.

I sat in the new desk on the first day of fifth grade, watching my new teacher pass out textbooks. It was all I could do to sit still for so long; I had been waiting for this day all summer. The new pencils and paper and folders I'd saved my fifty cent allowance for were already arranged in my tray, and I placed each new textbook that Mrs. Crane handed out beside them, feeling very mature. The first day of school was like a clean slate for me; all of the mistakes from fourth grade left safely behind me in Mr. Smith's room and in Mr. Smith's mind. I watched my new teacher as she handed out books; she was a woman of about fifty, and very pretty in a hard sort of pancake makeup way. She walked more purposefully than any woman I had ever known, her posture perfect as she slowly, deliberately put one high-heeled shoe out and placed it carefully in front of her before shifting her weight directly onto it. Her careful, composed walk would be something I would never forget—the way her shoulders moved as she walked, the way her hair didn't, the angle at which she held her chin. I knew instantly that I wanted her to like me, that I wanted to do well in her class, to please this woman whose authority radiated from her every gesture, rang clear in her every word. I rode the bus home that afternoon, bursting with excitement, anxious to tell my mother all about my new teacher.

My students stare at me the first day. Some of them look at me directly; others avert their gaze in case my eyes meet theirs. They are sizing me up. That's okay; I am sizing them up, too. I pass out the syllabus, and discuss classroom policy and course requirements with them. I tell them they must have a C in order to pass my class. They say nothing until I ask them to introduce themselves to the class and say where they are from. After much shifting in their seats, and mumbling out their introduction sentence, they gratefully return their eyes to me. I try hard not to smile too much on the first day, although it is hard. I try to encourage them to understand how my class will help them with all of their classes; I try hard to make them understand that they all have something important to say, that they are all unique and no single other person has the perspective they do. They look at me. I look back at them. I don't know if they believe me or not when it is time to dismiss them, but I watch them file out, and feel hopeful.

I stood in the dime store for maybe thirty minutes, wondering what Mrs. Crane's favorite color was. The folders were there on the shelf—pink, yellow, green, blue, red. On another shelf sat the folders I wished for: clear, plastic binders with front picture slots on the cover. I could just see a collage of Abraham Lincoln underneath those picture slots— Mrs. Crane would like that for sure. But I had only fifty cents, and the clear plastic binders were ninety-nine cents, while the colored cardboard folders were thirty-nine cents. Mrs. Crane wore a lot of blue—navy blue—but since the dime store only carried a cornflower color of blue—and because it seemed the only color suitable for Abraham Lincoln of the colors available, I took one blue folder to the counter, and watched the lady ring it up. I was sad. What could I do with a plain blue folder that would make Mrs. Crane notice it? I wanted her to know how hard I'd worked on my report, and how much I wanted to do everything right for her. I wanted her to like me.

Holly comes to my office at least once a week. She worries all the time; so much so, that she is terrified to commit anything to paper. She is careful to meet all of the requirements in an assignment, yet she is so careful that it stifles all of the creativity in her expression. She always asks me what I want her to write. Today, her curly brown hair is pulled back in a bun, and above her ruddy cheeks, her eyes are tired and bloodshot, no doubt from staying up all night working, or worrying that she should be working. She is a perfectionist to the point of self-destruction, and although I am pleased with her work, I know she could be more expressive if she were not so afraid of making mistakes.

The assignment I give today is to freewrite about what they want to say in their coming papers. I tell them I won't be grading these and that the only thing that matters is what they discover about their topic. I give them thirty minutes, and I watch Holly hunch over her desk and begin writing. After class, I ask her to stay behind a moment so I can look at her writing. It is thoughtful and original, and much better than what she has been turning in to me on a regular basis. I tell her I want to see her this week, knowing I will anyway. I am hopeful that we can make some progress.

Mrs. Crane stood regally before the class, holding a stack of reports in her hand. I could hardly wait to get mine back and read what she had written. I had worked so hard, and had so carefully and creatively constructed the cover, that I was sure that she would love it. "Class," she began, "why don't we take a look at some of the reports you handed in to me?" I was even more excited—I just knew she would pick mine as a good example for a creative cover, and I could hardly wait to see what she said about it when she held it up. "This is James' report—see how he pasted a mapped picture of Michigan on the cover of his folder for his Michigan report? Very nice . . . .". Next, she held up a crumpled sheet of paper which was half written on in pencil. "This . . ." she paused and her voice fell, as she extended the paper away from her body and pinched it between two fingers, as if it were dirty, or smelled bad, ". . . is Kevin's report." She quickly put Kevin's report on the bottom of the pile, and picked up the next one, commenting favorably on the reports she liked, and giving the same disdainful look and treatment as Kevin's report got to those she did not appreciate. I waited excitedly. I could see the blue edge of my folder sticking out of the pile . . . closer and closer it came to the top . . . and then it was in her hand. "This is Mary Beth's report," she said quickly, and made no comment on it at all, quickly replacing it on the bottom of the pile. I was crushed. My blue folder, with the pennies glued on to form the letters A and L, looked pitiful in the light of Mrs. Crane's disinterest in it. I had been so proud of it, had so carefully selected the shiniest pennies in my father's penny jar to use for the lettering, had handed it in with such confidence; now it seemed a pathetic idea, and I felt embarrassed as my cheeks glowed hotly, wondering how many students were looking at my flushed face, my burning ears.

Jonathan demands a lot of attention. He sits in the front row of my 9:00 class, and has assumed the role and voice of ringleader for the class. He is very entertaining, and I enjoy having him in class most of the time. His constant need to prove that he is the "best" or the most intelligent student in my class, however, is frustrating, because when the class gets into a debate over a particular issue, he cannot let a subject go until he feels he has won. I try to remain a neutral facilitator, although I have at times had to interrupt when Jonathan gets out of hand. I can tell this frustrates him, and I struggle to understand this unfulfilled need he has to be in the spotlight at all times.

Today, I hand back all of the papers except for one that I have saved to read to the class. It is well written, funny, and it meets the assignment's requirements. I choose it because it is a good example, but I have another motive. "I have a paper I'd like to read to you," I tell them. "I enjoyed it and I think all of you will, too." As I read, the class laughs appreciatively, and I do, too. When I am finished, I launch into a description of the next assignment. The students bend over their notes and begin writing, and I casually set Jonathan's paper on his desk. He is smiling, and beads of sweat have formed on his forehead. He is happy, and I am glad. For the rest of the period, things go well.

When Mrs. Crane handed back the folders, I had a second flash of hope: maybe she had only disliked the cover—maybe she had liked the report itself. I watched the other students read her comments, and when my folder was finally in my hands, I flipped through the pages, anxiously looking for her scrawling red script. I couldn't find anything, except for a check mark to signify that she had read it. I looked again, more frantically, and then realized that she had written nothing at all.

Nicole sits in the fifth row, hidden behind Drew, who is tall, and Thomas, who is large. I can just see the top of her blonde head peering at me occasionally as I teach; she is tentative, curious, nervous. Sometimes when class is over and she is on her way out the door, she will glance at me shyly and smile, a blush travelling from her ears to her nose. Nicole works very hard at my assignments; all of her in-class writing is printed, perfectly neat and straight. She is always the last to finish writing. Her papers are very well done, and she is meticulous about meeting every requirement I ask for in each paper. Her writing also reflects the deep thought she puts into the ideas we discuss in class. In Freshman Composition, I could not ask for a better student.

I like to watch her when I hand back papers. On this particular day, what little of her face I can see is lit up, and I am glad for what I have written on the bottom of her paper. "Nicole—this is excellent. Again, I commend you. You meet all of the requirements for this paper, and express your depth of thought on these issues very well. This is the highest grade I have given on this paper, so you should feel proud." I can see all the way from the front of the room that she does.

My name was on the blackboard. Mrs. Crane posted the names of students who had misspelled words in their weekly assignments there until those students could find the correct spelling for the words they had missed. On Monday, my name stood out among the other names simply because it was my name and it had never been on that list before. Then, as the names were gradually erased, those spelling ex-convicts were allowed to join the ranks of the anonymous students who had spelled perfectly that week. Slowly, the list dwindled, and by Thursday, my name was the only one left. I was frustrated. The word was "no one" and it was not one word, as I later learned, but two. I had written "noone," and Mrs. Crane had circled it. I had stared at it for a long time, and then fetched a dictionary from the back shelf of the room. I knew that "someone" and "anyone" and "somebody" and "anybody" and "nobody" were all words. Where was "noone"? I tried "noon," thinking it could be used two ways. Still, it came back marked wrong. I tried "nowan," and again it was marked wrong. On Thursday, I showed Mrs. Crane that it was not in the dictionary. "Well," she had replied frostily, "I can't do anything about that, Mary Beth. The ways you have tried are all wrong." She then dismissed me. I walked back to my desk with heavy heart and burning cheeks, staring at my name on the board. All of the other names were gone, and now everyone knew that I was the stupid girl who couldn't spell. For two long weeks, I stared at my name on the board, the chalky white letters seeming to jump off the blackboard and proclaim to the class my ignorance. Every night, I would hope that some diligent custodian would erase my name by accident. Every morning, my mark of shame would still be there. And every day, Mrs. Crane told me, "It's still wrong."

Darrin sits in the second row of my 9:00 class. I have just returned his paper, and I can see the disappointment that registers on his face. Most mornings, Darrin hides beneath a baseball cap, watching me furtively from beneath it, retreating turtle-like under the visor if my gaze lands momentarily on him. He is a hard worker, and shows up regularly to my office hours to ask for help. I am sorry when I receive his work to have to give it a C+ because of his errors. Darrin has difficulty with spelling and commas, but his work in general is often entertaining and interesting. On the bottom of this particular paper, I have written, "Darrin— this is very funny—I enjoyed reading it. I can see that you are improving the orga- nization and maintenance of focus in your writing. Keep it up (smiley face)! I am still concerned about your use of commas and number of spelling errors that have appeared here. Come see me and we'll talk about it. Good work overall." I know that Darrin will come to my office hours after class. I know what I will say to him. I know how he will respond. And regardless of whether or not he uses the dictio- nary or spellcheck, regardless of whether the exercises with commas that I will cover with him improve his writing, I know that he will leave my office feeling that he is a good writer who needs a little brushing up, rather than feeling he is a bad writer who is hopeless. He will leave knowing he is capable of doing better, and hopefully this will drive him to improve on his next paper.

On the day before Christmas vacation, we'd made ornaments in Mrs. Crane's class. My ornaments did not look like everyone else's. I had taken the pastry dough and twisted strips together to form candy canes, like the cookies my mother sometimes made at home. I loved art lessons, and I was happy with my ornaments. Mrs. Crane strolled up and down the aisle and paused to compliment those ornaments that she liked. She paused at my desk, and I waited, hopeful that she liked mine. She looked confused for a moment, and then walked quickly up to the front of the room and said, "Now class, let me show you again how to use the cookie cutters. Remember, these ornaments are going to hang on the tree in the big hallway, so we want them to look nice and neat." She searched for a particular cut- ter. "See," she said with false brightness, as she showed us how to cut the starchy dough, leaving a row of perfectly straight Gingerbread Men in her wake, "they all come out ex- actly the same if you use a cookie cutter."

Eric is angry. Ever since the first day he walked into my class, it has radi- ated from him, the aura of anger that surrounds him reminding me of the cloud of dust that follows the *Peanuts* character Pigpen everywhere he goes. With his long, red ponytail and goatee, he sits, withdrawn from the rest of the class, in the back corner, hiding behind his black leather jacket. Eric is brilliant; his forcefully written, anti-establishment, rebellious papers are testimony to this. He is by far the most openly creative student I have, and I handle him carefully because I know he is volatile. However, when he misses several classes in a row, I decide to take action. I stop him on his way out the door and ask him if he will make an appointment with me. He says yes, and we agree on a time. I don't know what I will say to him yet, or whether he will even show up. I only know that I do not want to lose this incredibly bright student, to let him slip through the cracks and disappear, never to return to my class. I am hoping that all he needs is some encouragement.

On the last day of fifth grade, we were allowed to take our brown bag lunches outside and sit on the lawn in front of the school. I sat with my class and watched Mrs. Crane talk to the students who sat around her. I sat far on the outside of the circle with another girl, and we traded Lifesavers and halves of our sandwiches. When the buses pulled up to take us home that day, Mrs. Crane stood by the door, and hugged each of us. I waited, dreading the hug, but knowing I couldn't get past her. She made a big show out of it, telling the students how much she would miss all of them. When my turn came, she put her mushy arms around me and my cheek burned where it touched her neck. When she finished hugging me, she put her hands on my shoulders and shook me a little. "I'm expecting big things from you, Mary Beth." My eyes filled up with tears. I managed good-bye and followed the other students on to the bus. I hated her even more for lying like that in front of all of my friends. As I stood behind the other students in line for my bus, I wondered why she would say such a thing. The way she had treated me all year told me everything I ever wanted to know about what she expected from me.

Mark sits in the back row of my classroom with Walter and Jonathan. All three are football players, and while Walter and Jonathan often doze or talk disruptively, Mark tries to listen closely to what I have to say. He asks questions in class and comes to my office regularly. He is creative and earnest, and usually manages to separate himself, if only in attention span, from his teammates.

I hand his paper back without a grade. While his writing is nearly error free, and might have been an "A" for another assignment, he has not met any of the requirements for this paper. Were I to grade it, it would have failed. I know he is a good writer and I do not want to discourage him, so I write on the bottom of his paper, "Mark—your writing, in terms of mechanics and style, is excellent. As a creative piece, this would have received an "A." However, for this assignment, you haven't met the requirements I needed to see. I know you are busy, but I'd like to meet with you and discuss what you need to change here. This is very good writing, Mark, but it doesn't meet the criteria I spelled out in class. You can take your time with it. See me first and we'll talk." Mark reads my comments and looks confused for a moment, but he nods slowly, and I know he understands. I know I haven't crushed him, and I know he will come see me and do better the next time.

Composing "Teacher Training"

Mary Elizabeth Pope

The idea for the "Teacher Training" piece came out of a journal activity assigned in a graduate nonfiction class asking each of us to make a list of all of the topics we would never write about and why. I wrote down "Mrs. Crane" [not her real name] among other things, because even though I was in fifth grade when I had her for a teacher, she was still affecting me in a negative way as a graduate student. The reason, though, that she had made it on the list of things I would never write about was because several months after I'd had her for a teacher, she'd been killed in a car accident. Although I'd never admitted it to anyone but my mother, I had gone home every day in fifth grade praying she would die somehow. I was still harboring a lot of guilt over that, because for years after she was killed, I had nightmares about her; I was convinced that God had answered my prayers and that I was responsible for her death. I still won't ever write about that aspect of my relationship with her, but the exercise got me thinking.

The third paper was to be a personal, non-fiction essay and we were all encouraged to experiment with a format we hadn't used very often. I wasn't sure what to write about, so I went back to my list of things I would never write about, took her name, put it in the middle of a blank page and did some clustering, just to see what would happen. As I clustered, I realized that I had a lot to say about this woman; from the clustering page, I started to freewrite and couldn't believe how angry I was getting just thinking about the things she used to do to me in class. She was the kind of teacher who used humiliation tactics to teach her students, and she really disliked me, even though I tried hard to be a good, hard-working, well-behaved student. I wasn't sure of what aspect of her teaching I wanted to focus on, or if I really wanted to focus more on my reaction to her techniques, but I knew I had a lot to say because I couldn't stop writing.

Another circumstance enters into this topic and my choosing to write about it—at the time I began to write this piece, I was in my second semester teaching freshman composition as a graduate assistant. The whole time I was scribbling

453

about the things she used to do me in class, I was thinking about myself as a teacher and couldn't imagine ever treating my students the way she treated me. My own teaching position had given me a new perspective on the whole Mrs. Crane issue, and it was one I could never have had before then, because I'd never taught. So as I "freewrote," I kept thinking about that aspect of it, although it didn't enter into any of my initial writing.

It actually took me a long time to determine what I wanted to do with this piece, because I knew I had a lot to say about it, and it felt really good getting it on paper. I'd been carrying it around for about thirteen years and had never really discussed it in detail with anyone, except for my mother at the time Mrs. Crane was killed. She had had a profound effect on my confidence as a student. Before I had her for a teacher, my other teachers always made me feel like I was really bright and put me in advanced reading groups and had given me higher level workbooks; I'd always assumed that I was one of the "smart kids," I guess. Before I had her as a teacher, I'd never questioned my abilities or my intelligence; after I had her, I always questioned it, even into graduate school. Getting it out on paper gave me a sense of relief, but at the same time, there was this urgency to do something with it because I needed to make sense of it.

I started with a segmented essay. Although I knew I wanted to use specific episodes from my year in her classroom—I had most of those written—I wasn't sure what to juxtapose with them. I thought of, and actually played around with, a speech I'd been forced to give about her at a tree dedication ceremony. The circumstances were odd—no other student was available to give the speech, and so my sixth grade teacher asked me to do it and gave me about two weeks to prepare. So I had to think about what I could say. No matter what I said about her, if it was nice, it would be a lie. My mother and I worked out a way where I could give the speech without actually saying that I had liked her or that I missed her. And so I played around with juxtaposing the day I gave that speech and the episodes in her classroom. One of the segments went like this:

> "My name is Mary Beth Pope," I began hesitantly, and swallowed out of fear involuntarily. "I was a student in Mrs. Crane's class last year." I paused, thinking of the things I was about to say, and looked at my first notecard. "Mrs. Crane taught us to sing The Grand Old Flag," I said, thinking that all she really taught us was to doubt ourselves, to be afraid, to never put yourself into anything you did lest it be rejected utterly and completely. "She . . . she, uh, liked us to push our . . . uh, chairs in . . ." She also liked to push us until we cried. I looked out at the crowd, and the principal, and at her husband and sisters who sat directly below me. I did not belong here, giving this speech. The wind blew my dress and made me shiver. My voice broke and I began, "She also . . ." I stopped.

It worked okay, but it wasn't really saying what I needed it to say.

After I had done that first freewriting, I prepared for this piece further by visiting the school and classroom where I'd had her for a teacher. The building wasn't being used as an elementary school at the time; it was part of an adult education site, and so there were big desks and bulletin boards with announcements instead of seasonal decorations. But the green shag carpet was still there, and the low chalkboards, and the same heaters where we used to dry our mittens under the window ledges. And the smell was exactly the same. I just stood there and looked. I couldn't breathe very well and the whole thing felt very claustrophobic. I couldn't believe how nothing had changed in terms of my reaction to the room; I instantly felt stupid and ashamed and on guard just by walking through that door at the age of 23, as intensely as I had felt it every morning when I would get off the bus and head for the room when I was ten. It was wild—it really triggered a lot of memories that helped me to remember more specific details in the segments from fifth grade.

After I made that visit to the classroom I talked to my mom about it. We talked about different days that I had come home crying because of something she'd done to me, and Mom even remembered things I had forgotten. The combination of the visit to the classroom and the discussion with Mom helped me to gel some of the ideas that had been brewing or seemed disconnected, and really got me going on the Mrs. Crane segments, although I still was playing around with the "speech" contrast idea and not feeling like it was going in the right direction.

What ultimately happened was that in a peer workshop session, I brought up my concerns about it, and a fellow graduate assistant and I talked about how awful some of our teachers were, and how, now that we were teachers, we couldn't imagine treating our students the way we'd been treated. This was very much an issue for me as I'd been working on the piece, and my friend suggested that maybe I should focus on that aspect of it and drop the whole "speech" thing. Everything fell into place when she said that, and I went home that night after class and just wrote it all out, using different students to compare my teaching style with Mrs. Crane's. I started with a clustering exercise using a few students who struggled with things similar to the issues I struggled with in Mrs. Crane's class, and tried to line up my fifth grade issues with their issues in my class. Then I did a journal entry on how to put it together in the essay, which went like this:

> What I need to do with this paper is show how having been through Mrs. Crane's class, I am much more sensitive to their feelings—I see the defenses, I see the fear, I see the need for approval in them. What I need to do is match one incident from fifth grade with one I've had with my students. For instance, match Darrin with my spelling, Nicole with my need for Mrs. Crane to like me, Mark with the math problems, Jonathan with my need to be admired, Brian with my frustration level, Eric with my need to be understood and accepted, Jason with my need for freedom and creativity within an assignment.
>
> I need to show the little fight I have every day trying to build their confidence while improve their writing skills.
>
> A final paragraph might be me, hunched over a stack of papers late at night. My comments are long—I write at the very least a half a page per student. I am tired. It would be easier to pick out the wrong things and scribble all over their pages, but I cannot.

I still wasn't sure about the exact structure the paper would take—like what student or incident in Mrs. Crane's class to use first, second, etc., but I knew what direction I wanted to go with it, and started writing and rearranging.

Once I had that figured out, the major problem I ran into was how to introduce the piece and how to conclude. I wasn't even sure what exactly I was trying to say, except that having a teacher who made me feel badly about myself helped me to be more sensitive to my own students—I remembered how it felt when she would ignore me or downplay my efforts or tell me I was stupid or wrong. I figured that a logical way to begin would be with the beginning of my first semester teaching, or at the end, looking back on how I had felt at the beginning. I had worried a lot about having had no training in teaching, only in English, and it had bothered me that whole first semester. Over the course of the semester I realized that I had plenty of experience with teaching because I'd been a student my whole life, watching teachers teach. I would think about my favorite English teachers (which was easy because all of my favorite teachers in high school and college taught English) and how they did things, and I'd try and be like them. It never occurred to me that I might have learned the most about how to teach from the worst teacher I'd ever had.

Also, I wanted to conclude by saying that having Mrs. Crane for a teacher made *me* a better teacher—that I had a better understanding of student needs because I'd had experience with my own needs not being met. The problem was how to get it across without making it sound like, "Mrs. Crane was a terrible teacher and I'm a great teacher because I don't do things the way she did," as that wasn't the point. The point was to show that I was able to turn that negative experience into something positive for both my students and myself. I also was hoping that it would be the kind of thing that other teachers could read which would make them think about teachers *they'd* had who'd hurt *them,* and get in touch with their own perspectives as former students. It's kind of a universal experience—I mean, we've all had bad teachers—and I was banking on that so I wouldn't have to do so much explaining.

Actually, I did a lot of explaining anyway in the first draft of the paper—the first paragraph began at the end of the semester of teaching, looking back, and sort of telling what I had learned. This is what it looked like:

> For weeks before my first semester of teaching began, I suffered from severe nausea. My main concern was that I had no experience with teaching—no classes, no training, no nothing. I walked into class on the first day, opened my mouth to speak, and before I knew it the semester was over. I wondered where I had learned to teach, and it was only after that first semester was over, and I had time to think about it, that I realized that I had been a student my whole life. I realized that my real training began in the fifth grade with Mrs. Crane. I have come to believe that only so much of teaching is curriculum; the rest is instinct. For most of my life I have hated this woman who destroyed my self-esteem and all the confidence I'd ever had in myself as a student at the age of eleven. Now, I thank her. Perhaps because of her—or maybe in spite of her—I am too sensitive to my students' needs, and at times I worry that I am too gentle

with them. But I am not sorry; in fact, I prefer to be that way, because I know now that my experiences in her classroom that year have made me a better teacher.

It's awful, when I look at it now, because I manage to sound exactly the way I didn't want to. I concluded the same way, with the teaching evaluations the students wrote at the end of the semester, and I used examples of what they said about me to confirm what I "said" in the body of the paper, comparing my experience with Mrs. Crane to my experience as a teacher. The truth is that when I got back the evaluation sheets that the students had written at the end of that first semester, I sat on the floor of my kitchen and was terrified to open them. When I finally did, and I read the nice things that the students had said about my teaching, I realized that maybe I was a good teacher and that I hadn't done the horrible job that I thought I had. I cried for about two hours that day because the whole semester I'd been afraid I wasn't a good teacher and that my inexperience showed. A lot of them said that they felt like I really cared about them, and that made me think about Mrs. Crane, and how she hadn't cared at all. So when I wrote the conclusion, all that went into it because it was exactly what I was experiencing at the time.

I didn't recognize immediately that both the introduction and conclusion were too self-conscious, and told more than they showed. I didn't really need either—I'd made my point by virtue of the contrast—but I felt obligated to set up some kind of a chronology and demonstrate what I'd learned about my teaching. When my composition instructor handed back the first draft, he said that he liked all of it except the introduction paragraph, which he felt "covered too much ground," and so I took that out and changed it to a scene of me waiting outside my classroom on the first day of class, worried about how I would manage to teach fifty students when I had no experience with teaching at all. Once I did that, I was really happy with it—it gave it the feeling that the reader was going to be there with me, walking into the classroom, scared to death like I was, and it removed that filter of my self-consciousness. I also did some major revisions on what my students said to me in the evaluations—because although I'd taken the quotes right off the evaluations, they were so unbelievably positive and sweet that it made me sound like I was bragging which, again, wasn't the point. What I was trying to do with the evaluations was to give the reader the same sense of "wow" and relief that I'd felt when I read them myself on the floor of the kitchen that day.

That was the point the paper was at when I handed it in for a final grade at the end of the semester, and that was close to the form it was in when I submitted it to the *Language Arts Journal of Michigan.* I did feel at one point that the sections on Mrs. Crane were too wordy, too self-pitying, and that the segments about my teaching were too self-righteous; however, when I was writing it, it felt good to discover something positive had come from that terrible year, and I got really excited about it. Before I submitted it to *LAJM,* I tried to tone it down a little, although after I went back and read it again, I realized I didn't need to make as many changes as I thought.

The draft I sent out ended with the following segments (I had chosen to distinguish past and present by putting the experiences with Mrs. Crane in past tense and italics and my experiences as a teaching assistant in present tense and plain text):

The tears in my eyes blurred the long division problems together until I couldn't see anymore. This was the best day of the month—free morning—and all of the other kids were down in the gym playing games and having fun. Three times I had redone the missed problems, eight of the forty she had given us, and run excitedly down the three flights of stairs to the gym, anxious to join my friends. Three times I had trudged back up the stairs, and been made to sit and rework the problems. I was so frustrated that I couldn't even see the paper, which had been erased so many times that I could see the pattern on my desk through what was left of the paper. Added to this were the tears that now made the page not only wet, but the answers I had gotten right, blurry. I couldn't bring myself to face her again, and I just knew that I could never do it right for her. I hated long division. Mrs. Crane hated me. And I had no idea what to do about it. I couldn't understand why she had singled me out to rework my missed problems—after all, I had worked as hard as all of the other students. And how was it that they all had answered their questions right? Was I the only one who couldn't get the problems right? Maybe it had nothing to do with the work, I thought. Maybe I wasn't pretty enough. She liked Erin and Laurie, who were both pretty. That had to be it—I worked as hard as both of them, but she still didn't like me. Or maybe it really was that I was the only one who didn't know how to do long division exactly right every time. I gave up wondering, and forgot about the gym. It hurt too much to hope that she would let me be like everyone else, so I abandoned my problems and went to look out the window instead.

Mark sits in the back row of my classroom with Walter and Jonathan. All three are football players, and while Walter and Jonathan often doze or talk disruptively, Mark tries to listen closely to what I have to say. He asks questions in class and comes to my office regularly. He is creative and earnest, and usually manages to separate himself, if only in attention span, from his teammates.

I hand his paper back without a grade. While his writing is nearly error free, and might have been an "A" for another assignment, he has not met any of the requirements for this paper. Were I to grade it, it would have failed. I know he is a good writer and I do not want to discourage him, so I write on the bottom of his paper, "Mark—your writing, in terms of mechanics and style, is excellent. As a creative piece, this would have received an "A". However, for this assignment, you haven't met the requirements I needed to see. I know you are busy, but I'd like to meet with you and discuss what you need to change here. This is very good writing, Mark, but it doesn't meet the criteria I spelled out in class. You can take your time with it. See me first and we'll talk." Mark reads my comments and looks confused for a moment, but he nods slowly, and I know he understands. I know I haven't crushed him, and I know he will come see me and do better the next time.

On the last day of fifth grade, we were allowed to take our brown bag lunches outside and sit on the lawn in front of the school. I sat with my class and watched Mrs. Crane talk to the students who sat around her. I sat far on the outside of the circle with another girl, and we traded lifesavers and halves of our sandwiches. When the buses pulled up to take us home that day, Mrs. Crane stood by the door, and hugged each of us. I waited, dreading the hug, but knowing I couldn't get past her. She made a big show out of it, telling the students how much she would miss all of them. When my turn came, she put her mushy arms around me and my cheek burned where it touched her neck. When she finished hugging me, she put her hands on my shoulders and shook me a little. "I'm expecting big things from you, Mary Beth." My eyes filled up with tears. I managed good-bye and followed the other students on to the bus. I hated her even more for lying like that in front of all of my friends. As I stood behind the other students in line for my bus, I wondered why she would say such a thing. The way she had treated me all year told me everything I ever wanted to know about what she expected from me.

I sit on the floor of the living room on the day I receive my student evaluations back. I have no idea what they have said, and I wonder if after reading them I will feel better or worse about my performance this past semester. I open them slowly, afraid of what they could say. I can remember really giving it to some of my teachers; I wonder if anyone has done that to me. I pick up the first one and read what it says: "I really liked this class and teacher. She was always so chipper in the morning." I smile, wondering who wrote it. I pick up the next one: "Miss Pope was a very good teacher. This was a great class, even though it was at 8:00 in the morning. The journals were fun—maybe you could do more of those in your next class." The next one reads: "This is the only class I didn't drop." I laugh, flattered by this student who chose to stick with me, and read another one. "Miss Pope really cares about her students and always has something positive to say about our work, even when we get a low grade." I pick up the next one, and the next. I smile until I come to the one that reads: "Miss Pope's class was my favorite class of all—and the only reason I got up for any of my classes." I don't recognize the writing, but I don't care. It is then that I realize my face is wet from my tears. I think about Mrs. Crane. And I thank her.

When the editors at *LAJM* wrote to me and told me they wanted to publish it, they asked that I make a few changes—essentially, take out two segments: one about the math exercise Mrs. Crane had made me rework instead of letting me play with the other kids in the gym, and the conclusion. I felt kind of funny chopping out the math segment part because I was so angry at her for that—and I think it showed, too, because it was long (probably why they wanted it out). Taking out the conclusion was fine with me, though, because once I realized that it was going to be published and other people besides my composition instructor and classmates would read it, it occurred to me that the conclusion could seem exaggerated or too slanted toward glorifying my teaching success that semester.

The editors also asked me to make the last day of school the final segment for fifth grade, and finish with a segment about my student, Mark. In the passage above, then, I was dropping the first and last segments and reversing the order of the middle two. I was actually really happy with that revision because it gave the piece a nice feeling of continuity, instead of closure, which made it seem as if there had been an end to what I'd learned. And for the purposes of the journal, I could see why they wanted it that way.

When the journal came out, and I saw it in print, and read it again, I realized that I was really happy with the way that it was written. The whole experience of writing it and revising it and then seeing it in print was important for me for a couple of reasons. The first was that I felt like it was okay for me to have really disliked Mrs. Crane as much as I had—I'd never wanted to admit that after she died because it seemed like such an awful thing to say about someone who was dead (especially since I'd wished her that way so often before it happened). Also, it helped me to see that I had left that year in her class with something important— that she really did teach me something significant by not giving me the things that I needed, and that though it was difficult to endure at the ages of ten and eleven, it had become a really significant learning experience for me.

There has been some carryover from writing this piece into the writing I am doing now indirectly. I learned that when I am writing, I need to watch myself think, and not try so hard to make everything go in a particular direction right away. For instance, if I had paid attention to the fact that I kept thinking "I would never treat a student that way" as I was writing the segments about Mrs. Crane, maybe it wouldn't have taken me so long to recognize that *that* was the direction the writing really wanted to go. A lot of times, I will sit down with what seems like a great idea, but then I can't figure out where to go with it. If I just pay attention to what I am thinking, and trust it, and not dismiss it as just an external observation about the work I'm doing, I can get a better perspective on how I really feel about what I am writing. It's hard to do, but I've been trying.

Zion

Maureen Stanton

Sometimes I wake up in the middle of the night and I don't know where I am. My bed is a flying carpet. Flat on my back, I am looking up at the stars, whizzing around in blackness. Then I slow down, the carpet lands. I figure out which direction I am facing and get a map of the room in my head. I recognize the window and the streetlight. The bed, the door, the lamp. I remember where I am, the longitude and latitude of my life. Fixed to locale, nailed to a place, I can begin to make order.

I am dozing in the hospital bed with Steve when he pulls me.

"Mo, something is happening to me. My head is shrinking."

"What do you mean? What does it feel like?"

"It feels like it's the size of a grapefruit." He starts to cry, the first time since all this started. I run to the nurses' station. "Help. Something weird is happening to Steve." Fay and Dora come and give Steve a shot, but this causes his tongue to swell and his eyes to roll back in their sockets. Fay holds his mouth open, while Dora gets a doctor who injects something into Steve's bicep, and after a few seconds he breathes normally.

"It was just a reaction to the new pain medicine," Fay tells us, like it was nothing more than a bee sting. I stand near Steve's head and try not to touch him too much. The feeling that his head is small stays with him the whole night.

We are at the hospital of last resort, a small brick building in Zion, Illinois, an hour north of Chicago. It's a hospital where the bedspreads are worn thin and have holes. A hospital that serves carrot and celery juice, and offers alternative treatments for cancer. One week a month we come here. Steve gets his poison. I bleed.

The doctors here are different than at the hospital Steve checked out of back in Michigan. For one thing, most of them are Filipino. It unnerves Steve's parents who discourage our decision (false hopes, grasping at straws). But here the doctors don't give up as easily. Steve's first oncologist wrote a note on his chart which we read during our flight to Chicago. *It is very sad to see that the patient cannot accept the poor prognosis.* Two months, she predicted for a twenty-nine-year-old man with three small children, then patted his hand and walked out of the room, dry as a desert, tearless, leaving us in the starkness of Steve's future.

Dr. Sanchez and Dr. Melijor give us information, allow us to see Steve's nuclear scans. Married to gray film, Steve's skeleton glows. Small black dots are sprayed from his skull to his kneecaps as if someone plugged him with bird shot. Cranium, sternum, ribs, vertebrae, pelvis, femur. It is a frightening lesson in anatomy. I try not to act shocked, but the black dots are more numerous than I had envisioned when the previous doctors spoke of "widespread metastases" and "multiple tumors." "Multiple" meant six or seven, a six-pack, a touchdown, a number we could beat. I count more than two dozen specks on the little x-ray man that is Steve—malignancies humming inside his flesh. Not to mention his liver, marbleized like a high priced cut of beef, with cancer cells. Now it is real.

I arrive at the hospital at nine in the morning and climb in bed with Steve as if I am joining him in his body, unzipping his skin like it's a space suit, and snuggling in. His roommates, Greg and Chuck, don't seem to mind. Greg is an insect exterminator from South Carolina with testicular cancer. He sleeps most of the time, or reads his Bible. The only noises he makes are vomiting, or buzzing for the nurses. Hand him his urine jug, fix his pillow, bring him a drink. He thinks he is at a resort.

Chuck is in the other bed. He has a clear tube taped inside his nose that pumps oxygen from tanks on the side of his bed into his drowning, malignant lungs. He is an earthbound scuba diver. Chuck breathes loud and heavy, and coughs wet, phlegmy coughs which temporarily paralyze his wife's kinetic fingers as she sits in a chair by his bed and knits violently, like she is weaving Chuck a new set of lungs.

Days pass by slowly. Flowers arrive for Steve from his parents. *When God closes a door, he opens a window.* I put the card on the nightstand, open the curtains and watch activity below, cars and people. Fat, slow winter flies buzz against the sealed glass. They appear out of nowhere, it seems, these retarded creatures, and now they are desperate to get out, as if they know they are trapped, as if they have some power of cognition. That's what I learn when I accompany Steve to the hospital. Empty hours. Time to think.

We walk around the hallways, Steve holding onto his pole like a staff. Bottles are suspended from the pole, clear liquids that feed the catheter in Steve's chest and flow into the big subclavian vein direct to his heart, like a fast underground train. Nitrogen mustard, 5-FU, methotrexate. The names remind me of the defoliants that were dropped on Vietnamese jungles. They cause hair to fall out of Steve's head, off his chest. His underarms and legs are bare. His eyebrows are missing. His pubic hair is gone. He looks like a fetus, a tall, skinny fetus. Still, he is handsome with his heavy eyelashes and soupy blue eyes, purple hollows below them, like watercolor. His eyes look bigger with his face so thin and his skin wrapped so tightly over his bones. Delicate bones.

Visitation ends at eight, but the nurses understand that hours matter and allow me to stay until midnight. Then I walk to the room I have rented from a notice I saw posted in the hospital cafeteria. Three blocks away and ten dollars a night. The couple who own the house are up when I arrive.

"Wipe down the shower before you get out. Don't use too much toilet paper. And use the towel more than once." Noma scolds me before I have transgressed. She is a tiny woman with messy gray hair and one sharp, pointy tooth, like an egg tooth a baby bird uses to peck its way out of a shell.

"Who've ya got in the hospital?" she asks.

"My boyfriend."

"Isn't that a shame." She asks me where I am from, and then says, "Emil's got a cousin in Detroit."

Emil has filmy blue eyes and hair that is sugar white with bangs cut straight across his forehead. He looks like an old angel.

"They come from all over to go to that hospital. We've had people from Florida, Kentucky . . . New Zealand! Staying right in your room," he says, as if I am privileged.

"We're blessed with good health, thank the Lord," Noma cuts in. "Emil broke his ankle forty years ago. It was healed by a miracle at our church and it never bothered him since, right, Em?"

"Still march with the Brothers of Zion band sixty years now. I'm the oldest clarinet player." Emil opens a closet and pulls out a red, wooly coat and matching pants with gold braiding up the seams.

"It's no coincidence you're in Zion," he says. "This is a holy town. Miracles take place all the time."

"That's very nice," I say, and manage to excuse myself. Behind the bedroom door, I flop onto the lumpy single bed and cry. I do every night. It's part of my sleep.

Later I am poked awake by noises in the kitchen: a spoon clinking against a dish, footsteps, cupboards opening and shutting, a toilet flushing. Then the sequence repeats. I can hear snoring from Noma and Emil's room. They would have had to pass me to get to the kitchen, but I didn't hear anyone in the hall. I become convinced there is a ghost just outside my door, making that last meal over and over again, unable to let go. I pull my blankets up around my chin. My heart is pounding, pushing my tired blood, echoing in the small room. I pray. *Please, God, don't let it come in here.* I lie in stiff fear until gray light when spirits are banished, then wake up at eleven, groggy. Emil's white toupee is on a styrofoam head on the kitchen table and his teeth in a jar of water on the bathroom sink. I ask Noma if she heard noises in the night.

"Just me eating my cereal," she says. "I get up about three every morning and have some cereal."

"What about the flushing?"

"Oh, that's the pump clearing water out of the basement."

In the daytime, I can get along. There are objects, events, people to hold on to, give texture to time, divide up space. But at night, I lose my way, lose my mind. It's easy.

The next month I find a room for $75 a week at the Harbor Hotel. The office is the living room of a small house that smells like curry. A boy is playing on the rug in the fuzzy penumbra of the television. A woman with a red dot on her forehead gives me a key and says there are no refunds, then directs me to their other hotel down the street.

The rooms are in the basement of a small, brick apartment building. There is no front desk, only a broken pay phone, and leaves blowing around the hallway. A disheveled man is loitering near the telephone. As far as I can tell, I am the only guest.

Ramona and Sue and Estherine and Georgia are on the same chemotherapy schedule as Steve, so we see them every month. Steve flirts with them, bald and in their bathrobes. They laugh when he tells them he is going to wear his camouflage hunting shirt and fatigues for his upper G. I. test. He likes the audience, but I don't care to share him much. Of what little he has left, I want it all. I am with him most of the time, in the bathroom even, keeping him company. He sits on the toilet and rests his head on the back of a fold-up chair. I sit on the chair and touch his back lightly. His skin is hot all the time now and I like to put my cold hands on it. We sit there in silence waiting for him to pee.

Steve naps and I read. Mysteries. Cheap little stories that completely absorb me, simple words I can eat, pages I can bend and fold. Perry Mason novels are the main staple of my diet. Perry always finds the killer, always wins his cases. I like the surety of that. There isn't anything in the stories to disturb me, or throw me off balance. They ask nothing of me.

At night I read to Steve, poems, clips about U.F.O.'s from *Omni* magazine, and stories from supermarket tabloids. GIANT FLYING CATS TERRIFY TOWN. WOMAN ABDUCTED BY ALIENS CAN NOW TALK TO ANIMALS. CANCER MAN'S LAST REQUEST: A JAGUAR CAR PARTS CATALOGUE. I envision a man in a leotard and cape with a big "C" on his chest, an action hero defying death. Cancer Man.

This month Cancer Man is undergoing an experimental treatment—whole body hyperthermia. His body temperature will be raised to 108 degrees Fahrenheit. The theory is that abnormal, mutant cancer cells slough off at 107 degrees, while healthy cells, skin, organs, muscle, brain tissue, begin to die at temperatures just above 108. It is a precarious balancing act to reach the right temperature, sustain it long enough to do specific damage, then lower it again. Steve has signed a liability waiver, a disclaimer of some kind that contains the words "result in possible death."

Dr. Kim, the anesthesiologist, brings me into the treatment room to see Steve. He has been stripped naked and wrapped head to toe in gauze like a mummy. To raise his temperature, he is wrapped in a heated plastic blanket filled with water and alcohol. A thermometer in his mouth, one in his rectum, and two others will monitor his fever for the next eight hours.

I spend the day wandering along Lake Michigan, the Illinois side which is not as sandy and beautiful as the Michigan side. Blame it on the wind, I think, noticing this habit I have of searching for culprits. I go to the library and draft a letter to Steve's insurance company pleading with them to pay for the hyperthermia. In the park, a large bird boldly garbed in a blood red hood and black and white tuxedo clings to the bark of a tree, a red-headed woodpecker. It stands out among the muted browns and greens and feels like a gift, blatant beauty. When I return Steve is knocked out, in intensive care, sleeping it off. He wakes later delirious, mumbling like a drunk, lashing out with his hands, yanking at the tubes and bandages. Wild. For two days Steve sleeps fitfully. Finally, he recognizes me. I say, "Tell yourself each day you are going to get better and better." He says, "I'm going to get better and better. I'll be the best."

These treatments—chemicals, radiation, hyperthermia—attempt to murder Steve each time; push him to the brink, lull him back, give him time to fortify then zonk him again. It's a tease, an oxymoron, Orwellian doublespeak. We must kill you to cure you, make you sick to make you better. It's a lie, a trick with fun house mirrors. We don't trust anyone.

The Harbor Hotel is quiet all week. Then late Friday night I hear people yelling and kicking the doors to the rooms, moving towards mine. I click off my lamp so they won't see a sliver of light leaching under my door into the hallway. I'm afraid that if they find me they will kill me. It is my nighttime logic. I practice saying "Who's there?" in a deep, male voice. After a while, they manage to break into a room a couple of doors down and party all night. I make myself small and quiet like the tiny baby cockroaches that scatter whenever I turn on the fluorescent light in the bathroom. I plan my escape out the small casement window above the television, level with the ground. Finally I sleep hard and wake up to the sounds of Big Wheels on pavement.

Outside, I blink at the sunlight. Mothers sit on the brick steps smoking cigarettes. They stare at me like I am an alien, out of my country, away from my land. Timeless, placeless, bodiless.

When I get to the hospital Chuck's bed is empty. He died during the night after a long coughing fit. His wife, Carol, is gone without a trace, not one thread left behind. Steve has gotten scorched from the hyperthermia. Bad wrapping job. The soles of his feet and his scrotum are tender. He's pissed off about this, but when Jane, a volunteer, comes around he forgets for a while. Steve and I stare at her round and bouncy firm flesh encased in stretchy nylon like she is wearing beach balls, at her unruly white hair and huge blurry eyes behind thick glasses. She hands out newspapers and carnations, and speaks in a flat, nasally voice, yogic, like a Sufi chant. "I have five dogs, two cats, a mallard (now in my freezer waiting for the Guinness Book of World Records to verify it as the oldest albino duck—seventeen years, as old as my niece), and a pet starling that barks like a dog and shouts 'thief' every time a stranger comes in my house."

Jane invites me to eat with her in the hospital cafeteria. She talks while she chews, projecting bullets of deviled ham and masticated bread bits. One lands on my cheek and it is all I can focus on, don't know what words she is saying. I avoid her after that. I give Steve enemas, put my fingers in his rectum, mop up his vomit, swab the raw, pink flesh around his catheter site, but none of that fazes me the way having to eat with Jane seems an insurmountable task. Everything seems odd. Off.

This life develops a rhythm: three weeks home, one in Zion. Months go by this way. I dial a number pinned to the hospital bulletin board and a woman named Martha says she has an extra room in her apartment. When I get there Martha is gone and her son, Jeff, is playing chess on a small hand-held computer, smoking a cigarette with a puddle of gray cat on his lap. He explains that Martha was called to take care of someone for the week. She is a home-care aide.

"Bummer," he says, after he asks why I am there. He is in his early twenties with long hair parted in the middle and scruffy sideburns zigging down his jaw line.

"I'm trying to quit drinking," he says. "I haven't had a drink in over two weeks."

"Good." I feel my head bobbing up and down like one of those spring-necked ceramic cats you see on dashboards. I've noticed this: when you tell people your boyfriend has cancer they feel they must ante up their own pain and lay it on the table. At first, I thought it was nice, a kind of offering, but now it just makes me mad. Nobody's pain is equal to ours. I feel self-righteous and chosen. Anointed and doomed at the same time.

When I get up the next day, Jeff is mixing a glass of lemonade, smoking a cigarette and playing chess.

"I guess you like to play chess." I feel obliged to address this man in whose living room I am a stranger.

"Keeps me out of trouble," he replies. "I'm on probation for dealing drugs."

"Good luck," I say. Fucking wingnut, I think. Who cares? It feels good to be mean.

Put your troubles in the hands of the Lord and he will help you. Steve flings this month's card from his parents across the room. I pick it up and set it on the nightstand. I can't stomach the tension of a thing being where it doesn't belong, throwing off order, tempting chaos. I fill a plastic urine jug with water for the flowers and arrange them. I check selections on Steve's menu card, cut his toenails, get ice from the machine down the hall for his pitcher, try to keep busy before succumbing, inevitably, to watching television. Nothing airs in the morning except for talk shows, game shows, and odd sports, like curling, a bizarre contest involving a puck and a broom, a tight little silly game. Lunch arrives. Steve looks at it and puts the metal lid back on. I walk across the street and pick up some Kentucky Fried Chicken.

Later Steve unhooks himself from the tubes and we escape from the hospital. Outside it is cold and gray. We walk around holding hands. I like Steve's hands, his long, slender fingers, nails brittle and yellowed, his palms still rough and callused though he has not worked in over a year. He has two warts on his left hand, stubborn, rubbery bumps that I like to bite. They're large, these hands, but deft as he glues a part on a model car with his son, or takes an eyelash out of my eye. Steve used to stand behind me and press my nipples between his fingers while I stirred spaghetti sauce, and when we slept, his leg draped over mine, clinging like sweaty children, he cupped my breast in his palm like it was a dove. Now touching hurts him, so the only kisses I give are little brush strokes.

Steve makes it one block to a park near the hospital before he tires. We sit on a bench and watch a mother absentmindedly hand bread to her daughter. The little girl stuffs fistfuls of the bread into her mouth, every now and then flinging a crust at the ducks. Steve laughs, and I kiss his knuckles as the girl fills her cheeks and her mother stares at something else across the pond.

Friday night Jeff is playing chess with the television shouting in the background. I crawl into bed and stare at squares of light on the wall. Street lights, window panes, simple inanimate objects make me feel sad.

Hours later I am awakened by a cat screeching, then Jeff laughing loudly. The sound is distorted, like in a tunnel. Too loud for laughing alone, I think. My eyes are wide open, sucking in the dim light. I hear Jeff's maniacal laugh again and the cat yelps painfully. I envision Jeff screwed up on hallucinogens, torturing the cat. Greenish street light burnishes the door knob, which I expect to rotate at any moment, Jeff entering my room to rape me and carve me up with a knife, laughing that wild, enormous laugh the whole time. I stuff the corner of the pillow in my mouth to muffle sobs.

Nights can be like this—scenes from frightening horror films. Disaster is no longer an abstract concept. Anything is possible and danger is everywhere. I have a hard time differentiating the real from the imagined. Steve used to scare me, curling his index finger and growling, "redrum redrum redrum" like the little boy in *The Shining*, amused by how I had to skulk from light switch to light switch to pee in the middle of the night. I have asked him not to come back and haunt me, even if it is just a joke. He has asked me not to write about him, wants to disappear. I am terrified of his leaving, waking up next to a stiff corpse. I think about it every night when I lie down beside him, of being left alone, abandoned.

I wake up at seven stiff-necked, and for a second surprised to be alive and okay. Lines pressed into my face from the wrinkled sheets make a map, look like a place. I gather my stuff, don't stop to wash. Downstairs, Jeff is gone. I leave the key on the table and walk to the hospital. The nurses break the rules and let me sleep in Chuck's old bed for one night. In the morning, the long black hospital limousine delivers Steve and me to the airport. People in cars pass us on the highway and stare into our opaque windows like we are celebrities. We can see them, but they can't see us, as if we are ghosts. We exist in a parallel life: we can see our peers (getting married, having babies, buying houses), but we can't touch them anymore. We are headed somewhere else.

On Writing "Zion"

Maureen Stanton

"Zion" began as journal entries made in 1986 when the events in the essay were taking place. I wasn't thinking then that in the future this might be a story or an essay, but was writing for the same reason I record anything in my journal—to understand what is happening in my life. (This isn't always the case. There are other experiences that I know I will want to turn into an essay, so I keep specific notes, though they are mostly facts, ideas, and observations rather than the "talking to myself" of journal writing.)

I didn't look at the journal until probably two years after the experience. Grief over the death of Steve, the subject of this essay, consumed me, and I was busy trying to figure out how to fill up my life, which had revolved around Steve's cancer for eighteen months. Also, Steve had asked me not to write about him and I was struggling with this issue. When I started to write Zion as a "piece," I talked with a counselor who had helped me through this period about whether I could write about Steve. She was blunt and logical. Steve was dead, and this was my story too so I had a right to tell it.

After the fogginess of grief started to lift I began to remember interesting details of the experience, interactions and events I couldn't seem to recall when I was engulfed by emotions. The lifting of the veil of grief brought a flurry of raw material forward and I jotted notes everywhere, often waking up at night to write down a sentence that would later trigger a whole episode.

This has become my modus operandi for writing. I get very excited about an idea and become preoccupied with it. My mind is constantly tugged back to that subject whenever it is not engaged (usually when I am trying to sleep, but I will always sacrifice sleep for inspiration, even when it means arriving at work the next day a bit exhausted).

These scribbled thoughts, observations, words, and memories are stashed in a file because they seem somehow related. The file thickens and at some point reaches a critical mass. Visually, I think of it as a bunch of free-floating atoms and molecules ranging around in their own individual orbits, then something like the Big Bang happens, a tiny pop perhaps, and these particles react to one another and begin to attract and repel, combine and multiply to create a cluster of raw material. This is accompanied by an almost physical restlessness to write the piece, and suddenly (it often seems) I begin to work on it in earnest (leaving other pieces I am working on half-finished).

For this piece, which at various times was titled, "Cancer Man," "The Rooms I Stayed In" (thankfully that one didn't last long), then "Dreaming in Zion," the critical mass occurred about three years after Steve died. I pulled the piece together and brought it to a fiction workshop at the Iowa Summer Writing Program. I had been writing short stories exclusively, largely because that is what I focused on in creative writing classes in college. No one ever mentioned anything about essays. In fact, in four undergraduate and one graduate creative writing classes, I never heard the word essay mentioned, nor was it offered as a course on its own. Even in the writing groups I joined everyone seemed to be writing fiction.

The version of "Zion" I took to the workshop was only slightly different than this final version, yet I was naively trying to pass it off as a short story. That version was straight narrative, factual recitation with detailed description but little reflection. The workshop attendants wanted to see more of "me" in the piece, and they thought that, although it was moving, it was not complete and was not a successful short story. As with nearly all of my writing at that time, I didn't know what it was or what to do with it. I wasn't really writing short stories but I kept trying to squash my pieces into that mold.

I tried to put more "me" into the story but what came out, I see now, was not poignant reflection but raw emotion, untempered anger and resentment mostly. The piece took on a maudlin and self-pitying tone. I did not know what to do with Zion at this point, so I did nothing. It sat for a while before I decided to bring it to a living room writing group I participated in (after removing the added "me"). Two of the members of the writing group were professors of English and accomplished writers, and the others were professionals of all ages, all good writers and critics. This group felt the piece was flat, and although the writing was good, it lacked something. I still did not know what to do with the piece, so it landed back in hibernation, this time for about three years. But it was in that living room group that I first heard the term creative nonfiction from Mike Steinberg. I didn't grasp immediately what he was talking about, but as I slowly began to open up to this genre, I felt like I was finding my way home. This was the type of writing I naturally tended to and I was excited about it, but I still didn't know what made good creative nonfiction.

Having been somewhat liberated from my fixation with short stories and the constraints of trying to fit my personal experiences into that format (and feeling like a liar and a fraud doing so), I began to write about whatever stirred me without trying to set up dialogue, point of view and develop characters. (Although I think what I learned in fiction workshops helped me with pacing, tone, freshness of language, and precision.) I wrote two more essays, both about Steve, who managed to work himself into nearly everything I was writing regardless of how remotely related he seemed to be to the subject at hand. Both of these essays were published, but I felt that it was dumb luck, that I had stumbled into something that I couldn't sustain or duplicate as I was unaware of how I did it or why people liked the essays.

At this time, I began to get increasingly frustrated with my demanding job, which was eclipsing my free time and energy to write. (Writing had always been my umbilical cord to a meaningful existence.) I saved money for over a year, quit my job, and moved to the homes of friends and family members where I could live inexpensively. (Although this was frightening financially, as soon as I did this part-time and consulting opportunities began to fall into my lap. It was uncanny.) This is significant because if I had not done this, I feel strongly that "Zion" and many other pieces would never have been resurrected at all. (More importantly, continuing to live an artless, passionless existence and working a thankless, dull job would have caused my soul to wither on the vine, the marrow in my bones to dry up.) With the luxury of time I could put my heart and soul into creating more finished works that gave me a greater sense of satisfaction.

Having bought myself time to write (I envisioned a big parking meter into which I deposited my hard-won savings that now registered one year of time, ticking, ticking . . .), I began to work on my essays and to read other essayists in literary journals, collections, and magazines. It was this reading that helped to bring me along. Who knows how long it would have taken for me to discover truths about writing creative nonfiction on my own? Although I did not retrieve "Zion" to work on right away, in this incubation period I was beginning to get a sense of what makes a good essay, and why people bother to write essays after all. (I do think that it was good, though, to write creative nonfiction without formally studying it at first. There was a terrific freedom about not knowing what I was trying to do, to let the writing range freely. I think it allowed my voice to emerge.)

I attended a creative nonfiction workshop at the Stonecoast Writers' Conference in 1996, encouraged by Mike Steinberg, the man who had first introduced me to the term "creative nonfiction." This was the first time I had ever taken a workshop in this genre. The workshop was excellent. It reminded me of a trip I took to Brazil where I was immersed in the Portuguese language, yet could only pick up a word or two from each exchange. Then, after three weeks there, something happened, some leap of understanding, where I began to be able to interpret whole sentences and chunks of conversation. I liken that experience to Stonecoast because afterwards, instead of moving towards the writing blindfolded, occasionally glimpsing into some secret chamber of knowledge, I began to comprehend holistically the concept of creative nonfiction so that I could now purposefully sculpt the subconscious or "blind" part of my writing.

After the workshop, I pulled "Zion" from its entombment. It had been one of my favorite subjects, the surrealness of the experience, and I wanted to perfect it as much as I could. I didn't want it to sit in my file drawer forever. I wanted people to read it, like most anything I write. I wanted to create a thing of beauty, a story that intrigued and moved people. A decade had passed since the actual experiences in Zion, but writing it in the present tense returned me to the scene, placed me squarely back in the hospital and those seedy rooms where I slept. I cried every time I read each revision. It was biologically ordained, this weeping, from a deep, forgotten place inside me.

My process is to work on a computer draft, then to rearrange paragraphs, edit, and mark up the text by hand, then back to the computer, only to repeat the process. I revised the manuscript probably two dozen times over the course of a month or so, sometimes setting the piece aside for a day or two and working on something else, or gardening, which is my form of meditation. I originally intended to change the piece from present to past tense after getting it all down. I was only using the present to make the experience come alive for me again, to sharpen details, but as the writing progressed, I began to grow attached to the piece the way it was. I liked the immediacy of the story, the sense of being transported into the hospital or hotel room. And I had a strong desire to preserve the authenticity of that section of my life, to keep it intact, like a clipping from a film reel. I wanted to keep the memory pure, not to muddy the events with thoughts that represent how I feel now rather than how I felt then.

I can become obsessed with a piece, and lately I am fortunate enough to have time for obsessions. With Zion, the prose seemed sparse, pared down (compared to all that happened in real life and compared to earlier drafts). Every word mattered so I often spent a half-hour on one word, going back and forth, changing my mind then changing it back to the way it was originally. I realized I needed to be exact about Steve's chemotherapy instead of relying on my memory. Staring at the names of cancer drugs in the library released waves of memories about this experience. Sometimes I would go in search of metaphors, once sitting in the library all afternoon reading the Biblical references to Zion (which I didn't import into the essay after all since they felt forced). Sometimes I think I was trying too hard to create a "thing" instead of letting the "thing" create itself, but I usually recognized the artificial passages after a few days time and removed them (no matter how fond I was of the phrase or image I wanted to push into the piece).

I dug back into my original journals of a decade before, reread my old letters from Steve and listened to a tape of his voice. In the end, I added little to the factual bulk of the piece. I reviewed earlier drafts with comments made by my peers at the Iowa Workshop and in my writers' group. My typed out questions to the living room group at the bottom of the essay demonstrate my confusion about what I was attempting. These "questions for the group" were: what tense should the story be told in? Should this be a short story or an essay? Is there such a thing as true fiction? It seems I was still leaning towards writing fiction.

I found the copy of the manuscript from Mike Steinberg. His comments, thoughtfully offered four years prior to this rewrite, were exactly what the piece needed. He liked a lot of the external description, but said, "I'd like to see you get more reflective about the experience . . . and yes, we'll talk about your questions regarding autobiographical essay/fiction." He pointed out places where the piece could be "opened up." It appears I wasn't ready for his comments when he gave them to me years ago, but after the Stonecoast workshop, I finally understood what he was getting at. (I have saved all the manuscripts from workshop reviewers over the years because I value their comments, but interestingly, Mike Steinberg was the only one who referred to Zion as an "essay" and treated it as such when critiquing it.)

When it was obvious that I was doing nothing more than fiddling with prepositions and articles, the tiniest bits of text, I decided the piece was done. In any event, I simply didn't know where else to go with it and called it done. I may someday rewrite this piece in past tense, as I have been encouraged to do, and maybe this will strengthen the story and give it more weight and relevance. But more time will have to pass. When I work on something as intensely as I did this, I get weary of it. I start to feel ridiculous about the amount of time I am spending on it (which feels disproportionate to things taking place in the larger world around me). This happens often with my writing. I tire of pieces (they wear me out), so I put them away, which usually turns out to be a good thing. When I return to them later, what is missing, what is false or contrived, what is sloppy or sophomoric becomes more obvious. And I, for the distance passed (often years), am wiser in my approach to the piece. Unfortunately, this does not make me a prolific writer, only a careful one.

Overall "Zion" has not changed dramatically since its original incarnation nearly a decade ago and many, many hours of labor later. The format turned out to be the same, and the opening and ending paragraphs are similar. Some passages are verbatim from the original draft. But the difference lies in telling phrases, observations, and reflections, which give the narrative facts a luminescence that only distance and learning can yield. It seems that finally, after a decade, I could look with relative detachment at this experience and see it for what it really was, and in subtle ways, infuse these small epiphanies into the essay.

In looking back, I see four stages that this, and most of my other essays, passed through. The first is the molecular stage, that early collection of bits of information, what I find fascinating, unusual, funny or poignant at the time it occurs, whether I retain it in memory or in a physical form on pieces of paper. The critical mass stage is next. The particles are vibrating on their own in proximity to one another until they reach a critical mass and a reaction occurs. The writing begins in a fury, raw data, raw memory, stream of consciousness writing.

Incubation happens throughout the writing when I walk away from the piece and it sits inside me, silently arranging itself, so that when I next visit it, I have made important connections. Then I edit and rewrite. The placement of events and observations creates irony, mood, pathos, humor. Events are taken out of the chronological or random order and purposefully placed, refined, commented on. With Zion, incubation occurred over ten years as I intermittently resuscitated the piece, but also during the active writing periods, each night when I turned off my computer and went to bed with the essay on my mind. This seems important, that the essay was written only partially at the desk. Much of it was written while I gardened or walked or lay in bed mulling it over.

Insight is the last thing to come, what the story is really about. I often don't know until very late in the process, and the story is frequently about something other than I intended, if I let the piece take the path it wants (which I did not do when I was forcing it to be a short story). The sensation I get when taking a train from Grand Central station, sitting in a seat facing where you just came from (not being able to see where you are headed) is the same one I feel when I read Zion. Distance. Perspective. It took me ten years to learn how that experience sculpted me, to tell the story, to locate its pulsing heart.

Alternative Contents

Approaches to Writing and Discussing Creative Nonfiction

Writers on Their Work

Memoir

Mary Clearman Blew, "The Unwanted Child"
Mary Clearman Blew, "The Art of Memoir"
Patricia Hampl, "Red Sky at Morning"
Patricia Hampl, "Memory and Imagination"
Mimi Schwartz, "My Father Always Said"
Mimi Schwartz, "Memoir? Fiction? Where's the Line?"
Maureen Stanton, "Zion"
Maureen Stanton, "On Writing 'Zion'"
Michael Steinberg, "Chin Music"
Michael Steinberg, "Finding the Inner Story in Memoirs and Personal Essays"

Personal Essay

Phillip Lopate, "Portrait of My Body"
Phillip Lopate, "What Happened to the Personal Essay?"
Mary Elizabeth Pope, "Teacher Training"
Mary Elizabeth Pope, "Composing 'Teacher Training'"
Robert L. Root, Jr, "Knowing Where You've Been"

Robert L. Root, Jr, "Collage, Montage, Mosaic, Vignette, Episode, Segment"
Scott Russell Sanders, "Cloud Crossing"
Scott Russell Sanders, "The Singular First Person"

Personal Cultural Criticism and Literary Journalism

Emily Chase, "Warping Time with Montaigne" (literature)
Emily Chase, "Notes from a Journey toward 'Warping Time'"
Tracy Kidder, "Courting the Approval of the Dead"
Marianna Torgovnick, "Experiment Critical Writing"

On Composing Processes

Emily Chase, "Notes from a Journey toward 'Warping Time'"
Patricia Foster, "The Intelligent Heart"
Vivian Gornick, "A Narrator Leaps Past Journalism"
Dustin Michael, "Advice to My Friend Beth's Undergraduate Nonfiction Students"
Mary Elizabeth Pope, "Composing 'Teacher Training'"
Robert L. Root, Jr, "Collage, Montage, Mosaic, Vignette, Episode, Segment"
Michael Steinberg, "Finding the Inner Story in Memoirs and Personal Essays"
Maureen Stanton, "On Writing 'Zion'"

On Form and Genre in Nonfiction

Jocelyn Bartkevicius, "The Landscape of Nonfiction"
Vivian Gornick, "A Narrator Leaps Past Journalism"
Steven Harvey, "The Art of Self"
Sonya Huber-Humes, "The Real Who, What, Where, Why of Journalism"
Judith Kitchen, "Mending Wall"
Brenda Miller, " 'Brenda Miller Has a Cold,' or, How the Lyric Essay Happens"
Michael Pearson, "The Other Creative Writing"
Robert L. Root, Jr, "Collage, Montage, Mosaic, Vignette, Episode, Segment"
Mimi Schwartz, "Memoir? Fiction? Where's the Line?"
Michael Steinberg, "Finding the Inner Story in Memoirs and Personal Essays"
Marianna Torgovnick, "Experimental Critical Writing"

On Family

Angela M. Balcita, "Dumpling"
Robin Black, "The Answer That Increasingly Appeals"
Mary Clearman Blew, "The Unwanted Child"
Lisa Groen Braner, "Soundtrack"
Steven Church, "I'm Just Getting to the Disturbing Part"
Judith Ortiz Cofer, "Silent Dancing"
Hillary Frank, "The Color of Monday"
Nicole Lamy, "Life in Motion"
Bret Lott, "Brothers"
Jared Jacang Maher, "Listen to the Sounds of the House"
Debra Marquart, "Some Things About That Day"
Mimi Schwartz, "My Father Always Said"
Christine White, "Reflection Rag: Uncle Joe, Roberto Clemente and I"

On Ethnicity

Angela M. Balcita, "Dumpling"
Lisa D. Chavez, "Independence Day, Manley Hot Springs, Alaska"
Judith Ortiz Cofer, "Silent Dancing"
Michelle Otero, "Quinto Sol"
Carol Paik, "A Few Things I Know About Softball"
Mimi Schwartz, "My Father Always Said"
Michael Steinberg, "Chin Music"

On Relationships

Meghan Daum, "On the Fringes of the Physical World"
Debra Marquart, "Some Things About That Day"
Michele Morano, "Grammar Lessons: The Subjunctive Mood"
Kate Petersen, "To All Those Who Say Write What You Know"
Wendy Rawlings, "Virtually Romance: A Discourse on Love in the Information Age"
Susan Allen Toth, "Going to the Movies"

On Others and Public Space

Jo Ann Beard, "Out There"

John Calderazzo, "Lost on Colfax Avenue"

Lisa D. Chavez, "Independence Day, Manley Hot Springs, Alaska"

Dagoberto Gilb, "Northeast Direct"

Adam Gopnick, "The People on the Bus"

Vivian Gornick, "On the Bus"

Patricia Hampl, "Red Sky at Morning"

Richard Hoffman, "Neighbors"

Pico Iyer, "Where Worlds Collide"

On the Body

Jennifer Kahn, "Stripped for Parts"

Phillip Lopate, "Portrait of My Body"

On Aspects of Culture

Lisa Groen Braner, "Soundtrack"

Shari Caudron, "Befriending Barbie"

Emily Gould, "The Death of the Personal Blog"

Jonathan Lethem, "13, 1977, 21"

John McPhee, "The Search for Marvin Gardens"

Susan Orlean, "Lifelike"

Chet Raymo, "Celebrating Creation"

Richard Rodriguez, "Disappointment"

Susan Allen Toth, "Going to the Movies"

Erika Vidal, "Undressing Victoria"

Christine White, "Reflection Rag: Uncle Joe, Roberto Clemente and I"

On Nature

Nancy Lord, "I Met a Man Who Has Seen the Ivory-Billed Woodpecker and This Is What He Told Me"

Tom Montgomery-Fate, "In Plain Sight"

Robert L. Root, Jr, "Knowing Where You've Been"
Scott Russell Sanders, "Cloud Crossing"

On Sports and Games

J. D. Dolan, "Pool, A Love Story"
John McPhee, "The Search for Marvin Gardens"
Carol Paik, "A Few Things I Know About Softball"
Michael Steinberg, "Chin Music"

On the Quarter-Life Crisis

Matt Farwell, "Welcome to Afghanistan"
Jared Jacang Maher, "Listen to the Sounds of the House"
Kate Torgovnick, "How I Became a Bed-Maker"
Erika Vidal, "Undressing Victoria"

Notes on Authors

Angela M. Balcita is the author of the memoir, *Moonface*.

Jocelyn Bartkevicius is the editor of *The Florida Review* and winner of the Annie Dillard and *Missouri Review* awards for the essay.

Jo Ann Beard is the author of the essay collection *The Boys of My Youth*.

Robin Black's personal essays and fiction appear in such literary journals as *Colorado Review*, *Alaska Quarterly Review*, *Bellevue Literary Review*, and *Indiana Review*.

Mary Clearman Blew, University of Idaho, wrote *All But The Waltz*, *Balsamroot: A Memoir*, and *Bone Deep in Landscape*.

Lisa Groen Braner is the author of *The Mother's Book of Well-Being*.

John Calderazzo, Colorado State University, is the author of *Writing from Scratch: Freelancing* and *Rising Fire: Volcanoes and Our Inner Lives*.

Shari Caudron, a freelance writer and teacher, is the author of *What Really Happened: Unexpected Insights from Life's Uncomfortable Moments* and *Who Are You People?*

Emily Chase is a ferrier in Michigan.

Lisa D. Chavez teaches at the University of New Mexico and is the author of two books of poetry, *Destruction Bay* and *In an Angry Season*.

Steven Church, California State University at Fresno, is the author of *The Guinness Book of Me: A Memoir of Record* and editor of *The Normal School: A Literary Magazine*.

Judith Ortiz Cofer is the author of *Silent Dancing: A Partial Remembrance of a Puerto Rican Childhood* and *Woman In Front of the Sun: On Becoming a Writer*.

Meghan Daum is the author of the essay collection *My Misspent Youth*.

J. D. Dolan, Western Michigan University, is the author of the memoir, *Phoenix: A Brother's Life*.

Matt Farwell is a sergeant in the United States Army, 10th Mountain Division.

Patricia Foster, University of Iowa, is the author of *All the Lost Girls: Confessions of a Southern Daughter*.

Hillary Frank's work has aired on *This American Life*, *Morning Edition*, and other radio programs.

Dagoberto Gilb is the author of the essay collection *Gritos*.

Adam Gopnick writes for *The New Yorker* and is the author of *Paris to the Moon* and *Through the Children's Gate*.

Vivian Gornick is the author of *Fierce Attachments*, *Approaching Eye Level*, and *The Situation and the Story: The Art of the Personal Narrative*.

Emily Gould is the Galley Cat Blogger for MediaBistro.com and editor/blogger for EmilyMagazine.com.

Patricia Hampl is the author of *A Romantic Education, Spillville, Virgin Time, I Could Tell You Stories: Sojourns in the Land of Memory, Blue Arabesque,* and *The Florist's Daughter.*

Steven Harvey's essays are collected in *A Geometry of Lilies, Lost in Translation,* and *Bound for Glory;* he teaches at Young-Harris College.

Richard Hoffman is the author of *Half the House: A Memoir,* writer-in-residence at Emerson College, and faculty member in the Stonecoast MFA Program.

Sonya Huber-Humes is the author of *Opa Nobody* and teaches at Georgia Southern University and the MFA in Creative Writing Program at Ashland University.

Pico Iyer is the author of *The Lady and the Monk, Global Soul, Falling Off the Map, Video Night in Kathmandu,* and *Tropical Classical.*

Jennifer Khan is a contributing editor for *Wired Magazine.*

Tracy Kidder is the author of *The Soul of a New Machine, House, Among Schoolchildren, Old Friends, Hometown,* and *Mountains Beyond Mountains.*

Judith Kitchen, Rainier Writing Workshop, is the editor of *In Short, In Brief,* and *Short Takes* and the author of two essay collections, *Only the Dance* and *Distance and Directions.*

Nicole Lamy is the former Managing Editor of the *Boston Book Review* and a freelance writer.

Jonathan Lethem is the author of a collection of essays, *The Disappointment Artist,* and several novels.

Phillip Lopate is the author of *Bachelorhood, Against Joie de Vivre, Portrait of My Body, Waterfront,* and *Getting Personal* and editor of *The Art of the Personal Essay.*

Nancy Lord's books of creative nonfiction include *Fishcamp: Life on an Alaskan Shore* and *Green Alaska: Dreams from the Far Coast.*

Bret Lott is the author of *Fathers, Sons, and Brothers: The Men in My Family* and the co-editor of the essay collection *A Year in Place.*

Jared Jacang Maher is a writer for *Westword Magazine* in Denver, Colorado.

Debra Marquart, Iowa State University, is the author of *The Horizontal World: Growing Up Wild in the Middle of Nowhere,* a memoir.

John McPhee has published twenty-six books, including the Pulitzer Prize-winning *Annals of the Former World.*

Dustin Michael is a doctoral student in English at the University of Missouri Columbia.

Brenda Miller, Western Washington University, is the author of *Seasons of the Body,* editor-in-chief of *The Bellingham Review,* and co-author of *Tell It Slant: Writing and Shaping Creative Nonfiction.*

Tom Montgomery-Fate, College of DuPage, is the author of *Steady & Trembling: Art, Faith, and Family in an Uncertain World.*

Michele Morano, DePaul University, is the author of the essay collection *Grammar Lessons: Translating a Life in Spain.*

Susan Orlean is a staff writer for *The New Yorker* and author of *The Orchid Thief, The Bullfighter Checks Her Makeup,* and *My Kind of Place.*

Michelle Otero is the author of *Malinche's Daughter,* an essay collection.

Carol Paik is a freelance writer based in New York City.

Michael Pearson, Director of the Creative Writing Program at Old Dominion, is the author of *A Place That's Known* and *Dreaming of Columbus*.

Kate Petersen lives in Boston. Her non-fiction has appeared in *The Iowa Review, Brevity*, and *Hayden's Ferry Review*.

Mary Elizabeth Pope, Emmanuel College, writes nonfiction and fiction.

Wendy Rawlings teaches creative writing at the University of Alabama and is a widely published essayist.

Chet Raymo's nonfiction includes *Honey From Stone: A Naturalist's Search for God, The Soul of Night, Natural Prayers*, and *The Path: A One-Mile Walk Through the Universe*.

Richard Rodriguez is the author of *Hunger of Memory, Days of Obligation*, and *Brown*.

Robert L. Root, Jr., Ashland University MFA Program, is the author of *The Nonfictionist's Guide* and editor of *Landscapes with Figures*.

Scott Russell Sanders's books include *Writing From the Center, Hunting for Hope, The Country of Language*, and *The Force of Spirit*.

Mimi Schwartz is the author of *Good Neighbors, Bad Times: Echoes of My Father's German Village* and *Thoughts from a Queen-Sized Bed* and the co-editor of *Writing True*.

Peggy Shumaker, Rainier Writing Workshop, wrote *Blaze*, a collaboration with the painter Kesler Woodward, and *Just Breathe Normally*, a lyrical memoir.

Maureen Stanton, University of Missouri at Columbia, is an award-winning essayist and associate editor of the journal *Fourth Genre: Explorations in Nonfiction*.

Michael Steinberg, author of *Still Pitching*, is the founding editor of *Fourth Genre: Explorations in Nonfiction*, and writer-in-residence at the Solstice/Pine Manor College MFA Program.

Kate Torgovnick is the author of *Cheer! Three Teams on a Quest for College Cheerleading's Ultimate Prize*.

Marianna Torgovnick's essays are in *Crossing Ocean Parkway: Readings by an Italian-American Daughter* and she edited *Eloquent Obsessions: Writing Cultural Criticism*.

Susan Allen Toth is the author of *Blooming: A Small Town Girlhood* and *Ivy Days: Making My Way Out East*.

Erika Vidal has an MFA in Creative Nonfiction from Goucher College and writes for the *St. Petersburg Times*.

Christine White, whose MFA Thesis in Creative Nonfiction at Goucher College is titled *Grace Notes: Syncopated Musings on the Journey Home*, died in a plane crash in June 2001.

Credits

Index

"Advice to My Friend Beth's Undergraduate Creative Nonfiction Students" (Michael), 376–377

"Answer That Increasingly Appeals, The" (Black), 15–22

"Art of Memoir, The" (Blew), 324–327

"Art of Self, The" (Harvey), 344–345

Balcita, Angela M., 5–9

Bartkevicius, Jocelyn, 317–323

Beard, Jo Ann, 10–14

"Befriending Barbie" (Caudron), 38–48

Black, Robin, 15–22

Blew, Mary Clearman, 23–33, 324–327

Braner, Lisa Groen, 34–36

"'Brenda Miller Has a Cold,' or, How the Lyric Essay Happens" (Miller), 378–384

"Brothers" (Lott), 166–169

Calderazzo, John, 37

Caudron, Shari, 38–48

"Celebrating Creation" (Raymo), 233–236

Chase, Emily, 433–438, 439–446

Chavez, Lisa D., 49–55

"Chin Music" (Steinberg), 268–277

Church, Steven, 56–63

"Cloud Crossing" (Sanders), 254–259

Cofer, Judith Ortiz, 64–70

"Collage, Montage, Mosaic, Vignette, Episode, Segment" (Root), 390–401

"Color of Monday, The" (Frank), 95–99

"Composing 'Teacher Training'" (Pope), 453–460

"Courting the Approval of the Dead" (Kidder), 350–363

Daum, Meghan, 71–79

"Death of the Personal Blog, The" (Gould), 114–115

"Disappointment" (Rodriguez), 237–246

Dolan, J. D., 80–88

"Dumpling" (Balcita), 5–9

"Experimental Critical Writing" (Torgovnick), 424–428

Farwell, Matt, 89–94

"Few Things I Know About Softball, A" (Paik), 212–220

"Finding the Inner Story in Memoirs and Personal Essays" (Steinberg), 420–423

Foster, Patricia, 328–330

Frank, Hillary, 95–99

Gilb, Dagoberto, 100–103

"Going to the Movies" (Toth), 283–285

Gopnick, Adam, 104–109

Gornick, Vivian, 110–113, 331–333

Gould, Emily, 114–115

"Grammar Lessons: The Subjunctive Mood" (Morano), 192–202

Hampl, Patricia, 116–119, 334–343

Harvey, Steven, 344–345

Hoffman, Richard, 120–127

"How I Became a Bed-Maker" (Torgovnick), 278–282

Huber-Humes, Sonya, 346–349

"I Met a Man Who Has Seen the Ivory-Billed Woodpecker and This Is What He Told Me" (Lord), 163–165

"I'm Just Getting to the Disturbing Part" (Church), 56–63

"In Plain Sight" (Montgomery-Fate), 188–191

"Independence Day, Manley Hot Springs, Alaska" (Chavez), 49–55

"Intelligent Heart, The" (Foster), 328–330

Introduction (Root, Steinberg), xxiii–xxxvi

Iyer, Pico, 128–137

Kahn, Jennifer, 138–143

Kidder, Tracy, 350–363

Kitchen, Judith, 364–367

"Knowing Where You've Been" (Root), 247–253

Lamy, Nicole, 144–148

"Landscape of Nonfiction, The" (Bartkevicius), 317–323

Lethem, Jonathan, 149–154

"Life in Motion" (Lamy), 144–148

"Lifelike" (Orlean), 203–209
"Listen to the Sounds of the House" (Maher), 170–176
Lopate, Phillip, 155–162, 368–375
Lord, Nancy, 163–165
"Lost on Colfax Avenue" (Calderazzo), 37
Lott, Bret, 166–169

Maher, Jared Jacang, 170–176
Marquart, Debra, 177–178
McPhee, John, 179–187
"Mending Wall" (Kitchen), 364–367
"Memoir? Fiction? Where's The Line?" (Schwartz), 411–416
"Memory and Imagination" (Hampl), 334–343
Michael, Dustin, 376–377
Miller, Brenda, 378–384
Montgomery-Fate, Tom, 188–191
Morano, Michele, 192–202
"My Father Always Said" (Schwartz), 260–267

"Narrator Leaps Past Journalism, A" (Gornick), 331–333
"Neighbors" (Hoffman), 120–127
"Northeast Direct" (Gilb), 100–103
"Notes from a Journey toward 'Warping Time'" (Chase), 439–446

"On the Bus" (Gornick), 110–113
"On the Fringes of the Physical World" (Daum), 71–79
"On Writing 'Zion'" (Stanton), 469–474
Orlean, Susan, 203–209
Otero, Michelle, 210–211
"Other Creative Writing, The" (Pearson), 385–389
"Out There" (Beard), 10–14

Paik, Carol, 212–220
Pearson, Michael, 385–389
"People on the Bus, The"(Gopnick), 104–109
Petersen, Kate, 221–222
"Pool, A Love Story" (Dolan), 80–88
Pope, Mary Elizabeth, 447–452, 453–460
"Portrait of My Body" (Lopate), 155–162
Preface (Steinberg, Root), xv–xxii
"Prose Poems, Paragraphs, Brief Lyric Nonfiction" (Shumaker), 417–419

"Quinto Sol" (Otero), 210–211

Rawlings, Wendy, 223–232
Raymo, Chet, 233–236

"Real Who, What, When and Why of Journalism, The" (Huber-Humes), 346–349
"Red Sky at Morning" (Hampl), 116–119
"Reflection Rag: Uncle Joe, Roberto Clemente and I" (White), 298–313
Rodriguez, Richard, 237–246
Root, Robert L. Jr., xv–xxii, xxiii–xxxvi, 247–253, 390–401

Sanders, Scott Russell, 254–259, 402–410
Schwartz, Mimi, 260–267, 411–416
"Search for Marvin Gardens, The" (McPhee), 179–187
Shumaker, Peggy, 417–419
"Silent Dancing" (Cofer), 64–70
"Singular First Person, The" (Sanders), 402–410
"Some Things About That Day" (Marquart), 177–178
"Soundtrack" (Braner), 34–36
Stanton, Maureen, 461–468, 469–474
Steinberg, Michael, xv–xxii, xxiii–xxxvi, 268–277, 420–423
"Stripped for Parts" (Kahn), 138–143

"Teacher Training" (Pope), 447–452
"13,1977,21" (Lethem), 149–154
"To All Those Who Say Write What You Know" (Petersen), 221–222
Torgovnick, Kate, 278–282
Torgovnick, Marianna, 424–428
Toth, Susan Allen, 283–285

"Undressing Victoria" (Vidal), 286–297
"Unwanted Child, The" (Blew), 23–33

Vidal, Erika, 286–297
"Virtually Romance: A Discourse on Love in the Information Age" (Rawlings), 223–232

"Warping Time with Montaigne" (Chase), 433–438
"Welcome to Afghanistan" (Farwell), 89–94
"What Happened to the Personal Essay?" (Lopate), 368–375
"Where Worlds Collide" (Iyer), 128–137
White, Christine, 298–313

"Zion" (Stanton), 461–468